Everyman, I will go with thee,
and be thy guide

THE BEGGAR'S OPERA

AND OTHER EIGHTEENTH-CENTURY PLAYS

Introduced by
DAVID W. LINDSAY
University of Wales, Bangor

EVERYMAN
J. M. DENT · LONDON
CHARLES E. TUTTLE
VERMONT

Introduction, chronology, biographies and reading list
© J. M. Dent 1993
Notes © J. M. Dent 1995

First published in Everyman's Library 1928

Reprinted with revisions and additions 1995
Reprinted 1997, 1998, 2000

J.M.Dent
Orion Publishing Group
Orion House
5 Upper St Martin's Lane,
London WC2H 9EA
and
Charles E. Tuttle Co., Inc.
28 South Main Street,
Rutland, Vermont 05701, USA

Printed in Great Britain by
The Guernsey Press Co. Ltd
Guernsey
Channel Islands

British Library Cataloguing-in-Publication Data
is available upon request.

ISBN 0 460 87314 8

CONTENTS

BIOGRAPHICAL NOTES

Lancelot Addison, the father of the essayist, served as military chaplain first in Dunkirk and then in Tangier. In 1672, when his eldest son Joseph was born, he was rector of Milston in Wiltshire; and in 1683 he became Dean of Lichfield. His many publications included a history of Morocco, in which he commented obliquely on the history of England.

Joseph Addison was educated at Lichfield Grammar School, Charterhouse, and Queen's College, Oxford. He became a proficient writer of Latin and English verse, and, while touring France and Italy in the years 1699–1703, extolled the classical associations of the places he visited. On his return to England he celebrated Marlborough's victory at Blenheim in an accomplished poem entitled *The Campaign*, the success of which earned him the patronage of the Whig administration; and in 1706 he responded to the popularity of Italian opera by writing the libretto for an English opera called *Rosamund*.

In 1708 Addison became Secretary to the Lord-Lieutenant of Ireland, but the downfall of the Whigs interrupted his political career, and under the Tory administration of 1710–14 he devoted his energies to literary work. His greatest achievement was in the new genre of the periodical essay, on which he collaborated with Richard Steele. Addison contributed 46 essays to *The Tatler* in 1709–11, 274 essays to *The Spectator* in 1711–12, and 51 essays to *The Guardian* in 1713. His tragedy *Cato*, received with enthusiasm at Drury Lane in 1713, acquired a European reputation.

Having re-entered public life after the accession of George I, Addison showed less interest in literary fame: his comedy *The Drummer* was produced anonymously at Drury Lane in 1716, and achieved popularity only when its authorship was acknowledged after his death. His political career reached its climax in

1717–18, when he served for eleven months as Secretary of State. He died in 1719 and was buried in Westminster Abbey.

SIR RICHARD STEELE

Richard Steele described himself as 'an *Englishman* born in the City of *Dublin*'; the year of his birth was 1672. Though his parents died about 1677, his uncle sent him to Charterhouse and to the University of Oxford. Having left Oxford without taking a degree, he served from 1695 to 1700 first as Ensign and then as Captain in the Coldstream Guards. In 1700 he fought a duel and wounded his opponent.

In 1701 Steele published a didactic work entitled *The Christian Hero*. His commitment to moral reformation in the theatre is manifest in his first three comedies: *The Funeral or Grief à la Mode* (1702), *The Lying Lover or The Ladies' Friendship* (1703), and *The Tender Husband or The Accomplished Fools* (1705). He was appointed Gazetteer in 1707, but lost this position after the Tory victory of 1710.

Steele's greatest contribution to literature was the invention of the periodical essay. He was the initiator and leading writer of *The Tatler* from 1709 to 1711, and he collaborated with Addison on *The Spectator* in 1711–12 and on *The Guardian* in 1713. He was elected to Parliament in 1713, but expelled in the following year because of his activities as a pamphleteer.

After the death of Queen Anne, Steele became Supervisor of the Drury Lane theatre, and in 1715 he re-entered Parliament and was knighted by George I. In 1717, as a member of the Forfeited Estates Commission, he made the first of several visits to Scotland.

In 1719 Steele played an active role in the controversy over the Peerage Bill, and in 1720 he defended his position at Drury Lane in a periodical entitled *The Theatre*. His last and best play, *The Conscious Lovers*, was acted at Drury Lane in 1722. Ill-health and financial problems caused him to withdraw from political and theatrical affairs, and he spent his last years in Carmarthen, where he died in 1729.

JOHN GAY

John Gay was born in 1685 at Barnstaple in Devon, and was educated at the local grammar school. From about 1702 to about 1706 he was apprenticed to a silk mercer in London, and about 1707 he became secretary to Aaron Hill. His first poem, a blank-verse georgic entitled *Wine*, was published in 1708. In the years 1711–14, when he was closely associated with Swift and Pope in the Scriblerus Club, he produced two dramatic works, but his main publications during this period were a georgic called *Rural Sports*, a mock-epic called *The Fan*, and a volume of burlesque pastorals called *The Shepherd's Week*. The influence of Pope is apparent in all these poems.

Queen Anne's death ended Gay's hopes of preferment, but the following years saw the appearance of some of his most original work. His 'tragi-comi-pastoral farce' *The What D'Ye Call It* was produced in 1715. His best poem, the mock-georgic entitled *Trivia or The Art of Walking the Streets of London*, was published in 1716. The comedy *Three Hours after Marriage*, written jointly by Gay, Pope and Arbuthnot, was acted in 1717.

In 1720 a collected edition of Gay's poems brought in substantial profit, but he invested in South Sea stock, which was soon worthless. In 1727 he published his most popular book of verse, a collection of Aesopic fables addressed to the young Duke of Cumberland, and in 1728 his masterpiece, *The Beggar's Opera*, began its triumphant progress at Lincoln's Inn Fields. The Walpole government prevented the performance of a sequel entitled *Polly*, but Gay's Tory friends ensured that the printed text sold well.

Gay's serenata *Acis and Galatea* was performed, with music by Handel, in 1732. He died later in the same year. His posthumously published works included a ballad-opera, two comedies, and a second collection of fables.

HENRY FIELDING

Henry Fielding, whose father fought under Marlborough and gambled in London coffee-houses, was born in the West Country in 1707. After his mother's death in 1718 he was sent to Eton College. In 1728 his first play, *Love in Several Masques*, was produced at Drury Lane. After a short period at the University of Leyden, he returned to London in 1729 and committed himself to the theatre.

Fielding's first successful play was a burlesque entitled *The*

Author's Farce, which was acted at the Little Theatre in the Haymarket in 1730. It was followed in the same year by *Tom Thumb*, which was expanded in 1731 as *The Tragedy of Tragedies*. Fielding's career as a political satirist began in 1731 with the production at the Haymarket of *The Welsh Opera*, which was later expanded as *The Grub-Street Opera*. His plays for Drury Lane included adaptations of Molière entitled *The Mock Doctor* (1732) and *The Miser* (1733). In 1736 he assumed new responsibilities as manager of 'the Great Mogul's Company of Comedians'. The texts he provided for this company included his best political satires, *Pasquin* and *The Historical Register*, which were acted at the Haymarket in 1736 and 1737 respectively. His theatrical career ended in 1737 with the passing of Walpole's Licensing Act.

In his later years Fielding was active as a lawyer and a political journalist, but his greatest achievement was in the field of prose fiction. In 1741 he satirised Richardson's *Pamela* in *An Apology for the Life of Mrs Shamela Andrews*, and in 1742 he published *The History of Joseph Andrews*. *The Life of Mr Jonathan Wild the Great* was published in 1743 and expanded in 1754. Fielding's masterpiece, *The History of Tom Jones, a Foundling*, appeared in 1749, and his last major work, *Amelia*, in 1752. He died in Lisbon in 1754, and his *Journal of a Voyage to Lisbon* was published posthumously in 1755.

GEORGE LILLO

George Lillo was born in London in 1693, the son of a Dutch jeweller and his English wife. He was a Dissenter, and for some years he was a partner in his father's business. He embarked on a theatrical career at the age of thirty-seven, when his ballad-opera *Silvia or The Country Burial* was performed in 1730 at Drury Lane.

Lillo's first and greatest success, *The London Merchant or The History of George Barnwell*, was produced at Drury Lane in 1731 with Colley Cibber's son Theophilus in the leading role. It was based on an old ballad, later reprinted in Percy's *Reliques*, and besides winning the approval of the royal family and the city merchants, it was admired and imitated in France and Germany.

In 1734 Lillo celebrated the marriage of Princess Anne to the

Prince of Orange with a masque entitled *Britannia or the Royal Lovers*; this was subsequently printed as *Britannia and Batavia*. In 1735 he produced at Drury Lane a historical drama entitled *The Christian Hero*, which was based on the life of the Albanian chieftain Scanderbeg.

In 1736 Lillo returned to the tragedy of common life with *Guilt Its Own Punishment or Fatal Curiosity*, which was produced at the Little Theatre in the Haymarket. This play, which may have been based on an old ballad about events in Cornwall in 1618, offers a powerfully simple story about a poor couple who murder a young man for his money, not realising that he is their long-lost son.

In 1738 Lillo's adaptation of the last two acts of Shakespeare's *Pericles* was performed at Covent Garden under the title *Marina*. When he died in 1739, he left the completed text of a historical tragedy entitled *Elmerick or Justice Triumphant*, and an uncompleted adaptation of the Elizabethan domestic tragedy *Arden of Faversham*.

OLIVER GOLDSMITH

Oliver Goldsmith was born in Ireland about 1730 and grew up near Lissoy, in County Westmeath, where his father was a curate. He studied medicine in Dublin, Edinburgh and Leyden, and spent two years travelling on the Continent. He arrived in England in 1756, and found a post at a boys' school at Peckham. He began writing for London periodicals in 1757, and from 1759 onwards he made a precarious living by working for booksellers.

An Enquiry into the Present State of Polite Learning in Europe appeared in 1759. In the years 1760–61 Goldsmith published a series of letters offering the response of a Chinese visitor to English society, and in 1762 these were collected as *The Citizen of the World*. He made the acquaintance of Johnson and Boswell, and in 1764 became a member of the Literary Club. In that year also he published a two-volume *History of England* and his first important poem, *The Traveller or A Prospect of Society*.

Goldsmith's novel *The Vicar of Wakefield* came out in 1766, and in 1768 his first play, *The Good-Natured Man*, was produced at Covent Garden. A two-volume *Roman History* appeared in 1769, his best poem *The Deserted Village* in 1770, and a four-volume *History of England to the Death of George II* in 1771. In 1773 he returned to the theatre with *She Stoops to Conquer or The Mistakes of a Night*.

Goldsmith's most interesting publication of 1774 is *Retaliation: A Poem*, which offers entertaining portraits of Garrick, Reynolds, Burke and others. His other works of that year included a two-volume *Grecian History* and an eight-volume *History of the Earth and Animated Nature*. Goldsmith's historical and scientific writings are now little read, but his versatility is sufficiently demonstrated by his essays, his novel, his two comedies, and his two major poems. He died in 1774.

RICHARD BRINSLEY SHERIDAN

Richard Brinsley Sheridan was born in Dublin in 1751. His father, Thomas Sheridan, was an actor and teacher of elocution, and his mother, Frances Sheridan, was a dramatist and novelist. He attended Harrow School from 1762 to about 1768, and in 1770 he took up residence in Bath. In 1773 he travelled to France with the singer Elizabeth Linley, whose broken engagement to Walter Long had been dramatised in Foote's play *The Maid of Bath*. After his return to England Sheridan fought two duels with Thomas Matthews, and in 1774 Sheridan and Elizabeth Linley were married.

Sheridan's comedy *The Rivals* was produced at Covent Garden in 1775, and later in that year his comic opera *The Duenna* began a long run at the same theatre. In 1776 Garrick retired, and Sheridan assumed managerial control of Drury Lane. In February 1777 his adaptation of Vanbrugh's *The Relapse* was acted there, and in March he became a member of the Literary Club. His greatest play, *The School for Scandal*, had its first performance at Drury Lane in May 1777, and his burlesque play *The Critic* was produced there in 1779.

In 1780 Sheridan was elected to Parliament. He became Under-Secretary of State for Foreign Affairs in 1782 and Secretary to the Treasury in 1783. In 1788 he earned a high reputation as an orator through his speeches during the trial of Warren Hastings in Westminster Hall. The Drury Lane theatre was rebuilt on an enlarged scale in 1794, and in 1799 Sheridan achieved a spectacular success there with his adaptation of two plays by August von Kotzebue under the title *Pizarro*. In 1806 he succeeded Charles James Fox as Member for Westminster, and in 1806–7 he served as Treasurer of the Navy. After the burning down of Drury Lane in 1809, he faced financial ruin; he lost his parliamentary seat in 1812, and was later arrested for debt. He died in 1816.

CHRONOLOGY OF HISTORICAL AND LITERARY EVENTS

Year	Historical Events	Literary Events
1660	Restoration of Charles II	Theatre patents granted
1672	Declaration of Indulgence	Birth of Addison and Steele
1675	Wren's St Paul's begun	
1676	Secret treaty with France	
1677	William marries Mary	
1682	Flight of Shaftesbury	Dryden, *MacFlecknoe*
1685	Death of Charles II	Birth of Gay
1690	Battle of the Boyne	Locke, *Human Understanding*
1693	Purcell, *The Fairy Queen*	Birth of Lillo
1697	Treaty of Ryswick	Dryden's *Virgil*
1700	Partition Treaty	Death of Dryden
1701	Act of Settlement	Defoe, *The True-Born Englishman*
1702	Death of William III	Defoe, *The Shortest Way*
1703	Founding of St Petersburg	Defoe, *A Hymn to the Pillory*
1704	Battle of Blenheim	Swift, *A Tale of a Tub*
1705	Blenheim Palace begun	Mandeville, *The Grumbling Hive*
1707	Union of the Parliaments	Birth of Fielding
1708	Battle of Oudenarde	Union of acting companies
1709	Battle of Malplaquet	*The Tatler* begun
1710	Tory election victory	Swift, *The Examiner*
1711	Dismissal of Marlborough	*The Spectator* begun
1712	Barrier Treaty	Blackmore, *Creation*
1713	Treaty of Utrecht	Dennis, *Remarks upon Cato*
1714	Death of Queen Anne	Gay, *The Shepherd's Week*
	Accession of George I	Pope, *The Rape of the Lock*
1715	Jacobite rebellion	Pope, *The Temple of Fame*
	Death of Louis XIV	Pope's *Homer*, I
		Watts, *Divine Songs*
1716	Septennial Act	Gay, *Trivia*
1717	Bangorian Controversy	Addison Secretary of State
	Triple Alliance	Birth of Garrick

CHRONOLOGY OF NEW PLAYS ACTED
IN LONDON

Year	Historical Events	Literary Events
1718	Quadruple Alliance	Prior, *Poems*
1719	Peace concluded	Death of Addison
	Silk mill in Derby	Defoe, *Robinson Crusoe*
1720	South Sea Bubble	Defoe, *Captain Singleton*
1721	Walpole Lord Treasurer	Dennis, *Original Letters*
1722	Death of Marlborough	Defoe, *Moll Flanders*
	Guy's Hospital founded	Dennis, defence of Etherege
1723	Bach, *St John Passion*	Dennis, attack on Steele
1725	Death of Peter the Great	
1726	St Martin's-in-the-Fields	Swift, *Gulliver's Travels*
1727	Death of George I	Newton, *Principia* (English tr.)
1728		Pope, *The Dunciad* (3 books)
		Savage, *The Bastard*
1729	Treaty of Seville	Death of Steele
1730	Resignation of Townshend	Thomson, *The Seasons*
	Methodist Society founded	Birth of Goldsmith
	Senate House, Cambridge	
1731		Death of Defoe
		Gentleman's Magazine founded
1732		Death of Gay
1736	Porteous Riots	
	Handel, *Alexander's Feast*	
1737	Licensing Act	
1739	War with Spain	Death of Lillo
1740	Prussia invades Silesia	Cibber, *Apology*
1742	Walpole resigns	Young, *Night Thoughts* (begun)
1743	Handel, *The Messiah*	Pope, *The Dunciad* (4 books)
1745	Battle of Prestonpans	Death of Swift
1746	Battle of Culloden	Collins, *Odes*
1747	British naval victories	Richardson, *Clarissa*, 1-2
1749	Bach, *The Art of Fugue*	Fielding, *Tom Jones*
1751	Clive takes Arcot	Birth of Sheridan
1753		Sarah Fielding, *David Simple*
		Hogarth, *Analysis of Beauty*
1754	War in North America	Death of Fielding
1755	Lisbon earthquake	Johnson, *Dictionary*
1757	Admiral Byng shot	Gray, *Odes*
1758	British naval victories	
1759	Capture of Quebec	Johnson, *Rasselas*
1760	Death of George II	Goldsmith, *Chinese Letters*
	Accession of George III	Sterne, *Tristram Shandy*, 1-2
1761	Resignation of Pitt	Churchill, *The Rosciad*
1762	Bute ministry	Macpherson, *Fingal*

Year	Historical Events	Literary Events
1765	*Encyclopédie* completed	Percy, *Reliques*
1766	Repeal of Stamp Act	Goldsmith, *Vicar of Wakefield*
1767	Royal Crescent, Bath	
1768	Royal Academy founded	Sterne, *A Sentimental Journey*
	Resignation of Chatham	Boswell, *An Account of Corsica*
1771		Smollett, *Humphry Clinker*
1773	Boston Tea Party	
1774	First American Congress	Death of Goldsmith
1775	Battle of Lexington	Johnson, *Western Islands*
	Battle of Bunker Hill	Burke, *Speech on Conciliation*
1776	American Independence	Gibbon, *Decline and Fall*, 1
1777		Chatterton, *Rowley Poems*
1779	Crompton's spinning mule	Death of Garrick
1784	Balloon ascent by Lunardi	Cowper, *The Task*
1789	Fall of the Bastille	Blake, *Songs of Innocence*
1799	Beethoven, first symphony	
1815	Battle of Waterloo	Scott, *Guy Mannering*
1816	Napoleon on St Helena	Death of Sheridan

Year	Author and Title
1765	Samuel Foote, *The Commissary*
1766	George Colman and David Garrick, *The Clandestine Marriage*
1767	Gotthold Ephraim Lessing, *Minna von Barnhelm* (Hamburg)
1768	Oliver Goldsmith, *The Good-Natured Man*
	Hugh Kelly, *False Delicacy*
1771	Richard Cumberland, *The West Indian*
1773	Oliver Goldsmith, *She Stoops to Conquer*
1775	Richard Brinsley Sheridan, *The Rivals*
	Richard Brinsley Sheridan, *The Duenna*
1777	Richard Brinsley Sheridan, *The School for Scandal*
1779	Richard Brinsley Sheridan, *The Critic*
1784	P.–A. de Beaumarchais, *Le mariage de Figaro* (Paris)
1799	Richard Brinsley Sheridan, *Pizarro*

INTRODUCTION

The seven plays included in this anthology were all performed for the first time in London theatres between 1708 and 1780. Two of them at least are dramatic masterpieces, and the selection as a whole represents both the historical development and the generic variety of English drama during this period. Although they originated within a continuous and coherent theatrical tradition, these plays reflect many aspects of political and cultural conflict. Their differing perspectives on social change are closely connected, too, with their use of various literary and dramatic conventions. Although the generic divisions are never absolute, it can plausibly be said that this volume contains a neo-classical tragedy, a sentimental comedy, a ballad-opera, a dramatic burlesque, a bourgeois tragedy, a laughing comedy and a satirical comedy. Each of these forms has its place in the complex history of eighteenth-century drama, and each has its distinctive ideological implications.

The theatrical context in which English dramatists worked between 1708 and 1780 was in great measure determined by the institutional structures which they inherited from the Restoration. When theatres reopened in 1660, Charles II granted the right to perform spoken drama in London to two companies of actors. The system established at that time underwent some modification as companies later amalgamated and divided, but the concept of the patent theatre survived. The acting companies of the Restoration broke immediately with English histrionic tradition by assigning female roles to actresses, and they also pioneered a new stagecraft which made extensive provision for representational scenery. As the size of the forestage was gradually reduced, a dramaturgy which incorporated human figures in a series of stage pictures increasingly invited audiences to acknowledge the controlling influence of temporal and spatial circumstance on human behaviour.

The reign of Charles II saw the flowering of a drama responsive both to the public ideology of the restored monarchy and to the deep-rooted scepticism of a materialistic era. The heroic play in rhyming couplets flourished from 1664 to 1676, but yielded after the production of Dryden's *All for Love* to neo-Shakespearean tragedy in blank verse. The varieties of comedy written at this time included the neo-Fletcherian drama with comic and tragi-comic plots, the comedy of humours in the manner of Ben Jonson, and the comedy of intrigue in the tradition of the Spanish cloak-and-sword play; but the comic masterpieces of the age were created not in those modes but rather in the comedy of sexual manners, which was cultivated in particular by Sir George Etherege and William Wycherley.

The ten years from 1683 to 1692 were relatively unproductive in terms of new dramatic texts; but the Williamite Revolution of 1688–90 created a new situation for the theatre by reducing the importance of royal patronage and promoting a moral reformation in English society. The dramatic masterpieces of Restoration drama's second creative phase, from 1693 to 1707, are characterised not by heroic extravagance and aggressive scepticism, but rather by a renewal of the pathetic note in blank-verse tragedy and a complex interaction between theatrical convention and the new morality in the comedy of manners. The Restoration tradition of sexual comedy was maintained by William Congreve and in a modified form by Sir John Vanbrugh and George Farquhar; but it was attacked, notably by Sir Richard Blackmore and Jeremy Collier, for its 'immorality and profaneness'. In the years 1701–5 an alternative mode of sentimental comedy was developed by the young Richard Steele.

The death of Farquhar in 1707 marks the end of the Restoration tradition in English drama. With the union of the acting companies in 1708 the London theatre entered a twenty-year period of stability and comparative prosperity under the guidance of the three actor-managers at Drury Lane. The power exercised by Colley Cibber and his associates was resented by many dramatists; but, despite the challenge posed from 1714 by Lincoln's Inn Fields, and from 1720 by the Little Theatre in the Haymarket, Drury Lane remained the principal centre in London for the production of non-musical drama. Whig taste in this period inclined to neo-classical tragedy and sentimental comedy, Tory taste to satirical comedy and to burlesque; but all genres were affected by the drift towards bourgeois values, and the Restoration stereotype of the foolish citizen was superseded by a new image of the responsible merchant. The most important innovative force, both in dramatic criticism and in the drama itself, was the bourgeois classicism of Joseph Addison and Sir Richard Steele; and the most interesting opposition to that ideology was offered by the irascible and principled conservatism of John Dennis.

The new tragedies of the years 1708–27 are not entirely homogeneous, and they offer some interesting echoes and anticipations. Edward Young's *The Revenge* (1712) recalls *Othello* and foreshadows later Gothic plays; and in *The Distressed Mother* (1712) Ambrose Philips offers a neo-classical adaptation of Racine's *Andromaque*. Nicholas Rowe, after completing the first scholarly edition of Shakespeare, returned to the theatre with a skilful blend of Shakespearean pastiche and melodious pathos in *Jane Shore* (1714); and in the following year he reiterated his commitment to the Whig cause by celebrating a Protestant martyr in *Lady Jane Grey*. The production of Thomas Southerne's *The Spartan Dame* in 1719 reminded audiences that 'the race of Charles' reign' was not extinct; and *The Fatal Extravagance* (1721), a modernisation of *A Yorkshire Tragedy* by Aaron Hill or his protégé Joseph Mitchell, anticipated later tragedies of contemporary life.

The most important tragedy of the years 1708–27, however, was Addison's *Cato*, which was acted at Drury Lane in 1713 with Barton Booth in the central role. Writing a political play at a time of intense political conflict, Addison took some trouble to ensure that it would not be considered partisan. His own sympathies lay with the Whigs, but he consulted Henry Viscount Bolingbroke to ensure that his text was acceptable to the ministry. The prologue was supplied by a Tory poet, Alexander Pope, and the epilogue by a Whig poet, Samuel Garth. At the first performance, Whigs and Tories in the audience competed in applauding Addison's praise of liberty and virtue. There was a storm of Whig applause for the lines

> When vice prevails, and impious men bear sway,
> The post of honour is a private station;

but Bolingbroke, to show that he too endorsed Addison's principles, gave Booth a purse of fifty guineas. In a forceful and entertaining pamphlet entitled *Remarks upon Cato*, Dennis attacked the play for its neglect of poetic justice and for the absurdities produced by its adherence to the unity of place; but the high esteem in which it was held throughout the eighteenth century is demonstrated by the German adaptation of J. C. Gottsched and the resonant praise of Samuel Johnson. Later readers have found the play's characterisation unconvincing, and have reacted unfavourably to its insistent celebration of political virtue; but Addison's linguistic authority remains impressive, and the triumph of the defeated Cato over the victorious Caesar is often articulated with an epigrammatic vigour reminiscent of Lucan.

The most actable and entertaining comedies of the years 1708–27 were those of Susanna Centlivre: *The Busy Body* (1709), *The Wonder* (1714) and *A Bold Stroke for a Wife* (1718) show a mastery of theatrical technique which still evoked 'incessant peals of laughter and applause' in the age of Hazlitt. A sharper and more aggressive mode is represented by two plays acted at Drury Lane in 1717, the Gay-Pope-Arbuthnot comedy *Three Hours after Marriage* and Cibber's adaptation of Molière's *Tartuffe* under the title *The Non-Juror*. More typical of the age were a number of plays which innocently continued the Farquhar tradition of provincial comedy: these included Charles Shadwell's *The Fair Quaker of Deal* (1710), Charles Johnson's *The Country Lasses* (1715), John Gay's 'tragi-comipastoral farce' *The What D'Ye Call It* (1715), and Addison's country-house comedy *The Drummer* (1716), which was adapted in both France and Germany. A more distinctive brand of rural drama appeared in Allan Ramsay's Scots pastoral comedy *The Gentle Shepherd* (published 1725).

The most ambitious comedy of the years 1708–27, however, was Steele's *The Conscious Lovers*, whose production at Drury Lane in 1722 occasioned an important critical debate. The social and cultural ideal embodied in Steele's play is concisely stated in Leonard Welsted's prologue, which expresses the hope that its success will 'Chasten Wit, and Moralize the Stage'. In transposing the *Andria* of Terence to contemporary London, Steele employs some of the standard devices of English intrigue comedy; but his reformist purpose ensures that even the back-chat among the servants is governed by notions of loyalty and propriety. He also exploits the Terentian plot to make two specific points about contemporary society: that the merchant class deserves as much respect as the landed aristocracy, and that the practice of duelling is uncivilised and morally indefensible. Steele's celebration of the humane wisdom which transcends stock responses is conveyed not only by his handling of these topical issues but also by his refashioning of an archetypal New Comedy motif in Act v Scene 3: it is the exercise of such wisdom by Sealand and Indiana that allows their relationship to emerge and thus makes the play's happy ending possible. Steele's associates saw *The Conscious Lovers* as the model for a reformation of comic drama, and their arguments provoked Dennis to vigorous dissent. In *A Defence of Sir Fopling Flutter* he sought to refute Steele's condemnation of Etherege, and in a hostile analysis of *The Conscious Lovers* he brought classical principles to bear on the reformist ideal. This argument between Dennis and Steele reflects an early phase in the eighteenth-century controversy between advocates of satirical comedy, which shows faults to be avoided, and advocates of sentimental comedy, which offers models for imitation.

The production of *The Beggar's Opera* at Lincoln's Inn Fields in 1728 initiated a period of confusion and innovation in the London theatre, and this lasted until the passing of Sir Robert Walpole's Licensing Act in 1737. Theatrical history in these years was closely involved with the propaganda battle between the Walpole regime and the 'patriotic' opposition: Gay's Macheath and Peachum were seen as caricatures of the 'Great Man', and Fielding's burlesques contained much anti-Government satire. Profits from ballad-opera and pantomime allowed the Lincoln's Inn Fields company to move in 1732 to a new theatre in Covent Garden; and the supremacy of Drury Lane was further challenged by unorthodox productions at the Little Theatre in the Haymarket. The conventions of Williamite comedy reasserted themselves in Cibber's *The Provoked Husband* (1728), a lively and intelligent play based on Vanbrugh's fragment *A Journey to London*; but, with that exception, the significant works of 1728–37 were in unconventional modes such as the ballad-opera, the theatrical burlesque and the bourgeois tragedy.

The Beggar's Opera, like *Gulliver's Travels* and *The Dunciad*, is a characteristic product of the Scriblerus Club; and one sees its mode of operation most clearly if one takes it in this context, exploring a network of implied comparisons such as one finds in Swift or Pope. It was Swift who suggested that Gay write a 'Newgate pastoral', thus combining the town pastoral and burlesque pastoral, which were among the new forms of the day. *The Beggar's Opera*, though far removed from eclogue, uses the pastoral method of oblique reference from one social world to another; and the incongruity of subject and form suggested by Swift's phrase is enforced by the linking of opera, which at this date involved legendary characters and an elevated tone, with the world of London's prisons and taverns. The version of opera which Gay invented replaces recitative with naturalistic prose and original arias with new words for well-known melodies; and this creates additional openings for ironic cross-reference, since Gay's lyrics are often ludicrously different from those familiar to the audience. Such incongruity is an important part of the dramatic effect when Macheath voices his delicate sentiments about womankind to the tune of a notoriously bawdy song, and when the highwaymen set off for the heath to the tune of a march from Handel's *Rinaldo*.

Gay's burlesque-allusive technique can be seen at its richest in the opera's central event, the arrest of Macheath. Coming after the satirical treatment of Peachum in the first act and the celebration of Macheath in the second, this arrest is clearly an emblem of heroic-romantic civilisation's defeat by market forces. It is a tragic event, but it is seen in burlesque terms, and Macheath's response to it is both noble and grotesque: 'Was this well done, Jenny? – Women are decoy Ducks; who can trust them! Beasts, Jades, Jilts, Harpies, Furies, Whores!' Cleopatra is there, of course; and so is the ranting warrior of heroic tragedy. The sequence of abusive terms, in fact, is very much that of a Restoration hero – except that the last term becomes comic and negates the whole statement because in this context it is literally appropriate. The absurdity is emphasised by Peachum's comparison of Macheath to the 'greatest heroes'; but this is still a martyrdom, and the kiss of betrayal and the reference to suffering on the tree associate it (tactfully) with the archetypal martyrdom. In addition, of course, it is a historical event; and if we want a gloss on this aspect of it we can find one in Macheath's final speech in Brecht's adaptation *Die Dreigroschenoper*: 'Was ist ein Dietrich gegen eine Aktie? (What are the tools of a criminal compared with the shares of a joint-stock company?)' Peachum's parting words, which appear unaltered in the Brechtian version, make the values of the new order clear: 'Ladies, I'll take care the reckoning shall be discharged.'

The Beggar's Opera is the greatest English play of this period; but the most versatile and productive dramatist of the time was Henry Fielding. The twenty-six dramatic works which Fielding composed in the years 1730–37 include ballad-operas, comedies of manners, and adaptations of Molière; but the best of them are the Haymarket burlesques in which he satirises first the contemporary theatre and then the Walpole government. The liveliness of his theatrical satire can be seen in *The Author's Farce* (1730), which combines a personal attack on the Drury Lane management with a sardonic review of current entertainments. On 24 April 1730 this work was followed by an afterpiece entitled *Tom Thumb*; and that afterpiece was subsequently enlarged as *The Tragedy of Tragedies* and then published in 1731 with elaborate notes in the manner of Pope's *The Dunciad Variorum*. Uniting the burlesque technique of Buckingham's *The Rehearsal* and Gay's *The What D'Ye Call It* with the Scriblerian mode of satire on false learning, this work effectively ridicules both contemporary tragedy and contemporary dramatic criticism. Fielding's talent for ridicule was deployed no less skilfully in the two political satires, *Pasquin* and *The Historical Register*, which he produced at the Little Theatre in the Haymarket in 1736–7; but the attacks on Walpole in these plays helped to provoke the 1737 Licensing Act, which brought Fielding's theatrical career to a premature end.

Many dramatists wrote ballad-operas in imitation of Gay, and among them was a London goldsmith named George Lillo. Lillo's ballad-opera was not a success, but he followed it in 1731 with a prose tragedy entitled *The London Merchant, or The History of George Barnwell*. Because this play was based on a popular ballad, the first-night audience came to Drury Lane prepared to laugh. 'Many gaily-disposed spirits brought the ballad with them ... intending to make ... ludicrous comparisons between the ancient ditty and the modern play .... But the play spoke so much to the heart, that ... they were drawn in to drop their ballads, and pull out their handkerchiefs.' Lillo's play, although conceived as a tragedy, was cast entirely in prose; and its central character, George Barnwell, was a London apprentice. It thus constituted a radical departure from the orthodox procedures of neo-classical tragedy; but it is not

a merely eccentric work, since it has important links both with
the sixteenth century and with the nineteenth. Lillo's knowledge
of Elizabethan literature was extensive, and in this play he
manifests it both through his choice of subject and through his
dramatic techniques. By temperament and social background,
he was well qualified to respond to such domestic dramas as
Arden of Faversham and *A Woman Killed with Kindness*; and
his desire to emulate them not only made him reject the currently
accepted principles of dramatic art but also led him towards a
new conception of tragedy. That conception was very different
from Addison's, and at a deeper level than that of articulated
theory it was more consonant with the spirit of the age. *The
London Merchant* deals in sober and sententious terms with the
career of an Elizabethan apprentice who is tempted first to fraud
and then to murder by his association with a harlot. It is marred
by frequent *longueurs* and by a tendency to moralistic rant, but
it differs from most eighteenth-century tragedies in being genu-
inely tragic and not merely pathetic or sensational. It remained
popular in the London theatre for many years, and by its impact
on Denis Diderot and Gotthold Lessing it affected the sub-
sequent development of European drama. Lillo's other plays
were less influential, but his later domestic tragedy *Fatal Curiosity*, acted at the Little Theatre in 1736, rivals *The London
Merchant* in emotional power.

Walpole's Licensing Act of 1737 established the patent theatres
of Drury Lane and Covent Garden as the only centres of
dramatic production in London; and it thus inaugurated a new
age of theatrical prosperity and dramatic mediocrity which was
to last for some thirty years. From 1738 to 1767 theatrical
audiences were less interested in new plays than in new productions of Shakespeare; and from 1741 onwards the prestige of
living dramatists was overshadowed by that of the actor David
Garrick. The authority of the patentees seems to have discour-
aged experimental writing; and the principal genres cultivated
were thus the blank-verse tragedy, the sentimentalised comedy
of manners, the comic opera which developed out of ballad-
opera, and the farcical or satirical afterpiece.

The most interesting new tragedies performed during the age
of Garrick were Edward Moore's *The Gamester* (1753), a
bourgeois drama in the manner of Lillo, and John Home's

Douglas (1757), which dramatised a ballad narrative and was first acted in Edinburgh. The new comedies of this period show little originality or individuality, but the best of them offer agreeable entertainment in a genteel and inoffensive mode. Benjamin Hoadly in *The Suspicious Husband* (1747) effected a skilful blend of libertinism and moral sentiment. Arthur Murphy in *The Way to Keep Him* (1760) offered a mildly amusing variation on the reformed-husband theme. George Colman in *The Jealous Wife* (1761) combined a drama of marital reconciliation with characters and plot-motifs from *Tom Jones*. Colman again, with some assistance from Garrick, offered in *The Clandestine Marriage* (1766) a genial picture of class hostility between an impoverished aristocrat and a wealthy bourgeois. There is even less substance in the comic operas of these years; but Isaac Bickerstaffe achieved a box-office triumph with *Love in a Village* (1762), a pleasantly escapist piece about the adventures of two young couples in the house of a country justice. The farcical and satirical elements of classical comedy maintained a precarious existence in the afterpiece: Murphy's *The Upholsterer* (1758) presented a man obsessively interested in newspapers, and Colman's *Polly Honeycombe* (1760) a girl obsessively interested in romantic fiction. In such works as *The Commissary* (1765) the accomplished mimic Samuel Foote used the afterpiece as a vehicle for satire on individuals.

Garrick's influence continued to dominate the theatrical world until his retirement in 1776, but from 1768 onwards the uncreative consensus of the mid-century was broken by a significant renewal of critical controversy and dramatic experiment. English tragedy remained comatose, and there was no major development either in comic opera or in the afterpiece; but the genteel mediocrity of the sentimentalised comedy of manners was disrupted in January 1768, when Hugh Kelly's sentimental comedy *False Delicacy* was performed at Drury Lane and Oliver Goldsmith's laughing comedy *The Good-Natured Man* was performed at Covent Garden. Although these works have many features in common, their authors' programmatic statements reveal a marked difference of intention: whereas a sympathetic character in Kelly's play declares that 'the stage should be a school of morality', Goldsmith's preface condemns 'genteel comedy' and affirms the dramatist's right to explore 'the recesses of the mean'.

The sentimental mode was further developed in Richard Cumberland's *The West Indian* (1771), which used the imprudent-hero motif with some inventiveness to criticise theatrically traditional assumptions about national character. The reaction against sentimentalism was encouraged by Voltaire's attack on the *comédie larmoyante* and by Samuel Foote's satirical 'puppet show' *The Handsome Housemaid*; and in 1773 Goldsmith published in the *Westminster Magazine* an 'Essay on the Theatre' subtitled 'A Comparison between Laughing and Sentimental Comedy'. Condemning sentimental comedy as a 'new species of Dramatic Composition' which seeks rather to exhibit virtues than to expose vices, this essay reaffirms classical generic principles by stressing the importance of laughter in comic drama. The implied standard is the comedy of the Williamite period, and especially the work of Farquhar.

The ideal propounded in this essay was largely realised in Goldsmith's second comedy *She Stoops to Conquer*, which was acted at Covent Garden in 1773. The heroine compares her plain dress with that of Cherry in *The Beaux' Stratagem*, and the two plays have many features in common: a rural world in which the main centres are the inn and the great house, two young men who have come down from London in search of wives, two plots kept going by the sustained invention of plausible absurdities, fantastic situations made comically real by naturalistic characterisation and exuberantly colloquial speech. Within the decorum of laughing comedy the parallel love stories of Goldsmith's play explore the unsettling complexities of sexual feeling as it interacts with money and with class; and in this context the erotic psychology echoes not only Farquhar but also Pierre de Marivaux. Even more than *The Beaux' Stratagem*, however, this is a comic celebration of rural England, a revivification of polite society by rustic energy: it is Tony Lumpkin, the central figure of Goldsmith's admirably planned double plot, who first initiates the deception which heals Marlow's split personality and then manages the midnight journey which earns Hastings his bride and her fortune.

Goldsmith's campaign against sentimentalism was continued by Richard Brinsley Sheridan, whose theatrical career began in 1775 with the production of *The Rivals* at Covent Garden. This notably stylish and conservative play, which originated as an afterpiece mocking sentimental fiction, combined a drama of duels and elopements set in contemporary Bath with an anti-romantic subplot attacking sentimental comedy. It was followed in the same year by an elegant but insubstantial comic opera entitled *The Duenna*, which achieved an unprecedented run of seventy-five nights. These successes enabled Sheridan to succeed Garrick in 1776 as manager of Drury Lane, and in that capacity he produced modified versions of two comedies by Congreve and one by Vanbrugh. The inspiration of Congreve in particular is manifest in Sheridan's brand of anti-sentimental drama, which aspires not to the Goldsmithian ideals of 'nature and humour' but rather to a sophisticated mastery of plot-construction, dialogue and stagecraft.

The School for Scandal, which was acted at Drury Lane in 1777, was the most accomplished comedy written in English since Congreve's *The Way of the World*. The topical subject of slanderous journalism had already been explored in plays by Colman and Foote, but Sheridan's invention of a full-scale 'scandalous college' under the presidency of Lady Sneerwell adds an ominous note of surrealistic nightmare. Besides functioning as an Aristophanic animal chorus, the slanderers infiltrate the human world of two traditional plots which Sheridan has refashioned in contemporary terms. The sentimental-comedy motif of marital conflict and reconciliation is sharpened by echoes of Wycherley, and acquires an extra dimension through Lady Teazle's entry into and withdrawal from the college. Insights from *Tom Jones* enrich the Terentian contest between the Surface brothers for the love of Maria and the money of Sir Oliver; and Sheridan complicates this opposition by making Joseph a hypocritical dispenser of moral platitudes and Charles an extravagant libertine with a heart of gold. As the sentimental hero is at last rewarded thanks to the approval of the *deus ex machina*, so the sentimental villain is ultimately destroyed by his association with the slanderers. The play's intricate plot is realised in superbly theatrical terms, the double-disguise motif opening the way for the drinking scene and the auction of family portraits. In Act IV Scene 3, when a doubling of the interruption-concealment-exposure pattern has enlightened the Teazles about the true characters of the brothers, the breakthrough from deception to reality is magnificently symbolised in the collapse of the screen.

The first production of *The School for Scandal* was greeted by

Horace Walpole as 'a marvellous resurrection of the stage', but in reality it heralded a period of decline in English dramatic literature. In 1779 Sheridan produced a hilarious burlesque drama entitled *The Critic*, in which he satirised Richard Cumberland and ridiculed the patriotic spectacles being performed at Sadler's Wells; but in 1780 he entered Parliament, and thereafter most of his energies were devoted to oratory and politics. Over the following half-century the social context of English drama was rapidly transformed by the expansion of London, the rebuilding of the patent theatres, the proliferation of minor and suburban theatres, the spread of democratic sentiment, and the growing appetite for Gothic sensation. Similar developments in other countries evoked a new productive relationship between literature and the theatre; but their immediate consequence in England was a dissociation of literary and theatrical talent which took many years to heal.

DAVID W. LINDSAY

DAVID W. LINDSAY was born in Dunfermline in 1936, and was educated at schools in Cupar and at the Universities of Edinburgh and Aberdeen. He has taught in the University of Aberdeen and the Queen's University of Belfast, and since 1966 has been a member of the English Department at the University of Wales, Bangor. His academic interests include Middle Scots poetry, eighteenth-century poetry and drama, German influences in Scottish literature, the literary and artistic work of William Blake, and modern African literature. He is married to an economic historian, and has two grown-up children now living in Londonderry and in Hungary.

CATO

Prologue

BY MR POPE

Spoken by Mr Wilks.

To wake the soul by tender strokes of art,
To raise the genius, and to mend the heart,
To make mankind in conscious virtue bold,
Live o'er each scene, and be what they behold:
For this the Tragic Muse first trod the stage,
Commanding tears to stream thro' every age;
Tyrants no more their savage nature kept,
And foes to virtue wondered how they wept.
Our author shuns by vulgar springs to move,
The hero's glory, or the virgin's love;
In pitying love we but our weakness show,
And wild ambition well deserves its woe.
Here tears shall flow from a more gen'rous cause,
Such tears as patriots shed for dying laws:
He bids your breasts with ancient ardour rise,
And calls forth Roman drops from British eyes.
Virtue confessed in human shape he draws,
What Plato thought, and godlike Cato was:
No common object to your sight displays,
But what with pleasure Heav'n itself surveys;
A brave man struggling in the storms of fate
And greatly falling with a falling state!
While Cato gives his little Senate laws,
What bosom beats not in his country's cause?
Who sees him act, but envies ev'ry deed?
Who hears him groan, and does not wish to bleed?
Ev'n when proud Cæsar 'midst triumphal cars,
The spoils of nations, and the pomp of wars,

Ignobly vain, and impotently great,
Showed Rome her Cato's figure drawn in state;
As her dead father's rev'rend image passed
The pomp was darkened and the day o'ercast,
The triumph ceased – tears gushed from ev'ry eye;
The world's great victor passed unheeded by;
Her last good man dejected Rome adored,
And honoured Cæsar's less than Cato's sword.
Britons, attend; be worth like this approved,
And show you have the virtue to be moved.
With honest scorn the first famed Cato viewed
Rome learning arts from Greece, whom she subdued;
Our scene precariously subsists too long
On French translation, and Italian song.
Dare to have sense yourselves; assert the stage,
Be justly warmed with your own native rage.
Such plays alone should please a British ear,
As Cato's self had not disdained to hear.

Dramatis Personæ

MEN

CATO	Mr Booth
LUCIUS, *a senator*	Mr Keen
SEMPRONIUS, *a senator*	Mr Mills
JUBA, *Prince of Numidia*	Mr Wilks
SYPHAX, *General of the Numidians*	Mr Cibber
PORTIUS } *sons of Cato* {	Mr Powell
MARCUS	Mr Ryan
DECIUS, *Ambassador from Cæsar*	Mr Bowman

Mutineers, Guards, etc.

WOMEN

MARCIA, *daughter to Cato*	Mrs Oldfield
LUCIA, *daughter to Lucius*	Mrs Porter

SCENE

A large hall in the Governor's Palace of Utica.

It will be noted that the first edition, which is followed here, abandons the French method of scene-division after Act I.

CATO

Act I

SCENE I

Portius, Marcus.

PORTIUS The dawn is overcast, the morning lowers,
    And heavily in clouds brings on the day,
    The great, the important day, big with the fate
    Of Cato and of Rome. Our father's death
    Would fill up all the guilt of civil war,
    And close the scene of blood. Already Cæsar
    Has ravaged more than half the globe, and sees
    Mankind grown thin by his destructive sword:
    Should he go further, numbers would be wanting
    To form new battles, and support his crimes.
    Ye gods, what havoc does ambition make
    Among your works!
MARCUS   Thy steady temper, Portius,
    Can look on guilt, rebellion, fraud, and Cæsar,
    In the calm lights of mild philosophy;
    I'm tortured, even to madness, when I think
    On the proud victor – ev'ry time he's named
    Pharsalia rises to my view! – I see
    The insulting tyrant, prancing o'er the field,
    Strewed with Rome's citizens, and drenched in slaughter;
    His horse's hoofs wet with patrician blood!
    Oh, Portius! is there not some chosen curse,
    Some hidden thunder in the stores of Heaven,
    Red with uncommon wrath, to blast the man,
    Who owes his greatness to his country's ruin?
PORTIUS Believe me, Marcus, 'tis an impious greatness,
    And mixed with too much horror to be envied:
    How does the lustre of our father's actions,

Through the dark cloud of ills that cover him,
Break out, and burn with more triumphant brightness!
His sufferings shine, and spread a glory round him;
Greatly unfortunate, he fights the cause
Of honour, virtue, liberty, and Rome.
His sword ne'er fell, but on the guilty head;
Oppression, tyranny, and power usurped,
Draw all the vengeance of his arm upon 'em.

MARCUS Who knows not this? But what can Cato do
Against a world, a base, degenerate world,
That courts the yoke, and bows the neck to Cæsar?
Pent up in Utica, he vainly forms
A poor epitome of Roman greatness,
And, covered with Numidian guards, directs
A feeble army, and an empty senate,
Remnants of mighty battles fought in vain.
By Heaven, such virtue, joined with such success,
Distract my very soul! our father's fortune
Would almost tempt us to renounce his precepts.

PORTIUS Remember what our father oft has told us!
The ways of Heaven are dark and intricate,
Puzzled in mazes, and perplexed with errors,
Our understanding traces them in vain,
Lost and bewildered in the fruitless search;
Nor sees with how much art the windings run,
Nor where the regular confusion ends.

MARCUS These are suggestions of a mind at ease:
Oh, Portius, didst thou taste but half the griefs
That wring my soul, thou couldst not talk thus coldly.
Passion unpitied, and successless love,
Plant daggers in my heart, and aggravate
My other griefs. — Were but my Lucia kind —

PORTIUS Thou seest not that thy brother is thy rival;
But I must hide it, for I know thy temper.   *Aside.*
Now, Marcus, now, thy virtue's on the proof;
Put forth thy utmost strength, work every nerve
And call up all thy father in thy soul:
To quell the tyrant Love, and guard thy heart
On this weak side, where most our nature fails,
Would be a conquest worthy Cato's son.

MARCUS Portius, the counsel which I cannot take,

Instead of healing, but upbraids my weakness.
Bid me for honour plunge into a war
Of thickest foes, and rush on certain death,
Then shalt thou see that Marcus is not slow
To follow glory, and confess his father.
Love is not to be reasoned down, or lost
In high ambition, in a thirst for greatness;
'Tis second life, it grows into the soul,
Warms every vein and beats in every pulse;
I feel it here, my resolution melts –

PORTIUS Behold young Juba, the Numidian prince,
    With how much care he forms himself to glory,
    And breaks the fierceness of his native temper,
    To copy out our father's bright example.
    He loves our sister Marcia, greatly loves her;
    His eyes, his looks, his actions, all betray it;
    But still the smothered fondness burns within him;
    When most it swells, and labours for a vent,
    The sense of honour, and desire of fame,
    Drive the big passion back into his heart.
    What! shall an African, shall Juba's heir
    Reproach great Cato's son, and show the world
    A virtue wanting in a Roman soul?

MARCUS Portius, no more! your words leave stings behind
    them.
    Whene'er did Juba, or did Portius, show
    A virtue that has cast me at a distance,
    And thrown me out in the pursuits of honour?

PORTIUS Marcus, I know thy gen'rous temper well;
    Fling but the appearance of dishonour on it,
    It straight takes fire, and mounts into a blaze.

MARCUS A brother's sufferings claim a brother's pity.

PORTIUS Heaven knows, I pity thee. Behold my eyes,
    Ev'n whilst I speak – do they not swim in tears?
    Were but my heart as naked to thy view,
    Marcus would see it bleed in his behalf.

MARCUS Why then dost treat me with rebukes, instead
    Of kind condoling cares, and friendly sorrow?

PORTIUS Oh, Marcus! did I know the way to ease
    Thy troubled heart, and mitigate thy pains,
    Marcus, believe me, I could die to do it.

MARCUS Thou best of brothers, and thou best of friends!
Pardon a weak, distempered soul, that swells
With sudden gusts, and sinks as soon in calms,
The sport of passions. But Sempronius comes:
He must not find this softness hanging on me.   *Exit.*

SCENE 2

Sempronius solus.

SEMPRONIUS Conspiracies no sooner should be formed
Than executed. What means Portius here?
I like not that cold youth. I must dissemble,
And speak a language foreign to my heart.

Sempronius, Portius.

Good morrow, Portius; let us once embrace,
Once more embrace, while yet we both are free.
To-morrow, should we thus express our friendship,
Each might receive a slave into his arms.
This sun, perhaps, this morning sun's the last
That e'er shall rise on Roman liberty.
PORTIUS My father has this morning call'd together
To this poor hall, his little Roman senate,
(The leavings of Pharsalia) to consult
If yet he can oppose the mighty torrent
That bears down Rome, and all her gods before it,
Or must at length give up the world to Cæsar.
SEMPRONIUS Not all this pomp and majesty of Rome
Can raise her senate more than Cato's presence.
His virtues render our assembly awful,
They strike with something like religious fear,
And make even Cæsar tremble at the head
Of armies flushed with conquest. Oh, my Portius!
Could I but call that wondrous man my father,
Would but thy sister Marcia be propitious
To thy friend's vows, I might be blest indeed!
PORTIUS Alas, Sempronius! wouldst thou talk of love
To Marcia, whilst her father's life's in danger;
Thou mightst as well court the pale, trembling vestal,
When she beholds the holy flame expiring.

SEMPRONIUS The more I see the wonders of thy race,
  The more I'm charmed. Thou must take heed, my Portius;
  The world has all its eyes on Cato's son;
  Thy father's merit sets thee up to view,
  And shows thee in the fairest point of light,
  To make thy virtues or thy faults conspicuous.
PORTIUS Well dost thou seem to check my lingering here
  On this important hour – I'll straight away,
  And while the fathers of the senate meet
  In close debate, to weigh the events of war,
  I'll animate the soldiers' drooping courage
  With love of freedom, and contempt of life;
  I'll thunder in their ears their country's cause,
  And try to rouse up all that's Roman in them.
  'Tis not in mortals to command success,
  But we'll do more, Sempronius, we'll deserve it.   *Exit.*
SEMPRONIUS (*Solus.*) Curse on the stripling! how he apes his
      sire!
  Ambitiously sententious – But I wonder
  Old Syphax comes not; his Numidian genius
  Is well disposed to mischief, were he prompt
  And eager on it; but he must be spurred,
  And every moment quickened to the course.
  Cato has used me ill; he has refused
  His daughter Marcia to my ardent vows.
  Besides, his baffled arms, and ruined cause,
  Are bars to my ambition. Cæsar's favour,
  That showers down greatness on his friends, will raise me
  To Rome's first honours. If I give up Cato,
  I claim, in my reward, his captive daughter.
  But Syphax comes –

SCENE 3

Syphax, Sempronius.

SYPHAX Sempronius, all is ready;
  I've sounded my Numidians, man by man,
  And find them ripe for a revolt: they all
  Complain aloud of Cato's discipline,
  And wait but the command to change their master.

SEMPRONIUS Believe me, Syphax, there's no time to waste;
　Ev'n whilst we speak, our conqueror comes on,
　And gathers ground upon us every moment.
　Alas! thou know'st not Cæsar's active soul,
　With what a dreadful course he rushes on
　From war to war. In vain has nature formed
　Mountains and oceans to oppose his passage;
　He bounds o'er all, victorious in his march,
　The Alps and Pyreneans sink before him;
　Through winds and waves and storms he works his way
　Impatient for the battle: one day more
　Will set the victor thundering at our gates.
　But tell me, hast thou yet drawn o'er young Juba?
　That still would recommend thee more to Cæsar,
　And challenge better terms.

SYPHAX　　　　　　　Alas! he's lost!
　He's lost, Sempronius; all his thoughts are full
　Of Cato's virtues. But I'll try once more
　(For every instant I expect him here)
　If yet I can subdue those stubborn principles
　Of faith and honour, and I know not what,
　That have corrupted his Numidian temper,
　And struck the infection into all his soul.

SEMPRONIUS Be sure to press upon him every motive.
　Juba's surrender, since his father's death,
　Would give up Afric into Cæsar's hands,
　And make him lord of half the burning zone.

SYPHAX But is it true, Sempronius, that your senate
　Is called together? Gods! thou must be cautious;
　Cato has piercing eyes, and will discern
　Our frauds, unless they're covered thick with art.

SEMPRONIUS Let me alone, good Syphax; I'll conceal
　My thoughts in passion ('tis the surest way);
　I'll bellow out for Rome, and for my country,
　And mouth at Cæsar, till I shake the senate.
　Your cold hypocrisy's a stale device,
　A worn-out trick: would'st thou be thought in earnest,
　Clothe thy feign'd zeal in rage, in fire, in fury!

SYPHAX In troth, thou'rt able to instruct grey hairs,
　And teach the wily African deceit.

SEMPRONIUS Once more be sure to try thy skill on Juba.

Meanwhile I'll hasten to my Roman soldiers,
Inflame the mutiny, and underhand
Blow up their discontents, till they break out
Unlooked for, and discharge themselves on Cato.
Remember, Syphax, we must work in haste;
Oh, think what anxious moments pass between
The birth of plots, and their last fatal periods!
Oh, 'tis a dreadful interval of time,
Fill'd up with horror all, and big with death!
Destruction hangs on every word we speak,
On every thought, till the concluding stroke
Determines all, and closes our design.   *Exit.*

SYPHAX (*Solus.*) I'll try if yet I can reduce to reason
This headstrong youth, and make him spurn at Cato.
The time is short; Cæsar comes rushing on us –
But hold! young Juba sees me, and approaches!

SCENE 4

Juba, Syphax.

JUBA Syphax, I joy to meet thee thus alone.
I have observed of late thy looks are fall'n,
O'ercast with gloomy cares and discontent;
Then tell me, Syphax, I conjure thee, tell me,
What are the thoughts that knit thy brow in frowns,
And turn thine eye thus coldly on thy prince?

SYPHAX 'Tis not my talent to conceal my thoughts,
Or carry smiles and sunshines in my face,
When discontent sits heavy at my heart:
I have not yet so much the Roman in me.

JUBA Why dost thou cast out such ungenerous terms
Against the lords and sovereigns of the world?
Dost thou not see mankind fall down before them,
And own the force of their superior virtue?
Is there a nation in the wilds of Afric,
Amidst our barren rocks, and burning sands,
That does not tremble at the Roman name?

SYPHAX Gods! where's the worth that sets this people up
Above your own Numidia's tawny sons?
Do they with tougher sinews bend the bow?

Or flies the javelin swifter to its mark,
Launched from the vigour of a Roman arm?
Who like our active African instructs
The fiery steed, and trains him to his hand?
Or guides in troops the embattled elephant
Loaden with war? These, these are arts, my prince,
In which your Zama does not stoop to Rome.

JUBA These are all virtues of a meaner rank:
Perfections that are placed in bones and nerves.
A Roman soul is bent on higher views:
To civilise the rude unpolished world,
And lay it under the restraint of laws;
To make man mild and sociable to man;
To cultivate the wild licentious savage
With wisdom, discipline, and liberal arts —
The embellishments of life; virtues like these
Make human nature shine, reform the soul,
And break our fierce barbarians into men.

SYPHAX Patience, kind heavens! — excuse an old man's
    warmth,
What are these wondrous civilising arts,
This Roman polish, and this smooth behaviour,
That render man thus tractable and tame?
Are they not wholly to disguise our passions,
To set our looks at variance with our thoughts,
To check the starts and sallies of the soul,
And break off all its commerce with the tongue;
In short, to change us into other creatures
Than what our nature and the gods designed us?

JUBA To strike thee dumb, turn up thy eyes to Cato!
There mayest thou see to what a godlike height
The Roman virtues lift up mortal man,
While good, and just, and anxious for his friends,
He's still severely bent against himself;
Renouncing sleep, and rest, and food, and ease,
He strives with thirst and hunger, toil and heat;
And when his fortune sets before him all
The pomps and pleasures that his soul can wish,
His rigid virtue will accept of none.

SYPHAX Believe me, Prince, there's not an African
That traverses our vast Numidian deserts

In quest of prey, and lives upon his bow,
But better practises those boasted virtues.
Coarse are his meals, the fortune of the chase;
Amidst the running stream he slakes his thirst;
Toils all the day, and at the approach of night,
On the first friendly bank he throws him down,
Or rests his head upon a rock till morn;
Then rises fresh, pursues his wonted game,
And if the following day he chance to find
A new repast, or an untasted spring,
Blesses his stars, and thinks it luxury.

JUBA Thy prejudices, Syphax, won't discern
What virtues grow from ignorance and choice,
Nor how the hero differs from the brute.
But grant that others could with equal glory
Look down on pleasures, and the baits of sense;
Where shall we find the man that bears affliction,
Great and majestic in his griefs, like Cato?
Heavens, with what strength, what steadiness of mind,
He triumphs in the midst of all his sufferings!
How does he rise against a load of woes,
And thank the gods that throw the weight upon him!

SYPHAX 'Tis pride, rank pride, and haughtiness of soul;
I think the Romans call it stoicism.
Had not your royal father thought so highly
Of Roman virtue, and of Cato's cause,
He had not fallen by a slave's hand inglorious;
Nor would his slaughtered army now have lain
On Afric's sands, disfigured with their wounds,
To gorge the wolves and vultures of Numidia.

JUBA Why dost thou call my sorrows up afresh?
My father's name brings tears into my eyes.

SYPHAX O that you'd profit by your father's ills!

JUBA What wouldst thou have me do?

SYPHAX   Abandon Cato.

JUBA Syphax, I should be more than twice an orphan
By such a loss.

SYPHAX   Aye, there's the tie that binds you!
You long to call him father. Marcia's charms
Work in your heart unseen, and plead for Cato.
No wonder you are deaf to all I say.

JUBA Syphax, your zeal becomes importunate;
  I've hitherto permitted it to rave,
  And talk at large; but learn to keep it in,
  Lest it should take more freedom than I'll give it.
SYPHAX Sir, your great father never used me thus.
  Alas, he's dead! but can you e'er forget
  The tender sorrows, and the pangs of nature,
  The fond embraces, and repeated blessings
  Which you drew from him in your last farewell?
  Still must I cherish the dear sad remembrance,
  At once to torture and to please my soul.
  The good old king, at parting, wrung my hand
  (His eyes brimful of tears), then sighing cried,
  Prithee be careful of my son! – His grief
  Swelled up so high, he could not utter more.
JUBA Alas! thy story melts away my soul!
  That best of fathers! how shall I discharge
  The gratitude and duty which I owe him?
SYPHAX By laying up his counsels in your heart.
JUBA His counsels bade me yield to thy directions:
  Then, Syphax, chide me in severest terms,
  Vent all thy passion, and I'll stand its shock,
  Calm and unruffled as a summer sea,
  When not a breath of wind flies o'er its surface.
SYPHAX Alas! my prince, I'd guide you to your safety.
JUBA I do believe thou wouldst; but tell me how?
SYPHAX Fly from the fate that follows Cæsar's foes.
JUBA My father scorn'd to do it.
SYPHAX   And therefore died.
JUBA Better to die ten thousand thousand deaths,
  Than wound my honour.
SYPHAX   Rather say, your love.
JUBA Syphax, I've promised to preserve my temper.
  Why wilt thou urge me to confess a flame
  I long have stifled, and would fain conceal?
SYPHAX Believe me, prince, 'tis hard to conquer love,
  But easy to divert and break its force.
  Absence might cure it, or a second mistress
  Light up another flame, and put out this.
  The glowing dames of Zama's royal court
  Have faces flush'd with more exalted charms;

The sun that rolls his chariot o'er their heads,
Works up more fire and colour in their cheeks:
Were you with these, my prince, you'd soon forget
The pale, unripened beauties of the north.
JUBA 'Tis not a set of features, or complexion,
The tincture of a skin, that I admire:
Beauty soon grows familiar to the lover,
Fades in his eye, and palls upon the sense.
The virtuous Marcia towers above her sex:
True, she is fair (oh, how divinely fair!),
But still the lovely maid improves her charms
With inward greatness, unaffected wisdom,
And sanctity of manners; Cato's soul
Shines out in everything she acts or speaks.
While winning mildness and attractive smiles
Dwell in her looks, and with becoming grace,
Soften the rigour of her father's virtues.
SYPHAX How does your tongue grow wanton in her praise!
But on my knees, I beg you would consider –

Enter Marcia and Lucia.

JUBA Ha! Syphax, is't not she? – She moves this way;
And with her Lucia, Lucius's fair daughter.
My heart beats thick – I prithee, Syphax, leave me.
SYPHAX Ten thousand curses fasten on them both!
Now will this woman, with a single glance,
Undo what I've been lab'ring all this while.   *Exit.*

Juba, Marcia, Lucia.

JUBA Hail, charming maid! How does thy beauty smooth
The face of war, and make even horror smile!
At sight of thee my heart shakes off its sorrows;
I feel a dawn of joy break in upon me,
And for a while forget the approach of Cæsar.
MARCIA I should be grieved, young prince, to think my
    presence
Unbent your thoughts, and slackened 'em to arms,
While, warm with slaughter, our victorious foe
Threatens aloud, and calls you to the field.
JUBA Oh, Marcia, let me hope thy kind concerns
And gentle wishes follow me to battle!

    The thought will give new vigour to my arm,
    Add strength and weight to my descending sword,
    And drive it in a tempest on the foe.
MARCIA My prayers and wishes always shall attend
    The friends of Rome, the glorious cause of virtue,
    And men approved of by the gods and Cato.
JUBA That Juba may deserve thy pious cares,
    I'll gaze for ever on thy godlike father,
    Transplanting one by one, into my life,
    His bright perfections, till I shine like him.
MARCIA My father never, at a time like this,
    Would lay out his great soul in words, and waste
    Such precious moments.
JUBA   Thy reproofs are just,
    Thou virtuous maid; I'll hasten to my troops,
    And fire their languid souls with Cato's virtue.
    If e'er I lead them to the field, when all
    The war shall stand ranged in its just array,
    And dreadful pomp, then will I think on thee;
    Oh, lovely maid! then will I think on thee;
    And in the shock of charging hosts, remember
    What glorious deeds should grace the man who hopes
    For Marcia's love.   *Exit*
LUCIA   Marcia, you're too severe;
    How could you chide the young good-natured prince,
    And drive him from you with so stern an air,
    A prince that loves, and dotes on you to death?
MARCIA 'Tis therefore, Lucia, that I chide him from me:
    His air, his voice, his looks, and honest soul,
    Speak all so movingly in his behalf,
    I dare not trust myself to hear him talk.
LUCIA Why will you fight against so sweet a passion.
    And steel your heart to such a world of charms?
MARCIA How, Lucia! wouldst thou have me sink away
    In pleasing dreams, and lose myself in love,
    When every moment Cato's life's at stake?
    Cæsar comes armed with terror and revenge,
    And aims his thunder at my father's head.
    Should not the sad occasion swallow up
    My other cares and draw them all into it?
LUCIA Why have not I this constancy of mind,

Who have so many griefs to try its force?
Sure, Nature formed me of her softest mould,
Enfeebled all my soul with tender passions,
And sunk me even below my own weak sex:
Pity and love, by turns, oppress my heart.

MARCIA Lucia, disburden all thy cares on me,
And let me share thy most retired distress.
Tell me, who raises up this conflict in thee?

LUCIA I need not blush to name them, when I tell thee
They're Marcia's brothers, and the sons of Cato.

MARCIA They both behold thee with their sister's eyes,
And often have revealed their passion to me.
But tell me whose address thou favourest most;
I long to know and yet I dread to hear it.

LUCIA Which is it Marcia wishes for?

MARCIA   For neither –
And yet for both; the youths have equal share
In Marcia's wishes, and divide their sister:
But tell me which of them is Lucia's choice.

LUCIA Marcia, they both are high in my esteem;
But in my love – why wilt thou make me name him?
Thou know'st it is a blind and foolish passion,
Pleased and disgusted with it knows not what –

MARCIA Oh, Lucia, I'm perplexed. Oh, tell me which
I must hereafter call my happy brother.

LUCIA Suppose 'twere Portius, could you blame my choice? –
Oh, Portius, thou has stolen away my soul!
With what a graceful tenderness he loves!
And breathes the softest, the sincerest vows!
Complacency, and truth, and manly sweetness
Dwell ever on his tongue and smooth his thoughts.
Marcus is over-warm, his fond complaints
Have so much earnestness and passion in them,
I hear him with a secret kind of horror,
And tremble at his vehemence of temper.

MARCIA Alas, poor youth! How canst thou throw him from
     thee?
Lucia, thou know'st not half the love he bears thee;
Whene'er he speaks of thee, his heart's in flames,
He sends out all his soul in every word,
And thinks, and talks, and looks like one transported.

Unhappy youth! How will thy coldness raise
Tempests and storms in his afflicted bosom!
I dread the consequence.

LUCIA   You seem to plead
Against your brother Portius.

MARCIA   Heaven forbid!
Had Portius been the unsuccessful lover,
The same compassion would have fallen on him.

LUCIA Was ever virgin love distressed like mine!
Portius himself oft falls in tears before me,
As if he mourned his rival's ill success;
Then bids me hide the motions of my heart,
Nor show which way it turns. So much he fears
The sad effects that it would have on Marcus.

MARCIA He knows too well how easily he's fired,
And would not plunge his brother in despair,
But waits for happier times, and kinder moments.

LUCIA Alas! Too late I find myself involved
In endless griefs and labyrinths of woe,
Born to afflict my Marcia's family,
And sow dissension in the hearts of brothers.
Tormenting thought! It cuts into my soul.

MARCIA Let us not, Lucia, aggravate our sorrows,
But to the gods permit the events of things.
Our lives, discolour'd with our present woes,
May still grow white, and smile with happier hours.

So the pure limpid stream, when foul with stains
Of rushing torrents, and descending rains,
Works itself clear, and, as it runs, refines,
Till, by degrees, the floating mirror shines,
Reflects each flower that on the border grows,
And a new heaven in its fair bosom shows.   *Exeunt.*

Act II

The Senate, sitting.

SEMPRONIUS Rome still survives in this assembled senate!
    Let us remember we are Cato's friends,
    And act like men who claim that glorious title.
LUCIUS Cato will soon be here, and open to us
    The occasion of our meeting. Hark! He comes!

                                    A sound of trumpets.

    May all the guardian gods of Rome direct him!

Enter Cato.

CATO Fathers, we once again are met in council;
    Cæsar's approach has summoned us together,
    And Rome attends her fate from our resolves.
    How shall we treat this bold aspiring man?
    Success still follows him, and backs his crimes;
    Pharsalia gave him Rome, Egypt has since
    Received his yoke, and the whole Nile is Cæsar's.
    Why should I mention Juba's overthrow,
    And Scipio's death? Numidia's burning sands
    Still smoke with blood. 'Tis time we should decree
    What course to take. Our foe advances on us,
    And envies us even Libya's sultry deserts.
    Fathers, pronounce your thoughts: are they still fixed
    To hold it out, and fight it to the last?
    Or are your hearts subdued at length, and wrought,
    By time and ill success, to a submission?
    Sempronius speak.
SEMPRONIUS   My voice is still for war.
    Gods! can a Roman senate long debate

Which of the two to choose, slavery or death!
No; let us rise at once, gird on our swords,
And, at the head of our remaining troops,
Attack the foe, break through the thick array
Of his thronged legions, and charge home upon him.
Perhaps some arm, more lucky than the rest,
May reach his heart, and free the world from bondage.
Rise, fathers, rise! 'tis Rome demands your help;
Rise, and revenge her slaughtered citizens,
Or share their fate. The corps of half her senate
Manure the fields of Thessaly, while we
Sit here, deliberating in cold debates,
If we should sacrifice our lives to honour,
Or wear them out in servitude and chains.
Rouse up, for shame! Our brothers of Pharsalia
Point at their wounds, and cry aloud — To battle!
Great Pompey's shade complains that we are slow;
And Scipio's ghost walks unrevenged amongst us.

CATO Let not a torrent of impetuous zeal
Transport thee thus beyond the bounds of reason;
True fortitude is seen in great exploits,
That justice warrants, and that wisdom guides;
All else is towering frenzy and distraction.
Are not the lives of those who draw the sword
In Rome's defence entrusted to our care?
Should we thus lead them to a field of slaughter,
Might not the impartial world with reason say
We lavished at our deaths the blood of thousands,
To grace our fall and make our ruin glorious?
Lucius, we next would know what's your opinion.

LUCIUS My thoughts, I must confess, are turned to peace.
Already have our quarrels filled the world
With widows and with orphans: Scythia mourns
Our guilty wars, and earth's remotest regions
Lie half unpeopled by the feuds of Rome:
'Tis time to sheathe the sword, and spare mankind.
It is not Cæsar, but the gods, my fathers,
The gods declare against us, and repel
Our vain attempts. To urge the foe to battle
(Prompted by blind revenge and wild despair)
Were to refuse the awards of Providence,

And not to rest in heaven's determination.
Already we have shown our love to Rome,
Now let us show submission to the gods.
We took up arms, not to revenge ourselves,
But free the commonwealth; when this end fails,
Arms have no further use. Our country's cause,
That drew our swords, now wrests them from our hands,
And bids us not delight in Roman blood,
Unprofitably shed. What men could do,
Is done already: Heaven and earth will witness,
If Rome must fall, that we are innocent.

SEMPRONIUS This smooth discourse and mild behaviour oft
Conceal a traitor – something whispers me
All is not right – Cato, beware of Lucius.   *Aside to Cato.*

CATO Let us appear nor rash nor diffident;
Immod'rate valour swells into a fault;
And fear, admitted into public councils,
Betrays like treason. Let us shun 'em both.
Fathers, I cannot see that our affairs
Are grown thus desperate: we have bulwarks round us;
Within our walls are troops inur'd to toil
In Afric's heat, and season'd to the sun;
Numidia's spacious kingdom lies behind us,
Ready to rise at its young prince's call.
While there is hope, do not distrust the gods;
But wait, at least, till Cæsar's near approach
Force us to yield. 'Twill never be too late
To sue for chains, and own a conqueror.
Why should Rome fall a moment ere her time?
No, let us draw her term of freedom out
In its full length, and spin it to the last,
So shall we gain still one day's liberty:
And let me perish, but, in Cato's judgment,
A day, an hour, of virtuous liberty
Is worth a whole eternity in bondage.

Enter Marcus.

MARCUS Fathers, this moment, as I watch'd the gate,
Lodged on my post, a herald is arrived
From Cæsar's camp, and with him comes old Decius,
The Roman knight: he carries in his looks

Impatience, and demands to speak with Cato.
CATO By your permission, fathers – bid him enter.

Exit Marcus.

Decius was once my friend, but other prospects
Have loosed those ties, and bound him fast to Cæsar.
His message may determine our resolves.

Enter Decius.

DECIUS Cæsar sends health to Cato –
CATO   Could he send it
To Cato's slaughtered friends, it would be welcome.
Are not your orders to address the senate?
DECIUS My business is with Cato; Cæsar sees
The straits to which you're driven; and, as he knows
Cato's high worth, is anxious for your life.
CATO My life is grafted on the fate of Rome.
Would he save Cato, bid him spare his country.
Tell your dictator this; and tell him, Cato
Disdains a life which he has power to offer.
DECIUS Rome and her senators submit to Cæsar;
Her gen'rals and her consuls are no more,
Who checked his conquests and denied his triumphs.
Why will not Cato be this Cæsar's friend?
CATO Those very reasons, thou hast urged, forbid it.
DECIUS Cato, I've orders to expostulate
And reason with you, as from friend to friend:
Think on the storm that gathers o'er your head,
And threatens every hour to burst upon it;
Still may you stand high in your country's honours,
Do but comply, and make your peace with Cæsar,
Rome will rejoice, and cast its eyes on Cato,
As on the second of mankind.
CATO   No more;
I must not think of life on such conditions.
DECIUS Cæsar is well acquainted with your virtues,
And therefore sets this value on your life.
Let him but know the price of Cato's friendship,
And name your terms.
CATO   Bid him disband his legions,
Restore the commonwealth to liberty,
Submit his actions to the public censure,

And stand the judgment of a Roman senate.
Bid him do this, and Cato is his friend.
DECIUS Cato, the world talks loudly of your wisdom –
CATO Nay, more, though Cato's voice was ne'er employed
To clear the guilty, and to varnish crimes,
Myself will mount the rostrum in his favour,
And strive to gain his pardon from the people.
DECIUS A style like this becomes a conqueror.
CATO Decius, a style like this becomes a Roman.
DECIUS What is a Roman, that is Cæsar's foe?
CATO Greater than Cæsar: he's a friend to virtue.
DECIUS Consider, Cato, you're in Utica,
And at the head of your own little senate:
You don't now thunder in the Capitol,
With all the mouths of Rome to second you.
CATO Let him consider that, who drives us hither.
'Tis Cæsar's sword has made Rome's senate little,
And thinn'd its ranks. Alas! thy dazzled eye
Beholds this man in a false glaring light,
Which conquest and success have thrown upon him;
Didst thou but view him right, thou'dst see him black
With murder, treason, sacrilege, and crimes,
That strike my soul with horror but to name 'em.
I know thou lookst on me as on a wretch
Beset with ills, and covered with misfortunes;
But, by the gods I swear, millions of worlds
Should never buy me to be like that Cæsar.
DECIUS Does Cato send this answer back to Cæsar,
For all his gen'rous cares and proffer'd friendship?
CATO His cares for me are insolent and vain:
Presumptuous man! the gods take care of Cato.
Would Cæsar show the greatness of his soul,
Bid him employ his care for these my friends,
And make good use of his ill-gotten power,
By sheltering men much better than himself.
DECIUS Your high, unconquered heart makes you forget
You are a man. You rush on your destruction.
But I have done. When I relate hereafter
The tale of this unhappy embassy,
All Rome will be in tears.   *Exit*.
SEMPRONIUS   Cato, we thank thee.

The mighty genius of immortal Rome
Speaks in thy voice; thy soul breathes liberty.
Cæsar will shrink to hear the words thou utterest,
And shudder in the midst of all his conquests.

LUCIUS The senate owes its gratitude to Cato,
Who with so great a soul consults its safety,
And guards our lives, while he neglects his own.

SEMPRONIUS Sempronius gives no thanks on this account.
Lucius seems fond of life; but what is life?
'Tis not to stalk about, and draw fresh air
From time to time, or gaze upon the sun;
'Tis to be free. When liberty is gone,
Life grows insipid, and has lost its relish.
Oh, could my dying hand but lodge a sword
In Cæsar's bosom, and revenge my country,
By heavens, I could enjoy the pangs of death,
And smile in agony.

LUCIUS   Others perhaps
May serve their country with as warm a zeal,
Though 'tis not kindled into so much rage.

SEMPRONIUS This sober conduct is a mighty virtue
In lukewarm patriots.

CATO   Come! no more, Sempronius.
All here are friends to Rome, and to each other.
Let us not weaken still the weaker side
By our divisions.

SEMPRONIUS   Cato, my resentments
Are sacrificed to Rome – I stand reproved.

CATO Fathers, 'tis time you come to a resolve.

LUCIUS Cato, we all go in to your opinion;
Cæsar's behaviour has convinced the senate,
We ought to hold it out till terms arrive.

SEMPRONIUS We ought to hold it out till death; but, Cato,
My private voice is drowned amid the senate's.

CATO Then let us rise, my friends, and strive to fill
This little interval, this pause of life
(While yet our liberty and fates are doubtful),
With resolution, friendship, Roman bravery,
And all the virtues we can crowd into it;
That Heaven may say, it ought to be prolonged.
Fathers, farewell – the young Numidian prince

Comes forward, and expects to know our counsels.
                                        Exeunt Senators.

                    Enter Juba.

CATO Juba, the Roman senate has resolved,
    Till time give better prospects, still to keep
    The sword unsheathed, and turn its edge on Cæsar.
JUBA The resolution fits a Roman senate.
    But, Cato, lend me for a while thy patience,
    And condescend to hear a young man speak.
    My father, when, some days before his death,
    He ordered me to march for Utica
    (Alas! I thought not then his death so near!),
    Wept o'er me, pressed me in his aged arms,
    And, as his griefs gave way, 'My son,' said he,
    'Whatever fortune shall befall thy father,
    Be Cato's friend; he'll train thee up to great
    And virtuous deeds; do but observe him well,
    Thou'lt shun misfortunes, or thou'lt learn to bear 'em.'
CATO Juba, thy father was a worthy prince,
    And merited, alas! a better fate;
    But Heaven thought otherwise.
JUBA   My father's fate,
    In spite of all the fortitude that shines
    Before my face, in Cato's great example,
    Subdues my soul, and fills my eyes with tears.
CATO It is an honest sorrow, and becomes thee.
JUBA My father drew respect from foreign climes!
    The kings of Afric sought him for their friend;
    Kings far remote, that rule, as fame reports,
    Behind the hidden sources of the Nile,
    In distant worlds, on t'other side the sun;
    Oft have their black ambassadors appeared,
    Loaden with gifts, and filled the courts of Zama.
CATO I am no stranger to thy father's greatness.
JUBA I would not boast the greatness of my father,
    But point out new alliances to Cato.
    Had we not better leave this Utica,
    To arm Numidia in our cause, and court
    The assistance of my father's powerful friends?
    Did they know Cato, our remotest kings

Would pour embattled multitudes about him;
Their swarthy hosts would darken all our plains,
Doubling the native horror of the war,
And making death more grim.

CATO   And canst thou think
Cato will fly before the sword of Cæsar!
Reduced, like Hannibal, to seek relief
From court to court, and wander up and down
A vagabond in Afric?

JUBA   Cato, perhaps
I'm too officious; but my forward cares
Would fain preserve a life of so much value.
My heart is wounded when I see such virtue
Afflicted by the weight of such misfortunes.

CATO Thy nobleness of soul obliges me.
But know, young prince, that valour soars above
What the world calls misfortune and affliction.
These are not ills; else would they never fall
On Heaven's first favourites, and the best of men.
The gods, in bounty, work up storms about us,
That give mankind occasion to exert
Their hidden strength, and throw out into practice
Virtues, which shun the day, and lie concealed
In the smooth seasons and the calms of life.

JUBA I'm charmed whene'er thou talk'st; I pant for virtue;
And all my soul endeavours at perfection.

CATO Dost thou love watchings, abstinence, and toil,
Laborious virtues all? Learn them from Cato:
Success and fortune must thou learn from Cæsar.

JUBA The best good fortune that can fall on Juba,
The whole success at which my heart aspires,
Depends on Cato.

CATO   What does Juba say?
Thy words confound me.

JUBA   I would fain retract them.
Give 'em me back again: they aimed at nothing.

CATO Tell me thy wish, young prince; make not my ear
A stranger to thy thoughts.

JUBA   Oh! they're extravagant;
Still let me hide them.

CATO   What can Juba ask

That Cato will refuse?
JUBA   I fear to name it.
  Marcia – inherits all her father's virtues.
CATO What wouldst thou say?
JUBA   Cato, thou hast a daughter.
CATO Adieu, young prince; I would not hear a word
  Should lessen thee in my esteem. Remember,
  The hand of fate is over us, and Heaven
  Exacts severity from all our thoughts.
  It is not now a time to talk of aught
  But chains, or conquest; liberty, or death.   *Exit.*

Enter Syphax.

SYPHAX How's this, my prince? What, covered with confusion?
  You look as if yon stern philosopher
  Had just now chid you.
JUBA   Syphax, I'm undone!
SYPHAX I know it well.
JUBA   Cato thinks meanly of me.
SYPHAX And so will all mankind.
JUBA   I've opened to him
  The weakness of my soul, my love for Marcia.
SYPHAX Cato's a proper person to entrust
  A love tale with!
JUBA   Oh, I could pierce my heart,
  My foolish heart! Was ever wretch like Juba?
SYPHAX Alas, my prince, how are you changed of late!
  I've known young Juba rise before the sun,
  To beat the thicket, where the tiger slept,
  Or seek the lion in his dreadful haunts:
  How did the colour mount into your cheeks,
  When first you roused him to the chase! I've seen you,
  Even in the Libyan dog-days, hunt him down,
  Then charge him close, provoke him to the rage
  Of fangs and claws, and stooping from your horse
  Rivet the panting savage to the ground.
JUBA   Prithee, no more.
SYPHAX How would the old king smile,
  To see you weigh the paws, when tipped with gold,
  And throw the shaggy spoils about your shoulders!
JUBA Syphax, this old man's talk, though honey flowed

In every word, would now lose all its sweetness.
Cato's displeased, and Marcia lost for ever.

SYPHAX Young prince, I yet could give you good advice;
Marcia might still be yours.

JUBA   What say'st thou, Syphax?
By heavens, thou turnest me all into attention.

SYPHAX Marcia might still be yours.

JUBA   As how, dear Syphax?

SYPHAX Juba commands Numidia's hardy troops,
Mounted on steeds unused to the restraint
Of curbs or bits, and fleeter than the winds:
Give but the word, we snatch this damsel up,
And bear her off.

JUBA   Can such dishonest thoughts
Rise up in man? Wouldst thou seduce my youth
To do an act that would destroy mine honour?

SYPHAX Gods, I could tear my beard to hear you talk!
Honour's a fine imaginary notion,
That draws in raw and inexperienced men
To real mischiefs, while they hunt a shadow.

JUBA Wouldst thou degrade thy prince into a ruffian?

SYPHAX The boasted ancestors of these great men,
Whose virtues you admire, were all such ruffians.
This dread of nations, this almighty Rome,
That comprehends in her wide empire's bounds
All under heaven, was founded on a rape;
Your Scipios, Cæsars, Pompeys, and your Catos
(These gods on earth) are all the spurious brood
Of violated maids, of ravish'd Sabines.

JUBA Syphax, I fear that hoary head of thine
Abounds too much in our Numidian wiles.

SYPHAX Indeed, my prince, you want to know the world;
You have not read mankind; your youth admires
The throws and swellings of a Roman soul,
Cato's bold fights, the extravagance of virtue.

JUBA If knowledge of the world makes men perfidious,
May Juba ever live in ignorance!

SYPHAX Go, go; you're young.

JUBA   Gods, must I tamely bear
This arrogance unanswered! thou'rt a traitor,
A false old traitor.

SYPHAX   I have gone too far.   *Aside.*
JUBA Cato shall know the baseness of thy soul.
SYPHAX I must appease this storm, or perish in it.   *Aside.*
  Young prince, behold these locks, that are grown white
  Beneath a helmet in your father's battles.
JUBA Those locks shall ne'er protect thy insolence.
SYPHAX Must one rash word, the infirmity of age,
  Throw down the merit of my better years?
  This the reward of a whole life of service!
  Curse on the boy! how steadily he hears me!   *Aside.*
JUBA Is it because the throne of my forefathers
  Still stands unfilled, and that Numidia's crown
  Hangs doubtful yet whose head it shall enclose,
  Thou thus presum'st to treat thy prince with scorn?
SYPHAX Why will you rive my heart with such expressions?
  Does not old Syphax follow you to war?
  What are his aims? Why does he load with darts
  His trembling hand, and crush beneath a casque
  His wrinkled brows? What is it he aspires to?
  Is it not this, to shed the slow remains,
  His last poor ebb of blood, in your defence?
JUBA Syphax, no more! I would not hear you talk.
SYPHAX Not hear me talk! what, when my faith to Juba,
  My royal master's son, is called in question?
  My prince may strike me dead, and I'll be dumb;
  But whilst I live I must not hold my tongue,
  And languish out old age in his displeasure.
JUBA Thou know'st the way too well into my heart.
  I do believe thee loyal to thy prince.
SYPHAX What greater instance can I give? I've offer'd
  To do an action which my soul abhors,
  And gain you whom you love, at any price.
JUBA Was this thy motive? I have been too hasty.
SYPHAX And 'tis for this my prince has called me traitor.
JUBA Sure thou mistakest; I did not call thee so.
SYPHAS You did, indeed, my prince, you called me traitor.
  Nay, further, threatened you'd complain to Cato.
  Of what, my prince, would you complain to Cato?
  That Syphax loves you, and would sacrifice
  His life, nay more, his honour, in your service?
JUBA Syphax, I know thou lovest me; but indeed

Thy zeal for Juba carried thee too far.
Honour's a sacred tie, the law of kings,
The noble mind's distinguishing perfection,
That aids and strengthens virtue, where it meets her,
And imitates her actions, where she is not;
It ought not to be sported with.

SYPHAX   By heavens,
I'm ravished when you talk thus, though you chide me!
Alas! I've hitherto been used to think
A blind officious zeal to serve my king
The ruling principle that ought to burn
And quench all others in a subject's heart.
Happy the people who preserve their honour
By the same duties that oblige their prince!

JUBA Syphax, thou now begin'st to speak thyself.
Numidia's grown a scorn among the nations
For breach of public vows. Our Punic faith
Is infamous, and branded to a proverb.
Syphax, we'll join our cares, to purge away
Our country's crimes, and clear her reputation.

SYPHAX Believe me, prince, you make old Syphax weep
To hear you talk – but 'tis with tears of joy.
If e'er your father's crown adorn your brows,
Numidia will be blest by Cato's lectures.

JUBA Syphax, thy hand; we'll mutually forget
The warmth of youth, and frowardness of age:
Thy prince esteems thy worth, and loves thy person.
If e'er the sceptre comes into my hand,
Syphax shall stand the second in my kingdom.

SYPHAX Why will you overwhelm my age with kindness?
My joy grows burdensome, I shan't support it.

JUBA Syphax, farewell. I'll hence, and try to find
Some blest occasion that may set me right
In Cato's thoughts. I'd rather have that man
Approve my deed, than worlds for my admirers.   *Exit.*

SYPHAX (*Solus.*) Young men soon give, and soon forget, affronts;
Old age is slow in both – A false old traitor! –
Those words, rash boy, may chance to cost thee dear.
My heart had still some foolish fondness for thee,
But hence, 'tis gone! I give it to the winds:
Cæsar, I'm wholly thine. –

Enter Sempronius.

SYPHAX   All hail, Sempronius!
  Well, Cato's senate is resolved to wait
  The fury of a siege, before it yields.
SEMPRONIUS Syphax, we both were on the verge of fate;
  Lucius declared for peace, and terms were offer'd
  To Cato, by a messenger from Cæsar.
  Should they submit, ere our designs are ripe,
  We both must perish in the common wreck,
  Lost in a general, undistinguished ruin.
SYPHAX But how stands Cato?
SEMPRONIUS   Thou hast seen mount Atlas:
  Whilst storms and tempests thunder on its brows,
  And oceans break their billows at its feet,
  It stands unmoved, and glories in its height;
  Such is that haughty man; his towering soul,
  'Midst all the shocks and injuries of fortune,
  Rises superior, and looks down on Cæsar.
SYPHAX But what's this messenger?
SEMPRONIUS   I've practised with him,
  And found a means to let the victor know
  That Syphax and Sempronius are his friends.
  But let me now examine in my turn;
  Is Juba fixed?
SYPHAX   Yes – but it is to Cato.
  I've tried the force of every reason on him,
  Soothed and caressed; been angry, soothed again;
  Laid safety, life, and interest in his sight.
  But all are in vain, he scorns them all for Cato.
SEMPRONIUS Come, 'tis no matter; we shall do without him.
  He'll make a pretty figure in a triumph,
  And serve to trip before the victor's chariot.
  Syphax, I now may hope thou hast forsook
  Thy Juba's cause, and wishest Marcia mine.
SYPHAX May she be thine as fast as thou wouldst have her.
SEMPRONIUS Syphax, I love that woman; though I curse
  Her and myself, yet, spite of me, I love her.
SYPHAX Make Cato sure, and give up Utica,
  Cæsar will ne'er refuse thee such a trifle.
  But are thy troops prepared for a revolt?

Does the sedition catch from man to man,
And run among the ranks?

SEMPRONIUS   All, all is ready;
The factious leaders are our friends, that spread
Murmurs and discontents among the soldiers;
They count their toilsome marches, long fatigues,
Unusual fastings, and will bear no more
This medley of philosophy and war.
Within an hour they'll storm the senate house.

SYPHAX   Meanwhile I'll draw up my Numidian troops
Within the square, to exercise their arms,
And, as I see occasion, favour thee.
I laugh to think how your unshaken Cato
Will look aghast, while unforeseen destruction
Pours in upon him thus from every side.
So, where our wide Numidian wastes extend,
Sudden the impetuous hurricanes descend,
Wheel through the air, in circling eddies play,
Tear up the sands, and sweep whole plains away.
The helpless traveller, with wild surprise,
Sees the dry desert all around him rise,
And, smothered in the dusty whirlwind, dies.   *Exeunt.*

Act III

SCENE I

Marcus and Portius.

MARCUS Thanks to my stars, I have not ranged about
   The wilds of life, ere I could find a friend;
   Nature first pointed out my Portius to me,
   And early taught me, by her secret force,
   To love thy person, ere I knew thy merit,
   Till what was instinct, grew up into friendship.
PORTIUS Marcus, the friendships of the world are oft
   Confed'racies in vice, or leagues of pleasure;
   Ours has severest virtue for its basis,
   And such a friendship ends not but with life.
MARCUS Portius, thou know'st my soul in all its weakness;
   Then prithee spare me on its tender side;
   Indulge me but in love, my other passions
   Shall rise and fall by virtue's nicest rules.
PORTIUS When love's well timed, 'tis not a fault to love.
   The strong, the brave, the virtuous, and the wise,
   Sink in the soft captivity together.
   I would not urge thee to dismiss thy passion
   (I know 'twere vain), but to suppress its force,
   Till better times may make it look more graceful.
MARCUS Alas! thou talk'st like one who never felt
   The impatient throbs and longings of a soul
   That pants and reaches after distant good!
   A lover does not live by vulgar time;
   Believe me, Portius, in my Lucia's absence
   Life hangs upon me, and becomes a burden;
   And yet, when I behold the charming maid,
   I'm ten times more undone; while hope and fear,

And grief and rage, and love, rise up at once,
And with variety of pain distract me.
PORTIUS What can thy Portius do to give thee help?
MARCUS Portius, thou oft enjoy'st the fair one's presence,
Then undertake my cause, and plead it to her
With all the strength and heats of eloquence
Fraternal love and friendship can inspire.
Tell her, thy brother languishes to death,
And fades away, and withers in his bloom;
That he forgets his sleep, and loathes his food;
That youth, and health, and war are joyless to him;
Describe his anxious days, and restless nights,
And all the torments that thou seest me suffer.
PORTIUS Marcus, I beg thee give me not an office
That suits with me so ill. Thou knowest my temper.
MARCUS Wilt thou behold me sinking in my woes,
And wilt thou not reach out a friendly arm
To raise me from amidst this plunge of sorrows?
PORTIUS Marcus, thou canst not ask what I'd refuse;
But here, believe me, I've a thousand reasons –
MARCUS I know thou'lt say, my passion's out of season,
That Cato's great example and misfortunes
Should both conspire to drive it from my thoughts.
But what's all this to one who loves like me?
Oh, Portius, Portius, from my soul I wish
Thou didst but know thyself what 'tis to love!
Then wouldst thou pity and assist thy brother.
PORTIUS What should I do? If I disclose my passion,
Our friendship's at an end: if I conceal it,
The world will call me false to a friend and brother.

                                                         Aside.

MARCUS But see where Lucia, at her wonted hour,
Amid the cool of yon high marble arch,
Enjoys the noonday breeze! Observe her, Portius;
That face, that shape, those eyes, that heaven of beauty!
Observe her well, and blame me if thou canst.
PORTIUS She sees us, and advances –
MARCUS   I'll withdraw,
And leave you for a while. Remember, Portius,
Thy brother's life depends upon thy tongue.   *Exit.*

Enter Lucia.

LUCIA Did not I see your brother Marcus here?
Why did he fly the place, and shun my presence?
PORTIUS Oh, Lucia, language is too faint to show
His rage of love; it preys upon his life;
He pines, he sickens, he despairs, he dies:
His passions and his virtues lie confused,
And mixed together in so wild a tumult,
That the whole man is quite disfigured in him.
Heavens! Would one think 'twere possible for love
To make such ravage in a noble soul!
Oh, Lucia, I'm distressed! My heart bleeds for him;
Ev'n now, while thus I stand blest in thy presence,
A secret damp of grief comes o'er my thoughts,
And I'm unhappy, though thou smil'st upon me.
LUCIA How wilt thou guard thy honour in the shock
Of love and friendship! Think betimes, my Portius,
Think how the nuptial tie, that might ensure
Our mutual bliss, would raise to such a height
Thy brother's griefs, as might perhaps destroy him.
PORTIUS Alas, poor youth! What dost thou think, my Lucia?
His generous, open, undesigning heart
Has begged his rival to solicit for him!
Then do not strike him dead with a denial,
But hold him up in life, and cheer his soul
With the faint glimmering of a doubtful hope;
Perhaps when we have passed these gloomy hours,
And weathered out the storm that beats upon us —
LUCIA No, Portius, no; I see thy sister's tears,
Thy father's anguish, and thy brother's death,
In the pursuit of our ill-fated loves;
And, Portius, here I swear; to Heaven I swear,
To Heaven, and all the powers that judge mankind,
Never to mix my plighted hands with thine,
While such a cloud of mischief hangs upon us,
But to forget our loves, and drive thee out
From all my thoughts — as far as I am able.
PORTIUS What hast thou said? I'm thunderstruck — recall
Those hasty words, or I am lost for ever.
LUCIA Has not the vow already passed my lips?

The gods have heard it, and 'tis sealed in heaven.
May all the vengeance, that was ever poured
On perjured heads, o'erwhelm me, if I break it!

After a pause.

PORTIUS Fixed in astonishment, I gaze upon thee
Like one just blasted by a stroke from Heaven,
Who pants for breath, and stiffens, yet alive,
In dreadful looks, a monument of wrath!
LUCIA At length I've acted my severest part,
I feel the woman breaking in upon me,
And melt about my heart! My tears will flow.
But oh, I'll think no more! The hand of fate
Has torn thee from me, and I must forget thee.
PORTIUS Hard-hearted cruel maid!
LUCIA   Oh, stop those sounds,
Those killing sounds! Why dost thou frown upon me?
My blood runs cold, my heart forgets to heave,
And life itself goes out at thy displeasure.
The gods forbid us to indulge our loves,
But oh! I cannot bear thy hate and live!
PORTIUS Talk not of love, thou never knew'st its force.
I've been deluded, led into a dream
Of fancied bliss. Oh, Lucia, cruel maid!
Thy dreadful vow, loaden with death, still sounds
In my stunned ears. What shall I say or do?
Quick, let us part! Perdition's in thy presence,
And horror dwells about thee! Hah, she faints!
Wretch that I am! What has my rashness done!
Lucia, thou injured innocence! Thou best
And loveliest of thy sex! Awake, my Lucia,
Or Portius rushes on his sword to join thee.
– Her imprecations reach not to the tomb,
They shut not out society in death –
But, hah! She moves! Life wanders up and down
Through all her face, and lights up every charm.
LUCIA Oh, Portius, was this well! To frown on her
That lives upon thy smiles! To call in doubt
The faith of one expiring at thy feet,
That loves thee more than ever woman loved!
– What do I say? My half-recovered sense

Forgets the vow in which my soul is bound.
Destruction stands betwixt us! We must part.
PORTIUS Name not the word, my frighted thoughts run back
And startle into madness at the sound.
LUCIA What wouldst thou have me do? Consider well
The train of ills our love would draw behind it.
Think, Portius, think thou seest thy dying brother
Stabbed at his heart, and all besmeared with blood,
Storming at Heaven and thee! Thy awful sire
Sternly demands the cause, th' accursed cause,
That robs him of his son; poor Marcia trembles,
Then tears her hair, and, frantic in her griefs,
Calls out on Lucia. What could Lucia answer,
Or how stand up in such a scene of sorrow?
PORTIUS To my confusion and eternal grief,
I must approve the sentence that destroys me.
The mist that hung about my mind clears up;
And now athwart the terrors that thy vow
Has planted round thee, thou appearest more fair,
More amiable, and risest in thy charms.
Loveliest of women! Heaven is in thy soul,
Beauty and virtue shine for ever round thee,
Brightening each other! Thou art all divine!
LUCIA Portius, no more; thy words shoot through my heart,
Melt my resolves, and turn me all to love.
Why are those tears of fondness in thy eyes?
Why heaves thy heart? Why swells thy soul with sorrow?
It softens me too much – farewell, my Portius!
Farewell, though death is in the word, – for ever!
PORTIUS Stay, Lucia, stay! What dost thou say? For ever?
LUCIA Have I not sworn? If, Portius, thy success
Must throw thy brother on his fate, farewell –
Oh, how shall I repeat the word? – For ever!
PORTIUS Thus o'er the dying lamp the unsteady flame
Hangs quivering on a point, leaps off by fits,
And falls again, as loath to quit its hold.
Thou must not go; my soul still hovers o'er thee,
And can't get loose.
LUCIA   If the firm Portius shake
To hear of parting, thinks what Lucia suffers!
PORTIUS 'Tis true, unruffled and serene, I've met

The common accidents of life, but here
Such an unlooked-for storm of ills falls on me,
It beats down all my strength, I cannot bear it.
We must not part.

LUCIA   What dost thou say? Not part!
Hast thou forgot the vow that I have made?
Are not there heavens, and gods, that thunder o'er us!
– But see, thy brother Marcus bends this way;
I sicken at the sight. Once more farewell.
Farewell, and know thou wrong'st me, if thou think'st
Ever was love, or ever grief like mine.   *Exit.*

Enter Marcus.

MARCUS Portius, what hopes? How stands she? Am I doom'd
To life or death?

PORTIUS   What wouldst thou have me say?

MARCUS What means this pensive posture? Thou appear'st
Like one amazed and terrified.

PORTIUS   I've reason.

MARCUS Thy downcast looks, and thy disordered thoughts,
Tell me my fate. I ask not the success
My cause has found.

PORTIUS   I'm grieved I undertook it.

MARCUS What, does the barbarous maid insult my heart,
My aching heart, and triumph in my pains?
That I could cast her from my thoughts for ever!

PORTIUS Away! you're too suspicious in your griefs;
Lucia, though sworn never to think of love,
Compassionates your pains, and pities you.

MARCUS Compassionates my pains, and pities me!
What is compassion, when 'tis void of love!
Fool that I was, to choose so cold a friend
To urge my cause! – Compassionate my pains!
Prithee what art, what rhetoric didst thou use
To gain this mighty boon? – She pities me!
To one that asks the warm return of love,
Compassion's cruelty, 'tis scorn, 'tis death –

PORTIUS Marcus, no more; have I deserved this treatment?

MARCUS What have I said? Oh! Portius, oh, forgive me!
A soul, exasperated in ills, falls out
With everything – its friend, itself – But hah!

What means that shout, big with the sounds of war?
What new alarm?

PORTIUS   A second, louder yet,
Swells in the wind, and comes more full upon us.

MARCUS Oh, for some glorious cause to fall in battle!
Lucia, thou hast undone me: thy disdain
Has broke my heart; 'tis death must give me ease.

PORTIUS Quick, let us hence. Who knows if Cato's life
Stands sure? Oh, Marcus, I am warmed; my heart
Leaps at the trumpet's voice, and burns for glory.   *Exeunt.*

Enter Sempronius, with the Leaders of the Mutiny.

SEMPRONIUS At length the winds are raised, the storm blows
    high,
Be it your care, my friends, to keep it up
In its full fury, and direct it right,
Till it has spent itself on Cato's head.
Meanwhile, I'll herd among his friends, and seem
One of the number, that, whate'er arrive,
My friends, and fellow-soldiers, may be safe.

FIRST LEADER We all are safe; Sempronius is our friend.
Sempronius is as brave a man as Cato.
But, hark, he enters. Bear up boldly to him;
Be sure you beat him down, and bind him fast.
This day will end our toils and give us rest.
Fear nothing, for Sempronius is our friend.

Enter Cato, Lucius, Portius, Marcus, etc.

CATO Where are those bold, intrepid sons of war,
That greatly turn their backs upon the foe,
And to their general send a brave defiance?

SEMPRONIUS Curse on their dastard souls, they stand
    astonished!   *Aside.*

CATO Perfidious men! And will you thus dishonour
Your past exploits, and sully all your wars?
Do you confess 'twas not a zeal for Rome,
Nor love of liberty, nor thirst of honour,
Drew you thus far; but hopes to share the spoil
Of conquered towns and plundered provinces?
Fired with such motives you do well to join
With Cato's foes and follow Cæsar's banners.

Why did I 'scape the envenomed aspic's rage,
And all the fiery monsters of the desert,
To see this day? Why could not Cato fall
Without your guilt! Behold, ungrateful men,
Behold my bosom naked to your swords,
And let the man that's injured strike the blow.
Which of you all suspects that he is wronged?
Or thinks he suffers greater ills than Cato?
Am I distinguished from you but by toils,
Superior toils, and heavier weight of cares?
Painful pre-eminence!

SEMPRONIUS By heavens, they droop!
  Confusion to the villains! all is lost!   *Aside.*

CATO Have you forgotten Libya's burning waste,
Its barren rocks, parched earth, and hills of sand,
Its tainted air, and all its broods of poison?
Who was the first to explore the untrodden path,
When life was hazarded in every step?
Or, fainting in the long laborious march,
When, on the banks of an unlooked for stream,
You sunk the river with repeated draughts,
Who was the last in all your host that thirsted?

SEMPRONIUS If some penurious source by chance appeared,
Scanty of waters, when you scooped it dry,
And offered the full helmet up to Cato,
Did he not dash the untasted moisture from him?
Did he not lead you through the midday sun,
And clouds of dust? Did not his temples glow
In the same sultry winds and scorching heats?

CATO Hence, worthless men! hence! and complain to Cæsar,
You could not undergo the toil of war,
Nor bear the hardships that your leader bore.

LUCIUS See, Cato, see the unhappy men; they weep!
Fear, and remorse, and sorrow for their crime,
Appear in every look, and plead for mercy.

CATO Learn to be honest men, give up your leaders.
And pardon shall descend on all the rest.

SEMPRONIUS Cato, commit these wretches to my care:
First let 'em each be broken on the rack,
Then, with what life remains, impaled, and left
To writhe at leisure round the bloody stake,

There let 'em hang, and taint the southern wind.
The partners of their crime will learn obedience,
When they look up and see their fellow-traitors
Stuck on a fork, and blackening in the sun.

LUCIUS Sempronius, why, why wilt thou urge the fate
Of wretched men?

SEMPRONIUS How! Wouldst thou clear rebellion?
Lucius (good man) pities the poor offenders.
That would imbrue their hands in Cato's blood.

CATO Forbear, Sempronius! — see they suffer death,
But in their deaths remember they are men;
Strain not the laws, to make their tortures grievous.
Lucius, the base, degenerate age requires
Severity, and justice in its rigour;
This awes an impious, bold, offending world,
Commands obedience and gives force to laws.
When by just vengeance guilty mortals perish,
The gods behold their punishment with pleasure,
And lay the uplifted thunderbolt aside.

SEMPRONIUS Cato, I execute thy will with pleasure.

CATO Meanwhile we'll sacrifice to liberty.
Remember, O my friends! the laws, the rights,
The generous plan of power delivered down
From age to age by your renowned forefathers
(So dearly bought, the price of so much blood):
Oh, let it never perish in your hands!
But piously transmit it to your children.
Do thou, great Liberty, inspire our souls,
And make our lives in thy possession happy,
Or our deaths glorious in thy just defence. *Exeunt Cato, etc.*

FIRST LEADER Sempronius, you have acted like yourself.
One would have thought you had been half in earnest.

SEMPRONIUS Villain, stand off; base, grov'ling, worthless
wretches,
Mongrels in faction, poor faint-hearted traitors!

SECOND LEADER Nay, now you carry it too far, Sempronius!
Throw off the mask, there are none here but friends.

SEMPRONIUS Know, villains, when such paltry slaves presume
To mix in treason, if the plot succeeds,
They're thrown neglected by; but, if it fails,
They're sure to die like dogs, as you shall do.

Here, take these factious monsters, drag 'em forth
To sudden death.   *Enter Guards.*
FIRST LEADER   Nay, since it comes to this —
SEMPRONIUS Dispatch 'em quick, but first pluck out their
    tongues,
Lest with their dying breath they sow sedition.
                          Exeunt Guards, with the Leaders.

Enter Syphax.

SYPHAX Our first design, my friend, has proved abortive:
    Still there remains an after-game to play;
    My troops are mounted; their Numidian steeds
    Snuff up the wind and long to scour the desert:
    Let but Sempronius head us in our flight,
    We'll force the gate, where Marcus keeps his guard,
    And hew down all that would oppose our passage.
    A day will bring us into Cæsar's camp.
SEMPRONIUS Confusion! I have failed of half my purpose:
    Marcia, the charming Marcia's left behind!
SYPHAX How! will Sempronius turn a woman's slave?
SEMPRONIUS Think not thy friend can ever feel the soft
    Unmanly warmth and tenderness of love.
    Syphax, I long to clasp that haughty maid
    And bend her stubborn virtue to my passion:
    When I have gone thus far, I'd cast her off.
SYPHAX Well said! that's spoken like thyself, Sempronius!
    What hinders, then, but that thou find her out,
    And hurry her away by manly force?
SEMPRONIUS But how to gain admission? For access
    Is given to none but Juba, and her brothers.
SYPHAX Thou shalt have Juba's dress and Juba's guards,
    The doors will open when Numidia's prince
    Seems to appear before the slaves that watch them.
SEMPRONIUS Heavens, what a thought is there! Marcia's my
    own!
    How will my bosom swell with anxious joy
    When I behold her struggling in my arms,
    With glowing beauty and disordered charms,
    While fear and anger, with alternate grace,
    Pant in her breast, and vary in her face!

So Pluto, seized of Proserpine, conveyed
To hell's tremendous gloom the affrighted maid,
There grimly smiled, pleased with the beauteous prize,
Nor envied Jove his sunshine and his skies.   *Exeunt.*

Act IV

Lucia and Marcia.

LUCIA Now tell me, Marcia, tell me from thy soul,
   If thou believ'st 'tis possible for woman
   To suffer greater ills than Lucia suffers?
MARCIA Oh, Lucia, Lucia, might my big swol'n heart
   Vent all its griefs, and give a loose to sorrow,
   Marcia could answer thee in sighs, keep pace
   With all thy woes, and count out tear for tear.
LUCIA I know thou'rt doomed alike to be belov'd
   By Juba, and thy father's friend, Sempronius:
   But which of these has power to charm like Portius?
MARCIA Still, I must beg thee not to name Sempronius.
   Lucia, I like not that loud, boisterous man;
   Juba, to all the bravery of a hero,
   Adds softest love, and more than female sweetness;
   Juba might make the proudest of our sex,
   Any of womankind, but Marcia, happy.
LUCIA And why not Marcia? Come, you strive in vain
   To hide your thoughts from one who knows too well
   The inward glowings of a heart in love.
MARCIA While Cato lives, his daughter has no right
   To love or hate, but as his choice directs.
LUCIA But should this father give you to Sempronius?
MARCIA I dare not think he will; but if he should —
   Why wilt thou add to all the griefs I suffer
   Imaginary ills, and fancied tortures?
   I hear the sound of feet! They march this way!
   Let us retire, and try if we can drown
   Each softer thought in sense of present danger:

When love once pleads admission to our hearts,
In spite of all the virtue we can boast,
The woman that deliberates is lost.   *Exeunt.*

Enter Sempronius, dressed like Juba, with Numidian Guards.

SEMPRONIUS The deer is lodg'd, I've tracked her to her covert.
Be sure you mind the word, and when I give it,
Rush in at once, and seize upon your prey.
Let not her cries or tears have force to move you.
How will the young Numidian rave to see
His mistress lost! If aught could glad my soul
Beyond the enjoyment of so bright a prize,
'Twould be to torture that young, gay barbarian.
– But, hark! what noise! Death to my hopes! 'tis he,
'Tis Juba's self! There is but one way left –
He must be murdered and a passage cut
Through those his guards. – Hah! dastards, do you tremble!
Or act like men, or by yon azure heaven –

Enter Juba.

JUBA What do I see? Who's this, that dare usurp
The guards and habit of Numidia's prince?
SEMPRONIUS One that was born to scourge thy arrogance,
Presumptuous youth!
JUBA What can this mean? Sempronius!
SEMPRONIUS My sword shall answer thee. Have at thy heart.
JUBA Nay, then, beware thy own, proud, barbarous man.

Sempronius falls; his Guards surrender.

SEMPRONIUS Curse on my stars! Am I then doomed to fall
By a boy's hand, disfigured in a vile
Numidian dress, and for a worthless woman?
Gods, I'm distracted! this my close of life!
O for a peal of thunder that would make
Earth, sea, and air, and Heaven, and Cato tremble!   *Dies.*
JUBA With what a spring his furious soul broke loose
And left the limbs still quivering on the ground!
Hence, let us carry off those slaves to Cato.
That we may there at length unravel all
This dark design, this mystery of fate.
                                    Exit Juba with Prisoners, etc.

Enter Lucia and Marcia.

LUCIA Sure 'twas the clash of swords; my troubled heart
Is so cast down, and sunk amidst its sorrows,
It throbs with fear, and aches at every sound.
Oh, Marcia, should thy brothers, for my sake —
I die away with horror at the thought!

MARCIA See, Lucia, see! here's blood! here's blood and murder!
Ha! a Numidian! Heavens preserve the prince!
The face lies muffled up within the garment;
But ah! death to my sight! a diadem,
And purple robes! O gods! 'tis he, 'tis he!
Juba, the loveliest youth that ever warmed
A virgin's heart, Juba, lies dead before us!

LUCIA Now, Marcia now, call up to thy assistance,
Thy wonted strength and constancy of mind,
Thou canst not put it to a greater trial.

MARCIA Lucia, look there, and wonder at my patience;
Have I not cause to rave, and beat my breast,
To rend my heart with grief, and run distracted?

LUCIA What can I think, or say, to give thee comfort?

MARCIA Talk not of comfort, 'tis for lighter ills:
Behold a sight that strikes all comfort dead.

Enter Juba, listening.

I will indulge my sorrows, and give way
To all the pangs and fury of despair;
That man, that best of men, deserved it from me.

JUBA What do I hear? And was the false Sempronius
That best of men? Oh, had I fallen like him,
And could have thus been mourned, I had been happy.

LUCIA Here will I stand companion in thy woes
And help thee with my tears! When I behold
A loss like thine I half forget my own.

MARCIA 'Tis not in fate to ease my tortured breast.
This empty world, to me a joyless desert,
Has nothing left to make poor Marcia happy.

JUBA I'm on the rack! Was he so near her heart?

MARCIA Oh, he was all made up of love and charms!
Whatever maid could wish, or man admire:
Delight of every eye; when he appeared,

    A secret pleasure gladdened all that saw him;
    But when he talked, the proudest Roman blushed
    To hear his virtues, and old age grew wise.
JUBA I shall run mad!
MARCIA   Oh, Juba! Juba! Juba!
JUBA What means that voice? Did she not call on Juba?
MARCIA Why do I think on what he was? He's dead!
    He's dead, and never knew how much I loved him!
    Lucia, who knows but his poor bleeding heart,
    Amidst its agonies, remembered Marcia,
    And the last words he uttered called me cruel!
    Alas! he knew not, hapless youth, he knew not
    Marcia's whole soul was full of love and Juba!
JUBA Where am I? Do I live: or am indeed
    What Marcia thinks? All is Elysium round me!
MARCIA Ye dear remains of the most loved of men,
    Nor modesty nor virtue here forbid
    A last embrace, while thus —
JUBA   See, Marcia, see,
    The happy Juba lives! he lives to catch
    That dear embrace, and to return it too,
    With mutual warmth, and eagerness of love.
MARCIA With pleasure and amaze I stand transported!
    Sure 'tis a dream! dead and alive at once!
    If thou art Juba, who lives there?
JUBA   A wretch,
    Disguised like Juba on a cursed design.
    The tale is long, nor have I heard it out;
    Thy father knows it all. I could not bear
    To leave thee in the neighbourhood of death,
    But flew, in all the haste of love, to find thee;
    I found thee weeping, and confess this once,
    Am rapt with joy to see my Marcia's tears.
MARCIA I've been surprised in an unguarded hour,
    But must not now go back; the love, that lay
    Half smothered in my breast, has broke through all
    Its weak restraints, and burns in its full lustre.
    I cannot, if I would, conceal it from thee.
JUBA I'm lost in ecstasy! And dost thou love,
    Thou charming maid?
MARCIA   And dost thou live to ask it?

JUBA This, this is life indeed! Life worth preserving,
  Such life as Juba never felt till now.
MARCIA Believe me, prince, before I thought thee dead,
  I did not know myself how much I loved thee.
JUBA O fortunate mistake!
MARCIA   O happy Marcia!
JUBA My joy! my best beloved, my only wish!
  How shall I speak the transport of my soul!
MARCIA Lucia, thy arm! Oh, let me rest upon it –
  The vital blood, that had forsook my heart,
  Returns again in such tumultuous tide,
  It quite o'ercomes me. Lead to my apartment.
  Oh, prince! I blush to think what I have said,
  But fate has wrested the confession from me;
  Go on, and prosper in the paths of honour.
  Thy virtues will excuse my passion for thee.
  And make the gods propitious to our love.
                     Exeunt Lucia and Marcia.
JUBA I am so blest, I fear 'tis all a dream.
  Fortune, thou now hast made amends for all
  Thy past unkindness: I absolve my stars.
  What though Numidia add her conquered towns
  And provinces to swell the victor's triumph,
  Juba will never at his fate repine:
  Let Cæsar have the world, if Marcia's mine.   *Exit.*

A march at a distance.

Enter Cato and Lucius.

LUCIUS I stand astonished! What, the bold Sempronius,
  That still broke foremost through the crowd of patriots,
  As with a hurricane of zeal transported,
  And virtuous even to madness –
CATO   Trust me, Lucius,
  Our civil discords have produced such crimes,
  Such monstrous crimes, I am surprised at nothing.
  – Oh, Lucius, I am sick of this bad world!
  The daylight and the sun grow painful to me.

Enter Portius.

But see where Portius comes: what means this haste?
Why are thy looks thus changed?

PORTIUS   My heart is grieved,
  I bring such news as will afflict my father.
CATO Has Cæsar shed more Roman blood?
PORTIUS   Not so.
  The traitor Syphax, as within the square
  He exercised his troops, the signal given,
  Flew off at once with his Numidian horse
  To the south gate, where Marcus holds the watch;
  I saw, and called to stop him, but in vain:
  He tossed his arm aloft, and proudly told me
  He would not stay, and perish, like Sempronius.
CATO Perfidious men! But haste, my son, and see
  Thy brother Marcus acts a Roman's part.   *Exit Portius.*
  – Lucius, the torrent bears too hard upon me:
  Justice gives way to force: the conquered world
  Is Cæsar's! Cato has no business in it.
LUCIUS While pride, oppression, and injustice reign,
  The world will still demand her Cato's presence.
  In pity to mankind submit to Cæsar,
  And reconcile thy mighty soul to life.
CATO Would Lucius have me live to swell the number
  Of Cæsar's slaves, or by a base submission
  Give up the cause of Rome, and own a tyrant?
LUCIUS The victor never will impose on Cato
  Ungenerous terms. His enemies confess
  The virtues of humanity are Cæsar's.
CATO Curse on his virtues! they've undone his country.
  Such popular humanity is treason –
  But see young Juba; the good youth appears
  Full of the guilt of his perfidious subjects!
LUCIUS Alas, poor prince! his fate deserves compassion.

Enter Juba.

JUBA I blush, and am confounded to appear
  Before thy presence, Cato.
CATO   What's thy crime?
JUBA I'm a Numidian.
CATO   And a brave one, too.
  Thou hast a Roman soul.
JUBA   Hast thou not heard
  Of my false countrymen?

CATO   Alas, young prince!
  Falsehood and fraud shoot up in every soil,
  The product of all climes — Rome has its Cæsars.
JUBA 'Tis generous thus to comfort the distressed.
CATO 'Tis just to give applause where 'tis deserved:
  Thy virtue, prince, has stood the test of fortune,
  Like purest gold, that, tortured in the furnace,
  Comes out more bright, and brings forth all its weight.
JUBA What shall I answer thee? My ravished heart
  O'erflows with secret joy: I'd rather gain
  Thy praise, O Cato! than Numidia's empire.

Enter Portius hastily.

PORTIUS Misfortune on misfortune! grief on grief!
  My brother Marcus —
CATO   Ha! what has he done?
  Has he forsook his post? Has he given way?
  Did he look tamely on, and let 'em pass?
PORTIUS Scarce had I left my father, but I met him
  Borne on the shields of his surviving soldiers,
  Breathless and pale, and covered o'er with wounds.
  Long, at the head of his few faithful friends,
  He stood the shock of a whole host of foes,
  Till, obstinately brave, and bent on death,
  Oppress'd with multitudes, he greatly fell.
CATO I'm satisfied.
PORTIUS   Nor did he fall before
  His sword had pierced through the false heart of Syphax.
  Yonder he lies. I saw the hoary traitor
  Grin in the pangs of death, and bite the ground.
CATO Thanks to the gods, my boy has done his duty.
  — Portius, when I am dead, be sure thou place
  His urn near mine.
PORTIUS   Long may they keep asunder!
LUCIUS Oh, Cato, arm thy soul with all its patience;
  See where the corpse of thy dead son approaches!
  The citizens and senators, alarmed,
  Have gathered round it, and attend it weeping.

Cato meeting the Corpse.

CATO Welcome, my son! Here lay him down, my friends
  Full in my sight, that I may view at leisure

The bloody corpse, and count these glorious wounds.
– How beautiful is death when earned by virtue!
Who would not be that youth? What pity is it,
That we can die but once to serve our country!
– Why sits this sadness on your brows, my friends?
I should have blushed, if Cato's house had stood
Secure, and flourished in a civil war.
Portius, behold thy brother, and remember,
Thy life is not thine own when Rome demands it.

JUBA Was ever man like this!   *Aside.*

CATO   Alas! my friends,
Why mourn you thus? Let not a private loss
Afflict your hearts. 'Tis Rome requires our tears,
The mistress of the world, the seat of empire,
The nurse of heroes, the delight of gods,
That humbled the proud tyrants of the earth,
And set the nations free; Rome is no more.
Oh, liberty! Oh, virtue! Oh, my country!

JUBA Behold that upright man! Rome fills his eyes
With tears, that flowed not o'er his own dead son.   *Aside.*

CATO Whate'er the Roman virtue has subdued,
The sun's whole course, the day and year, are Cæsar's:
For him the self-devoted Decii died,
The Fabii fell, and the great Scipios conquered:
Even Pompey fought for Cæsar. Oh, my friends,
How is the toil of fate, the work of ages,
The Roman empire, fallen! Oh, cursed ambition!
Fallen into Cæsar's hands! Our great forefathers
Had left him naught to conquer but his country.

JUBA While Cato lives, Cæsar will blush to see
Mankind enslaved, and be ashamed of empire.

CATO Cæsar ashamed! Has not he seen Pharsalia!

LUCIUS Cato, 'tis time thou save thyself and us.

CATO Lose not a thought on me; I'm out of danger;
Heaven will not leave me in the victor's hand.
Cæsar shall never say, I conquered Cato.
But oh, my friends! your safety fills my heart
With anxious thoughts; a thousand secret terrors
Rise in my soul. How shall I save my friends?
'Tis now, O Cæsar, I begin to fear thee!

LUCIUS Cæsar has mercy, if we ask it of him.
CATO Then ask it, I conjure you; let him know,
   Whate'er was done against him, Cato did it.
   Add, if you please, that I request it of him, –
   That I myself, with tears, request it of him, –
   The virtue of my friends may pass unpunished.
   Juba, my heart is troubled for thy sake.
   Should I advise thee to regain Numidia,
   Or seek the conqueror?
JUBA   If I forsake thee
   Whilst I have life, may Heaven abandon Juba!
CATO Thy virtues, prince, if I foresee aright,
   Will one day make thee great; at Rome, hereafter,
   'Twill be no crime to have been Cato's friend.
   Portius, draw near: my son, thou oft has seen
   Thy sire engaged in a corrupted state,
   Wrestling with vice and faction: now thou seest me
   Spent, overpowered, despairing of success;
   Let me advise thee to retreat betimes
   To thy paternal seat, the Sabine field;
   Where the great Censor toiled with his own hands,
   And all our frugal ancestors were blessed
   In humble virtues, and a rural life;
   There live retired, pray for the peace of Rome;
   Content thyself to be obscurely good.
   When vice prevails, and impious men bear sway,
   The post of honour is a private station.
PORTIUS I hope my father does not recommend
   A life to Portius that he scorns himself.
CATO Farewell, my friends! If there be any of you
   Who dare not trust the victor's clemency,
   Know there are ships prepared, by my command,
   Their sails already opening to the winds,
   That shall convey you to the wished-for port.
   Is there aught else, my friends, I can do for you?
   The conqueror draws near. Once more, farewell!
   If e'er we meet hereafter, we shall meet
   In happier climes, and on a safer shore,
   Where Cæsar never shall approach us more.
   There, the brave youth, with love of virtue fired,

Pointing to the body of his dead son.

Who greatly in his country's cause expired,
Shall know he conquered. The firm patriot there,
Who made the welfare of mankind his care,
Though still by faction, vice, and fortune crossed,
Shall find the generous labour was not lost.

Act V

Cato, solus, sitting in a thoughtful posture; in his hand, Plato's book on the Immortality of the Soul. A drawn sword on the table by him.

It must be so – Plato, thou reasonest well –
Else whence this pleasing hope, this fond desire,
This longing after immortality?
Or whence this secret dread, and inward horror
Of falling into naught? Why shrinks the soul
Back on herself, and startles at destruction?
'Tis the divinity that stirs within us:
'Tis Heaven itself that points out an hereafter,
And intimates eternity to man.
Eternity! thou pleasing, dreadful thought!
Through what variety of untried being,
Through what new scenes and changes must we pass?
The wide, the unbounded prospect lies before me;
But shadows, clouds, and darkness, rest upon it.
Here will I hold. If there's a Power above us
(And that there is, all nature cries aloud
Through all her works), he must delight in virtue;
And that which he delights in, must be happy.
But when, or where? – This world was made for Cæsar:
I'm weary of conjectures – this must end 'em.

                              Laying his hand on his sword.

Thus am I doubly armed: my death and life,
My bane and antidote are both before me.
This in a moment brings me to an end;
But this informs me I shall never die.
The soul, secured in her existence, smiles

At the drawn dagger, and defies its point.
The stars shall fade away, the sun himself
Grow dim with age, and nature sink in years,
But thou shalt flourish in immortal youth,
Unhurt amidst the wars of elements,
The wrecks of matter, and the crush of worlds.
What means this heaviness that hangs upon me?
This lethargy that creeps through all my senses?
Nature, oppressed and harassed out with care,
Sinks down to rest. This once I'll favour her,
That my awakened soul may take her flight,
Renewed in all her strength, and fresh with life,
An offering fit for Heaven. Let guilt or fear
Disturb man's rest, Cato knows neither of 'em,
Indifferent in his choice to sleep or die.

Enter Portius.

But, hah! how's this? my son! Why this intrusion?
Were not my orders that I would be private?
Why am I disobeyed?
PORTIUS   Alas! my father!
What means this sword, this instrument of death?
Let me convey it hence.
CATO   Rash youth, forbear!
PORTIUS Oh, let the prayers, the entreaties of your friends,
Their tears, their common danger, wrest it from you!
CATO Wouldst thou betray me? Would'st thou give me up
A slave, a captive, into Cæsar's hands?
Retire, and learn obedience to a father,
Or know, young man! –
PORTIUS   Look not thus sternly on me;
You know I'd rather die than disobey you.
CATO 'Tis well! again I'm master of myself.
Now, Cæsar, let thy troops beset our gates,
And bar each avenue; thy gathering fleets
O'erspread the sea, and stop up every port;
Cato shall open to himself a passage,
And mock thy hopes. –
PORTIUS   Oh, sir! forgive your son,
Whose grief hangs heavy on him. Oh, my father!
How am I sure it is not the last time

I e'er shall call you so? Be not displeased,
Oh, be not angry with me whilst I weep,
And, in the anguish of my heart, beseech you
To quit the dreadful purpose of your soul!
CATO Thou hast been ever good and dutiful.

Embracing him.

Weep not, my son, all will be well again;
The righteous gods, whom I have sought to please,
Will succour Cato, and preserve his children.
PORTIUS Your words give comfort to my drooping heart.
CATO Portius, thou mayest rely upon my conduct:
Thy father will not act what misbecomes him.
But go, my son, and see if aught be wanting
Among thy father's friends; see them embarked,
And tell me if the winds and seas befriend them.
My soul is quite weighed down with care, and asks
The soft refreshment of a moment's sleep.   *Exit.*
PORTIUS My thoughts are more at ease, my heart revives –

Enter Marcia.

Oh, Marcia! Oh, my sister, still there's hope
Our father will not cast away a life
So needful to us all, and to his country.
He is retired to rest, and seems to cherish
Thoughts full of peace. – He has dispatched me hence
With orders that bespeak a mind composed,
And studious for the safety of his friends.
Marcia, take care that none disturb his slumbers.   *Exit.*
MARCIA Oh, ye immortal powers that guard the just,
Watch round his couch, and soften his repose,
Banish his sorrows, and becalm his soul
With easy dreams; remember all his virtues,
And show mankind that goodness is your care!

Enter Lucia.

LUCIA Where is your father, Marcia, where is Cato?
MARCIA Lucia, speak low, he is retired to rest.
Lucia, I feel a gently dawning hope
Rise in my soul. We shall be happy still.
LUCIA Alas, I tremble when I think on Cato!
In every view, in every thought, I tremble!

Cato is stern and awful as a god;
He knows not how to wink at human frailty,
Or pardons weakness that he never felt.
MARCIA Though stern and awful to the foes of Rome,
  He is all goodness, Lucia, always mild;
  Compassionate and gentle to his friends:
  Filled with domestic tenderness, the best,
  The kindest father; I have ever found him
  Easy and good, and bounteous to my wishes.
LUCIA 'Tis his consent alone can make us blest.
  Marcia, we both are equally involved
  In the same intricate, perplexed distress.
  The cruel hand of fate, that has destroyed
  Thy brother Marcus, whom we both lament –
MARCIA And ever shall lament; unhappy youth!
LUCIA Has set my soul at large, and now I stand
  Loose of my vow. But who knows Cato's thoughts?
  Who knows how yet he may dispose of Portius,
  Or how he has determined of thyself?
MARCIA Let him but live, commit the rest to Heaven.

Enter Lucius.

LUCIUS Sweet are the slumbers of the virtuous man!
  Oh, Marcia, I have seen thy godlike father:
  Some power invisible supports his soul,
  And bears it up, in all its wonted greatness.
  A kind, refreshing sleep is fallen upon him:
  I saw him stretched at ease; his fancy lost
  In pleasing dreams; as I drew near his couch,
  He smiled, and cried, 'Cæsar, thou canst not hurt me.'
MARCIA His mind still labours with some dreadful thought.
LUCIUS Lucia, why all this grief, these floods of sorrow?
  Dry up thy tears, my child, we all are safe
  While Cato lives – his presence will protect us.

Enter Juba.

JUBA Lucius, the horsemen are returned from viewing
  The number, strength, and posture of our foes,
  Who now encamp within a short hour's march;
  On the high point of yon bright western tower
  We ken them from afar; the setting sun

Plays on their shining arms and burnished helmets,
And covers all the field with gleams of fire.

LUCIUS Marcia, 'tis time we should awake thy father.
Cæsar is still disposed to give us terms,
And waits at distance, till he hears from Cato.

Enter Portius.

Portius, thy looks speak somewhat of importance.
What tidings dost thou bring? Methinks I see
Unusual gladness sparkling in thy eyes.

PORTIUS As I was hasting to the port, where now
My father's friends, impatient for a passage,
Accuse the lingering winds, a sail arrived
From Pompey's son, who, through the realms of Spain,
Calls out for vengeance on his father's death,
And rouses the whole nation up to arms.
Were Cato at their head, once more might Rome
Assert her rights, and claim her liberty.
But, hark! what means that groan! – Oh, give me way
And let me fly into my father's presence!   *Exit.*

LUCIUS Cato, amidst his slumbers, thinks on Rome,
And, in the wild disorder of his soul,
Mourns o'er his country. – Ah! a second groan –
Heaven guard us all!

MARCIA   Alas! 'tis not the voice
Of one who sleeps; 'tis agonising pain –
'Tis death is in that sound –

Re-enter Portius.

PORTIUS   Oh, sight of woe!
Oh, Marcia, what we feared, is come to pass! –
Cato is fallen upon his sword –

LUCIUS   Oh, Portius!
Hide all the horrors of thy mournful tale,
And let us guess the rest.

PORTIUS   I've raised him up,
And placed him in his chair; where, pale and faint,
He gasps for breath, and, as his life flows from him,
Demands to see his friends. His servants, weeping,
Obsequious to his orders, bear him hither! –

               The back scene opens and discovers Cato.

MARCIA Oh, Heaven! assist me in this dreadful hour,
  To pay the last sad duties to my father!
JUBA These are thy triumphs, thy exploits, O Cæsar!
LUCIUS Now is Rome fallen indeed!
                              Cato brought forward in his chair.
CATO   Here set me down —
  Portius, come near me. Are my friends embarked?
  Can anything be thought of for their service?
  Whilst I yet live, let me not live in vain —
  Oh, Lucius, art thou here? Thou art too good.
  Let this our friendship live between our children —
  Make Portius happy in thy daughter Lucia —
  Alas! poor man, he weeps. Marcia, my daughter —
  Oh, bend me forward! — Juba loves thee, Marcia —
  A senator of Rome, while Rome survived,
  Would not have matched his daughter with a king —
  But Cæsar's arms have thrown down all distinction —
  I'm sick to death — Oh, when shall I get loose
  From this vain world, the abode of guilt and sorrow!
  And yet, methinks, a beam of light breaks in
  On my departing soul — Alas, I fear
  I've been too hasty! — Oh, ye powers that search
  The heart of man, and weigh his inmost thoughts,
  If I have done amiss, impute it not —
  The best may err, but you are good, and — Oh!   *Dies.*
LUCIUS There fled the greatest soul that ever warmed
  A Roman breast. O Cato! O my friend!
  Thy will shall be religiously observed.
  But let us bear this awful corpse to Cæsar,
  And lay it in his sight, that it may stand
  A fence betwixt us and the victor's wrath;
  Cato, though dead, shall still protect his friends.
  From hence, let fierce contending nations know
  What dire effects from civil discord flow:
  'Tis this that shakes our country with alarms,
  And gives up Rome a prey to Roman arms;
  Produces fraud, and cruelty, and strife,
  And robs the guilty world of Cato's life.   *Exeunt Omnes.*

Epilogue

BY DR GARTH

Spoken by Mrs Porter.

What odd fantastic things we women do!
Who would not listen when young lovers woo?
But die a maid, yet have the choice of two!
Ladies are often cruel to their cost;
To give you pain themselves they punish most.
Vows of virginity should well be weighed;
Too oft they're cancelled though in convents made.
Would you revenge such rash resolves – you may:
Be spiteful – and believe the thing we say;
We hate you when you're easily said nay.
How needless, if you knew us, were your fears!
Let Love have eyes and Beauty will have ears.
Our hearts are formed, as you yourselves would choose,
Too proud to ask, too humble to refuse:
We give to merit and to wealth we sell;
He sighs with most success that settles well.
The woes of wedlock with the joys we mix;
'Tis best repenting in a coach and six.
Blame not our conduct, since we but pursue
Those lively lessons we have learned from you;
Your breasts no more the fire of beauty warms,
But wicked wealth usurps the power of charms;
What pains to get the gaudy thing you hate,
To swell in show and be a wretch in state!
At plays you ogle, at the Ring you bow;
Even churches are no sanctuaries now.
There, golden idols all your vows receive;
She is no goddess that has naught to give.

Oh, may once more the happy age appear
When words were artless and the thoughts sincere;
When gold and grandeur were unenvied things,
And courts less coveted than groves and springs.
Love then shall only mourn when Truth complains,
And Constancy feel transport in its chains.
Sighs with success their own soft anguish tell,
And eyes shall utter what the lips conceal:
Virtue again to its bright station climb,
And Beauty fear no enemy but Time.
The fair shall listen to desert alone,
And every Lucia find a Cato's son.

THE CONSCIOUS LOVERS

To the King

May it please Your Majesty,

After having aspir'd to the Highest and most Laudable Ambition, that of following the Cause of Liberty, I should not have humbly petition'd Your Majesty for a Direction of the Theatre, had I not believ'd Success in that Providence an Happiness much to be wish'd by an Honest Man, and highly conducing to the Prosperity of the Commonwealth. It is in this View I lay before Your Majesty a Comedy, which the audience, in Justice to themselves, has supported and encouraged, and is the Prelude of what, by Your Majesty's Influence and Favour, may be attempted in future Representations.

The Imperial Mantle, the Royal Vestment, and the shining Diadem are what strike ordinary Minds; But Your Majesty's Native Goodness, Your Passion for Justice, and Her constant Assessor Mercy, is what continually surrounds You, in the View of intelligent Spirits, and gives Hope to the Suppliant, who sees he has more than succeeded in giving Your Majesty an Opportunity of doing Good. Our King is above the Greatness of Royalty, and every Act of His Will which makes another Man happy, has ten times more Charms in it, than one that makes Himself appear rais'd above the Condition of others; but even this carries Unhappiness with it; for, Calm Dominion, Equal Grandeur and Familiar Greatness do not easily affect the Imagination of the Vulgar, who cannot see Power but in Terror; and as Fear moves mean Spirits, and Love prompts Great ones to obey, the Insinuations of Malecontents are directed accordingly; and the unhappy People are insnar'd, from Want of Reflection, into Disrespectful Ideas of their Gracious and Amiable Sovereign; and then only begin to apprehend the Greatness of their Master, when they have incurr'd his Displeasure.

As Your Majesty was invited to the Throne of a Willing People, for their own sakes, and has ever enjoy'd it with Contempt of the Ostentation of it, we beseech You to Protect us who revere Your Title as we love Your Person. 'Tis to be a Savage to be a Rebel, and they who have fall'n from You have not so much forfeited their Allegiance, as lost their Humanity.

And therefore, if it were only to preserve myself from the Imputation of being amongst the Insensible and Abandon'd, I would beg Permission in the most publick manner possible, to profess my self, with the utmost Sincerity and Zeal,

Sire,
Your Majesty's
Most Devoted Subject
and Servant,
RICHARD STEELE

The Preface

This Comedy has been receiv'd with universal Acceptance, for it was in every Part excellently perform'd; and there needs no other Applause of the Actors, but that they excell'd according to the Dignity and Difficulty of the Character they represented. But this great Favour done to the Work in Acting, renders the Expectation still the greatest from the Author, to keep up the Spirit in the Representation of the Closet, or any other Circumstance of the Reader, whether alone or in Company: To which I can only say, that it must be remember'd a Play is to be Seen, and is made to be Represented with the Advantage of Action, nor can appear but with half the Spirit, without it; for the greatest Effect of a Play in reading is to excite the Reader to go see it; and when he does so, it is then a Play has the Effect of Example and Precept.

The chief Design of this was to be an innocent Performance, and the Audience have abundantly show'd how ready they are to support what is visibly intended that way; nor do I make any Difficulty to acknowledge, that the whole was writ for the sake of the Scene of the Fourth Act, wherein Mr *Bevill* evades the Quarrel with his Friend; and hope it may have some Effect upon the *Goths* and *Vandals* that frequent the Theatres, or a more polite Audience may supply their Absence.

But this Incident, and the Case of the Father and Daughter, are esteem'd by some People no Subjects of Comedy; but I cannot be of their Mind: for any thing that has its Foundation in Happiness and Success, must be allow'd to be the Object of Comedy; and sure it must be an Improvement of it, to introduce a Joy too exquisite for Laughter, that can have no Spring but in delight, which is the Case of this young Lady. I must therefore contend, that the Tears which were shed on that Occasion flow'd from Reason and good sense, and that Men ought not to be laugh'd at for weeping, till we are come to a more clear Notion of what is to be imputed to the Hardness of the Head, and the Softness of the Heart; and I think it was very politely said of Mr *Wilks* to one who told him there was a *General* weeping for *Indiana*, I'll warrant he'll fight ne'er the worse for that. To be apt to give way to the Impressions of Humanity is the Excellence of a right Disposition, and the natural Working of a well-turn'd Spirit. But as I have suffer'd by Criticks who are got no farther than to enquire whether they ought to be pleas'd or not, I would willingly find them properer Matter for their Employment, and revive here a Song which was omitted for want of a Performer, and design'd for the Entertainment of *Indiana*; Sig. *Carbonelli* instead of it play'd on the Fiddle, and it is for want of a Singer that such advantageous things are said of an Instrument which were design'd for a Voice. The Song is the Distress of a Love-sick Maid, and may be a fit Entertainment for some small Criticks to examine whether the Passion is just, or the Distress Male or Female.

I

From Place to Place forlorn I go,
   With downcast Eyes a silent Shade;
Forbidden to declare my Woe;
   To speak, till spoken to, afraid.

II

My inward Pangs, my secret Grief,
   My soft consenting Looks betray:
He Loves, but gives me no Relief:
   Why speaks not he who may?

It remains to say a Word concerning *Terence*, and I am extremely surpriz'd to find what Mr *Cibber* told me, prove a Truth, That what I valued my self so much upon, the Translation of him, should be imputed to me as a Reproach. Mr *Cibber's* Zeal for the Work, his Care and Application in instructing the Actors, and altering the Disposition of the Scenes, when I was, through Sickness, unable to cultivate such Things my self, has been a very obliging Favour and Friendship to me. For this Reason, I was very hardly persuaded to throw away *Terence's* celebrated Funeral, and take only the bare Authority of the young Man's Character, and how I have work'd it into an *Englishman*, and made Use of the same Circumstances of discovering a Daughter, when we least hop'd for one, is humbly submitted to the Learned Reader.

Prologue

BY MR WELSTED

Spoken by Mr Wilks.

To win your Hearts, and to secure your Praise,
The Comic-Writers strive by various Ways:
By subtil Stratagems they act their Game,
And leave untry'd no Avenue to Fame.
One writes the Spouse a beating from his Wife,
And says, Each stroke was Copy'd from the Life;
Some fix all Wit and Humour in Grimace,
And make a Livelyhood of Pinkey's Face:
Here, One gay Shew and costly Habits tries,
Confiding to the Judgment of your Eyes:
Another smuts his Scene (a cunning Shaver)
Sure of the Rakes and of the Wenches Favour.
Oft have these Arts prevail'd; and one may guess,
If practis'd o'er again, would find Success.
But the bold Sage, the Poet of To-night,
By new and desp'rate Rules resolv'd to Write;
Fain would he give more just Applauses Rise,
And please by Wit that scorns the Aids of Vice;
The Praise he seeks, from worthier Motives springs,
Such Praise, as Praise to those that give it, brings.
Your aid, most humbly sought, then Britons lend,
And Lib'ral Mirth, like Lib'ral Men, defend:
No more let Ribaldry, with Licence writ,
Usurp the Name of Eloquence or Wit;
No more let lawless Farce uncensur'd go,
The lewd dull Gleanings of a Smithfield Show.
'Tis yours, with Breeding to refine the Age,
To Chasten Wit, and Moralize the Stage.

Ye Modest, Wise and Good, ye Fair, ye Brave,
To-night the Champion of your Virtues save,
Redeem from long Contempt the Comic Name,
And Judge Politely for your Countrey's Fame.

Dramatis Personæ

MEN

SIR JOHN BEVIL	Mr Mills
MR SEALAND	Mr Williams
BEVIL JUNIOR, *in love with Indiana*	Mr Booth
MYRTLE, *in love with Lucinda*	Mr Wilks
CIMBERTON, *a coxcomb*	Mr Griffin
HUMPHRY, *an old servant to Sir John*	Mr Shepard
TOM, *servant to Bevil junior*	Mr Cibber
DANIEL, *a country boy, servant to Indiana*	Mr Theo. Cibber

WOMEN

MRS SEALAND, *second wife to Sealand*	Mrs Moore
ISABELLA, *sister to Sealand*	Mrs Thurmond
INDIANA, *Sealand's daughter by his first wife*	Mrs Oldfield
LUCINDA, *Sealand's daughter by his second wife*	Mrs Booth
PHILLIS, *maid to Lucinda*	Mrs Younger

SCENE
London

Act I

SCENE I

SCENE: *Sir John Bevil's house.*

Enter Sir John Bevil, and Humphrey.

SIR J. BEVIL Have you order'd that I should not be interrupted while I am dressing?

HUMPHREY Yes, Sir: I believ'd you had something of moment to say to me.

SIR J. BEVIL Let me see, Humphrey; I think it is now full forty years since I first took thee, to be about my self.

HUMPHREY I thank you, Sir, it has been an easy forty years; and I have pass'd 'em without much sickness, care, or labour.

SIR J. BEVIL Thou hast a brave constitution; you are a year or two older than I am, Sirrah.

HUMPHREY You have ever been of that mind, Sir.

SIR J. BEVIL You knave, you know it; I took thee for thy gravity and sobriety, in my wild years.

HUMPHREY Ah Sir! our manners were form'd from our different fortunes, not our different age. Wealth gave a loose to your youth, and poverty put a restraint upon mine.

SIR J. BEVIL Well, Humphrey, you know I have been a kind master to you; I have us'd you, for the ingenuous nature I observ'd in you from the beginning, more like an humble friend than a servant.

HUMPHREY I humbly beg you'll be so tender of me, as to explain your commands, Sir, without any farther preparation.

SIR J. BEVIL I'll tell thee then. In the first place this wedding of my son's, in all probability, (shut the door) will never be at all.

HUMPHREY How, Sir! not be at all? for what reason is it carry'd on in appearance?

SIR J. BEVIL Honest Humphrey, have patience; and I'll tell thee all in order. I have my self, in some part of my life, liv'd (indeed) with freedom, but, I hope, without reproach: Now, I thought liberty wou'd be as little injurious to my son; therefore, as soon as he grew towards man, I indulg'd him in living after his own manner: I knew not how, otherwise, to judge of his inclination; for what can be concluded from a behaviour under restraint and fear? But what charms me above all expression is, that my son has never in the least action, the most distant hint or word, valued himself upon that great estate of his mother's, which, according to our marriage settlement, he has had ever since he came to age.

HUMPHREY No, Sir; on the contrary, he seems afraid of appearing to enjoy it, before you or any belonging to you – He is as dependent and resign'd to your will, as if he had not a farthing but what must come from your immediate bounty – You have ever acted like a good and generous father, and he like an obedient and grateful son.

SIR J. BEVIL Nay, his carriage is so easy to all with whom he converses, that he is never assuming, never prefers himself to others, nor ever is guilty of that rough sincerity which a man is not call'd to, and certainly disobliges most of his acquaintance; to be short, Humphrey, his reputation was so fair in the world, that Old Sealand, the great India Merchant, has offer'd his only daughter, and sole heiress to that vast estate of his, as a wife for him; you may be sure I made no difficulties, the match was agreed on, and this very day named for the wedding.

HUMPHREY What hinders the proceeding?

SIR J. BEVIL Don't interrupt me. You know, I was last Thursday at the masquerade; my son, you may remember, soon found us out – He knew his grandfather's habit, which I then wore; and tho' it was the mode, in the last age, yet the maskers, you know, follow'd us as if we had been the most monstrous figures in that whole assembly.

HUMPHREY I remember indeed a young man of quality in the habit of a clown, that was particularly troublesome.

SIR J. BEVIL Right – He was too much what he seem'd to be. You remember how impertinently he follow'd, and teiz'd us, and wou'd know who we were.

HUMPHREY I know he has a mind to come into that particular.

Aside.

SIR J. BEVIL Ay, he follow'd us, till the gentleman who led the lady in the Indian mantle presented that gay creature to the rustick, and bid him (like Cymon in the Fable) grow polite, by falling in love, and let that worthy old gentleman alone, meaning me: The clown was not reform'd, but rudely persisted, and offer'd to force off my mask; with that the gentleman throwing off his own, appear'd to be my son, and in his concern for me, tore off that of the nobleman; at this they seiz'd each other; the company call'd the guards: and in the surprize, the lady swoon'd away: upon which my son quitted his adversary, and had now no care but of the lady, – when raising her in his arms, Art thou gone, cry'd he, for ever – forbid it Heav'n! – She revives at his known voice, – and with the most familiar tho' modest gesture hangs in safety over his shoulder weeping, but wept as in the arms of one before whom she could give her self a loose, were she not under observation: while she hides her face in his neck, he carefully conveys her from the company.

HUMPHREY I have observ'd this accident has dwelt upon you very strongly.

SIR J. BEVIL Her uncommon air, her noble modesty, the dignity of her person, and the occasion it self, drew the whole assembly together; and I soon heard it buzz'd about, she was the adopted daughter of a famous sea-officer, who had serv'd in France. Now this unexpected and publick discovery of my son's so deep concern for her –

HUMPHREY Was what I suppose alarm'd Mr Sealand, in behalf of his daughter, to break off the match.

SIR J. BEVIL You are right – He came to me yesterday, and said, he thought himself disengag'd from the bargain; being credibly informed my son was already marry'd, or worse, to the lady at the masquerade. I palliated matters, and insisted on our agreement; but we parted with little less than a direct breach between us.

HUMPHREY Well, Sir; and what notice have you taken of all this to my young master?

SIR J. BEVIL That's what I wanted to debate with you – I have said nothing to him yet – But look you, Humphrey – if there is so much in this amour of his, that he denies upon my summons to marry, I have cause enough to be offended; and then by my insisting upon his marrying to-day, I shall know how far he is engag'd to this lady in masquerade, and from thence only shall be able take my measures: in the mean time I would have you find out how far that rogue his man is let into his secret – He, I know, will play tricks as much to cross me, as to serve his master.

HUMPHREY Why do you think so of him, Sir? I believe he is no worse than I was for you, at your son's age.

SIR J. BEVIL I see it in the rascal's looks. But I have dwelt on these things too long; I'll go to my son immediately, and while I'm gone, your part is to convince his rogue Tom that I am in earnest. I'll leave him to you.   *Exit Sir John Bevil.*

HUMPHREY Well, tho' this father and son live as well together as possible, yet their fear of giving each other pain, is attended with constant mutual uneasiness. I'm sure I have enough to do to be honest, and yet keep well with them both: But they know I love 'em, and that makes the task less painful however – Oh, here's the prince of poor coxcombs, the representative of all the better fed than taught. – Ho! ho! Tom, whither so gay and so airy this morning?

Enter Tom, singing.

TOM Sir, we servants of single gentlemen are another kind of people than you domestick ordinary drudges that do business: we are rais'd above you: The pleasures of board-wages, tavern-dinners, and many a clear gain; vails, alas! you never heard or dreamt of.

HUMPHREY Thou hast follies and vices enough for a man of ten thousand a year, tho' 'tis but as t'other day that I sent for you to town, to put you into Mr Sealand's family, that you might learn a little before I put you to my young master, who is too gentle for training such a rude thing as you were into proper obedience – You then pull'd off your hat to every one you met in the street, like a bashful great aukward cub as you were. But your great oaken cudgel when you were a booby, became you much better than that dangling stick at your button now you are a fop. That's fit for nothing, except it hangs there to be ready for your master's hand when you are impertinent.

TOM Uncle Humphrey, you know my master scorns to strike

his servants. You talk as if the world was now, just as it was when my old master and you were in your youth – when you went to dinner because it was so much a clock, when the great blow was given in the hall at the pantrey-door, and all the family came out of their holes in such strange dresses and formal faces as you see in the pictures in our long gallery in the country.

HUMPHREY Why, you wild rogue!

TOM You could not fall to your dinner till a formal fellow in a black gown said something over the meat, as if the cook had not made it ready enough.

HUMPHREY Sirrah, who do you prate after? – Despising men of sacred characters! I hope you never heard my good young master talk so like a profligate.

TOM Sir, I say you put upon me, when I first came to town, about being orderly, and the doctrine of wearing shams to make linnen last clean a fortnight, keeping my cloaths fresh, and wearing a frock within doors.

HUMPHREY Sirrah, I gave you those lessons, because I suppos'd at that time your master and you might have din'd at home every day, and cost you nothing; then you might have made a good family servant. But the gang you have frequented since at chocolate houses and taverns, in a continual sound of noise and extravagance –

TOM I don't know what you heavy inmates call noise and extravagance; but we gentlemen, who are well fed, and cut a figure, Sir, think it a fine life, and that we must be very pretty fellows who are kept only to be looked at.

HUMPHREY Very well, Sir, – I hope the fashion of being lewd and extravagant, despising of decency and order, is almost at an end, since it is arrived at persons of your quality.

TOM Master Humphrey, Ha! ha! you were an unhappy lad to be sent up to town in such queer days as you were: Why now, Sir, the Lacquies are the men of pleasure of the age; the top-gamesters; and many a lac'd coat about town have had their education in our party-colour'd regiment, – We are false lovers; have a taste of musick, poetry, billet-doux, dress, politicks; ruin damsels; and when we are weary of this lewd town, and have a mind to take up, whip into our masters whigs and linnen, and marry fortunes.

HUMPHREY Hey-day!

TOM Nay, Sir! our order is carry'd up to the highest dignities and distinctions; step but into the Painted Chamber – and by our titles you'd take us all for men of quality – then again come down to the Court of Requests, and you see us all laying our broken heads together for the good of the nation: and tho' we never carry a question *nemine contradicente*, yet this I can say with a safe conscience, (and I wish every gentleman of our cloth could lay his hand upon his heart and say the same) that I never took so much as a single mug of beer for my vote in all my life.

HUMPHREY Sirrah, there is no enduring your extravagance; I'll hear you prate no longer. I wanted to see you, to enquire how things go with your master, as far as you understand them; I suppose he knows he is to be married to-day.

TOM Ay, Sir, he knows it, and is dress'd as gay as the sun; but, between you and I, my dear, he has a very heavy heart under all that gayety. As soon as he was dress'd I retir'd, but overheard him sigh in the most heavy manner. He walk'd thoughtfully to and fro in the room, then went into his closet; when he came out, he gave me this for his mistress, whose maid you know –

HUMPHREY Is passionately fond of your fine person.

TOM The poor fool is so tender, and loves to hear me talk of the world, and the plays, opera's, and Ridotto's, for the winter; the parks and Bellsize, for our summer diversions; and lard! says she, you are so wild – but you have a world of humour –

HUMPHREY Coxcomb! Well, but why don't you run with your master's letter to Mrs Lucinda, as he order'd you?

TOM Because Mrs Lucinda is not so easily come at as you think for.

HUMPHREY Not easily come at? Why Sirrah, are not her father and my old master agreed, that she and Mr Bevil are to be one flesh before to-morrow morning?

TOM It's no matter for that; her mother, it seems, Mrs Sealand, has not agreed to it: and you must know, Mr Humphrey, that in that family the grey mare is the better horse.

HUMPHREY What do'st thou mean?

TOM In one word, Mrs Sealand pretends to have a will of her own, and has provided a relation of hers, a stiff, starch'd philosopher, and a wise fool for her daughter; for which reason for these ten days past, she has suffer'd no message nor letter from my master to come near her.

HUMPHREY And where had you this intelligence?

TOM From a foolish fond soul, that can keep nothing from me — One that will deliver this letter too, if she is rightly manag'd.

HUMPHREY What! Her pretty hand-maid, Mrs Phillis?

TOM Even she, Sir; this is the very hour, you know, she usually comes hither, under a pretence of a visit to your housekeeper forsooth, but in reality to have a glance at —

HUMPHREY Your sweet face, I warrant you.

TOM Nothing else in nature; you must know, I love to fret, and play with the little wanton. —

HUMPHREY Play with the little wanton! What will this world come to!

TOM I met her, this morning, in a new manteau and petticoat, not a bit the worse for her lady's wearing: and she has always new thoughts and new airs with new cloaths — then she never fails to steal some glance or gesture from every visitant at their house; and is indeed the whole town of coquets at second hand. But here she comes; in one motion she speaks and describes herself better than all the words in the world can.

HUMPHREY Then I hope, dear Sir, when your own affair is over, you will be so good as to mind your master's with her.

TOM Dear Humphrey, you know my master is my friend, and those are people I never forget. —

HUMPHREY Sawciness itself! but I'll leave you to do your best for him.   *Exit.*

Enter Phillis.

PHILLIS Oh, Mr Thomas, is Mrs Sugar-key at home? — Lard, one is almost asham'd to pass along the streets. The town is quite empty, and no body of fashion left in it; and the ordinary people do so stare to see any thing dress'd like a woman of condition (as it were on the same floor with them) pass by. Alas! Alas! it is a sad thing to walk. Oh Fortune! Fortune!

TOM What! a sad thing to walk? Why, Madam Phillis, do you wish your self lame?

PHILLIS No, Mr Tom, but I wish I were generally carry'd on a coach or chair, and of a fortune neither to stand nor go, but to totter, or slide, to be short-sighted, or stare, to fleer in the face, to look distant, to observe, to overlook, yet all become me; and, if I was rich, I could twire and loll as well as the best of them. Oh Tom! Tom! is it not a pity, that you shou'd be so great a coxcomb, and I so great a coquet, and yet be such poor devils as we are?

TOM Mrs Phillis, I am your humble servant for that –

PHILLIS Yes, Mr Thomas, I know how much you are my humble servant, and know what you said to Mrs Judy, upon seeing her in one of her lady's cast manteaus; that any one wou'd have thought her the lady, and that she had ordered the other to wear it till it sat easy – for now only it was becoming: – To my lady it was only a covering, to Mrs Judy it was a habit. This you said, after some body or other. Oh, Tom! Tom! thou art as false and as base, as the best gentleman of them all: but, you wretch, talk to me no more on the old odious subject. Don't, I say.

TOM I know not how to resist your commands, Madam.

In a submissive tone, retiring.

PHILLIS Commands about parting are grown mighty easy to you of late.

TOM O, I have her; I have nettled and put her into the right temper to be wrought upon, and set a prating. (*Aside.*) – Why truly, to be plain with you, Mrs Phillis, I can take little comfort of late in frequenting your house.

PHILLIS Pray, Mr Thomas, what is it all of a sudden offends your nicety at our house?

TOM I don't care to speak particulars, but I dislike the whole.

PHILLIS I thank you, Sir, I am a part of that whole.

TOM Mistake me not, good Phillis.

PHILLIS Good Phillis! Saucy enough. But however –

TOM I say, it is that thou art a part, which gives me pain for the disposition of the whole. You must know, Madam, to be serious, I am a man, at the bottom, of prodigious nice honour. You are too much expos'd to company at your house: To be plain, I don't like so many, that wou'd be your mistress's lovers, whispering to you.

PHILLIS Don't think to put that upon me. You say this, because I wrung you to the heart, when I touch'd your guilty conscience about Judy.

TOM Ah Phillis! Phillis! if you but knew my heart!

PHILLIS I know too much on't.

TOM Nay then, poor Crispo's fate and mine are one – Therefore give me leave to say, or sing at least, as he does upon the same occasion –

Se vedette, etc., sings.

PHILLIS What, do you think I'm to be fob'd off with a song? I don't question but you have sung the same to Mrs Judy too.

TOM Don't disparage your charms, good Phillis, with jealousy of so worthless an object; besides, she is a poor hussey, and if you doubt the sincerity of my love, you will allow me true to my interest. You are a fortune, Phillis –

PHILLIS What wou'd the fop be at now? In good time indeed, you shall be setting up for a fortune!

TOM Dear Mrs Phillis, you have such a spirit that we shall never be dull in marriage, when we come together. But I tell you, you are a fortune, and you have an estate in my hands.

He pulls out a purse, she eyes it.

PHILLIS What pretence have I to what is in your hands, Mr Tom?

TOM As thus: there are hours, you know, when a lady is neither pleas'd nor displeas'd, neither sick nor well, when she lolls or loiters, when she's without desires, from having more of every thing than she knows what to do with.

PHILLIS Well, what then?

TOM When she has not life enough to keep her bright eyes quite open, to look at her own dear image in the glass.

PHILLIS Explain thy self, and don't be so fond of thy own prating.

TOM There are also prosperous and good-natur'd moments, as when a knot or a patch is happily fix'd; when the complexion particularly flourishes.

PHILLIS Well, what then? I have not patience!

TOM Why then – or on the like occasions – we servants who have skill to know how to time business, see when such a pretty folded thing as this (*shews a letter*) may be presented, laid, or dropp'd, as best suits the present humour. And, Madam, because it is a long wearisome journey to run through all the several stages of a lady's temper, my master, who is the most reasonable man in the world, presents you this to bear your charges on the road.   *Gives her the purse.*

PHILLIS Now, you think me a corrupt hussey.

TOM Oh fie, I only think you'll take the letter.

PHILLIS Nay, I know you do, but I know my own innocence; I take it for my mistress's sake.

TOM I know it, my pretty one, I know it.

PHILLIS Yes, I say I do it, because I wou'd not have my mistress deluded by one who gives no proof of his passion; but I'll talk more of this, as you see me on my way home – No, Tom, I assure thee, I take this trash of thy master's, not for the value of the thing, but as it convinces me he has a true respect for my mistress. I remember a verse to the purpose.

They may be false who languish and complain,
But they who part with money never feign.   *Exeunt.*

SCENE 2

SCENE: *Bevil junior's lodgings.*

Bevil junior, reading.

BEVIL JUNIOR These moral writers practise virtue after death: This charming vision of Mirza! Such an author consulted in a morning, sets the spirit for the vicissitudes of the day, better than the glass does a man's person: But what a day have I to go thro'! to put on an easy look with an aking heart. – If this lady my father urges me to marry should not refuse me, my dilemma is insupportable. But why should I fear it? is not she in equal distress with me? has not the letter, I have sent her this morning, confest my inclination to another? Nay, have I not moral assurances of her engagements too, to my friend Myrtle? It's impossible but she must give in to it: For, sure to be deny'd is a favour any man may pretend to. It must be so – Well then, with the assurance of being rejected, I think I may confidently say to my father, I am ready to marry her – Then let me resolve upon (what I am not very good at, tho' it is) an honest dissimulation.

Enter Tom.

TOM Sir John Bevil, Sir, is in the next room.

BEVIL JUNIOR Dunce! Why did not you bring him in?

TOM I told him, Sir, you were in your closet.

BEVIL JUNIOR I thought you had known, Sir, it was my duty to see my father any where. *Going himself to the door.*

TOM The devil's in my master! he has always more wit than I have. *Aside.*

Bevil Junior introducing Sir John.

BEVIL JUNIOR Sir, you are the most gallant, the most complaisant of all parents – Sure 'tis not a compliment to say these lodgings are yours – Why wou'd you not walk in, Sir?

SIR J. BEVIL I was loth to interrupt you unseasonably on your wedding-day.

BEVIL JUNIOR One to whom I am beholden for my birth-day, might have used less ceremony.

SIR J. BEVIL Well, son, I have intelligence you have writ to your mistress this morning: it would please my curiosity to know the contents of a wedding-day letter; for courtship must then be over.

BEVIL JUNIOR I assure you, Sir, there was no insolence in it, upon the prospect of such a vast fortune's being added to our family; but much acknowledgment of the lady's greater desert.

SIR J. BEVIL But, dear Jack, are you in earnest in all this? And will you really marry her?

BEVIL JUNIOR Did I ever disobey any command of yours, Sir? nay, any inclination that I saw you bent upon?

SIR J. BEVIL Why, I can't say you have, son; but methinks in this whole business, you have not been so warm as I could have wish'd you: You have visited her, it's true, but you have not been particular. Every one knows you can say and do as handsome things as any man; but you have done nothing, but liv'd in the general; been complaisant only.

BEVIL JUNIOR As I am ever prepar'd to marry if you bid me, so I am ready to let it alone if you will have me.

Humphrey enters unobserv'd.

SIR J. BEVIL Look you there now! why what am I to think of this so absolute and so indifferent a resignation?

BEVIL JUNIOR Think? That I am still your son, Sir – Sir, – you have been married, and I have not. And you have, Sir, found the inconvenience there is, when a man weds with too much love in his head. I have been told, Sir, that at the time you married, you made a mighty bustle on the occasion. There was challenging and fighting, scaling walls – locking up the lady – and the gallant under an arrest for fear of killing all his rivals – Now, Sir, I suppose you having found the ill consequences of these strong passions and prejudices, in preference of one woman to another, in case of a man's becoming a widower –

SIR J. BEVIL How is this!

BEVIL JUNIOR I say Sir, experience has made you wiser in your care of me – for, Sir, since you lost my dear mother, your time has been so heavy, so lonely, and so tasteless, that you are so good as to guard me against the like unhappiness, by marrying me prudentially by way of bargain and sale. For, as you well judge, a woman that is espous'd for a fortune, is yet a better bargain, if she dies; for then a man still enjoys what he did marry, the money; and is disencumber'd of what he did not marry, the woman.

SIR J. BEVIL But pray, Sir, do you think Lucinda then a woman of such little merit?

BEVIL JUNIOR Pardon me, Sir, I don't carry it so far neither; I am rather afraid I shall like her too well; she has, for one of her fortune, a great many needless and superfluous good qualities.

SIR J. BEVIL I am afraid, Son, there's something I don't see yet, something that's smother'd under all this raillery.

BEVIL JUNIOR Not in the least, Sir: If the lady is dress'd and ready, you see I am. I suppose the lawyers are ready too.

HUMPHREY This may grow warm, if I don't interpose.   *Aside.*
Sir, Mr Sealand is at the coffee-house, and has sent to speak with you.

SIR J. BEVIL Oh! that's well! Then I warrant the lawyers are ready. Son, you'll be in the way, you say –

BEVIL JUNIOR If you please, Sir, I'll take a chair, and go to Mr Sealand's, where the young lady and I will wait your leisure.

SIR J. BEVIL By no means – The old fellow will be so vain, if he sees –

BEVIL JUNIOR Ay – But the young lady, Sir, will think me so indifferent –

HUMPHREY Ay – there you are right – press your readiness to go to the bride – he won't let you.   *Aside to Bevil junior.*

BEVIL JUNIOR Are you sure of that?   *Aside to Humphrey.*

HUMPHREY How he likes being prevented.   *Aside.*

SIR J. BEVIL No, no: You are an hour or two too early.

Looking at his watch.

BEVIL JUNIOR You'll allow me, Sir, to think it too late to visit a beautiful, virtuous young woman, in the pride and bloom of life, ready to give her self to my arms: and to place her happiness or misery, for the future, in being agreeable or displeasing to me, is a – call a chair.

SIR J. BEVIL No, no, no, dear Jack; this Sealand is a moody old fellow: There's no dealing with some people, but by managing with indifference. We must leave to him the conduct of this day. It is the last of his commanding his daughter.

BEVIL JUNIOR Sir, he can't take it ill, that I am impatient to be hers.

SIR J. BEVIL Pray let me govern in this matter: you can't tell how humoursome old fellows are: There's no offering reason to some of 'em, especially when they are rich – If my son should see him, before I've brought old Sealand into better temper, the match would be impracticable.   *Aside.*

HUMPHREY Pray, Sir, let me beg you, to let Mr Bevil go. – See whether he will or not. (*Aside to Sir John.*) – (*Then to Bevil.*) Pray, Sir, command your self; since you see my master is positive, it is better you should not go.

BEVIL JUNIOR My father commands me, as to the object of my affections; but I hope he will not, as to the warmth and height of them.

SIR J. BEVIL So! I must even leave things as I found them: And in the mean time, at least, keep old Sealand out of sight. – Well, son, I'll go myself and take orders in your affair – You'll be in the way, I suppose, if I send to you – I'll leave your old friend with you. – Humphrey – don't let him stir, d'ye hear: your servant, your servant.   *Exit Sir John.*

HUMPHREY I have a sad time on't, Sir, between you and my master – I see you are unwilling, and I know his violent inclinations for the match – I must betray neither, and yet deceive you both, for your common good – Heav'n grant a good end of this matter: But there is a lady, Sir, that gives your father much trouble and sorrow – You'll pardon me.

BEVIL JUNIOR Humphrey, I know thou art a friend to both; and in that confidence, I dare tell thee – That lady – is a woman of honour and virtue. You may assure your self, I never will marry without my father's consent: But give me leave to say too, this declaration does not come up to a promise, that I will take whomsoever he pleases.

HUMPHREY Come Sir, I wholly understand you: You would engage my services to free you from this woman, whom my master intends you, to make way, in time, for the woman you have really a mind to.

BEVIL JUNIOR Honest Humphrey, you have always been an useful friend to my father, and my self; I beg you to continue your good offices, and don't let us come to the necessity of a dispute; for, if we should dispute, I must either part with more than life, or lose the best of fathers.

HUMPHREY My dear master, were I but worthy to know this secret, that so near concerns you, my life, my all should be engag'd to serve you. This, Sir, I dare promise, that I am sure I will and can be secret: your trust, at worst, but leaves you where you were; and if I cannot serve you, I will at once be plain, and tell you so.

BEVIL JUNIOR That's all I ask: Thou hast made it now my interest to trust thee — Be patient then, and hear the story of my heart.

HUMPHREY I am all attention, Sir.

BEVIL JUNIOR You may remember, Humphrey, that in my last travels, my father grew uneasy at my making so long a stay at Toulon.

HUMPHREY I remember it; he was apprehensive some woman had laid hold of you.

BEVIL JUNIOR His fears were just; for there I first saw this lady: She is of English birth: her father's name was Danvers, a younger brother of an ancient family, and originally an eminent merchant of Bristol; who, upon repeated misfortunes, was reduced to go privately to the Indies. In this retreat providence again grew favourable to his industry, and, in six years time, restored him to his former fortunes: On this he sent directions over, that his wife and little family should follow him to the Indies. His wife, impatient to obey such welcome orders, would not wait the leisure of a convoy, but took the first occasion of a single ship, and with her husband's sister only, and this daughter, then scarce seven years old, undertook the fatal voyage: For here, poor creature, she lost her liberty, and life; she, and her family, with all they had, were unfortunately taken by a privateer from Toulon. Being thus made a prisoner, though, as such, not ill treated, yet the fright, the shock, and cruel disappointment, seiz'd with such violence upon her unhealthy frame, she sicken'd, pined and died at sea.

HUMPHREY Poor soul! O the helpless infant!

BEVIL JUNIOR Her sister yet surviv'd, and had the care of her: The captain too proved to have humanity, and became a father to her; for having himself married an English woman, and being childless, he brought home into Toulon this her little country-woman; presenting her, with all her dead mother's moveables of value, to his wife, to be educated as his own adopted daughter.

HUMPHREY Fortune here seem'd, again, to smile on her.

BEVIL JUNIOR Only to make her frowns more terrible: For in his height of fortune, this captain too, her benefactor, unfortunately was kill'd at sea, and dying intestate, his estate fell wholly to an advocate his brother, who coming soon to take possession, there found (among his other riches) this blooming virgin, at his mercy.

HUMPHREY He durst not, sure, abuse his power!

BEVIL JUNIOR No wonder if his pamper'd blood was fired at the sight of her – in short, he lov'd: but, when all arts and gentle means had fail'd to move, he offer'd too his menaces in vain, denouncing vengeance on her cruelty; demanding her to account for all her maintenance, from her childhood; seiz'd on her little fortune, as his own inheritance, and was dragging her by violence to prison; when providence at the instant interpos'd, and sent me, by miracle, to relieve her.

HUMPHREY 'Twas providence indeed; But pray, Sir, after all this trouble, how came this lady at last to England?

BEVIL JUNIOR The disappointed advocate, finding she had so unexpected a support, on cooler thoughts, descended to a composition; which I, without her knowledge, secretly discharg'd.

HUMPHREY That generous concealment made the obligation double.

BEVIL JUNIOR Having thus obtain'd her liberty, I prevail'd, not without some difficulty, to see her safe to England; where no sooner arrived, but my father, jealous of my being imprudently engaged, immediately proposed this other fatal match that hangs upon my quiet.

HUMPHREY I find, Sir, you are irrecoverably fix'd upon this lady.

BEVIL JUNIOR As my vital life dwells in my heart – and yet you see – what I do to please my father: walk in this pageantry of dress, this splendid covering of sorrow – But, Humphrey, you have your lesson.

HUMPHREY Now, Sir, I have but one material question –

BEVIL JUNIOR Ask it freely.

HUMPHREY Is it, then, your own passion for this secret lady, or hers for you, that gives you this aversion to the match your father has proposed you?

BEVIL JUNIOR I shall appear, Humphrey, more romantick in my answer, than in all the rest of my story: For tho' I doat on her to death, and have no little reason to believe she has the same thoughts for me; yet in all my acquaintance, and utmost privacies with her, I never once directly told her, that I loved.

HUMPHREY How was it possible to avoid it?

BEVIL JUNIOR My tender obligations to my father have laid so inviolable a restraint upon my conduct, that 'till I have his consent to speak, I am determin'd, on that subject, to be dumb for ever –

HUMPHREY Well Sir, to your praise be it spoken, you are certainly the most unfashionable lover in Great Britain.

Enter Tom.

TOM Sir, Mr Myrtle's at the next door, and, if you are at leisure, will be glad to wait on you.

BEVIL JUNIOR Whenever he pleases – hold, Tom! did you receive no answer to my letter?

TOM Sir, I was desir'd to call again; for I was told her mother would not let her be out of her sight; but about an hour hence, Mrs Lettice said, I should certainly have one.

BEVIL JUNIOR Very well.

HUMPHREY Sir, I will take another opportunity: in the mean time, I only think it proper to tell you, that from a secret I know, you may appear to your father as forward as you please, to marry Lucinda, without the least hazard of its coming to a conclusion – Sir, your most obedient servant.

BEVIL JUNIOR Honest Humphrey, continue but my friend, in this exigence, and you shall always find me yours.

Exit Humphrey.

I long to hear how my letter has succeeded with Lucinda –
but I think, it cannot fail: for, at worst, were it possible she
could take it ill, her resentment of my indifference may as
probably occasion a delay, as her taking it right. – Poor
Myrtle, what terrors must he be in all this while? – Since he
knows she is offer'd to me, and refused to him, there is no
conversing, or taking any measures, with him, for his own
service – But I ought to bear with my friend, and use him as
one in adversity;

> All his disquiets by my own I prove,
> The greatest grief's perplexity in love.   *Exeunt*.

Act II

SCENE: *Continues.*

Enter Bevil junior and Tom.

TOM Sir, Mr Myrtle.

BEVIL JUNIOR Very well, – do you step again, and wait for an answer to my letter.

Enter Myrtle.

BEVIL JUNIOR Well Charles, why so much care in thy countenance. Is there any thing in this world deserves it? You, who used to be so gay, so open, so vacant!

MYRTLE I think we have of late chang'd complexions. You, who us'd to be much the graver man, are now all air in your behaviour – But the cause of my concern, may, for ought I know, be the same object that gives you all this satisfaction. In a word, I am told that you are this very day (and your dress confirms me in it) to be married to Lucinda.

BEVIL JUNIOR You are not misinform'd. – Nay, put not on the terrors of a rival, till you hear me out. I shall disoblige the best of fathers, if I don't seem ready to marry Lucinda. And you know I have ever told you, you might make use of my secret resolution never to marry her, for your own service, as you please. But I am now driven to the extremity of immediately refusing, or complying, unless you help me to escape the match.

MYRTLE Escape? Sir, neither her merit nor her fortune are below your acceptance. – Escaping, do you call it!

BEVIL JUNIOR Dear Sir, do you wish I should desire the match?

MYRTLE No – but such is my humorous and sickly state of mind, since it has been able to relish nothing but Lucinda, that tho' I must owe my happiness to your aversion to this marriage, I can't bear to hear her spoken of with levity or unconcern.

BEVIL JUNIOR Pardon me, Sir; I shall transgress that way no more. She has understanding, beauty, shape, complexion, wit —

MYRTLE Nay, dear Bevil, don't speak of her as if you lov'd her, neither.

BEVIL JUNIOR Why then, to give you ease at once, tho' I allow Lucinda to have good sense, wit, beauty and virtue; I know another, in whom these qualities appear to me more amiable than in her.

MYRTLE There you spoke like a reasonable and good-natur'd friend. When you acknowledge her merit, and own your prepossession for another, at once, you gratify my fondness, and cure my jealousie.

BEVIL JUNIOR But all this while you take no notice, you have no apprehension of another man, that has twice the fortune of either of us.

MYRTLE Cimberton! Hang him, a formal, philosophical, pedantick coxcomb — For the sot, with all these crude notions of divers things, under the direction of great vanity, and very little judgment, shews his strongest biass is avarice; which is so predominant in him, that he will examine the limbs of his mistress with the caution of a jockey, and pays no more compliment to her personal charms, than if she were a meer breeding animal.

BEVIL JUNIOR Are you sure that is not affected? I have known some women sooner set on fire by that sort of negligence, than by —

MYRTLE No, no; hang him, the rogue has no art, it is pure simple insolence and stupidity.

BEVIL JUNIOR Yet, with all this, I don't take him for a fool.

MYRTLE I own the man is not a natural; he has a very quick sense, tho' very slow understanding — He says indeed many things, that want only the circumstances of time and place to be very just and agreeable.

BEVIL JUNIOR Well, you may be sure of me, if you can disappoint him; but my intelligence says, the mother has actually sent for the conveyancer, to draw articles for his marriage with Lucinda; tho' those for mine with her, are, by her father's order, ready for signing: but it seems she has not thought fit to consult either him or his daughter in the matter.

MYRTLE Pshaw! A poor troublesome woman – Neither Lucinda nor her father will ever be brought to comply with it, – besides, I am sure Cimberton can make no settlement upon her, without the concurrence of his great Uncle Sir Geoffry in the west.

BEVIL JUNIOR Well Sir, and I can tell you, that's the very point that is now laid before her council; to know whether a firm settlement can be made, without this uncle's actual joyning in it. – Now pray consider, Sir, when my affair with Lucinda comes, as it soon must, to an open rupture, how are you sure that Cimberton's fortune may not then tempt her father too, to hear his proposals?

MYRTLE There you are right indeed, that must be provided against. – Do you know who are her council?

BEVIL JUNIOR Yes, for your service I have found out that too, they are Serjeant Bramble and old Target – by the way, they are neither of 'em known in the family; now I was thinking why you might not put a couple of false council upon her, to delay and confound matters a little – besides, it may probably let you into the bottom of her whole design against you.

MYRTLE As how pray?

BEVIL JUNIOR Why, can't you slip on a black wig and a gown, and be old Bramble your self?

MYRTLE Ha! I don't dislike it – but what shall I do for a brother in the case?

BEVIL JUNIOR What think you of my fellow, Tom? The rogue's intelligent, and is a good mimick; all his part will be but to stutter heartily, for that's old Target's case – Nay, it would be an immoral thing to mock him, were it not that his impertin-ence is the occasion of its breaking out to that degree – the conduct of the scene will chiefly lye upon you.

MYRTLE I like it of all things; if you'll send Tom to my chambers, I will give him full instructions: this will certainly give me occasion to raise difficulties, to puzzle, or confound her project for a while, at least.

BEVIL JUNIOR I'll warrant you success: so far we are right then: And now, Charles, your apprehension of my marrying her, is all you have to get over.

MYRTLE Dear Bevil! tho' I know you are my friend, yet when I abstract my self from my own interest in the thing, I know no objection she can make to you, or you to her, and therefore hope –

BEVIL JUNIOR Dear Myrtle, I am as much obliged to you for the cause of your suspicion, as I am offended at the effect: but be assured, I am taking measures for your certain security, and that all things with regard to me will end in your entire satisfaction.

MYRTLE Well, I'll promise you to be as easy and as confident as I can; tho' I cannot but remember that I have more than life at stake on your fidelity.   *Going.*

BEVIL JUNIOR Then depend upon it, you have no chance against you.

MYRTLE Nay, no ceremony, you know I must be going.

Exit Myrtle.

BEVIL Well! this is another instance of the perplexities which arise too, in faithful friendship: We must often, in this life, go on in our good offices, even under the displeasure of those to whom we do them, in compassion to their weaknesses and mistakes – But all this while poor Indiana is tortured with the doubt of me! she has no support or comfort, but in my fidelity, yet sees me daily press'd to marriage with another! How painful, in such a crisis, must be every hour she thinks on me! I'll let her see, at least, my conduct to her is not chang'd: I'll take this opportunity to visit her; for tho' the religious vow, I have made to my father, restrains me from ever marrying, without his approbation, yet that confines me not from seeing a virtuous woman, that is the pure delight of my eyes, and the guiltless joy of my heart: But the best condition of human life is but a gentler misery.

> To hope for perfect happiness is vain,
> And love has ever its allays of pain.   *Exit.*

SCENE 2

Enter Isabella, and Indiana in her own lodgings.

ISABELLA Yes – I say 'tis artifice, dear child; I say to thee again and again, 'tis all skill and management.

INDIANA Will you persuade me there can be an ill design, in supporting me in the condition of a woman of quality?

attended, dress'd, and lodg'd like one; in my appearance abroad, and my furniture at home, every way in the most sumptuous manner, and he that does it has an artifice, a design in it?

ISABELLA Yes, yes.

INDIANA And all this without so much as explaining to me, that all about me comes from him!

ISABELLA Ay, ay, – the more for that – that keeps the title to all you have, the more in him.

INDIANA The more in him! – He scorns the thought –

ISABELLA Then he – he – he –

INDIANA Well, be not so eager. – If he is an ill man, let us look into his stratagems. Here is another of them. (*Shewing a letter.*) Here's two hundred and fifty pound in bank notes, with these words, 'To pay for the set of dressing-plate, which will be brought home to-morrow.' Why dear aunt, now here's another piece of skill for you, which I own I cannot comprehend – and it is with a bleeding heart I hear you say any thing to the disadvantage of Mr Bevil. When he is present, I look upon him as one to whom I owe my life, and the support of it; then again, as the man who loves me with sincerity and honour. When his eyes are cast another way, and I dare survey him, my heart is painfully divided between shame and love – Oh! cou'd I tell you: –

ISABELLA Ah! You need not: I imagine all this for you.

INDIANA This is my state of mind in his presence; and when he is absent, you are ever dinning my ears with notions of the arts of men; that his hidden bounty, his respectful conduct, his careful provision for me, after his preserving me from utmost misery, are certain signs he means nothing, but to make I know not what of me?

ISABELLA Oh! You have a sweet opinion of him, truly.

INDIANA I have, when I am with him, ten thousand things, besides my sex's natural decency and shame, to suppress my heart, that yearns to thank, to praise, to say it loves him: I say, thus it is with me while I see him; and in his absence I am entertain'd with nothing but your endeavours to tear this amiable image from my heart; and in its stead, to place a base dissembler, an artful invader of my happiness, my innocence, my honour.

ISABELLA Ah poor soul! has not his plot taken? don't you die for him? has not the way he has taken, been the most proper with you? Oh! oh! He has sense, and has judg'd the thing right.

INDIANA Go on then, since nothing can answer you: say what you will of him. Heigh! ho!

ISABELLA Heigh! ho! indeed. It is better to say so, as you are now, than as many others are. There are, among the destroyers of women, the gentle, the generous, the mild, the affable, the humble, who all, soon after their success in their designs, turn to the contrary of those characters. I will own to you, Mr Bevil carries his hypocrisie the best of any man living, but still he is a man, and therefore a hypocrite. They have usurp'd an exemption from shame, for any baseness, any cruelty towards us. They embrace without love; they make vows, without conscience of obligation; they are partners, nay, seducers to the crime, wherein they pretend to be less guilty.

INDIANA That's truly observ'd.   *Aside*.
But what's all this to Bevil?

ISABELLA This it is to Bevil, and all mankind. Trust not those, who will think the worse of you for your confidence in them. Serpents, who lie in wait for doves. Won't you be on your guard against those who would betray you? Won't you doubt those who would contemn you for believing 'em? Take it from me: fair and natural dealing is to invite injuries, 'tis bleating to escape wolves who would devour you! Such is the world, – and such (since the behaviour of one man to my self) have I believ'd all the rest of the sex.   *Aside*.

INDIANA I will not doubt the truth of Bevil, I will not doubt it; He has not spoke it by an organ that is given to lying: His eyes are all that have ever told me that he was mine: I know his virtue, I know his filial piety, and ought to trust his management with a father, to whom he has uncommon obligations. What have I to be concern'd for? my lesson is very short. If he takes me for ever, my purpose of life is only to please him. If he leaves me (which heaven avert) I know he'll do it nobly; and I shall have nothing to do but to learn to die, after worse than death has happen'd to me.

ISABELLA Ay, do, persist in your credulity! flatter your self that a man of his figure and fortune will make himself the jest of the town, and marry a handsome beggar for love.

INDIANA The town! I must tell you, Madam, the fools that

laugh at Mr Bevil, will but make themselves more ridiculous; his actions are the result of thinking, and he has sense enough to make even virtue fashionable.

ISABELLA O' my conscience he has turn'd her head – Come, come; if he were the honest fool you take him for, why has he kept you here these three weeks, without sending you to Bristol, in search of your father, your family, and your relations?

INDIANA I am convinc'd he still designs it; and that nothing keeps him here, but the necessity of not coming to a breach with his father, in regard to the match he has propos'd him: besides, has he not writ to Bristol? and has not he advice that my father has not been heard of there, almost these twenty years?

ISABELLA All sham, meer evasion; he is afraid, if he should carry you thither, your honest relations may take you out of his hands, and so blow up all his wicked hopes at once.

INDIANA Wicked hopes! did I ever give him any such?

ISABELLA Has he ever given you any honest ones? can you say, in your conscience, he has ever once offer'd to marry you?

INDIANA No! but by his behaviour I am convinc'd he will offer it, the moment 'tis in his power, or consistent with his honour, to make such a promise good to me.

ISABELLA His honour!

INDIANA I will rely upon it; therefore desire you will not make my life uneasie, by these ungrateful jealousies of one, to whom I am, and wish to be oblig'd: For from his integrity alone, I have resolv'd to hope for happiness.

ISABELLA Nay, I have done my duty; if you won't see, at your peril be it –

INDIANA Let it be – This is his hour of visiting me.

ISABELLA Oh! to be sure, keep up your form; don't see him in a bed-chamber: This is pure prudence, when she is liable, where-ever he meets her, to be convey'd where-e'er he pleases.   *Apart.*

INDIANA All the rest of my life is but waiting till he comes: I live only when I'm with him.   *Exit.*

ISABELLA Well, go thy ways, thou willful innocent! I once had almost as much love for a man, who poorly left me, to marry an estate – And I am now, against my will, what they call an old maid – but I will not let the peevishness of that condition grow upon me – only keep up the suspicion of it, to prevent this creature's being any other than a virgin, except upon proper terms.   *Exit.*

Re-enter Indiana speaking to a servant.

INDIANA Desire Mr Bevil to walk in – Design! impossible! A base designing mind could never think of what he hourly puts in practice – And yet, since the late rumour of his marriage, he seems more reserv'd than formerly – he sends in too, before he sees me, to know if I am at leisure – such new respect may cover coldness in the heart – it certainly makes me thoughtful – I'll know the worst, at once; I'll lay such fair occasions in his way, that it shall be impossible to avoid an explanation – for these doubts are insupportable! – But see! he comes and clears them all.

Enter Bevil junior.

BEVIL JUNIOR Madam, your most obedient – I am afraid I broke in upon your rest last night – 'twas very late before we parted; but 'twas your own fault: I never saw you in such agreeable humour.

INDIANA I am extremely glad we were both pleas'd; so I thought I never saw you better company.

BEVIL JUNIOR Me, Madam! you rally; I said very little.

INDIANA But, I am afraid, you heard me say a great deal; and when a woman is in the talking vein, the most agreeable thing a man can do, you know, is to have patience, to hear her.

BEVIL JUNIOR Then it's pity, Madam, you should ever be silent, that we might be always agreeable to one another.

INDIANA If I had your talent, or power, to make my actions speak for me, I might indeed be silent, and yet pretend to something more than the agreeable.

BEVIL JUNIOR If I might be vain of any thing, in my power, Madam, 'tis that my understanding, from all your sex, has mark'd you out, as the most deserving object of my esteem.

INDIANA Should I think I deserve this, 'twere enough to make my vanity forfeit the very esteem you offer me.

BEVIL JUNIOR How so, Madam?

INDIANA Because esteem is the result of reason, and to deserve it from good sense, the height of human glory: nay, I had rather a man of honour should pay me that, than all the homage of a sincere and humble love.

BEVIL JUNIOR You certainly distinguish right, Madam; love often kindles from external merit only —

INDIANA But esteem arises from a higher source, the merit of the soul —

BEVIL JUNIOR True — And great souls only can deserve it.

Bowing respectfully.

INDIANA Now, I think, they are greater still, that can so charitably part with it.

BEVIL JUNIOR Now, Madam, you make me vain, since the utmost pride, and pleasure of my life is, that I esteem you — as I ought.

INDIANA (*Aside.*) As he ought! still more perplexing! he neither saves, nor kills my hope.

BEVIL JUNIOR But Madam, we grow grave methinks — Let's find some other subject — Pray how did you like the opera last night?

INDIANA First give me leave to thank you, for my tickets.

BEVIL JUNIOR O! your servant, Madam — But pray tell me, you now, who are never partial to the fashion, I fancy, must be the properest judge of a mighty dispute among the ladies, that is, whether Crispo or Griselda is the more agreeable entertainment.

INDIANA With submission now, I cannot be a proper judge of this question.

BEVIL How so, Madam?

INDIANA Because I find I have a partiality for one of them.

BEVIL JUNIOR Pray which is that?

INDIANA I do not know — there's something in that rural cottage of Griselda, her forlorn condition, her poverty, her solitude, her resignation, her innocent slumbers, and that lulling *dolce sogno* that's sung over her; it had an effect upon me, that — in short I never was so well deceiv'd, at any of them.

BEVIL JUNIOR O! Now then, I can account for the dispute: Griselda, it seems, is the distress of an injur'd innocent woman: Crispo, that only of a man in the same condition; therefore the men are mostly concern'd for Crispo, and, by a natural indulgence, both sexes for Griselda.

INDIANA So that judgment, you think, ought to be for one, tho' fancy and complaisance have got ground for the other. Well!

I believe you will never give me leave to dispute with you on any subject; for I own, Crispo has its charms for me too: Though in the main, all the pleasure the best opera gives us, is but meer sensation – Methinks it's pity the mind can't have a little more share in the entertainment. – The musick's certainly fine; but, in my thoughts, there's none of your composers come up to old Shakespear and Otway.

BEVIL JUNIOR How, Madam! why if a woman of your sense were to say this in the drawing-room –

Enter a Servant.

SERVANT Sir, here's Signior Carbonelli says he waits your commands, in the next room.

BEVIL JUNIOR A propos! You were saying yesterday, Madam, you had a mind to hear him – will you give him leave to entertain you now?

INDIANA By all means: desire the gentleman to walk in.

Exit servant.

BEVIL JUNIOR I fancy you will find something in this hand, that is uncommon.

INDIANA You are always finding ways, Mr Bevil, to make life seem less tedious to me. –

Enter Musick Master.

When the gentleman pleases.

After a sonata is play'd, Bevil junior waits on the master to the door, etc.

BEVIL JUNIOR You smile, Madam, to see me so complaisant to one, whom I pay for his visit: Now, I own, I think it is not enough barely to pay those, whose talents are superior to our own (I mean such talents, as would become our condition, if we had them). Methinks we ought to do something more, than barely gratify them, for what they do at our command, only because their fortune is below us.

INDIANA You say I smile: I assure you it was a smile of approbation; for indeed, I cannot but think it the distinguishing part of a gentleman, to make his superiority of fortune as easy to his inferiors, as he can. – Now once more to try him. (*Aside.*) – I was saying just now, I believed you would never let me dispute with you, and I dare say, it will always be so:

However I must have your opinion upon a subject, which created a debate between my aunt and me, just before you came hither; she would needs have it, that no man ever does any extraordinary kindness or service for a woman, but for his own sake.

BEVIL JUNIOR Well Madam! Indeed I can't but be of her mind.

INDIANA What, tho' he should maintain, and support her, without demanding any thing of her, on her part?

BEVIL JUNIOR Why, Madam, is making an expence, in the service of a valuable woman (for such I must suppose her) though she should never do him any favour, nay, though she should never know who did her such service, such a mighty heroick business?

INDIANA Certainly! I should think he must be a man of an uncommon mold.

BEVIL JUNIOR Dear Madam, why so? 'tis but, at best, a better taste in expence: To bestow upon one, whom he may think one of the ornaments of the whole creation, to be conscious, that from his superfluity, an innocent, a virtuous spirit is supported above the temptations and sorrows of life! That he sees satisfaction, health and gladness in her countenance, while he enjoys the happiness of seeing her (as that I will suppose too, or he must be too abstracted, too insensible) I say, if he is allowed to delight in that prospect; alas! what mighty matter is there, in all this?

INDIANA No mighty matter, in so disinterested a friendship!

BEVIL JUNIOR Disinterested! I can't think him so; your hero, Madam, is no more, than what every gentleman ought to be, and I believe very many are — he is only one, who takes more delight in reflections, than in sensations: he is more pleased with thinking, than eating; that's the utmost you can say of him — Why, Madam, a greater expence, than all this, men lay out upon an unnecessary stable of horses.

INDIANA Can you be sincere, in what you say?

BEVIL JUNIOR You may depend upon it, if you know any such man, he does not love dogs inordinately.

INDIANA No, that he does not.

BEVIL JUNIOR Nor cards, nor dice.

INDIANA No.

BEVIL JUNIOR Nor bottle companions.

INDIANA No.

BEVIL JUNIOR Nor loose women.

INDIANA No, I'm sure he does not.

BEVIL JUNIOR Take my word then, if your admired hero is not liable to any of these kind of demands, there's no such preheminence in this, as you imagine: Nay this way of expence you speak of, is what exalts and raises him, that has a taste for it: And, at the same time, his delight is incapable of satiety, disgust, or penitence.

INDIANA But still I insist his having no private interest in the action, makes it prodigious, almost incredible.

BEVIL JUNIOR Dear Madam, I never knew you more mistaken: Why, who can be more an usurer, than he, who lays out his money in such valuable purchases? If pleasure be worth purchasing, how great a pleasure is it to him, who has a true taste of life, to ease an aking heart, to see the humane countenance lighted up, into smiles of joy, on the receipt of a bit of oar, which is superfluous, and otherwise useless in a man's own pocket? What could a man do better with his cash? This is the effect of an humane disposition, where there is only a general tye of nature, and common necessity. What then must it be, when we serve an object of merit, of admiration!

INDIANA Well! the more you argue against it, the more I shall admire the generosity.

BEVIL JUNIOR Nay, nay – Then, Madam, 'tis time to fly, after a declaration, that my opinion strengthens my adversary's argument – I had best hasten to my appointment with Mr Myrtle, and begone, while we are friends, and – before things are brought to an extremity – *Exit carelessly*.

Enter Isabella.

ISABELLA Well, Madam, what think you of him now, pray?

INDIANA I protest, I begin to fear he is wholly disinterested, in what he does for me. On my heart, he has no other view, but the meer pleasure of doing it, and has neither good or bad designs upon me.

ISABELLA Ah! dear neice! don't be in fear of both! I'll warrant you, you will know time enough, that he is not indifferent.

INDIANA You please me, when you tell me so: For, if he has any wishes towards me, I know he will not pursue them, but with honour.

ISABELLA I wish, I were as confident of one, as t'other – I saw the respectful downcast of his eye, when you catcht him gazing at you during the musick: He, I warrant, was surpriz'd, as if he had been taken stealing your watch. O! the undissembled guilty look!

INDIANA But did you observe any such thing, really? I thought he look'd most charmingly graceful! How engaging is modesty, in a man, when one knows there is a great mind within – So tender a confusion! and yet, in other respects, so much himself, so collected, so dauntless, so determin'd!

ISABELLA Ah! Niece! there is a sort of bashfulness, which is the best engine to carry on a shameless purpose: some men's modesty serves their wickedness, as hypocrisy gains the respect due to piety: but I will own to you, there is one hopeful symptom, if there could be such a thing, as a disinterested lover; But it's all a perplexity, till – till – till –

INDIANA Till what?

ISABELLA Till I know whether Mr Myrtle and Mr Bevil are really friends, or foes – And that I will be convinced of, before I sleep: For you shall not be deceiv'd.

INDIANA I'm sure, I never shall, if your fears can guard me: In the mean time, I'll wrap my self up, in the integrity of my own heart, nor dare to doubt of his.

> As conscious honour all his actions steers;
> So conscious innocence dispels my fears.   *Exit.*

Act III

SCENE I

SCENE: *Sealand's house.*

Enter Tom meeting Phillis.

TOM Well, Phillis! — what, with a face, as if you had never seen
me before — What a work have I to do now? She has seen
some new visitant, at their house, whose airs she has catch'd,
and is resolv'd to practise them upon me. Numberless are the
changes she'll dance thro', before she'll answer this plain
question; videlicet, Have you deliver'd my master's letter to
your lady? Nay, I know her too well, to ask an account of it,
in an ordinary way; I'll be in my airs as well as she. *Aside.*
— Well, Madam, as unhappy as you are, at present pleased to
make me, I would not, in the general be any other than what
I am; I would not be a bit wiser, a bit richer, a bit taller, a bit
shorter, than I am at this instant.

Looking stedfastly at her.

PHILLIS Did ever any body doubt, Master Thomas, but that
you were extremely satisfied with your sweet self?

TOM I am indeed — The thing I have least reason to be satisfied
with, is my fortune, and I am glad of my poverty; Perhaps, if
I were rich, I should overlook the finest woman in the world,
that wants nothing but riches, to be thought so.

PHILLIS How prettily was that said? But, I'll have a great deal
more, before I'll say one word. *Aside.*

TOM I should, perhaps, have been stupidly above her, had I not
been her equal; and by not being her equal, never had
opportunity of being her slave. I am my master's servant, for
hire; I am my mistress's from choice; wou'd she but approve
my passion.

PHILLIS I think, it's the first time I ever heard you speak of it, with any sense of the anguish, if you really do suffer any.

TOM Ah! Phillis, can you doubt after what you have seen?

PHILLIS I know not what I have seen, nor what I have heard; but since I'm at leisure, you may tell me, When you fell in love with me; How you fell in love with me; and what you have suffer'd, or are ready to suffer for me.

TOM Oh! the unmerciful jade! when I'm in haste about my master's letter – But, I must go thro' it. (*Aside*.) – Ah! too well I remember when, and how, and on what occasion I was first surpriz'd. It was on the first of April, one thousand seven hundred and fifteen, I came into Mr Sealand's service; I was then a hobble de-hoy, and you a pretty little tight girl, a favourite handmaid of the housekeeper – At that time, we neither of us knew what was in us: I remember, I was order'd to get out of the window, one pair of stairs, to rub the sashes clean, – the person employ'd, on the innerside, was your charming self, whom I had never seen before.

PHILLIS I think, I remember the silly accident: What made ye, you oaf, ready to fall down into the street?

TOM You know not, I warrant you – You could not guess what surpriz'd me. You took no delight, when you immediately grew wanton, in your conquest, and put your lips close, and breath'd upon the glass, and when my lips approach'd, a dirty cloth you rubb'd against my face, and hid your beauteous form; when I again drew near, you spit, and rubb'd, and smil'd at my undoing.

PHILLIS What silly thoughts you men have!

TOM We were Pyramus and Thisbe – but ten times harder was my fate; Pyramus could peep only through a wall, I saw her, saw my Thisbe in all her beauty, but as much kept from her as if a hundred walls between, for there was more, there was her will against me – Would she but yet relent! – Oh, Phillis! Phillis! shorten my torment, and declare you pity me.

PHILLIS I believe, it's very sufferable; the pain is not so exquisite, but that you may bear it, a little longer.

TOM Oh! my charming Phillis, if all depended on my fair one's will, I could with glory suffer – But, dearest creature, consider our miserable state.

PHILLIS How! Miserable!

TOM We are miserable to be in love, and under the command

of others than those we love – with that generous passion in
the heart, to be sent to and fro on errands, call'd, check'd and
rated for the meanest trifles. Oh, Phillis, you don't know how
many China cups, and glasses, my passion for you has made
me break: you have broke my fortune, as well as my heart.

PHILLIS Well, Mr Thomas, I cannot but own to you, that I
believe, your master writes and you speak the best of any men
in the world. Never was woman so well pleas'd with a letter,
as my young lady was with his, and this is an answer to it.

Gives him a letter.

TOM This was well done, my dearest; consider, we must strike
out some pretty livelyhood for our selves, by closing their
affairs: It will be nothing for them to give us a little being of
our own, some small tenement, out of their large possessions:
whatever they give us, 'twill be more than what they keep for
themselves: one acre, with Phillis, wou'd be worth a whole
county without her.

PHILLIS O, could I but believe you!

TOM If not the utterance, believe the touch of my lips.

Kisses her.

PHILLIS There's no contradicting you; how closely you argue,
Tom!

TOM And will closer, in due time. But I must hasten with this
letter, to hasten towards the possession of you. – Then, Phillis,
consider, how I must be reveng'd, look to it, of all your
skittishness, shy looks, and at best but coy compliances.

PHILLIS Oh! Tom, you grow wanton, and sensual, as my lady
calls it, I must not endure it; Oh! Foh! you are a man, an
odious filthy male creature; you should behave, if you had a
right sense, or were a man of sense, like Mr Cimberton, with
distance, and indifference; or, let me see, some other becoming
hard word, with seeming in-in-inadvertency, and not rush on
one as if you were seizing a prey. But hush – the ladies are
coming – Good Tom, don't kiss me above once, and be gone
– Lard, we have been fooling and toying, and not consider'd
the main business of our masters and mistresses.

TOM Why, their business is to be fooling and toying, as soon as
the parchments are ready.

PHILLIS Well remember'd – parchments – . My lady, to my
knowledge, is preparing writings between her coxcomb cousin
Cimberton, and my mistress; though my master has an eye to

the parchments already prepar'd between your master Mr Bevil, and my mistress; and I believe, my mistress herself has sign'd and seal'd in her heart, to Mr Myrtle — Did I not bid you kiss me but once, and be gone? but I know you won't be satisfy'd.

TOM No, you smooth creature, how should I!

Kissing her hand.

PHILLIS Well, since you are so humble, or so cool, as to ravish my hand only, I'll take my leave of you like a great lady, and you a man of quality.   *They salute formally.*

TOM Pox of all this state.   *Offers to kiss her more closely.*

PHILLIS No, pr'ythee, Tom, mind your business. We must follow that interest which will take; but endeavour at that which will be most for us, and we like most — O here's my young mistress! (*Tom taps her neck behind, and kisses his fingers.*) Go, ye, liquorish fool.   *Exit Tom.*

Enter Lucinda.

LUCINDA Who was that you was hurrying away?

PHILLIS One that I had no mind to part with.

LUCINDA Why did you turn him away then?

PHILLIS For your ladyship's service, to carry your ladyship's letter to his master: I could hardly get the rogue away.

LUCINDA Why, has he so little love for his master?

PHILLIS No; but he hath so much love for his mistress.

LUCINDA But, I thought, I heard him kiss you. Why do you suffer that?

PHILLIS Why, Madam, we vulgar take it to be a sign of love; we servants, we poor people, that have nothing but our persons to bestow, or treat for, are forc'd to deal, and bargain by way of sample; and therefore, as we have no parchments, or wax necessary in our agreements, we squeeze with our hands, and seal with our lips, to ratifie vows and promises.

LUCINDA But can't you trust one another, without such earnest down?

PHILLIS We don't think it safe, any more than you gentry, to come together without deeds executed.

LUCINDA Thou art a pert merry hussy.

PHILLIS I wish, Madam, your lover and you were as happy, as Tom and your servant are.

LUCINDA You grow impertinent.

PHILLIS I have done, Madam; and I won't ask you, what you intend to do with Mr Myrtle, what your father will do with Mr Bevil, nor what you all, especially my lady, mean by admitting Mr Cimberton as particularly here, as if he were married to you already; nay, you are married actually as far as people of quality are.

LUCINDA How's that?

PHILLIS You have different beds in the same house.

LUCINDA Pshaw! I have a very great value for Mr Bevil, but have absolutely put an end to his pretensions, in the letter I gave you for him: But, my father, in his heart, still has a mind to him, were it not for this woman they talk of; and, I am apt to imagine he is married to her, or never designs to marry at all.

PHILLIS Then Mr Myrtle –

LUCINDA He had my parents leave to apply to me, and by that he has won me, and my affections: who is to have this body of mine, without 'em, it seems, is nothing to me; my mother says, 'tis indecent for me to let my thoughts stray about the person of my husband: nay, she says, a maid, rigidly virtuous, tho' she may have been where her lover was a thousand times, should not have made observations enough, to know him from another man, when she sees him in a third place.

PHILLIS That is more than the severity of a nun, for not to see, when one may, is hardly possible; not to see when one can't, is very easy: at this rate, madam, there are a great many whom you have not seen who –

LUCINDA Mamma says, the first time you see your husband should be at that instant he is made so; when your father, with the help of the minister, gives you to him; then you are to see him, then you are to observe and take notice of him, because then you are to obey him.

PHILLIS But does not my lady remember, you are to love, as well as obey?

LUCINDA To love is a passion, 'tis a desire, and we must have no desires. Oh! I cannot endure the reflection! With what insensibility on my part, with what more than patience, have I been expos'd, and offer'd to some aukward booby or other, in every county of Great Britain?

PHILLIS Indeed, Madam, I wonder, I never heard you speak of it before, with this indignation.

LUCINDA Every corner of the land has presented me with a wealthy coxcomb. As fast as one treaty has gone off, another has come on, till my name and person have been the tittle tattle of the whole town: What is this world come to! No shame left! To be barter'd for, like the beasts of the fields, and that, in such an instance, as coming together, to an intire familiarity, and union of soul and body; Oh! and this, without being so much as well-wishers to each other, but for encrease of fortune.

PHILLIS But, Madam, all these vexations will end very soon, in one for all: Mr Cimberton is your mother's kinsman, and three hundred years an older gentleman than any lover you ever had; for which reason, with that of his prodigious large estate, she is resolved on him, and has sent to consult the lawyers accordingly. Nay, has (whether you know it or no) been in treaty with Sir Geoffry, who, to join in the settlement, has accepted of a sum to do it, and is every moment expected in town for that purpose.

LUCINDA How do you get all this intelligence?

PHILLIS By an art I have, I thank my stars, beyond all the waiting-maids in Great Britain; the art of list'ning, Madam, for your ladyship's service.

LUCINDA I shall soon know as much as you do; leave me, leave me, Phillis, be gone: Here, here, I'll turn you out. My mother says I must not converse with my servants; tho' I must converse with no one else. (*Exit Phillis.*) How unhappy are we, who are born to great fortunes! No one looks at us, with indifference, or acts towards us on the foot of plain dealing; yet, by all I have been heretofore offer'd to, or treated for, I have been us'd with the most agreeable of all abuses, flattery; but now, by this flegmatick fool, I'm us'd as nothing, or a meer thing; He, forsooth! is too wise, too learned to have any regard to desires, and, I know not what the learned oaf calls sentiments of love and passion – Here he comes with my mother – It's much if he looks at me; or if he does, takes no more notice of me, than of any other moveable in the room.

Enter Mrs Sealand, and Mr Cimberton.

MRS SEALAND How do I admire this noble, this learned taste of yours, and the worthy regard you have to our own ancient and honourable house, in consulting a means, to keep the blood as pure, and as regularly descended as may be.

CIMBERTON Why, really Madam, the young women of this age are treated with discourses of such a tendency, and their imaginations so bewilder'd in flesh and blood, that a man of reason can't talk to be understood: They have no ideas of happiness, but what are more gross than the gratification of hunger and thirst.

LUCINDA With how much reflection he is a coxcomb!   *Aside*.

CIMBERTON And in truth, Madam, I have consider'd it, as a most brutal custom, that persons, of the first character in the world, should go as ordinarily, and with as little shame, to bed, as to dinner with one another. They proceed to the propagation of the species, as openly, as to the preservation of the individual.

LUCINDA She that willingly goes to bed to thee, must have no shame, I'm sure.   *Aside*.

MRS SEALAND Oh cousin Cimberton! cousin Cimberton! how abstracted, how refin'd, is your sense of things! But, indeed, it is too true, there is nothing so ordinary as to say, in the best govern'd families, my master and lady are gone to bed; one does not know but it might have been said of one's self.

Hiding her face with her fan.

CIMBERTON Lycurgus, Madam, instituted otherwise; among the Lacedæmonians, the whole female world was pregnant, but none, but the mothers themselves, knew by whom; their meetings were secret, and the amorous congress always by stealth; and no such professed doings between the sexes, as are tolerated among us, under the audacious word, marriage.

MRS SEALAND Oh! had I liv'd, in those days, and been a matron of Sparta, one might, with less indecency, have had ten children, according to that modest institution, than one, under the confusion of our modern, barefac'd manner.

LUCINDA And yet, poor woman, she has gone thro' the whole ceremony, and here I stand a melancholy proof of it.   *Aside*.

MRS SEALAND We will talk then of business. That girl walking about the room there is to be your wife. She has, I confess, no ideas, no sentiments, that speak her born of a thinking mother.

CIMBERTON I have observ'd her; her lively look, free air, and disengag'd countenance speak her very –

LUCINDA Very, what?

CIMBERTON If you please, Madam – to set her a little that way.

MRS SEALAND Lucinda, say nothing to him, you are not a match for him; when you are married, you may speak to such a husband, when you're spoken to. But, I am disposing of you, above your self, every way.

CIMBERTON Madam, you cannot but observe the inconveniences I expose my self to, in hopes that your ladyship will be the consort of my better part: As for the young woman, she is rather an impediment, than a help, to a man of letters and speculation. Madam, there is no reflection, no philosophy, can, at all times, subdue the sensitive life, but the animal shall sometimes carry away the man: Ha! ay, the vermilion of her lips.

LUCINDA Pray, don't talk to me thus.

CIMBERTON The pretty enough – pant of her bosom.

LUCINDA Sir; Madam, don't you hear him?

CIMBERTON Her forward chest.

LUCINDA Intollerable!

CIMBERTON High health.

LUCINDA The grave, easy impudence of him!

CIMBERTON Proud heart.

LUCINDA Stupid coxcomb!

CIMBERTON I say, Madam, her impatience, while we are looking at her, throws out all attractions – her arms – her neck – what a spring in her step!

LUCINDA Don't you run me over thus, you strange unaccountable!

CIMBERTON What an elasticity in her veins and arteries!

LUCINDA I have no veins, no arteries.

MRS SEALAND Oh, child, hear him, he talks finely, he's a scholar, he knows what you have.

CIMBERTON The speaking invitation of her shape, the gathering of her self up, and the indignation you see in the pretty little thing – now, I am considering her, on this occasion, but as one that is to be pregnant.

LUCINDA The familiar, learned, unseasonable puppy!   *Aside.*

CIMBERTON And pregnant undoubtedly she will be yearly. I fear, I shan't, for many years, have discretion enough to give her one fallow season.

LUCINDA Monster! there's no bearing it. The hideous sot! – there's no enduring it, to be thus survey'd like a steed at sale.

CIMBERTON At sale! she's very illiterate – But she's very well limb'd too; turn her in; I see what she is.

Exit Lucinda in a rage.

MRS SEALAND Go, you creature, I am asham'd of you.

CIMBERTON No harm done – you know, Madam, the better sort of people, as I observ'd to you, treat by their lawyers of weddings (*adjusting himself at the glass*) and the woman in the bargain, like the mansion-house in the sale of the estate, is thrown in, and what that is, whether good or bad, is not at all consider'd.

MRS SEALAND I grant it, and therefore make no demand for her youth, and beauty, and every other accomplishment, as the common world think 'em, because she is not polite.

CIMBERTON Madam, I know, your exalted understanding, abstracted, as it is, from vulgar prejudices, will not be offended, when I declare to you, I marry to have an heir to my estate, and not to beget a colony, or a plantation: This young woman's beauty, and constitution, will demand provision for a tenth child at least.

MRS SEALAND With all that wit, and learning, how considerate! What an oeconomist! (*Aside.*) – Sir, I cannot make her any other than she is; or say she is much better than the other young women of this age, or fit for much, besides being a mother; but I have given directions for the marriage settlements, and Sir Geoffrey Cimberton's council is to meet ours here, at this hour, concerning his joyning in the deed, which when executed, makes you capable of settling what is due to Lucinda's fortune: Her self, as I told you, I say nothing of.

CIMBERTON No, no, no, indeed, Madam, it is not usual, and I must depend upon my own reflection, and philosophy, not to overstock my family.

MRS SEALAND I cannot help her, cousin Cimberton; but she is, for ought I see, as well as the daughter of any body else.

CIMBERTON That is very true, Madam.

Enter a Servant, who whispers Mrs Sealand.

MRS SEALAND The lawyers are come, and now we are to hear what they have resolv'd as to the point whether it's necessary that Sir Geoffrey should join in the settlement, as being what they call in the remainder. But, good cousin, you must have patience with 'em. These lawyers, I am told, are of a different kind, one is what they call a chamber-council, the other a pleader: The conveyancer is slow, from an imperfection in his speech, and therefore shun'd the bar, but extremely passionate, and impatient of contradiction: The other is as warm as he; but has a tongue so voluble, and a head so conceited, he will suffer no body to speak but himself.

CIMBERTON You mean old Serjeant Target, and Counsellor Bramble? I have heard of 'em.

MRS SEALAND The same: shew in the gentlemen. *Exit Servant.*

Re-enter Servant, introducing Myrtle and Tom, disguis'd as Bramble and Target.

MRS SEALAND Gentlemen, this is the party concern'd, Mr Cimberton; and I hope you have consider'd of the matter.

TARGET Yes, Madam, we have agreed that it must be by Indent – dent – dent – dent –

BRAMBLE Yes, Madam, Mr Serjeant and my self have agreed, as he is pleas'd to inform you, that it must be an indenture tripartite, and tripartite let it be, for Sir Geoffry must needs be a party; old Cimberton, in the year 1619, says, in that ancient roll, in Mr Serjeant's hands, as recourse thereto being had, will more at large appear –

TARGET Yes, and by the deed in your hands, it appears that –

BRAMBLE Mr Serjeant, I beg of you to make no inferences upon what is in our custody; but speak to the titles in your own deeds – I shall not show that deed till my client is in town.

CIMBERTON You know best your own methods.

MRS SEALAND The single question is, whether the intail is such, that my cousin Sir Geoffry is necessary in this affair?

BRAMBLE Yes, as to the lordship of Tretriplet, but not as to the messuage of Grimgribber.

TARGET I say that Gr – gr – that Gr – gr – Grimgribber, Grimgribber is in us. That is to say the Remainder thereof, as well as that of Tr – tr – Triplet.

BRAMBLE You go upon the deed of Sir Ralph, made in the middle of the last century, precedent to that in which old Cimberton made over the remainder, and made it pass to the heirs general, by which your client comes in; and I question whether the remainder even of Tretriplet is in him – But we

are willing to wave that, and give him a valuable consideration. But we shall not purchase what is in us for ever, as
Grimgribber is, at the rate as we guard against the contingent
of Mr Cimberton having no son – Then we know Sir Geoffry
is the first of the collateral male line in this family – Yet –

TARGET Sir, Gr – gr – ber is –

BRAMBLE I apprehend you very well, and your argument might
be of force, and we would be inclin'd to hear that in all its
parts – But, Sir, I see very plainly what you are going into – I
tell you, it is as probable a Contingent that Sir Geoffry may
die before Mr Cimberton, as that he may outlive him.

TARGET Sir, we are not ripe for that yet, but I must say –

BRAMBLE Sir, I allow you the whole extent of that argument;
but that will go no farther than as to the claimants under old
Cimberton, – I am of opinion, that according to the Instruc-
tion of Sir Ralph, he could not dock the entail, and then
create a new estate for the heirs general.

TARGET Sir, I have not patience to be told that, when Gr – gr –
ber –

BRAMBLE I will allow it you, Mr Serjeant; but there must be the
word heirs for ever, to make such an estate as you pretend.

CIMBERTON I must be impartial, tho' you are council for my
side of the question – Were it not that you are so good as to
allow him what he has not said, I should think it very hard
you should answer him without hearing him – But gentlemen,
I believe you have both consider'd this matter, and are firm in
your different opinions: 'Twere better therefore you proceeded according to the particular sense of each of you, and
gave your thoughts distinctly in writing – And do you see,
Sirs, pray let me have a copy of what you say, in English.

BRAMBLE Why, what is all we have been saying? – In English!
Oh! But I forgot my self, you're a wit – But however, to please
you, Sir, you shall have it, in as plain terms, as the law will
admit of.

CIMBERTON But I would have it, Sir, without delay.

BRAMBLE That, Sir, the law will not admit of: the courts are
sitting at Westminster, and I am this moment oblig'd to be at
every one of them, and 'twould be wrong if I should not be in
the hall to attend one of 'em at least, the rest would take it ill
else – Therefore, I must leave what I have said to Mr Serjeant's

consideration, and I will digest his arguments on my part, and you shall hear from me again, Sir.   *Exit Bramble.*

TARGET Agreed, agreed.

CIMBERTON Mr Bramble is very quick – He parted a little abruptly.

TARGET He could not bear my argument, I pincht him to the quick about that Gr – gr – ber.

MRS SEALAND I saw that, for he durst not so much as hear you – I shall send to you, Mr Serjeant, as soon as Sir Geoffry comes to town, and then I hope all may be adjusted.

TARGET I shall be at my chambers, at my usual hours.   *Exit.*

CIMBERTON Madam, if you please, I'll now attend you to the tea-table, where I shall hear from your ladyship, reason and good sense, after all this law and gibberish.

MRS SEALAND 'Tis a wonderful thing, Sir, that men of professions do not study to talk the substance of what they have to say, in the language of the rest of the world: Sure, they'd find their account in it.

CIMBERTON They might, perhaps, Madam, with people of your good sense; but, with the generality 'twould never do: The vulgar would have no respect for truth and knowledge, if they were exposed to naked view.

> Truth is too simple, of all Art bereav'd:
> Since the World will – why let it be deceiv'd.   *Exeunt.*

Act IV

SCENE I

SCENE: *Bevil junior's lodgings.*

Bevil junior with a letter in his hand, follow'd by Tom.

TOM Upon my life, Sir, I know nothing of the matter: I never open'd my lips to Mr Myrtle, about any thing of your honour's letter to Madam Lucinda.

BEVIL JUNIOR What's the fool in such a fright for? I don't suppose you did: What I would know is, whether Mr Myrtle shew'd any suspicion, or ask'd you any questions, to lead you to say casually, that you had carry'd any such letter, for me, this morning.

TOM Why, Sir, if he did ask me any questions, how could I help it?

BEVIL JUNIOR I don't say you could, oaf! I am not questioning you, but him: What did he say to you?

TOM Why, Sir, when I came to his chambers, to be dress'd for the lawyer's part, your honour was pleas'd to put me upon, he ask'd me, if I had been at Mr Sealand's this morning? – So I told him, Sir, I often went thither – because, Sir, if I had not said that, he might have thought, there was something more, in my going now, than at another time.

BEVIL JUNIOR Very well! – This fellow's caution, I find, has given him this jealousy. (*Aside*.) Did he ask you no other questions?

TOM Yes, Sir – now I remember, as we came away in the hackney coach, from Mr Sealand's, Tom, says he, as I came in to your master this morning, he bad you go for an answer to a letter he had sent. Pray did you bring him any? Says he – Ah! says I, Sir, your honour is pleas'd to joke with me, you have a mind to know whether I can keep a secret, or no?

BEVIL JUNIOR And so, by shewing him you could, you told him you had one?

TOM Sir —   *Confus'd.*

BEVIL JUNIOR What mean actions does jealousy make a man stoop to? How poorly has he us'd art, with a servant, to make him betray his master? Well! and when did he give you this letter for me?

TOM Sir, he writ it, before he pull'd off his lawyer's gown, at his own chambers.

BEVIL JUNIOR Very well; and what did he say, when you brought him my answer to it?

TOM He look'd a little out of humour, Sir, and said, It was very well.

BEVIL JUNIOR I knew he would be grave upon't, — wait without.

TOM Humh! 'gad, I don't like this; I am afraid we are all in the wrong box here. —   *Exit Tom.*

BEVIL JUNIOR I put on a serenity, while my fellow was present: But I have never been more thoroughly disturb'd; This hot man! to write me a challenge, on supposed artificial dealing, when I profess'd my self his friend! I can live contented without glory; but I cannot suffer shame. What's to be done? But first, let me consider, Lucinda's letter again.   *Reads.*

> Sir,
>
> I hope it is consistent with the laws a woman ought to impose upon her self, to acknowledge, that your manner of declining a treaty of marriage, in our family, and desiring the refusal may come from me, has something more engaging in it, than the courtship of him, who, I fear, will fall to my lot; except your friend exerts himself, for our common safety, and happiness: I have reasons for desiring Mr Myrtle may not know of this letter, till hereafter, and am your most oblig'd humble servant, Lucinda Sealand.

Well, but the postscript.   *Reads.*

> I won't, upon second thoughts, hide any thing from you. But, my reason for concealing this is, that Mr Myrtle has a jealousy in his temper, which gives me some terrors; but my esteem for him inclines me to hope that only an ill effect, which sometimes accompanies a tender love; and what may be cur'd, by a careful and unblameable conduct.

Thus has this lady made me her friend and confident, and put her self, in a kind, under my protection: I cannot tell him immediately the purport of her letter, except I could cure him of the violent and untractable passion of jealousy, and so serve him, and her, by disobeying her, in the article of secrecy, more than I should by complying with her directions. – But then this duelling, which custom has impos'd upon every man, who would live with reputation and honour in the world: – How must I preserve my self from imputations there? He'll, forsooth, call it, or think it fear, if I explain without fighting – But his letter – I'll read it again –

Sir,
You have us'd me basely, in corresponding, and carrying on a treaty, where you told me you were indifferent: I have chang'd my sword, since I saw you; which advertisement I thought proper to send you against the next meeting, between you, and the injur'd

Charles Myrtle.

Enter Tom.

TOM Mr Myrtle. Sir: would your honour please to see him?

BEVIL JUNIOR Why you stupid creature! Let Mr Myrtle wait at my lodgings! Shew him up. (*Exit Tom.*) Well! I am resolv'd upon my carriage to him – He is in love, and in every circumstance of life a little distrustful, which I must allow for – but here he is.

Enter Tom introducing Myrtle.

Sir, I am extremely oblig'd to you for this honour, – But, Sir, you, with your very discerning face, leave the room. (*Exit Tom.*) Well, Mr Myrtle, your commands with me?

MYRTLE The time, the place our long acquaintance, and many other circumstances, which affect me on this occasion, oblige me, without farther ceremony, or conference, to desire you would not only, as you already have, acknowledge the receipt of my letter, but also comply with the request in it. I must have farther notice taken of my message than these half lines, – I have yours, – I shall be at home. –

BEVIL JUNIOR Sir, I own, I have received a letter from you, in a very unusual style; But as I design every thing, in this matter, shall be your own action, your own seeking, I shall understand nothing, but what you are pleas'd to confirm, face to face, and I have already forgot the contents of your epistle.

MYRTLE This cool manner is very agreeable to the abuse you have already made of my simplicity and frankness; and I see your moderation tends to your own advantage, and not mine; your own safety, not consideration of your friend.

BEVIL JUNIOR My own safety, Mr Myrtle!

MYRTLE Your own safety, Mr Bevil.

BEVIL JUNIOR Look you, Mr Myrtle, there's no disguising that I understand what you would be at – But, Sir, you know, I have often dared to disapprove of the decisions a tyrant custom has introduc'd, to the breach of all laws, both divine and human.

MYRTLE Mr Bevil, Mr Bevil, it would be a good first principle, in those who have so tender a conscience that way, to have as much abhorrence of doing injuries, as –

BEVIL JUNIOR As what?

MYRTLE As fear of answering for 'em.

BEVIL JUNIOR As fear of answering for 'em! But that apprehension is just or blameable, according to the object of that fear. – I have often told you in confidence of heart, I abhorr'd the daring to offend the author of life, and rushing into his presence – I say, by the very same act, to commit the crime against him, and immediately to urge on to his tribunal.

MYRTLE Mr Bevil, I must tell you, this coolness, this gravity, this shew of conscience, shall never cheat me of my mistress. You have, indeed, the best excuse for life, the hopes of possessing Lucinda: But consider, Sir, I have as much reason to be weary of it, if I am to lose her; and my first attempt to recover her, shall be to let her see the dauntless man, who is to be her guardian and protector.

BEVIL JUNIOR Sir, shew me but the least glimpse of argument, that I am authoriz'd, by my own hand, to vindicate any lawless insult of this nature, and I will shew thee – to chastize thee – hardly deserves the name of courage – slight, inconsiderate man! – There is, Mr Myrtle, no such terror in quick anger; and you shall, you know not why, be cool, as you have, you know not why, been warm.

MYRTLE Is the woman one loves, so little an occasion of anger? You perhaps, who know not what it is to love, who have your ready, your commodious, your foreign trinket, for your loose hours; and from your fortune, your specious outward carriage, and other lucky circumstances, as easie a way to the possession of a woman of honour; you know nothing of what it is to be alarm'd, to be distracted, with anxiety and terror of losing more than life: Your marriage, happy man! goes on like common business, and in the interim, you have your rambling captive, your Indian princess, for your soft moments of dalliance, your convenient, your ready Indiana.

BEVIL JUNIOR You have touch'd me beyond the patience of a man; and I'm excusable, in the guard of innocence (or from the infirmity of human nature, which can bear no more) to accept your invitation, and observe your letter – Sir, I'll attend you.

Enter Tom.

TOM Did you call, Sir? I thought you did: I heard you speak aloud.

BEVIL JUNIOR Yes, go call a coach.

TOM Sir, – Master – Mr Myrtle – Friends – Gentlemen – what d'ye mean? I am but a servant, or –

BEVIL JUNIOR Call a coach.   *Exit Tom.*
                 A long pause, walking sullenly by each other.
(*Aside.*) Shall I (though provok'd to the uttermost) recover my self at the entrance of a third person, and that my servant too, and not have respect enough to all I have ever been receiving from infancy, the obligation to the best of Fathers, to an unhappy virgin too, whose life depends on mine.
                                    Shutting the door.
(*To Myrtle.*) I have, thank Heaven, had time to recollect my self, and shall not for fear of what such a rash man as you think of me, keep longer unexplain'd the false appearances, under which your infirmity of temper makes you suffer; when, perhaps, too much regard to a false point of honour, makes me prolong that suffering.

MYRTLE I am sure, Mr Bevil cannot doubt, but I had rather have satisfaction from his innocence, than his sword.

BEVIL JUNIOR Why then would you ask it first that way?

MYRTLE Consider, you kept your temper your self no longer than till I spoke to the disadvantage of her you lov'd.

BEVIL JUNIOR True. But let me tell you, I have sav'd you from the most exquisite distress, even tho' you had succeeded in the dispute: I know you so well, that I am sure, to have found this letter about a man you had kill'd, would have been worse than death to your self – Read it – . When he is thoroughly mortify'd, and shame has got the better of jealousie, when he has seen himself throughly, he will deserve to be assisted towards obtaining Lucinda.

MYRTLE With what a superiority has he turn'd the injury on me, as the aggressor? I begin to fear, I have been too far transported – *A treaty in our family!* is not that saying too much? I shall relapse – But, I find (on the postscript) *something like jealousie* – with what face can I see my benefactor? my advocate? whom I have treated like a betrayer. – Oh! Bevil, with what words shall I –

BEVIL JUNIOR There needs none; to convince, is much more than to conquer.

MYRTLE But can you –

BEVIL JUNIOR You have o'erpaid the inquietude you gave me, in the change I see in you towards me: Alas! what machines are we! thy face is alter'd to that of another man; to that of my companion, my friend.

MYRTLE That I could be such a precipitant wretch!

BEVIL JUNIOR Pray no more.

MYRTLE Let me reflect how many friends have died, by the hands of friends, for want of temper; and you must give me leave to say again, and again, how much I am beholden to that superior spirit you have subdu'd me with – what had become of one of us, or perhaps both, had you been as weak as I was, and as incapable of reason?

BEVIL JUNIOR I congratulate to us both the escape from our selves, and hope the memory of it will make us dearer friends than ever.

MYRTLE Dear Bevil, your friendly conduct has convinc'd me that there is nothing manly, but what is conducted by reason, and agreeable to the practice of virtue and justice. And yet, how many have been sacrific'd to that idol, the unreasonable opinion of men! Nay, they are so ridiculous in it, that they often use their swords against each other, with dissembled anger, and real fear.

> Betray'd by honour, and compell'd by shame,
> They hazard being, to preserve a name:
> Nor dare enquire into the dread mistake,
> 'Till plung'd in sad eternity they wake.   *Exeunt.*

SCENE 2

SCENE: *St James's Park.*

Enter Sir John Bevil, and Mr Sealand.

SIR J. BEVIL Give me leave, however, Mr Sealand, as we are upon a treaty for uniting our families, to mention only the business of an ancient house – genealogy and descent are to be of some consideration, in an affair of this sort –

MR SEALAND Genealogy, and descent! – Sir, There has been in our family a very large one. There was Galfrid the father of Edward, the father of Ptolomey, the father of Crassus, the father of Earl Richard, the father of Henry the Marquis, the father of Duke John –

SIR J. BEVIL What, do you rave, Mr Sealand? all these great names in your family?

MR SEALAND These? yes, Sir – I have heard my father name 'em all, and more.

SIR J. BEVIL Ay, Sir? – and did he say they were all in your family?

MR SEALAND Yes, Sir, he kept 'em all – he was the greatest cocker in England – he said, Duke John won him many battles, and never lost one.

SIR J. BEVIL Oh Sir, your servant, you are laughing at my laying any stress upon descent – but I must tell you, Sir, I never knew any one, but he that wanted that advantage, turn it into ridicule.

MR SEALAND And I never knew any one, who had many better advantages, put that into his account – But, Sir John, value your self as you please upon your ancient house, I am to talk freely of every thing, you are pleas'd to put into your bill of rates, on this occasion – yet, Sir, I have made no objections to your son's family – 'Tis his morals, that I doubt.

SIR J. BEVIL Sir, I can't help saying, that what might injure a citizen's credit, may be no stain to a gentleman's honour.

MR SEALAND Sir John, the honour of a gentleman is liable to be tainted, by as small a matter as the credit of a trader; we are talking of a marriage, and in such a case, the father of a young woman will not think it an addition, to the honour, or credit of her lover – that he is a keeper –

SIR J. BEVIL Mr Sealand, don't take upon you, to spoil my son's marriage, with any woman else.

MR SEALAND Sir John, let him apply to any woman else, and have as many mistresses as he pleases –

SIR J. BEVIL My son, Sir, is a discreet and sober gentleman –

MR SEALAND Sir, I never saw a man that wench'd soberly and discreetly, that ever left it off – the decency observ'd in the practice, hides, even from the sinner, the iniquity of it. They pursue it, not that their appetites hurry 'em away; but, I warrant you, because, 'tis their opinion, they may do it.

SIR J. BEVIL Were what you suspect a truth – do you design to keep your daughter a virgin, 'till you find a man unblemish'd that way?

MR SEALAND Sir, as much a cit as you take me for – I know the town, and the world – and give me leave to say, that we merchants are a species of gentry, that have grown into the world this last century, and are as honourable, and almost as useful, as you landed folks, that have always thought your selves so much above us; For your trading, forsooth! is extended no farther, than a load of hay, or a fat ox – You are pleasant people, indeed; because you are generally bred up to be lazy, therefore, I warrant you, industry is dishonourable.

SIR J. BEVIL Be not offended, Sir; let us go back to our point.

MR SEALAND Oh! not at all offended – but I don't love to leave any part of the account unclos'd – look you, Sir John, comparisons are odious, and more particularly so, on occasions of this kind, when we are projecting races, that are to be made out of both sides of the comparisons.

SIR J. BEVIL But, my son, Sir, is in the eye of the world, a gentleman of merit.

MR SEALAND I own to you, I think him so. – But, Sir John, I am a man exercis'd, and experienc'd in chances, and disasters; I lost, in my earlier years, a very fine wife, and with her a poor little infant; this makes me, perhaps, over cautious, to preserve the second bounty of providence to me, and be as careful, as I can, of this child – you'll pardon me, my poor girl, Sir, is as valuable to me, as your boasted son, to you.

SIR J. BEVIL Why, that's one very good reason, Mr Sealand, why I wish my son had her.

MR SEALAND There is nothing, but this strange lady here, this *incognita*, that can be objected to him – here and there a man

falls in love with an artful creature, and gives up all the
motives of life, to that one passion.

SIR J. BEVIL A man of my son's understanding, cannot be
suppos'd to be one of them.

MR SEALAND Very wise men have been so enslav'd; and, when
a man marries with one of them upon his hands, whether
mov'd from the demand of the world, or slighter reasons;
such a husband soils with his wife for a month perhaps – then
good B'w'y' Madam – the show's over – ah! John Dryden
points out such a husband to a hair, where he says,

> And while abroad so prodigal the dolt is,
> Poor spouse at home as ragged as a colt is.

Now in plain terms, Sir, I shall not care to have my poor girl
turn'd a grazing, and that must be the case, when –

SIR J. BEVIL But pray consider, Sir, my son –

MR SEALAND Look you Sir, I'll make the matter short. This
unknown lady, as I told you, is all the objection I have to
him: But, one way or other, he is, or has been, certainly
engag'd to her – I am therefore resolv'd, this very afternoon,
to visit her: Now from her behaviour, or appearance, I shall
soon be let into, what I may fear, or hope for.

SIR J. BEVIL Sir, I am very confident, there can be nothing
enquir'd into, relating to my son, that will not, upon being
understood, turn to his advantage.

MR SEALAND I hope that, as sincerely, as you believe it – Sir
John Bevil, when I am satisfied, in this great point, if your
son's conduct answers the character you give him, I shall wish
your alliance more than that of any gentleman in Great
Britain, and so your servant.   *Exit.*

SIR J. BEVIL He is gone, in a way but barely civil; but his great
wealth, and the merit of his only child, the heiress of it, are
not to be lost for a little peevishness –

Enter Humphrey.

Oh! Humphrey, you are come in a seasonable minute; I want
to talk to thee, and to tell thee, that my head and heart are on
the rack, about my son.

HUMPHREY Sir, you may trust his discretion, I am sure you may.

SIR J. BEVIL Why, I do believe I may, and yet I'm in a thousand
fears, when I lay this vast wealth before me: When I consider

his prepossessions, either generous, to a folly, in an honourable love; or abandon'd, past redemption, in a vicious one; and, from the one or the other, his insensibility to the fairest prospect, towards doubling our estate: a father, who knows how useful wealth is, and how necessary, even to those who despise it, I say a father, Humphrey, a father cannot bear it.

HUMPHREY Be not transported, Sir; you will grow incapable of taking any resolution, in your perplexity.

SIR J. BEVIL Yet, as angry as I am with him, I would not have him, surpriz'd in any thing – This mercantile rough man may go grosly into the examination of this matter, and talk to the gentlewoman so as to –

HUMPHREY No, I hope, not in an abrupt manner.

SIR J. BEVIL No, I hope not! Why, dost thou know any thing of her, or of him, or of any thing of it, or all of it?

HUMPHREY My dear master, I know so much, that I told him this very day, you had reason to be secretly out of humour about her.

SIR J. BEVIL Did you go so far? Well, what said he to that?

HUMPHREY His words were, looking upon me stedfastly; Humphrey, says he, that woman is a woman of honour.

SIR J. BEVIL How! Do you think he is married to her, or designs to marry her?

HUMPHREY I can say nothing to the latter – But he says, he can marry no one without your consent, while you are living.

SIR J. BEVIL If he said so much, I know he scorns to break his word with me.

HUMPHREY I am sure of that.

SIR J. BEVIL You are sure of that – Well! that's some comfort – Then I have nothing to do but to see the bottom of this matter, during this present ruffle – Oh, Humphrey –

HUMPHREY You are not ill, I hope, Sir.

SIR J. BEVIL Yes, a man is very ill, that's in a very ill humour: To be a father, is to be in care for one, whom you oftner disoblige, than please, by that very care – Oh! that sons could know the duty to a father, before they themselves are fathers – But, perhaps, you'll say now, that I am one of the happiest fathers in the world; but, I assure you, that of the very happiest is not a condition to be envied.

HUMPHREY Sir, your pain arises, not from the thing it self, but your particular sense of it – You are overfond, nay, give me leave to say, you are unjustly apprehensive from your fondness: My master Bevil never disoblig'd you, and he will, I know he will, do every thing you ought to expect.

SIR J. BEVIL He won't take all this money with this girl – For ought I know, he will, forsooth, have so much moderation, as to think he ought not to force his liking for any consideration.

HUMPHREY He is to marry her, not you; he is to live with her, not you, Sir.

SIR J. BEVIL I know not what to think: But, I know, nothing can be more miserable than to be in this doubt – Follow me; I must come to some resolution.   *Exeunt.*

SCENE 3

SCENE: *Bevil junior's lodgings.*

Enter Tom and Phillis.

TOM Well, Madam, if you must speak with Mr Myrtle, you shall; he is now with my master in the library.

PHILLIS But you must leave me alone with him, for he can't make me a present, nor I so handsomly take any thing from him, before you; it would not be decent.

TOM It will be very decent, indeed, for me to retire, and leave my mistress with another man.

PHILLIS He is a gentleman, and will treat one properly –

TOM I believe so – but, however, I won't be far off, and therefore will venture to trust you: I'll call him to you.

Exit Tom.

PHILLIS What a deal of pother, and sputter here is, between my mistress, and Mr Myrtle, from meer punctilio? I could any hour of the day get her to her lover, and would do it – But she, forsooth, will allow no plot to get him; but, if he can come to her, I know she would be glad of it: I must therefore do her an acceptable violence, and surprize her into his arms. I am sure I go by the best rule imaginable: If she were my maid, I should think her the best servant in the world for doing so by me.

Enter Myrtle and Tom.

Oh Sir! You and Mr Bevil are fine gentlemen, to let a lady remain under such difficulties as my poor mistress, and no attempt to set her at liberty, or release her from the danger of being instantly married to Cimberton.

MYRTLE Tom has been telling – But what is to be done?

PHILLIS What is to be done – when a man can't come at his mistress! – Why, can't you fire our house, or the next house to us, to make us run out, and you take us?

MYRTLE How, Mrs Phillis –

PHILLIS Ay – let me see that rogue deny to fire a house, make a riot, or any other little thing, when there were no other way to come at me.

TOM I am oblig'd to you, Madam.

PHILLIS Why, don't we hear every day of people's hanging themselves for love, and won't they venture the hazard of being hang'd for love? – Oh! were I man –

MYRTLE What manly thing would you have me undertake? according to your ladyship's notion of a man.

PHILLIS Only be at once, what, one time or other, you may be, and wish to be, or must be.

MYRTLE Dear girl, talk plainly to me, and consider, I, in my condition, can't be in very good humour – you say, to be at once what I must be.

PHILLIS Ay, ay, – I mean no more than to be an old man; I saw you do it very well at the masquerade: In a word, old Sir Geoffry Cimberton is every hour expected in town, to join in the deeds and settlements, for marrying Mr Cimberton – He is half blind, half lame, half deaf, half dumb, tho', as to his passions and desires, he is as warm and ridiculous as when in the heat of youth. –

TOM Come to the business, and don't keep the gentleman in suspense for the pleasure of being courted, as you serve me.

PHILLIS I saw you at the masquerade act such a one to perfection; Go, and put on that very habit, and come to our house as Sir Geoffry. There is not one there, but my self, knows his person; I was born in the parish where he is lord of the manor. I have seen him often and often at church in the country. Do not hesitate; but come thither; they will think you bring a certain security against Mr Myrtle, and you bring Mr Myrtle; leave the rest to me, I leave this with you, and expect – They don't, I told you, know you; they think you out of town, which you had as good be for ever, if you lose this opportunity. – I must be gone; I know I am wanted at home.

MYRTLE My dear Phillis!

Catches and kisses her, and gives her money.

PHILLIS O fie! my kisses are not my own; you have committed violence; but I'll carry 'em to the right owner. (*Tom kisses her.*) Come, see me down stairs, (*to Tom*) and leave the lover to think of his last game for the prize.

Exeunt Tom and Phillis.

MYRTLE I think I will instantly attempt this wild expedient – The extravagance of it will make me less suspected, and it will give me opportunity to assert my own right to Lucinda, without whom I cannot live: But I am so mortify'd at this conduct of mine, towards poor Bevil; He must think meanly of me – I know not how to reassume myself, and be in spirit enough, for such an adventure as this – Yet I must attempt it, if it be only to be near Lucinda, under her present perplexities; and sure –

The next delight to transport, with the fair,
Is to relieve her, in her hours of care.   *Exit.*

Act V

SCENE I

SCENE: *Sealand's house.*

Enter Phillis, with lights, before Myrtle, disguis'd like old Sir Geoffry; supported by Mrs Sealand, Lucinda, and Cimberton.

MRS SEALAND Now I have seen you thus far, Sir Geoffry, will you excuse me a moment, while I give my necessary orders for your accommodation?   *Exit Mrs Sealand.*

MYRTLE I have not seen you, cousin Cimberton, since you were ten years old; and as it is incumbent on you, to keep up our name and family, I shall, upon very reasonable terms, join with you, in a settlement to that purpose. Tho' I must tell you, cousin, this is the first merchant that has married into our house.

LUCINDA Deuce on 'em! am I a merchant, because my father is?
                                                                                Aside.

MYRTLE But is he directly a trader, at this time?

CIMBERTON There's no hiding the disgrace, Sir; he trades to all parts of the world.

MYRTLE We never had one of our family before, who descended from persons that did any thing.

CIMBERTON Sir, since it is a girl that they have, I am, for the honour of my family, willing to take it in again; and to sink her into our name, and no harm done.

MYRTLE 'Tis prudently, and generously resolv'd – Is this the young thing?

CIMBERTON Yes, Sir.

PHILLIS Good Madam, don't be out of humour, but let them run to the utmost of their extravagance – Hear them out.

MYRTLE Can't I see her nearer? My eyes are but weak.

PHILLIS Beside, I am sure the unkle has something worth your notice. I'll take care to get off the young one, and leave you to observe what may be wrought out of the old one for your good.   *Exit.*

CIMBERTON Madam, this old gentleman, your great unkle, desires to be introduced to you, and to see you nearer! – Approach, Sir.

MYRTLE By your leave, young lady – (*Puts on spectacles.*) – Cousin Cimberton! She has exactly that sort of neck, and bosom, for which my sister Gertrude was so much admir'd, in the year sixty one, before the French dresses first discovered any thing in women, below the chin.

LUCINDA (*Aside.*) What a very odd situation am I in? Tho' I cannot but be diverted, at the extravagance of their humours, equally unsuitable to their age – Chin, quotha – I don't believe my passionate lover there knows whether I have one or not. Ha! ha!

MYRTLE Madam, I would not willingly offend, but I have a better glass – *Pulls out a large one.*

Enter Phillis to Cimberton.

PHILLIS Sir, my lady desires to shew the apartment to you, that she intends for Sir Geoffry.

CIMBERTON Well Sir! by that time you have sufficiently gazed, and sunned your self in the beauties of my spouse there, I will wait on you again.   *Exeunt Cimberton and Phillis.*

MYRTLE Were it not, Madam, that I might be troublesome, there is something of importance, tho' we are alone, which I would say more safe from being heard.

LUCINDA There is something, in this old fellow methinks, that raises my curiosity.

MYRTLE To be free, Madam, I as heartily contemn this kinsman of mine, as you do, and am sorry to see so much beauty and merit devoted, by your parents, to so insensible a possessor.

LUCINDA Surprising! – I hope then, Sir, you will not contribute to the wrong you are so generous as to pity, whatever may be the interest of your family.

MYRTLE This hand of mine shall never be employ'd, to sign any thing, against your good and happiness.

LUCINDA I am sorry, Sir, it is not in my power to make you proper acknowledgments; but there is a gentleman in the world, whose gratitude will, I am sure, be worthy of the favour.

MYRTLE All the thanks I desire, Madam, are in your power to give.

LUCINDA Name them, and command them.

MYRTLE Only, Madam, that the first time you are alone with your lover, you will, with open arms, receive him.

LUCINDA As willingly as his heart could wish it.

MYRTLE Thus then he claims your promise! O Lucinda!

LUCINDA O! a cheat! a cheat! a cheat!

MYRTLE Hush! 'tis I, 'tis I, your lover, Myrtle himself, Madam.

LUCINDA O bless me! what a rashness, and folly to surprize me so – But hush – my mother –

Enter Mrs Sealand, Cimberton, and Phillis.

MRS SEALAND How now! what's the matter?

LUCINDA O Madam! as soon as you left the room, my uncle fell into a sudden fit, and – and – so I cry'd out for help, to support him, and conduct him to his chamber.

MRS SEALAND That was kindly done! Alas! Sir, how do you find your self?

MYRTLE Never was taken, in so odd a way in my life – pray lead me! Oh! I was talking here – (*pray carry me*) to my cousin Cimberton's young lady –

MRS SEALAND (*Aside.*) My cousin Cimberton's young lady! How zealous he is, even in his extremity, for the match! a right Cimberton.

Cimberton and Lucinda lead him, as one in pain, etc.

CIMBERTON Pox! Uncle, you will pull my ear off.

LUCINDA Pray Uncle! you will squeeze me to death.

MRS SEALAND No matter, no matter – he knows not what he does. Come, Sir, shall I help you out?

MYRTLE By no means; I'll trouble no body, but my young cousin here.   *They lead him off.*

PHILLIS But pray, Madam, does your ladyship intend that Mr Cimberton shall really marry my young mistress at last? I don't think he likes her.

MRS SEALAND That's not material! Men of his speculation are above desires – but be as it may; now I have given old Sir Geoffry the trouble of coming up to sign and seal, with what countenance can I be off?

PHILLIS As well as with twenty others, Madam; It is the glory and honour of a great fortune, to live in continual treaties, and still to break off: it looks great, Madam.

MRS SEALAND True, Phillis – yet to return our blood again into the Cimberton's, is an honour not to be rejected – but were not you saying, that Sir John Bevil's creature Humphrey has been with Mr Sealand?

PHILLIS Yes, Madam; I overheard them agree, that Mr Sealand should go himself, and visit this unknown lady that Mr Bevil is so great with; and if he found nothing there to fright him, that Mr Bevil should still marry my young mistress.

MRS SEALAND How! nay then he shall find she is my daughter, as well as his: I'll follow him this instant, and take the whole family along with me: The disputed power of disposing of my own daughter shall be at an end this very night – I'll live no longer in anxiety for a little hussey, that hurts my appearance, where-ever I carry her: and, for whose sake, I seem to be not at all regarded, and that in the best of my days.

PHILLIS Indeed, Madam, if she were married, your ladyship might very well be taken for Mr Sealand's daughter.

MRS SEALAND Nay, when the chit has not been with me, I have heard the men say as much – I'll no longer cut off the greatest pleasure of a woman's life (the shining in assemblies) by her forward anticipation of the respect, that's due to her superior – she shall down to Cimberton-Hall – she shall – she shall.

PHILLIS I hope, Madam, I shall stay with your ladyship.

MRS SEALAND Thou shalt, Phillis, and I'll place thee then more about me. – But order chairs immediately – I'll be gone this minute.   *Exeunt.*

SCENE 2

SCENE: *Charing Cross.*

Enter Mr Sealand, and Humphrey.

MR SEALAND I am very glad, Mr Humphrey, that you agree with me, that it is for our common good, I should look thoroughly into this matter.

HUMPHREY I am, indeed, of that opinion; for there is no artifice, nothing concealed, in our family, which ought in justice to be

known; I need not desire you, Sir, to treat the lady with care
and respect.

MR SEALAND Master Humphrey — I shall not be rude, tho' I
design to be a little abrupt, and come into the matter at once,
to see how she will bear, upon a surprize.

HUMPHREY That's the door, Sir I wish you success — (*while
Humphrey speaks, Sealand consults his table-book*) I am less
concern'd what happens there, because I hear Mr Myrtle is
well-lodg'd, as old Sir Geoffry, so I am willing to let this
gentleman employ himself here, to give them time at home:
for I am sure, 'tis necessary for the quiet of our family,
Lucinda were disposed of, out of it, since Mr Bevil's inclination is so much otherwise engaged.   *Exit.*

MR SEALAND I think this is the door — (*Knocks.*) I'll carry this
matter with an air of authority, to enquire, tho' I make an
errand, to begin discourse. (*Knocks again, and enter a Foot-
Boy.*) So young man! is your lady within?

BOY Alack, Sir! I am but a country boy — I dant know, whether
she is, or noa: but an you'll stay a bit, I'll goa, and ask the
gentlewoman that's with her.

MR SEALAND Why, Sirrah, tho' you are a country boy, you can
see, can't you? you know whether she is at home, when you
see her, don't you?

BOY Nay, nay, I'm not such a country lad neither, Master, to
think she's at home, because I see her: I have been in town
but a month, and I lost one place already, for believing my
own eyes.

MR SEALAND Why, Sirrah! have you learnt to lie already?

BOY Ah! Master! things that are lies in the country, are not lies
at London — I begin to know my business a little better than
so — but an you please to walk in, I'll call a gentlewoman to
you, that can tell you for certain — she can make bold to ask
my lady her self.

MR SEALAND O! then, she is within, I find, tho' you dare not say
so.

BOY Nay, nay! that's neither here, nor there: what's matter,
whether she is within or no, if she has not a mind to see any
body?

MR SEALAND I can't tell, Sirrah, whether you are arch, or simple,
but however get me a direct answer, and here's a shilling for
you.

BOY Will you please to walk in, I'll see what I can do for you.
MR SEALAND I see you will be fit for your business, in time, child. But I expect to meet with nothing but extraordinaries, in such a house.
BOY Such a house! Sir, you han't seen it yet: Pray walk in.
MR SEALAND Sir, I'll wait upon you.   *Exeunt.*

SCENE 3
SCENE: *Indiana's house.*

Enter Isabella.

ISABELLA What anxiety do I feel for this poor creature! What will be the end of her? Such a languishing unreserv'd passion, for a man, that at last must certainly leave, or ruin her! and perhaps both! then the aggravation of the distress is, that she does not believe he will – not but, I must own, if they are both what they would seem, they are made for one another, as much as Adam and Eve were, for there is no other, of their kind, but themselves.

Enter Boy.

So Daniel! what news with you?
BOY Madam, there's a gentleman below would speak with my lady.
ISABELLA Sirrah! don't you know Mr Bevil yet?
BOY Madam, 'tis not the gentleman who comes every day, and asks for you, and won't go in till he knows whether you are with her or no.
ISABELLA Ha! that's a particular I did not know before: Well! be it who it will, let him come up to me.
            Exit Boy; and re-enters with Mr Sealand.

Isabella looks amaz'd!

MR SEALAND Madam, I can't blame your being a little surpriz'd, to see a perfect stranger make a visit, and –
ISABELLA I am indeed surpriz'd! – I see he does not know me.
MR SEALAND You are very prettily lodg'd here, Madam; in troth you seem to have every thing in plenty – a thousand a year, I warrant you, upon this pretty nest of rooms, and the dainty one within them.   (*Aside, and looking about.*)

ISABELLA (*Apart.*) Twenty years, it seems, have less effect in the alteration of a man of thirty, than of a girl of fourteen – he's almost still the same; but alas! I find by other men, as well as himself, I am not what I was – As soon as he spoke, I was convinc'd 'twas He – How shall I contain my surprize and satisfaction! he must not know me yet.

MR SEALAND Madam, I hope I don't give you any disturbance; But there is a young lady here, with whom I have a particular business to discourse, and I hope she will admit me to that favour.

ISABELLA Why, Sir, have you had any notice concerning her? I wonder who could give it you.

MR SEALAND That, Madam, is fit only to be communicated to herself.

ISABELLA Well, Sir! you shall see her: – I find he knows nothing yet, nor shall from me: I am resolv'd, I will observe this interlude, this sport of nature, and of fortune – You shall see her presently, Sir; For now I am as a mother, and will trust her with you.   *Exit.*

MR SEALAND As a mother! right; that's the old phrase, for one of those commode ladies, who lend out beauty, for hire, to young gentlemen that have pressing occasions. But here comes the precious lady her self. In troth a very sightly woman –

Enter Indiana.

INDIANA I am told, Sir, you have some affair that requires your speaking with me.

MR SEALAND Yes, Madam: There came to my hands a bill drawn by Mr Bevil, which is payable to-morrow; and he, in the intercourse of business, sent it to me, who have cash of his, and desired me to send a servant with it; but I have made bold to bring you the money my self.

INDIANA Sir! was that necessary?

MR SEALAND No, Madam; but, to be free with you, the fame of your beauty, and the regard, which Mr Bevil is a little too well known to have for you, excited my curiosity.

INDIANA Too well known to have for me! Your sober appearance, Sir, which my friend describ'd, made me expect no rudeness, or absurdity, at least – Who's there? Sir, if you pay the money to a servant, 'twill be as well.

MR SEALAND Pray, Madam, be not offended; I came hither on

an innocent, nay a virtuous design; and, if you will have patience to hear me, it may be as useful to you, as you are in a friendship with Mr Bevil, as to my only daughter, whom I was this day disposing of.

INDIANA You make me hope, Sir, I have mistaken you; I am composed again; be free, say on – what I am afraid to hear –

Aside.

MR SEALAND I fear'd, indeed, an unwarranted passion here, but I did not think it was in abuse of so worthy an object, so accomplish'd a lady, as your sense and mien bespeak – but the youth of our age care not what merit and virtue they bring to shame, so they gratify –

INDIANA Sir – you are going into very great errors – but, as you are pleas'd to say you see something in me that has chang'd, at least, the colour of your suspicions; so has your appearance alter'd mine, and made me earnestly attentive to what has any way concern'd you, to enquire into my affairs, and character.

MR SEALAND How sensibly! with what an air she talks!

INDIANA Good Sir, be seated – and tell me tenderly – keep all your suspicions concerning me alive, that you may in a proper and prepared way – acquaint me why the care of your daughter obliges a person of your seeming worth and fortune, to be thus inquisitive about a wretched, helpless, friendless – (*Weeping.*) But I beg your Pardon – tho' I am an orphan, your child is not; and your concern for her, it seems, has brought you hither – I'll be composed – pray go on, Sir.

MR SEALAND How could Mr Bevil be such a monster, to injure such a woman?

INDIANA No, Sir – you wrong him – he has not injured me – my support is from his bounty.

MR SEALAND Bounty! when gluttons give high prices for delicates, they are prodigious bountiful.

INDIANA Still, still you will persist in that error – But my own fears tell me all – You are the gentleman, I suppose, for whose happy daughter he is design'd a husband, by his good father, and he has, perhaps, consented to the overture: He was here this morning, dress'd beyond his usual plainness, nay most sumptuously – and he is to be, perhaps, this night a bridegroom.

MR SEALAND I own he was intended such: But, Madam, on your account, I have determin'd to defer my daughter's marriage, till I am satisfied from your own mouth, of what nature are the obligations you are under to him.

INDIANA His actions, Sir, his eyes have only made me think, he design'd to make me the partner of his heart. The goodness and gentleness of his demeanour made me misinterpret all – 'Twas my own hope, my own passion, that deluded me – he never made one amorous advance to me – His large heart, and bestowing hand, have only helpt the miserable: Nor know I why, but from his mere delight in virtue, that I have been his care, the object on which to indulge and please himself, with pouring favours.

MR SEALAND Madam, I know not why it is, but I, as well as you, am methinks afraid of entring into the matter I came about; but 'tis the same thing, as if we had talk'd never so distinctly – he ne'er shall have a daughter of mine.

INDIANA If you say this from what you think of me, you wrong your self and him – Let not me, miserable tho' I may be, do injury to my benefactor – No, Sir, my treatment ought rather to reconcile you to his virtues – If to bestow, without a prospect of return; if to delight in supporting, what might, perhaps, be thought an object of desire, with no other view than to be her guard against those who would not be so disinterested; if these actions, Sir, can in a careful parent's eye commend him to a daughter, give yours, Sir, give her to my honest, generous Bevil – What have I to do, but sigh, and weep, to rave, run wild, a lunatick in chains, or hid in darkness, mutter in distracted starts, and broken accents, my strange, strange story!

MR SEALAND Take comfort, Madam.

INDIANA All my comfort must be to expostulate in madness, to relieve with frenzy my despair, and shrieking to demand of fate, why – why was I born to such variety of sorrows?

MR SEALAND If I have been the least occasion –

INDIANA No – 'twas Heaven's high will, I should be such – to be plunder'd in my cradle! Toss'd on the seas! and even there, an infant captive! to lose my mother, hear but of my father – To be adopted! lose my adopter! then plunged again in worse calamities!

MR SEALAND An infant captive!

INDIANA Yet then! to find the most charming of mankind, once more to set me free, (from what I thought the last distress) to load me with his services, his bounties, and his favours; to support my very life, in a way, that stole, at the same time, my very soul it self from me.

MR SEALAND And has young Bevil been this worthy man?

INDIANA Yet then again, this very man to take another! without leaving me the right, the pretence of easing my fond heart with tears! For oh! I can't reproach him, though the same hand that rais'd me to this height, now throws me down the precipice.

MR SEALAND Dear Lady! O yet one moment's patience: my heart grows full with your affliction: But yet, there's something in your story that —

INDIANA My portion here is bitterness, and sorrow.

MR SEALAND Do not think so: Pray answer me: Does Bevil know your name, and family?

INDIANA Alas! too well! O, could I be any other thing, than what I am — I'll tear away all traces of my former self, my little ornaments, the remains of my first state, the hints of what I ought to have been —

In her disorder she throws away a bracelet,
which Sealand takes up, and looks earnestly on it.

MR SEALAND Ha! what's this? my eyes are not deceiv'd! It is, it is the same! the very bracelet which I bequeath'd my wife, at our last mournful parting.

INDIANA What said you, Sir! Your wife! Whither does my fancy carry me? What means this unfelt motion at my heart? And yet again my fortune but deludes me; for if I err not, Sir, your name is Sealand: But my lost father's name was —

MR SEALAND Danvers! was it not?

INDIANA What new amazement! That is indeed my family.

MR SEALAND Know then, when my misfortunes drove me to the Indies, for reasons too tedious now to mention, I chang'd my name of Danvers into Sealand.

Enter Isabella.

ISABELLA If yet there wants an explanation of your wonder, examine well this face, (yours, Sir, I well remember) gaze on, and read, in me, your sister Isabella!

MR SEALAND My sister!

ISABELLA But here's a claim more tender yet — your Indiana, Sir, your long lost daughter.

MR SEALAND O my child! my child!

INDIANA All-gracious Heaven! is it possible! do I embrace my
father!

MR SEALAND And I do hold thee – These passions are too strong
for utterance – Rise, rise, my child, and give my tears their
way – O my sister!   *Embracing her.*

ISABELLA Now, dearest neice, my groundless fears, my painful
cares no more shall vex thee. If I have wrong'd thy noble
lover with too hard suspicions; my just concern for thee, I
hope, will plead my pardon.

MR SEALAND O! make him then the full amends, and be your
self the messenger of joy: Fly this instant! tell him all these
wondrous turns of providence in his favour! Tell him I have
now a daughter to bestow, which he no longer will decline:
that this day he still shall be a bridegroom: nor shall a fortune, the merit which his father seeks, be wanting: tell him
the reward of all his virtues waits on his acceptance.

Exit Isabella.

My dearest Indiana!   *Turns, and embraces her.*

INDIANA Have I then at last a father's sanction on my love! His
bounteous hand to give, and make my heart a present worthy
of Bevil's generosity?

MR SEALAND O my child! how are our sorrows past o'erpaid by
such a meeting! Though I have lost so many years of soft
paternal dalliance with thee, yet, in one day, to find thee thus,
and thus bestow thee, in such perfect happiness! is ample!
ample reparation! And yet again the merit of thy lover.

INDIANA O! had I spirits left to tell you of his actions! how
strongly filial duty has suppressed his love; and how concealment still has doubled all his obligations; the pride, the joy of
his alliance, Sir, would warm your heart, as he has conquer'd
mine.

MR SEALAND How laudable is love, when born of virtue! I burn
to embrace him –

INDIANA See, Sir, my aunt already has succeeded, and brought
him to your wishes.

*Enter Isabella, with Sir John Bevil, Bevil junior,
Mrs Sealand, Cimberton, Myrtle, and Lucinda.*

SIR J. BEVIL (*Entering.*) Where! where's this scene of wonder! –
Mr Sealand, I congratulate, on this occasion, our mutual

happiness – Your good sister, Sir, has with the story of your daughter's fortune, fill'd us with surprize and joy! Now, all exceptions are remov'd; my son has now avow'd his love, and turn'd all former jealousies and doubts to approbation, and, I am told, your goodness has consented to reward him.

MR SEALAND If, Sir, a fortune equal to his father's hopes, can make this object worthy his acceptance.

BEVIL JUNIOR I hear your mention, Sir, of fortune, with pleasure only, as it may prove the means to reconcile the best of fathers to my love – Let him be provident, but let me be happy – My ever-destin'd, my acknowledg'd wife!   *Embracing Indiana.*

INDIANA Wife! – O, my ever loved! my lord! my master!

SIR J. BEVIL I congratulate my self, as well as you, that I had a son, who could, under such disadvantages, discover your great merit.

MR SEALAND O! Sir John! how vain, how weak is humane prudence? What care, what foresight, what imagination could contrive such blest events, to make our children happy, as providence in one short hour has laid before us?

CIMBERTON (*To Mrs Sealand.*) I am afraid, Madam, Mr Sealand is a little too busy for our affair, if you please we'll take another opportunity.

MRS SEALAND Let us have patience, Sir.

CIMBERTON But we make Sir Geoffry wait, Madam.

MYRTLE O Sir! I am not in haste.

During this, Bevil junior presents Lucinda to Indiana.

MR SEALAND But here! here's our general benefactor! Excellent young man, that could be, at once, a lover to her beauty, and a parent to her virtue.

BEVIL JUNIOR If you think that an obligation, Sir, give me leave to overpay my self, in the only instance, that can now add to my felicity, by begging you to bestow this lady on Mr Myrtle.

MR SEALAND She is his without reserve, (I beg he may be sent for) – Mr Cimberton, notwithstanding you never had my consent, yet there is, since I last saw you, another objection to your marriage with my daughter.

CIMBERTON I hope, Sir, your lady has conceal'd nothing from me?

MR SEALAND Troth, Sir! nothing but what was conceal'd from

my self; another daughter, who has an undoubted title to half my estate.

CIMBERTON How! Mr Sealand! why then if half Mrs Lucinda's fortune is gone, you can't say, that any of my estate is settled upon her: I was in treaty for the whole; but if that is not to be come at, to be sure, there can be no bargain, – Sir, – I have nothing to do but to take my leave of your good lady, my cousin, and beg pardon for the trouble I have given this old gentleman.

MYRTLE That you have, Mr Cimberton, with all my heart.

Discovers himself.

OMNES Mr Myrtle!

MYRTLE And I beg pardon of the whole company, that I assume the person of Sir Geoffry, only to be present at the danger of this lady's being disposed of, and in her utmost exigence to assert my right to her: Which if her parents will ratifie, as they once favour'd my pretensions, no abatement of fortune shall lessen her value to me.

LUCINDA Generous man!

MR SEALAND If, Sir, you can overlook the injury of being in treaty with one, who as meanly left her, as you have generously asserted your right in her, she is yours.

LUCINDA Mr Myrtle, tho' you have ever had my heart, yet now I find I love you more, because I bring you less.

MYRTLE We have much more than we want, and I am glad any event has contributed to the discovery of our real inclinations to each other.

MRS SEALAND Well! however I'm glad the girl's disposed of any way. *Aside.*

BEVIL JUNIOR Myrtle! no longer rivals now, but brothers.

MYRTLE Dear Bevil! you are born to triumph over me! but now our competition ceases: I rejoyce in the preheminence of your virtue, and your alliance adds charms to Lucinda.

SIR J. BEVIL Now, ladies and gentlemen, you have set the world a fair example: Your happiness is owing to your constancy and merit: And the several difficulties you have struggled with, evidently shew

> Whate'er the generous Mind it self denies,
> The secret Care of Providence supplies.   *Exeunt.*

Epilogue

BY MR WELSTED

Intended to be spoken by Indiana.

Our author, whom intreaties cannot move,
Spight of the dear coquetry that you love,
Swears he'll not frustrate (so he plainly means)
By a loose epilogue, his decent scenes.
Is it not, Sirs, hard fate, I meet to-day,
To keep me rigid still beyond the play?
And yet I'm sav'd a world of pains that way.
I now can look, I now can move at ease,
Nor need I torture these poor limbs, to please;
Nor with the hand or foot attempt surprize,
Nor wrest my features, nor fatigue my eyes:
Bless me! What freakish gambols have I play'd!
What motions try'd, and wanton looks betray'd!
Out of pure kindness all! to over-rule
The threaten'd hiss, and screen some scribling fool.
With more respect I'm entertain'd to-night:
Our author thinks, I can with ease delight.
My artless looks while modest graces arm,
He says, I need but to appear; and charm.
A wife so form'd, by these examples bred,
Pours joy and gladness 'round the marriage bed;
Soft source of comfort, kind relief from care,
And 'tis her least perfection to be fair.
The nymph with Indiana's worth who vies,
A nation will behold with Bevil's eyes.

THE BEGGAR'S OPERA

Dramatis Personæ

PEACHUM		Mr Hippesley
LOCKIT		Mr Hall
MACHEATH		Mr Walker
FILCH		Mr Clark
JEMMY TWITCHER		Mr H. Bullock
CROOK-FINGERED JACK		Mr Houghton
WAT DREARY		Mr Smith
ROBIN OF BAGSHOT	*Macheath's*	Mr Lacy
NIMMING NED	*Gang*	Mr Pit
HARRY PADDINGTON		Mr Eaton
MAT OF THE MINT		Mr Spiller
BEN BUDGE		Mr Morgan
BEGGAR		Mr Chapman
PLAYER		Mr Milward

Constables, Drawer, Turnkey, etc.

WOMEN

MRS PEACHUM		Mrs Martin
POLLY PEACHUM		Miss Fenton
LUCY LOCKIT		Mrs Egleton
DIANA TRAPES		Mrs Martin
MRS COAXER		Mrs Holiday
DOLLY TRULL		Mrs Lacy
MRS VIXEN		Mrs Rice
BETTY DOXY	*Women of*	Mrs Rogers
JENNY DIVER	*the Town*	Mrs Clarke
MRS SLAMMEKIN		Mrs Morgan
SUKY TAWDRY		Mrs Palin
MOLLY BRAZEN		Mrs Sallee

Introduction

Beggar, Player.

BEGGAR If poverty be a title to poetry, I am sure nobody can dispute mine. I own myself of the company of beggars; and I make one at their weekly festivals at St Giles's; I have a small yearly salary for my catches, and am welcome to a dinner there whenever I please, which is more than most poets can say.

PLAYER As we live by the Muses, it is but gratitude in us to encourage poetical merit wherever we find it. The Muses, contrary to all other ladies, pay no distinction to dress, and never partially mistake the pertness of embroidery for wit, nor the modesty of want for dullness. Be the author who he will, we push his play as far as it will go. So, though you are in want, I wish you success heartily.

BEGGAR This piece I own was originally writ for the celebrating the marriage of James Chanter and Moll Lay, two most excellent ballad-singers. I have introduced the similes that are in all your celebrated operas; the Swallow, the Moth, the Bee, the Ship, the Flower, etc. Besides, I have a prison scene, which the ladies always reckon charmingly pathetic. As to the parts, I have observed such a nice impartiality to our two ladies, that it is impossible for either of them to take offence. I hope I may be forgiven that I have not made my opera throughout unnatural, like those in vogue; for I have no recitative; excepting this, as I have consented to have neither Prologue nor Epilogue, it must be allowed an opera in all its forms. The piece indeed hath been heretofore frequently represented by ourselves in our great room at St Giles's, so that I cannot too often acknowledge your charity in bringing it now on the stage.

PLAYER But I see 'tis time for us to withdraw; the actors are preparing to begin. Play away the overture.   *Exeunt.*

Act I

SCENE I

SCENE: *Peachum's house.*

Peachum sitting at a table, with a large book of accounts before him.

AIR I – 'An old woman, clothed in grey'.

PEACHUM *Through all the employments of life,*
    Each neighbour abuses his brother;
  Whore and rogue, they call husband and wife:
    All professions be-rogue one another.
  The priest calls the lawyer a cheat:
    The lawyer be-knaves the divine:
  And the statesman, because he's so great,
    Thinks his trade as honest as mine.

A lawyer is an honest employment, so is mine. Like me too, he acts in a double capacity, both against rogues, and for 'em; for 'tis but fitting that we should protect and encourage cheats, since we live by them.

SCENE 2

Peachum, Filch.

FILCH Sir, Black Moll hath sent word her trial comes on in the afternoon, and she hopes you will order matters so as to bring her off.

PEACHUM Why, she may plead her belly at worst; to my knowledge she hath taken care of that security. But, as the wench is very active and industrious, you may satisfy her that I'll soften the evidence.

FILCH Tom Gagg, sir, is found guilty.

PEACHUM A lazy dog! When I took him the time before, I told him what he would come to, if he did not mend his hand. This is death, without reprieve. I may venture to book him; (*Writes*.) for Tom Gagg, forty pounds. Let Betty Sly know that I'll save her from transportation, for I can get more by her staying in England.

FILCH Betty hath brought more goods into our lock to-year than any five of the gang; and, in truth, 'tis a pity to lose so good a customer.

PEACHUM If none of the gang take her off, she may, in the common course of business, live a twelvemonth longer. I love to let women 'scape. A good sportsman always lets the hen-partridges fly, because the breed of the game depends upon them. Besides, here the law allows us no reward: there is nothing to be got by the death of women – except our wives.

FILCH Without dispute, she is a fine woman! 'Twas to her I was obliged for my education, and (to say a bold word) she hath trained up more young fellows to the business than the gaming-table.

PEACHUM Truly, Filch, thy observation is right. We and the surgeons are more beholden to women than all the professions besides.

AIR 2 – 'The bonny grey-eyed morn', etc.

FILCH 'Tis woman that seduces all mankind;
    By her we first were taught the wheedling arts;
Her very eyes can cheat; when most she's kind,
    She tricks us of our money, with our hearts.
For her, like wolves by night, we roam for prey,
    And practise every fraud to bribe her charms;
For suits of love, like law, are won by pay,
    And beauty must be fee'd into our arms.

PEACHUM But make haste to Newgate, boy, and let my friends know what I intend; for I love to make them easy, one way or other.

FILCH When a gentleman is long kept in suspense, penitence may break his spirit ever after. Besides, certainty gives a man a good air upon his trial, and makes him risk another without fear or scruple. But I'll away, for 'tis a pleasure to be the messenger of comfort to friends in affliction.

SCENE 3

Peachum.

PEACHUM But 'tis now high time to look about me for a decent execution against next sessions. I hate a lazy rogue, by whom one can get nothing till he is hanged. A register of the gang. (*Reading.*) 'Crook-fingered Jack' – a year and a half in the service – let me see how much the stock owes to his industry: One, two, three, four, five gold watches, and seven silver ones – a mighty, clean-handed fellow! – sixteen snuff-boxes, five of them of true gold, six dozen of handkerchiefs, four silver-hilted swords, half a dozen of shirts, three tie-periwigs, and a piece of broad-cloth. Considering these are only the fruits of his leisure hours, I don't know a prettier fellow; for no man alive hath a more engaging presence of mind upon the road. 'Wat Dreary, alias Brown Will' – an irregular dog! who hath an underhand way of disposing of his goods; I'll try him only for a sessions or two longer, upon his good behaviour. 'Harry Paddington' – a poor, petty-larceny rascal, without the least genius! that fellow, though he were to live these six months, will never come to the gallows with any credit. 'Slippery Sam' – he goes off the next sessions; for the villain hath the impudence to have views of following his trade as a tailor, which he calls an honest employment. 'Mat of the Mint' – listed not above a month ago; a promising, sturdy fellow, and diligent in his way; somewhat too bold and hasty, and may raise good contributions on the public, if he does not cut himself short by murder. 'Tom Tipple' – a guzzling, soaking sot, who is always too drunk to stand himself, or to make others stand; a cart is absolutely necessary for him. 'Robin of Bagshot, alias Gorgon, alias Bluff Bob, alias Carbuncle, alias Bob Booty – '

SCENE 4

Peachum, Mrs Peachum.

MRS PEACHUM What of Bob Booty, husband? I hope nothing bad hath betided him. You know, my dear, he's a favourite customer of mine – 'twas he, made me a present of this ring.

PEACHUM I have set his name down in the black list, that's all, my dear; he spends his life among women, and, as soon as his money is gone, one or other of the ladies will hang him for the reward, and there's forty pound lost to us for ever!

MRS PEACHUM You know, my dear, I never meddle in matters of death; I always leave those affairs to you. Women, indeed, are bitter bad judges in these cases; for they are so partial to the brave, that they think every man handsome who is going to the camp, or the gallows.

AIR 3 – 'Cold and raw', etc.

If any wench Venus's girdle wear,
  Though she be never so ugly:
Lilies and roses will quickly appear
  And her face look wondrous smugly.
Beneath the left ear so fit but a cord
  (A rope so charming a zone is!),
The youth in his cart hath the air of a lord,
  And we cry, There dies an Adonis!

But, really, husband, you should not be too hard-hearted, for you never had a finer, braver set of men than at present. We have not had a murder among them all these seven months; and truly, my dear, that is a great blessing.

PEACHUM What a dickens is the woman always whimpering about murder for? No gentleman is ever looked upon the worse for killing a man in his own defence; and if business cannot be carried on without it, what would you have a gentleman do?

MRS PEACHUM If I am in the wrong, my dear, you must excuse me, for nobody can help the frailty of an over-scrupulous conscience.

PEACHUM Murder is as fashionable a crime as a man can be guilty of. How many fine gentlemen have we in Newgate every year, purely upon that article? If they have wherewithal to persuade the jury to bring in manslaughter, what are they the worse for it? So, my dear, have done upon this subject. Was Captain Macheath here this morning, for the banknotes he left with you last week?

MRS PEACHUM Yes, my dear; and though the bank hath stopped payment, he was so cheerful, and so agreeable! Sure, there is not a finer gentleman upon the road than the captain! If he comes from Bagshot at any reasonable hour, he hath promised to make one this evening with Polly and me, and Bob Booty, at a party of quadrille. Pray, my dear, is the captain rich?

PEACHUM The captain keeps too good company ever to grow rich. Marybone, and the chocolate-houses, are his undoing. The man that proposes to get money by play should have the education of a fine gentleman, and be trained up to it from his youth.

MRS PEACHUM Really, I am sorry, upon Polly's account, the captain hath not more discretion. What business hath he to keep company with lords and gentlemen? He should leave them to prey upon one another.

PEACHUM Upon Polly's account! What a plague does the woman mean? — Upon Polly's account!

MRS PEACHUM Captain Macheath is very fond of the girl.

PEACHUM And what then?

MRS PEACHUM If I have any skill in the ways of women, I am sure Polly thinks him a very pretty man.

PEACHUM And what then? You would not be so mad to have the wench marry him! Gamesters and highwaymen are, generally, very good to their whores, but they are very devils to their wives.

MRS PEACHUM But if Polly should be in love, how should we help her, or how can she help herself? Poor girl, I'm in the utmost concern about her!

AIR 4 – 'Why is your faithful slave disdained?' etc.

> *If love the virgin's heart invade,*
> *How, like a moth, the simple maid*
>   *Still plays about the flame!*
> *If soon she be not made a wife,*
> *Her honour's singed, and then for life*
>   *She's — what I dare not name.*

PEACHUM Lookye, wife, a handsome wench in our way of business is as profitable as at the bar of a Temple coffee-house, who looks upon it as her livelihood to grant every liberty but one. You see I would indulge the girl as far as prudently we can. In anything but marriage! After that, my dear, how shall we be safe? Are we not then in her husband's power? For a husband hath the absolute power over all a wife's secrets but her own. If the girl had the discretion of a court lady, who can have a dozen young fellows at her ear without complying with one, I should not matter it; but Polly is tinder, and a spark will at once set her on a flame. Married! If the wench does not know her own profit, sure she knows her own pleasure better than to make herself a property! My daughter, to me, should be like a court lady to a minister of state, a key to the whole gang. Married! if the affair is not already done, I'll terrify her from it by the example of our neighbours.

MRS PEACHUM Mayhap, my dear, you may injure the girl: she loves to imitate the fine ladies, and she may only allow the captain liberties in the view of interest.

PEACHUM But 'tis your duty, my dear, to warn the girl against her ruin, and to instruct her how to make the most of her beauty. I'll go to her this moment, and sift her. In the meantime, wife, rip out the coronets and marks of these dozen of cambric handkerchiefs, for I can dispose of them this afternoon to a chap in the city.

SCENE 5

Mrs Peachum.

MRS PEACHUM Never was a man more out of the way in an argument than my husband. Why must our Polly, forsooth, differ from her sex, and love only her husband? and why must our Polly's marriage, contrary to all observation, make her the less followed by other men? All men are thieves in love, and like a woman the better for being another's property.

AIR 5 – 'Of all the simple things we do', etc.

A maid is like the golden ore,
    Which hath guineas intrinsical in't,
Whose worth is never known, before
    It is tried and impressed in the mint.
A wife's like a guinea in gold,
    Stamped with the name of her spouse;
Now here, now there; is bought or is sold;
    And is current in every house.

SCENE 6

Mrs Peachum, Filch.

MRS PEACHUM Come hither, Filch. – I am as fond of this child as though my mind misgave me he were my own. He hath as fine a hand at picking a pocket as a woman, and is as nimble-fingered as a juggler. If an unlucky session does not cut the rope of thy life, I pronounce, boy, thou wilt be a great man in history. Where was your post last night, my boy?

FILCH I plied at the opera, madam; and, considering 'twas neither dark nor rainy, so that there was no great hurry in getting chairs and coaches, made a tolerable hand on't – these seven handkerchiefs, madam.

MRS PEACHUM Coloured ones, I see. They are of sure sale from our warehouse at Redriff, among the seamen.

FILCH And this snuff-box.

MRS PEACHUM Set in gold! A pretty encouragement, this, to a young beginner!

FILCH I had a fair tug at a charming gold watch. Pox take the tailors for making the fobs so deep and narrow! – it stuck by the way, and I was forced to make my escape under a coach. Really, madam, I fear I shall be cut off in the flower of my youth, so that, every now and then, since I was pumped, I have thoughts of taking up and going to sea.

MRS PEACHUM You should go to Hockley-in-the-Hole, and to Marybone, child, to learn valour; these are the schools that have bred so many brave men. I thought, boy, by this time, thou hadst lost fear as well as shame. Poor lad! how little does he know yet of the Old Bailey! For the first fact, I'll ensure thee from being hanged; and going to sea, Filch, will come time enough, upon a sentence of transportation. But now, since you have nothing better to do, even go to your book, and learn your catechism: for, really, a man makes but an ill figure in the ordinary's paper who cannot give a satisfactory answer to his questions. But, hark you, my lad, don't tell me a lie; for you know I hate a liar: – Do you know of anything that hath passed between Captain Macheath and our Polly?

FILCH I beg you, madam, don't ask me; for I must either tell a

lie to you or to Miss Polly; for I promised her I would not
tell.

MRS PEACHUM But when the honour of our family is concerned –

FILCH I shall lead a sad life with Miss Polly, if ever she come to
know I told you. Besides, I would not willingly forfeit my
own honour, by betraying anybody.

MRS PEACHUM Yonder comes my husband and Polly. Come,
Filch, you shall go with me into my own room, and tell me
the whole story. I'll give thee a glass of a most delicious
cordial that I keep for my own drinking.

SCENE 7

Peachum, Polly.

POLLY I know as well as any of the fine ladies how to make the
most of myself and of my man too. A woman knows how to
be mercenary, though she hath never been in a court or at an
assembly. We have it in our natures, papa. If I allow Captain
Macheath some trifling liberties, I have this watch and other
visible marks of his favour to show for it. A girl who cannot
grant some things, and refuse what is most material, will
make a poor hand of her beauty, and soon be thrown upon
the common.

AIR 6 – 'What shall I do to show how much I love her?' etc.

Virgins are like the fair flower in its lustre,
  Which in the garden enamels the ground,
Near it the bees in play flutter and cluster,
  And gaudy butterflies frolic around:

But when once plucked 'tis no longer alluring,
  To Covent Garden 'tis sent (as yet sweet),
There fades, and shrinks, and grows past all enduring,
  Rots, stinks, and dies, and is trod under feet.

PEACHUM You know, Polly, I am not against your toying and
trifling with a customer, in the way of business, or to get out
a secret or so; but if I find out that you have played the fool,
and are married, you jade you, I'll cut your throat, hussy.
Now, you know my mind.

SCENE 8

Peachum, Polly, Mrs Peachum.

AIR 7 – 'O London is a fine town'

MRS PEACHUM *(In a very great passion.)*
Our Polly is a sad slut! nor heeds what we have taught her,
I wonder any man alive will ever rear a daughter!
For she must have both hoods and gowns, and hoops to swell
her pride,
With scarves and stays, and gloves and lace, and she will have
men beside:
And when she's dressed with care and cost, all tempting, fine
and gay,
As men should serve a cowcumber, she flings herself away.

You baggage! you hussy! you inconsiderate jade! had you
been hanged it would not have vexed me; for that might have
been your misfortune; but to do such a mad thing by choice!
– The wench is married, husband.

PEACHUM Married! the captain is a bold man, and will risk
anything for money: to be sure he believes her a fortune. Do
you think your mother and I should have lived comfortably
so long together if ever we had been married? Baggage!

MRS PEACHUM I knew she was always a proud slut, and now
the wench hath played the fool and married, because, forsooth, she would do like the gentry! Can you support the
expense of a husband, hussy, in gaming, drinking and whor-
ing! Have you money enough to carry on the daily quarrels of
man and wife about who shall squander most? There are not
many husbands and wives who can bear the charges of
plaguing one another in a handsome way. If you must be
married, could you introduce nobody into our family but a
highwayman! Why, thou foolish jade, thou wilt be as ill-used
and as much neglected as if thou hadst married a lord!

PEACHUM Let not your anger, my dear, break through the rules
of decency; for the captain looks upon himself in the military
capacity as a gentleman by his profession. Besides what he
hath already, I know he is in a fair way of getting or of dying;
and both these ways, let me tell you, are most excellent
chances for a wife. Tell me, hussy, are you ruined or no?

MRS PEACHUM With Polly's fortune she might very well have gone off to a person of distinction: yes, that you might, you pouting slut.

PEACHUM What! is the wench dumb? Speak, or I'll make you plead by squeezing out an answer from you. Are you really bound wife to him, or are you only upon liking?

Pinches her.

POLLY Oh!   *Screaming.*

MRS PEACHUM How the mother is to be pitied who hath handsome daughters! Locks, bolts, bars, and lectures of morality, are nothing to them; they break through them all; they have as much pleasure in cheating a father and mother as in cheating at cards.

PEACHUM Why, Polly, I shall soon know if you are married, by Macheath's keeping from our house.

AIR 8 – 'Grim king of the ghosts', etc.

POLLY   *Can love be controlled by advice?*
Will Cupid our mothers obey?
Though my heart were as frozen as ice,
At his flame 'twould have melted away.
When he kissed me, so closely he pressed,
'Twas so sweet that I must have complied,
So I thought it both safest and best
To marry, for fear you should chide.

MRS PEACHUM Then all the hopes of our family are gone for ever and ever!

PEACHUM And Macheath may hang his father- and mother-in-law, in hope to get into their daughter's fortune.

POLLY I did not marry him (as 'tis the fashion) coolly and deliberately, for honour or money – but I love him.

MRS PEACHUM Love him! worse and worse! I thought the girl had been better bred. Oh, husband! husband! her folly makes me mad! my head swims! I'm distracted! I can't support myself – Oh!   *Faints.*

PEACHUM See, wench, to what a condition you have reduced your poor mother! A glass of cordial this instant! How the poor woman takes it to heart! (*Polly goes out, and returns with it.*) Ah, hussy, now this is the only comfort your mother has left.

POLLY Give her another glass, sir; my mamma drinks double the quantity whenever she is out of order. This you see fetches her.

MRS PEACHUM The girl shows such a readiness, and so much concern, that I could almost find in my heart to forgive her.

AIR 9 – 'O Jenny, O Jenny, where hast thou been?'

[MRS PEACHUM]   *O Polly, you might have toyed and kissed;*
By keeping men off you keep them on.
POLLY   *But he so teased me,*
                       And he so pleased me,
             What I did you must have done.

MRS PEACHUM Not with a highwayman – you sorry slut.

PEACHUM A word with you, wife. 'Tis no new thing for a wench to take man without consent of parents. You know 'tis the frailty of woman, my dear!

MRS PEACHUM Yes, indeed, the sex is frail; but the first time a woman is frail, she should be somewhat nice methinks, for then or never is the time to make her fortune: after that she hath nothing to do but to guard herself from being found out, and she may do what she pleases.

PEACHUM Make yourself a little easy; I have a thought shall soon set all matters again to rights. Why so melancholy, Polly? Since what is done cannot be undone, we must all endeavour to make the best of it.

MRS PEACHUM Well, Polly, as far as one woman can forgive another, I forgive thee. Your father is too fond of you, hussy.

POLLY Then all my sorrows are at an end.

MRS PEACHUM A mighty likely speech in troth for a wench who is just married!

AIR 10 – 'Thomas, I cannot', etc.

POLLY   *I like a ship in storms was tossed,*
                Yet afraid to put into land,
        For seized in the port the vessel's lost
               Whose treasure is contraband.
                     The waves are laid,
                     My duty's paid;
                  O joy beyond expression!
                  Thus safe ashore

I ask no more;
My all is in my possession.

PEACHUM I hear customers in t'other room; go talk with 'em. Polly; but come to us again as soon as they are gone. — But hark ye, child, if 'tis the gentleman who was here yesterday about the repeating watch, say you believe we can't get intelligence of it till to-morrow, for I lent it to Sukey Straddle, to make a figure with to-night at a tavern in Drury Lane. If t'other gentleman calls for the silver-hilted sword, you know beetle-browed Jemmy hath it on, and he doth not come from Tunbridge till Tuesday night, so that it cannot be had till then.

SCENE 9

Peachum, Mrs Peachum.

PEACHUM Dear wife! be a little pacified; don't let your passion run away with your senses: Polly, I grant you, has done a rash thing.

MRS PEACHUM If she had had only an intrigue with the fellow, why the very best families have excused and huddled up a frailty of that sort. 'Tis marriage, husband, that makes it a blemish.

PEACHUM But money, wife, is the true fuller's earth for reputations; there is not a spot or stain but what it can take out. A rich rogue nowadays is fit company for any gentleman; and the world, my dear, hath not such a contempt for roguery as you imagine. I tell you, wife, I can make this match turn to our advantage.

MRS PEACHUM I am very sensible, husband, that Captain Macheath is worth money, but I am in doubt whether he hath not two or three wives already, and then if he should die in a session or two, Polly's dower would come into dispute.

PEACHUM That indeed is a point which ought to be considered.

AIR 11 — 'A soldier and a sailor'.

A fox may steal your hens, sir,
A whore your health and pence, sir,
Your daughter rob your chest, sir,
Your wife may steal your rest, sir,

> *A thief your goods and plate.*
> *But this is all for picking,*
> *With rest, pence, chest and chicken;*
> *It ever was decreed, sir,*
> *If lawyer's hand is fee'd, sir,*
> *He steals your whole estate.*

The lawyers are bitter enemies to those in our way; they don't care that anybody should get a clandestine livelihood but themselves.

SCENE 10

Mrs Peachum, Peachum, Polly.

POLLY 'Twas only Nimming Ned: he brought in a damask window-curtain, a hoop-petticoat, a pair of silver candlesticks, a periwig, and one silk stocking, from the fire that happened last night.

PEACHUM There is not a fellow that is cleverer in his way, and saves more goods out of the fire, than Ned. But now, Polly, to your affair; for matters must not be left as they are. You are married then, it seems?

POLLY Yes, sir.

PEACHUM And how do you propose to live, child?

POLLY Like other women, sir; upon the industry of my husband.

MRS PEACHUM What! is the wench turned fool? A highwayman's wife, like a soldier's, hath as little of his pay as of his company.

PEACHUM And had not you the common views of a gentlewoman in your marriage, Polly?

POLLY I don't know what you mean, sir.

PEACHUM Of a jointure, and of being a widow.

POLLY But I love him, sir: how then could I have thoughts of parting with him?

PEACHUM Parting with him! why that is the whole scheme and intention of all marriage articles. The comfortable estate of widowhood is the only hope that keeps up a wife's spirits. Where is the woman who would scruple to be a wife, if she had it in her power to be a widow whenever she pleased? If you have any views of this sort, Polly, I shall think the match not so very unreasonable.

POLLY How I dread to hear your advice! Yet I must beg you to explain yourself.

PEACHUM Secure what he hath got, have him peached the next sessions, and then at once you are made a rich widow.

POLLY What! murder the man I love! The blood runs cold at my heart with the very thought of it.

PEACHUM Fie, Polly! what hath murder to do in the affair? Since the thing sooner or later must happen, I dare say that the captain himself would like that we should get the reward for his death sooner than a stranger. Why, Polly, the captain knows that as 'tis his employment to rob, so 'tis ours to take robbers; every man in his business: so that there is no malice in the case.

MRS PEACHUM Ay, husband, now you have nicked the matter. To have him peached is the only thing could ever make me forgive her.

AIR 12 — 'Now ponder well, ye parents dear'.

POLLY   *Oh ponder well! be not severe;*
                    So save a wretched wife,
            For on the rope that hangs my dear
                    Depends poor Polly's life.

MRS PEACHUM But your duty to your parents, hussy, obliges you to hang him. What would many a wife give for such an opportunity!

POLLY What is a jointure, what is widowhood, to me? I know my heart; I cannot survive him.

AIR 13 — '*Le printemps rappelle aux armes*'.

The turtle thus with plaintive crying,
        Her lover dying,
The turtle thus with plaintive crying
        Laments her dove.
Down she drops quite spent with sighing,
        Paired in death, as paired in love.

Thus, sir, it will happen to your poor Polly.

MRS PEACHUM What! is the fool in love in earnest then? I hate thee for being particular. Why, wench, thou art a shame to thy very sex!

POLLY But hear me, mother — if you ever loved —

MRS PEACHUM Those cursed play-books she reads have been her ruin! One word more, hussy, and I shall knock your brains out, if you have any.

PEACHUM Keep out of the way, Polly, for fear of mischief, and consider of what is proposed to you.

MRS PEACHUM Away, hussy! Hang your husband, and be dutiful.

SCENE 11

Mrs Peachum, Peachum.

Polly listening.

MRS PEACHUM The thing, husband, must and shall be done. For the sake of intelligence we must take other measures and have him peached the next session without her consent. If she will not know her duty, we know ours.

PEACHUM But really, my dear! it grieves one's heart to take off a great man. When I consider his personal bravery, his fine stratagems, how much we have already got by him, and how much more we may get, methinks I can't find in my heart to have a hand in his death: I wish you could have made Polly undertake it.

MRS PEACHUM But in a case of necessity – our own lives are in danger.

PEACHUM Then indeed we must comply with the customs of the world, and make gratitude give way to interest. – He shall be taken off.

MRS PEACHUM I'll undertake to manage Polly.

PEACHUM And I'll prepare matters for the Old Bailey.

SCENE 12

Polly.

POLLY Now I'm a wretch indeed! – Methinks I see him already in the cart, sweeter and more lovely than the nosegay in his hand! – I hear the crowd extolling his resolution and intrepidity! – What volleys of sighs are sent from the windows of Holborn, that so comely a youth should be brought to disgrace! I see him at the tree! the whole circle are in tears!

Even butchers weep! – Jack Ketch himself hesitates to perform
his duty and would be glad to lose his fee by a reprieve. –
What then will become of Polly? – As yet I may inform him
of their design, and aid him in his escape. – It shall be so. –
But then he flies, absents himself, and I bar myself from his
dear, dear conversation! That too will distract me. – If he
keeps out of the way my papa and mamma may in time relent,
and we may be happy. – If he stays, he is hanged, and then he
is lost for ever! – He intended to lie concealed in my room till
the dusk of the evening. If they are abroad I'll this instant let
him out, lest some accident should prevent him.

Exit, and returns.

SCENE 13

Polly, Macheath.

AIR 14 – 'Pretty parrot, say,' etc.

MACHEATH   *Pretty Polly, say,*
                          When I was away,
                    Did your fancy never stray
                          To some newer lover?

POLLY   *Without disguise,*
                          Heaving sighs,
                          Doting eyes,
                    My constant heart discover,
                          Fondly let me loll!

MACHEATH   *O pretty, pretty Poll!*

POLLY And are you as fond as ever, my dear?

MACHEATH Suspect my honour, my courage, suspect anything
but my love. May my pistols miss fire, and my mare slip her
shoulder while I am pursued, if I ever forsake thee!

POLLY Nay, my dear! I have no reason to doubt you, for I find
in the romance you lent me, none of the great heroes were
ever false in love.

AIR 15 – 'Pray, fair one, be kind'.

MACHEATH   *My heart was so free,*
                          It roved like the bee,

> *Till Polly my passion requited:*
>   *I sipped each flower,*
>   *I changed every hour,*
> *But here every flower is united.*

POLLY Were you sentenced to transportation, sure, my dear, you could not leave me behind you – could you?

MACHEATH Is there any power, any force, that could tear me from thee? You might sooner tear a pension out of the hands of a courtier, a fee from a lawyer, a pretty woman from a looking-glass, or any woman from quadrille. But to tear me from thee is impossible!

AIR 16 – 'Over the hills, and far away'.

> *Were I laid on Greenland's coast,*
>   *And in my arms embraced my lass,*
> *Warm amidst eternal frost,*
>   *Too soon the half-year's night would pass.*

POLLY
> *Were I sold on Indian soil,*
>   *Soon as the burning day was closed,*
> *I could mock the sultry toil*
>   *When on my charmer's breast reposed.*

MACHEATH *And I would love you all the day,*
POLLY *Every night would kiss and play,*
MACHEATH *If with me you'd fondly stray*
POLLY *Over the hills, and far away.*

POLLY Yes, I would go with thee. But oh! – how shall I speak it? I must be torn from thee! We must part!

MACHEATH How! part!

POLLY We must, we must! My papa and mamma are set against thy life: they now, even now, are in search after thee: they are preparing evidence against thee; thy life depends upon a moment!

AIR 17 – 'Gin thou wert mine awn thing'.

> *O, what pain it is to part!*
>   *Can I leave thee, can I leave thee?*
> *O, what pain it is to part!*
>   *Can thy Polly ever leave thee!*
> *But lest death my love should thwart,*
>   *And bring thee to the fatal cart,*

Thus I tear thee from my bleeding heart.
Fly hence, and let me leave thee.

One kiss, and then! – one kiss! – Begone! – Farewell!

MACHEATH My hand, my heart, my dear, is so riveted to thine, that I cannot unloose my hold!

POLLY But my papa may intercept thee, and then I should lose the very glimmering of hope. A few weeks, perhaps, may reconcile us. Shall thy Polly hear from thee?

MACHEATH Must I then go?

POLLY And will not absence change your love?

MACHEATH If you doubt it, let me stay – and be hanged.

POLLY Oh, how I fear! how I tremble! Go – but, when safety will give you leave, you will be sure to see me again; for, till then, Polly is wretched.

AIR 18 – 'O the broom', etc.

MACHEATH *The miser thus a shilling sees,*
Which he's obliged to pay,
With sighs resigns it by degrees,
And fear 'tis gone for ay.

(*Parting and looking back at each other with fondness:*
he at one door, she at another.)

POLLY *The boy thus, when his sparrow's flown,*
The bird in silence eyes:
But soon as out of sight 'tis gone,
Whines, whimpers, sobs, and cries.

Act II

SCENE: *A tavern near Newgate.*

Jemmy Twitcher, Crook-fingered Jack, Wat Dreary, Robin of Bagshot, Nimming Ned, Henry Paddington, Mat of the Mint, Ben Budge, and the rest of the Gang, at the table, with wine, brandy, and tobacco.

BEN But prithee, Mat, what is become of thy brother Tom? I have not seen him since my return from transportation.

MAT Poor brother Tom had an accident, this time twelve-month, and so clever made a fellow he was, I could not save him from these fleaing rascals, the surgeons; and now, poor man, he is among the otamies at Surgeons' Hall.

BEN So, it seems, his time was come.

JEMMY But the present time is ours, and nobody alive hath more. Why are the laws levelled at us? Are we more dishonest than the rest of mankind? What we win, gentlemen, is our own, by the law of arms and the right of conquest.

CROOK Where shall we find such another set of practical philosophers, who, to a man, are above the fear of death?

WAT Sound men, and true!

ROBIN Of tried courage, and indefatigable industry!

NED Who is there here that would not die for his friend?

HARRY Who is there here that would betray him for his interest?

MAT Show me a gang of courtiers that can say as much.

BEN We are for a just partition of the world; for every man hath a right to enjoy life.

MAT We retrench the superfluities of mankind. The world is avaricious, and I hate avarice. A covetous fellow, like a jackdaw, steals what he was never made to enjoy, for the sake of hiding it. These are the robbers of mankind; for money was made for the free-hearted and generous: and where is the injury of taking from another what he hath not the heart to make use of?

JEMMY Our several stations for the day are fixed. Good luck attend us all! Fill the glasses!

AIR 1 – 'Fill ev'ry glass', etc.

MAT   *Fill ev'ry glass, for wine inspires us,*
           And fires us
    With courage, love and joy.
    Women and wine should life employ;
           Is there aught else on earth desirous?

CHORUS   *Fill ev'ry glass, etc.*

SCENE 2

To them enter Macheath.

MACHEATH Gentlemen, well met; my heart hath been with you this hour, but an unexpected affair hath detained me. No ceremony, I beg you!

MAT We were just breaking up, to go upon duty. Am I to have the honour of taking the air with you, sir, this evening, upon the heath? I drink a dram, now and then, with the stage-coachmen, in the way of friendship and intelligence; and I know that, about this time, there will be passengers, upon the western road, who are worth speaking with.

MACHEATH I was to have been of that party – but –

MAT But what, sir?

MACHEATH Is there any man who suspects my courage?

MAT We have all been witnesses of it.

MACHEATH My honour and truth to the gang?

MAT I'll be answerable for it.

MACHEATH In the division of our booty, have I ever shown the least marks of avarice or injustice?

MAT By these questions, something seems to have ruffled you. Are any of us suspected?

MACHEATH I have a fixed confidence, gentlemen, in you all, as men of honour, and as such I value and respect you. Peachum is a man that is useful to us.

MAT Is he about to play us any foul play? I'll shoot him through the head.

MACHEATH I beg you, gentlemen, act with conduct and discretion. A pistol is your last resort.

MAT He knows nothing of this meeting.

MACHEATH Business cannot go on without him: he is a man who knows the world, and is a necessary agent to us. We have had a slight difference, and, till it is accommodated, I shall be obliged to keep out of his way. Any private dispute of mine shall be of no ill consequence to my friends. You must continue to act under his direction; for, the moment we break loose from him, our gang is ruined.

MAT As a bawd to a whore I grant you he is, to us, of great convenience.

MACHEATH Make him believe I have quitted the gang, which I can never do but with life. At our private quarters I will continue to meet you. A week, or so, will probably reconcile us.

MAT Your instructions shall be observed. 'Tis now high time for us to repair to our several duties; so, till the evening, at our quarters in Moorfields, we bid you farewell.

MACHEATH I shall wish myself with you. Success attend you.
                              Sits down, melancholy, at the table.

    AIR 2 – March in Rinaldo, with drums and trumpets.

MAT   *Let us take the road:*
         Hark! I hear the sound of coaches,
         The hour of attack approaches,
      To your arms, brave boys, and load.
         See the ball I hold!
      Let the chemists toil like asses,
         Our fire their fire surpasses,
         And turns all our lead to gold.

(The Gang, ranged in front of the stage, load their pistols, and stick them under their girdles, then go off, singing the first part in chorus.)

SCENE 3
Macheath, Drawer.

MACHEATH What a fool is a fond wench! Polly is most confoundedly bit. I love the sex; and a man who loves money might as well be contented with one guinea, as I with one woman. The town, perhaps, hath been as much obliged to me for recruiting it with free-hearted ladies, as to any recruiting-officer in the army. If it were not for us, and the other gentlemen of the sword, Drury Lane would be uninhabited.

AIR 3 — 'Would you have a young virgin', etc.

If the heart of a man is depressed with cares,
The mist is dispelled when a woman appears,
Like the notes of a fiddle, she sweetly, sweetly,
Raises the spirits, and charms our ears.
Roses and lilies her cheeks disclose,
But her ripe lips are more sweet than those;
  Press her,
  Caress her,
  With blisses,
  Her kisses
Dissolve us in pleasure and soft repose.

I must have women -- there is nothing unbends the mind like them: money is not so strong a cordial for the time. Drawer!

Enter Drawer.

Is the porter gone for all the ladies, according to my directions?

DRAWER I expect him back every minute; but you know, sir, you sent him as far as Hockley-in-the-Hole for three of the ladies; for one in Vinegar Yard, and for the rest of them somewhere about Lewkner's Lane. Sure some of them are below, for I hear the bar bell. As they come, I will show them up. Coming! coming!

SCENE 4

Macheath, Mrs Coaxer, Dolly Trull, Mrs Vixen, Betty Doxy, Jenny Diver, Mrs Slammekin, Sukey Tawdry, and Molly Brazen.

MACHEATH Dear Mrs Coaxer, you are welcome! you look charmingly to-day: I hope you don't want the repairs of quality, and lay on paint. — Dolly Trull! kiss me, you slut! are you as amorous as ever, hussy? You are always so taken up

with stealing hearts, that you don't allow yourself time to
steal anything else. Ah, Dolly! thou wilt ever be a coquette. –
Mrs Vixen, I'm yours! I always loved a woman of wit and
spirit; they make charming mistresses, but plaguy wives. –
Betty Doxy! come hither, hussy: do you drink as hard as ever?
You had better stick to good wholesome beer, for, in troth,
Betty, strong waters will, in time, ruin your constitution: you
should leave those to your betters. – What, and my pretty
Jenny Diver too! as prim and demure as ever! There is not
any prude, though ever so high bred, hath a more sanctified
look, with a more mischievous heart: ah, thou art a dear,
artful hypocrite! – Mrs Slammekin! as careless and genteel as
ever! All you fine ladies, who know your own beauty, affect
an undress. – But see! here's Sukey Tawdry come to contradict
what I was saying. Everything she gets one way, she lays out
upon her back. Why, Sukey, you must keep at least a dozen
tally-men. – Molly Brazen! (*She kisses him.*) That's well done:
I love a free-hearted wench: thou hast a most agreeable
assurance, girl, and art as willing as a turtle. – But hark! I
hear music! The harper is at the door. 'If music be the food of
love, play on!' Ere you seat yourselves, ladies, what think you
of a dance? Come in.

Enter Harper.

Play the French tune that Mrs Slammekin was so fond of.

*A dance à la ronde in the French manner: near the
end of it this Song and Chorus.*

AIR 4 – Cotillon.

> Youth's the season made for joys,
>   Love is then our duty:
> She alone who that employs,
>   Well deserves her beauty.
>   Let's be gay
>   While we may,
> Beauty's a flower despised in decay.

CHORUS   *Youth's the season, etc.*

> Let us drink and sport to-day,
>   Ours is not to-morrow:

> *Love with youth flies swift away,*
> *Age is naught but sorrow.*
> *Dance and sing,*
> *Time's on the wing,*
> *Life never knows the return of spring.*

CHORUS   *Let us drink, etc.*

MACHEATH Now, pray, ladies, take your places. Here, fellow. (*Pays the Harper.*) Bid the drawer bring us more wine. (*Exit Harper.*) If any of the ladies choose gin, I hope they will be so free as to call for it.

JENNY You look as if you meant me. Wine is strong enough for me. Indeed, sir, I never drink strong waters but when I have the colic.

MACHEATH Just the excuse of the fine ladies! why, a lady of quality is never without colic. I hope, Mrs Coaxer, you have had good success of late in your visits among the mercers?

MRS COAXER We have so many interlopers. Yet with industry, one may still have a little picking. I carried a silver-flowered lute-string and a piece of black padesoy to Mr Peachum's Lock but last week.

MRS VIXEN There's Molly Brazen hath the ogle of a rattlesnake. She riveted a linen-draper's eye so fast upon her, that he was nicked of three pieces of cambric before he could look off.

BRAZEN O dear madam! But sure nothing can come up to your handling of laces! And then you have such a sweet deluding tongue! To cheat a man is nothing; but the woman must have the fine parts indeed who cheats a woman!

MRS VIXEN Lace, madam, lies in a small compass, and is of easy conveyance. But you are apt, madam, to think too well of your friends.

MRS COAXER If any woman hath more art than another, to be sure 'tis Jenny Diver. Though her fellow be never so agreeable, she can pick his pocket as coolly as if money were her only pleasure. Now that is a command of the passions uncommon in a woman!

JENNY I never go to a tavern with a man but in the view of business. I have other hours, and other sort of men, for my pleasure. But had I your address, madam —

MACHEATH Have done with your compliments, ladies, and

drink about. You are not so fond of me, Jenny, as you used to be.

JENNY 'Tis not convenient, sir, to show my fondness among so many rivals. 'Tis your own choice, and not the warmth of my inclination, that will determine you.

AIR 5 – 'All in a misty morning', etc.

Before the barn-door crowing,
  The Cock by hens attended,
His eyes around him throwing,
  Stands for a while suspended;
Then one he singles from the crew,
  And cheers the happy hen:
With how do you do, and how do you do,
  And how do you do again.

MACHEATH Ah, Jenny! thou art a dear slut.

TRULL Pray, madam, were you ever in keeping?

TAWDRY I hope, madam, I han't been so long upon the town but I have met with some good fortune as well as my neighbours.

TRULL Pardon me, madam, I meant no harm by the question: 'twas only in the way of conversation.

TAWDRY Indeed, madam, if I had not been a fool, I might have lived very handsomely with my last friend. But upon his missing five guineas, he turned me off. Now I never suspected he had counted them.

MRS SLAMMEKIN Who do you look upon, madam, as your best sort of keepers?

TRULL That, madam, is thereafter as they be.

MRS SLAMMEKIN Madam was once kept by a Jew; and bating their religion, to women they are a good sort of people.

TAWDRY Now for my own part, I own I like an old fellow: for we always make them pay for what they can't do.

MRS VIXEN A spruce 'prentice, let me tell you, ladies, is no ill thing; they bleed freely. I have sent at least two or three dozen of them, in my time, to the Plantations.

JENNY But to be sure, sir, with so much good fortune as you have had upon the road, you must be grown immensely rich.

MACHEATH The road, indeed, hath done me justice, but the gaming-table hath been my ruin.

AIR 6 – 'When once I lay with another man's wife'.

JENNY *The gamesters and lawyers are jugglers alike:*
If they meddle, your all is in danger;
Like gipsies, if once they can finger a souse,
Your pockets they pick, and they pilfer your house,
And give your estate to a stranger.

These are the tools of a man of honour. Cards and dice are only fit for cowardly cheats, who prey upon their friends.
She takes up his pistol. Tawdry takes up the other.

TAWDRY This, sir, is fitter for your hand. Besides your loss of money, 'tis a loss to the ladies. Gaming takes you off from women. How fond could I be of you! but before company, 'tis ill-bred.

MACHEATH Wanton hussies!

JENNY I must and will have a kiss to give my wine a zest.
They take him about the neck, and make signs to
Peachum and Constables: who rush in upon him.

SCENE 5

To them Peachum and Constables.

PEACHUM I seize you, sir, as my prisoner.

MACHEATH Was this well done, Jenny? Women are decoy ducks; who can trust them! Beasts, jades, jilts, harpies, furies, whores!

PEACHUM Your case, Mr Macheath, is not particular. The greatest heroes have been ruined by women. But, to do them justice, I must own they are a pretty sort of creatures, if we could trust them. You must now, sir, take your leave of the ladies: and, if they have a mind to make you a visit, they will be sure to find you at home. The gentleman, ladies, lodges in Newgate. Constables, wait upon the captain to his lodgings.

AIR 7 – 'When first I laid siege to my Chloris', etc.

MACHEATH *At the tree I shall suffer with pleasure,*
At the tree I shall suffer with pleasure,
Let me go where I will,
In all kinds of ill,
I shall find no such furies as these are.

PEACHUM Ladies, I'll take care the reckoning shall be discharged.

Exit Macheath, guarded, with Peachum and Constables.

SCENE 6

The women remain.

MRS VIXEN Look, Mrs Jenny, though Mr Peachum may have made a private bargain with you and Sukey Tawdry for betraying the captain, as we were all assisting, we ought all to share alike.

MRS COAXER I think Mr Peachum, after so long an acquaintance, might have trusted me as well as Jenny Diver.

MRS SLAMMEKIN I am sure at least three men of his hanging, and in a year's time, too (if he did me justice), should be set down to my account.

TRULL Mrs Slammekin, that is not fair. For you know one of them was taken in bed with me.

JENNY As far as a bowl of punch or a treat, I believe Mrs Sukey will join with me. As for anything else, ladies, you cannot in conscience expect it.

MRS SLAMMEKIN Dear madam –

TRULL I would not for the world –

MRS SLAMMEKIN 'Tis impossible for me –

TRULL As I hope to be saved, madam –

MRS SLAMMEKIN Nay, then I must stay here all night –

TRULL Since you command me.   *Exeunt with great ceremony.*

SCENE 7

SCENE: *Newgate.*

Lockit, Turnkeys, Macheath, Constables.

LOCKIT Noble captain, you are welcome! you have not been a lodger of mine this year and half. You know the custom, sir; garnish, captain, garnish. Hand me down those fetters there.

MACHEATH Those, Mr Lockit, seem to be the heaviest of the whole set. With your leave, I should like the farther pair better.

LOCKIT Lookye, captain, we know what is fittest for our

prisoners. When a gentleman uses me with civility, I always do the best I can to please him. – Hand them down, I say. – We have them of all prices, from one guinea to ten; and 'tis fitting every gentleman should please himself.

MACHEATH I understand you, sir. (*Gives money.*) The fees here are so many, and so exorbitant, that few fortunes can bear the expense of getting off handsomely, or of dying like a gentleman.

LOCKIT Those, I see, will fit the captain better. Take down the farther pair. Do but examine them, sir – never was better work – how genteelly they are made! They will fit as easy as a glove, and the nicest man in England might not be ashamed to wear them. (*He puts on the chains.*) If I had the best gentleman in the land in my custody, I could not equip him more handsomely. And so, sir, I now leave you to your private meditations.

SCENE 8

Macheath.

AIR 8 – 'Courtiers, courtiers, think it no harm', etc.

MACHEATH *Man may escape from rope and gun,*
  Nay, some have outlived the doctor's pill:
 Who takes a woman, must be undone,
  That basilisk is sure to kill.
 The fly that sips treacle is lost in the sweets,
  So he that tastes woman, woman, woman,
 He that tastes woman, ruin meets.

To what a woeful plight have I brought myself! Here must I (all day long, till I am hanged) be confined to hear the reproaches of a wench who lays her ruin at my door. I am in the custody of her father; and, to be sure, if he knows of the matter, I shall have a fine time on't betwixt this and my execution. – But I promised the wench marriage. What signifies a promise to a woman? does not man, in marriage itself, promise a hundred things that he never means to perform? Do all we can, women will believe us: for they look upon a promise as an excuse for following their own inclinations. But here comes Lucy, and I cannot get from her – would I were deaf!

SCENE 9

Macheath, Lucy.

LUCY You base man, you! – how can you look me in the face, after what hath passed between us? See here, perfidious wretch, how I am forced to bear about the load of infamy you have laid upon me. Oh, Macheath! thou hast robbed me of my quiet – to see thee tortured would give me pleasure.

AIR 9 – 'A lovely lass to a friar came', etc.

> *Thus when a good housewife sees a rat*
> *In her trap in the morning taken,*
> *With pleasure her heart goes pit-a-pat,*
> *In revenge for her loss of bacon,*
> > *Then she throws him*
> > *To the dog or cat,*
> *To be worried, crushed, and shaken.*

MACHEATH Have you no bowels, no tenderness, my dear Lucy, to see a husband in these circumstances?

LUCY A husband!

MACHEATH In every respect but the form, and that, my dear, may be said over us at any time. Friends should not insist upon ceremonies. From a man of honour his word is as good as his bond.

LUCY It is the pleasure of all you fine men to insult the women you have ruined.

AIR 10 – ''Twas when the sea was roaring', etc.

> *How cruel are the traitors,*
> > *Who lie and swear in jest,*
> *To cheat unguarded creatures*
> > *Of virtue, fame, and rest!*
> *Whoever steals a shilling*
> > *Through shame the guilt conceals:*
> *In love the perjured villain*
> > *With boasts the theft reveals.*

MACHEATH The very first opportunity, my dear, (but have patience) you shall be my wife in whatever manner you please.

LUCY Insinuating monster! And so you think I know nothing of the affair of Miss Polly Peachum? I could tear thy eyes out.

MACHEATH Sure, Lucy, you can't be such a fool as to be jealous of Polly?

LUCY Are you not married to her, you brute, you?

MACHEATH Married! very good. The wench gives it out only to vex thee, and to ruin me in thy good opinion. 'Tis true I go to the house, I chat with the girl, I kiss her, I say a thousand things to her (as all gentlemen do) that mean nothing, to divert myself; and now the silly jade hath set it about that I am married to her, to let me know what she would be at. Indeed, my dear Lucy, these violent passions may be of ill consequence to a woman in your condition.

LUCY Come, come, captain, for all your assurance, you know that Miss Polly hath put it out of your power to do me the justice you promised me.

MACHEATH A jealous woman believes everything her passion suggests. To convince you of my sincerity, if we can find the ordinary, I shall have no scruples of making you my wife; and I know the consequence of having two at a time.

LUCY That you are only to be hanged, and so get rid of them both.

MACHEATH I am ready, my dear Lucy, to give you satisfaction – if you think there is any in marriage. What can a man of honour say more?

LUCY So then it seems you are not married to Miss Polly?

MACHEATH You know, Lucy, the girl is prodigiously conceited: no man can say a civil thing to her but (like other fine ladies) her vanity makes her think he's her own for ever and ever.

AIR 11 – 'The Sun hath loosed his weary teams', etc.

> The first time at the looking-glass
>   The mother sets her daughter,
> The image strikes the smiling lass
>   With self-love ever after.
> Each time she looks, she, fonder grown,
>   Thinks every charm grows stronger;
> But alas, vain maid! all eyes but your own
>   Can see you are not younger.

When women consider their own beauties, they are all alike unreasonable in their demands; for they expect their lovers should like them as long as they like themselves.

LUCY Yonder is my father. Perhaps this way we may light upon the ordinary, who shall try if you will be as good as your word — for I long to be made an honest woman.

SCENE 10

Peachum, Lockit with an account book.

LOCKIT In this last affair, brother Peachum, we are agreed. You have consented to go halves in Macheath.

PEACHUM We shall never fall out about an execution. But as to that article, pray how stands our last year's account?

LOCKIT If you will run your eye over it, you'll find 'tis fair and clearly stated.

PEACHUM This long arrear of the Government is very hard upon us. Can it be expected that we should hang our acquaintances for nothing, when our betters will hardly save theirs without being paid for it? Unless the people in employment pay better, I promise them for the future I shall let other rogues live beside their own.

LOCKIT Perhaps, brother, they are afraid these matters may be carried too far. We are treated, too, by them with contempt, as if our profession were not reputable.

PEACHUM In one respect indeed our employment may be reckoned dishonest, because, like great statesmen, we encourage those who betray their friends.

LOCKIT Such language, brother, anywhere else might turn to your prejudice. Learn to be more guarded, I beg you.

AIR 12 – 'How happy are we', etc.

> *When you censure the age,*
> *Be cautious and sage,*
> *Lest the courtiers offended should be:*
> *If you mention vice or bribe,*
> *'Tis so pat to all the tribe,*
> *Each cries – That was levelled at me.*

PEACHUM Here's poor Ned Clincher's name I see: sure, brother Lockit, there was a little unfair proceeding in Ned's case: for he told me in the condemned hold, that for value received you had promised him a session or two longer without molestation.

LOCKIT Mr Peachum, this is the first time my honour was ever called in question.

PEACHUM Business is at an end, if once we act dishonourably.

LOCKIT Who accuses me?

PEACHUM You are warm, brother.

LOCKIT He that attacks my honour, attacks my livelihood – and this usage, sir, is not to be borne.

PEACHUM Since you provoke me to speak, I must tell you, too, that Mrs Coaxer charges you with defrauding her of her information money for the apprehending of Curlpated Hugh. Indeed, indeed, brother, we must punctually pay our spies, or we shall have no information.

LOCKIT Is this language to me, sirrah – who have saved you from the gallows, sirrah!   *Collaring each other.*

PEACHUM If I am hanged, it shall be for ridding the world of an arrant rascal.

LOCKIT This hand shall do the office of the halter you deserve, and throttle you – you dog!

PEACHUM Brother, brother, we are both in the wrong – we shall be both losers in the dispute – for you know we have it in our power to hang each other. You should not be so passionate.

LOCKIT Nor you so provoking.

PEACHUM 'Tis our mutual interest, 'tis for the interest of the world, we should agree. If I said anything, brother, to the prejudice of your character, I ask pardon.

LOCKIT Brother Peachum, I can forgive as well as resent. Give me your hand: suspicion does not become a friend.

PEACHUM I only meant to give you occasion to justify yourself. But I must now step home, for I expect the gentleman about this snuff-box that Filch nimmed two nights ago in the park. I appointed him at this hour.

SCENE 11

Lockit, Lucy.

LOCKIT Whence come you, hussy?

LUCY My tears might answer that question.

LOCKIT You have then been whimpering and fondling like a spaniel over the fellow that hath abused you.

LUCY One can't help love; one can't cure it. 'Tis not in my power to obey you and hate him.

LOCKIT Learn to bear your husband's death like a reasonable woman; 'tis not the fashion nowadays so much as to affect sorrow upon these occasions. No woman would ever marry, if she had not the chance of mortality for a release. Act like a woman of spirit, hussy, and thank your father for what he is doing.

AIR 13 – 'Of a noble race was Shenkin'.

LUCY
Is then his fate decreed, sir,
Such a man can I think of quitting?
When first we met, so moves me yet,
O see how my heart is splitting!

LOCKIT Lookye, Lucy, there is no saving him, so I think you must even do like other widows – buy yourself weeds, and be cheerful.

AIR 14

You'll think, ere many days ensue,
This sentence not severe;
I hang your husband, child, 'tis true,
But with him hang your care.
Twang dang dillo dee.

Like a good wife, go moan over your dying husband; that, child, is your duty. Consider, girl, you can't have the man and the money, too – so make yourself as easy as you can, by getting all you can from him.

SCENE 12

Lucy, Macheath.

LUCY Though the ordinary was out of the way to-day, I hope, my dear, you will upon the first opportunity quiet my scruples. Oh, sir! my father's hard heart is not to be softened, and I am in the utmost despair.

MACHEATH But if I could raise a small sum – would not twenty guineas, think you, move him? Of all the arguments in the way of business, the perquisite is the most prevailing. Your father's perquisites for the escape of prisoners must amount to a considerable sum in the year. Money, well timed, and properly applied, will do anything.

AIR 15 – 'London Ladies'.

If you at an office solicit your due,
  And would not have matters neglected,
You must quicken the clerk with a perquisite too,
  To do what his duty directed.
Or would you the frowns of a lady prevent,
  She too has this palpable failing,
The perquisite softens her into consent;
  That reason with all is prevailing.

LUCY What love or money can do, shall be done; for all my comfort depends upon your safety.

SCENE 13

Lucy, Macheath, Polly.

POLLY Where is my dear husband! Was a rope ever intended for this neck! Oh, let me throw my arms about it, and throttle thee with love! Why dost thou turn away from me? – 'tis thy Polly – 'tis thy wife.

MACHEATH Was ever such an unfortunate rascal as I am!

LUCY Was there ever such another villain!

POLLY Oh, Macheath! was it for this we parted? Taken! imprisoned! tried! hanged! Cruel reflection! I'll stay with thee till death – no force shall tear thy dear wife from thee now. What means my love? – not one kind word! not one kind look! Think what thy Polly suffers to see thee in this condition.

AIR 16 – 'All in the Downs', etc.

Thus when the swallow, seeking prey,
  Within the sash is closely pent,
His consort with bemoaning lay
  Without sits pining for the event.
Her chattering lovers all around her skim;
She heeds them not, poor bird, her soul's with him.

MACHEATH I must disown her. (*Aside.*) The wench is distracted!

LUCY Am I then bilked of my virtue? Can I have no reparation? Sure men were born to lie, and women to believe them! Oh, villain! villain!

POLLY Am I not thy wife? Thy neglect of me, thy aversion to me, too severely proves it. Look on me – tell me, am I not thy wife?

LUCY Perfidious wretch!

POLLY Barbarous husband!

LUCY Hadst thou been hanged five months ago, I had been happy.

POLLY And I, too. If you had been kind to me till death, it would not have vexed me – and that's no very unreasonable request (though from a wife) to a man who hath not above seven or eight days to live.

LUCY Art thou, then, married to another? Hast thou two wives, monster?

MACHEATH If women's tongues can cease for an answer – hear me.

LUCY I won't. Flesh and blood can't bear my usage!

POLLY Shall not I claim my own? Justice bids me speak.

AIR 17 – 'Have you heard of a frolicsome ditty', etc.

MACHEATH   *How happy could I be with either,*
              Were t'other dear charmer away!
              But, while ye thus tease me together,
                 To neither a word will I say;
                 But toll de roll, etc.

POLLY Sure, my dear, there ought to be some preference shown to a wife – at least, she may claim the appearance of it. He must be distracted with misfortunes, or he could not use me thus.

LUCY Oh, villain! villain! thou hast deceived me! I could even inform against thee with pleasure. Not a prude wishes more heartily to have facts against her intimate acquaintance than I now wish to have facts against thee. I would have her satisfaction, and they should all out.

AIR 18 – 'Irish trot'.

POLLY *I'm bubbled.*
LUCY   *I'm bubbled.*

POLLY   *Oh, how I'm troubled!*
LUCY   *Bamboozled and bit!*
POLLY   *My distresses are doubled.*
LUCY   *When you come to the tree, should the hangman refuse,*
        These fingers, with pleasure, could fasten the noose.
POLLY   *I'm bubbled, etc.*

MACHEATH Be pacified, my dear Lucy — this is all a fetch of
    Polly's to make me desperate with you, in case I get off. If I
    am hanged, she would fain have the credit of being thought
    my widow. Really, Polly, this is no time for a dispute of this
    sort; for whenever you are talking of marriage, I am thinking
    of hanging.
POLLY   And hast thou the heart to persist in disowning me?
MACHEATH And hast thou the heart to persist in persuading me
    that I am married? Why, Polly, dost thou seek to aggravate
    my misfortunes?
LUCY   Really, Miss Peachum, you but expose yourself; besides,
    'tis barbarous in you to worry a gentleman in his circum-
    stances.

                              AIR 19

POLLY   *Cease your funning,*
                            Force or cunning,
                        Never shall my heart trepan;
                            All these sallies
                            Are but malice,
                        To seduce my constant man.

                            'Tis most certain,
                            By their flirting,
                        Women oft have envy shown;
                            Pleased to ruin
                            Others' wooing,
                        Never happy in their own!

    Decency, madam, methinks, might teach you to behave your-
    self with some reserve with the husband while his wife is
    present.
MACHEATH But, seriously, Polly, this is carrying the joke a little
    too far.
LUCY   If you are determined, madam, to raise a disturbance in

the prison, I shall be obliged to send for the turnkey to show you the door. I am sorry, madam, you force me to be so ill-bred.

POLLY Give me leave to tell you, madam, these forward airs don't become you in the least, madam; and my duty, madam, obliges me to stay with my husband, madam.

AIR 20 – 'Good morrow, Gossip Joan'.

LUCY *Why, how now, Madam Flirt?*
   If you thus must chatter,
   And are for flinging dirt,
    Let's try, who best can spatter,
        Madam Flirt!

POLLY *Why, how now, saucy jade!*
   Sure, the wench is tipsy!
   How can you see me made   (To him.)
   The scoff of such a gipsy?
      Saucy jade !   (To her.)

SCENE 14

Lucy, Macheath, Polly, Peachum.

PEACHUM Where's my wench? Ah, hussy, hussy! Come home, you slut! and when your fellow is hanged, hang yourself, to make your family some amends.

POLLY Dear, dear father! do not tear me from him. I must speak – I have more to say to him. Oh, twist thy fetters about me, that he may not haul me from thee!

PEACHUM Sure, all women are alike! if ever they commit the folly, they are sure to commit another, by exposing themselves. Away – not a word more! You are my prisoner now, hussy.

AIR 21 – 'Irish howl'.

POLLY *No power on earth can e'er divide*
   The knot that sacred love hath tied.
   When parents draw against our mind,
   The true love's knot they faster bind,
    Oh, oh, ray, oh Amborah – Oh, oh, etc.

     (Holding Macheath, Peachum pulling her.)

SCENE 15

Lucy, Macheath.

MACHEATH I am naturally compassionate, wife, so that I could not use the wench as she deserved, which made you, at first, suspect there was something in what she said.

LUCY Indeed, my dear, I was strangely puzzled!

MACHEATH If that had been the case, her father would never have brought me into this circumstance. No, Lucy, I had rather die than be false to thee!

LUCY How happy am I, if you say this from your heart! for I love thee so, that I could sooner bear to see thee hanged than in the arms of another.

MACHEATH But couldst thou bear to see me hanged?

LUCY Oh, Macheath! I could never live to see that day!

MACHEATH You see, Lucy, in the account of love, you are in my debt. And you must now be convinced that I rather choose to die than be another's. Make me, if possible, love thee more, and let me owe my life to thee. If you refuse to assist me, Peachum and your father will immediately put me beyond all means of escape.

LUCY My father, I know, hath been drinking hard with the prisoners, and, I fancy, he is now taking his nap in his own room. If I can procure the keys, shall I go off with thee, my dear?

MACHEATH If we are together, 'twill be impossible to lie concealed. As soon as the search begins to be a little cool, I will send to thee; till then, my heart is thy prisoner.

LUCY Come, then, my dear husband, owe thy life to me; and, though you love me not, be grateful. But that Polly runs in my head strangely.

MACHEATH A moment of time may make us unhappy for ever.

AIR 22 – 'The Lass of Patie's Mill'.

LUCY

I like the fox shall grieve,
    Whose mate hath left her side;
Whom hounds, from morn to eve,
    Chase o'er the country wide.

Where can my lover hide?
    Where cheat the wary pack?
If love be not his guide,
    He never will come back.

Act III

SCENE: *Newgate.*

Lockit, Lucy.

LOCKIT To be sure, wench, you must have been aiding and abetting to help him to this escape?

LUCY Sir, here hath been Peachum and his daughter Polly, and, to be sure, they know the ways of Newgate as well as if they have been born and bred in the place all their lives. Why must all your suspicion light upon me?

LOCKIT Lucy, Lucy, I will have none of these shuffling answers!

LUCY Well, then, if I know anything of him, I wish I may be burned!

LOCKIT Keep your temper, Lucy, or I shall pronounce you guilty.

LUCY Keep yours, sir – I do wish I may be burned, I do, and what can I say more to convince you?

LOCKIT Did he tip handsomely? How much did he come down with? Come, hussy, don't cheat your father, and I shall not be angry with you. Perhaps you have made a better bargain with him than I could have done. How much, my good girl?

LUCY You know, sir, I am fond of him, and would have given money to have kept him with me.

LOCKIT Ah, Lucy! thy education might have put thee more upon thy guard: for a girl in the bar of an ale-house is always besieged.

LUCY Dear sir, mention not my education, for 'twas to that I owe my ruin.

AIR I – 'If love's a sweet passion', etc.

When young at the bar you first taught me to score
And bid me be free with my lips, and no more;

I was kissed by the parson, the squire, and the sot;
When the guest was departed, the kiss was forgot.
But his kiss was so sweet, and so closely he pressed,
That I languished and pined till I granted the rest.

If you can forgive me, sir, I will make a fair confession; for, to be sure, he hath been a most barbarous villain to me!

LOCKIT And so you have let him escape, hussy – have you?

LUCY When a woman loves, a kind look, a tender word, can persuade her to anything, and I could ask no other bribe.

LOCKIT Thou wilt always be a vulgar slut, Lucy. If you would not be looked upon as a fool, you should never do anything but upon the foot of interest. Those that act otherwise are their own bubbles.

LUCY But love, sir, is a misfortune that may happen to the most discreet woman, and in love we are all fools alike. Notwithstanding all he swore, I am now fully convinced that Polly Peachum is actually his wife. Did I let him escape, fool that I was! to go to her? Polly will wheedle herself into his money; and then Peachum will hang him, and cheat us both.

LOCKIT So I am to be ruined because, forsooth, you must be in love! A very pretty excuse!

LUCY I could murder that impudent, happy strumpet! I gave him his life, and that creature enjoys the sweets of it. Ungrateful Macheath!

AIR 2 – 'South Sea Ballad'.

My love is all madness and folly;
Alone I lie,
Toss, tumble, and cry,
What a happy creature is Polly!
Was e'er such a wretch as I?
With rage I redden like scarlet,
That my dear inconstant varlet,
Stark blind to my charms,
Is lost in the arms
Of that jilt, that inveigling harlot!
Stark blind to my charms,
Is lost in the arms
Of that jilt, that inveigling harlot!
This, this my resentment alarms.

LOCKIT And so, after all this mischief, I must stay here to be
entertained with your caterwauling, Mistress Puss! Out of my
sight, wanton strumpet! You shall fast, and mortify yourself
into reason, with, now and then, a little handsome discipline,
to bring you to your senses. Go!

SCENE 2

Lockit.

LOCKIT Peachum then intends to outwit me in this affair; but
I'll be even with him. The dog is leaky in his liquor, so I'll ply
him that way, get the secret from him, and turn this affair to
my own advantage. Lions, wolves, and vultures don't live
together in herds, droves or flocks. Of all animals of prey,
man is the only sociable one. Every one of us preys upon his
neighbour, and yet we herd together. Peachum is my companion, my friend – according to the custom of the world,
indeed, he may quote thousands of precedents for cheating
me – and shall not I make use of the privilege of friendship to
make him a return!

AIR 3 – 'Packington's Pound'.

Thus gamesters united in friendship are found,
  Though they know that their industry all is a cheat;
They flock to their prey at the dice-box's sound,
  And join to promote one another's deceit.
    But if by mishap
    They fail of a chap,
To keep in their hands, they each other entrap.
Like pikes, lank with hunger, who miss of their ends,
They bite their companions, and prey on their friends.

Now, Peachum, you and I, like honest tradesmen, are to have
a fair trial which of us two can overreach the other. Lucy!

Enter Lucy.

Are there any of Peachum's people now in the house?
LUCY Filch, sir, is drinking a quartern of strong waters in the
next room with Black Moll.
LOCKIT Bid him come to me.

SCENE 3

Lockit, Filch.

LOCKIT Why, boy, thou lookest as if thou wert half starved; like a shotten herring.

FILCH One had need have the constitution of a horse to go through the business. Since the favourite child-getter was disabled by a mishap, I have picked up a little money by helping the ladies to a pregnancy against their being called down to sentence. But if a man cannot get an honest livelihood any easier way, I am sure 'tis what I can't undertake for another session.

LOCKIT Truly, if that great man should tip off, 'twould be an irreparable loss. The vigour and prowess of a knight-errant never saved half the ladies in distress that he hath done. But, boy, canst thou tell me where thy master is to be found?

FILCH At his Lock, sir, at the Crooked Billet.

LOCKIT Very well. I have nothing more with you. (*Exit Filch.*) I'll go to him there, for I have many important affairs to settle with him; and in the way of those transactions, I'll artfully get into his secret. So that Macheath shall not remain a day longer out of my clutches.

SCENE 4

SCENE: *A gaming house.*

Macheath, in a fine tarnished coat, Ben Budge,
Mat of the Mint.

MACHEATH I am sorry, gentlemen, the road was so barren of money. When my friends are in difficulties, I am always glad that my fortune can be serviceable to them. (*Gives them money.*) You see, gentlemen, I am not a mere Court friend, who professes everything and will do nothing.

AIR 4 – 'Lillibulero'.

The modes of the Court so common are grown,
*   That a true friend can hardly be met;*
Friendship for interest is but a loan,
*   Which they let out for what they can get.*

> 'Tis true, you find
> Some friends so kind,
> Who will give you good counsel themselves to defend.
> In sorrowful ditty,
> They promise, they pity,
> But shift you for money from friend to friend.

But we, gentlemen, have still honour enough to break through the corruptions of the world. And while I can serve you, you may command me.

BEN It grieves my heart that so generous a man should be involved in such difficulties as oblige him to live with such ill company and herd with gamesters.

MAT See the partiality of mankind! One man may steal a horse better than another look over a hedge. Of all mechanics, of all servile handicrafts, a gamester is the vilest. But yet, as many of the quality are of the profession, he is admitted amongst the politest company. I wonder we are not more respected.

MACHEATH There will be deep play to-night at Marybone, and consequently money may be picked up upon the road. Meet me there, and I'll give you the hint who is worth setting.

MAT The fellow with a brown coat with a narrow gold binding, I am told, is never without money.

MACHEATH What do you mean, Mat? Sure you will not think of meddling with him! He's a good honest kind of a fellow and one of us.

BEN To be sure, sir, we will put ourselves under your direction.

MACHEATH Have an eye upon the money-lenders. A rouleau or two would prove a pretty sort of an expedition. I hate extortion.

MAT Those rouleaux are very pretty things. I hate your bank bills – there is such a hazard in putting them off.

MACHEATH There is a certain man of distinction who in his time has nicked me out of a great deal of the ready. He is my cash, Ben; I'll point him out to you this evening, and you shall draw upon him for the debt. The company are met; I hear the dice-box in the other room. So, gentlemen, your servant. You'll meet me at Marybone.

SCENE 5

SCENE: *Peachum's lock.*

A table with wine, brandy, pipes and tobacco.

Peachum, Lockit.

LOCKIT The Coronation account, brother Peachum, is of so intricate a nature, that I believe it will never be settled.

PEACHUM It consists indeed of a great variety of articles. It was worth to our people, in fees of different kinds, above ten instalments. This is part of the account, brother, that lies open before us.

LOCKIT A lady's tail of rich brocade – that I see is disposed of.

PEACHUM To Mrs Diana Trapes, the tally-woman, and she will make a good hand on't in shoes and slippers, to trick out young ladies upon their going into keeping.

LOCKIT But I don't see any article of the jewels.

PEACHUM Those are so well known that they must be sent abroad – you'll find them entered under the article of exportation. As for the snuff-boxes, watches, swords, etc., I thought it best to enter them under their several heads.

LOCKIT Seven and twenty women's pockets complete; with the several things therein contained; all sealed, numbered and entered.

PEACHUM But, brother, it is impossible for us now to enter upon this affair. We should have the whole day before us. Besides, the account of the last half-year's plate is in a book by itself, which lies at the other office.

LOCKIT Bring us then more liquor. To-day shall be for pleasure – to-morrow for business. Ah, brother, those daughters of ours are two slippery hussies – keep a watchful eye upon Polly, and Macheath in a day or two shall be our own again.

AIR 5 – 'Down in the North Country', etc.

LOCKIT
> *What gudgeons are we men!*
>   *Every woman's easy prey.*
> *Though we have felt the hook, agen*
>   *We bite, and they betray.*
>
> *The bird that has been trapped,*
>   *When he hears his calling mate,*

To her he flies, again he's clipped
  Within the wiry grate.

PEACHUM But what signifies catching the bird, if your daughter
Lucy will set open the door of the cage?

LOCKIT If men were answerable for the follies and frailties of
their wives and daughters, no friends could keep a good
correspondence together for two days. This is unkind of you,
brother; for among good friends, what they say or do goes
for nothing.

Enter a Servant.

SERVANT Sir, here's Mrs Diana Trapes wants to speak with you.

PEACHUM Shall we admit her, brother Lockit?

LOCKIT By all means – she's a good customer, and a fine-spoken
woman, and a woman who drinks and talks so freely will
enliven the conversation.

PEACHUM Desire her to walk in.   *Exit Servant.*

SCENE 6

Peachum, Lockit, Mrs Trapes.

PEACHUM Dear Mrs Dye, your servant – one may know by
your kiss that your gin is excellent.

MRS TRAPES I was always very curious in my liquors.

LOCKIT There is no perfumed breath like it – I have been long
acquainted with the flavour of those lips – han't I, Mrs Dye?

MRS TRAPES Fill it up. I take as large draughts of liquor as I did
of love. I hate a flincher in either.

AIR 6 – 'A shepherd kept sheep', etc.

In the days of my youth I could bill like a dove,
      fa, la, la, etc.
Like a sparrow at all times was ready for love,
      fa, la, la, etc.
The life of all mortals in kissing should pass,
Lip to lip while we're young – then the lip to the glass,
      fa, la, la, etc.

But now, Mr Peachum, to our business. If you have blacks of
any kind, brought in of late, mantoes, velvet scarfs, petticoats,

let it be what it will, I am your chap, for all my ladies are very fond of mourning.

PEACHUM Why, look, Mrs Dye, you deal so hard with us that we can afford to give the gentlemen who venture their lives for the goods little or nothing.

MRS TRAPES The hard times oblige me to go very near in my dealing. To be sure, of late years I have been a great sufferer by the Parliament. Three thousand pounds would hardly make me amends. The Act for destroying the mint was a severe cut upon our business – till then, if a customer stepped out of the way, we knew where to have her. No doubt, you know Mrs Coaxer – there's a wench now (till to-day) with a good suit of clothes of mine upon her back, and I could never set eyes upon her for three months together. Since the Act too against imprisonment for small sums, my loss there, too, has been very considerable, and it must be so, when a lady can borrow a handsome petticoat, or a clean gown, and I not have the least hank upon her! And o' my conscience, nowadays most ladies take a delight in cheating, when they can do it with safety.

PEACHUM Madam, you had a handsome gold watch of us t'other day for seven guineas. Considering we must have our profit, to a gentleman upon the road, a gold watch will be scarce worth the taking.

MRS TRAPES Consider, Mr Peachum, that watch was remarkable, and not of very safe sale. If you have any black velvet scarfs, they are a handsome winter wear, and take with most gentlemen who deal with my customers. 'Tis I that put the ladies upon a good foot. 'Tis not youth or beauty that fixes the price. The gentlemen always pay according to their dress, from half a crown to two guineas; and yet those hussies make nothing of bilking me. Then, too, allowing for accidents, I have eleven fine customers now down under the surgeons' hands; what with fees and other expenses, there are great goings-out and no comings-in, and not a farthing to pay for at least a month's clothing. We run great risks, great risks indeed.

PEACHUM As I remember, you said something just now of Mrs Coaxer.

MRS TRAPES Yes, sir – to be sure, I stripped her of a suit of my own clothes about two hours ago; and have left her as she should be, in her shift, with a lover of hers at my house. She called him upstairs as he was going to Marybone in a hackney-coach. And I hope for her own sake and mine, she will persuade the captain to redeem her, for the captain is very generous to the ladies.

LOCKIT What captain?

MRS TRAPES He thought I did not know him. An intimate acquaintance of yours, Mr Peachum – only Captain Macheath – as fine as a lord.

PEACHUM To-morrow, dear Mrs Dye, you shall get your own price upon any of the goods you like – we have at least half a dozen velvet scarfs and all at your service. Will you give me leave to make you a present of this suit of night-clothes for your own wearing? But are you sure it is Captain Macheath?

MRS TRAPES Though he thinks I have forgot him, nobody knows him better. I have taken a great deal of the captain's money in my time at second-hand, for he always loved to have his ladies well dressed.

PEACHUM Mr Lockit and I have a little business with the captain; you understand me – and we will satisfy you for Mrs Coaxer's debt.

LOCKIT Depend upon it – we will deal like men of honour.

MRS TRAPES I don't inquire after your affairs – so whatever happens, I wash my hands on it. It has always been my maxim, that one friend should assist another. But if you please, I'll take one of the scarfs home with me, 'tis always good to have something in hand.

SCENE 7

SCENE: *Newgate.*

Lucy.

Jealousy, rage, love, and fear, are at once tearing me to pieces. How am I weather-beaten and shattered with distresses!

AIR 7 – 'One evening having lost my way', etc.

I'm like a skiff on the ocean tossed,
  Now high, now low, with each billow borne,
With her rudder broke and her anchor lost,
  Deserted and all forlorn.

While thus I lie rolling and tossing all night,
That Polly lies sporting on seas of delight!
  Revenge, revenge, revenge,
Shall appease my restless sprite.

I have the ratsbane ready — I run no risk; for I can lay her death upon the gin, and so many die of that naturally, that I shall never be called in question. But say I were to be hanged — I never could be hanged for anything that would give me greater comfort than the poisoning that slut.

Enter Filch.

FILCH Madam, here's our Miss Polly come to wait upon you.
LUCY Show her in.

SCENE 8

Lucy, Polly.

LUCY Dear madam! your servant. I hope you will pardon my passion when I was so happy to see you last — I was so overrun with the spleen, that I was perfectly out of myself; and really when one hath the spleen, everything is to be excused by a friend.

AIR 8 — 'Now, Roger, I'll tell thee, because thou'rt my son'.

When a wife's in her pout
(As she's sometimes, no doubt),
  The good husband, as meek as a lamb,
    Her vapours to still,
    First grants her her will,
  And the quieting draught is a dram;
Poor man! and the quieting draught is a dram.

— I wish all our quarrels might have so comfortable a reconciliation.
POLLY I have no excuse for my own behaviour, madam, but my misfortunes — and really, madam, I suffer too upon your account.
LUCY But, Miss Polly, in the way of friendship, will you give me leave to propose a glass of cordial to you?

POLLY Strong waters are apt to give me the headache. I hope, madam, you will excuse me?

LUCY Not the greatest lady in the land could have better in her closet for her own private drinking. You seem mighty low in spirits, my dear!

POLLY I am sorry, madam, my health will not allow me to accept of your offer. I should not have left you in the rude manner I did when we met last, madam, had not my papa hauled me away so unexpectedly. I was indeed somewhat provoked, and perhaps might use some expressions that were disrespectful – but really, madam, the captain treated me with so much contempt and cruelty, that I deserved your pity rather than your resentment.

LUCY But since his escape, no doubt, all matters are made up again. Ah, Polly! Polly! 'tis I am the unhappy wife, and he loves you as if you were only his mistress.

POLLY Sure, madam, you cannot think me so happy as to be the object of your jealousy. A man is always afraid of a woman who loves him too well. So that I must expect to be neglected and avoided.

LUCY Then our cases, my dear Polly, are exactly alike. Both of us indeed have been too fond.

AIR 9 – 'O Bessy Bell'.

POLLY   *A curse attends that woman's love*
           Who always would be pleasing.
LUCY   *The pertness of the billing dove,*
           Like tickling is but teasing.
POLLY   *What then in love can woman do?*
LUCY   *If we grow fond they shun us.*
POLLY   *And when we fly them, they pursue:*
LUCY   *But leave us when they've won us.*

LUCY Love is so very whimsical in both sexes, that it is impossible to be lasting. But my heart is particular, and contradicts my own observation.

POLLY But really, mistress Lucy, by his last behaviour I think I ought to envy you. When I was forced from him he did not show the least tenderness. But perhaps he hath a heart not capable of it.

AIR 10 – 'Would fate to me Belinda give'.

> *Among the men coquets we find,*
> *Who court by turns all womankind:*
> *And we grant all their hearts desired*
> *When they are flattered and admired.*

The coquets of both sexes are self-lovers, and that is a love no other whatever can dispossess. I fear, my dear Lucy, our husband is one of those.

LUCY Away with these melancholy reflections! Indeed, my dear Polly, we are both of us a cup too low; let me prevail upon you to accept of my offer.

AIR 11 – 'Come, sweet lass'.

> *Come, sweet lass,*
> *Let's banish sorrow*
> *Till to-morrow:*
> *Come, sweet lass,*
> *Let's take a chirping glass*
> *Wine can clear*
> *The vapours of despair,*
> *And make us light as air;*
> *Then drink and banish care.*

I can't bear, child, to see you in such low spirits – and I must persuade you to what I know will do you good. – I shall now soon be even with the hypocritical strumpet.   *Aside.*

SCENE 9

Polly.

POLLY All this wheedling of Lucy cannot be for nothing – at this time too, when I know she hates me! The dissembling of a woman is always the forerunner of mischief. By pouring strong waters down my throat she thinks to pump some secrets out of me. I'll be upon my guard, and won't taste a drop of her liquor, I'm resolved.

SCENE 10

Lucy, with strong waters. Polly.

LUCY Come, Miss Polly.

POLLY Indeed, child, you have given yourself trouble to no purpose. You must, my dear, excuse me.

LUCY Really, Miss Polly, you are so squeamishly affected about taking a cup of strong waters as a lady before company. I vow, Polly, I shall take it monstrously ill if you refuse me. Brandy and men, though women love them never so well, are always taken by us with some reluctance — unless 'tis in private.

POLLY I protest, madam, it goes against me — What do I see! Macheath again in custody! Now every glimmering of happiness is lost!   *Drops the glass of liquor on the ground.*

LUCY Since things are thus, I am glad the wench hath escaped, for by this event 'tis plain she was not happy enough to deserve to be poisoned.   *Aside.*

SCENE 11

Lockit, Macheath, Peachum, Lucy, Polly.

LOCKIT Set your heart at rest, captain. You have neither the chance of love nor money for another escape, for you are ordered to be called down upon your trial immediately.

PEACHUM Away, hussies! This is not a time for a man to be hampered with his wives — you see the gentleman is in chains already.

LUCY O husband, husband! my heart longed to see thee, but to see thee thus distracts me!

POLLY Will not my dear husband look upon his Polly? Why hadst thou not flown to me for protection? With me thou hadst been safe.

AIR 12 — 'The last time I went o'er the moor'.

POLLY   *Hither, dear husband, turn your eyes!*
LUCY   *Bestow one glance to cheer me.*
POLLY   *Think, with that look, thy Polly dies.*
LUCY   *Oh, shun me not, but hear me!*
POLLY   *'Tis Polly sues.*

LUCY	*'Tis Lucy speaks.*
POLLY	*Is thus true love requited?*
LUCY	*My heart is bursting.*
POLLY	*Mine, too, breaks.*
LUCY	*Must I —*
POLLY	*Must I be slighted?*

MACHEATH What would you have me say, ladies? You see, this affair will soon be at an end, without my disobliging either of you.

PEACHUM But the settling of this point, captain, might prevent a lawsuit between your two widows.

AIR 13 – 'Tom Tinker's my true love'.

MACHEATH *Which way shall I turn me? how can I decide?*
Wives, the day of our death, are as fond as a bride.
One wife is too much for most husbands to hear,
But two at a time there's no mortal can bear.
This way, and that way, and which way I will,
What would comfort the one, t'other wife would
    take ill.

POLLY But, if his own misfortunes have made him insensible to mine, a father, sure, will be more compassionate! – Dear, dear, sir! sink the material evidence, and bring him off at his trial – Polly, upon her knees, begs it of you.

AIR 14 – 'I am a poor shepherd, undone'.

When my hero in court appears,
    And stands arraigned for his life,
Then think of poor Polly's tears,
    For ah! poor Polly's his wife.
Like the sailor, he holds up his hand,
    Distressed, on the dashing wave;
To die a dry death at land,
    Is as bad as a watery grave.
        And alas, poor Polly!
            Alack, and well-a-day!
        Before I was in love,
            Oh, every month was May.

LUCY If Peachum's heart is hardened, sure, sir, you will have more compassion on a daughter. I know the evidence is in your power. How, then, can you be a tyrant to me?

Kneeling.

AIR 15 – 'Ianthe the lovely', etc.

When he holds up his hand arraigned for his life,
O think of your daughter, and think I'm his wife!
What are cannons, or bombs, or clashing of swords?
For death is more certain by witnesses' words.
Then nail up their lips; that dread thunder allay;
And each month of my life will hereafter be May.

LOCKIT Macheath's time is come, Lucy. We know our own affairs, therefore let us have no more whimpering or whining.

AIR 16 – 'A cobbler there was', etc.

Ourselves, like the great, to secure a retreat,
When matters require it, must give up our gang:
    And good reason why,
    Or, instead of the fry,
    Even Peachum and I,
Like poor petty rascals, might hang, hang;
Like poor petty rascals, might hang.

PEACHUM Set your heart at rest, Polly – your husband is to die to-day; therefore, if you are not already provided, 'tis high time to look about for another. There's comfort for you, you slut!

LOCKIT We are ready, sir, to conduct you to the Old Bailey.

AIR 17 – 'Bonny Dundee'.

MACHEATH *The charge is prepared, the lawyers are met,*
        The judges all ranged (a terrible show!).
    I go undismayed, for death is a debt –
        A debt on demand, so take what I owe.
    Then farewell, my love – dear charmers, adieu!
    Contented I die – 'tis the better for you.
    Here ends all dispute for the rest of our lives,
    For this way, at once, I please all my wives.

Now, gentlemen, I am ready to attend you.

SCENE 12

Lucy, Polly, Filch.

POLLY Follow them, Filch, to the court. And when the trial is over, bring me a particular account of his behaviour, and of everything that happened. You'll find me here with Miss Lucy. (*Exit Filch.*) But why is all this music?

LUCY The prisoners whose trials are put off till next session are diverting themselves.

POLLY Sure there is nothing so charming as music! I'm fond of it to distraction. But alas! now all mirth seems an insult upon my affliction. Let us retire, my dear Lucy, and indulge our sorrows. The noisy crew you see are coming upon us

Exeunt.

A dance of prisoners in chains, etc.

SCENE 13

SCENE: *The condemned hold.*

Macheath, in a melancholy posture.

AIR 18 – 'Happy Groves'.

Oh, cruel, cruel, cruel case!
Must I suffer this disgrace?

AIR 19 – 'Of all the girls that are so smart'.

Of all the friends in time of grief,
    When threatening death looks grimmer,
Not one so sure can bring relief
    As this best friend, a brimmer.   (*Drinks.*)

AIR 20 – 'Britons, strike home'.

Since I must swing – I scorn, I scorn to wince or whine.
                                                    (*Rises.*)

AIR 21 – 'Chevy Chase'.

But now again my spirits sink,
I'll raise them high with wine.
                              (*Drinks a glass of wine.*)

AIR 22 – 'To old Sir Simon, the king'.

But valour the stronger grows,
  The stronger liquor we're drinking,
And how can we feel our woes,
  When we've lost the trouble of thinking? (*Drinks.*)

AIR 23 – 'Joy to great Cæsar'.

  If thus, a man can die
  Much bolder with brandy.
                   (*Pours out a bumper of brandy.*)

AIR 24 – 'There was an old woman'.

So I take off this bumper – and now I can stand the test,
And my comrades shall see that I die as brave as the best.
                                              (*Drinks.*)

AIR 25 – 'Did you ever hear of a gallant sailor?'

  But can I leave my pretty hussies,
  Without one tear, or tender sigh?

AIR 26 – 'Why are mine eyes still flowing?'

  Their eyes, their lips, their busses,
  Recall my love – Ah! must I die?

AIR 27 – 'Green Sleeves'.

Since laws were made, for every degree,
To curb vice in others, as well as me,
I wonder we han't better company
    Upon Tyburn tree.
But gold from law can take out the sting;
And if rich men, like us, were to swing,
'Twould thin the land, such numbers to string
    Upon Tyburn tree.

JAILER Some friends of yours, captain, desire to be admitted – I
leave you together.

SCENE 14

Macheath, Ben Budge, Mat of the Mint.

MACHEATH For my having broke prison, you see, gentlemen, I
am ordered immediate execution. The sheriff's officers, I

believe, are now at the door. That Jemmy Twitcher should 'peach me, I own, surprised me. 'Tis a plain proof that the world is all alike, and that even our gang can no more trust one another than other people; therefore, I beg you, gentlemen, to look well to yourselves, for, in all probability, you may live some months longer.

MAT We are heartily sorry, captain, for your misfortune, but 'tis what we must all come to.

MACHEATH Peachum and Lockit, you know, are infamous scoundrels – their lives are as much in your power, as yours are in theirs. Remember your dying friend – 'tis my last request. Bring those villains to the gallows before you, and I am satisfied.

MAT We'll do it.

JAILER Miss Polly and Miss Lucy entreat a word with you.

MACHEATH Gentlemen, adieu!

SCENE 15

Lucy, Macheath, Polly.

MACHEATH My dear Lucy! my dear Polly! whatsoever hath passed between us is now at an end. If you are fond of marrying again, the best advice I can give you is to ship yourselves off for the West Indies, where you'll have a fair chance of getting a husband apiece; or by good luck, two or three, as you like best.

POLLY How can I support this sight!

LUCY There is nothing moves one so much as a great man in distress.

AIR 28 – 'All you that must take a leap', etc.

LUCY *'Would I might be hanged!*

POLLY *And I would so too!*

LUCY *To be hanged with you,*

POLLY *My dear, with you.*

MACHEATH *Oh, leave me to thought! I fear, I doubt!*
I tremble – I droop! – See, my courage is out!
(Turns up the empty bottle.)

POLLY *No token of love?*

MACHEATH	*See, my courage is out!*
	(Turns up the empty pot.)
LUCY	*No token of love?*
POLLY	*Adieu!*
LUCY	*Farewell!*
MACHEATH	*But hark! I hear the toll of the bell.*
CHORUS	*Tol de rol lol, etc.*

JAILER Four women more, captain, with a child apiece. See, here they come!

Enter women and children.

MACHEATH What! four wives more! this is too much. Here, tell the sheriff's officers I am ready.   *Exit Macheath, guarded.*

SCENE 16

To them enter Player and Beggar.

PLAYER But, honest friend, I hope you don't intend that Macheath shall be really executed.

BEGGAR Most certainly, sir. To make the piece perfect, I was for doing strict poetical justice. Macheath is to be hanged; and for the other personages of the drama, the audience must have supposed they were all either hanged or transported.

PLAYER Why then, friend, this is a downright deep tragedy. The catastrophe is manifestly wrong, for an opera must end happily.

BEGGAR Your objection, sir, is very just; and is easily removed. For you must allow that, in this kind of drama, 'tis no matter how absurdly things are brought about — so — you rabble there — run and cry a reprieve — let the prisoner be brought back to his wives in triumph.

PLAYER All this we must do, to comply with the taste of the town.

BEGGAR Through the whole piece you may observe such a similitude of manners in high and low life, that it is difficult to determine whether (in the fashionable vices) the fine gentlemen imitate the gentlemen of the road, or the gentlemen of the road the fine gentlemen. Had the play remained as I at first intended, it would have carried a most excellent moral. 'Twould have shown that the lower sort of people have their vices in a degree as well as the rich: and that they are punished for them.

SCENE 17

To them Macheath, with rabble, etc.

MACHEATH So, it seems, I am not left to my choice, but must have a wife at last. Lookye, my dears, we will have no controversy now. Let us give this day to mirth, and I am sure, she who thinks herself my wife will testify her joy by a dance.

ALL Come, a dance! a dance!

MACHEATH Ladies, I hope you will give me leave to present a partner to each of you; and (if I may without offence) for this time, I take Polly for mine — and for life, you slut, for we were really married. As for the rest — But, at present, keep your own secret. *To Polly.*

A DANCE

AIR 29 – 'Lumps of Pudding', etc.

Thus I stand like a Turk, with his doxies around,
From all sides their glances his passion confound;
For black, brown, and fair, his inconstancy burns,
And the different beauties subdue him by turns:
Each calls forth her charms to provoke his desires,
Though willing to all, with but one he retires:
But think of this maxim, and put off your sorrow,
The wretch of to-day, may be happy to-morrow.

CHORUS

But think of this maxim, etc.

THE TRAGEDY OF TRAGEDIES,
OR
THE LIFE AND DEATH
OF
TOM THUMB THE GREAT

H. Scriblerus Secundus;

HIS PREFACE

The town hath seldom been more divided in its opinion than concerning the merit of the following scenes. Whilst some publicly affirmed, That no author could produce so fine a piece but Mr P[ope], others have with as much vehemence insisted, That no one could write anything so bad but Mr F[ielding].

Nor can we wonder at this dissension about its merit, when the learned world have not unanimously decided even the very nature of this tragedy. For though most of the universities in Europe have honoured it with the name of *egregium et maximi pretii opus, Tragœdiis tam antiquis quàm novis longe anteponendum*; nay, Dr B – hath pronounced, *Citiùs Mœvii Æneadem quam Scribleri istius tragœdiam hanc crediderim, cujus autorem Senecam ipsum tradidisse haud dubitârim*'; and the great Professor Burman hath styled Tom Thumb, *Heroum omnium tragicorum facile principem*. Nay, though it hath, among other languages, been translated into Dutch, and celebrated with great applause at Amsterdam (where burlesque never came) by the title of *Mynheer Vander Thumb*, the burgomasters receiving it with that reverent and silent attention which becometh an audience at a deep tragedy: notwithstanding all this, there have not been wanting some who have represented these scenes in a ludicrous light; and Mr D – hath been heard to say, with some concern, That he wondered a tragical and Christian nation would permit a representation on its theatre, so visibly designed to ridicule and extirpate everything that is great and solemn among us.

This learned critic and his followers were led into so great an error by that surreptitious and piratical copy which stole last year into the world; with what injustice and prejudice to our author will be acknowledged, I hope, by everyone who shall happily peruse this genuine and original copy. Nor can I help remarking, to the great praise of our author, that however imperfect the former was, even that faint resemblance of the true *Tom Thumb* contained sufficient beauties to give it a run of upwards of forty nights to the politest audiences. But, notwithstanding that applause which it received from all the best judges, it was as severely censured by some few bad ones, and, I believe rather maliciously than ignorantly, reported to have been intended a burlesque on the loftiest parts of tragedy, and designed to banish what we generally call fine things from the stage.

Now, if I can set my country right in an affair of this importance, I shall lightly esteem any labour which it may cost. And this I the rather undertake, first, as it is indeed in some measure incumbent on me to vindicate myself from the surreptitious copy before mentioned, published by some ill-meaning people under my name: secondly, as knowing myself more capable of doing justice to our author than any other man, as I have given myself more pains to arrive at a thorough understanding of this little piece, having for ten years together read nothing else; in which time, I think I may modestly presume, with the help of my English dictionary, to comprehend all the meanings of every word in it.

But should any error of my pen awaken Clariss. Bentleium to enlighten the world with his annotations on our author, I shall not think that the least reward or happiness arising to me from these my endeavours.

I shall waive at present what hath caused such feuds in the learned world, whether this piece was originally written by Shakespeare, though certainly that, were it true, must add a considerable share to its merit; especially with such who are so generous as to buy and to commend what they never read, from an implicit faith in the author only: a faith which our age abounds in as much as it can be called deficient in any other.

Let it suffice, that *The Tragedy of Tragedies, or The Life and Death of Tom Thumb* was written in the reign of Queen Elizabeth. Nor can the objection made by Mr D—, that the tragedy must then have been antecedent to the history, have any weight, when we consider, that though the *History of Tom Thumb*, printed by and for Edward M—r, at the Looking-Glass on London Bridge, be of a later date, still must we suppose this history to have been transcribed from some other, unless we suppose the writer thereof to be inspired: a gift very faintly contended for by the writers of our age. As to this history not bearing the stamp of second, third, or fourth edition, I see but little in that objection; editions being very uncertain lights to judge of books by: and perhaps Mr M—r may have joined twenty editions in one, as Mr C—l hath ere now divided one into twenty.

Nor doth the other argument, drawn from the little care our author hath taken to keep up to the letter of the history, carry any greater force. Are there not instances of plays wherein the history is so perverted, that we can know the heroes whom they celebrate by no other marks than their names: nay, do we not find the same character placed by different poets in such different lights, that we can discover not the least sameness or even likeness in the features? The Sophonisba of Mairet, and of Lee, is a tender, passionate, amorous mistress of Masinissa; Corneille and Mr Thomson give her no other passion but the love of her country, and make her as cool in her affection to Masinissa as to Syphax. In the two latter, she resembles the character of Queen Elizabeth; in the two former she is the picture of Mary Queen of Scotland. In short, the one Sophonisba is as different from the other as the Brutus of Voltaire is from the Marius Jun. of Otway; or as the Minerva is from the Venus of the Ancients.

Let us now proceed to a regular examination of the tragedy before us, in which I shall treat separately of the Fable, the Moral, the Characters, the Sentiments, and the Diction. And first of the *Fable*, which I take to be the most simple imaginable; and, to use the words of an eminent author, 'One regular, and uniform, not charged with a multiplicity of incidents, and yet affording several revolutions of fortune; by which the passions may be excited, varied, and driven to their full tumult of emotion.' Nor is the action of this tragedy less great than uniform. The spring of all is the love of Tom Thumb for Huncamunca, which causeth the quarrel between their Majesties in the first act; the passion of Lord Grizzle in the second; the rebellion, fall of Lord Grizzle and Glumdalca, devouring of Tom Thumb by the cow, and that bloody catastrophe in the third.

Nor is the *Moral* of this excellent tragedy less noble than the *Fable*; it teaches these two instructive lessons, viz. That human happiness is exceeding transient, and, That death is the certain end of all men; the former whereof is inculcated by the fatal end of Tom Thumb; the latter by that of all the other personages.

The *Characters* are, I think, sufficiently described in the Dramatis Personæ; and I believe we shall find few plays where greater care is taken to maintain them throughout, and to preserve in every speech that characteristical mark which distinguishes them from each other. 'But,' says Mr D——, 'how well doth the character of Tom Thumb, whom we must call the hero of this tragedy, if it hath any hero, agree with the precepts of Aristotle, who defineth "Tragedy" to be the imitation of a short, but perfect action, containing a just greatness in itself, etc. What greatness can be in a fellow whom history relateth to have been no higher than a span?' This gentleman seemeth to think, with Sergeant Kite, that the greatness of a man's soul is in proportion to that of his body, the contrary of which is affirmed by our English physiognominical writers. Besides, if I understand Aristotle right, he speaketh only of the greatness of the action, and not of the person.

As for the *Sentiments* and the *Diction*, which now only remain to be spoken to; I thought I could afford them no stronger justification than by producing parallel passages out of the best of our English writers. Whether this sameness of thought and expression, which I have quoted from them, proceeded from an agreement in their way of thinking, or whether they have borrowed from our author, I leave the reader to determine. I shall adventure to affirm this of the *Sentiments* of our author: that they are generally the most familiar which I have ever met with, and at the same time delivered with the highest dignity of phrase; which brings me to speak of his *Diction*. Here I shall only beg one postulatum, viz. That the greatest perfection of the language of a tragedy is, that it is not to be understood; which granted (as I think it must be) it will necessarily follow, that the only ways to avoid this is by being too high or too low for the understanding, which will comprehend everything within its reach. Those two extremities of style Mr Dryden illustrates by the familiar image of two inns, which I shall term the Aerial and the Subterrestrial.

Horace goes farther, and showeth when it is proper to call at one of these inns, and when at the other:

Telephus & Peleus, cum pauper & exul uterque,
Projicit Ampullas & sesquipedalia verba.

That he approveth of the *sesquipedalia verba* is plain; for had
not Telephus and Peleus used this sort of diction in prosperity,
they could not have dropped it in adversity. The Aerial Inn,
therefore (says Horace), is proper only to be frequented by
princes and other great men, in the highest affluence of fortune;
the Subterrestrial is appointed for the entertainment of the
poorer sort of people only, whom Horace advises:

– *dolere sermone pedestri.*

The true meaning of both which citations is, that bombast is the
proper language for joy, and doggerel for grief, the latter of
which is literally implied in the *sermo pedestris*, as the former is
in the *sesquipedalia verba.*

Cicero recommendeth the former of these. *Quid est tam
furiosum vel tragicum quām verborum sonitus inanis, nullā
subjectā sententiā neque scientiā.*' What can be so proper for
tragedy as a set of big-sounding words, so contrived together as
to convey no meaning? which I shall one day or other prove to
be the sublime of Longinus. Ovid declareth absolutely for the
latter inn:

Omne genus scripti gravitate tragœdia vincit.

Tragedy hath of all writings the greatest share in the Bathos,
which is the profound of Scriblerus.

I shall not presume to determine which of these two styles be
properer for tragedy. It sufficeth that our author excelleth in
both. He is very rarely within sight through the whole play,
either rising higher than the eye of your understanding can soar,
or sinking lower than it careth to stoop. But here it may perhaps
be observed, that I have given more frequent instances of
authora who have imitated him in the sublime, than in the
contrary. To which I answer, first, bombast being properly a
redundancy of genius, instances of this nature occur in poets
whose names do more honour to our author than the writers in
the doggerel, which proceeds from a cool, calm, weighty way of
thinking. Instances whereof are most frequently to be found in
authors of a lower class. Secondly, that the works of such
authors are difficultly found at all. Thirdly, that it is a very hard

task to read them, in order to extract these flowers from them. And lastly, it is very often difficult to transplant them at all; they being like some flowers of a very nice nature, which will flourish in no soil but their own: for it is easy to transcribe a thought, but not the want of one. The *Earl of Essex*, for instance, is a little garden of choice rarities, whence you can scarce transplant one line so as to preserve its original beauty. This must account to the reader for his missing the names of several of his acquaintance, which he had certainly found here, had I ever read their works; for which, if I have not a just esteem, I can at least say with Cicero, *Quæ non contemno, quippè quæ nunquam legerim.* However, that the reader may meet with due satisfaction in this point, I have a young commentator from the university, who is reading over all the modern tragedies, at five shillings a dozen, and collecting all that they have stole from our author, which shall shortly be added as an appendix to this work.

Dramatis Personæ

MEN

KING ARTHUR, *a passionate sort of King, husband to Queen Dollallolla, of whom he stands a little in fear; father to Huncamunca, whom he is very fond of; and in love with Glumdalca*	Mr Mullart
TOM THUMB THE GREAT, *a little hero with a great soul, something violent in his temper, which is a little abated by his love for Huncamunca*	Young Verhuyck
GHOST OF GAFFER THUMB, *a whimsical sort of ghost*	Mr Lacy
LORD GRIZZLE, *extremely zealous for the liberty of the subject, very choleric in his temper, and in love with Huncamunca*	Mr Jones
MERLIN, *a conjurer, and in some sort father to Tom Thumb*	Mr Hallam
NOODLE ⎱ *Courtiers in place, and consequently of that party*	Mr Reynolds
DOODLE ⎰ *that is uppermost*	Mr Wathan
FOODLE, *a courtier that is out of place, and consequently of that party that is undermost*	Mr Ayres
BAILIFF, and FOLLOWER ⎱ *of the party of the Plaintiff*	Mr Peterson / Mr Hicks
PARSON, *of the side of the Church*	Mr Watson

WOMEN

QUEEN DOLLALLOLLA, *wife to King Arthur,
and mother to Huncamunca, a woman
entirely faultless, saving that she is a little
given to drink; a little too much a virago
towards her husband, and in love with Tom
Thumb*   Mrs Mullart

THE PRINCESS HUNCAMUNCA, *daughter to
their Majesties King Arthur and Queen
Dollallolla, of a very sweet, gentle, and
amorous disposition, equally in love with
Lord Grizzle and Tom Thumb, and
desirous to be married to them both*   Mrs Jones

GLUMDALCA, *of the Giants, a captive queen,
beloved by the King, but in love with Tom
Thumb*   Mrs Dove

CLEORA   } *Maids of Honour, in* { Noodle
MUSTACHA } *love with*   { Doodle

Courtiers, Guards, Rebels, Drums, Trumpets, Thunder and
Lightning.

SCENE:
The Court of King Arthur, and a plain thereabouts.

Act I

SCENE I

SCENE: *The Palace.*

Doodle, Noodle.

DOODLE Sure such a day as this was never seen!
   The sun himself, on this auspicious day,
   Shines like a beau in a new birthday suit:
   This down the seams embroidered, that the beams,
   All nature wears one universal grin.[1]

---

[1] Corneille recommends some very remarkable day wherein to fix the action of a tragedy. This the best of our tragical writers have understood to mean a day remarkable for the serenity of the sky, or what we generally call a fine summer's day. So that, according to this their exposition, the same months are proper for tragedy which are proper for pastoral. Most of our celebrated English tragedies, as *Cato*, *Mariamne*, *Tamerlane*, etc., begin with their observations on the morning. Lee seems to have come the nearest to this beautiful description of our author's:

> *The morning dawns with an unwonted crimson,*
> *The flowers all odorous seem, the garden birds*
> *Sing louder, and the laughing sun ascends*
> *The gaudy earth with an unusual brightness,*
> *All nature smiles.*   Cæs Borg.

Masinissa in the new *Sophonisba* is also a favourite of the sun:

> — *The sun too seems*
> *As conscious of my joy, with broader eye*
> *To look abroad the world, and all things smile*
> *Like Sophonisba.*

Memnon in the *Persian Princess* makes the sun decline rising, that he may not peep on objects which would profane his brightness.

> — *The morning rises slow,*
> *And all those ruddy streaks that us'd to paint*
> *The day's approach are lost in clouds, as if*
> *The horrors of the night had sent 'em back,*
> *To warn the sun he should not leave the sea,*
> *To peep, etc.*

NOODLE This day, O Mr Doodle, is a day
  Indeed! – ; A day we never saw before.[1]
  The mighty Thomas Thumb[2] victorious comes;
  Millions of giants crowd his chariot wheels,
  Giants[3] to whom the giants in Guildhall
  Are infant dwarfs. They frown, and foam, and roar,
  While Thumb, regardless of their noise, rides on.
  So some cock-sparrow, in a farmer's yard,
  Hops at the head of an huge flock of turkeys.
DOODLE When Goody Thumb first brought this Thomas forth,
  The genius of our land triumphant reigned;
  Then, then, O Arthur! did thy genius reign.
NOODLE They tell me it is whispered in the books[4]

---

[1] This line is highly conformable to the beautiful simplicity of the ancients. It hath been copied by almost every modern:

Not to be is not to be in woe.	State of Innocence.
Love is not sin but where 'tis sinful love.	Don Sebastian.
Nature is nature, Lælius.	Sophonisba.
Men are but men, we did not make ourselves.	Revenge.

[2] Dr B—y reads: 'The mighty Tall-mast Thumb'. Mr D—s: 'The mighty thumping Thumb'. Mr T—d reads: 'Thundering'. I think 'Thomas' more agreeable to the great simplicity so apparent in our author.

[3] That learned historian Mr S—n, in the third number of his criticism on our author, takes great pains to explode this passage. 'It is,' says he, 'difficult to guess what Giants are here meant, unless the Giant Despair in the *Pilgrim's Progress*, or the Giant Greatness in the *Royal Villain*; for I have heard of no other sort of giants in the reign of King Arthur.' Petrus Burmanus makes three Tom Thumbs, one whereof he supposes to have been the same person whom the Greeks called Hercules, and that by these giants are to be understood the centaurs slain by that hero. Another Tom Thumb he contends to have been no other than the Hermes Trismegistus of the ancients. The third Tom Thumb he places under the reign of King Arthur, to which third Tom Thumb, says he, the actions of the other two were attributed. Now, tho' I know that this opinion is supported by an assertion of Justus Lipsius, *Thomam illum Thumbum non alium quàm Herculem fuisse satis constat*, yet shall I venture to oppose one line of Mr Midwinter against them all:

  In Arthur's Court Tom Thumb did live.

'But then,' says Dr B—y, 'if we place Tom Thumb in the Court of King Arthur it will be proper to place that Court out of Britain, where no giants were ever heard of.' Spenser, in his *Faërie Queene*, is of another opinion, where describing Albion he says:

  – Far within, a savage nation dwelt
  Of hideous giants.

And in the same canto:

  Then Elfar; who two brethren giants had,
  The one of which had two heads –
  The other three.

Risum teneatis, Amici.

[4] 'To whisper in books,' says Mr D—s, 'is arrant nonsense.' I am afraid this learned man does not sufficiently understand the extensive meaning of the word *whisper*. If he had rightly understood what is meant by the 'senses whisp'ring the soul' in the *Persian Princess*, or what 'whisp'ring like winds' is in *Aurengzebe*, or like thunder in another author, he would have understood this. Emmeline in Dryden sees a voice, but she was born blind,

Of all our sages, that this mighty hero,
By Merlin's art begot, hath not a bone
Within his skin, but is a lump of gristle.
DOODLE Then 'tis a gristle of no mortal kind;
Some god, my Noodle, stept into the place
Of Gaffer Thumb, and more than half begot
This mighty Tom.[1]
NOODLE   Sure he was sent express
From Heaven to be the pillar of our State.[2]
Though small his body be, so very small
A chairman's leg is more than twice as large,
Yet is his soul like any mountain big,
And as a mountain once brought forth a mouse,
So doth this mouse contain a mighty mountain.[3]
DOODLE Mountain indeed! So terrible his name,
The giant nurses frighten children with it,[4]
And cry Tom Thumb is come, and if you are
Naughty will surely take the child away.
NOODLE But hark! these trumpets speak the King's approach.[5]
DOODLE He comes most luckily for my petition.   *Flourish*.

which is an excuse Panthea cannot plead in *Cyrus*, who hears a sight:
> *– Your description will surpass*
> *All fiction, painting, or dumb show of horror,*
> *That ever ears yet heard, or eyes beheld.*

When Mr D—s understands these he will understand whispering in books.

[1]
> *Some ruffian stepped into his father's place,*
> *And more than half begot him.*   Mary Queen of Scots.

[2]
> *For Ulamar seems sent express from heaven,*
> *To civilise this rugged Indian clime.*   Liberty Asserted.

[3] '*Omne majus continet in se minus, sed minus non in se majus continere potest*', says Scaliger in *Thumbo*. – I suppose he would have cavilled at these beautiful lines in the *Earl of Essex*:
> *– Thy most inveterate soul,*
> *That looks through the foul prison of thy body.*

And at those of Dryden:
> *The palace is without too well design'd,*
> *Conduct me in, for I will view thy mind.*   Aurengzebe.

[4] Mr Banks has copied this almost verbatim:
> *It was enough to say, here's Essex come,*
> *And nurses stilled their children with the fright.*   Earl of Essex.

[5] The Trumpet in a tragedy is generally as much as to say 'Enter King', which makes Mr Banks in one of his plays call it the 'trumpet's formal sound'.

SCENE 2

King, Queen, Grizzle, Noodle, Doodle, Foodle.

KING Let nothing but a face of joy appear;[1]
The man who frowns this day shall lose his head,
That he may have no face to frown withal.
Smile, Dollallolla – Ha! what wrinkled sorrow
Hangs, sits, lies, frowns upon thy knitted brow?[2]
Whence flow those tears fast down thy blubbered cheeks,
Like a swoll'n gutter, gushing through the streets?
QUEEN Excess of joy, my lord, I've heard folks say,
Gives tears as certain as excess of grief.[3]
KING If it be so, let all men cry for joy,
Till my whole Court be drowned with their tears;
Nay, till they overflow my utmost land,
And leave me nothing but the sea to rule.[4]

---

[1] Phraortes in the *Captives* seems to have been acquainted with King Arthur.
> *Proclaim a festival for seven days' space,*
> *Let the Court shine in all its pomp and lustre,*
> *Let all our streets resound with shouts of joy;*
> *Let music's care-dispelling voice be heard;*
> *The sumptuous banquet and the flowing goblet*
> *Shall warm the cheek, and fill the heart with gladness.*
> *Astarbe shall sit mistress of the feast.*

[2]
> *Repentance frowns on thy contracted brow.*   Sophonisba.
> *Hung on his clouded brow, I mark'd despair.*   Ibid.
> *– A sullen gloom*
> *Scowls on his brow.*   Busiris.

[3] Plato is of this opinion, and so is Mr Banks:
> *Behold these tears sprung from fresh pain and joy.*   Earl of Essex.

[4] These floods are very frequent in the tragic authors:
> *Near to some murmuring brook I'll lay me down,*
> *Whose waters, if they should too shallow flow,*
> *My tears shall swell them up till I will drown.*   Lee's Sophonisba.
> *Pouring forth tears at such a lavish rate,*
> *That were the world on fire they might have drowned*
> *The wrath of Heaven, and quenched the mighty ruin.*   Mithridates.

One author changes the waters of grief to those of joy:
> *– These tears, that sprung from tides of grief,*
> *Are now augmented to a flood of joy.*   Cyrus the Great.

Another:
> *Turns all the streams of hate, and makes them flow*
> *In pity's channel.*   Royal Villain.

One drowns himself:
> *– Pity like a torrent pours me down,*
> *Now I am drowning all within a deluge.*   Anna Bullen.

Cyrus drowns the whole world:

DOODLE My liege, I a petition have here got.

KING Petition me no petitions, sir, to-day;
　Let other hours be set apart for business.
　To-day it is our pleasure to be drunk,[1]
　And this our Queen shall be as drunk as we.

QUEEN (Though I already half seas over am)[2]
　If the capacious goblet overflow
　With arrack-punch – 'fore George! I'll see it out;
　Of rum and brandy I'll not taste a drop.

KING Though rack, in punch, eight shillings be a quart,
　And rum and brandy be no more than six,
　Rather than quarrel you shall have your will.　　*Trumpets.*
　But, ha! the warrior comes; the Great Tom Thumb,
　The little hero, giant-killing boy,
　Preserver of my kingdom, is arrived.

SCENE 3

Tom Thumb, to them with Officers, Prisoners and Attendants.

KING Oh! welcome most, most welcome[3] to my arms.
　What gratitude can thank away the debt
　Your valour lays upon me?

　　　Our swelling grief
　　　Shall melt into a deluge, and the world
　　　Shall drown in tears.　　　　　　　　　　　Cyrus the Great.

[1] 'An expression vastly beneath the dignity of tragedy,' says Mr D—s, yet we find the word he cavils at in the mouth of Mithridates less properly used, and applied to a more terrible idea:

　　　I would be drunk with death.　　　　　　　Mithridates.

The author of the new *Sophonisba* taketh hold of this monosyllable and uses it pretty much to the same purpose:

　　　The Carthaginian sword with Roman blood
　　　Was drunk.

I would ask Mr D—s, which gives him the best idea, a drunken king, or a drunken sword? Mr Tate dresses up King Arthur's resolution in heroics:

　　　Merry, my lord, o' th' captain's humour right,
　　　I am resolved to be dead drunk to-night.

Lee also uses this charming word:

　　　Love's the drunkenness of the mind.　　　　Gloriana.

[2] Dryden has borrowed this, and applied it improperly:

　　　I'm half seas o'er in death.　　　　　　　Cleomenes.

[3] This figure is in great use among the tragedians:

　　　'Tis therefore, therefore 'tis.　　　　　　Victim.
　　　I long, repent, repent and long again.　　　Busiris.

QUEEN   – Oh! ye gods![1]   *Aside.*

THUMB When I'm not thanked at all I'm thanked enough,
I've done my duty, and I've done no more.[2]

QUEEN Was ever such a godlike creature seen!   *Aside.*

KING Thy modesty's a candle to thy merit,[3]
It shines itself, and shows thy merit too.
But say, my boy, where didst thou leave the giants?

THUMB My liege, without the castle gates they stand,
The castle gates too low for their admittance.

KING What look they like?

THUMB   Like nothing but themselves.

QUEEN And sure thou art like nothing but thyself.[4]   *Aside.*

KING Enough! the vast idea fills my soul.
I see them, yes, I see them now before me:
The monstrous, ugly, barb'rous sons of whores.
But, ha! what form majestic strikes our eyes?
So perfect, that it seems to have been drawn
By all the gods in council: so fair she is,
That surely at her birth the council paused,
And then at length cried out, This is a woman![5]

THUMB Then were the gods mistaken. She is not
A woman, but a giantess whom we,
With much ado, have made a shift to haul[6]

---

[1] A tragical exclamation.
[2] This line is copied verbatim in the *Captives*.
[3] We find a candlestick for this candle in two celebrated authors:

> – Each star withdraws
> His golden head, and burns within the socket.   Nero.
> A soul grown old and sunk in the socket.   Sebastian.

[4] This simile occurs very frequently among the dramatic writers of both kinds.
[5] Mr Lee hath stolen this thought from our author:

> – This perfect face, drawn by the gods in council,
> Which they were long a-making.   Lu. Jun. Brut.
> – At his birth the heavenly council paused,
> And then at last cry'd out, 'This is a man!'

Dryden hath improved this hint to the utmost perfection:

> So perfect that the very gods, who formed you, wondered
> At their own skill, and cried, 'A lucky hit
> Has mended our design!' Their envy hindered,
> Or you had been immortal, and a pattern,
> When heaven would work for ostentation sake,
> To copy out again.   All for Love.

Banks prefers the works of Michael Angelo to that of the gods:

> A pattern for the gods to make a man by,
> Or Michael Angelo to form a statue.

[6] 'It is impossible,' says Mr W—, 'sufficiently to admire this natural easy line.'

Within the town; for she is by a foot
Shorter than all her subject giants were.[1]

GLUMDALCA We yesterday were both a queen and wife,
One hundred thousand giants owned our sway,
Twenty whereof were married to ourself.

QUEEN Oh! happy state of giantism — where husbands
Like mushrooms grow, whilst hapless we are forced
To be content, nay, happy thought with one.

GLUMDALCA But then to lose them all in one black day!
That the same sun which, rising, saw me wife
To twenty giants, setting, should behold
Me widowed of them all! My worn out heart,
That ship, leaks fast, and the great heavy lading,
My soul, will quickly sink.[2]

QUEEN   Madam, believe
I view your sorrows with a woman's eye;
But learn to bear them with what strength you may,
To-morrow we will have our grenadiers
Drawn out before you, and you then shall choose
What husbands you think fit.

GLUMDALCA   Madam, I am
Your most obedient, and most humble servant.[3]

KING Think, mighty Princess, think this Court your own,
Nor think the landlord me, this house my inn;
Call for whate'er you will, you'll nothing pay.
I feel a sudden pain within my breast,
Nor know I whether it arise from love,
Or only the wind-colic.[4] Time must show.
O Thumb! what do we to thy valour owe?

---

[1] This tragedy, which in most points resembles the ancients, differs from them in this, that it assigns the same honour to lowness of stature which they did to height. The gods and heroes in Homer and Virgil are continually described higher by the head than their followers, the contrary of which is observed by our author. In short to exceed, on either side is equally admirable, and a man of three foot is as wonderful a sight as a man of nine.

[2]   *My blood leaks fast, and the great heavy lading*
                My soul will quickly sink.   Mithridates.
                My soul is like a ship.   Injured Love.

[3] This well-bred line seems to be copied in the *Persian Princess*:
                To be your humblest, and most faithful slave.

[4] This doubt of the king puts me in mind of a passage in the *Captives*, where the noise of feet is mistaken for the rustling of leaves:
                — Methinks I hear
                The sound of feet;
                No, 'twas the wind that shook yon cypress boughs.

Ask some reward, great as we can bestow.

THUMB I ask not kingdoms, I can conquer those,
I ask not money, money I've enough;
For what I've done, and what I mean to do,
For giants slain, and giants yet unborn,
Which I will slay — if this be called a debt,
Take my receipt in full — I ask but this,[1]
To sun myself in Huncamunca's eyes.[2]

KING Prodigious bold request!   ⎱
QUEEN Be still, my soul![3]   ⎰   *Aside.*

THUMB My heart is at the threshold of your mouth,
And waits its answer there. Oh! do not frown;
I've tried, to reason's tune, to tune my soul,
But love did overwind and crack the string.
Though Jove in thunder had cried out, You shan't,
I should have loved her still — for oh, strange fate,
Then when I loved her least I loved her most![4]

KING It is resolved — the Princess is your own.

THUMB Oh! happy, happy, happy, happy Thumb.[5]

QUEEN Consider, sir, reward your soldier's merit,
But give not Huncamunca to Tom Thumb.

KING Tom Thumb! Odzooks, my wide-extended realm
Knows not a name so glorious as Tom Thumb.
Let Macedonia, Alexander boast,
Let Rome her Cæsars and her Scipios show,
Her Messieurs France, let Holland boast Mynheers,
Ireland her O's, her Macs let Scotland boast,

---

[1] Mr Dryden seems to have had this passage in his eye in the first page of *Love Triumphant*.

[2] Don Carlos in the *Revenge* suns himself in the charms of his mistress:
> *While in the lustre of her charms I lay.*

[3] A tragical phrase much in use.

[4] This speech hath been taken to pieces by several tragical authors, who seem to have rifled it and shared its beauties among them.
> *My soul waits at the portal of thy breast,*
> *   To ravish from thy lips the welcome news.*   Anna Bullen.
> *My soul stands list'ning at my ears.*   Cyrus the Great.
> *Love to his tune my jarring heart would bring,*
> *But reason overwinds and cracks the string.*   Duke of Guise.
> *   — I should have loved,*
> *Though Jove in muttering thunder had forbid it.*   New Sophonisba.
> *And when it (my heart) wild resolves to love no more,*
> *Then is the triumph of excessive love.*   Ibidem.

[5] Masinissa is one-fourth less happy than Tom Thumb:
> *Oh! happy, happy, happy.*   New Sophonisba.

Let England boast no other than Tom Thumb.
QUEEN Though greater yet his boasted merit was,
    He shall not have my daughter, that is pos'.
KING Ha! sayst thou, Dollallolla?
QUEEN   I say he shan't.
KING Then by our royal self we swear you lie.[1]
QUEEN Who but a dog, who but a dog[2]
    Would use me as thou dost? Me, who have lain
    These twenty years so loving by thy side![3]
    But I will be revenged. I'll hang myself,
    Then tremble all who did this match persuade,
    For riding on a cat from high I'll fall,
    And squirt down royal vengeance on you all.[4]
FOODLE Her Majesty the Queen is in a passion.[5]
KING Be she or be she not[6] — I'll to the girl
    And pave thy way, O Thumb. Now, by ourself,
    We were indeed a pretty king of clouts
    To truckle to her will. For when by force
    Or art the wife her husband overreaches,
    Give him the petticoat, and her the breeches.
THUMB Whisper, ye winds that Huncamunca's mine!
    Echoes repeat, that Huncamunca's mine!
    The dreadful business of the war is o'er,
    And beauty, heavenly beauty! crowns my toils;
    I've thrown the bloody garment now aside,
    And Hymeneal sweets invite my bride.
      So when some chimney-sweeper, all the day,
    Hath through dark paths pursued the sooty way,
    At night, to wash his hands and face he flies,
    And in his t'other shirt with his Brickdusta lies.[7]

1
2   No by myself.   *Anna Bullen.*
                        — *Who caused*
              This dreadful revolution in my fate?
              Ulamar. Who but a dog, who but a dog?   *Liberty Asserted.*
3   — *A bride*
              Who twenty years lay loving by your side.   *Banks.*
4   *For borne upon a cloud from high I'll fall,*
              And rain down royal vengeance on you all.   Albion Queens.
[5] An information very like this we have in the *Tragedy of Love*, where Cyrus having
stormed in the most violent manner, Cyaxares observes very calmly:
              Why, nephew Cyrus — you are moved.
6   *'Tis in your choice,*
              Love me, or love me not.   Conquest of Granada.
[7] There is not one beauty in this charming speech but hath been borrowed by almost
every tragic writer.

SCENE 4

Grizzle, solus.

Where art thou, Grizzle! where are now thy glories?
Where are the drums that wakened thee to honour?
Greatness is a laced coat from Monmouth Street,
Which fortune lends us for a day to wear,
To-morrow puts it on another's back.
The spiteful sun but yesterday surveyed
His rival high as Saint Paul's cupola;
Now may he see me as Fleet Ditch laid low.[1]

SCENE 5

Queen, Grizzle.

QUEEN Teach me to scold, prodigious-minded Grizzle,
　　Mountain of treason, ugly as the devil,
　　Teach this confounded hateful mouth of mine
　　To spout forth words malicious as thyself,
　　Words which might shame all Billingsgate to speak.[2]
GRIZZLE Far be it from my pride to think my tongue
　　Your royal lips can in that art instruct,
　　Wherein you so excel. But may I ask,
　　Without offence, wherefore my queen would scold?
QUEEN Wherefore? Oh! Blood and thunder! han't thou heard
　　(What ev'ry corner of the Court resounds)
　　That little Thumb will be a great man made?
GRIZZLE I heard it, I confess — for who, alas!
　　Can always stop his ears?[3] — but would my teeth,
　　By grinding knives, had first been set on edge.
QUEEN Would I had heard, at the still noon of night,
　　The hallaloo of fire in every street!
　　Odsbobs! I have a mind to hang myself,

---

[1] Mr Banks has (I wish I could not say too servilely) imitated this of Grizzle in his *Earl of Essex*:
　　　　　　Where art thou, Essex, etc.
[2] The Countess of Nottingham in the *Earl of Essex* is apparently acquainted with Dollallolla.
[3] Grizzle was not probably possessed of that glue of which Mr Banks speaks in his *Cyrus*:
　　　　　　I'll glue my ears to every word.

To think I should a grandmother be made
By such a rascal. Sure the King forgets,
When in a pudding, by his mother put,
The bastard, by a tinker, on a stile
Was dropped. – O good Lord Grizzle! can I bear
To see him from a pudding mount the throne?
Or can, oh can! my Huncamunca bear
To take a pudding's offspring to her arms?

GRIZZLE Oh Horror! Horror! Horror! Cease, my Queen,
Thy voice, like twenty screech-owls, wracks my brain.[1]

QUEEN Then rouse thy spirit – we may yet prevent
This hated match.

GRIZZLE   We will; not Fate itself,[2]
Should it conspire with Thomas Thumb, should cause it.
I'll swim through seas; I'll ride upon the clouds;
I'll dig the earth; I'll blow out ev'ry fire;
I'll rave; I'll rant; I'll rise; I'll rush; I'll roar;
Fierce as the man whom smiling[3] dolphins bore
From the prosaic to the poetic shore.
I'll tear the scoundrel into twenty pieces.

QUEEN Oh, no! prevent the match, but hurt him not;
For, though I would not have him have my daughter,
Yet can we kill the man that killed the giants?

GRIZZLE I tell you, madam, it was all a trick.
He made the giants first, and then he killed them;
As fox-hunters bring foxes to the wood,
And then with hounds they drive them out again.

QUEEN How! have you seen no giants? Are there not
Now, in the yard, ten thousand proper giants?

GRIZZLE Indeed I cannot positively tell,
But firmly do believe there is not one.[4]

---

[1]   Screech-owls, dark ravens and amphibious monsters
             Are screaming in that voice.   Mary Queen of Scots.
[2] The reader may see all the beauties of this speech in a late ode called the *Naval Lyric*.
[3] This epithet to a dolphin doth not give one so clear an idea as were to be wished, a
smiling fish seeming a little more difficult to be imagined than a flying fish. Mr Dryden is of
the opinion, that smiling is the property of reason, and that no irrational creature can smile.
             Smiles not allowed to beasts from reason move.
                                                      State of Innocence.
[4] These lines are written in the same key with those in the *Earl of Essex*:
             Why sayest thou so? I love thee well, indeed
             I do, and thou shalt find by this, 'tis true.
Or with this in *Cyrus*:
             The most heroic mind that ever was.
And with above half of the modern tragedies.

QUEEN Hence! from my sight! thou traitor, hie away!
  By all my stars! thou enviest Tom Thumb.
  Go, sirrah! go, hie away! hie! — thou art
  A setting dog. Begone![1]
GRIZZLE   Madam, I go.
  Tom Thumb shall feel the vengeance you have raised:
  So, when two dogs are fighting in the streets,
  With a third dog, one of the two dogs meets,
  With angry teeth he bites him to the bone,
  And this dog smarts for what that dog had done.

SCENE 6

Queen, sola.

And whither shall I go? — Alack-a-day!
I love Tom Thumb — but must not tell him so;
For what's a woman when her virtue's gone?
A coat without its lace; wig out of buckle;
A stocking with a hole in't. I can't live
Without my virtue, or without Tom Thumb.
Then let me weigh them in two equal scales,[2]
In this scale put my virtue, that, Tom Thumb.
Alas! Tom Thumb is heavier than my virtue.
But hold! — perhaps I may be left a widow:
This match prevented, then Tom Thumb is mine:
In that dear hope I will forget my pain.
  So, when some wench to Tothill-Bridewell's sent,
With beating hemp and flogging she's content;
She hopes in time to ease her present pain,
At length is free, and walks the streets again.

---

[1] Aristotle in that excellent work of his, which is very justly styled his masterpiece, earnestly recommends using the terms of art, however coarse or even indecent they may be. Mr Tate is of the same opinion.
> Bru. *Do not, like young hawks, fetch a course about,*
> *Your fame flies fair.*
> Fra. *Do not fear it.*
> *He answers you in your own hawking phrase.*   Injured Love.

I think these two great authorities are sufficient to justify Dollallolla in the use of the phrase, 'Hie away! hie!' when in the same line she says she is speaking to a setting dog.

[2] We meet with such another pair of scales in Dryden's *King Arthur*:
> *Arthur and Oswald, and their different fates*
> *Are weighing now within the scales of Heaven.*

Also in *Sebastian*:
> *This hour my lot is weighting in the scales.*

Act II

SCENE: *The street.*

Bailiff, Follower.

BAILIFF Come on, my trusty Follower, come on,
This day discharge thy duty, and at night
A double mug of beer and beer shall glad thee.
Stand here by me, this way must Noodle pass.
FOLLOWER No more, no more, O Bailiff! every word
Inspires my soul with virtue. Oh! I long
To meet the enemy in the street — and nab him:
To lay arresting hands upon his back,
And drag him trembling to the sponging-house.
BAILIFF There, when I have him, I will sponge upon him.
O glorious thought! by the sun, moon and stars,
I will enjoy it, though it be in thought!
Yes, yes, my Follower, I will enjoy it.[1]
FOLLOWER Enjoy it then some other time, for now
Our prey approaches.
BAILIFF   Let us retire.

SCENE 2

Tom Thumb, Noodle, Bailiff, Follower.

THUMB Trust me, my Noodle, I am wondrous sick;
For though I love the gentle Huncamunca,

---

[1] Mr Rowe is generally imagined to have taken some hints from this scene in his character of Bajazet; but as he, of all the tragic writers, bears the least resemblance to our author in his diction, I am unwilling to imagine he would condescend to copy him in this particular.

Yet at the thought of marriage I grow pale;
For oh! – but swear thou'lt keep it ever secret,[1]
I will unfold a tale will make thee stare.

NOODLE I swear by lovely Huncamunca's charms.

THUMB Then know – my grandmamma hath often said,
Tom Thumb, beware of marriage.[2]

NOODLE   Sir, I blush
To think a warrior, great in arms as you,
Should be affrighted by his grandmamma;
Can an old woman's empty dreams deter
The blooming hero from the virgin's arms?
Think of the joy that will your soul alarm
When in her fond embraces clasped you lie,
While on her panting breast dissolved in bliss,
You pour out all Tom Thumb in every kiss.

THUMB O Noodle, thou hast fired my eager soul;
Spite of my grandmother she shall be mine;
I'll hug, caress, I'll eat her up with love;
Whole days, and nights, and years shall be too short
For our enjoyment; every sun shall rise
Blushing, to see us in our bed together.[3]

NOODLE Oh, sir! this purpose of your soul pursue.

BAILIFF Oh sir! I have an action against you.

NOODLE At whose suit is it?

BAILIFF   At your tailor's, sir.

---

[1] This method of surprising an audience by raising their expectation to the highest pitch, and then balking it, hath been practised with great success by most of our tragical authors.

[2] Almeyda in *Sebastian* is in the same distress:

> Sometimes methinks I hear the groan of ghosts,
> Thin hollow sounds and lamentable screams;
> Then, like a dying echo from afar,
> My mother's voice that cries: Wed not, Almeyda!
> Forewarned, Almeyda, marriage is thy crime.

[3] 'As very well he may if he hath any modesty in him,' says Mr D—s. The author of *Busiris* is extremely zealous to prevent the sun's blushing at any indecent object; and therefore on all such occasions he addresses himself to the sun, and desires him to keep out of the way:

> Rise never more, O sun! let night prevail,
> Eternal darkness close the world's wide scene.   *Busiris.*
> Sun, hide thy face, and put the world in mourning.   *Ibid.*

Mr Banks makes the sun perform the office of Hymen; and therefore not likely to be disgusted at such a sight:

> The sun sets forth like a gay brideman with you.
>   *Mary Queen of Scots.*

Your tailor put this warrant in my hands,
And I arrest you, sir, at his commands.
THUMB Ha! dogs! Arrest my friend before my face!
Think you Tom Thumb will suffer this disgrace!
But let vain cowards threaten by their word,
Tom Thumb shall show his anger by his sword.
                    Kills the Bailiff and his Follower.
BAILIFF Oh, I am slain!
FOLLOWER   I am murdered also,
And to the shades, the dismal shades below,
My Bailiff's faithful Follower I go.
NOODLE Go then to Hell like rascals as you are,
And give our service to the bailiffs there.[1]
THUMB Thus perish all the bailiffs in the land,
Till debtors at noonday shall walk the streets,
And no one fear a bailiff or his writ.

SCENE 3

SCENE: *The Princess Huncamunca's apartment.*

Huncamunca, Cleora, Mustacha.

HUNCAMUNCA Give me some music — see that it be sad.[2]

                Cleora sings.

> *Cupid, ease a love-sick maid,*
> *Bring thy quiver to her aid;*
> *With equal ardour wound the swain;*
> *Beauty should never sigh in vain.*

            II
> *Let him feel the pleasing smart,*
> *Drive thy arrow through his heart;*
> *When one you wound, you then destroy;*
> *When both you kill, you kill with joy.*

---

[1] Neurmahal sends the same message to Heaven:
> *For I would have you, when you upwards move,*
> *Speak kindly of us to our friends above.*   Aurengzebe.
We find another to Hell in the *Persian Princess*:
> *Villain, get thee down*
> *To Hell, and tell them that the fray's begun.*
[2] Anthony gives the same command in the same words.

HUNCAMUNCA Oh, Tom Thumb! Tom Thumb! wherefore art
   thou Tom Thumb?[1]
   Why hadst thou not been born of royal race?
   Why had not mighty Bantam been thy father?
   Or else the King of Brentford, Old or New?
MUSTACHA I am surprised that your Highness can give yourself
   a moment's uneasiness about that little insignificant fellow,
   Tom Thumb the Great[2] – one properer for a plaything than
   a husband. Were he my husband his horns should be as long
   as his body. If you had fallen in love with a grenadier, I should
   not have wondered at it – if you had fallen in love with
   something; but to fall in love with nothing!
HUNCAMUNCA Cease, my Mustacha, on thy duty cease.
   The zephyr, when in flowery vales it plays,
   Is not so soft, so sweet as Thummy's breath.
   The dove is not so gentle to its mate.
MUSTACHA The dove is every bit as proper for a husband. Alas!
   madam, there's not a beau about the Court looks so little like
   a man. He is a perfect butterfly, a thing without substance,
   and almost without shadow too.
HUNCAMUNCA This rudeness is unseasonable; desist
   Or I shall think this railing comes from love.
   Tom Thumb's a creature of that charming form
   That no one can abuse, unless they love him.
MUSTACHA Madam, the King.

SCENE 4

King, Huncamunca.

KING Let all but Huncamunca leave the room.
                              Exeunt Cleora and Mustacha.
   Daughter, I have observed of late some grief
   Unusual in your countenance – your eyes,

---

[1]   *Oh! Marius, Marius; wherefore art thou Marius?* Otway's Marius.
[2] Nothing is more common than these seeming contradictions, such as:
             Haughty Weakness   Victim.
             Great small world   Noah's Flood.

That, like two open windows,[1] used to show
The lovely beauty of the rooms within,
Have now two blinds before them. What is the cause?
Say, have you not enough of meat and drink?[2]
We've given strict orders not to have you stinted.

HUNCAMUNCA Alas! my lord, I value not myself,
  That once I eat two fowls and half a pig;
  Small is that praise: but oh! a maid may want
  What she can neither eat nor drink.

KING   What's that?

HUNCAMUNCA Oh! spare my blushes; but I mean a husband.[3]

KING If that be all, I have provided one,
  A husband great in arms, whose warlike sword
  Streams with the yellow blood of slaughtered giants.
  Whose name in Terrâ Incognitâ is known,
  Whose valour, wisdom, virtue make a noise
  Great as the kettle-drums of twenty armies.

HUNCAMUNCA Whom does my royal father mean?

KING   Tom Thumb.

HUNCAMUNCA Is it possible?

KING   Ha! the window-blinds are gone,

---

[1] Lee hath improved this metaphor:
> Dost thou not view joy peeping from my eyes,
> The casements opened wide to gaze on thee?
> So Rome's glad citizens to windows rise,
> When they some young triumpher fain would see.   Gloriana.

[2] Almahide hath the same contempt for these appetites:
> To eat and drink can no perfection be.   Conquest of Granada.

The Earl of Essex is of a different opinion, and seems to place the chief happiness of a general therein:
> Were but commanders half so well regarded,
> Then they might eat.   Banks's Earl of Essex.

But if we may believe one, who knows more than either, the devil himself, we shall find eating to be an affair of more moment than is generally imagined.
> Gods are immortal only by their food.
>   Lucifer in the State of Innocence.

[3] This expression is enough of itself (says Mr D—s) utterly to destroy the character of Huncamunca; yet we find a woman of no abandoned character in Dryden adventuring farther, and thus excusing herself:
> To speak our wishes first, forbid it pride,
> Forbid it modesty. True, they forbid it,
> But nature does not. When we are athirst,
> Or hungry, will imperious nature stay,
> Nor eat, nor drink, before 'tis bid fall on.   Cleomenes.

Cassandra speaks before she is asked, Huncamunca afterwards. Cassandra speaks her wishes to her lover, Huncamunca only to her father.

A country-dance of joy is in your face,
Your eyes spit fire, your cheeks grow red as beef.[1]

HUNCAMUNCA Oh! there's a magic music in that sound,
Enough to turn me into beef indeed.
Yes, I will own, since licensed by your word,
I'll own Tom Thumb the cause of all my grief.
For him I've sighed, I've wept, I've gnawed my sheets.

KING Oh! thou shalt gnaw thy tender sheets no more,
A husband thou shalt have to mumble now.

HUNCAMUNCA Oh! happy sound! henceforth let no one tell
That Huncamunca shall lead apes in hell.
Oh! I am overjoyed!

KING　　　　　　　　I see thou art.
Joy lightens in thy eyes, and thunders from thy brows;
Transports, like lightning, dart along thy soul,[2]
As small-shot through a hedge.

HUNCAMUNCA　　　　　Oh! say not small.

KING This happy news shall on our tongue ride post,
Ourself will bear the happy news to Thumb.
Yet think not, daughter, that your powerful charms
Must still detain the hero from his arms;
Various his duty, various his delight;
Now is his turn to kiss, and now to fight;
And now to kiss again. So mighty Jove,
When with excessive thund'ring tired above,
Comes down to earth, and takes a bit – and then
Flies to his trade of thund'ring back again.[3]

---

[1]　　*Her eyes resistless magic bear,*
　　　Angels I see, and gods are dancing there.　　　Lee's *Sophonisba.*

[2] Mr Dennis, in that excellent tragedy called *Liberty Asserted*, which is thought to have given so great a stroke to the late French king, hath frequent imitations of this beautiful speech of King Arthur:
　　　Conquest light'ning in his eyes, and thund'ring in his arm.
　　　Joy lightened in her eyes.
　　　Joys like lightning dart along my soul.

[3]　　*Jove, with excessive thund'ring tired above,*
　　　Comes down for ease, enjoys a nymph, and then
　　　Mounts dreadful, and to thund'ring goes again.　　　Gloriana.

SCENE 5

Grizzle, Huncamunca.

GRIZZLE Oh! Huncamunca, Huncamunca, oh![1]
Thy pouting breasts, like kettle-drums of brass,
Beat everlasting loud alarms of joy;
As bright as brass they are, and oh! as hard;
Oh! Huncamunca, Huncamunca, oh!

HUNCAMUNCA Ha! dost thou know me, Princess as I am,
That thus of me you dare to make your game?[2]

GRIZZLE Oh, Huncamunca, well I know that you
A Princess are, and a king's daughter, too;
But love no meanness scorns, no grandeur fears;
Love often lords into the cellar bears,
And bids the sturdy porter come upstairs.
For what's too high for love, or what's too low?
Oh! Huncamunca, Huncamunca, oh!

HUNCAMUNCA But granting all you say of love were true,
My love, alas! is to another due!
In vain to me a-suitoring you come,
For I'm already promised to Tom Thumb.

GRIZZLE And can my Princess such a durgen wed,
One fitter for your pocket than your bed!
Advised by me, the worthless baby shun,
Or you will ne'er be brought to bed of one.
Oh! take me to thy arms, and never flinch,
Who am a man, by Jupiter, ev'ry inch.
Then while in joys together lost we lie,
I'll press thy soul while gods stand wishing by.[3]

HUNCAMUNCA If, sir, what you insinuate you prove,

---

[1] This beautiful line, which ought, says Mr W—, to be written in gold, is imitated in the new *Sophonisba*:

> *Oh! Sophonisba, Sophonisba, oh!*
> *Oh! Narva, Narva, oh!*

The author of a song called *Duke upon Duke* hath improved it:

> *Alas! O Nick, O Nick, alas!*

Where, by the help of a little false spelling, you have two meanings in the repeated words.

[2] Edith, in the *Bloody Brother*, speaks to her lover in the same familiar language:

> *Your grace is full of game.*

[3]

> *Traverse the glittering chambers of the sky,*
> *Borne on a cloud in view of fate I'll lie,*
> *And press her soul while gods stand wishing by.*   Hannibal.

All obstacles of promise you remove;
For all engagements to a man must fall,
Whene'er that man is proved no man at all.

GRIZZLE Oh! let him seek some dwarf, some fairy miss,
Where no joint-stool must lift him to the kiss.
But by the stars and glory you appear
Much fitter for a Prussian Grenadier;
One globe alone on Atlas' shoulders rests,
Two globes are less than Huncamunca's breasts:
The Milky Way is not so white, that's flat,
And sure thy breasts are full as large as that.

HUNCAMUNCA Oh, sir, so strong your eloquence I find,
It is impossible to be unkind.

GRIZZLE Ah! speak that o'er again, and let the sound
From one pole to another pole rebound;
The earth and sky each be a battledoor,
And keep the sound, that shuttlecock, up an hour;[1]
To Doctors Commons for a licence I
Swift as an arrow from a bow will fly.

HUNCAMUNCA Oh no! lest some disaster we should meet,
'Twere better to be married at the Fleet.

GRIZZLE Forbid it, all ye powers, a Princess should
By that vile place contaminate her blood;
My quick return shall to my charmer prove,
I travel on the post-horses of love.[2]

HUNCAMUNCA Those post-horses to me will seem too slow,
Though they should fly swift as the gods, when they
Ride on behind that post-boy, Opportunity.

---

[1]
> Let the four winds from distant corners meet,
> And on their wings first bear it into France;
> Then back again to Edina's proud walls,
> Till victim to the sound the aspiring city falls.   Albion Queens.

[2] I do not remember any metaphors so frequent in the tragic poets as those borrowed from riding post:
> The gods and opportunity ride post.   Hannibal.
> – Let's rush together,
> For Death rides post.   Duke of Guise.
> Destruction gallops to thy murder post.   Gloriana.

SCENE 6

Tom Thumb, Huncamunca.

THUMB Where is my Princess, where's my Huncamunca?
  Where are those eyes, those cardmatches of love,
  That light up all with love my waxen soul?[1]
  Where is that face, which artful nature made
  In the same moulds where Venus self was cast?[2]
HUNCAMUNCA Oh! what is music to the ear that's deaf,[3]
  Or a goose-pie to him that has no taste?
  What are these praises now to me, since I
  Am promised to another?
THUMB   Ha! promised?

---

[1] This image too very often occurs:

  — *Bright as when thy eye*
  First lighted up our loves.   Aurengzebe.
  This is not a crown alone lights up my name.   Busiris.

[2] There is great dissension among the poets concerning the method of making man. One tells his mistress that the mould she was made in being lost, Heaven cannot form such another. Lucifer, in Dryden, gives a merry description of his own formation:

  Whom Heaven neglecting, made and scarce designed,
  But threw me in for number to the rest.   State of Innocence.

In one place the same poet supposes man to be made of metal:

  I was formed
  Of that coarse metal, which when she was made,
  The gods threw by for rubbish.   All for Love.

In another of dough:

  When the gods moulded up the paste of man,
  Some of their clay was left upon their hands,
  And so they made Egyptians.   Cleomenes.

In another of clay:

  — *Rubbish of remaining clay.*   Sebastian.

One makes the soul of wax:

  Her waxen soul begins to melt apace.   Anna Bullen.

Another of flint:

  Sure our two souls have somewhere been acquainted
  In former beings, or struck out together,
  One spark to Afric flew, and one to Portugal. Sebastian.

To omit the great quantities of iron, brazen and leaden souls which are so plenty in modern authors — I cannot omit the dress of a soul as we find it in Dryden:

  Souls shirted but with air.   King Arthur.

Nor can I pass by a particular sort of soul in a particular sort of description in the new *Sophonisba*:

  Ye mysterious powers,
  — *Whether through your gloomy depths I wander,*
  Or on the mountains walk, give me the calm,
  The steady smiling soul, where wisdom sheds
  Eternal sunshine, and eternal joy.

[3] This line Mr Banks has plundered entire in his *Anna Bullen*.

HUNCAMUNCA Too sure; it's written in the Book of Fate.

THUMB Then I will tear away the leaf
  Wherein it's writ, or if Fate won't allow
  So large a gap within its journal-book,
  I'll blot it out at least.[1]

SCENE 7

Glumdalca, Tom Thumb, Huncamunca.

GLUMDALCA I need not ask if you are Huncamunca,[2]
  Your brandy-nose proclaims –

HUNCAMUNCA   I am a Princess;
  Nor need I ask who you are.

GLUMDALCA   A giantess;
  The Queen of those who made and unmade queens.

HUNCAMUNCA The man, whose chief ambition is to be
  My sweetheart, hath destroyed these mighty giants.

GLUMDALCA Your sweetheart? Dost thou think the man who
  once
  Hath worn my easy chains, will e'er wear thine?

HUNCAMUNCA Well may your chains be easy, since, if fame
  Says true, they have been tried on twenty husbands.
  The glove or boot, so many times pulled on,[3]
  May well fit easy on the hand or foot.

GLUMDALCA I glory in the number, and when I
  Sit poorly down, like thee, content with one,
  Heaven change this face for one as bad as thine.

---

[1]   *Good Heaven! the book of fate before me lay,*
     But to tear out the journal of that day,
     Or if the order of the world below,
     Will not the gap of one whole day allow,
     Give me that minute when she made her vow.
                               Conquest of Granada.

[2] I know some of the commentators have imagined that Mr Dryden, in the altercative scene between Cleopatra and Octavia, a scene which Mr Addison inveighs against with great bitterness, is much beholden to our author. How just this their observation is I will not presume to determine.

[3] 'A cobbling poet indeed,' says Mr D—. And yet I believe we may find as monstrous images in the tragic authors. I'll put down one:
    Untie your folded thoughts, and let them dangle loose as a bride's hair.
                                   Injured Love.
Which line seems to have as much title to a milliner's shop as our author's to a shoemaker's.

HUNCAMUNCA Let me see nearer what this beauty is,
  That captivates the heart of men by scores.

                        Holds a candle to her face.

Oh! Heaven, thou art as ugly as the devil.

GLUMDALCA You'd give the best of shoes within your shop
  To be but half so handsome.

HUNCAMUNCA   Since you come
  To that, I'll put my beauty to the test;[1]
  Tom Thumb, I'm yours, if you with me will go.

GLUMDALCA Oh! stay, Tom Thumb, and you alone shall fill
  That bed where twenty giants used to lie.

THUMB In the balcony that o'erhangs the stage,
  I've seen a whore two 'prentices engage;
  One half a crown does in his fingers hold,
  The other shows a little piece of gold;
  She the half-guinea wisely does purloin,
  And leaves the larger and the baser coin.

GLUMDALCA Left, scorned, and loathed for such a chit as this;
  I feel the storm that's rising in my mind,
  Tempests and whirlwinds rise, and roll and roar.[2]
  I'm all within a hurricane, as if
  The world's four winds were pent within my carcass.[3]
  Confusion, horror, murder, guts and death.[4]

SCENE 8

King, Glumdalca.

KING Sure never was so sad a king as I,[5]
  My life is worn as ragged as a coat

---

[1] Mr L— takes occasion in this place to commend the great care of our author to preserve the metre of blank verse, in which Shakespeare, Jonson and Fletcher were so notoriously negligent; and the moderns in imitation of our author, so laudably observant:

                – Then does
      Your majesty believe that he can be
      A traitor!   Earl of Essex.

Every page of *Sophonisba* gives us instances of this excellence.

[2]   *Love mounts and rolls about my stormy mind.*   Aurengzebe.
      Tempests and whirlwinds through my bosom move.   Cleomenes.

[3]   *With such a furious tempest on his brow,*
      As if the world's four winds were pent within
      His blustering carcass.   Anna Bullen.

[4] *Verba tragica.*

[5] This speech hath been terribly mauled by the poets.

A beggar wears; a prince should put it off,[1]
To love a captive and a giantess.
O Love! O Love! how great a king art thou!
My tongue's thy trumpet, and thou trumpetest,
Unknown to me, within me.[2] Oh, Glumdalca!
Heaven thee designed a giantess to make,
But an angelic soul was shuffled in.[3]
I am a multitude of walking griefs,[4]
And only on her lips the balm is found,[5]
To spread a plaster that might cure them all.

GLUMDALCA   What do I hear?

KING   What do I see?

GLUMDALCA   Oh!

KING   Ah!

GLUMDALCA   Ah, wretched queen!

KING   Oh! wretched king![6]

GLUMDALCA   Ah!

KING   Oh![7]

---

[1]   — My life is worn to rags;
                    Not worth a prince's wearing.   Love Triumph.
[2]   Must I beg the pity of my slave?
             Must a king beg! But Love's a greater king,
             A tyrant, nay a devil that possesses me.
             He tunes the organ of my voice and speaks,
             Unknown to me, within me.   Sebastian.
[3]   When thou wert formed Heaven did a man begin;
             But a brute soul by chance was shuffled in.   Aurengzebe.
[4]   — I am a multitude
             Of walking griefs.   New Sophonisba.
[5]   I will take thy scorpion blood,
             And lay it to my grief till I have ease.   Anna Bullen.

[6] Our author, who everywhere shows his great penetration into human nature, here outdoes himself; where a less judicious poet would have raised a long scene of whining love. He, who understood the passions better, and that so violent an affection as this must be too big for utterance, chooses rather to send his characters off in this sullen and doleful manner; in which admirable conduct he is imitated by the author of the justly celebrated *Eurydice*. Dr Young seems to point at this violence of passion:

                    — passion chokes
             Their words, and they're the statues of despair.

And Seneca tells us, *Curæ leves loquuntur, ingentes stupent*. The story of the Egyptian king in Herodotus is too well known to need to be inserted. I refer the more curious reader to the excellent Montaigne, who hath written an essay on this subject.

[7]   To part is death —
                    'Tis death to part.
             — Ah.
             — Oh.   Don Carlos.

SCENE 9

Tom Thumb, Huncamunca, Parson.

PARSON Happy's the wooing that's not long a-doing;
　For, if I guess aright, Tom Thumb this night
　Shall give a being to a new Tom Thumb.
THUMB It shall be my endeavour so to do.
HUNCAMUNCA Oh! fie upon you, sir, you make me blush.
THUMB It is the virgin's sign, and suits you well:
　I know not where, nor how, nor what I am;[1]
　I'm so transported I have lost myself.[2]
HUNCAMUNCA Forbid it, all ye stars, for you're so small,
　That were you lost you'd find yourself no more.
　So the unhappy sempstress once, they say,
　Her needle in a pottle, lost, of hay;
　In vain she looked, and looked, and made her moan,
　For ah! the needle was for ever gone.

---

[1]　　　　Nor know I whether,
　　　　What am I, who or where.　　　　　　　　　　*Busiris.*
　　　　I was I know not what, and am I know not how.　　*Gloriana.*
[2] To understand sufficiently the beauty of this passage it will be necessary that we comprehend every man to contain two selves. I shall not attempt to prove this from philosophy, which the poets make so plainly evident.
　One runs away from the other:
　　　　– Let me demand your majesty,
　　　　Why fly you from yourself?　　　　　　　　*Duke of Guise.*
In a second, one self is a guardian to the other:
　　　　Leave me the care of me.　　　　　*Conquest of Granada.*
Again:
　　　　Myself am to myself less near.　　　　　　　　*Ibid.*
In the same, the first self is proud of the second:
　　　　I myself am proud of me.　　　　　　*State of Innocence.*
In a third, distrustful of him:
　　　　Fain I would tell, but whisper it in mine ear,
　　　　That none besides might hear, nay not myself.　*Earl of Essex.*
In a fourth, honours him:
　　　　I honour Rome,
　　　　But honour too myself.　　　　　　　　*Sophonisba.*
In a fifth, at variance with him:
　　　　Leave me not thus at variance with myself.　　*Busiris.*
Again, in a sixth:
　　　　I find myself divided from myself.　　　　　　*Medea.*
　　　　She seemed the sad effigies of herself.　　　　*Banks.*
　　　　Assist me, Zulema, if thou wouldst be
　　　　The friend thou seemest, assist me against me.　*Albion Queens.*
From all which it appears that there are two selves; and therefore Tom Thumb's losing himself is no such solecism as it hath been represented by men, rather ambitious of criticising than qualified to criticise.

PARSON Long may they live, and love, and propagate,
  Till the whole land be peopled with Tom Thumbs.
  So when the Cheshire cheese a maggot breeds,[1]
  Another and another still succeeds:
  By thousands, and ten thousands they increase,
  Till one continued maggot fills the rotten cheese.

SCENE 10

Noodle, and then Grizzle.

NOODLE Sure Nature means to break her solid chain,
  Or else unfix the world, and in a rage
  To hurl it from its axle-tree and hinges;[2]
  All things are so confused, the King's in love,
  Till Queen is drunk, the Princess married is.
GRIZZLE Oh! Noodle, hast thou Huncamunca seen?
NOODLE I've seen a thousand sights this day, where none
  Are by the wonderful bitch herself outdone,
  The King, the Queen, and all the Court are sights.
GRIZZLE D—n your delay, you trifler, are you drunk, ha?
  I will not hear one word but Huncamunca.[3]
NOODLE By this time she is married to Tom Thumb.
GRIZZLE My Huncamunca.[4]
NOODLE   Your Huncamunca,
  Tom Thumb's Huncamunca, every man's Huncamunca.
GRIZZLE If this be true, all womankind are damned.
NOODLE If it be not, may I be so myself.
GRIZZLE See where she comes! I'll not believe a word
  Against that face, upon whose ample brow
  Sits innocence with majesty enthroned.[5]

---

[1] Mr F— imagines this parson to have been a Welsh one from his simile.
[2] Our author hath been plundered here according to custom:
>   Great Nature break thy chain that links together
>   The fabric of the world, and make a chaos,
>   Like that within my soul.   Love Triumphant.
>   – Startle Nature, unfix the globe,
>   And hurl it from its axle-tree and hinges.   Albion Queens.
>   The tottering earth seems sliding off its props.
>   D—n your delay, ye torturers proceed,
>   I will not hear one word but Almahide.   Conquest of Granada.
[4] Mr Dryden hath imitated this in All for Love.
[5] This Miltonic style abounds in the new Sophonisba:
>   – And on her ample brow
>   Sat majesty.

Grizzle, Huncamunca.

GRIZZLE Where has my Huncamunca been? See here
The licence in my hand!
HUNCAMUNCA   Alas! Tom Thumb.
GRIZZLE Why dost thou mention him?
HUNCAMUNCA   Ah me! Tom Thumb.
GRIZZLE What means my lovely Huncamunca?
HUNCAMUNCA   Hum!
GRIZZLE Oh! Speak.
HUNCAMUNCA   Hum!
GRIZZLE   Ha! your every word is Hum:
You force me still to answer you, Tom Thumb.[1]
Tom Thumb, I'm on the rack, I'm in a flame,
Tom Thumb, Tom Thumb, Tom Thumb, you love the name;[2]
So pleasing is that sound, that were you dumb
You still would find a voice to cry, Tom Thumb!
HUNCAMUNCA Oh! Be not hasty to proclaim my doom,
My ample heart for more than one has room,
A maid, like me, Heaven formed at least for two,
I married him, and now I'll marry you.[3]
GRIZZLE Ha! dost thou own thy falsehood to my face?
Think'st thou that I will share thy husband's place,
Since to that office one cannot suffice,
And since you scorn to dine one single dish on,
Go, get your husband put into commission,
Commissioners to discharge (ye gods), it fine is,
The duty of a husband to your Highness;
Yet think not long I will my rival bear,
Or unrevenged the slighted willow wear;
The gloomy, brooding tempest, now confined
Within the hollow caverns of my mind,

---

[1]   *Your every answer still so ends in that,*
              You force me still to answer you Morat.   Aurengzebe.
[2]   *Morat, Morat, Morat, you love the name.*   Ibid.
[3] 'Here is a sentiment for the virtuous Huncamunca,' says Mr D—s. And yet, with the
leave of this great man, the virtuous Panthea in *Cyrus* hath an heart every whit as ample:
              For two I must confess are gods to me,
              Which is my Abradatus first, and thee.   Cyrus the Great.
Nor is the lady in *Love Triumphant* more reserved, though not so intelligible:
              – I am so divided,
              That I grieve most for both, and love both most.

In dreadful whirl shall roll along the coasts,
Shall thin the land of all the men it boasts,
And cram up ev'ry chink of hell with ghosts.[1]
So I have seen, in some dark winter's day,
A sudden storm rush down the sky's highway,
Sweep through the streets with terrible ding-dong,
Gush through the spouts, and wash whole crowds along.
The crowded shops the thronging vermin screen,
Together cram the dirty and the clean,
And not one shoe-boy in the street is seen.[2]

HUNCAMUNCA Oh! fatal rashness should his fury slay
My hapless bridegroom on his wedding-day;
I, who this morn of two chose which to wed,
May go again this night alone to bed;
So have I seen some wild unsettled fool,
Who had her choice of this and that joint-stool;
To give the preference to either loath,
And fondly coveting to sit on both:
While the two stools her sitting-part confound,
Between 'em both fall squat upon the ground.[3]

---

[1] A ridiculous supposition to anyone who considers the great and extensive largeness of hell, says a commentator. But not so to those who consider the great expansion of immaterial substance. Mr Banks makes one soul to be so expanded that heaven could not contain it:

> The heavens are all too narrow for her soul.   Virtue Betrayed.

The *Persian Princess* hath a passage not unlike the author of this:

> We will send such shoals of murdered slaves,
> Shall glut hell's empty regions.

This threatens to fill hell even though it were empty; Lord Grizzle only to fill up the chinks, supposing the rest already full.

[2] Mr Addison is generally thought to have had this simile in his eye when he wrote that beautiful one at the end of the third act of his *Cato*.

[3] This beautiful simile is founded on a proverb which does honour to the English language:

> Between two stools the breech falls to the ground.

I am not so well pleased with any written remains of the ancients, as with those little aphorisms which verbal tradition hath delivered down to us, under the title of proverbs. It were to be wished that instead of filling their pages with the fabulous theology of the pagans, our modern poets would think it worth their while to enrich their works with the proverbial sayings of their ancestors. Mr Dryden hath chronicled one in heroic:

> Two ifs scarce make one possibility.   Conquest of Granada.

My Lord Bacon is of opinion, that whatever is known of arts and sciences might be proved to have lurked in the Proverbs of Solomon. I am of the same opinion in relation to those above mentioned. At least I am confident that a more perfect system of ethics, as well as economy, might be compiled out of them than is at present extant, either in the works of the ancient philosophers, or those more valuable, as more voluminous, ones of the modern divines.

Act III

SCENE 1

SCENE: *King Arthur's Palace.*

Ghost, solus.[1]

Hail! ye black horrors of midnight's midnoon!
Ye fairies, goblins, bats and screech-owls, hail!
And oh! ye mortal watchmen, whose hoarse throats
The immortal ghosts dread croaking counterfeit,
All hail! — Ye dancing phantoms, who by day
Are some condemned to fast, some feast in fire;
Now play in churchyards, skipping o'er the graves,
To the loud music of the silent bell.[2]
All hail!

SCENE 2

King and Ghost.

KING What noise is this — what villain dares,
  At this dread hour, with feet and voice profane,

[1] Of all the particulars in which the modern stage falls short of the ancient, there is none so much to be lamented as the great scarcity of ghosts in the latter. Whence this proceeds I will not presume to determine. Some are of opinion that the moderns are unequal to that sublime language which a ghost ought to speak. One says ludicrously that ghosts are out of fashion; another that they are properer for comedy; forgetting, I suppose, that Aristotle hath told us that a ghost is the soul of tragedy; for so I render the ψυχὴ ὁ μῦθος τῆς τραγῳδίας, which M Dacier, amongst others, hath mistaken; I suppose misled by not understanding the *fabula* of the Latins, which signifies a ghost as well as a fable.
  — *Te premet nox, fabulæque manes.*   Hor.
  Of all the ghosts that have ever appeared on the stage, a very learned and judicious foreign critic gives the preference to this of our author. These are his words, speaking of this tragedy: . . . *Nec quidquam in illâ admirabilius quam phasma quoddam horrendum, quod omnibus aliis spectris, quibuscum scatet Anglorum tragædia, longè* (*pace D—isii* V. *Doctiss. dixerim*) *prætulerim.*
[2] We have already given instances of this figure.

Disturb our royal walls?

GHOST   One who defies
Thy empty power to hurt him; one who dares
Walk in thy bedchamber.[1]

KING   Presumptuous slave!
Thou diest.

GHOST   Threaten others with that word,
I am a ghost, and am already dead.[2]

KING Ye stars! 'tis well; were thy last hour to come
This moment had been it; yet by thy shroud
I'll pull thee backward, squeeze thee to a bladder,
Till thou dost groan thy nothingness away.[3]
Thou fliest! 'Tis well.   *Ghost retires.*
I thought what was the courage of a ghost![4]
Yet dare not, on thy life – Why say I that,
Since life thou hast not? – Dare not walk again
Within these walls, on pain of the Red Sea.
For, if henceforth I ever find thee here,
As sure, sure as a gun, I'll have thee laid –

GHOST Were the Red Sea a sea of Hollands gin,
The liquor (when alive) whose very smell
I did detest, did loathe – yet, for the sake
Of Thomas Thumb, I would be laid therein.

---

[1] Almanzor reasons in the same manner:
     – A ghost I'll be,
     And from a ghost, you know, no place is free.
                                Conquest of Granada.

[2] 'The man who writ this wretched pun,' says Mr D—, 'would have picked your pocket.' Which he proceeds to show not only bad in itself, but doubly so on so solemn an occasion. And yet in that excellent play of *Liberty Asserted* we find something very much resembling a pun in the mouth of a mistress, who is parting with the lover she is fond of:
     Ul. *Oh, mortal woe! one kiss, and then farewell.*
     Irene. *The gods have given to others to fare well.*
     O miserably must Irene fare.

[3] Agamemnon, in the *Victim*, is full as facetious on the most solemn occasion, that of sacrificing his daughter:
     Yes, daughter, yes; you will assist the priest;
     Yes, you must offer up your – vows for Greece.

     I'll pull thee backwards by thy shroud to light,
     Or else I'll squeeze thee, like a bladder, there,
     And make thee groan thyself away to air.   Conquest of Granada.
     Snatch me, ye gods, this moment into nothing.   Cyrus the Great.

[4]   *So art thou gone? Thou canst no conquest boast,*
     I thought what was the courage of a ghost.   Conquest of Granada.
King Arthur seems to be as brave a fellow as Almanzor, who says most heroically:
     – In spite of ghosts I'll on

KING Ha! said you?

GHOST   Yes, my liege, I said Tom Thumb,
  Whose father's ghost I am – once not unknown
  To mighty Arthur. But, I see, 'tis true,
  The dearest friend, when dead, we all forget.

KING 'Tis he, it is the honest Gaffer Thumb!
  Oh! let me press thee in my eager arms,
  Thou best of ghosts! Thou something more than ghost!

GHOST Would I were something more, that we again
  Might feel each other in the warm embrace.
  But now I have the advantage of my King,
  For I feel thee, whilst thou dost not feel me.[1]

KING But say, thou dearest air,[2] oh! say what dread,
  Important business sends thee back to earth?

GHOST Oh! then prepare to hear – which but to hear,
  Is full enough to send thy spirit hence.
  Thy subjects up in arms, by Grizzle led,
  Will, ere the rosy-fingered morn shall ope
  The shutters of the sky, before the gate
  Of this thy royal palace swarming spread;
  So have I seen the bees in clusters swarm,
  So have I seen the stars in frosty nights,
  So have I seen the sand in windy days,
  So have I seen the ghosts on Pluto's shore,
  So have I seen the flowers in spring arise,
  So have I seen the leaves in autumn fall,
  So have I seen the fruits in summer smile,
  So have I seen the snow in winter frown.[3]

KING D—n all thou'st seen! – Dost thou, beneath the shape
  Of Gaffer Thumb, come hither to abuse me
  With similes to keep me on the rack?
  Hence – or, by all the torments of thy hell,
  I'll run thee through the body, though thou'st none.[4]

[1] The ghost of Lausaria in *Cyrus* is a plain copy of this, and is therefore worth reading:
  > *Ah, Cyrus!*
  > *Thou mayest as well grasp water, or fleet air,*
  > *As think of touching my immortal shade.*   Cyrus the Great.

[2]   *Thou better part of heavenly air.*   Conquest of Granada.

[3] 'A string of similes,' says one, 'proper to be hung up in the cabinet of a prince.'

[4] This passage hath been understood several different ways by the commentators. For my part I find it difficult to understand it at all. Mr Dryden says:
  > *I have heard something how two bodies meet,*
  > *But how two souls join I know not.*

So that till the body of a spirit is better understood, it will be difficult to understand how it is possible to run him through it.

GHOST Arthur, beware; I must this moment hence,
Not frighted by your voice, but by the cocks;
Arthur, beware, beware, beware, beware!
Strive to avert thy yet impending fate;
For if thou'rt killed to-day,
To-morrow all thy care will come too late.

SCENE 3

King, solus.

KING Oh! stay, and leave me not uncertain thus!
And whilst thou tellest me what's like my fate,
Oh! teach me how I may avert it too!
Curst be the man who first a simile made!
Curst ev'ry bard who writes! – So have I seen
Those whose comparisons are just and true,
And those who liken things not like at all.
The devil is happy that the whole creation
Can furnish out no simile to his fortune.

SCENE 4

King, Queen.

QUEEN What is the cause, my Arthur, that you steal
Thus silently from Dollallolla's breast?
Why dost thou leave me in the dark alone,[1]
When well thou know'st I am afraid of sprites?
KING Oh, Dollallolla! do not blame my love;
I hoped the fumes of last night's punch had laid
Thy lovely eyelids fast. But, oh! I find
There is no power in drams to quiet wives;
Each morn, as the returning sun, they wake,
And shine upon their husbands.
QUEEN Think, oh! think
What a surprise it must be to the sun,
Rising, to find the vanished world away.
What less can be the wretched wife's surprise

---

[1] Cydaria is of the same fearful temper with Dollallolla:
  I never durst in darkness be alone.   Ind. Emp.

When, stretching out her arms to fold thee fast,
She folds her useless bolster in her arms!
Think, think on that – oh! think, think well on that![1]
I do remember also to have read
In Dryden's *Ovid's Metamorphoses*,
That Jove in form inanimate did lie
With beauteous Danae;[2] and trust me, love,
I feared the bolster might have been a Jove.[3]
KING   Come to my arms, most virtuous of thy sex;
Oh, Dollallolla! were all wives like thee,
So many husbands never had worn horns.
Should Huncamunca of thy worth partake,
Tom Thumb indeed were blest. – Oh fatal name!
For didst thou know one quarter what I know,
Then wouldst thou know – alas! what thou wouldst know!
QUEEN   What can I gather hence? Why dost thou speak
Like men who carry raree-shows about!
Now you shall see, gentlemen, what you shall see.
O tell me more, or thou hast told too much.

SCENE 5

King, Queen, Noodle.

NOODLE   Long life attend your Majesties serene,
Great Arthur, King, and Dollallolla, Queen!
Lord Grizzle, with a bold rebellious crowd,
Advances to the palace, threat'ning loud,
Unless the Princess be delivered straight,
And the victorious Thumb, without his pate,
They are resolved to batter down the gate.

---

[1]   *Think well of this, think that, think every way.*   Sophonisba.
[2] These quotations are more usual in the comic than in the tragic writers.
[3] 'This distress,' says Mr D—, 'I must allow to be extremely beautiful, and tends to heighten the virtuous character of Dollallolla, who is so exceedingly delicate, that she is in the highest apprehension from the inanimate embrace of a bolster. An example worthy of imitation from all our writers of tragedy.'

SCENE 6

King, Queen, Huncamunca, Noodle.

KING See where the Princess comes! Where is Tom Thumb?

HUNCAMUNCA Oh! sir, about an hour and half ago
    He sallied out to encounter with the foe,
    And swore, unless his fate had him misled,
    From Grizzle's shoulders to cut off his head,
    And serv't up with your chocolate in bed.

KING 'Tis well, I find one devil told us both.
    Come, Dollallolla, Huncamunca, come,
    Within we'll wait for the victorious Thumb;
    In peace and safety we secure may stay,
    While to his arm we trust the bloody fray;
    Though men and giants should conspire with gods,
    He is alone equal to all these odds.[1]

QUEEN He is, indeed, a helmet[2] to us all,
    While he supports we need not fear to fall;
    His arm dispatches all things to our wish,
    And serves up ev'ry foe's head in a dish.
    Void is the mistress of the house of care,

---

[1] *Credat Judæus Apella.*

'*Non ego –* ', says Mr D—. 'For, passing over the absurdity of being equal to odds, can we possibly suppose a little insignificant fellow – I say again, a little insignificant fellow – able to vie with a strength which all the Samsons and Herculeses of antiquity would be unable to encounter?'

I shall refer this incredulous critic to Mr Dryden's defence of his Almanzor; and lest that should not satisify him, I shall quote a few lines from the speech of a much braver fellow than Almanzor, Mr Johnson's Achilles:

> *Though human race rise in embattled hosts,*
> *To force her from my arms – O son of Atreus*
> *By that immortal power, whose deathless spirit*
> *Informs this earth, I will oppose them all.*   Victim.

[2] 'I have heard of being supported by a staff,' says Mr D—, 'but never of being supported by a helmet.' I believe he never heard of sailing with wings, which he may read in no less a poet than Mr Dryden:

> *Unless we borrow wings, and sail through air.*   Love Triumph.

What will he say to a kneeling valley!

> *– I'll stand*
> *Like a safe valley, that low bends the knee*
> *To some aspiring mountain.*   Injured Love.

I am ashamed of so ignorant a carper, who doth not know that an epithet in tragedy is very often no other than an expletive. Do not we read in the new *Sophonisba* of 'grinding chains', 'blue plagues', 'white occasions', and 'blue serenity'? Nay, 'tis not the adjective only, but sometimes half a sentence is put by way of expletive, as 'Beauty pointed high with spirit', in the same play, and 'In the lap of blessing, to be most cursed', in the *Revenge*.

While the good cook presents the bill of fare;
Whether the cod, that northern king of fish,
Or duck, or goose, or pig, adorn the dish,
No fears the number of her guests afford,
But at her hour she sees the dinner on the board.

SCENE 7

SCENE: *A plain.*

Lord Grizzle, Foodle, and Rebels.

GRIZZLE Thus far our arms with victory are crowned;
　　For though we have not fought, yet we have found
　　No enemy to fight withal.[1]
FOODLE　　　　　　　Yet I,
　　Methinks, would willingly avoid this day,
　　This first of April, to engage our foes.[2]
GRIZZLE This day, of all the days of the year, I'd choose,
　　For on this day my grandmother was born.
　　Gods! I will make Tom Thumb an April fool;
　　Will teach his wit an errand it ne'er knew,
　　And send it post to the Elysian shades.[3]
FOODLE I'm glad to find our army is so stout,
　　Nor does it move my wonder less than joy.
GRIZZLE What friends we have, and how we came so strong,
　　I'll softly tell you as we march along.[4]

SCENE 8

SCENE: *Thunder and lightning.*

Tom Thumb, Glumdalca, cum suis.

THUMB Oh, Noodle! hast thou seen a day like this?
　　The unborn thunder rumbles o'er our heads,[5]

[1] A victory like that of Almanzor:
　　　　　　Almanzor is victorious without fight.　　Conq. of Granada.
[2]　　　　　*Well have we chose an happy day for fight,*
　　　　　　For every man in course of time has found,
　　　　　　Some days are lucky, some unfortunate.　　K. Arthur.
[3] We read of such another in Lee:
　　　　　　Teach his rude wit a flight she never made,
　　　　　　And sent her post to the Elysian shade.　　Gloriana.
[4] These lines are copied verbatim in the *Indian Emperor.*
[5]　　　　　*Unborn thunder rolling in a cloud.*　　Conq. of Granada.

As if the gods meant to unhinge the world;
And heaven and earth in wild confusion hurl;
Yet I will boldly tread the tott'ring ball.[1]

MERLIN Tom Thumb!

THUMB What voice is this I hear?

MERLIN Tom Thumb!

THUMB Again it calls.

MERLIN Tom Thumb!

GLUMDALCA It calls again.

THUMB Appear, whoe'er thou art, I fear thee not.

MERLIN Thou hast no cause to fear, I am thy friend.
Merlin by name, a conjurer by trade,
And to my art thou dost thy being owe.

THUMB How!

MERLIN Hear then the mystic getting of Tom Thumb.

> His father was a ploughman plain,
> His mother milked the cow:
> And yet the way to get a son,
> This couple knew not how.
> Until such time the good old man
> To learned Merlin goes,
> And there to him, in great distress,
> In secret manner shows,
> How in his heart he wished to have
> A child, in time to come,
> To be his heir, though it might be
> No bigger than his thumb:
> Of which old Merlin was foretold,
> That he his wish should have
> And so a son of stature small,
> The charmer to him gave.[2]

Thou'st heard the past, look up and see the future.

THUMB Lost in amazement's gulf my senses sink;[3]

---

[1]
> Were heaven and earth in wild confusion hurled,
> Should the rash gods unhinge the rolling world,
> Undaunted would I tread the tott'ring ball,
> Crushed, but unconquered, in the dreadful fall.   Female Warrior.

[2] See the History of Tom Thumb, page 2.

[3]
> – Amazement swallows up my sense,
> And in th' impetuous whirl of circling fate
> Drinks down my reason.   Persian Princess.

See there, Glumdalca, see another me![1]

GLUMDALCA O sight of horror! see, you are devoured
By the expanded jaws of a red cow.

MERLIN Let not these sights deter thy noble mind,
For lo! a sight more glorious courts thy eyes;
See from afar a theatre arise;
There ages yet unborn shall tribute pay
To the heroic actions of this day:
Then buskin tragedy at length shall choose
Thy name the best supporter of her muse.[2]

THUMB Enough, let every warlike music sound,
We fall contented, if we fall renowned.

SCENE 9

*Lord Grizzle, Foodle, Rebels, on one side. Tom Thumb,
Glumdalca, on the other.*

FOODLE At length the enemy advances nigh,
I hear them with my ear, and see them with my eye.[3]

GRIZZLE Draw all your swords; for liberty we fight,
And liberty the mustard[4] is of life.

THUMB Are you the man whom men famed Grizzle name?

GRIZZLE Are you the much more famed Tom Thumb?[5]

THUMB   The same.

GRIZZLE Come on, our worth upon ourselves we'll prove,
For liberty I fight.

THUMB   And I for love.

---

[1]   – *I have outfaced myself,*
          What! am I two? Is there another me?   K. Arthur.

[2] The character of Merlin is wonderful throughout, but most so in this prophetic part.
We find several of these prophecies in the tragic authors, who frequently take this
opportunity to pay a compliment to their country, and sometimes to their prince. None but
our author (who seems to have detested the least appearance of flattery) would have passed
by such an opportunity of being a political prophet.

[3]   *I saw the villain, Myron, with these eyes I saw him.*   Busiris.
In both which places it is intimated that it is sometime possible to see with other eyes than
your own.

[4] 'This mustard,' says Mr D—, 'is enough to turn one's stomach. I would be glad to
know what idea the author had in his head when he wrote it.' This will be, I believe, best
explained by a line of Mr Dennis:

          And gave him liberty, the salt of life.   Liberty Asserted.
The understanding that can digest the one, will not rise at the other.

[5]   Han. *Are you the chief whom men famed Scipio call?*
          Scip. *Are you the much more famous Hannibal?*   Hannibal.

A bloody engagement between the two armies here; drums beating, trumpets sounding, thunder and lightning. They fight off and on several times. Some fall. Grizzle and Glumdalca remain.

GLUMDALCA Turn, coward, turn, nor from a woman fly.

GRIZZLE Away – thou art too ignoble for my arm.

GLUMDALCA Have at thy heart.

GRIZZLE   Nay, then I thrust at thine.

GLUMDALCA You push too well, you've run me through the guts,
And I am dead.

GRIZZLE   Then there's an end of one.

THUMB When thou art dead, then there's an end of two,
Villain!

GRIZZLE Tom Thumb!

THUMB Rebel!

GRIZZLE Tom Thumb!

THUMB Hell!

GRIZZLE Huncamunca!¹

THUMB Thou hast it there.

GRIZZLE   Too sure I feel it.

THUMB To Hell then, like a rebel as you are,
And give my service to the rebels there.

GRIZZLE Triumph not, Thumb, nor think thou shalt enjoy
Thy Huncamunca undisturbed; I'll send
My ghost to fetch her to the other world;²
It shall but bait at Heaven, and then return.³

---

¹ Dr Young seems to have copied this engagement in his *Busiris*:
> Myr. *Villain!*
> Mem. *Myron!*
> Myr. *Rebel!*
> Mem. *Myron!*
> Myr. *Hell!*
> Mem. *Mandane.*

² This last speech of my Lord Grizzle hath been of great service to our poets:
> – *I'll hold it fast*
> *As life, and when life's gone I'll hold this last;*
> *And if thou tak'st it from me when I'm slain,*
> *I'll send my ghost and fetch it back again.*   Conq. of Granada.

³
> *My soul should with such speed obey,*
> *It should not bait at heaven to stop its way.*

Lee seems to have had this last in his eye:
> *'Twas not my purpose, sir, to tarry there,*
> *I would but go to heaven to take the air.*   Gloriana.

But, ha! I feel Death rumbling in my brains,[1]
Some kinder sprite knocks softly at my soul,[2]
And gently whispers it to haste away:
I come, I come, most willingly I come.
So when some city wife for country air,
To Hampstead or to Highgate does repair;[3]
Her, to make haste, her husband does implore,
And cries, 'My dear, the coach is at the door.'
With equal wish, desirous to be gone,
She gets into the coach, and then she cries: 'Drive on!'
THUMB With those last words he vomited his soul,[4]
Which, like whipped cream, the devil will swallow down.[5]
Bear off the body, and cut off the head,
Which I will to the King in triumph lug!
Rebellion's dead, and now I'll go to breakfast.

SCENE 10

King, Queen, Huncamunca, and Courtiers.

KING Open the prisons, set the wretched free,
And bid our treasurer disburse six pounds
To pay their debts. Let no one weep to-day.
Come, Dollallolla; curse that odious name!
It is so long it asks an hour to speak it.
By heavens! I'll change it into Doll, or Loll,
Or any other civil monosyllable
That will not tire my tongue.[6] – Come, sit thee down.
Here seated let us view the dancer's sports;
Bid 'em advance. This is the wedding-day
Of Princess Huncamunca and Tom Thumb;

---

[1]   *A rising vapour rumbling in my brains.*   Cleomenes.
[2]   *Some kind sprite knocks softly at my soul,*
           To tell me Fate's at hand.
[3] Mr Dryden seems to have had this simile in his eye when he says:
               My soul is packing up, and just on wing.   Conq. of Granada.
[4]   *And in a purple vomit poured his soul.*
[5]   *The devil swallows vulgar souls*
           Like whipped cream.
[6]   *How I could curse my name of Ptolemy!*   Sebastian.
           It is so long it asks an hour to write it.
           By heaven! I'll change it into Jove, or Mars,
           Or any other civil monosyllable,
           That will not tire my hand.   Cleomenes.

Tom Thumb! who wins two victories to-day,[1]
And this way marches, bearing Grizzle's head.

A dance here.

NOODLE Oh! monstrous, dreadful, terrible! Oh! Oh!
  Deaf be my ears, for ever blind my eyes!
  Dumb be my tongue! feet lame! all senses lost!
  Howl wolves, grunt bears, hiss snakes, shriek all ye ghosts![2]
KING What does the blockhead mean?
NOODLE   I mean, my liege,
  Only to grace my tale with decent horror;[3]
  Whilst from my garret, twice two stories high,
  I looked abroad into the streets below,
  I saw Tom Thumb attended by the mob,
  Twice twenty shoe-boys, twice two dozen links,
  Chairmen and porters, hackney-coachmen, whores;
  Aloft he bore the grizly head of Grizzle;
  When of a sudden through the streets there came
  A cow, of larger than the usual size,
  And in a moment – guess, oh! guess the rest!
  And in a moment swallowed up Tom Thumb.
KING Shut up again the prisons, bid my treasurer
  Not give three farthings out – hang all the culprits,
  Guilty or not, no matter – ravish virgins.
  Go bid the schoolmasters whip all their boys;
  Let lawyers, parsons, and physicians loose,
  To rob, impose on, and to kill the world.
NOODLE Her Majesty the Queen is in a swoon.
QUEEN Not so much in a swoon, but I have still
  Strength to reward the messenger of ill news.   *Kills Noodle.*
NOODLE Oh! I am slain.
CLEORA My lover's killed, I will revenge him so.
                                          Kills the Queen.

---

  [1] Here is a visible conjunction of two days in one, by which our author may have either intended an emblem of a wedding, or to insinuate that men in the honeymoon are apt to imagine time shorter than it is. It brings into my mind a passage in the comedy called the *Coffee-House Politician*:
          We will celebrate this day at my house to-morrow.
  [2] These beautiful phrases are all to be found in one single speech of *King Arthur*, or *The British Worthy*.
  [3]   *I was but teaching him to grace his tale*
             With decent horror.   Cleomenes.

ACT III   257

HUNCAMUNCA My mamma killed! vile murderers, beware.
                                                   Kills Cleora.

DOODLE This for an old grudge, to thy heart.
                                             Kills Huncamunca.

MUSTACHA   And this
I drive to thine, O Doodle! for a new one.   *Kills Doodle.*
KING Ha! Murderess vile, take that.   *Kills Mustacha.*
           And take thou this.   *Kills himself, and falls.*
So when the child whom nurse from danger guards,
Sends Jack for mustard with a pack of cards;
Kings, queens and knaves throw one another down,
Till the whole pack lies scattered and o'erthrown;
So all our pack upon the floor is cast,
And all I boast is – that I fall the last.[1]   *Dies.*

[1] We may say with Dryden:
> *Death did at length so many slain forget,*
> *And left the tale, and took them by the great.*

I know of no tragedy which comes nearer to this charming and bloody catastrophe than *Cleomenes*, where the curtain covers five principal characters dead on the stage. These lines, too,
> *I ask no questions then, of Who killed who?*
> *The bodies tell the story as they lie,*

seem to have belonged more properly to this scene of our author. – Nor can I help imagining they were originally his. The *Rival Ladies*, too, seems beholden to this scene:
> *We're now a chain of lovers linked in death,*
> *Julia goes first, Gonsalvo hangs on her,*
> *And Angelina hangs upon Gonsalvo,*
> *As I on Angelina.*

No scene, I believe, ever received greater honours than this. It was applauded by several encores, a word very unusual in tragedy – and it was very difficult for the actors to escape without a second slaughter. This I take to be a lively assurance of that fierce spirit of liberty which remains among us, and which Mr Dryden, in his *Essay on Dramatic Poetry*, hath observed: 'Whether custom,' says he, 'hath so insinuated itself into our countrymen, or Nature hath so formed them to fierceness, I know not, but they will scarely suffer combats, and other objects of horror, to be taken from them.' And indeed I am for having them encouraged in this martial disposition. Nor do I believe our victories over the French have been owing to anything more than to those bloody spectacles daily exhibited in our tragedies, of which the French stage is so entirely clear.

THE LONDON MERCHANT,
OR
THE HISTORY OF
GEORGE BARNWELL

To Sir John Eyles, Bar.

Member of Parliament for, and Alderman of the City of London, and sub-Governor of the South-Sea Company.

Sir,

If tragic poetry be, as Mr Dryden has somewhere said, the most excellent and most useful kind of writing, the more extensively useful the moral of any tragedy is, the more excellent that piece must be of its kind.

I hope I shall not be thought to insinuate that this, to which I have presumed to prefix your name, is such; that depends on its fitness to answer the end of tragedy, the exciting of the passions, in order to the correcting such of them as are criminal, either in their nature, or through their excess. Whether the following scenes do this in any tolerable degree, is, with the deference that becomes one who would not be thought vain, submitted to your candid and impartial judgment.

What I would infer is this, I think, evident truth; that tragedy is so far from losing its dignity, by being accommodated to the circumstances of the generality of mankind, that it is more truly august in proportion to the extent of its influence, and the numbers that are properly affected by it. As it is more truly great to be the instrument of good to many, who stand in need of our assistance, than to a very small part of that number.

If princes etc., were alone liable to misfortune, arising from vice or weakness in themselves or others, there would be good reason for confining the characters in tragedy to those of superior rank; but, since the contrary is evident, nothing can be more reasonable than to proportion the remedy to the disease.

I am far from denying that tragedies, founded on any instructive and extraordinary events in history, or a well-invented fable, where the persons introduced are of the highest rank, are without their use, even to the bulk of the audience. The strong contrast between a Tamerlane and a Bajazet, may have its weight with an unsteady people, and contribute to the fixing of them in the interest of a prince of the character of the former, when through their own levity, or the arts of designing men, they are rendered factious and uneasy, though they have the highest reason to be satisfied. The sentiments and example of a Cato may inspire his spectators with a just sense of the value of liberty, when they see that honest patriot prefer death to an obligation from a tyrant who would sacrifice the constitution of his country, and the liberties of mankind, to his ambition or revenge. I have attempted, indeed, to enlarge the province of the graver kind of poetry, and should be glad to see it carried on by some abler hand. Plays founded on moral tales in private life may be of admirable use, by carrying conviction to the mind with such irresistible force as to engage all the faculties and powers of the soul in the cause of virtue, by stifling vice in its first principles. They who imagine this to be too much to be attributed to tragedy, must be strangers to the energy of that noble species of poetry. Shakespeare, who has given such amazing proofs of his genius, in that as well as in comedy, in his *Hamlet* has the following lines:

> *Had he the motive and the cause for passion*
> *That I have, he would drown the stage with tears*
> *And cleave the general ear with horrid speech;*
> *Make mad the guilty, and appal the free,*
> *Confound the ignorant; and amaze indeed*
> *The very faculty of eyes and ears.*

and farther in the same speech:

> *I've heard that guilty creatures at a play*
> *Have, by the very cunning of the scene,*
> *Been so struck to the soul, that presently*
> *They have proclaimed their malefactions.*

Prodigious! yet strictly just. But I shan't take up your valuable time with my remarks; only give me leave just to observe, that he seems so firmly persuaded of the power of a well-wrote piece to produce the effect here ascribed to it, as to make Hamlet venture his soul on the event, and rather trust that than a messenger from the other world, though it assumed, as he expresses it, his noble father's form, and assured him that it was his spirit. 'I'll have,' says Hamlet, 'grounds more relative;

> . . . *The Play's the thing,*
> *Wherein I'll catch the conscience of the King.*'

Such plays are the best answers to them who deny the lawfulness of the stage.

Considering the novelty of this attempt, I thought it would be expected from me to say something in its excuse; and I was unwilling to lose the opportunity of saying something of the usefulness of tragedy in general, and what may be reasonably expected from the farther improvement of this excellent kind of poetry.

Sir, I hope you will not think I have said too much of an art, a mean specimen of which I am ambitious enough to recommend to your favour and protection. A mind, conscious of superior worth, as much despises flattery as it is above it. Had I found in myself an inclination to so contemptible a vice, I should not have chosen Sir JOHN EYLES for my patron. And indeed the best writ panegyric, though strictly true, must place you in a light much inferior to that in which you have long been fixed by the love and esteem of your fellow-citizens; whose choice of you for one of their representatives in Parliament has sufficiently declared their sense of your merit. Nor hath the knowledge of your worth been confined to the city. The proprietors in the South Sea Company, in which are included numbers of persons as considerable for their rank, fortune, and understanding, as any in the kingdom, gave the greatest proof of their confidence in your capacity and probity, when they chose you Sub-Governor of their Company, at a time when their affairs were in the utmost confusion, and their properties in the greatest danger. Nor is the Court insensible of your importance. I shall not, therefore, attempt your character, nor pretend to add anything to a reputation so well established.

Whatever others may think of a Dedication wherein there is so much said of other things, and so little of the person to whom it is addressed, I have reason to believe that you will the more easily pardon it on that very account.

> I am, Sir,
> Your most obedient
> humble servant,
> GEORGE LILLO

Prologue

Spoken by Mr Cibber, junior.

The tragic muse, sublime, delights to show
Princes distressed, and scenes of royal woe;
In awful pomp, majestic, to relate
The fall of nations, or some hero's fate;
That sceptred chiefs may, by example, know
The strange vicissitude of things below;
What dangers on security attend;
How pride and cruelty in ruin end;
Hence, Providence supreme to know, and own
Humanity, adds glory to a throne.
In ev'ry former age, and foreign tongue,
With native grandeur thus the goddess sung.
Upon our stage, indeed, with wished success,
You've sometimes seen her in a humbler dress –
Great only in distress. When she complains
In Southerne's, Rowe's, or Otway's moving strains,
The brilliant drops that fall from each bright eye,
The absent pomp with brighter gems supply.
Forgive us, then, if we attempt to show,
In artless strains, a tale of private woe.
A London 'prentice ruined is our theme,
Drawn from the famed old song that bears his name.
We hope your taste is not so high, to scorn
A moral tale esteemed ere you were born;
Which, for a century of rolling years,
Has filled a thousand, thousand eyes with tears.
If thoughtless youth to warn, and shame the age
From vice destructive, well becomes the stage;
If this example innocence secure,
Prevent our guilt, or by reflection cure;

If Millwood's dreadful guilt, and sad despair,
Commend the virtue of the good and fair;
Though art be wanting, and our numbers fail,
Indulge th' attempt in justice to the tale.

Dramatis Personæ

MEN

THOROWGOOD	Mr Bridgwater
BARNWELL, *Uncle to George*	Mr Roberts
GEORGE BARNWELL	Mr Cibber, Jun.
TRUEMAN	Mr W. Mills
BLUNT	Mr R. Wetherilt

WOMEN

MARIA	Mrs Cibber
MILLWOOD	Mrs Butler
LUCY	Mrs Charke

Officers with their Attendants, Keeper and Footmen.

SCENE
London, and an adjacent village

Act I

SCENE I

SCENE: *A room in Thorowgood's house.*

Thorowgood and Trueman.

TRUEMAN Sir, the packet from Genoa is arrived.

Gives letters.

THOROWGOOD Heaven be praised! The storm that threatened our royal mistress, pure religion, liberty, and laws, is for a time diverted. The haughty and revengeful Spaniard, disappointed of the loan on which he depended from Genoa, must now attend the slow return of wealth from his new world, to supply his empty coffers, ere he can execute his purposed invasion of our happy island. By which means time is gained to make such preparations on our part, as may, Heaven concurring, prevent his malice, or turn the meditated mischief on himself.

TRUEMAN He must be insensible indeed, who is not affected when the safety of his country is concerned. Sir, may I know by what means? If am too bold —

THOROWGOOD Your curiosity is laudable; and I gratify it with the greater pleasure, because from thence you may learn how honest merchants, as such, may sometimes contribute to the safety of their country, as they do at all times to its happiness; that if hereafter you should be tempted to any action that has the appearance of vice or meanness in it, upon reflecting on the dignity of our profession, you may, with honest scorn, reject whatever is unworthy of it.

TRUEMAN Should Barnwell, or I, who have the benefit of your example, by our ill-conduct bring any imputation on that honourable name, we must be left without excuse.

THOROWGOOD You compliment, young man. (*Trueman bows*

respectfully). Nay, I am not offended. As the name of merchant never degrades the gentleman, so by no means does it exclude him; only take heed not to purchase the character of complaisant at the expense of your sincerity. But to answer your question: The bank of Genoa had agreed, at excessive interest, and on good security, to advance the King of Spain a sum of money sufficient to equip his vast Armada; of which our peerless Elizabeth (more than in name the mother of her people) being well informed, sent Walsingham, her wise and faithful secretary, to consult the merchants of this loyal city; who all agreed to direct their several agents to influence, if possible, the Genoese to break their contract with the Spanish Court. 'Tis done; the state and bank of Genoa, having maturely weighed, and rightly judged of their true interest, prefer the friendship of the merchants of London to that of the monarch who proudly styles himself King of both Indies.

TRUEMAN Happy success of prudent counsels! What an expense of blood and treasure is here saved! Excellent queen! O how unlike to former princes, who made the danger of foreign enemies a pretence to oppress their subjects by taxes great and grievous to be borne.

THOROWGOOD Not so our gracious queen, whose richest exchequer is her people's love, as their happiness her greatest glory.

TRUEMAN On these terms to defend us, is to make our protection a benefit worthy her who confers it, and well worth our acceptance. Sir, have you any commands for me at this time?

THOROWGOOD Only to look carefully over the files, to see whether there are any tradesmen's bills unpaid; if there are, to send and discharge 'em. We must not let artificers lose their time, so useful to the public and their families, in unnecessary attendance.

SCENE 2

Thorowgood and Maria.

Well, Maria, have you given orders for the entertainment? I would have it in some measure worthy the guests. Let there be plenty, and of the best, that the courtiers, though they should deny us citizens politeness, may at least commend our hospitality.

MARIA Sir, I have endeavoured not to wrong your well-known generosity by an ill-timed parsimony.

THOROWGOOD Nay, 'twas a needless caution: I have no cause to doubt your prudence.

MARIA Sir, I find myself unfit for conversation at present; I should but increase the number of the company, without adding to their satisfaction.

THOROWGOOD Nay, my child, this melancholy must not be indulged.

MARIA Company will but increase it: I wish you would dispense with my absence. Solitude best suits my present temper.

THOROWGOOD You are not insensible that it is chiefly on your account these noble lords do me the honour so frequently to grace my board. Should you be absent, the disappointment may make them repent their condescension, and think their labour lost.

MARIA He that shall think his time or honour lost in visiting you, can set no real value on your daughter's company; whose only merit is, that she is yours. The man of quality who chooses to converse with a gentleman and merchant of your worth and character, may confer honour by so doing, but he loses none.

THOROWGOOD Come, come, Maria; I need not tell you that a young gentleman may prefer your conversation to mine, yet intend me no disrespect at all; for though he may lose no honour in my company, 'tis very natural for him to expect more pleasure in yours. I remember the time when the company of the greatest and wisest man in the kingdom would have been insipid and tiresome to me, if it had deprived me of an opportunity of enjoying your mother's.

MARIA Yours, no doubt, was as agreeable to her; for generous minds know no pleasure in society but where 'tis mutual.

THOROWGOOD Thou knowest I have no heir, no child, but thee; the fruits of many years' successful industry must all be thine. Now it would give me pleasure, great as my love, to see on whom you will bestow it. I am daily solicited by men of the greatest rank and merit for leave to address you; but I have hitherto declined it, in hopes that, by observation, I should learn which way your inclination tends; for, as I know love to be essential to happiness in the marriage state, I had rather my approbation should confirm your choice than direct it.

MARIA What can I say! How shall I answer, as I ought, this tenderness, so uncommon even in the best of parents! But you are without example; yet, had you been less indulgent, I had been most wretched. That I look on the crowd of courtiers that visit here, with equal esteem, but equal indifference, you have observed, and I must needs confess; yet, had you asserted your authority, and insisted on a parent's right to be obeyed, I had submitted, and to my duty sacrificed my peace.

THOROWGOOD From your perfect obedience in every other instance, I feared as much; and therefore would leave you without a bias, in an affair wherein your happiness is so immediately concerned.

MARIA Whether from a want of that just ambition that would become your daughter, or from some other cause, I know not; but I find high birth and titles don't recommend the man who owns them to my affection.

THOROWGOOD I would not that they should, unless his merit recommends him more. A noble birth and fortune, though they make not a bad man good, yet they are a real advantage to a worthy one, and place his virtues in the fairest light.

MARIA I cannot answer for my inclinations; but they shall ever be submitted to your wisdom and authority. And as you will not compel me to marry where I cannot love, so love shall never make me act contrary to my duty – Sir, have I your permission to retire?

THOROWGOOD I'll see you to your chamber.

SCENE 3

SCENE: *A room in Millwood's house.*

Millwood, Lucy waiting.

MILLWOOD How do I look to-day, Lucy?

LUCY Oh, killingly, madam? A little more red, and you'll be irresistible! But why this more than ordinary care of your dress and complexion? What new conquest are you aiming at?

MILLWOOD A conquest would be new, indeed!

LUCY Not to you, who make 'em every day – but to me – Well!

'tis what I'm never to expect, unfortunate as I am. But your wit and beauty —

MILLWOOD First made me a wretch, and still continue me so. Men, however generous or sincere to one another, are all selfish hypocrites in their affairs with us; we are no otherwise esteemed or regarded by them, but as we contribute to their satisfaction.

LUCY You are certainly, madam, on the wrong side in this argument. Is not the expense all theirs? And I am sure it is our own fault, if we han't our share of the pleasure.

MILLWOOD We are but slaves to men.

LUCY Nay, 'tis they that are slaves, most certainly, for we lay them under contribution.

MILLWOOD Slaves have no property; no, not even in themselves: all is the victor's.

LUCY You are strangely arbitrary in your principles, madam.

MILLWOOD I would have my conquests complete, like those of the Spaniards in the New World; who first plundered the natives of all the wealth they had, and then condemned the wretches to the mines for life, to work for more.

LUCY Well, I shall never approve of your scheme of government: I should think it much more politic, as well as just, to find my subjects an easier employment.

MILLWOOD It is a general maxim among the knowing part of mankind, that a woman without virtue, like a man without honour or honesty, is capable of any action, though never so vile. And yet what pains will they not take, what arts not use, to seduce us from our innocence, and make us contemptible and wicked, even, in their own opinion? Then is it not just, the villains to their cost should find us so? But guilt makes them suspicious, and keeps them on their guard; therefore we can take advantage only of the young and innocent part of the sex; who, having never injured women, apprehend no injury from them.

LUCY Ay, they must be young indeed!

MILLWOOD Such a one, I think, I have found. As I've passed through the city, I have often observed him receiving and paying considerable sums of money; from thence I conclude he is employed in affairs of consequence.

LUCY Is he handsome?

MILLWOOD Ay, ay, the stripling is well made.

LUCY About —

MILLWOOD Eighteen.

LUCY Innocent, handsome, and about eighteen! You'll be vastly happy. Why, if you manage well, you may keep him to yourself these two or three years.

MILLWOOD If I manage well, I shall have done with him much sooner. Having long had a design on him, and meeting him yesterday, I made a full stop, and gazing wishfully on his face, asked him his name. He blushed; and, bowing very low, answered, George Barnwell. I begged his pardon for the freedom I had taken, and told him that he was the person I had long wished to see, and to whom I had an affair of importance to communicate at a proper time and place. He named a tavern; I talked of honour and reputation, and invited him to my house. He swallowed the bait, promised to come, and this is the time I expect him. (*Knocking at the door.*) Somebody knocks — D'ye hear; I am at home to nobody to-day but him.

SCENE 4

Millwood.

MILLWOOD Less affairs must give way to those of more consequence; and I am strangely mistaken if this does not prove of great importance to me and him too, before I have done with him. Now, after what manner shall I receive him? Let me consider — what manner of person am I to receive? He is young, innocent, and bashful; therefore I must take care not to shock him at first. But then, if I have any skill in physiognomy, he is amorous, and, with a little assistance, will soon get the better of his modesty. I'll trust to nature, who does wonders in these matters. If to seem what one is not, in order to be the better liked for what one really is; if to speak one thing, and mean the direct contrary, be art in a woman, — I know nothing of nature.

SCENE 5

To her Barnwell, bowing very low. Lucy at a distance.

MILLWOOD Sir! the surprise and joy —

BARNWELL Madam —

MILLWOOD This is such a favour.   *Advancing.*

BARNWELL Pardon me, madam.

MILLWOOD So unhoped for.   *Still advances.*

             Barnwell salutes her, and retires in confusion.
To see you here. Excuse the confusion –

BARNWELL I fear I am too bold.

MILLWOOD Alas, sir! All my apprehensions proceed from my
fears of your thinking me so. Please, sir, to sit. I am as much
at a loss how to receive this honour as I ought, as I am
surprised at your goodness in conferring it.

BARNWELL I thought you had expected me: I promised to come.

MILLWOOD That is the more surprising; few men are such
religious observers of their word.

BARNWELL All, who are honest, are.

MILLWOOD To one another; but we silly women are seldom
thought of consequence enough to gain a place in your
remembrance.   *Laying her hand on his, as by accident.*

BARNWELL Her disorder is so great, she don't perceive she has
laid her hand on mine. Heaven! how she trembles! What can
this mean?   *Aside.*

MILLWOOD The interest I have in all that relates to you (the
reason of which you shall know hereafter) excites my curiosity; and were I sure you would pardon my presumption, I
should desire to know your real sentiments on a very particular affair.

BARNWELL Madam, you may command my poor thoughts on
any subject. I have none that I would conceal.

MILLWOOD You'll think me bold.

BARNWELL No, indeed.

MILLWOOD What, then, are your thoughts of love?

BARNWELL If you mean the love of women, I have not thought
of it [at] all. My youth and circumstances make such thoughts
improper in me yet. But if you mean the general love we owe
to mankind, I think no one has more of it in his temper than
myself. I don't know that person in the world whose happiness I don't wish, and wouldn't promote were it in my power.
In an especial manner I love my uncle, and my master; but
above all, my friend.

MILLWOOD You have a friend, then, whom you love?

BARNWELL As he does me, sincerely.

MILLWOOD He is, no doubt, often blessed with your company and conversation.

BARNWELL We live in one house together, and both serve the same worthy merchant.

MILLWOOD Happy, happy youth! Whoe'er thou art, I envy thee, and so must all who see and know this youth. What have I lost, by being formed a woman! I hate my sex, my self. Had I been a man, I might, perhaps, have been as happy in your friendship, as he who now enjoys it, but as it is – Oh! –

BARNWELL (*Aside.*) I never observed women before; or this is, sure, the most beautiful of her sex. You seem disordered, madam. May I know the cause?

MILLWOOD Do not ask me – I can never speak it, whatever is the cause. I wish for things impossible. I would be a servant, bound to the same master as you are, to live in one house with you.

BARNWELL (*Aside.*) How strange, and yet how kind, her words and actions are! And the effect they have on me is as strange. I feel desires I never knew before. I must be gone, while I have power to go. Madam, I humbly take my leave.

MILLWOOD You will not, sure, leave me so soon!

BARNWELL Indeed I must.

MILLWOOD You cannot be so cruel! I have prepared a poor supper, at which I promised myself your company.

BARNWELL I am sorry I must refuse the honour that you designed me: but my duty to my master calls me hence. I never yet neglected his service. He is so gentle and so good a master, that should I wrong him, though he might forgive me, I never should forgive myself.

MILLWOOD Am I refused by the first man, the second favour I ever stooped to ask? Go, then, thou proud, hard-hearted youth; but know, you are the only man that could be found who would let me sue twice for greater favours.

BARNWELL What shall I do! How shall I go, or stay!

MILLWOOD Yet do not, do not leave me! I wish my sex's pride would meet your scorn; but when I look upon you, when I behold those eyes – Oh! spare my tongue, and let my blushes speak – this flood of tears to[o], that will force its way, and declare – what woman's modesty should hide.

BARNWELL Oh, heaven! she loves me, worthless as I am. Her looks, her words, her flowing tears confess it. And can I leave

her, then? Oh, never, never! – Madam, dry up those tears:
you shall command me always; I will stay here for ever, if
you'd have me.

LUCY So! she has wheedled him out of his virtue of obedience
already, and will strip him of all the rest, one after another,
till she has left him as few as her ladyship or myself.   *Aside.*

MILLWOOD Now you are kind, indeed! but I mean not to detain
you always: I would have you shake off all slavish obedience
to your master; but you may serve him still.

LUCY Serve him still! Ay, or he'll have no opportunity of
fingering his cash; and then he'll not serve your end, I'll be
sworn.   *Aside.*

SCENE 6

To them Blunt.

BLUNT Madam, supper's on the table.

MILLWOOD Come, sir, you'll excuse all defects. My thoughts
were too much employed on my guest to observe the entertainment.   *Exeunt Millwood and Barnwell.*

SCENE 7

Lucy and Blunt.

BLUNT What! is all this preparation, this elegant supper, variety
of wines, and music, for the entertainment of that young
fellow?

LUCY So it seems.

BLUNT What! is our mistress turned fool at last! She's in love
with him, I suppose.

LUCY I suppose not. But she designs to make him in love with
her, if she can.

BLUNT What will she get by that? He seems under age, and
can't be supposed to have much money.

LUCY But his master has; and that's the same thing, as she'll
manage it.

BLUNT I don't like this fooling with a handsome young fellow;
while she's endeavouring to ensnare him, she may be caught
herself.

LUCY Nay, were she like me, that would certainly be the

consequence; for, I confess, there is something in youth and innocence that moves me mightily.

BLUNT Yes; so does the smoothness and plumpness of a partridge move a mighty desire in the hawk to be the destruction of it.

LUCY Why, birds are their prey, as men are ours; though, as you observed, we are sometimes caught ourselves. But that, I dare say, will never be the case with our mistress.

BLUNT I wish it may prove so; for you know we all depend upon her. Should she trifle away her time with a young fellow that there's nothing to be got by, we must all starve.

LUCY There's no danger of that; for I am sure she has no view in this affair but interest.

BLUNT Well, and what hopes are there of success in that?

LUCY The most promising that can be. 'Tis true the youth has his scruples; but she'll soon teach him to answer them, by stifling his conscience. Oh, the lad is in a hopeful way, depend upon it.

SCENE 8

Barnwell and Millwood at an entertainment.

BARNWELL What can I answer? All that I know is, that you are fair, and I am miserable.

MILLWOOD We are both so; and yet the fault is in ourselves.

BARNWELL To ease our present anguish, by plunging into guilt, is to buy a moment's pleasure with an age of pain.

MILLWOOD I should have thought the joys of love as lasting as they are great; if ours prove otherwise, 'tis your inconstancy must make them so.

BARNWELL The law of heaven will not be reversed, and that requires us to govern our passions.

MILLWOOD To give us sense of beauty and desires, and yet forbid us to taste and be happy, is a cruelty to nature. Have we passions only to torment us?

BARNWELL To hear you talk, though in the cause of vice – to gaze upon your beauty – press your hand – and see your snow-white bosom heave and fall – enflames my wishes. My pulse beats high – my senses all are in a hurry, and I am on the rack of wild desire. Yet, for a moment's guilty pleasure, shall I lose my innocence, my peace of mind, and hopes of solid happiness?

MILLWOOD *Chimeras all! – Come on with me and prove*
No joy's like woman kind, nor Heaven like love.

BARNWELL I would not, yet must on –
Reluctant thus, the merchant quits his ease,
And trusts to rocks, and sands, and stormy seas;
In hopes some unknown golden coast to find;
Commits himself, though doubtful, to the wind;
Longs much for joys to come, yet mourns those left behind.

Act II

SCENE: *A room in Thorowgood's house.*

Barnwell.

BARNWELL How strange are all things round me! Like some thief, who treads forbidden ground, fearful I enter each apartment of this well-known house. To guilty love, as if it was too little, already have I added breach of trust. A thief! Can I know myself that wretched thing, and look my honest friend and injured master in the face? Though hypocrisy may awhile conceal my guilt, at length it will be known, and public shame and ruin must ensue. In the meantime, what must be my life? Ever to speak a language foreign to my heart; hourly to add to the number of my crimes, in order to conceal 'em. Sure such was the condition of the grand apostate, when first he lost his purity. Like me, disconsolate, he wandered; and, while yet in heaven, bore all his future hell about him.

SCENE 2

Barnwell and Trueman.

TRUEMAN Barnwell, oh, how I rejoice to see you safe! So will our master, and his gentle daughter; who, during your absence, often inquired after you.

BARNWELL (*Aside.*) Would he were gone! His officious love will pry into the secrets of my soul.

TRUEMAN Unless you knew the pain the whole family has felt on your account, you can't conceive how much you are beloved. But why thus cold and silent? When my heart is full of joy for your return, why do you turn away; why thus avoid me? What have I done? How am I altered since you saw me last? Or rather, what have you done; and why are you thus changed? for I am still the same.

BARNWELL (*Aside.*) What have I done, indeed!

TRUEMAN Not speak! – nor look upon me! –

BARNWELL (*Aside.*) By my face he would discover all I would conceal; methinks already I begin to hate him.

TRUEMAN I cannot bear this usage from a friend; one whom till now I ever found so loving; whom yet I love; though this unkindness strikes at the root of friendship, and might destroy it in any breast but mine.

BARNWELL I am not well. (*Turning to him.*) Sleep has been a stranger to these eyes since you beheld them last.

TRUEMAN Heavy they look, indeed, and swollen with tears; – now they o'erflow. Rightly did my sympathising heart forebode last night, when thou wast absent, something fatal to our peace.

BARNWELL Your friendship engages you too far. My troubles whatever they are, are mine alone, you have no interest in them; nor ought your concern for me give you a moment's pain.

TRUEMAN You speak as if you knew of friendship nothing but the name. Before I saw your grief I felt it. Since we parted last I have slept no more than you, but pensive in my chamber sat alone, and spent the tedious night in wishes for your safety and return; e'en now, though ignorant of the cause, your sorrow wounds me to the heart.

BARNWELL 'Twill not be always thus. Friendship and all engagements cease, as circumstances and occasions vary; and since you once may hate me, perhaps it might be better for us both that now you loved me less.

TRUEMAN Sure I but dream! Without a cause would Barnwell use me thus? Ungenerous and ungrateful youth, farewell; I shall endeavour to follow your advice. (*Going.*) (*Aside.*) Yet stay; perhaps I am too rash; and angry, when the cause demands compassion. Some unforeseen calamity may have befallen him, too great to bear.

BARNWELL (*Aside.*) What part am I reduced to act! 'Tis vile and base to move his temper thus, the best of friends and men.

TRUEMAN I am to blame; prithee forgive me, Barnwell. Try to compose your ruffled mind; and let me know the cause that thus transports you from yourself. My friendly counsel may restore your peace.

BARNWELL All that is possible for man to do for man, your generous friendship may effect; but here even that's in vain.

TRUEMAN Something dreadful is labouring in your breast; Oh, give it vent, and let me share your grief; 'twill ease your pain, should it admit no cure, and make it lighter by the part I bear.

BARNWELL Vain supposition! my woes increase by being observed; should the cause be known, they would exceed all bounds.

TRUEMAN So well I know thy honest heart, guilt cannot harbour there.

BARNWELL (*Aside.*) Oh, torture insupportable!

TRUEMAN Then why am I excluded? Have I a thought I would conceal from you?

BARNWELL If still you urge me on this hated subject, I'll never enter more beneath this roof, nor see your face again.

TRUEMAN 'Tis strange — but I have done, say but you hate me not.

BARNWELL Hate you! I am not that monster yet.

TRUEMAN Shall our friendship still continue?

BARNWELL It's a blessing I never was worthy of, yet now must stand on terms; and but upon conditions can confirm it.

TRUEMAN What are they?

BARNWELL Never hereafter, though you should wonder at my conduct, desire to know more than I am willing to reveal.

TRUEMAN 'Tis hard; but upon any conditions I must be your friend.

BARNWELL Then, as much as one lost to himself can be another's, I am yours.   *Embracing.*

TRUEMAN Be ever so, and may Heaven restore your peace!

BARNWELL Will yesterday return? We have heard the glorious sun, that till then incessant rolled, once stopped his rapid course, and once went back. The dead have risen, and parched rocks poured forth a liquid stream to quench a people's thirst; the sea divided, and formed walls of water, while a whole nation passed in safety through its sandy bosom; hungry lions have refused their prey, and men unhurt have walked amidst consuming flames. But never yet did time, once past, return.

TRUEMAN Though the continued chain of time has never once been broke, nor ever will, but uninterrupted must keep on its course, till lost in eternity it ends there where it first begun: yet, as Heaven can repair whatever evils time can bring upon us, he who trusts Heaven ought never to despair. But business requires our attendance – business, the youth's best preservative from ill, as idleness his worst of snares. Will you go with me?

BARNWELL I'll take a little time to reflect on what has passed, and follow you.

SCENE 3

Barnwell.

BARNWELL I might have trusted Trueman to have applied to my uncle to have repaired the wrong I have done my master – but what of Millwood? Must I expose her, too? Ungenerous and base! Then Heaven requires it not. But Heaven requires that I forsake her. What! never see her more! Does Heaven require that? I hope I may see her, and Heaven not be offended. Presumptuous hope – dearly already have I proved my frailty; should I once more tempt Heaven, I may be left to fall never to rise again. Yet shall I leave her, for ever leave her, and not let her know the cause? She who loves me with such a boundless passion! Can cruelty be duty? I judge of what she then must feel, by what I now endure. The love of life, and fear of shame, opposed by inclination strong as death or shame, like wind and tide in raging conflict met, when neither can prevail, keep me in doubt. How then can I determine!

SCENE 4

Thorowgood and Barnwell.

THOROWGOOD Without a cause assigned, or notice given, to absent yourself last night was a fault, young man, and I came to chide you for it, but hope I am prevented. That modest blush, the confusion so visible in your face, speak grief and shame. When we have offended Heaven, It requires no more; and shall man, who needs himself to be forgiven, be harder to appease? If my pardon or love be of moment to your peace, look up secure of both.

BARNWELL *(Aside.)* This goodness has o'ercome me. Oh, sir,

you know not the nature and extent of my offence; and I should abuse your mistaken bounty to receive 'em. Though I had rather die than speak my shame; though racks could not have forced the guilty secret from my breast, your kindness has.

THOROWGOOD Enough, enough, whate'er it be; this concern shows you're convinced, and I am satisfied. How painful is the sense of guilt to an ingenuous mind! Some youthful folly, which it were prudent not to inquire into. When we consider the frail condition of humanity, it may raise our pity, not our wonder, that youth should go astray; when reason, weak at the best when opposed to inclination, scarce formed, and wholly unassisted by experience, faintly contends, or willingly becomes the slave of sense. The state of youth is much to be deplored; and the more so, because they see it not; they being then to danger most exposed when they are least prepared for their defence.

BARNWELL It will be known, and you recall your pardon and abhor me.

THOROWGOOD I never will; so Heaven confirm to me the pardon of my offences! Yet be upon your guard in this gay, thoughtless season of your life; now, when the sense of pleasure's quick, and passion high, the voluptuous appetites raging and fierce demand the strongest curb, take heed of a relapse: when vice becomes habitual, the very power of leaving it is lost.

BARNWELL Hear me, then, on my knees, confess –

THOROWGOOD I will not hear a syllable more upon this subject; it were not mercy, but cruelty, to hear what must give you such torment to reveal.

BARNWELL This generosity amazes and distracts me.

THOROWGOOD This remorse makes thee dearer to me than if thou hadst never offended. Whatever is your fault, of this I am certain, 'twas harder for you to offend, than me to pardon.

SCENE 5

Barnwell.

BARNWELL Villain! Villain! Villain! basely to wrong so excellent a man. Should I again return to folly? – Detested thought! –

But what of Millwood then? – Why, I renounce her; I give her up. The struggle's over, and virtue has prevailed. Reason may convince, but gratitude compels. This unlooked for generosity has saved me from destruction.   *Going.*

SCENE 6

To him a Footman.

FOOTMAN Sir, two ladies from your uncle in the country desire to see you.

BARNWELL (*Aside.*) Who should they be? – Tell them I'll wait upon them.

SCENE 7

Barnwell.

BARNWELL Methinks I dread to see them. Guilt, what a coward hast thou made me! Now everything alarms me.

SCENE 8

SCENE: *Another room in Thorowgood's house.*

Millwood and Lucy; and to them a Footman.

FOOTMAN Ladies, he'll wait upon you immediately.

MILLWOOD 'Tis very well. I thank you.

SCENE 9

Barnwell, Millwood and Lucy.

BARNWELL Confusion! Millwood!

MILLWOOD That angry look tells me that here I'm an unwelcome guest; I feared as much; the unhappy are so everywhere.

BARNWELL Will nothing but my utter ruin content you?

MILLWOOD Unkind and cruel! Lost myself, your happiness is now my only care.

BARNWELL How did you gain admission?

MILLWOOD Saying we were desired by your uncle to visit and

deliver a message to you, we were received by the family without suspicion, and with much respect directed here.

BARNWELL Why did you come at all?

MILLWOOD I never shall trouble you more. I'm come to take my leave for ever. Such is the malice of my fate: I go hopeless, despairing ever to return. This hour is all I have left me; one short hour is all I have to bestow on love and you, for whom I thought the longest life too short.

BARNWELL Then we are met to part for ever?

MILLWOOD It must be so. Yet think not that time or absence ever shall put a period to my grief, or make me love you less. Though I must leave you, yet condemn me not.

BARNWELL Condemn you! No; I approve your resolution, and rejoice to hear it; 'tis just — 'tis necessary — I have well weighed, and found it so.

LUCY (Aside.) I am afraid the young man has more sense than she thought he had.

BARNWELL Before you came, I had determined never to see you more.

MILLWOOD (Aside.) Confusion!

LUCY (Aside.) Ay, we are all out! This is a turn so unexpected, that I shall make nothing of my part; they must e'en play the scene betwixt themselves.

MILLWOOD It was some relief to think, though absent, you would love me still. But to find, though fortune had been kind, that you, more cruel and inconstant, had resolved to cast me off — this, as I never could expect, I have not learnt to bear.

BARNWELL I am sorry to hear you blame in me a resolution that so well becomes us both.

MILLWOOD I have reason for what I do, but you have none.

BARNWELL Can we want a reason for parting, who have so many to wish we never had met?

MILLWOOD Look on me, Barnwell. Am I deformed or old, that satiety so soon succeeds enjoyment? Nay, look again; am I not she whom yesterday you thought the fairest and the kindest of her sex, whose hand, trembling with ecstasy, you pressed and moulded thus, while on my eyes you gazed with such delight as if desire increased by being fed?

BARNWELL No more; let me repent my former follies, if possible, without remembering what they were.

MILLWOOD Why?

BARNWELL Such is my frailty, that 'tis dangerous.

MILLWOOD Where is the danger, since we are to part?

BARNWELL The thought of that already is too painful.

MILLWOOD If it be painful to part, then I may hope, at least, you do not hate me?

BARNWELL No, no, I never said I did. Oh, my heart!

MILLWOOD Perhaps you pity me?

BARNWELL I do – I do. Indeed, I do.

MILLWOOD You'll think upon me?

BARNWELL Doubt it not, while I can think at all.

MILLWOOD You may judge an embrace at parting too great a favour – though it would be the last. (*He draws back.*) A look shall then suffice. Farewell – for ever.

SCENE 10

Barnwell.

BARNWELL If to resolve to suffer be to conquer, I have conquered. Painful victory!

SCENE 11

Barnwell, Millwood and Lucy.

MILLWOOD One thing I had forgot; – I never must return to my own house again. This I thought proper to let you know, lest your mind should change, and you should seek in vain to find me there. Forgive me this second intrusion; I only came to give you this caution, and that, perhaps, was needless.

BARNWELL I hope it was; yet it is kind, and I must thank you for it.

MILLWOOD (*To Lucy.*) My friend, your arm. Now I am gone for ever.   *Going.*

BARNWELL One more thing. Sure there's no danger in my knowing where you go? If you think otherwise –

MILLWOOD (*Weeping.*) Alas!

LUCY (*Aside.*) We are right, I find that's my cue. Ah, dear sir, she's going she knows not whither; but go she must.

BARNWELL Humanity obliges me to wish you well; why will you thus expose yourself to needless troubles?

LUCY Nay, there's no help for it: she must quit the town immediately, and the kingdom as soon as possible. It was no small matter, you may be sure, that could make her resolve to leave you.

MILLWOOD No more, my friend; since he for whose dear sake alone I suffer, and am content to suffer, is kind and pities me; where'er I wander, through wilds and deserts, benighted and forlorn, that thought shall give me comfort.

BARNWELL For my sake! – Oh, tell me how! which way am I so cursed, as to bring such ruin on thee?

MILLWOOD No matter; I am contented with my lot.

BARNWELL Leave me not in this uncertainty.

MILLWOOD I have said too much.

BARNWELL How, how am I the cause of your undoing?

MILLWOOD 'Twill but increase your troubles.

BARNWELL My troubles can't be greater than they are.

LUCY Well, well, sir, if she won't satisfy you, I will.

BARNWELL I am bound to you beyond expression.

MILLWOOD Remember, sir, that I desired you not to hear it.

BARNWELL Begin, and ease my racking expectation.

LUCY Why, you must know, my lady here was an only child; but her parents dying while she was young, left her and her fortune (no inconsiderable one, I assure you) to the care of a gentleman who has a good estate of his own.

MILLWOOD Ay, ay, the barbarous man is rich enough; but what are riches when compared to love?

LUCY For a while he performed the office of a faithful guardian, settled her in a house, hired her servants – But you have seen in what manner she lived, so I need say no more of that.

MILLWOOD How I shall live hereafter, Heaven knows!

LUCY All things went on as one could wish; till some time ago, his wife dying, he fell violently in love with his charge, and would fain have married her. Now the man is neither old nor ugly, but a good personable sort of a man; but I don't know how it was, she could never endure him. In short, her ill-usage so provoked him, that he brought in an account of his executorship, wherein he makes her debtor to him –

MILLWOOD A trifle in itself, but more than enough to ruin me, whom, by this unjust account, he had stripped of all before.

LUCY Now, she having neither money nor friend, except me, who am as unfortunate as herself, he compelled her to pass his account, and give bond for the sum he demanded; but still provided handsomely for her, and continued his courtship, till being informed by his spies (truly I suspect some in her own family) that you were entertained at her house, and stayed with her all night, he came this morning raving and storming like a madman, talks no more of marriage (so there's no hopes of making up matters that way) but vows her ruin, unless she'll allow him the same favour that he supposes she granted you.

BARNWELL Must she be ruined, or find her refuge in another's arms?

MILLWOOD He gave me but an hour to resolve in; that's happily spent with you. And now I go —

BARNWELL To be exposed to all the rigours of the various seasons; the summer's parching heat, and winter's cold; unhoused, to wander, friendless, through the unhospitable world, in misery and want; attended with fear and danger, and pursued by malice and revenge. Wouldst thou endure all this for me, and can I do nothing, nothing to prevent it?

LUCY 'Tis really a pity there can be no way found out.

BARNWELL Oh, where are all my resolutions now? Like early vapours, or the morning dew, chased by the sun's warm beams, they're vanished and lost, as though they had never been.

LUCY Now, I advise her, sir, to comply with the gentleman; that would not only put an end to her troubles, but make her fortune at once.

BARNWELL Tormenting fiend, away! I had rather perish, nay, see her perish, than have her saved by him. I will, myself, prevent her ruin, though with my own. A moment's patience; I'll return immediately.

SCENE 12

Millwood and Lucy.

LUCY 'Twas well you came; or, by what I can perceive, you had lost him.

MILLWOOD That, I must confess, was a danger I did not foresee; I was only afraid he should have come without money. You know, a house of entertainment, like mine, is not kept with nothing.

LUCY That's very true; but then you should be reasonable in your demands; 'tis pity to discourage a young man.

SCENE 13

Barnwell, Millwood and Lucy.

BARNWELL (*Aside.*) What am I about to do? – Now you, who boast your reason all-sufficient, suppose yourselves in my condition, and determine for me, whether it's right to let her suffer for my faults, or, by this small addition to my guilt, prevent the ill-effects of what is past.

LUCY These young sinners think everything in the ways of wickedness so strange! But I could tell him that this is nothing but what's very common; for one vice as naturally begets another, as a father a son. But he'll find out that himself, if he lives long enough.

BARNWELL Here, take this, and with it purchase your deliverance; return to your house, and live in peace and safety.

MILLWOOD So, I may hope to see you there again?

BARNWELL Answer me not, but fly; lest, in the agonies of my remorse, I take again what is not mine to give, and abandon thee to want and misery.

MILLWOOD Say but you'll come.

BARNWELL You are my fate, my heaven or my hell; only leave me now, dispose of me hereafter as you please.

SCENE 14

Barnwell.

BARNWELL What have I done! Were my resolutions founded on reason, and sincerely made – why then has Heaven suffered me to fall? I sought not the occasion; and, if my heart deceives me not, compassion and generosity were my motives. Is virtue inconsistent with itself, or are vice and virtue only empty names? Or do they depend on accidents, beyond our power to produce or to prevent – wherein we have no part, and yet must be determined by the event? But why should I attempt to reason? All is confusion, horror and remorse. I find I am

lost, cast down from all my late-erected hopes, and plunged
again in guilt, yet scarce know how or why:

Such undistinguished horrors make my brain,
Like hell, the seat of darkness and of pain.

Act III

SCENE I

SCENE: *Thorowgood's house.*

Thorowgood and Trueman (Discovered with account books, seated at a table.)

THOROWGOOD Methinks I would not have you only learn the method of merchandise, and practise it hereafter, merely as a means of getting wealth. 'Twill be well worth your pains to study it as a science. See how it is founded in reason, and the nature of things; how it has promoted humanity, as it has opened and yet keeps up an intercourse between nations, far remote from one another in situation, customs and religion; promoting arts, industry, peace and plenty; by mutual benefits diffusing mutual love from pole to pole.

TRUEMAN Something of this I have considered, and hope, by your assistance, to extend my thoughts much farther. I have observed those countries, where trade is promoted and encouraged, do not make discoveries to destroy, but to improve mankind by love and friendship; to tame the fierce and polish the most savage; to teach them the advantage of honest traffic, by taking from them, with their own consent, their useless superfluities, and giving them, in return, what, from their ignorance in manual arts, their situation, or some other accident, they stand in need of.

THOROWGOOD 'Tis justly observed: the populous East, luxuriant, abounds with glittering gems, bright pearls, aromatic spices, and health-restoring drugs. The late found Western world glows with unnumbered veins of gold and silver ore. On every climate and on every country, Heaven has bestowed some good peculiar to itself. It is the industrious merchant's business to collect the various blessings of each soil and climate, and, with the product of the whole, to enrich his native country. – Well! I have examined your accounts: they are not only just, as I have always found them, but regularly kept, and fairly entered. I commend your diligence. Method in business is the surest guide. He who neglects it frequently stumbles, and always wanders perplexed, uncertain, and in danger. – Are Barnwell's accounts ready for my inspection? He does not use to be the last on these occasions.

TRUEMAN Upon receiving your orders he retired, I thought, in some confusion. If you please, I'll go and hasten him. I hope he has not been guilty of any neglect.

THOROWGOOD I'm now going to the Exchange; let him know, at my return I expect to find him ready.

SCENE 2

Maria with a book. Sits and reads.

MARIA How forcible is truth! The weakest mind, inspired with love of that, fixed and collected in itself, with indifference beholds the united force of earth and hell opposing. Such souls are raised above the sense of pain, or so supported that they regard it not. The martyr cheaply purchases his Heaven; small are his sufferings, great is his reward. Not so the wretch who combats love with duty: when the mind, weakened and dissolved by the soft passion, feeble and hopeless, opposes its own desires – what is an hour, a day, a year of pain, to a whole life of tortures such as these?

SCENE 3

Trueman and Maria.

TRUEMAN Oh, Barnwell! Oh, my friend! how art thou fallen!

MARIA Ha! Barnwell! What of him? Speak! say, what of Barnwell?

TRUEMAN 'Tis not to be concealed: I've news to tell of him that will afflict your generous father, yourself, and all who knew him.

MARIA Defend us, Heaven!

TRUEMAN I cannot speak it. See there.

Gives a letter, Maria reads.

'Trueman, I know my absence will surprise my honoured master and yourself; and the more, when you shall understand that the reason of my withdrawing is my having embezzled part of the cash with which I was entrusted. After this, 'tis needless to inform you, that I intend never to return again. Though this might have been known by examining my accounts, yet to prevent that unnecessary trouble, and to cut off all fruitless expectations of my return, I have left this from the lost GEORGE BARNWELL.'

TRUEMAN Lost indeed! Yet how he should be guilty of what he there charges himself withal, raises my wonder equal to my grief. Never had youth a higher sense of virtue. Justly he thought, and as he thought he practised; never was life more regular than his. An understanding uncommon at his years; an open, generous manliness of temper; his manners easy, unaffected, and engaging.

MARIA This, and much more, you might have said with truth. He was the delight of every eye, and joy of every heart that knew him.

TRUEMAN Since such he was, and was my friend, can I support his loss? See, the fairest and happiest maid this wealthy city boasts, kindly condescends to weep for thy unhappy fate, poor, ruined Barnwell!

MARIA Trueman, do you think a soul so delicate as his, so sensible of shame, can e'er submit to live a slave to vice?

TRUEMAN Never, never. So well I know him, I'm sure this act of his, so contrary to his nature, must have been caused by some unavoidable necessity.

MARIA Is there no means yet to preserve him?

TRUEMAN Oh, that there were! But few men recover reputation lost, a merchant never. Nor would he, I fear, though I should find him, ever be brought to look his injured master in the face.

MARIA I fear as much, and therefore would never have my father know it.

TRUEMAN That's impossible.

MARIA What's the sum?

TRUEMAN 'Tis considerable; I've marked it here, to show it, with the letter, to your father, at his return.

MARIA If I should supply the money, could you so dispose of that and the account, as to conceal this unhappy mismanagement from my father?

TRUEMAN Nothing more easy. But can you intend it? Will you save a helpless wretch from ruin? Oh, 'twere an act worthy such exalted virtue as Maria's! Sure Heaven, in mercy to my friend, inspired the generous thought.

MARIA Doubt not but I would purchase so great a happiness at a much dearer price. But how shall he be found?

TRUEMAN Trust to my diligence for that. In the meantime, I'll conceal his absence from your father, or find such excuses for it, that the real cause shall never be suspected.

MARIA In attempting to save from shame one whom we hope may yet return to virtue, to Heaven and you, the judges of this action, I appeal, whether I have done anything misbecoming my sex and character.

TRUEMAN Earth must approve the deed, and Heaven, I doubt not, will reward it.

MARIA If Heaven succeed it, I am well rewarded. A virgin's fame is sullied by suspicion's slightest breath; and therefore, as this must be a secret from my father and the world for Barnwell's sake, for mine let it be so to him.

SCENE 4

SCENE: *Millwood's house.*

Lucy and Blunt.

LUCY Well, what do you think of Millwood's conduct now?

BLUNT I own it is surprising. I don't know which to admire most, her feigned or his real passion; though I have sometimes been afraid that her avarice would discover her. But his youth and want of experience make it the easier to impose on him.

LUCY No, it is his love. To do him justice, notwithstanding his youth, he don't want understanding. But you men are much easier imposed on in these affairs, than your vanity will allow you to believe. Let me see the wisest of you all as much in love with me as Barnwell is with Millwood, and I'll engage to make as great a fool of him.

BLUNT And, all circumstances considered, to make as much money of him too?

LUCY I can't answer for that. Her artifice, in making him rob his master at first, and the various stratagems by which she has obliged him to continue in that course, astonish even me, who know her so well.

BLUNT But then you are to consider that the money was his master's.

LUCY There was the difficulty of it. Had it been his own, it had been nothing. Were the world his, she might have it for a smile. But those golden days are done; he's ruined, and Millwood's hopes of further profits there are at an end.

BLUNT That's no more than we all expected.

LUCY Being called by his master to make up his accounts, he was forced to quit his house and service; and wisely flies to Millwood for relief and entertainment.

BLUNT I have not heard of this before: how did she receive him?

LUCY As you would expect. She wondered what he meant; was astonished at his impudence; and, with an air of modesty peculiar to herself, swore so heartily that she never saw him before, that she put me out of countenance.

BLUNT That's much indeed! But how did Barnwell behave?

LUCY He grieved; and at length, enraged at this barbarous treatment, was preparing to be gone, and making toward the door showed a bag of money which he had stolen from his master, the last he is ever like to have from thence.

BLUNT But then, Millwood?

LUCY Ay, she, with her usual address, returned to her old arts of lying, swearing, and dissembling; hung on his neck and wept, and swore 'twas meant in jest, till the easy fool melted into tears, threw the money into her lap, and swore he had rather die than think her false.

BLUNT Strange infatuation!

LUCY But what followed was stranger still. As doubts and fears, followed by reconcilement, ever increase love where the passion is sincere, so in him it caused so wild a transport of excessive fondness, such joy, such grief, such pleasure, and such anguish, that nature in him seemed sinking with the weight, and the charmed soul disposed to quit his breast for hers. Just then, when every passion with lawless anarchy prevailed, and reason was in the raging tempest lost, the cruel, artful Millwood prevailed upon the wretched youth to promise – what I tremble to but think on.

BLUNT I am amazed! What can it be?

LUCY You will be more so, to hear it is to attempt the life of his nearest relation and best benefactor.

BLUNT His uncle! whom we have often heard him speak of, as a gentleman of a large estate, and fair character, in the country where he lives!

LUCY The same. She was no sooner possessed of the last dear purchase of his ruin, but her avarice, insatiate as the grave, demands this horrid sacrifice – Barnwell's near relation; and unsuspected virtue must give too easy means to seize the good man's treasure, whose blood must seal the dreadful secret, and prevent the terrors of her guilty fears.

BLUNT Is it possible she could persuade him to do an act like that? He is, by nature, honest, grateful, compassionate, and generous; and though his love and her artful persuasions have wrought him to practise what he most abhors, yet we all can witness for him with what reluctance he has still complied! So many tears he shed o'er each offence, as might, if possible, sanctify theft, and make a merit of a crime.

LUCY 'Tis true, at the naming the murder of his uncle, he started into rage; and, breaking from her arms (where she till then had held him with well-dissembled love, and false endearments), called her cruel monster, devil! and told her she was born for his destruction. She thought it not for her purpose to meet his rage with rage, but affected a most passionate fit of grief, railed at her fate, and cursed her wayward stars, that still her wants should force her to press him to act such deeds as she must needs abhor as well as he; but told him necessity had no law, and love no bounds; that therefore he never truly loved, but meant, in her necessity, to forsake her; then kneeled and swore, that since by his refusal he had given her cause to doubt his love, she never would see him more, unless, to prove it true, he robbed his uncle to supply her wants, and murdered him to keep it from discovery.

BLUNT I am astonished! What said he?

LUCY Speechless he stood; but in his face you might have read that various passions tore his very soul. Oft he in anguish threw his eyes towards Heaven, and then as often bent their beams on her, then wept and groaned, and beat his breast; at length, with horror not to be expressed, he cried, Thou cursed fair, have I not given dreadful proofs of love? What drew me from my youthful innocence to stain my then unspotted soul, but love?

What caused me to rob my gentle master, but cursed love! What makes me now a fugitive from his service, loathed by myself, and scorned by all the world, but love? What fills my eyes with tears, my soul with torture never felt on this side death before? Why, love, love, love! And why, above all, do I resolve (for, tearing his hair, he cried, I do resolve) to kill my uncle?

BLUNT Was she not moved? It makes me weep to hear the sad relation.

LUCY Yes – with joy, that she had gained her point. She gave him no time to cool, but urged him to attempt it instantly. He's now gone. If he performs it, and escapes, there's more money for her; if not, he'll ne'er return, and then she's fairly rid of him.

BLUNT 'Tis time the world was rid of such a monster.

LUCY If we don't do our endeavours to prevent this murder, we are as bad as she.

BLUNT I am afraid it is too late.

LUCY Perhaps not. Her barbarity to Barnwell makes me hate her. We have run too great a length with her already. I did not think her or myself so wicked, as I find, upon reflection, we are.

BLUNT 'Tis true, we have all been too much so. But there is something so horrid in murder, that all other crimes seem nothing when compared to that; I would not be involved in the guilt of that for all the world.

LUCY Nor I, Heaven knows. Therefore let us clear ourselves, by doing all that is in our power to prevent it. I have just thought of a way that to me seems probable. Will you join with me to detect this cursed design?

BLUNT With all my heart. How else shall I clear myself? He who knows of a murder intended to be committed, and does not discover it, in the eye of the law and reason is a murderer.

LUCY Let us lose no time; I'll acquaint you with the particulars as we go.

SCENE 5

SCENE: *A walk at some distance from a country-seat.*

Barnwell.

BARNWELL A dismal gloom obscures the face of day. Either the sun has slipped behind a cloud, or journeys down the west of heaven with more than common speed, to avoid the sight of what I am doomed to act. Since I set forth on this accursed design, where'er I tread, methinks the solid earth trembles beneath my feet. Yonder limpid stream, whose hoary fall has made a natural cascade, as I passed by, in doleful accents seemed to murmur 'Murder!' The earth, the air and water seem concerned, but that's not strange: the world is punished, and Nature feels the shock, when Providence permits a good man's fall. Just Heaven! Then what should I be! For him that was my father's only brother – and, since his death, has been to me a father; who took me up an infant and an orphan, reared me with tenderest care, and still indulged me with most paternal fondness? Yet here I stand avowed his destined murderer – I stiffen with horror at my own impiety. 'Tis yet unperformed – what if I quit my bloody purpose, and fly the place? (*Going, then stops.*) – But whither, oh, whither shall I fly? My master's once friendly doors are ever shut against me; and without money Millwood will never see me more; and life is not to be endured without her. She's got such firm possession of my heart and governs there with such despotic sway. – Ay, there's the cause of all my sin and sorrow: 'tis more than love; 'tis the fever of the soul and madness of desire. In vain does nature, reason, conscience, all oppose it; the impetuous passion bears down all before it, and drives me on to lust, to theft, and murder. Oh, conscience! feeble guide to virtue! who only shows us when we go astray, but wants the power to stop us in our course! – Ha! in yonder shady walk I see my uncle. He's alone. Now for my disguise. (*Plucks out a visor.*) – This is his hour of private meditation. Thus daily he prepares his soul for Heaven; whilst I – But what have I to do with Heaven? Ha! no struggles, conscience –

    Hence, hence, remorse, and ev'ry thought that's good:
    The storm that lust began must end in blood.

                Puts on the visor, draws a pistol and exit.

SCENE 6

SCENE: *A close walk in a wood.*

Uncle.

UNCLE If I were superstitious, I should fear some danger lurked unseen, or death were nigh. A heavy melancholy clouds my spirits. My imagination is filled with ghastly forms of dreary graves, and bodies changed by death; when the pale length-ened visage attracts each weeping eye, and fills the musing soul at once with grief and horror, pity and aversion – I will indulge the thought. The wise man prepares himself for death by making it familiar to his mind. When strong reflections hold the mirror near, and the living in the dead behold their future selves, how does each inordinate passion and desire cease, or sicken at the view! The mind scarce moves; the blood, curdling and chilled, creeps slowly through the veins; fixed still, and motionless like the solemn object of our thoughts, we are almost at present what we must be hereafter; till curiosity awakes the soul, and sets it on inquiry.

SCENE 7

Uncle. George Barnwell at a distance.

UNCLE O Death! thou strange mysterious power, seen every day, yet never understood but by the incommunicative dead, what art thou? The extensive mind of man, that with a thought circles the earth's vast globe, sinks to the centre, or ascends above the stars; that worlds exotic finds, or thinks it finds, thy thick clouds attempts to pass in vain, lost and bewildered in the horrid gloom; defeated, she returns more doubtful than before; of nothing certain but of labour lost.

During this speech, Barnwell sometimes presents the pistol, and draws it back again; at last he drops it, at which his uncle starts and draws his sword.

BARNWELL Oh, 'tis impossible!
UNCLE A man so near me! armed and masked –
BARNWELL Nay, then there's no retreat.
         Plucks a poignard from his bosom, and stabs him.
UNCLE Oh, I am slain! All-gracious Heaven, regard the prayer of thy dying servant; bless, with thy choicest blessings, my dearest nephew; forgive my murderer, and take my fleeting soul to endless mercy.

Barnwell, throws off his mask; runs to him; and kneeling by him, raises and chafes him.

BARNWELL Expiring saint! Oh, murdered, martyred uncle! lift up your dying eyes, and view your nephew in your murderer! – Oh, do not look so tenderly upon me! – Let indignation lighten from your eyes, and blast me ere you die! – By Heaven, he weeps, in pity of my woes! – Tears, tears, for blood! – The murdered, in the agonies of death, weeps for his murderer. – Oh, speak your pious purpose; pronounce my pardon, then, and take me with you! – He would, but cannot. – Oh, why, with such fond affection, do you press my murdering hand? – What! will you kiss me! (*Kisses him. Uncle groans and dies.*) He is gone for ever – and oh! I follow. (*Swoons away upon his uncle's dead body*.) Do I still live to press the suffering bosom of the earth? Do I still breathe, and taint with my infectious breath the wholesome air! Let Heaven from its high throne, in justice or in mercy, now look down on that dear murdered saint, and me the murderer. And, if his vengeance spares, let pity strike and end my wretched being! – Murder the worst of crimes, and parricide the worst of murders, and this the worst of parricides! Cain, who stands on record from the birth of time, and must to its last final period, as accursed, slew a brother favoured above him. Detested Nero by another's hand dispatched a mother that he feared and hated. But I, with my own hand, have murdered a brother, mother, father, and a friend, most loving and beloved. This execrable act of mine's without a parallel. O may it ever stand alone – the last of murders, as it is the worst!

> *The rich man thus, in torment and despair,*
> *Preferred his vain, but charitable prayer.*
> *The fool, his own soul lost, would fain be wise*
> *For other's good; but Heaven his suit denies.*
> *By laws and means well known we stand or fall,*
> *And one eternal rule remains for all.*

Act IV

SCENE: *A room in Thorowgood's house.*

Maria.

MARIA How falsely do they judge who censure or applaud as we're afflicted or rewarded here! I know I am unhappy, yet cannot charge myself with any crime, more than the common frailties of our kind, that should provoke just Heaven to mark me out for sufferings so uncommon and severe. Falsely to accuse ourselves, Heaven must abhor; then it is just and right that innocence should suffer, for Heaven must be just in all its ways. Perhaps by that they are kept from moral evils much worse than penal, or more improved in virtue; or may not the lesser ills that they sustain be the means of greater good to others? Might all the joyless days and sleepless nights that I have passed but purchase peace for thee –

> *Thou dear, dear cause of all my grief and pain,*
> *Small were the loss, and infinite the gain;*
> *Though to the grave in secret love I pine,*
> *So life, and fame, and happiness were thine.*

SCENE 2

Trueman and Maria.

MARIA What news of Barnwell?

TRUEMAN None. I have sought him with the greatest diligence, but all in vain.

MARIA Doth my father yet suspect the cause of his absenting himself?

TRUEMAN All appeared so just and fair to him, it is not possible he ever should; but his absence will no longer be concealed. Your father's wise; and, though he seems to hearken to the friendly excuses I would make for Barnwell, yet I am afraid he regards them only as such, without suffering them to influence his judgment.

MARIA How does the unhappy youth defeat all our designs to serve him! Yet I can never repent what we have done. Should he return, 'twill make his reconciliation with my father easier, and preserve him from future reproach from a malicious, unforgiving world.

SCENE 3

To them Thorowgood and Lucy.

THOROWGOOD This woman here has given me a sad and (bating some circumstance) too probable account of Barnwell's defection.

LUCY I am sorry, sir, that my frank confession of my former unhappy course of life, should cause you to suspect my truth on this occasion.

THOROWGOOD It is not that; your confession has in it all the appearance of truth. (*To them.*) Among many other particulars, she informs me that Barnwell has been influenced to break his trust and wrong me at several times of considerable sums of money. Now as I know this to be false, I would fain doubt the whole of her relation; too dreadful to be willingly believed.

MARIA Sir, your pardon; I find myself on a sudden so indisposed that I must retire. (*Aside.*) Providence opposes all attempts to save him. Poor ruined Barnwell! Wretched, lost Maria!

SCENE 4

Thorowgood, Trueman, and Lucy.

THOROWGOOD How I am distressed on every side! Pity for that unhappy youth, fear for the life of a much valued friend – and then, my child – the only joy and hope of my declining life! – Her melancholy increases hourly, and gives me painful apprehensions of her loss. – Oh, Trueman, this person informs me that your friend, at the instigation of an impious woman, is gone to rob and murder his venerable uncle.

TRUEMAN Oh, execrable deed! I am blasted with the horror of the thought!

LUCY This delay may ruin all.

THOROWGOOD What to do or think, I know not. That he ever wronged me, I know is false; the rest may be so too; there's all my hope.

TRUEMAN Trust not to that; rather suppose all true, than lose a moment's time. Even now the horrid deed may be a-doing — dreadful imagination! — or it may be done, and we are vainly debating on the means to prevent what is already past.

THOROWGOOD This earnestness convinces me that he knows more than he had yet discovered. What, ho! without there, who waits?

SCENE 5

To them a Servant.

THOROWGOOD Order the groom to saddle the swiftest horse, and prepare himself to set out with speed! — An affair of life and death demands his diligence.

SCENE 6

Thorowgood, Trueman and Lucy.

THOROWGOOD For you, whose behaviour on this occasion I have no time to commend as it deserves, I must engage your farther assistance. Return and observe this Millwood till I come. I have your directions, and will follow you as soon as possible.

SCENE 7

Thorowgood and Trueman.

THOROWGOOD Trueman, you I am sure would not be idle on this occasion.

SCENE 8

Trueman.

TRUEMAN He only who is a friend can judge of my distress.

SCENE 9

SCENE: *Millwood's house.*

Millwood.

MILLWOOD I wish I knew the event of his design. The attempt without success would ruin him. Well, what have I to apprehend from that? I fear too much. The mischief being only intended, his friends, in pity of his youth, turn all their rage on me. I should have thought of that before. Suppose the deed done; then, and then only, I shall be secure. Or what if he returns without attempting it at all?

SCENE 10

Millwood, and Barnwell, bloody.

MILLWOOD But he is here, and I have done him wrong. His bloody hands show he has done the deed, but show he wants the prudence to conceal it.

BARNWELL Where shall I hide me? Whither shall I fly, to avoid the swift unerring hand of justice?

MILLWOOD Dismiss those fears: though thousands had pursued you to the door, yet being entered here, you are safe as innocence. I have such a cavern, by art so cunningly contrived, that the piercing eyes of jealousy and revenge may search in vain nor find the entrance to the safe retreat. There will I hide you, if any danger's near.

BARNWELL Oh, hide me – from myself, if it be possible; for while I bear my conscience in my bosom, though I were hid where man's eye never saw, nor light e'er dawned, 'twere all in vain. For that inmate, that impartial judge, will try, convict, and sentence me for murder, and execute me with never-ending torments. Behold these hands, all crimsoned o'er with my dear uncle's blood. Here's a sight to make a statue start with horror, or turn a living man into a statue!

MILLWOOD Ridiculous! Then it seems you are afraid of your own shadow; or, what's less than a shadow, your conscience.

BARNWELL Though to man unknown I did the accursed act, what can we hide from Heaven's omniscient eye?

MILLWOOD No more of this stuff. What advantage have you made of his death; or what advantage may yet be made of it? Did you secure the keys of his treasure? Those, no doubt, were about him? What gold, what jewels, or what else of value have you brought me?

BARNWELL Think you, I added sacrilege to murder? Oh, had you seen him as his life flowed from him in a crimson flood, and heard him praying for me by the double name of nephew and of murderer; alas, alas! he knew not then that his nephew was his murderer: how would you have wished, as I did, though you had a thousand years of life to come, to have given them all to have lengthened his one hour! But being dead, I fled the sight of what my hands had done; nor could I, to have gained the empire of the world, have violated, by theft, his sacred corpse.

MILLWOOD Whining, preposterous, canting villain! to murder your uncle, rob him of life, nature's first, last, dear prerogative, after which there's no injury, then fear to take what he no longer wanted, and bring to me your penury and guilt. Do you think I'll hazard my reputation, nay, my life, to entertain you?

BARNWELL Oh, Millwood! — this from thee? — But I have done. If you hate me, if you wish me dead, then you are happy; for, oh, 'tis sure my grief will quickly end me.

MILLWOOD (*Aside*.) In his madness he will discover all, and involve me in his ruin. We are on a precipice from whence there's no retreat for both. Then, to preserve myself — (*Pauses*.) — There is no other way — 'tis dreadful, but reflection comes too late when danger's pressing, and there's no room for choice. It must be done. *Stamps*.

SCENE II

To them a Servant.

MILLWOOD Fetch me an officer, and seize this villain, he has confessed himself a murderer. Should I let him escape, I justly might be thought as bad as he.

SCENE 12

Millwood and Barnwell.

BARNWELL Oh Millwood! sure thou dost not, cannot mean it. Stop the messenger; upon my knees, I beg you call him back. 'Tis fit I die indeed, but not by you. I will this instant deliver myself into the hands of justice, indeed I will; for death is all I wish. But thy ingratitude so tears my wounded soul, 'tis worse ten thousand times than death with torture.

MILLWOOD Call it what you will; I am willing to live, and live secure, which nothing but your death can warrant.

BARNWELL If there be a pitch of wickedness that seats the author beyond the reach of vengeance, you must be secure. But what remains for me, but a dismal dungeon, hard galling fetters, an awful trial, and ignominious death – justly to fall unpitied and abhorred; after death to be suspended between heaven and earth, a dreadful spectacle, the warning and horror of a gaping crowd. This I could bear, nay, wish not to avoid, had it come from any hand but thine.

SCENE 13

Millwood, Barnwell, Blunt, Officer and Attendants.

MILLWOOD Heaven defend me! Conceal a murderer! Here, sir; take this youth into your custody. I accuse him of murder, and will appear to make good my charge.   *They seize him.*

BARNWELL To whom, of what, or how shall I complain? I'll not accuse her: the hand of Heaven is in it, and this the punishment of lust and parricide. Yet Heaven, that justly cuts me off, still suffers her to live, perhaps to punish others. Tremendous mercy! so fiends are cursed with immortality, to be the executioners of Heaven:

> Be warned, ye youths, who see my sad despair,
> Avoid lewd women, false as they are fair;
> By reason guided, honest joys pursue;
> The fair, to honour and to virtue true,
> Just to herself, will ne'er be false to you.
> By my example learn to shun my fate
> (How wretched is the man who's wise too late!);

Ere innocence, and fame, and life, be lost,
Here purchase wisdom, cheaply, at my cost!

Officers take him out.

SCENE 14

Millwood and Blunt.

MILLWOOD Where is Lucy? Why is she absent at such a time?
BLUNT Would I had been so, too, thou devil!
MILLWOOD Insolent! This to me!
BLUNT The worst that we know of the devil is, that he first seduces to sin and then betrays to punishment.

SCENE 15

Millwood.

They disapprove of my conduct, and mean to take this opportunity to set up for themselves. My ruin is resolved. I see my danger, but scorn it and them. I was not born to fall by such weak instruments.   *Going.*

SCENE 16

Thorowgood and Millwood.

THOROWGOOD Where is this scandal of her own sex, and curse of ours?
MILLWOOD What means this insolence? Who do you seek?
THOROWGOOD Millwood.
MILLWOOD Well, you have found her then. I am Millwood.
THOROWGOOD Then you are the most impious wretch that e'er the sun beheld.
MILLWOOD From your appearance I should have expected wisdom and moderation, but your manners belie your aspect. What is your business here? I know you not.
THOROWGOOD Hereafter you may know me better; I am Barnwell's master.
MILLWOOD Then you are master to a villain; which, I think, is not much to your credit.

THOROWGOOD Had he been as much above thy arts as my credit is superior to thy malice, I need not blush to own him.

MILLWOOD My arts! I don't understand you, sir. If he has done amiss what's that to me? Was he my servant, or yours? You should have taught him better.

THOROWGOOD Why should I wonder to find such uncommon impudence in one arrived to such a height of wickedness! When innocence is banished, modesty soon follows. Know, sorceress, I'm not ignorant of any of your arts by which you first deceived the unwary youth. I know how, step by step, you've led him on, reluctant and unwilling, from crime to crime, to this last horrid act; which you contrived, and by your cursed wiles even forced him to commit, and then betrayed him.

MILLWOOD (*Aside.*) Ha! Lucy has got the advantage of me, and accused me first. Unless I can turn the accusation, and fix it upon her and Blunt, I am lost.

THOROWGOOD Had I known your cruel design sooner, it had been prevented. To see you punished, as the law directs, is all that now remains. Poor satisfaction! for he, innocent as he is compared to you, must suffer too. But Heaven, who knows our frame, and graciously distinguishes between frailty and presumption, will make a difference though man cannot, who sees not the heart, but only judges by the outward action.

MILLWOOD I find, sir, we are both unhappy in our servants. I was surprised at such ill-treatment from a gentleman of your appearance without cause; and therefore too hastily returned it; for which I ask your pardon. I now perceive you have been so far imposed on, as to think me engaged in a former correspondence with your servant, and some way or other accessary to his undoing.

THOROWGOOD I charge you as the cause, the sole cause of all his guilt, and all his suffering; of all he now endures, and must endure, till a violent and shameful death shall put a dreadful period to his life and miseries together.

MILLWOOD 'Tis very strange! But who's secure from scandal and detraction? So far from contributing to his ruin, I never spoke to him till since that fatal accident, which I lament as much as you. 'Tis true I have a servant, on whose account he has of late frequented my house. If she has abused my good opinion of her, am I to blame? Hasn't Barnwell done the same by you?

THOROWGOOD I hear you; pray go on.

MILLWOOD I have been informed he had a violent passion for her, and she for him: but I always thought it innocent. I know her poor, and given to expensive pleasures. Now, who can tell but she may have influenced the amorous youth to commit this murder to supply her extravagancies? – It must be so. I now recollect a thousand circumstances that confirm it. I'll have her, and a man-servant that I suspect as an accomplice, secured immediately. I hope, sir, you will lay aside your ill-grounded suspicions of me, and join to punish the real contrivers of this bloody deed.   *Offers to go.*

THOROWGOOD Madam, you pass not this way: I see your design, but shall protect them from your malice.

MILLWOOD I hope you will not use your influence, and the credit of your name, to screen such guilty wretches. Consider, sir, the wickedness of persuading a thoughtless youth to such a crime.

THOROWGOOD I do – and of betraying him when it was done.

MILLWOOD That which you call betraying him may convince you of my innocence. She who loves him, though she contrived the murder, would never have delivered him into the hands of justice, as I, struck with horror at his crimes, have done.

THOROWGOOD How should an unexperienced youth escape her snares? The powerful magic of her wit and form might betray the wisest to simple dotage, and fire the blood that age had froze long since. Even I, that with just prejudice came prepared, had by her artful story been deceived, but that my strong conviction of her guilt makes even a doubt impossible! Those whom subtly you would accuse, you know are your accusers; and, what proves unanswerably their innocence and your guilt, they accused you before the deed was done, and did all that was in their power to have prevented it.

MILLWOOD Sir, you are very hard to be convinced; but I have such a proof, which, when produced, will silence all objections.   *Exit.*

SCENE 17

Thorowgood, Lucy, Trueman, Blunt, Officers, etc.

LUCY Gentlemen, pray place yourselves, some on one side of that door, and some on the other; watch her entrance, and act as your prudence shall direct you. This way (*To Thorowgood.*) and note her behaviour. I have observed her; she's driven to the last extremity, and is forming some desperate resolution. I guess at her design.

SCENE 18

To them Millwood with a pistol. Trueman secures her.

TRUEMAN Here thy power of doing mischief ends; deceitful, cruel, bloody woman!

MILLWOOD Fool, hypocrite, villain; man! thou canst not call me that.

TRUEMAN To call thee woman were to wrong the sex, thou devil!

MILLWOOD That imaginary being is an emblem of thy cursed sex collected; a mirror wherein each particular man may see his own likeness, and that of all mankind.

TRUEMAN Think not, by aggravating the fault of others to extenuate thy own, of which the abuse of such uncommon perfections of mind and body is not the least.

MILLWOOD If such I had, well may I curse your barbarous sex, who robbed me of 'em ere I knew their worth; then left me, too late, to count their value by their loss. Another and another spoiler came, and all my gain was poverty and reproach. My soul disdained, and yet disdains, dependence and contempt. Riches, no matter by what means obtained, I saw secured the worst of men from both. I found it, therefore, necessary to be rich, and to that end I summoned all my arts. You call 'em wicked, be it so; they were such as my conversation with your sex had furnished me withal.

THOROWGOOD Sure none but the worst of men conversed with thee.

MILLWOOD Men of all degrees, and all professions, I have known, yet found no difference but in their several capacities; all were alike wicked, to the utmost of their power. In pride, contention, avarice, cruelty and revenge, the reverend priest-hood were my unerring guides. From suburb-magistrates, who live by ruined reputations, as the unhospitable natives of Cornwall do by shipwrecks, I learned that to charge my innocent neighbours with my crimes, was to merit their protection; for to screen the guilty is the less scandalous when many are suspected, and detraction, like darkness and death, blackens all objects and levels all distinction. Such are your venal magistrates, who favour none but such as, by their office, they are sworn to punish. With them, not to be guilty is the worst of crimes; and large fees privately paid is every needful virtue.

THOROWGOOD Your practice has sufficiently discovered your contempt of laws, both human and divine; no wonder then that you should hate the officers of both.

MILLWOOD I hate you all; I know you, and expect no mercy. Nay, I ask for none; I have done nothing that I am sorry for; I followed my inclinations, and that the best of you does every day. All actions are alike natural and indifferent to man and beast, who devour, or are devoured, as they meet with others weaker or stronger than themselves.

THOROWGOOD What pity it is, a mind so comprehensive, daring and inquisitive should be a stranger to religion's sweet, but powerful charms.

MILLWOOD I am not fool enough to be an atheist, though I have known enough of men's hypocrisy to make a thousand simple women so. Whatever religion is in itself – as practised by mankind, it has caused the evils you say it was designed to cure. War, plague and famine, has not destroyed so many of the human race as this pretended piety has done, and with such barbarous cruelty – as if the only way to honour Heaven were to turn the present world into hell.

THOROWGOOD Truth is truth, though from an enemy and spoke in malice. You bloody, blind, and superstitious bigots, how will you answer this?

MILLWOOD What are your laws, of which you make your boast, but the fool's wisdom, and the coward's valour; the instrument and screen of all your villainies, by which you punish in others what you act yourselves, or would have acted had you been in their circumstances. The judge who condemns the poor man for being a thief, had been a thief himself had he been poor. Thus you go on, deceiving and being deceived, harassing, and plaguing, and destroying one another. But women are your universal prey.

> *Women, by whom you are, the source of joy,*
> *With cruel arts you labour to destroy;*
> *A thousand ways our ruin you pursue,*
> *Yet blame in us those arts first taught by you.*
> *Oh, may from hence each violated maid,*
> *By flattering, faithless, barb'rous man betrayed,*
> *When robbed of innocence and virgin fame,*
> *From your destruction raise a nobler name;*
> *To right their sex's wrongs devote their mind,*
> *And future Millwoods prove to plague mankind.*

Act V

SCENE: *A room in a prison.*

Thorowgood, Blunt and Lucy.

THOROWGOOD I have recommended to Barnwell a reverend divine, whose judgment and integrity I am well acquainted with. Nor has Millwood been neglected; but she, unhappy woman, still obstinate, refuses his assistance.

LUCY This pious charity to the afflicted well becomes your character; yet pardon me, sir, if I wonder you were not at their trial.

THOROWGOOD I knew it was impossible to save him, and I and my family bear so great a part in his distress, that to have been present would have aggravated our sorrows without relieving his.

BLUNT It was mournful indeed. Barnwell's youth and modest deportment, as he passed, drew tears from every eye: when placed at the bar, and arraigned before the reverend judges, with many tears and interrupting sobs he confessed and aggravated his offences, without accusing or once reflecting on Millwood, the shameless author of his ruin; who dauntless and unconcerned stood by his side, viewing with visible pride and contempt the vast assembly, who all with sympathising sorrow wept for the wretched youth. Millwood, when called upon to answer, loudly insisted upon her innocence, and made an artful and bold defence; but, finding all in vain, the impartial jury and the learned bench concurring to find her guilty, how did she curse herself, poor Barnwell, us, her judges, all mankind! But what could that avail? She was condemned, and is this day to suffer with him.

THOROWGOOD The time draws on. I am going to visit Barnwell, as you are Millwood.

LUCY We have not wronged her, yet I dread this interview. She is proud, impatient, wrathful, and unforgiving. To be the branded instruments of vengeance, to suffer in her shame, and sympathise with her in all she suffers, is the tribute we must pay for our former ill-spent lives, and long confederacy with her in wickedness.

THOROWGOOD Happy for you it ended when it did! What you have done against Millwood, I know, proceeded from a just abhorrence of her crimes, free from interest, malice, or revenge. Proselytes to virtue should be encouraged. Pursue your proposed reformation, and know me hereafter for your friend.

LUCY This is a blessing as unhoped for as unmerited; but Heaven, that snatched us from impending ruin, sure intends you as its instrument to secure us from apostasy.

THOROWGOOD With gratitude to impute your deliverance to Heaven is just. Many, less virtuously disposed than Barnwell was, have never fallen in the manner he has done; may not such owe their safety rather to Providence than to themselves? With pity and compassion let us judge him! Great were his faults, but strong was the temptation. Let his ruin learn us diffidence, humanity and circumspection; for we, who wonder at his fate – perhaps, had we like him been tried, like him we had fallen too.

SCENE 2

SCENE: *A dungeon. A table and lamp.*

Thorowgood, Barnwell reading.

THOROWGOOD See there the bitter fruits of passion's detested reign, and sensual appetite indulged; severe reflections, penitence, and tears.

BARNWELL My honoured, injured master, whose goodness has covered me a thousand times with shame, forgive this last unwilling disrespect. Indeed I saw you not.

THOROWGOOD 'Tis well; I hope you are better employed in viewing of yourself. Your journey's long, your time for preparation almost spent. I sent a reverend divine to teach you to improve it, and should be glad to hear of his success.

BARNWELL The word of truth, which he recommended for my constant companion in this my sad retirement, has at length removed the doubts I laboured under. From thence I've learned the infinite extent of heavenly mercy; that my offences, though great, are not unpardonable: and that 'tis not my interest only, but my duty, to believe and to rejoice in that hope. So shall Heaven receive the glory, and future penitents the profit of my example.

THOROWGOOD Go on! How happy am I who live to see this!

BARNWELL 'Tis wonderful that words should charm despair, speak peace and pardon to a murderer's conscience; but truth and mercy flow in every sentence, attended with force and energy divine. How shall I describe my present state of mind? I hope in doubt, and trembling I rejoice; I feel my grief increase, even as my fears give way. Joy and gratitude now supply more tears than the horror and anguish of despair before.

THOROWGOOD These are the genuine signs of true repentance; the only preparatory, certain way to everlasting peace. O the joy it gives to see a soul formed and prepared for heaven! For this the faithful minister devotes himself to meditation, abstinence and prayer, shunning the vain delights of sensual joys, and daily dies that others may live for ever. For this he turns the sacred volumes o'er, and spends his life in painful search of truth. The love of riches and the lust of power he looks on with just contempt and detestation, who only counts for wealth the souls he wins, and whose highest ambition is to serve mankind. If the reward of all his pains be to preserve one soul from wandering, or turn one from the error of his ways, how does he then rejoice, and own his little labours over-paid!

BARNWELL What do I owe for all your generous kindness! But though I cannot, Heaven can and will reward you.

THOROWGOOD To see thee thus, is joy too great for words. Farewell! – Heaven strengthen thee. – Farewell!

BARNWELL Oh, sir, there's something I could say, if my sad swelling heart would give me leave.

THOROWGOOD Give it vent a while, and try.

BARNWELL I had a friend – 'tis true I am unworthy – yet

methinks your generous example might persuade – Could I not see him once before I go from whence there's no return?

THOROWGOOD He's coming, and as much thy friend as ever. But I'll not anticipate his sorrow; too soon he'll see the sad effect of this contagious ruin. This torrent of domestic misery bears too hard upon me. I must retire to indulge a weakness I find impossible to overcome. Much loved – and much lamented youth! – Farewell! – Heaven strengthen thee. – Eternally farewell!

BARNWELL The best of masters and of men – Farewell. While I live, let me not want your prayers.

THOROWGOOD Thou shalt not. Thy peace being made with Heaven, death's already vanquished. Bear a little longer the pains that attend this transitory life, and cease from pain for ever.

SCENE 3

Barnwell.

BARNWELL I find a power within that bears my soul above the fears of death, and, spite of conscious shame and guilt, gives me a taste of pleasure more than mortal.

SCENE 4

To him Trueman and Keeper.

KEEPER Sir, there's the prisoner.

SCENE 5

Barnwell and Trueman.

BARNWELL Trueman! – My friend, whom I so wished to see! yet now he's here, I dare not look upon him.   *Weeps.*

TRUEMAN Oh, Barnwell! Barnwell!

BARNWELL Mercy! Mercy! gracious Heaven! For death, but not for this, was I prepared.

TRUEMAN What have I suffered since I saw thee last! What pain has absence given me! – But, oh, to see thee thus! –

BARNWELL I know it is dreadful! I feel the anguish of thy

generous soul: — But I was born to murder all who love me.   *Both weep*.

TRUEMAN I came not to reproach you; I thought to bring you comfort; but I am deceived, for I have none to give. I came to share thy sorrow, but cannot bear my own.

BARNWELL My sense of guilt, indeed, you cannot know; 'tis what the good and innocent, like you, can ne'er conceive: but other griefs at present I have none, but what I feel for you. In your sorrow I read you love me still; but yet, methinks, 'tis strange, when I consider what I am.

TRUEMAN No more of that; I can remember nothing but thy virtues; thy honest, tender friendship, our former happy state, and present misery. Oh, had you trusted me when first the fair seducer tempted you, all might have been prevented.

BARNWELL Alas! thou knowest not what a wretch I've been. Breach of friendship was my first and least offence. So far was I lost to goodness, so devoted to the author of my ruin, that had she insisted on my murdering thee — I think I should have done it.

TRUEMAN Prithee aggravate thy faults no more.

BARNWELL I think I should! Thus good and generous as you are, I should have murdered you!

TRUEMAN We have not yet embraced, and may be interrupted. Come to my arms.

BARNWELL Never, never will I taste such joys on earth; never will I so soothe my just remorse. Are those honest arms and faithful bosom fit to embrace and to support a murderer? These iron fetters only shall clasp, and flinty pavement bear me. (*Throwing himself on the ground*.) Even these too good for such a bloody monster.

TRUEMAN Shall fortune sever those whom friendship joined? Thy miseries cannot lay thee so low but love will find thee. (*Lies down beside him*.) Upon this rugged couch then let us lie; for well it suits our most deplorable condition. Here will we offer to stern calamity; this earth the altar, and ourselves the sacrifice. Our mutual groans shall echo to each other through the dreary vault; our sighs shall number the moments as they pass, and mingling tears communicate such anguish, as words were never made to express.

BARNWELL Then be it so. Since you propose an intercourse of woe, pour all your griefs into my breast, and in exchange take mine. (*Embracing*.) Where's now the anguish that you promised? You've taken mine, and make me no return. Sure peace and comfort dwell within these arms, and sorrow can't approach me while I'm here. This too is the work of Heaven, who, having before spoke peace and pardon to me, now sends thee to confirm it. O take, take some of the joy that overflows my breast!

TRUEMAN I do, I do. Almighty Power, how have you made us capable to bear, at once, the extremes of pleasure and of pain?

SCENE 6

To them, Keeper.

KEEPER Sir!

TRUEMAN I come.

SCENE 7

Barnwell and Trueman.

BARNWELL Must you leave me? Death would soon have parted us for ever.

TRUEMAN Oh, my Barnwell! there's yet another talk behind. Again your heart must bleed for others' woes.

BARNWELL To meet and part with you I thought was all I had to do on earth. What is there more for me to do, or suffer?

TRUEMAN I dread to tell thee, yet it must be known! Maria —

BARNWELL Our master's fair and virtuous daughter?

TRUEMAN The same.

BARNWELL No misfortune, I hope, has reached that lovely maid! Preserve her, Heaven, from every will, to show mankind that goodness is your care!

TRUEMAN Thy, thy misfortunes, my unhappy friend, have reached her. Whatever you and I have felt, and more, if more be possible, she feels for you.

BARNWELL (*Aside*). I know he doth abhor a lie, and would not trifle with his dying friend. This is, indeed, the bitterness of death.

TRUEMAN You must remember, for we all observed it, for some time past, a heavy melancholy weighed her down. Disconsolate she seemed, and pined and languished from a cause unknown; till, hearing of your dreadful fate, the long-stifled flame blazed out. She wept, she wrung her hands, and tore her hair, and, in the transport of her grief, discovered her own lost state, whilst she lamented yours.

BARNWELL Will all the pain I feel restore thy ease, lovely unhappy maid! (*Weeping.*) Why didn't you let me die and never know it?

TRUEMAN It was impossible; she makes no secret of her passion for you, and is determined to see you ere you die. She waits for me to introduce her.

SCENE 8

Barnwell.

BARNWELL Vain, busy thoughts, be still! What avails it to think on what I might have been? I now am what I've made myself.

SCENE 9

To him, Trueman and Maria.

TRUEMAN Madam, reluctant I lead you to this dismal scene. This is the seat of misery and guilt. Here awful justice reserves her public victims. This is the entrance to shameful death.

MARIA To this sad place, then, no improper guest, the abandoned, lost Maria brings despair – and see the subject and the cause of all this world of woe! Silent and motionless he stands, as if his soul had quitted her abode, and the lifeless form alone was left behind – yet that so perfect that beauty and death, ever at enmity, now seem united there.

BARNWELL I groan, but murmur not. Just Heaven, I am your own; do with me what you please.

MARIA Why are your streaming eyes still fixed below, as though thou didst give the greedy earth thy sorrows, and rob me of my due? Were happiness within your power, you should bestow it where you pleased; but in your misery I must and will partake!

BARNWELL Oh, say not so, but fly, abhor, and leave me to my fate! Consider what you are – how vast your fortune, and how bright your fame; have pity on your youth, your beauty, and unequalled virtue, for which so many noble peers have

sighed in vain! Bless with your charms some honourable lord!
Adorn with your beauty, and by your example improve, the
English Court, that justly claims such merit: so shall I quickly
be to you as though I had never been.

MARIA When I forget you, I must be so indeed. Reason, choice,
virtue, all forbid it. Let women, like Millwood, if there be
more such women, smile in prosperity, and in adversity
forsake! Be it the pride of virtue to repair, or to partake, the
ruin such have made.

TRUEMAN Lovely, ill-fated maid! Was there ever such generous
distress before? How must this pierce his grateful heart, and
aggravate his woes!

BARNWELL Ere I knew guilt or shame – when fortune smiled,
and when my youthful hopes were at the highest – if then to
have raised my thoughts to you, had been presumption in me,
never to have been pardoned: think how much beneath
yourself you condescend, to regard me now!

MARIA Let her blush, who, professing love, invades the freedom
of your sex's choice, and meanly sues in hopes of a return!
Your inevitable fate hath rendered hope impossible as vain.
Then, why should I fear to avow a passion so just and so
disinterested?

TRUEMAN If any should take occasion, from Millwood's crimes,
to libel the best and fairest part of the creation, here let them
see their error! The most distant hopes of such a tender
passion from so bright a maid add to the happiness of the
most happy, and make the greatest proud. Yet here 'tis
lavished in vain: though by the rich present the generous
donor is undone, he on whom it is bestowed receives no
benefit.

BARNWELL So the aromatic spices of the East, which all the
living covet and esteem, are, with unavailing kindness, wasted
on the dead.

MARIA Yes, fruitless is my love, and unavailing all my sighs and
tears. Can they save thee from approaching death – from such
a death? Oh, terrible idea! What is her misery and distress,
who sees the first last object of her love, for whom alone she'd
live – for whom she'd die a thousand, thousand deaths, if it
were possible – expiring in her arms? Yet she is happy, when
compared to me. Were millions of worlds mine, I'd gladly
give them in exchange for her condition. The most consum-

mate woe is light to mine. The last of curses to other miserable maids is all I ask; and that's denied me.

TRUEMAN Time and reflections cure all ills.

MARIA All but this, this dreadful catastrophe virtue herself abhors. To give a holiday to suburb slaves, and passing entertain the savage herd, who elbowing each other for a sight, pursue and press upon him like his fate! A mind with piety and resolution armed may smile on death. But public ignominy, everlasting shame – shame, the death of souls, to die a thousand times, and yet survive even death itself, in never dying infamy – is this to be endured? Can I who live in him, and must, each hour of my devoted life, feel all these woes renewed, can I endure this?

TRUEMAN Grief has impaired her spirits; she pants as in the agonies of death.

BARNWELL Preserve her, Heaven, and restore her peace; nor let her death be added to my crime! (*Bell tolls.*) I am summoned to my fate.

SCENE 10

To *them, Keeper.*

KEEPER The officers attend you, sir. Mrs Millwood is already summoned.

BARNWELL Tell 'em I am ready. And now, my friend, farewell! (*Embracing.*) Support and comfort the best you can this mourning fair. – No more! Forget not to pray for me! (*Turning to Maria.*) Would you, bright excellence, permit me the honour of a chaste embrace, the last happiness this world could give were mine. (*She inclines towards him; they embrace.*) Exalted goodness! O turn your eyes from earth, and me, to Heaven, where virtue, like yours, is ever heard. Pray for the peace of my departing soul! Early my race of wickedness began, and soon has reached the summit. Ere Nature has finished her work, and stamped me man – just at the time that others begin to stray – my course is finished. Though short my span of life, and few my days, yet, count my crimes for years, and I have lived whole ages. Justice and mercy are in Heaven the same: its utmost severity is mercy to the whole, thereby to cure man's folly and presumption,

which else would render even infinite mercy vain and ineffec-
tual. Thus justice, in compassion to mankind, cuts off a
wretch like me, by one such example to secure thousands
from future ruin.

> *If any youth, like you, in future times*
> *Shall mourn my fate, though he abhor my crimes;*
> *Or tender maid, like you, my tale shall hear,*
> *And to my sorrows give a pitying tear;*
> *To each such melting eye, and throbbing heart,*
> *Would gracious Heaven this benefit impart*
> *Never to know my guilt, nor feel my pain:*
> *Then must you own, you ought not to complain:*
> *Since you nor weep, nor shall I die, in vain.*

SCENE 11

SCENE: *The place of execution. The gallows and ladders*
at farther end of the stage. A crowd of spectators.

Blunt and Lucy.

LUCY Heavens! what a throng!

BLUNT How terrible is death, when thus prepared!

LUCY Support them, Heaven; thou only can support them; all
other help is vain.

OFFICER (*Within.*) Make way there; make way, and give the
prisoners room!

LUCY They are here; observe them well! How humble and
composed young Barnwell seems! But Millwood looks wild,
ruffled with passion, confounded and amazed.

Enter Barnwell, Millwood, Officers and Executioners.

BARNWELL See, Millwood, see: our journey's at an end. Life,
like a tale that is told, is passed away; that short but dark and
unknown passage, death, is all the space between us and
endless joys, or woes eternal.

MILLWOOD Is this the end of all my flattering hopes? Were
youth and beauty given me for a curse, and wisdom only to
insure my ruin? They were, they were! Heaven, thou hast
done thy worst. Or, if thou hast in store some untried plague
– somewhat that's worse than shame, despair and death,

unpitied death, confirmed despair and soul-confounding shame – something that men and angels can't describe, and only fiends, who bear it, can conceive: now pour it now on this devoted head, that I may feel the worst thou canst inflict, and bid defiance to thy utmost power!

BARNWELL Yet, ere we pass the dreadful gulf of death – yet, ere you're plunged in everlasting woe: O bend your stubborn knees and harder heart, humbly to deprecate the wrath divine! Who knows but Heaven, in your dying moments, may bestow that grace and mercy which your life despised!

MILLWOOD Why name you mercy to a wretch like me! Mercy's beyond my hope – almost beyond my wish. I can't repent, nor ask to be forgiven.

BARNWELL Oh, think what 'tis to be for ever, ever miserable! nor with vain pride oppose a Power that's able to destroy you!

MILLWOOD That will destroy me; I feel it will. A deluge of wrath is pouring on my soul. Chains, darkness, wheels, racks, sharp-stinging scorpions, molten lead, and seas of sulphur, are light to what I feel.

BARNWELL Oh, add not to your vast account despair! a sin more injurious to Heaven than all you've yet committed.

MILLWOOD Oh, I have sinned beyond the reach of mercy!

BARNWELL Oh, say not so! 'tis blasphemy to think it. As yon bright roof is higher than the earth, so, and much more, does Heaven's goodness pass our apprehension. Oh! what created being shall presume to circumscribe mercy, that knows no bounds?

MILLWOOD This yields no hope. Though mercy may be boundless, yet 'tis free; and I was doomed, before the world began, to endless pains, and thou to joys eternal.

BARNWELL O gracious Heaven! extend thy pity to her! Let thy rich mercy flow in plenteous streams, to chase her fears and heal her wounded soul!

MILLWOOD It will not be. Your prayers are lost in air, or else returned, perhaps with double blessing, to your bosom; but me they help not.

BARNWELL Yet hear me, Millwood!

MILLWOOD Away! I will not hear thee. I tell thee, youth, I am by Heaven devoted a dreadful instance of its power to punish. (*Barnwell seems to pray.*) If thou wilt pray, pray for thyself, not me! How doth his fervent soul mount with his words, and both ascend to Heaven — that Heaven whose gates are shut with adamantine bars against my prayers, had I the will to pray. I cannot bear it! Sure, 'tis the worst of torments to behold others enjoy that bliss that we must never taste!

OFFICER The utmost limit of your time's expired.

MILLWOOD Incompassed with horror, whither must I go? I would not live — nor die. That I could cease to be, or ne'er had been!

BARNWELL Since peace and comfort are denied her here, may she find mercy where she least expects it, and this be all her hell! From our example may all be taught to fly the first approach of vice, but, if o'ertaken:

> By strong temptation, weakness, or surprise,
> Lament their guilt and by repentance rise!
> The impenitent alone die unforgiven:
> To sin's like man, and to forgive like Heaven.   Exeunt.

SCENE 12

Trueman, Blunt and Lucy.

LUCY Heart-breaking sight! O wretched, wretched Millwood!

TRUEMAN You came from her, then; how is she disposed to meet her fate?

BLUNT Who can describe unalterable woe?

LUCY She goes to death incompassed with horror, loathing life, and yet afraid to die; no tongue can tell her anguish and despair.

TRUEMAN Heaven be better to her than her fears; may she prove a warning to others, a monument of mercy in herself!

LUCY O sorrow insupportable! Break, break, my heart!

TRUEMAN In vain

> With bleeding hearts and weeping eyes we show
> A human gen'rous sense of others' woe,
> Unless we mark what drew their ruin on,
> And, by avoiding that, prevent our own.

Epilogue

BY COLLEY CIBBER, ESQ.

Spoken by Mrs Cibber.

Since fate has robbed me of the hapless youth
For whom my heart had boarded up its truth;
By all the laws of love and honour, now
I'm free again to choose — and one of you.
But soft — With caution first I'll round me peep;
Maids, in my case, should look before they leap.
Here's choice enough, of various sorts and hue, ⎫
The cit, the wit, the rake cocked up in cue, ⎬
The fair spruce mercer, and the tawny Jew. ⎭

   Suppose I search the sober gallery? — No; ⎫
There's none but 'prentices and cuckolds all a-row; ⎬
And these, I doubt, are those that make 'em so. ⎭

Pointing to the boxes.

   'Tis very well, enjoy the jest — But you, ⎫
Fine powdered sparks — nay, I am told 'tis true, ⎬
Your happy spouses — can make cuckolds too. ⎭
'Twixt you and them the difference this, perhaps;
The cit's ashamed whene'er his duck he traps;
But you, when Madam's tripping, let her fall,
Cock up your hats, and take no shame at all.

   What if some favoured poet I could meet,
Whose love would lay his laurels at my feet.
No — painted passion real love abhors —
His flame would prove the suit of creditors.

   Not to detain you, then, with longer pause,
In short, my heart to this conclusion draws —
I yield it to the hand that's loudest in applause.

SHE STOOPS TO CONQUER,
OR
THE MISTAKES OF THE NIGHT

Dramatis Personæ

MEN

SIR CHARLES MARLOW	Mr Gardner
YOUNG MARLOW, *his son*	Mr Lewes
HARDCASTLE	Mr Shuter
HASTINGS	Mr Dubellamy
TONY LUMPKIN	Mr Quick
DIGGORY	Mr Saunders

WOMEN

MRS HARDCASTLE	Mrs Green
MISS HARDCASTLE	Mrs Bulkely
MISS NEVILLE	Mrs Kniveton
MAID	Miss Willems

Landlord, Servants, etc.

To Samuel Johnson, L.L.D.

Dear Sir,

By inscribing this slight performance to you, I do not mean so much to compliment you as myself. It may do me some honour to inform the public, that I have lived many years in intimacy with you. It may serve the interests of mankind also to inform them, that the greatest wit may be found in a character, without impairing the most unaffected piety.

I have, particularly, reason to thank you for your partiality to this performance. The undertaking a comedy, not merely sentimental, was very dangerous; and Mr Colman, who saw this piece in its various stages, always thought it so. However I ventured to trust it to the public; and though it was necessarily delayed till late in the season, I have every reason to be grateful.

I am, Dear Sir,
Your most sincere friend
and admirer,
OLIVER GOLDSMITH

Prologue

BY DAVID GARRICK, ESQ.

Enter Mr Woodward,
Dressed in black, and holding a handkerchief to his eyes.

Excuse me, Sirs, I pray – I can't yet speak –
I'm crying now – and have been all the week!
'Tis not alone this mourning suit, good masters;
I've that within – for which there are no plaisters!
Pray wou'd you know the reason why I'm crying?
The Comic muse, long sick, is now a dying!
And if she goes, my tears will never stop;
For as a play'r, I can't squeeze out one drop:
I am undone, that's all – shall lose my bread –
I'd rather, but that's nothing – lose my head.
When the sweet maid is laid upon the bier,
Shuter and *I* shall be chief mourners here.
To *her* a mawkish drab of spurious breed,
Who deals in *sentimentals* will succeed!
Poor *Ned* and I are dead to all intents,
We can as soon speak *Greek* as *sentiments!*
Both nervous grown, to keep our spirits up,
We now and then take down a hearty cup.
What shall we do? – If Comedy forsake us!
They'll turn us out, and no one else will take us,
But why can't I be moral? – Let me try –
My heart thus pressing – fix'd my face and eye –
With a sententious look, that nothing means,
(Faces are blocks, in sentimental scenes)
Thus I begin – *All is not gold that glitters,*
Pleasure seems sweet, but proves a glass of bitters.
When ign'rance enters, folly is at hand;

Learning is better far than house and land:
Let not your virtue trip, who trips may stumble,
And virtue is not virtue, if she tumble.
  I give it up – morals won't do for me;
To make you laugh I must play tragedy.
One hope remains – hearing the maid was ill,
A *doctor* comes this night to shew his skill.
To cheer her heart, and give your muscles motion,
He in *five draughts* prepar'd, presents a potion:
A kind of magic charm – for be assur'd,
If you will *swallow it*, the maid is cur'd:
But desperate the Doctor, and her case is,
If you reject the dose, and make wry faces!
This truth he boasts, will boast it while he lives,
No *Pois'nous drugs* are mix'd in what he gives;
Should he succeed, you'll give him his degree;
If not, within he will receive no fee!
The college *you*, must his pretensions back,
Pronounce him *regular*, or dub him *quack*.

Act I

SCENE: *A chamber in an old fashioned house.*

Enter Mrs Hardcastle and Mr Hardcastle.

MRS HARDCASTLE I vow, Mr Hardcastle, you're very particular. Is there a creature in the whole country, but ourselves, that does not take a trip to town now and then, to rub off the rust a little? There's the two Miss Hoggs, and our neighbour, Mrs Grigsby, go to take a month's polishing every winter.

HARDCASTLE Ay, and bring back vanity and affectation to last them the whole year. I wonder why London cannot keep its own fools at home. In my time, the follies of the town crept slowly among us, but now they travel faster than a stage-coach. Its fopperies come down, not only as inside passengers, but in the very basket.

MRS HARDCASTLE Ay, *your* times were fine times, indeed; you have been telling us of *them* for many a long year. Here we live in an old rumbling mansion, that looks for all the world like an inn, but that we never see company. Our best visitors are old Mrs Oddfish, the curate's wife, and little Cripplegate, the lame dancing-master: And all our entertainment your old stories of Prince Eugene and the Duke of Marlborough. I hate such old-fashioned trumpery.

HARDCASTLE And I love it. I love every thing that's old: old friends, old times, old manners, old books, old wine; and, I believe, Dorothy, (*taking her hand*) you'll own I have been pretty fond of an old wife.

MRS HARDCASTLE Lord, Mr Hardcastle, you're for ever at your Dorothy's and your old wife's. You may be a Darby, but I'll be no Joan, I promise you. I'm not so old as you'd make me, by more than one good year. Add twenty to twenty, and make money of that.

HARDCASTLE Let me see; twenty added to twenty, makes just fifty and seven.

MRS HARDCASTLE It's false, Mr Hardcastle: I was but twenty when I was brought to bed of Tony, that I had my Mr Lumpkin, my first husband; and he's not come to years of discretion yet.

HARDCASTLE Nor ever will, I dare answer for him. Ay, you have taught *him* finely.

MRS HARDCASTLE No matter, Tony Lumpkin has a good fortune. My son is not to live by his learning. I don't think a boy wants much learning to spend fifteen hundred a year.

HARDCASTLE Learning, quotha! A mere composition of tricks and mischief.

MRS HARDCASTLE Humour, my dear: nothing but humour. Come, Mr Hardcastle, you must allow the boy a little humour.

HARDCASTLE I'd sooner allow him an horse-pond. If burning the footmen's shoes, frighting the maids, and worrying the kittens, be humour, he has it. It was but yesterday he fastened my wig to the back of my chair, and when I went to make a bow, I popt my bald head in Mrs Frizzle's face.

MRS HARDCASTLE And am I to blame? The poor boy has always too sickly to do any good. A school would be his death. When he comes to be a little stronger, who knows what a year or two's Latin may do for him?

HARDCASTLE Latin for him! A cat and fiddle. No, no, the alehouse and the stable are the only schools he'll ever go to.

MRS HARDCASTLE Well, we must not snub the poor boy now, for I believe we shan't have him long among us. Any body that looks in his face may see he's consumptive.

HARDCASTLE Ay, if growing too fat be one of the symptoms.

MRS HARDCASTLE He coughs sometimes.

HARDCASTLE Yes, when his liquor goes the wrong way.

MRS HARDCASTLE I'm actually afraid of his lungs.

HARDCASTLE And truly so am I; for he sometimes whoops like a speaking trumpet – (*Tony hallooing behind the scenes.*) – O there he goes – A very consumptive figure, truly.

Enter Tony, crossing the stage.

MRS HARDCASTLE Tony, where are you going, my charmer? Won't you give papa and I a little of your company, lovee?

TONY I'm in haste, mother, I cannot stay.

MRS HARDCASTLE You shan't venture out this raw evening, my dear: You look most shockingly.

TONY I can't stay, I tell you. The Three Pigeons expects me down every moment. There's some fun going forward.

HARDCASTLE Ay; the ale-house, the old place: I thought so.

MRS HARDCASTLE A low, paltry set of fellows.

TONY Not so low neither. There's Dick Muggins the exciseman, Jack Slang the horse doctor, Little Aminadab that grinds the music box, and Tom Twist that spins the pewter platter.

MRS HARDCASTLE Pray, my dear, disappoint them for one night at least.

TONY As for disappointing *them*, I should not so much mind; but I can't abide to disappoint *myself*.

MRS HARDCASTLE (*Detaining him.*) You shan't go.

TONY I will, I tell you.

MRS HARDCASTLE I say you shan't.

TONY We'll see which is strongest, you or I.

Exit, hawling her out.

Hardcastle, solus.

HARDCASTLE Ay, there goes a pair that only spoil each other. But is not the whole age in a combination to drive sense and discretion out of doors? There's my pretty darling Kate; the fashions of the times have almost infected her too. By living a year or two in town, she is as fond of gauze, and French frippery, as the best of them.

Enter Miss Hardcastle.

HARDCASTLE Blessings on my pretty innocence! Drest out as usual my Kate. Goodness! What a quantity of superfluous silk hast thou got about thee, girl! I could never teach the fools of this age, that the indigent world could be cloathed out of the trimmings of the vain.

MISS HARDCASTLE You know our agreement, Sir. You allow me the morning to receive and pay visits, and to dress in my own manner; and in the evening, I put on my housewife's dress to please you.

HARDCASTLE Well, remember I insist on the terms of our agreement; and, by the bye, I believe I shall have occasion to try your obedience this very evening.

MISS HARDCASTLE I protest, Sir, I don't comprehend your meaning.

HARDCASTLE Then, to be plain with you, Kate, I expect the young gentleman I have chosen to be your husband from town this very day. I have his father's letter, in which he informs me his son is set out, and that he intends to follow himself shortly after.

MISS HARDCASTLE Indeed! I wish I had known something of this before. Bless me, how shall I behave? It's a thousand to one I shan't like him; our meeting will be so formal, and so like a thing of business, that I shall find no room for friendship or esteem.

HARDCASTLE Depend upon it, child, I'll never controul your choice; but Mr Marlow, whom I have pitched upon, is the son of my old friend, Sir Charles Marlow, of whom you have heard me talk so often. The young gentleman has been bred a scholar, and is designed for an employment in the service of his country. I am told he's a man of an excellent understanding.

MISS HARDCASTLE Is he?

HARDCASTLE Very generous.

MISS HARDCASTLE I believe I shall like him.

HARDCASTLE Young and brave.

MISS HARDCASTLE I'm sure I shall like him.

HARDCASTLE And very handsome.

MISS HARDCASTLE My dear Papa, say no more (*kissing his hand*) he's mine, I'll have him.

HARDCASTLE And to crown all, Kate, he's one of the most bashful and reserved young fellows in all the world.

MISS HARDCASTLE Eh! you have frozen me to death again. That word reserved, has undone all the rest of his accomplishments. A reserved lover, it is said, always makes a suspicious husband.

HARDCASTLE On the contrary, modesty seldom resides in a breast that is not enriched with nobler virtues. It was the very feature in his character that first struck me.

MISS HARDCASTLE He must have more striking features to catch me, I promise you. However, if he be so young, so handsome, and so every thing, as you mention, I believe he'll do still. I think I'll have him.

HARDCASTLE Ay, Kate, but there is still an obstacle. Its more than an even wager, he may not have *you*.

MISS HARDCASTLE My dear Papa, why will you mortify one so? – Well, if he refuses, instead of breaking my heart at his indifference, I'll only break my glass for its flattery. Set my cap to some newer fashion, and look out for some less difficult admirer.

HARDCASTLE Bravely resolved! In the mean time I'll go prepare the servants for his reception; as we seldom see company they want as much training as a company of recruits, the first day's muster.   *Exit.*

Miss Hardcastle, sola.

MISS HARDCASTLE Lud, this news of Papa's, puts me all in a flutter. Young, handsome; these he put last; but I put them foremost. Sensible, good-natured; I like all that. But then reserved, and sheepish, that's much against him. Yet can't he be cured of his timidity, by being taught to be proud of his wife? Yes, and can't I – But I vow I'm disposing of the husband, before I have secured the lover.

Enter Miss Neville.

MISS HARDCASTLE I'm glad you're come, Neville, my dear. Tell me, Constance, how do I look this evening? Is there any thing whimsical about me? Is it one of my well looking days, child? Am I in face to day?

MISS NEVILLE Perfectly, my dear. Yet now I look again – bless me! – sure no accident has happened among the canary birds or the gold fishes. Has your brother or the cat been meddling? Or has the last novel been too moving?

MISS HARDCASTLE No; nothing of all this. I have been threatened – I can scarce get it out – I have been threatened with a lover.

MISS NEVILLE And his name –

MISS HARDCASTLE Is Marlow.

MISS NEVILLE Indeed!

MISS HARDCASTLE The son of Sir Charles Marlow.

MISS NEVILLE As I live, the most intimate friend of Mr Hastings, *my* admirer. They are never asunder. I believe you must have seen him when we lived in town.

MISS HARDCASTLE Never.

MISS NEVILLE He's a very singular character, I assure you. Among women of reputation and virtue, he is the modestest man alive; but his acquaintance give him a very different character among creatures of another stamp: you understand me.

MISS HARDCASTLE An odd character, indeed. I shall never be able to manage him. What shall I do? Pshaw, think no more of him, but trust to occurrences for success. But how goes on your own affair my dear, has my mother been courting you for my brother Tony, as usual?

MISS NEVILLE I have just come from one of our agreeable tête-à-têtes. She has been saying a hundred tender things, and setting off her pretty monster as the very pink of perfection.

MISS HARDCASTLE And her partiality is such, that she actually thinks him so. A fortune like your's is no small temptation. Besides, as she has the sole management of it, I'm not surprized to see her unwilling to let it go out of the family.

MISS NEVILLE A fortune like mine, which chiefly consists in jewels, is no such mighty temptation. But at any rate if my dear Hastings be but constant, I make no doubt to be too hard for her at last. However, I let her suppose that I am in love with her son, and she never once dreams that my affections are fixed upon another.

MISS HARDCASTLE My good brother holds out stoutly. I could almost love him for hating you so.

MISS NEVILLE It is a good natured creature at bottom, and I'm sure would wish to see me married to any body but himself. But my aunt's bell rings for our afternoon's walk round the improvements. Allons. Courage is necessary as our affairs are critical.

MISS HARDCASTLE Would it were bed time and all were well.

Exeunt.

SCENE: *An alehouse room. Several shabby fellows, with punch and tobacco. Tony at the head of the table, a little higher than the rest: a mallet in his hand.*

OMNES Hurrea, hurrea, hurrea, bravo.

FIRST FELLOW Now, gentlemen, silence for a song. The 'Squire is going to knock himself down for a song.

OMNES Ay, a song, a song.

TONY Then I'll sing you, gentlemen, a song I made upon this
ale-house, the Three Pigeons.

SONG

> Let school-masters puzzle their brain,
>   With grammar, and nonsense, and learning;
> Good liquor, I stoutly maintain,
>   Gives genus a better discerning.
> Let them brag of their Heathenish Gods,
>   Their Lethes, their Styxes, and Stygians;
> Their Quis, and their Quæs, and their Quods,
>   They're all but a parcel of Pigeons.
> Toroddle, toroddle, toroll.
>
> When Methodist preachers come down,
>   A preaching that drinking is sinful,
> I'll wager the rascals a crown,
>   They always preach best with a skinful.
> But when you come down with your pence,
>   For a slice of their scurvy religion,
> I'll leave it to all men of sense,
>   But you my good friend are the pigeon.
> Toroddle, toroddle, toroll.
>
> Then come, put the jorum about,
>   And let us be merry and clever,
> Our hearts and our liquors are stout,
>   Here's the Three Jolly Pigeons for ever.
> Let some cry up woodcock or hare,
>   Your bustards, your ducks, and your widgeons;
> But of all the birds in the air,
>   Here's a health to the Three Jolly Pigeons.
> Toroddle, toroddle, toroll.

OMNES Bravo, bravo.

FIRST FELLOW The 'Squire has got spunk in him.

SECOND FELLOW I love to hear him sing, bekeays he never gives
us nothing that's *low*.

THIRD FELLOW O damn any thing that's *low*, I cannot bear it.

FOURTH FELLOW The genteel thing is the genteel thing at any time. If so be that a gentleman bees in a concatenation accordingly.

THIRD FELLOW I like the maxum of it, Master Muggins. What, tho' I am obligated to dance a bear, a man may be a gentleman for all that. May this be my poison if my bear ever dances but to the very genteelest of tunes. Water Parted, or the minuet in Ariadne.

SECOND FELLOW What a pity it is the 'Squire is not come to his own. It would be well for all the publicans within ten miles round of him.

TONY Ecod and so it would Master Slang. I'd then shew what it was to keep choice of company.

SECOND FELLOW O he takes after his own father for that. To be sure old 'Squire Lumpkin was the finest gentleman I ever set my eyes on. For winding the streight horn, or beating a thicket for a hare, or a wench, he never had his fellow. It was a saying in the place, that he kept the best horses, dogs, and girls in the whole county.

TONY Ecod, and when I'm of age I'll be no bastard I promise you. I have been thinking of Bett Bouncer and the miller's grey mare to begin with. But come, my boys, drink about and be merry, for you pay no reckoning. Well, Stingo, what's the matter?

Enter Landlord.

LANDLORD There be two gentlemen in a post-chaise at the door. They have lost their way upo' the forest; and they are talking something about Mr Hardcastle.

TONY As sure as can be one of them must be the gentleman that's coming down to court my sister. Do they seem to be Londoners?

LANDLORD I believe they may. They look woundily like Frenchmen.

TONY Then desire them to step this way, and I'll set them right in a twinkling. (*Exit Landlord.*) Gentlemen, as they mayn't be good enough company for you, step down for a moment, and I'll be with you in the squeezing of a lemon.   *Exeunt Mob.*

Tony solus.

TONY Father-in-law has been calling me whelp, and hound, this half year. Now if I pleased, I could be so revenged upon the old grumbletonian. But then I'm afraid – afraid of what! I shall soon be worth fifteen hundred a year, and let him frighten me out of *that* if he can.

Enter Landlord, conducting Marlow and Hastings.

MARLOW What a tedious uncomfortable day have we had of it! We were told it was but forty miles across the country, and we have come above threescore.

HASTINGS And all Marlow, from that unaccountable reserve of yours, that would not let us enquire more frequently on the way.

MARLOW I own, Hastings, I am unwilling to lay myself under an obligation to every one I meet; and often, stand the chance of an unmannerly answer.

HASTINGS At present, however, we are not likely to receive any answer.

TONY No offence, gentlemen. But I'm told you have been enquiring for one Mr Hardcastle, in these parts. Do you know what part of the country you are in?

HASTINGS Not in the least Sir, but should thank you for information.

TONY Nor the way you came?

HASTINGS No, Sir; but you can inform us –

TONY Why, gentlemen, if you know neither the road you are going, nor where you are, nor the road you came, the first thing I have to inform you is that – You have lost your way.

MARLOW We wanted no ghost to tell us that.

TONY Pray, gentlemen, may I be so bold as to ask the place from whence you came?

MARLOW That's not necessary towards directing us where we are to go.

TONY No offence; but question for question is all fair, you know. Pray gentlemen, is not this same Hardcastle a cross-grain'd, old-fashion'd, whimsical fellow, with an ugly face; a daughter, and a pretty son?

HASTINGS We have not seen the gentleman, but he has the family you mention.

TONY The daughter, a tall trapesing, trolloping, talkative may-pole – The son, a pretty, well-bred, agreeable youth, that every body is fond of.

MARLOW Our information differs in this. The daughter is said to be well-bred and beautiful; the son, an aukward booby, reared up, and spoiled at his mother's apron-string.

TONY He-he-hem – Then, gentlemen, all I have to tell you is, that you won't reach Mr Hardcastle's house this night, I believe.

HASTINGS Unfortunate!

TONY It's a damn'd long, dark, boggy, dirty, dangerous way. Stingo, tell the gentlemen the way to Mr Hardcastle's; (*winking upon the Landlord*) Mr Hardcastle's, of Quagmire Marsh, you understand me.

LANDLORD Master Hardcastle's! Lock-a-daisy, my masters, you're come a deadly deal wrong! When you came to the bottom of the hill, you should have cross'd down Squash-lane.

MARLOW Cross down Squash-lane!

LANDLORD Then you were to keep streight forward, 'till you come to four roads.

MARLOW Come to where four roads meet!

TONY Ay; but you must be sure to take only one of them.

MARLOW O Sir, you're facetious.

TONY Then keeping to the right, you are to go side-ways till you come upon Crack-skull common: there you must look sharp for the track of the wheel, and go forward, 'till you come to farmer Murrain's barn. Coming to the farmer's barn, you are to turn to the right, and then to the left, and then to the right about again, till you find out the old mill –

MARLOW Zounds, man! we could as soon find out the longitude!

HASTINGS What's to be done, Marlow?

MARLOW This house promises but a poor reception; though perhaps the Landlord can accommodate us.

LANDLORD Alack, master, we have but one spare bed in the whole house.

TONY And to my knowledge, that's taken up by three lodgers already. (*After a pause, in which the rest seem disconcerted.*) I have hit it. Don't you think, Stingo, our landlady could accommodate the gentlemen by the fire-side, with – three chairs and a bolster?

HASTINGS I hate sleeping by the fire-side.

MARLOW And I detest your three chairs and a bolster.

TONY You do, do you? – then let me see – what if you go on a mile further, to the Buck's Head; the old Buck's Head on the hill, one of the best inns in the whole country?

HASTINGS O ho! so we have escaped an adventure for this night, however.

LANDLORD (*Apart to Tony.*) Sure, you ben't sending them to your father's as an inn, be you?

TONY Mum, you fool you. Let *them* find that out. (*To them.*) You have only to keep on streight forward, till you come to a large old house by the road side. You'll see a pair of large horns over the door. That's the sign. Drive up the yard, and call stoutly about you.

HASTINGS Sir, we are obliged to you. The servants can't miss the way?

TONY No, no: But I tell you though, the landlord is rich, and going to leave off business; so he wants to be thought a Gentleman, saving your presence, he! he! he! He'll be for giving you his company, and ecod if you mind him, he'll persuade you that his mother was an alderman, and his aunt a justice of peace.

LANDLORD A troublesome old blade to be sure; but a keeps as good wines and beds as any in the whole country.

MARLOW Well, if he supplies us with these, we shall want no further connexion. We are to turn to the right, did you say?

TONY No, no, streight forward. I'll just step myself, and shew you a piece of the way. (*To the Landlord.*) Mum.

LANDLORD Ah, bless your heart, for a sweet, pleasant — damn'd mischievous son of a whore.   *Exeunt.*

Act II

SCENE: *An old-fashioned house.*

Enter Hardcastle, followed by three or four aukward Servants.

HARDCASTLE Well, I hope you're perfect in the table exercise I have been teaching you these three days. You all know your posts and your places, and can shew that you have been used to good company, without ever stirring from home.

OMNES Ay, ay.

HARDCASTLE When company comes, you are not to pop out and stare, and then run in again, like frighted rabbits in a warren.

OMNES No, no.

HARDCASTLE You, Diggory, whom I have taken from the barn, are to make a shew at the side-table; and you, Roger, whom I have advanced from the plough, are to place yourself behind *my* chair. But you're not to stand so, with your hands in your pockets. Take your hands from your pockets, Roger; and from your head, you blockhead you. See how Diggory carries his hands. They're a little too stiff, indeed, but that's no great matter.

DIGGORY Ay, mind how I hold them. I learned to hold my hands this way, when I was upon drill for the militia. And so being upon drill –

HARDCASTLE You must not be so talkative, Diggory. You must be all attention to the guests. You must hear us talk, and not think of talking; you must see us drink, and not think of drinking; you must see us eat, and not think of eating.

DIGGORY By the laws, your worship, that's parfectly unpossible. Whenever Diggory sees yeating going forward, ecod he's always wishing for a mouthful himself.

HARDCASTLE Blockhead! Is not a belly-full in the kitchen as good as a belly-full in the parlour? Stay your stomach with that reflection.

DIGGORY Ecod I thank your worship, I'll make a shift to stay my stomach with a slice of cold beef in the pantry.

HARDCASTLE Diggory, you are too talkative. Then if I happen to say a good thing, or tell a good story at table, you must not all burst out a-laughing, as if you made part of the company.

DIGGORY Then ecod your worship must not tell the story of Ould Grouse in the gun-room: I can't help laughing at that – he! he! he! – for the soul of me. We have laughed at that these twenty years – ha! ha! ha!

HARDCASTLE Ha! ha! ha! The story is a good one. Well, honest Diggory, you may laugh at that – but still remember to be attentive. Suppose one of the company should call for a glass of wine, how will you behave? A glass of wine, Sir, if you please (*to Diggory*) – Eh, why don't you move?

DIGGORY Ecod, your worship, I never have courage till I see the eatables and drinkables brought upo' the table, and then I'm as bauld as a lion.

HARDCASTLE What, will no body move?

FIRST SERVANT I'm not to leave this pleace.

SECOND SERVANT I'm sure it's no pleace of mine.

THIRD SERVANT Nor mine, for sartain.

DIGGORY Wauns, and I'm sure it canna be mine.

HARDCASTLE You numbskulls! and so while, like your betters, you are quarrelling for places, the guests must be starved. O you dunces! I find I must begin all over again – But don't I hear a coach drive into the yard? To your posts, you block-heads. I'll go in the mean time and give my old friend's son a hearty reception at the gate.   *Exit Hardcastle.*

DIGGORY By the elevens, my pleace is gone quite out of my head.

ROGER I know that my pleace is to be every where.

FIRST SERVANT Where the devil is mine?

SECOND SERVANT My pleace is to be no where at all; and so Ize go about my business.

Exeunt Servants, running about as if frighted, different ways.

Enter Servant with candles, shewing in Marlow and Hastings.

SERVANT Welcome, gentlemen, very welcome. This way.

HASTINGS After the disappointments of the day, welcome once

more, Charles, to the comforts of a clean room and a good fire. Upon my word, a very well-looking house, antique, but creditable.

MARLOW The usual fate of a large mansion. Having first ruined the master by good housekeeping, it at last comes to levy contributions as an inn.

HASTINGS As you say, we passengers are to be taxed to pay all these fineries. I have often seen a good sideboard, or a marble chimney-piece, tho' not actually put in the bill, enflame a reckoning confoundedly.

MARLOW Travellers, George, must pay in all places. The only difference is, that in good inns, you pay dearly for luxuries; in bad ones, you are fleeced and starved.

HASTINGS You have lived pretty much among them. In truth, I have been often surprized, that you who have seen so much of the world, with your natural good sense, and your many opportunities, could never yet acquire a requisite share of assurance.

MARLOW The Englishman's malady. But tell me, George, where could I have learned that assurance you talk of? My life has been chiefly spent in a college, or an inn, in seclusion from that lovely part of the creation that chiefly teach men confidence. I don't know that I was ever familiarly acquainted with a single modest woman – except my mother – But among females of another class you know –

HASTINGS Ay, among them you are impudent enough of all conscience.

MARLOW They are of *us* you know.

HASTINGS But in the company of women of reputation I never saw such an idiot, such a trembler; you look for all the world as if you wanted an opportunity of stealing out of the room.

MARLOW Why man that's because I *do* want to steal out of the room. Faith, I have often formed a resolution to break the ice, and rattle away at any rate. But I don't know how, a single glance from a pair of fine eyes has totally overset my resolution. An impudent fellow may counterfeit modesty, but I'll be hanged if a modest man can ever counterfeit impudence.

HASTINGS If you could but say half the fine things to them that I have heard you lavish upon the bar-maid of an inn, or even a college bed maker –

MARLOW Why, George, I can't say fine things to them. They freeze, they petrify me. They may talk of a comet, or a burning mountain, or some such bagatelle. But to me, a modest woman, drest out in all her finery, is the most tremendous object of the whole creation.

HASTINGS Ha! ha! ha! At this rate, man, how can you ever expect to marry!

MARLOW Never, unless as among kings and princes, my bride were to be courted by proxy. If, indeed, like an Eastern bridegroom, one were to be introduced to a wife he never saw before, it might be endured. But to go through all the terrors of a formal courtship, together with the episode of aunts, grandmothers and cousins, and at last to blurt out the broad staring question, of, *madam will you marry me*? No, no, that's a strain much above me I assure you.

HASTINGS I pity you. But how do you intend behaving to the lady you are come down to visit at the request of your father?

MARLOW As I behave to all other ladies. Bow very low. Answer yes, or no, to all her demands — But for the rest, I don't think I shall venture to look in her face, till I see my father's again.

HASTINGS I'm surprized that one who is so warm a friend can be so cool a lover.

MARLOW To be explicit, my dear Hastings, my chief inducement down was to be instrumental in forwarding your happiness, not my own. Miss Neville loves you, the family don't know you, as my friend you are sure of a reception, and let honour do the rest.

HASTINGS My dear Marlow! But I'll suppress the emotion. Were I a wretch, meanly seeking to carry off a fortune, you should be the last man in the world I would apply to for assistance. But Miss Neville's person is all I ask, and that is mine, both from her deceased father's consent, and her own inclination.

MARLOW Happy man! You have talents and art to captivate any woman. I'm doom'd to adore the sex, and yet to converse with the only part of it I despise. This stammer in my address, and this aukward prepossessing visage of mine, can never permit me to soar above the reach of a milliner's 'prentice, or one of the dutchesses of Drury-lane. Pshaw! this fellow here to interrupt us.

Enter Hardcastle.

HARDCASTLE Gentlemen, once more you are heartily welcome. Which is Mr Marlow? Sir, you're heartily welcome. It's not my way, you see, to receive my friends with my back to the fire. I like to give them a hearty reception in the old stile at my gate. I like to see their horses and trunks taken care of.

MARLOW (*Aside.*) He has got our names from the servants already. (*To him.*) We approve your caution and hospitality, Sir. (*To Hastings.*) I have been thinking, George, of changing our travelling dresses in the morning. I am grown confoundedly ashamed of mine.

HARDCASTLE I beg, Mr Marlow, you'll use no ceremony in this house.

HASTINGS I fancy, Charles, you're right: the first blow is half the battle. I intend opening the campaign with the white and gold.

HARDCASTLE Mr Marlow — Mr Hastings — gentlemen — pray be under no constraint in this house. This is Liberty-hall, gentlemen. You may do just as you please here.

MARLOW Yet, George, if we open the campaign too fiercely at first, we may want ammunition before it is over. I think to reserve the embroidery to secure a retreat.

HARDCASTLE Your talking of a retreat, Mr Marlow, puts me in mind of the Duke of Marlborough, when we went to besiege Denain. He first summoned the garrison.

MARLOW Don't you think the *ventre d'or* waistcoat will do with the plain brown?

HARDCASTLE He first summoned the garrison, which might consist of about five thousand men —

HASTINGS I think not: Brown and yellow mix but very poorly.

HARDCASTLE I say, gentlemen, as I was telling you, he summoned the garrison, which might consist of about five thousand men —

MARLOW The girls like finery.

HARDCASTLE Which might consist of about five thousand men, well appointed with stores, ammunition, and other implements of war. Now, says the Duke of Marlborough, to George Brooks, that stood next to him — You must have heard of George Brooks; I'll pawn my Dukedom, says he, but I take that garrison without spilling a drop of blood. So —

MARLOW What, my good friend, if you gave us a glass of punch in the mean time, it would help us to carry on the siege with vigour.

HARDCASTLE Punch, Sir! (*Aside.*) This is the most unaccountable kind of modesty I ever met with.

MARLOW Yes, Sir, Punch. A glass of warm punch, after our journey, will be comfortable. This is Liberty-hall, you know.

HARDCASTLE Here's cup, Sir.

MARLOW (*Aside.*) So this fellow, in his Liberty-hall, will only let us have just what he pleases.

HARDCASTLE (*Taking the cup.*) I hope you'll find it to your mind. I have prepared it with my own hands, and I believe you'll own the ingredients are tolerable. Will you, be so good as to pledge me, Sir? Here, Mr Marlow, here is to our better acquaintance. (*Drinks.*)

MARLOW (*Aside.*) A very impudent fellow this! but he's a character, and I'll humour him a little. Sir, my service to you. (*Drinks.*)

HASTINGS (*Aside.*) I see this fellow wants to give us his company, and forgets that he's an innkeeper, before he has learned to be a gentleman.

MARLOW From the excellence of your cup, my old friend, I suppose you have a good deal of business in this part of the country. Warm work, now and then, at elections, I suppose.

HARDCASTLE No, Sir, I have long given that work over. Since our betters have hit upon the expedient of electing each other, there's no business *for us that sell ale.*

HASTINGS So, then you have no turn for politics I find.

HARDCASTLE Not in the least. There was a time, indeed, I fretted myself about the mistakes of government, like other people; but finding myself every day grow more angry, and the government growing no better, I left it to mend itself. Since that, I no more trouble my head about *Heyder Ally*, or *Ally Cawn*, than about *Ally Croaker*. Sir, my service to you.

HASTINGS So that with eating above stairs, and drinking below, with receiving your friends without, and amusing them within, you lead a good pleasant bustling life of it.

HARDCASTLE I do stir about a great deal, that's certain. Half the differences of the parish are adjusted in this very parlour.

MARLOW (*After drinking.*) And you have an argument in your cup, old gentleman, better than any in Westminster-hall.

HARDCASTLE Ay, young gentleman, that, and a little philosophy.

MARLOW (*Aside.*) Well, this is the first time I ever heard of an inn-keeper's philosophy.

HASTINGS So then, like an experienced general, you attack them on every quarter. If you find their reason manageable, you attack it with your philosophy; if you find they have no reason, you attack them with this. Here's your health, my philosopher. (*Drinks.*)

HARDCASTLE Good, very good, thank you; ha, ha. Your Generalship puts me in mind of Prince Eugene, when he fought the Turks at the battle of Belgrade. You shall hear.

MARLOW Instead of the battle of Belgrade, I believe it's almost time to talk about supper. What has your philosophy got in the house for supper?

HARDCASTLE For supper, Sir! (*Aside.*) Was ever such a request to a man in his own house!

MARLOW Yes, Sir, supper Sir; I begin to feel an appetite. I shall make devilish work to-night in the larder, I promise you.

HARDCASTLE (*Aside.*) Such a brazen dog sure never my eyes beheld. (*To him.*) Why really, Sir, as for supper I can't well tell. My Dorothy, and the cook maid, settle these things between them. I leave these kind of things entirely to them.

MARLOW You do, do you?

HARDCASTLE Entirely. By-the-bye, I believe they are in actual consultation upon what's for supper this moment in the kitchen.

MARLOW Then I beg they'll admit *me* as one of their privy council. It's a way I have got. When I travel, I always chuse to regulate my own supper. Let the cook be called. No offence I hope, Sir.

HARDCASTLE O no, Sir, none in the least; yet I don't know how: our Bridget, the cook maid, is not very communicative upon these occasions. Should we send for her, she might scold us all out of the house.

HASTINGS Let's see your list of the larder then. I ask it as a favour. I always match my appetite to my bill of fare.

MARLOW (*To Hardcastle, who looks at them with surprize.*) Sir, he's very right, and it's my way too.

HARDCASTLE Sir, you have a right to command here. Here, Roger, bring us the bill of fare for to-night's supper. I believe it's drawn out. Your manner, Mr Hastings, puts me in mind of my uncle, Colonel Wallop. It was a saying of his, that no man was sure of his supper till he had eaten it.

Enter Roger, who gives a bill of fare.

HASTINGS (*Aside.*) All upon the high ropes! His uncle a Colonel! We shall soon hear of his mother being a justice of peace. But let's hear the bill of fare.

MARLOW (*Perusing.*) What's here? For the first course; for the second course; for the dessert. The devil, Sir, do you think we have brought down the whole Joiners Company, or the Corporation of Bedford, to eat up such a supper? Two or three little things, clean and comfortable, will do.

HASTINGS But, let's hear it.

MARLOW (*Reading.*) For the first course at the top, a pig, and pruin sauce.

HASTINGS Damn your pig, I say.

MARLOW And damn your pruin sauce, say I.

HARDCASTLE And yet, gentlemen, to men that are hungry, pig, with pruin sauce, is very good eating.

MARLOW At the bottom, a calve's tongue and brains.

HASTINGS Let your brains be knock'd out, my good Sir; I don't like them.

MARLOW Or you may clap them on a plate by themselves. I do.

HARDCASTLE (*Aside.*) Their impudence confounds me. (*To them.*) Gentlemen, you are my guests, make what alterations you please. Is there any thing else you wish to retrench or alter, gentlemen?

MARLOW Item. A pork pie, a boiled rabbet and sausages, a florentine, a shaking pudding, and a dish of tiff – taff – taffety cream!

HASTINGS Confound your made dishes, I shall be as much at a loss in this house as at a green and yellow dinner at the French ambassador's table. I'm for plain eating.

HARDCASTLE I'm sorry, gentlemen, that I have nothing you like, but if there be any thing you have a particular fancy to –

MARLOW Why, really, Sir, your bill of fare is so exquisite, that any one part of it is full as good as another. Send us what you please. So much for supper. And now to see that our beds are air'd, and properly taken care of.

HARDCASTLE I entreat you'll leave all that to me. You shall not stir a step.

MARLOW Leave that to you! I protest, Sir, you must excuse me, I always look at these things myself.

HARDCASTLE I must insist, Sir, you'll make yourself easy on that head.

MARLOW You see I'm resolved on it. (*Aside.*) A very troublesome fellow this, as ever I met with.

HARDCASTLE Well, Sir, I'm resolved at least to attend you. (*Aside.*) This may be modern modesty, but I never saw any thing look so like old-fashioned impudence.

Exeunt Marlow and Hardcastle.

Hastings solus.

HASTINGS So I find this fellow's civilities begin to grow troublesome. But who can be angry at those assiduities which are meant to please him? Ha! what do I see? Miss Neville, by all that's happy!

Enter Miss Neville.

MISS NEVILLE My dear Hastings! To what unexpected good fortune? to what accident am I to ascribe this happy meeting?

HASTINGS Rather let me ask the same question, as I could never have hoped to meet my dearest Constance at an inn.

MISS NEVILLE An inn! sure you mistake! my aunt, my guardian, lives here. What could induce you to think this house an inn?

HASTINGS My friend, Mr Marlow, with whom I came down, and I, have been sent here as to an inn, I assure you. A young fellow whom we accidentally met at a house hard by directed us hither.

MISS NEVILLE Certainly it must be one of my hopeful cousin's tricks, of whom you have heard me talk so often, ha! ha! ha! ha!

HASTINGS He whom your aunt intends for you? He of whom I have such just apprehensions?

MISS NEVILLE You have nothing to fear from him, I assure you. You'd adore him if you knew how heartily he depises me. My aunt knows it too, and has undertaken to court me for him, and actually begins to think she has made a conquest.

HASTINGS Thou dear dissembler! You must know, my Constance, I have just seized this happy opportunity of my friend's visit here to get admittance into the family. The horses that carried us down are now fatigued with their journey, but they'll soon be refreshed; and then if my dearest girl will trust in her faithful Hastings, we shall soon be landed in France, where even among slaves the laws of marriage are respected.

MISS NEVILLE I have often told you, that though ready to obey you, I yet should leave my little fortune behind with reluctance. The greatest part of it was left me by my uncle, the India Director, and chiefly consists in jewels. I have been for some time persuading my aunt to let me wear them. I fancy I'm very near succeeding. The instant they are put into my possession you shall find me ready to make them and myself yours.

HASTINGS Perish the baubles! Your person is all I desire. In the mean time, my friend Marlow must not be let into his mistake. I know the strange reserve of his temper is such, that if abruptly informed of it, he would instantly quit the house before our plan was ripe for execution.

MISS NEVILLE But how shall we keep him in the deception? Miss Hardcastle is just returned from walking; what if we still continue to deceive him? – This, this way –   *They confer.*

Enter Marlow.

MARLOW The assiduities of these good people teize me beyond bearing. My host seems to think it ill manners to leave me alone, and so he claps not only himself but his old-fashioned wife on my back. They talk of coming to sup with us too; and then, I suppose, we are to run the gauntlet thro' all the rest of the family. – What have we got here! –

HASTINGS My dear Charles! Let me congratulate you! – The most fortunate accident! – Who do you think is just alighted?

MARLOW Cannot guess.

HASTINGS Our mistresses my boy, Miss Hardcastle and Miss Neville. Give me leave to introduce Miss Constance Neville to your acquaintance. Happening to dine in the neighbourhood, they called on their return to take fresh horses here. Miss Hardcastle has just stept into the next room, and will be back in an instant. Wasn't it lucky? eh!

MARLOW (*Aside.*) I have just been mortified enough of all conscience, and here comes something to complete my embarrassment.

HASTINGS Well! but wasn't it the most fortunate thing in the world?

MARLOW Oh! yes. Very fortunate – a most joyful encounter –
But our dresses, George, you know, are in disorder – What if
we should postpone the happiness 'till to-morrow? – To-
morrow at her own house – It will be every bit as convenient
– And rather more respectful – To-morrow let it be.

Offering to go.

MISS NEVILLE By no means, Sir. Your ceremony will displease
her. The disorder of your dress will shew the ardour of your
impatience. Besides, she knows you are in the house, and will
permit you to see her.

MARLOW O! the devil! how shall I support it? Hem! hem!
Hastings, you must not go. You are to assist me, you know. I
shall be confoundedly ridiculous.

HASTINGS Pshaw man! it's but the first plunge, and all's over.
She's but a woman, you know.

MARLOW And of all women, she that I dread most to encounter!
Yet, hang it! I'll take courage. Hem!

Enter Miss Hardcastle as returned from walking, a bonnet, etc.

HASTINGS (*Introducing them.*) Miss Hardcastle, Mr Marlow,
I'm proud of bringing two persons of such merit together,
that only want to know, to esteem each other.

MISS HARDCASTLE (*Aside.*) Now, for meeting my modest gentleman with a demure face, and quite in his own manner. (*After
a pause, in which he appears very uneasy and disconcerted.*)
I'm glad of your safe arrival, Sir – I'm told you had some
accidents by the way.

MARLOW Only a few Madam. Yet, we had some. Yes, Madam,
a good many accidents, but should be sorry – Madam – or
rather glad of any accidents – that are so agreeably concluded.
Hem!

HASTINGS (*To him.*) You never spoke better in your whole life.
Keep it up, and I'll insure you the victory.

MISS HARDCASTLE I'm afraid you flatter, Sir. You that have seen
seen so much of the finest company can find little entertainment in an obscure corner of the country.

MARLOW (*Gathering courage.*) I have lived, indeed, in the
world, Madam; but I have kept very little company. I have
been but an observer upon life, Madam, while others were
enjoying it.

MISS NEVILLE But that, I am told, is the way to enjoy it at last.

HASTINGS *(To him.)* Cicero never spoke better. Once more, and you are confirm'd in assurance for ever.

MARLOW *(To him.)* Hem! Stand by me then, and when I'm down, throw in a word or two to set me up again.

MISS HARDCASTLE An observer, like you, upon life, were, I fear, disagreeably employed, since you must have had much more to censure than to approve.

MARLOW Pardon me, Madam. I was always willing to be amused. The folly of most people is rather an object of mirth than uneasiness.

HASTINGS *(To him.)* Bravo, Bravo. Never spoke so well in your whole life. Well! Miss Hardcastle, I see that you and Mr Marlow are going to be very good company. I believe our being here will but embarrass the interview.

MARLOW Not in the least, Mr Hastings. We like your company of all things. *(To him.)* Zounds! George, sure you won't go? How can you leave us?

HASTINGS Our presence will but spoil conversation, so we'll retire to the next room. *(To him.)* You don't consider, man, that we are to manage a little tête-à-tête of our own.

Exeunt.

MISS HARDCASTLE *(After a pause.)* But you have not been wholly an observer, I presume, Sir: The ladies I should hope have employed some part of your addresses.

MARLOW *(Relapsing into timidity.)* Pardon me, Madam, I – I – I – as yet have studied – only – to – deserve them.

MISS HARDCASTLE And that some say is the very worst way to obtain them.

MARLOW Perhaps so, Madam. But I love to converse only with the more grave and sensible part of the sex. – But I'm afraid I grow tiresome.

MISS HARDCASTLE Not at all, Sir; there is nothing I like so much as grave conversation myself; I could hear it for ever. Indeed I have often been surprized how a man of *sentiment* could ever admire those light airy pleasures, where nothing reaches the heart.

MARLOW It's – a disease – of the mind, Madam. In the variety of tastes there must be some who wanting a relish – for – um-a-um.

MISS HARDCASTLE I understand you, Sir. There must be some,

who wanting a relish for refined pleasures, pretend to despise what they are incapable of tasting.

MARLOW My meaning, Madam, but infinitely better expressed. And I can't help observing – a –

MISS HARDCASTLE (*Aside.*) Who could ever suppose this fellow impudent upon some occasions. (*To him.*) You were going to observe, Sir –

MARLOW I was observing, Madam – I protest, Madam, I forget what I was going to observe.

MISS HARDCASTLE (*Aside.*) I vow and so do I. (*To him.*) You were observing, Sir, that in this age of hypocrisy – something about hypocrisy, Sir.

MARLOW Yes, Madam. In this age of hypocrisy there are few who upon strict enquiry do not – a – a – a –

MISS HARDCASTLE I understand you perfectly, Sir.

MARLOW (*Aside.*) Egad! and that's more than I do myself.

MISS HARDCASTLE You mean that in this hypocritical age there are few that do not condemn in public what they practise in private, and think they pay every debt to virtue when they praise it.

MARLOW True, Madam; those who have most virtue in their mouths, have least of it in their bosoms. But I'm sure I tire you, Madam.

MISS HARDCASTLE Not in the least, Sir; there's something so agreeable and spirited in your manner, such life and force – pray, Sir, go on.

MARLOW Yes, Madam. I was saying – that there are some occasions – when a total want of courage, madam, destroys all the – and puts us – upon a – a – a –

MISS HARDCASTLE I agree with you entirely, a want of courage upon some occasions assumes the appearance of ignorance, and betrays us when we most want to excel. I beg you'll proceed.

MARLOW Yes, Madam. Morally speaking, Madam – But I see Miss Neville expecting us in the next room. I would not intrude for the world.

MISS HARDCASTLE I protest, Sir, I never was more agreeably entertained in all my life. Pray go on.

MARLOW Yes, Madam. I was – But she beckons us to join her. Madam, shall I do myself the honour to attend you?

MISS HARDCASTLE Well then, I'll follow.

MARLOW (*Aside.*) This pretty smooth dialogue has done for me

Exit.

Miss Hardcastle, sola.

MISS HARDCASTLE Ha! ha! ha! Was there ever such a sober
sentimental interview? I'm certain he scarce look'd in my face
the whole time. Yet the fellow, but for his unaccountable
bashfulness, is pretty well too. He has good sense, but then so
buried in his fears, that it fatigues one more than ignorance.
If I could teach him a little confidence, it would be doing
somebody that I know of a piece of service. But who is that
somebody? — that, faith, is a question I can scarce answer.

Exit.

*Enter Tony and Miss Neville, followed by Mrs Hardcastle and
Hastings.*

TONY What do you follow me for, cousin Con? I wonder you're
not ashamed to be so very engaging.

MISS NEVILLE I hope, cousin, one may speak to one's own
relations, and not be to blame.

TONY Ay, but I know what sort of a relation you want to make
me though; but it won't do. I tell you, cousin Con, it won't
do, so I beg you'll keep your distance, I want no nearer
relationship. *She follows coqueting him to the back scene.*

MRS HARDCASTLE Well! I vow, Mr Hastings, you are very
entertaining. There's nothing in the world I love to talk of so
much as London, and the fashions, though I was never there
myself.

HASTINGS Never there! You amaze me! From your air and
manner, I concluded you had been bred all your life either at
Ranelagh, St James's, or Tower Wharf.

MRS HARDCASTLE O! Sir, you're only pleased to say so. We
country persons can have no manner at all. I'm in love with
the town, and that serves to raise me above some of our
neighbouring rustics; but who can have a manner, that has
never seen the Pantheon, the Grotto Gardens, the Borough,
and such places where the Nobility chiefly resort? All I can
do, is to enjoy London at second-hand. I take care to know
every tête-à-tête from the Scandalous Magazine, and have all
the fashions, as they come out, in a letter from the two Miss

Rickets of Crooked-lane. Pray how do you like this head, Mr Hastings?

HASTINGS Extremely elegant and *degagée*, upon my word, Madam. Your *friseur* is a Frenchman, I suppose?

MRS HARDCASTLE I protest I dressed it myself from a print in the Ladies Memorandum-book for the last year.

HASTINGS Indeed. Such a head in a side-box, at the Playhouse, would draw as many gazers as my Lady May'ress at a City Ball.

MRS HARDCASTLE I vow, since inoculation began, there is no such thing to be seen as a plain woman; so one must dress a little particular or one may escape in the crowd.

HASTINGS But that can never be your case, Madam, in any dress.
(*Bowing.*)

MRS HARDCASTLE Yet, what signifies *my* dressing when I have such a piece of antiquity by my side as Mr Hardcastle: all I can say will never argue down a single button from his cloaths. I have often wanted him to throw off his great flaxen wig, and where he was bald, to plaister it over like my Lord Pately, with powder.

HASTINGS You are right, Madam; for, as among the ladies, there are none ugly, so among the men there are none old.

MRS HARDCASTLE But what do you think his answer was? Why, with his usual Gothic vivacity, he said I only wanted him to throw off his wig to convert it into a tête for my own wearing.

HASTINGS Intolerable! At your age you may wear what you please, and it must become you.

MRS HARDCASTLE Pray, Mr Hastings, what do you take to be the most fashionable age about town?

HASTINGS Some time ago, forty was all the mode; but I'm told the ladies intend to bring up fifty for the ensuing winter.

MRS HARDCASTLE Seriously? Then I shall be too young for the fashion.

HASTINGS No lady begins now to put on jewels 'till she's past forty. For instance, Miss there, in a polite circle, would be considered as a child, as a mere maker of samplers.

MRS HARDCASTLE And yet Mrs Niece thinks herself as much a woman, and is as fond of jewels as the oldest of us all.

HASTINGS Your niece, is she? And that young gentleman, a brother of yours, I should presume?

MRS HARDCASTLE My son, Sir. They are contracted to each

other. Observe their little sports. They fall in and out ten times a day, as if they were man and wife already. (*To them.*) Well Tony, child, what soft things are you saying to your cousin Constance this evening?

TONY I have been saying no soft things; but that it's very hard to be followed about so. Ecod! I've not a place in the house now that's left to myself but the stable.

MRS HARDCASTLE Never mind him, Con my dear. He's in another story behind your back.

MISS NEVILLE There's something generous in my cousin's manner. He falls out before faces to be forgiven in private.

TONY That's a damned confounded – crack.

MRS HARDCASTLE Ah! he's a sly one. Don't you think they're like each other about the mouth, Mr Hastings? The Blenkinsop mouth to a T. They're of a size too. Back to back, my pretties, that Mr Hastings may see you. Come Tony.

TONY You had as good not make me, I tell you.

(*Measuring.*)

MISS NEVILLE O lud! he has almost cracked my head.

MRS HARDCASTLE O the monster! For shame, Tony. You a man, and behave so!

TONY If I'm a man, let me have my fortin. Ecod! I'll not be made a fool of no longer.

MRS HARDCASTLE Is this, ungrateful boy, all that I'm to get for the pains I have taken in your education? I that have rock'd you in your cradle, and fed that pretty mouth with a spoon! Did not I work that waistcoat to make you genteel? Did not I prescribe for you every day, and weep while the receipt was operating?

TONY Ecod! you had reason to weep, for you have been dosing me ever since I was born. I have gone through every receipt in *The Complete Huswife* ten times over; and you have thoughts of coursing me through *Quincy* next spring. But, Ecod! I tell you, I'll not be made a fool of no longer.

MRS HARDCASTLE Wasn't it all for your good, viper? Wasn't it all for your good?

TONY I wish you'd let me and my good alone then. Snubbing this way when I'm in spirits. If I'm to have any good, let it come of itself; not to keep dinging it, dinging it into one so.

MRS HARDCASTLE That's false; I never see you when you're in spirits. No, Tony, you then go to the alehouse or the kennel.

I'm never to be delighted with your agreeable, wild notes, unfeeling monster!

TONY Ecod! Mamma, your own notes are the wildest of the two.

MRS HARDCASTLE Was ever the like? But I see he wants to break my heart, I see he does.

HASTINGS Dear Madam, permit me to lecture the young gentleman a little. I'm certain I can persuade him to his duty.

MRS HARDCASTLE Well! I must retire. Come, Constance, my love. You see Mr Hastings, the wretchedness of my situation: Was ever poor woman so plagued with a dear, sweet, pretty, provoking, undutiful boy.

Exeunt Mrs Hardcastle and Miss Neville.

Hastings, Tony.

TONY (*Singing.*) *There was a young man riding by, and fain would have his will. Rang do didlo dee.* Don't mind her. Let her cry. It's the comfort of her heart. I have seen her and sister cry over a book for an hour together, and they said, they liked the book the better the more it made them cry.

HASTINGS Then you're no friend to the ladies, I find, my pretty young gentleman?

TONY That's as I find 'um.

HASTINGS Not to her of your mother's chusing, I dare answer? And yet she appears to me a pretty well-tempered girl.

TONY That's because you don't know her as well as I. Ecod! I know every inch about her; and there's not a more bitter cantanckerous toad in all Christendom.

HASTINGS (*Aside.*) Pretty encouragement this for a lover!

TONY I have seen her since the height of that. She has as many tricks as a hare in a thicket, or a colt the first day's breaking.

HASTINGS To me she appears sensible and silent!

TONY Ay, before company. But when she's with her play-mates she's as loud as a hog in a gate.

HASTINGS But there is a meek modesty about her that charms me.

TONY Yes, but curb her never so little, she kicks up, and you're flung in a ditch.

HASTINGS Well, but you must allow her a little beauty. — Yes, you must allow her some beauty.

TONY Bandbox! She's all a made up thing, mun. Ah! could you

but see Bet Bouncer of these parts, you might then talk of beauty. Ecod, she has two eyes as black as sloes, and cheeks as broad and red as a pulpit cushion. She'd make two of she.

HASTINGS Well, what say you to a friend that would take this bitter bargain off your hands?

TONY Anon?

HASTINGS Would you thank him that would take Miss Neville and leave you to happiness and your dear Betsy?

TONY Ay; but where is there such a friend, for who would take *her*?

HASTINGS I am he. If you but assist me, I'll engage to whip her off to France, and you shall never hear more of her.

TONY Assist you! Ecod I will, to the last drop of my blood. I'll clap a pair of horses to your chaise that shall trundle you off in a twinkling, and may be get you a part of her fortin beside, in jewels, that you little dream of.

HASTINGS My dear squire, this looks like a lad of spirit.

TONY Come along then, and you shall see more of my spirit before you have done with me (*Singing.*) *We are the boys that fears no noise where the thundering cannons roar.*

Exeunt.

Act III

Enter Hardcastle solus.

HARDCASTLE What could my old friend Sir Charles mean by recommending his son as the modestest young man in town? To me he appears the most impudent piece of brass that ever spoke with a tongue. He has taken possession of the easy chair by the fire-side already. He took off his boots in the parlour, and desired me to see them taken care of. I'm desirous to know how his impudence affects my daughter. − She will certainly be shocked at it.

Enter Miss Hardcastle, plainly dress'd.

HARDCASTLE Well, my Kate, I see you have changed your dress as I bid you; and yet, I believe, there was no great occasion.

MISS HARDCASTLE I find such a pleasure, Sir, in obeying your commands, that I take care to observe them without ever debating their propriety.

HARDCASTLE And yet, Kate, I sometimes give you some cause, particularly when I recommended my *modest* gentleman to you as a lover to-day.

MISS HARDCASTLE You taught me to expect something extraordinary, and I find the original exceeds the description.

HARDCASTLE I was never so surprized in my life! He has quite confounded all my faculties!

MISS HARDCASTLE I never saw any thing like it: And a man of the world too!

HARDCASTLE Ay, he learned it all abroad, − what a fool was I, to think a young man could learn modesty by travelling. He might as soon learn wit at a masquerade.

MISS HARDCASTLE It seems all natural to him.

HARDCASTLE A good deal assisted by bad company and a French dancing-master.

MISS HARDCASTLE Sure you mistake, papa! A French dancing-master could never have taught him that timid look, – that aukward address, – that bashful manner –

HARDCASTLE Whose look? Whose manner? child!

MISS HARDCASTLE Mr Marlow's: his *mauvaise honte*, his timidity struck me at the first sight.

HARDCASTLE Then your first sight deceived you; for I think him one of the most brazen first sights that ever astonished my senses.

MISS HARDCASTLE Sure, Sir, you rally! I never saw any one so modest.

HARDCASTLE And can you be serious! I never saw such a bouncing swaggering puppy since I was born. Bully Dawson was but a fool to him.

MISS HARDCASTLE Surprizing! He met me with a respectful bow, a stammering voice, and a look fixed on the ground.

HARDCASTLE He met me with loud voice, a lordly air, and a familiarity that made my blood freeze again.

MISS HARDCASTLE He treated me with diffidence and respect; censured the manners of the age; admired the prudence of girls that never laughed; tired me with apologies for being tiresome; then left the room with a bow, and, Madam, I would not for the world detain you.

HARDCASTLE He spoke to me as if he knew me all his life before. Asked twenty questions, and never waited for an answer. Interrupted my best remarks with some silly pun, and when I was in my best story of the Duke of Marlborough and Prince Eugene, he asked if I had not a good hand at making punch. Yes, Kate, he ask'd your father if he was a maker of punch!

MISS HARDCASTLE One of us must certainly be mistaken.

HARDCASTLE If he be what he has shewn himself, I'm determined he shall never have my consent.

MISS HARDCASTLE And if he be the sullen thing I take him, he shall never have mine.

HARDCASTLE In one thing then we are agreed – to reject him.

MISS HARDCASTLE Yes. But upon conditions. For if you should find him less impudent, and I more presuming; if you find him more respectful, and I more importunate – I don't know – the fellow is well enough for a man – Certainly we don't meet many such at a horse race in the country.

HARDCASTLE If we should find him so — But that's impossible. The first appearance has done my business. I'm seldom deceived in that.

MISS HARDCASTLE And yet there may be many good qualities under that first appearance.

HARDCASTLE Ay, when a girl finds a fellow's outside to her taste, she then sets about guessing the rest of his furniture. With her, a smooth face stands for good sense, and a genteel figure for every virtue.

MISS HARDCASTLE I hope, Sir, a conversation begun with a compliment to my good sense won't end with a sneer at my understanding?

HARDCASTLE Pardon me, Kate. But if young Mr Brazen can find the art of reconciling contradictions, he may please us both, perhaps.

MISS HARDCASTLE And as one of us must be mistaken, what if we go to make further discoveries?

HARDCASTLE Agreed. But depend on't I'm in the right.

MISS HARDCASTLE And depend on't I'm not much in the wrong.
Exeunt.

Enter Tony running in with a casket.

TONY Ecod! I have got them. Here they are. My Cousin Con's necklaces, bobs and all. My mother shan't cheat the poor souls out of their fortune neither. O! my genus, is that you?

Enter Hastings.

HASTINGS My dear friend, how have you managed with your mother? I hope you have amused her with pretending love for your cousin, and that you are willing to be reconciled at last? Our horses will be refreshed in a short time, and we shall soon be ready to set off.

TONY And here's something to bear your charges by the way (*Giving the casket.*) Your sweetheart's jewels. Keep them, and hang those, I say, that would rob you of one of them.

HASTINGS But how have you procured them from your mother?

TONY Ask me no questions, and I'll tell you no fibs. I procured them by the rule of thumb. If I had not a key to every drawer in mother's bureau, how could I go to the alehouse so often as I do? An honest man may rob himself of his own at any time.

HASTINGS Thousands do it every day. But to be plain with you; Miss Neville is endeavouring to procure them from her aunt this very instant. If she succeeds, it will be the most delicate way at least of obtaining them.

TONY Well, keep them, till you know how it will be. But I know how it will be well enough, she'd as soon part with the only sound tooth in her head.

HASTINGS But I dread the effects of her resentment, when she finds she has lost them.

TONY Never you mind her resentment, leave *me* to manage that. I don't value her resentment the bounce of a cracker. Zounds! here they are. Morrice. Prance. *Exit Hastings.*

Tony, Mrs Hardcastle, Miss Neville.

MRS HARDCASTLE Indeed, Constance, you amaze me. Such a girl as you want jewels? It will be time enough for jewels, my dear, twenty years hence, when your beauty begins to want repairs.

MISS NEVILLE But what will repair beauty at forty, will certainly improve it at twenty, Madam.

MRS HARDCASTLE Yours, my dear, can admit of none. That natural blush is beyond a thousand ornaments. Besides, child, jewels are quite out at present. Don't you see half the ladies of our acquaintance, my Lady Kill-day-light, and Mrs Crump, and the rest of them, carry their jewels to town, and bring nothing but Paste and Marcasites back.

MISS NEVILLE But who knows, Madam, but somebody that shall be nameless would like me best with all my little finery about me?

MRS HARDCASTLE Consult your glass, my dear, and then see, if with such a pair of eyes, you want any better sparklers. What do you think, Tony, my dear, does your cousin Con want any jewels, in your eyes, to set off her beauty?

TONY That's as thereafter may be.

MISS NEVILLE My dear aunt, if you knew how it would oblige me.

MRS HARDCASTLE A parcel of old-fashioned rose and table-cut things. They would make you look like the court of king Solomon at a puppet-shew. Besides, I believe I can't readily come at them. They may be missing for aught I know to the contrary.

TONY (*Apart to Mrs Hardcastle.*) Then why don't you tell her so at once, as she's so longing for them. Tell her they're lost. It's the only way to quiet her. Say they're lost, and call me to bear witness.

MRS HARDCASTLE (*Apart to Tony.*) You know, my dear, I'm only keeping them for you. So if I say they're gone, you'll bear me witness, will you? He! he! he!

TONY Never fear me, Ecod! I'll say I saw them taken out with my own eyes.

MISS NEVILLE I desire them but for a day, Madam. Just to be permitted to shew them as relicks, and then they may be lock'd up again.

MRS HARDCASTLE To be plain with you, my dear Constance; if I could find them, you should have them. They're missing, I assure you. Lost, for aught I know; but we must have patience wherever they are.

MISS NEVILLE I'll not believe it; this is but a shallow pretence to deny me. I know they're too valuable to be so slightly kept, and as you are to answer for the loss.

MRS HARDCASTLE Don't be alarm'd, Constance. If they be lost, I must restore an equivalent. But my son knows they are missing, and not to be found.

TONY That I can bear witness to. They are missing, and not to be found, I'll take my oath on't.

MRS HARDCASTLE You must learn resignation, my dear; for tho' we lose our fortune, yet we should not lose our patience. See me, how calm I am.

MISS NEVILLE Ay, people are generally calm at the misfortunes of others.

MRS HARDCASTLE Now, I wonder a girl of your good sense should waste a thought upon such trumpery. We shall soon find them; and, in the mean time, you shall make use of my garnets till your jewels be found.

MISS NEVILLE I detest garnets.

MRS HARDCASTLE The most becoming things in the world to set off a clear complexion. You have often seen how well they look upon me. You *shall* have them.   *Exit.*

MISS NEVILLE I dislike them of all things. You shan't stir. – Was ever any thing so provoking to mislay my own jewels, and force me to wear her trumpery.

TONY Don't be a fool. If she gives you the garnets, take what you can get. The jewels are your own already. I have stolen them out of her bureau, and she does not know it. Fly to your spark, he'll tell you more of the matter. Leave me to manage *her*.

MISS NEVILLE My dear cousin.

TONY Vanish. She's here, and has missed them already. Zounds! how she fidgets and spits about like a Catharine wheel.

Enter Mrs Hardcastle.

MRS HARDCASTLE Confusion! thieves! robbers! We are cheated, plundered, broke open, undone.

TONY What's the matter, what's the matter, mamma? I hope nothing has happened to any of the good family!

MRS HARDCASTLE We are robbed. My bureau has been broke open, the jewels taken out, and I'm undone.

TONY Oh! is that all? Ha, ha, ha. By the laws, I never saw it better acted in my life. Ecod, I thought you was ruin'd in earnest, ha, ha, ha.

MRS HARDCASTLE Why boy, I *am* ruin'd in earnest. My bureau has been broke open, and all taken away.

TONY Stick to that; ha, ha, ha; stick to that. I'll bear witness, you know, call me to bear witness.

MRS HARDCASTLE I tell you, Tony, by all that's precious, the jewels are gone, and I shall be ruin'd for ever.

TONY Sure I know they're gone, and I am to say so.

MRS HARDCASTLE My dearest Tony, but hear me. They're gone, I say.

TONY By the laws, mamma, you make me for to laugh, ha, ha. I know who took them well enough, ha, ha, ha.

MRS HARDCASTLE Was there ever such a blockhead, that can't tell the difference between jest and earnest. I tell you I'm not in jest, booby.

TONY That's right, that's right: You must be in a bitter passion, and then nobody will suspect either of us. I'll bear witness that they are gone.

MRS HARDCASTLE Was there ever such a cross-grain'd brute, that won't hear me! Can you bear witness that you're no better than a fool? Was ever poor woman so beset with fools on one hand, and thieves on the other.

TONY I can bear witness to that.

MRS HARDCASTLE Bear witness again, you blockhead you, and

I'll turn you out of the room directly. My poor niece, what will become of *her*! Do you laugh, you unfeeling brute, as if you enjoy'd my distress?

TONY I can bear witness to that.

MRS HARDCASTLE Do you insult me, monster? I'll teach you to vex your mother, I will.

TONY I can bear witness to that.

He runs off, she follows him.

Enter Miss Hardcastle and Maid.

MISS HARDCASTLE What an unaccountable creature is that brother of mine, to send them to the house as an inn, ha, ha. I don't wonder at his impudence.

MAID But what is more, Madam, the young gentleman as you passed by in your present dress, ask'd me if you were the bar maid? He mistook you for the bar maid, Madam.

MISS HARDCASTLE Did he? Then as I live I'm resolved to keep up the delusion. Tell me, Pimple, how do you like my present dress. Don't you think I look something like Cherry in the Beaux Stratagem?

MAID It's the dress, Madam, that every lady wears in the country, but when she visits or receives company.

MISS HARDCASTLE And are you sure he does not remember my face or person?

MAID Certain of it.

MISS HARDCASTLE I vow I thought so; for though we spoke for some time together, yet his fears were such, that he never once looked up during the interview. Indeed, if he had, my bonnet would have kept him from seeing me.

MAID But what do you hope from keeping him in his mistake?

MISS HARDCASTLE In the first place, I shall be *seen*, and that is no small advantage to a girl who brings her face to market. Then I shall perhaps make an acquaintance and that's no small victory gained over one who never addresses any but the wildest of her sex. But my chief aim is to take my gentleman off his guard, and like an invisible champion of romance examine the giant's force before I offer to combat.

MAID But are you sure you can act your part, and disguise your voice, so that he may mistake that, as he has already mistaken your person?

MISS HARDCASTLE Never fear me. I think I have got the true bar

cant. – Did your honour call? – Attend the Lion there. – Pipes
and tobacco for the Angel. – The Lamb has been outrageous
this half hour.

MAID It will do, madam. But he's here.   *Exit Maid.*

Enter Marlow.

MARLOW What a bawling in every part of the house; I have
scarce a moment's repose. If I go to the best room, there I find
my host and his story. If I fly to the gallery, there we have my
hostess with her curtesy down to the ground. I have at last
got a moment to myself, and now for recollection.

Walks and muses.

MISS HARDCASTLE Did you call, Sir? did your honour call?

MARLOW (*Musing.*) As for Miss Hardcastle, she's too grave and
sentimental for me.

MISS HARDCASTLE Did your honour call?

She still places herself before him, he turning away.

MARLOW No, child. (*Musing.*) Besides from the glimpse I had
of her, I think she squints.

MISS HARDCASTLE I'm sure, Sir, I heard the bell ring.

MARLOW No, No. (*Musing.*) I have pleased my father, however,
by coming down, and I'll to-morrow please myself by returning.   *Taking out his tablets, and perusing.*

MISS HARDCASTLE Perhaps the other gentleman called, Sir.

MARLOW I tell you, no.

MISS HARDCASTLE I should be glad to know, Sir. We have such
a parcel of servants.

MARLOW No, no, I tell you. (*Looks full in her face.*) Yes, child,
I think I did call. I wanted – I wanted – I vow, child, you are
vastly handsome.

MISS HARDCASTLE O la, Sir, you'll make one asham'd.

MARLOW Never saw a more sprightly malicious eye. Yes, yes,
my dear, I did call. Have you got any of your – a – what d'ye
call it in the house?

MISS HARDCASTLE No, Sir, we have been out of that these ten
days.

MARLOW One may call in this house, I find, to very little
purpose. Suppose I should call for a taste, just by way of trial,
of the nectar of your lips; perhaps I might be disappointed in
that too.

MISS HARDCASTLE Nectar! nectar! that's a liquor there's no call for in these parts. French, I suppose. We keep no French wines here, Sir.

MARLOW Of true English growth, I assure you.

MISS HARDCASTLE Then it's odd I should not know it. We brew all sorts of wines in this house, and I have lived here these eighteen years.

MARLOW Eighteen years! Why one would think, child, you kept the bar before you were born. How old are you?

MISS HARDCASTLE O! Sir, I must not tell my age. They say women and music should never be dated.

MARLOW To guess at this distance, you can't be much above forty. (*Approaching.*) Yet nearer I don't think so much. (*Approaching.*) By coming close to some women they look younger still; but when we come very close indeed. (*Attempting to kiss her.*)

MISS HARDCASTLE Pray, Sir, keep your distance. One would think you wanted to know one's age as they do horses, by mark of mouth.

MARLOW I protest, child, you use me extremely ill. If you keep me at this distance, how is it possible you and I can be ever acquainted?

MISS HARDCASTLE And who wants to be acquainted with you? I want no such acquaintance, not I. I'm sure you did not treat Miss Hardcastle that was here awhile ago in this obstropalous manner. I'll warrant me, before her you look'd dash'd, and kept bowing to the ground, and talk'd, for all the world, as if you was before a justice of peace.

MARLOW (*Aside.*) Egad! she has hit it, sure enough. (*To her.*) In awe of her, child? Ha! ha! ha! A mere, aukward, squinting thing, no, no. I find you don't know me. I laugh'd, and rallied her a little; but I was unwilling to be too severe. No, I could not be too severe, *curse me*!

MISS HARDCASTLE O! then, Sir, you are a favourite, I find, among the ladies?

MARLOW Yes, my dear, a great favourite. And yet, hang me, I don't see what they find in me to follow. At the Ladies Club in town, I'm called their agreeable Rattle. Rattle, child, is not my real name, but one I'm known by. My name is Solomons. Mr Solomons, my dear, at your service. (*Offering to salute her.*)

MISS HARDCASTLE Hold, Sir; you were introducing me to your

club, not to yourself. And you're so great a favourite there you say?

MARLOW Yes, my dear. There's Mrs Mantrap, Lady Betty Blackleg, the Countess of Sligo, Mrs Langhorns, old Miss Biddy Buckskin, and your humble servant, keep up the spirit of the place.

MISS HARDCASTLE Then it's a very merry place, I suppose.

MARLOW Yes, as merry as cards, suppers, wine, and old women can make us.

MISS HARDCASTLE And their agreeable Rattle, ha! ha! ha!

MARLOW (*Aside.*)Egad! I don't quite like this chit. She looks knowing, methinks. You laugh, child!

MISS HARDCASTLE I can't but laugh to think what time they all have for minding their work or their family.

MARLOW (*Aside.*) All's well, she don't laugh at me. (*To her.*) Do *you* ever work, child?

MISS HARDCASTLE Ay, sure. There's not a screen or a quilt in the whole house but what can bear witness to that.

MARLOW Odso! Then you must shew me your embroidery. I embroider and draw patterns myself a little. If you want a judge of your work you must apply to me.

Seizing her hand.

MISS HARDCASTLE Ay, but the colours don't look well by candle light. You shall see all in the morning. *Struggling.*

MARLOW And why not now, my angel? Such beauty fires beyond the power of resistance – Pshaw! the father here! My old luck: I never nick'd seven that I did not throw ames ace three times following. *Exit Marlow.*

Enter Hardcastle, who stands in surprize.

HARDCASTLE So, Madam! So I find *this* is your *modest* lover. This is your humble admirer that kept his eyes fixed on the ground, and only ador'd at humble distance. Kate, Kate, art thou not asham'd to deceive your father so?

MISS HARDCASTLE Never trust me, dear papa, but he's still the modest man I first took him for, you'll be convinced of it as well as I.

HARDCASTLE By the hand of my body I believe his impudence is infectious! Didn't I see him seize your hand? Didn't I see him hawl you about like a milk maid? and now you talk of his respect and his modesty, forsooth!

MISS HARDCASTLE But if I shortly convince you of his modesty, that he has only the faults that will pass off with time, and the virtues that will improve with age, I hope you'll forgive him.

HARDCASTLE The girl would actually make one run mad! I tell you I'll not be convinced. I am convinced. He has scarcely been three hours in the house, and he has already encroached on all my prerogatives. You may like his impudence, and call it modesty. But my son-in-law, Madam, must have very different qualifications.

MISS HARDCASTLE Sir, I ask but this night to convince you.

HARDCASTLE You shall not have half the time, for I have thoughts of turning him out this very hour.

MISS HARDCASTLE Give me that hour then, and I hope to satisfy you.

HARDCASTLE Well, an hour let it be then. But I'll have no trifling with your father. All fair and open, do you mind me?

MISS HARDCASTLE I hope, Sir, you have ever found that I considered your commands as my pride; for your kindness is such, that my duty as yet has been inclination. *Exeunt.*

Act IV

Enter Hastings and Miss Neville.

HASTINGS You surprise me! Sir Charles Marlow expected here this night? Where have you had your information?

MISS NEVILLE You may depend upon it. I just saw his letter to Mr Hardcastle, in which he tells him he intends setting out a few hours after his son.

HASTINGS Then, my Constance, all must be completed before he arrives. He knows me; and should he find me here, would discover my name, and perhaps my designs, to the rest of the family.

MISS NEVILLE The jewels, I hope, are safe.

HASTINGS Yes, yes. I have sent them to Marlow, who keeps the keys of our baggage. In the mean time, I'll go to prepare matters for our elopement. I have had the Squire's promise of a fresh pair of horses; and, if I should not see him again, will write him further directions.   *Exit.*

MISS NEVILLE Well! success attend you. In the mean time, I'll go amuse my aunt with the old pretence of a violent passion for my cousin.   *Exit.*

Enter Marlow, followed by a Servant.

MARLOW I wonder what Hastings could mean by sending me so valuable a thing as a casket to keep for him, when he knows the only place I have is the seat of a post-coach at an Inn-door. Have you deposited the casket with the landlady, as I ordered you? Have you put it into her own hands?

SERVANT Yes, your honour.

MARLOW She said she'd keep it safe, did she?

SERVANT Yes, she said she'd keep it safe enough; she ask'd me how I came by it? and she said she had a great mind to make me give an account of myself.   *Exit Servant.*

MARLOW Ha! ha! ha! They're safe however. What an accountable set of beings have we got amongst! This little bar-maid though runs in my head most strangely, and drives out the absurdities of all the rest of the family. She's mine, she must be mine, or I'm greatly mistaken.

Enter Hastings.

HASTINGS Bless me! I quite forgot to tell her that I intended to prepare at the bottom of the garden. Marlow here, and in spirits too!

MARLOW Give my joy, George! Crown me, shadow me with laurels! Well, George, after all, we modest fellows don't want for success among the women.

HASTINGS Some women you mean. But what success has your honour's modesty been crowned with now, that it grows so insolent upon us?

MARLOW Didn't you see the tempting, brisk, lovely, little thing that runs about the house with a bunch of keys to its girdle?

HASTINGS Well! and what then?

MARLOW She's mine, you rogue you. Such fire, such motion, such eyes, such lips – but, egad! she would not let me kiss them though.

HASTINGS But are you so sure, so very sure of her?

MARLOW Why man, she talk'd of shewing me her work above-stairs, and I am to improve the pattern.

HASTINGS But how can *you*, Charles, go about to rob a woman of her honour?

MARLOW Pshaw! pshaw! we all know the honour of the bar-maid of an inn. I don't intend to *rob* her, take my word for it, there's nothing in this house, I shan't honestly *pay* for.

HASTINGS I believe the girl has virtue.

MARLOW And if she has, I should be the last man in the world that would attempt to corrupt it.

HASTINGS You have taken care, I hope, of the casket I sent you to lock up? It's in safety?

MARLOW Yes, yes. It's safe enough. I have taken care of it. But how could you think the seat of a post-coach at an Inn-door a place of safety? Ah! numbskull! I have taken better precautions for you than you did for yourself. – I have –

HASTINGS What!

MARLOW I have sent it to the landlady to keep for you.

HASTINGS To the landlady!

MARLOW The landlady.

HASTINGS You did.

MARLOW I did. She's to be answerable for its forth-coming, you know.

HASTINGS Yes, she'll bring it forth, with a witness.

MARLOW Wasn't I right? I believe you'll allow that I acted prudently upon this occasion?

HASTINGS (*Aside.*) He must not see my uneasiness.

MARLOW You seem a little disconcerted though, methinks. Sure nothing has happened?

HASTINGS No, nothing. Never was in better spirits in all my life. And so you left it with the landlady, who, no doubt, very readily undertook the charge?

MARLOW Rather too readily. For she not only kept the casket; but, thro' her great precaution, was going to keep the messenger too. Ha! ha! ha!

HASTINGS He! he! he! They're safe however.

MARLOW As a guinea in a miser's purse.

HASTINGS (*Aside.*) So now all hopes of fortune are at an end, and we must set off without it. (*To him.*) Well, Charles, I'll leave you to your meditations on the pretty bar-maid, and, he! he! he! may you be as successful for yourself as you have been for me.   *Exit.*

MARLOW Thank ye, George! I ask no more. Ha! ha! ha!

Enter Hardcastle.

HARDCASTLE I no longer know my own house. It's turned all topsey-turvey. His servants have got drunk already. I'll bear it no longer, and yet, from my respect for his father, I'll be calm. (*To him.*) Mr Marlow, your servant. I'm your very humble servant. (*Bowing low.*)

MARLOW Sir, your humble servant. (*Aside.*) What's to be the wonder now?

HARDCASTLE I believe, Sir, you must be sensible, Sir, that no man alive ought to be more welcome than your father's son, Sir. I hope you think so?

MARLOW I do from my soul, Sir. I don't want much intreaty. I generally make my father's son welcome wherever he goes.

HARDCASTLE I believe you do, from my soul, Sir. But tho' I say nothing to your own conduct, that of your Servants is insufferable. Their manner of drinking is setting a very bad example in this house, I assure you.

MARLOW I protest, my very good Sir, that's no fault of mine. If they don't drink as they ought *they* are to blame. I ordered them not to spare the cellar. I did, I assure you. (*To the side scene.*) Here, let one of my servants come up. (*To him.*) My positive directions were, that as I did not drink myself, they should make up for my deficiencies below.

HARDCASTLE Then they had your orders for what they do! I'm satisfied!

MARLOW They had, I assure you. You shall hear from one of themselves.

Enter Servant drunk.

MARLOW You, Jeremy! Come forward, sirrah! What were my orders? Were you not told to drink freely, and call for what you thought fit, for the good of the house?

HARDCASTLE (*Aside.*) I begin to lose my patience.

JEREMY Please your honour, liberty and Fleet-street for ever! Tho' I'm but a servant, I'm as good as another man. I'll drink for no man before supper, Sir, dammy! Good liquor will sit upon a good supper, but a good supper will not sit upon — hiccup — upon my conscience, Sir.

MARLOW You see, my old friend, the fellow is as drunk as he can possibly be. I don't know what you'd have more, unless you'd have the poor devil soused in a beer-barrel.

HARDCASTLE Zounds! He'll drive me distracted if I contain myself any longer. Mr Marlow, Sir; I have submitted to your insolence for more than four hours, and I see no likelihood of its coming to an end. I'm now resolved to be master here, Sir, and I desire that you and your drunken pack may leave my house directly.

MARLOW Leave your house! — Sure you jest, my good friend? What, when I'm doing what I can to please you.

HARDCASTLE I tell you, Sir, you don't please me; so I desire you'll leave my house.

MARLOW Sure you cannot be serious? At this time o'night, and such a night. You only mean to banter me?

HARDCASTLE I tell you, Sir, I'm serious; and, now that my passions are rouzed, I say this house is mine, Sir; this house is mine, and I command you to leave it directly.

MARLOW Ha! ha! ha! A puddle in a storm. I shan't stir a step, I assure you. (*In a serious tone.*) This, your house, fellow! It's my house. This is my house. Mine, while I chuse to stay. What right have you to bid me leave this house, Sir? I never met with such impudence, curse me, never in my whole life before.

HARDCASTLE Nor I, confound me if ever I did. To come to my house, to call for what he likes, to turn me out of my own chair, to insult the family, to order his servants to get drunk, and then to tell me *This house is mine, Sir.* By all that's impudent it makes me laugh. Ha! ha! ha! Pray, Sir, (*bantering*) as you take the house, what think you of taking the rest of the furniture? There's a pair of silver candlesticks, and there's a fire-screen, and here's a pair of brazen nosed bellows, perhaps you may take a fancy to them?

MARLOW Bring me your bill, Sir, bring me your bill, and let's make no more words about it.

HARDCASTLE There are a set of prints too. What think you of *The Rake's Progress* for your own apartment?

MARLOW Bring me your bill, I say; and I'll leave you and your infernal house directly.

HARDCASTLE Then there's a mahogany table, that you may see your own face in.

MARLOW My bill, I say.

HARDCASTLE I had forgot the great chair, for your own particular slumbers, after a hearty meal.

MARLOW Zounds! bring me my bill, I say, and let's hear no more on't.

HARDCASTLE Young man, young man, from your father's letter to me, I was taught to expect a well-bred modest man, as a visitor here, but now I find him no better than a coxcomb and a bully; but he will be down here presently, and shall hear more of it.   *Exit.*

MARLOW How's this! Sure I have not mistaken the house! Everything looks like an inn. The servants cry, *Coming.* The attendance is aukward; the bar-maid too to attend us. But she's here, and will further inform me. Whither so fast, child. A word with you.

Enter Miss Hardcastle.

MISS HARDCASTLE Let it be short then. I'm in a hurry. (*Aside.*) (I believe he begins to find out his mistake, but its too soon quite to undeceive him.)

MARLOW Pray, child, answer me one question. What are you, and what may your business in this house be?

MISS HARDCASTLE A relation of the family, Sir.

MARLOW What! A poor relation?

MISS HARDCASTLE Yes, Sir. A poor relation appointed to keep the keys, and to see that the guests want nothing in my power to give them.

MARLOW That is, you act as the bar-maid of this inn.

MISS HARDCASTLE Inn. O law – What brought that in your head. One of the best families in the country keep an inn. Ha, ha, ha, old Mr Hardcastle's house an inn.

MARLOW Mr Hardcastle's house! Is this house Mr Hardcastle's house, child!

MISS HARDCASTLE Ay, sure. Whose else should it be.

MARLOW So then all's out, and I have been damnably imposed on. O, confound my stupid head, I shall be laugh'd at over the whole town. I shall be stuck up in caricatura in all the print-shops. The Dullissimo Maccaroni. To mistake this house of all others for an inn, and my father's old friend for an inn-keeper. What a swaggering puppy must he take me for. What a silly puppy do I find myself. There again, may I be hang'd, my dear, but I mistook you for the bar-maid.

MISS HARDCASTLE Dear me! dear me! I'm sure there's nothing in my *behaviour* to put me upon a level with one of that stamp.

MARLOW Nothing, my dear, nothing. But I was in for a list of blunders, and could not help making you a subscriber. My stupidity saw every thing the wrong way. I mistook your assiduity for assurance, and your simplicity for allurement. But its over – This house I no more shew *my* face in.

MISS HARDCASTLE I hope, Sir, I have done nothing to disoblige you. I'm sure I should be sorry to affront any gentleman who has been so polite, and said so many civil things to me. I'm sure I should be sorry (*pretending to cry*) if he left the family upon my account. I'm sure I should be sorry people said any thing amiss, since I have no fortune but my character.

MARLOW (*Aside.*) By heaven, she weeps. This is the first mark of tenderness I ever had from a modest woman, and it touches me; (*to her*) Excuse me, my lovely girl, you are the only part of the family I leave with reluctance. But to be plain with you, the difference of our birth, fortune and education, make an honourable connexion impossible; and I can never harbour a thought of seducing simplicity that trusted in my honour, or bringing ruin upon one, whose only fault was being too lovely.

MISS HARDCASTLE (*Aside.*) Generous man! I now begin to admire him. (*To him.*) But I'm sure my family is as good as Miss Hardcastle's, and though I'm poor, that's no great misfortune to a contented mind, and, until this moment, I never thought that it was bad to want fortune.

MARLOW And why now, my pretty simplicity?

MISS HARDCASTLE Because it puts me at a distance from one, that if I had a thousand pound I would give it all to.

MARLOW (*Aside.*) This simplicity bewitches me, so that if I stay I'm undone. I must make one bold effort, and leave her. (*To her.*) Your partiality in my favour, my dear, touches me most sensibly, and were I to live for myself alone, I could easily fix my choice. But I owe too much to the opinion of the world, too much to the authority of a father, so that – I can scarcely speak it – it affects me. Farewell. *Exit.*

MISS HARDCASTLE I never knew half his merit till now. He shall not go, if I have power or art to detain him. I'll still preserve the character in which I stoop'd to conquer, but will undeceive my papa, who, perhaps, may laugh him out of his resolution.

Exit.

Enter Tony, Miss Neville.

TONY Ay, you may steal for yourselves the next time. I have done my duty. She has got the jewels again, that's a sure thing; but she believes it was all a mistake of the servants.

MISS NEVILLE But, my dear cousin, sure you won't forsake us in this distress. If she in the least suspects that I am going off, I shall certainly be locked up, or sent to my aunt Pedigree's, which is ten times worse.

TONY To be sure, aunts of all kinds are damn'd bad things. But what can I do? I have got you a pair of horses that will fly like Whistle-jacket, and I'm sure you can't say but I have courted you nicely before her face. Here she comes, we must court a bit or two more, for fear she should suspect us.

They retire, and seem to fondle.

Enter Mrs Hardcastle.

MRS HARDCASTLE Well, I was greatly fluttered, to be sure. But my son tells me it was all a mistake of the servants. I shan't be easy, however, till they are fairly married, and then let her keep her own fortune. But what do I see! Fondling together, as I'm alive. I never saw Tony so sprightly before. Ah! have I caught you, my pretty doves! What, billing, exchanging stolen glances, and broken murmurs. Ah!

TONY As for murmurs, mother, we grumble a little now and then, to be sure. But there's no love lost between us.

MRS HARDCASTLE A mere sprinkling, Tony, upon the flame, only to make it burn brighter.

MISS NEVILLE Cousin Tony promises to give us more of his company at home. Indeed, he shan't leave us any more. It won't leave us cousin Tony, will it?

TONY O! it's a pretty creature. No, I'd sooner leave my horse in a pound, than leave you when you smile upon one so. Your laugh makes you so becoming.

MISS NEVILLE Agreeable cousin! Who can help admiring that natural humour, that pleasant, broad, red, thoughtless, (*patting his cheek*) ah! it's a bold face.

MRS HARDCASTLE Pretty innocence.

TONY I'm sure I always lov'd cousin Con's hazel eyes, and her pretty long fingers, that she twists this way and that, over the haspicholls, like a parcel of bobbins.

MRS HARDCASTLE Ah, he could charm the bird from the tree. I was never so happy before. My boy takes after his father, poor Mr Lumpkin, exactly. The jewels, my dear Con, shall be your's incontinently. You shall have them. Isn't he a sweet boy, my dear? You shall be married to-morrow, and we'll put off the rest of his education, like Dr Drowsy's sermons, to a fitter opportunity.

Enter Diggory.

DIGGORY Where's the 'Squire? I have got a letter for your worship.

TONY Give it to my mamma. She reads all my letters first.

DIGGORY I had orders to deliver it into your own hands.

TONY Who does it come from?

DIGGORY Your worship mun ask that o' the letter itself.

TONY I could wish to know, tho' (*turning the letter, and gazing on it*).

MISS NEVILLE (*Aside.*) Undone, undone. A letter to him from Hastings. I know the hand. If my aunt sees it, we are ruined for ever. I'll keep her employ'd a little if I can. (*To Mrs Hardcastle.*) But I have not told you, Madam, of my cousin's smart answer just now to Mr Marlow. We so laugh'd — You must know, Madam — this way a little, for he must not hear us.   *They confer.*

TONY (*Still gazing.*) A damn'd cramp piece of penmanship, as ever I saw in my life. I can read your print-hand very well. But here there are such handles, and shanks, and dashes, that one can scarce tell the head from the tail. *To Anthony Lumpkin, Esquire.* It's very odd, I can read the outside of my letters, where my own name is, well enough. But when I come to open it, it's all — buzz. That's hard, very hard; for the inside of the letter is always the cream of the correspondence.

MRS HARDCASTLE Ha, ha, ha. Very well, very well. And so my son was too hard for the philosopher.

MISS NEVILLE Yes, Madam; but you must hear the rest, Madam. A little more this way, or he may hear us. You'll hear how he puzzled him again.

MRS HARDCASTLE He seems strangely puzzled now himself, methinks.

TONY (*Still gazing.*) A damn'd up and down hand, as if it was disguised in liquor. (*Reading.*) *Dear Sir.* Ay, that's that. Then there's an *M*, and a *T*, and an *S*, but whether the next be an *izzard* or an *R*, confound me, I cannot tell.

MRS HARDCASTLE What's that, my dear. Can I give you any assistance?

MISS NEVILLE Pray, aunt, let me read it. No body reads a cramp hand better than I. (*Twitching the letter from her.*) Do you know who it is from?

TONY Can't tell, except from Dick Ginger the feeder.

MISS NEVILLE Ay, so it is. (*Pretending to read.*) Dear 'Squire, Hoping that you're in health, as I am at this present. The gentlemen of the Shake-bag club has cut the gentlemen of Goose-green quite out of feather. The odds — um — odd battle — um — long fighting — um here, here, it's all about cocks, and fighting; it's of no consequence, here, put it up, put it up.

Thrusting the crumpled letter upon him.

TONY But I tell you, Miss, it's of all the consequence in the world. I would not lose the rest of it for a guinea. Here, mother, do you make it out. Of no consequence!

Giving Mrs Hardcastle the letter.

MRS HARDCASTLE How's this! (*Reads.*) Dear 'Squire, I'm now waiting for Miss Neville, with a post-chaise and pair, at the bottom of the garden, but I find my horses yet unable to perform the journey. I expect you'll assist us with a pair of fresh horses, as you promised. Dispatch is necessary, as the *hag* (ay the hag) your mother, will otherwise suspect us. Your's, Hastings. Grant me patience. I shall run distracted. My rage choaks me.

MISS NEVILLE I hope, Madam, you'll suspend your resentment for a few moments, and not impute to me any impertinence, or sinister design that belongs to another.

MRS HARDCASTLE (*Curtesying very low.*) Fine spoken, Madam, you are most miraculously polite and engaging, and quite the very pink of curtesy and circumspection, Madam. (*Changing her tone.*) And you, you great ill-fashioned oaf, with scarce sense enough to keep your mouth shut. Were you too join'd against me? But I'll defeat all your plots in a moment. As for you, Madam, since you have got a pair of fresh horses ready, it would be cruel to disappoint them. So, if you please, instead of running away with your spark, prepare, this very moment, to run off with *me.* Your old aunt Pedigree will keep you secure, I'll warrant me. You too, Sir, may mount your horse, and guard us upon the way. Here, Thomas, Roger, Diggory, I'll shew you that I wish you better than you do yourselves.   *Exit.*

MISS NEVILLE So now I'm completely ruined.

TONY Ay, that's a sure thing.

MISS NEVILLE What better could be expected from being connected with such a stupid fool, and after all the nods and signs I made him.

TONY By the laws, Miss, it was your own cleverness, and not my stupidity, that did your business. You were so nice and so busy with your Shake-bags and Goose-greens, that I thought you could never be making believe.

Enter Hastings.

HASTINGS So, Sir, I find by my servant, that you have shewn my letter, and betray'd us. Was this well done, young gentleman?

TONY Here's another. Ask Miss there who betray'd you. Ecod, it was her doing, not mine.

Enter Marlow.

MARLOW So I have been finely used here among you. Rendered contemptible, driven into ill manners, despised, insulted, laugh'd at.

TONY Here's another. We shall have old Bedlam broke loose presently.

MISS NEVILLE And there, Sir, is the gentleman to whom we all owe every obligation.

MARLOW What can I say to him, a mere boy, an ideot, whose ignorance and age are a protection.

HASTINGS A poor contemptible booby, that would but disgrace correction.

MISS NEVILLE Yet with cunning and malice enough to make himself merry with all our embarrassments.

HASTINGS An insensible cub.

MARLOW Replete with tricks and mischief.

TONY Baw! damme, but I'll fight you both one after the other, – with baskets.

MARLOW As for him, he's below resentment. But your conduct, Mr Hastings, requires an explanation. You knew of my mistakes, yet would not undeceive me.

HASTINGS Tortured as I am with my own disappointments, is this a time for explanations! It is not friendly, Mr Marlow.

MARLOW But, Sir –

MISS NEVILLE Mr Marlow, we never kept on your mistake, till it was too late to undeceive you. Be pacified.

Enter Servant.

SERVANT My mistress desires you'll get ready immediately, Madam. The horses are putting to. Your hat and things are in the next room. We are to go thirty miles before morning.

Exit Servant.

MISS NEVILLE Well, well; I'll come presently.

MARLOW (*To Hastings.*) Was it well done, Sir, to assist in rendering me ridiculous? To hang me out for the scorn of all my acquaintance. Depend upon it, Sir, I shall expect an explanation.

HASTINGS Was it well done, Sir, if you're upon that subject, to deliver what I entrusted to yourself, to the care of another, Sir?

MISS NEVILLE Mr Hastings. Mr Marlow. Why will you increase my distress by this groundless dispute? I implore, I intreat you —

Enter Servant.

SERVANT Your cloak, Madam. My mistress is impatient.

MISS NEVILLE I come. Pray be pacified. If I leave you thus, I shall die with apprehension.

SERVANT Your fan, muff, and gloves, Madam. The horses are waiting.

MISS NEVILLE O, Mr Marlow! if you knew what a scene of constraint and ill-nature lies before me, I'm sure it would convert your resentment into pity.

MARLOW I'm so distracted with a variety of passions, that I don't know what I do. Forgive me, Madam. George, forgive me. You know my hasty temper, and should not exasperate it.

HASTINGS The torture of my situation is my only excuse.

MISS NEVILLE Well, my dear Hastings, if you have that esteem for me that I think, that I am sure you have, your constancy for three years will but encrease the happiness of our future connexion. If —

MRS HARDCASTLE (*Within.*) Miss Neville. Constance, why Constance, I say.

MISS NEVILLE I'm coming. Well, constancy. Remember, constancy is the word.   *Exit.*

HASTINGS My heart! How can I support this. To be so near happiness, and such happiness.

MARLOW (*To Tony.*) You see now, young gentleman, the effects of your folly. What might be amusement to you, is here disappointment, and even distress.

TONY (*From a reverie.*) Ecod, I have hit it. Its here. Your hands. Yours and yours, my poor Sulky. My boots there, ho. Meet me two hours hence at the bottom of the garden; and if you don't find Tony Lumpkin a more good natur'd fellow than you thought for, I'll give you leave to take my best horse, and Bet Bouncer into the bargain. Come along. My boots, ho.

Exeunt.

Act V

Enter Hastings and Servant.

HASTINGS You saw the Old Lady and Miss Neville drive off, you say.

SERVANT Yes, your honour. They went off in a post coach, and the young 'Squire went on horseback. They're thirty miles off by this time.

HASTINGS Then all my hopes are over.

SERVANT Yes, Sir. Old Sir Charles is arrived. He and the Old Gentleman of the house have been laughing at Mr Marlow's mistake this half hour. They are coming this way.

HASTINGS Then I must not be seen. So now to my fruitless appointment at the bottom of the garden. This is about the time.   *Exit.*

Enter Sir Charles and Hardcastle.

HARDCASTLE Ha, ha, ha. The peremptory tone in which he sent forth his sublime commands.

SIR CHARLES And the reserve with which I suppose he treated all your advances.

HARDCASTLE And yet he might have seen something in me above a common inn-keeper, too.

SIR CHARLES Yes, Dick, but he mistook you for an uncommon inn-keeper, ha, ha, ha.

HARDCASTLE Well, I'm in too good spirits to think of any thing but joy. Yes, my dear friend, this union of our families will make our personal friendship hereditary; and tho' my daughter's fortune is but small —

SIR CHARLES Why, Dick, will you talk of fortune to *me*. My son is possessed of more than a competence already, and can want nothing but a good and virtuous girl to share his happiness and encrease it. If they like each other, as you say they do –

HARDCASTLE *If*, man. I tell you they *do* like each other. My daughter as good as told me so.

SIR CHARLES But girls are apt to flatter themselves, you know.

HARDCASTLE I saw him grasp her hand in the warmest manner myself; and here he comes to put you out of your *iffs*, I warrant him.

Enter Marlow.

MARLOW I come, Sir, once more, to ask pardon for my strange conduct. I can scarce reflect on my insolence without confusion.

HARDCASTLE Tut, boy, a trifle. You take it too gravely. An hour or two's laughing with my daughter will set all to rights again. She'll never like you the worse for it.

MARLOW Sir, I shall be always proud of her approbation.

HARDCASTLE Approbation is but a cold word, Mr Marlow; if I am not deceived, you have something more than approbation thereabouts. You take me.

MARLOW Really, Sir, I have not that happiness.

HARDCASTLE Come, boy, I'm an old fellow, and know what's what, as well as you that are younger. I know what has past between you; but mum.

MARLOW Sure, Sir, nothing has past between us but the most profound respect on my side, and the most distant reserve on her's. You don't think, Sir, that my impudence has been past upon all the rest of the family.

HARDCASTLE Impudence! No, I don't say that – Not quite impudence – Though girls like to be play'd with, and rumpled a little too sometimes. But she has told no tales, I assure you.

MARLOW I never gave her the slightest cause.

HARDCASTLE Well, well, I like modesty in its place well enough. But this is over-acting, young gentleman. You *may* be open. Your father and I will like you the better for it.

MARLOW May I die, Sir, if I ever –

HARDCASTLE I tell you, she don't dislike you; and as I'm sure you like her –

MARLOW Dear Sir – I protest, Sir –

HARDCASTLE I see no reason why you should not be joined as fast as the parson can tie you.

MARLOW But hear me, Sir –

HARDCASTLE Your father approves the match, I admire it, every moment's delay will be doing mischief, so –

MARLOW But why won't you hear me? By all that's just and true, I never gave Miss Hardcastle the slightest mark of my attachment, or even the most distant hint to suspect me of affection. We had but one interview, and that was formal, modest and uninteresting.

HARDCASTLE (*Aside*.) This fellow's formal modest impudence is beyond bearing.

SIR CHARLES And you never grasp'd her hand, or made any protestations!

MARLOW As heaven is my witness, I came down in obedience to your commands. I saw the lady without emotion, and parted without reluctance. I hope you'll exact no further proofs of my duty, nor prevent me from leaving a house in which I suffer so many mortifications.   *Exit*.

SIR CHARLES I'm astonish'd at the air of sincerity with which he parted.

HARDCASTLE And I'm astonish'd at the deliberate intrepidity of his assurance.

SIR CHARLES I dare pledge my life and honour upon his truth.

HARDCASTLE Here comes my daughter, and I would stake my happiness upon her veracity.

Enter Miss Hardcastle.

HARDCASTLE Kate, come hither, child. Answer us sincerely, and without reserve; has Mr Marlow made you any professions of love and affection?

MISS HARDCASTLE The question is very abrupt, Sir! But since you require unreserved sincerity, I think he has.

HARDCASTLE (*To Sir Charles*.) You see.

SIR CHARLES And pray, Madam, have you and my son had more than one interview?

MISS HARDCASTLE Yes, Sir, several.

HARDCASTLE (*To Sir Charles*.) You see.

SIR CHARLES But did he profess any attachment?

MISS HARDCASTLE A lasting one.

SIR CHARLES Did he talk of love?

MISS HARDCASTLE Much, Sir.

SIR CHARLES Amazing! And all this formally?

MISS HARDCASTLE Formally.

HARDCASTLE Now, my friend, I hope you are satisfied.

SIR CHARLES And how did he behave, Madam?

MISS HARDCASTLE As most profest admirers do. Said some civil things of my face, talked much of his want of merit, and the greatness of mine; mentioned his heart, gave a short tragedy speech, and ended with pretended rapture.

SIR CHARLES Now I'm perfectly convinced, indeed. I know his conversation among women to be modest and submissive. This forward canting ranting manner by no means describes him, and I am confident, he never sate for the picture.

MISS HARDCASTLE Then what, Sir, if I should convince you to your face of my sincerity? If you and my papa, in about half an hour, will place yourselves behind that screen, you shall hear him declare his passion to me in person.

SIR CHARLES Agreed. And if I find him what you describe, all my happiness in him must have an end.   *Exit.*

MISS HARDCASTLE And if you don't find him what I describe – I fear my happiness must never have a beginning.   *Exeunt.*

SCENE: *Changes to the back of the garden.*

Enter Hastings.

HASTINGS What an ideot am I, to wait here for a fellow, who probably takes a delight in mortifying me. He never intended to be punctual, and I'll wait no longer. What do I see. It is he, and perhaps with news of my Constance.

Enter Tony, booted and spattered.

HASTINGS My honest 'Squire! I now find you a man of your word. This looks like friendship.

TONY Ay, I'm your friend, and the best friend you have in the world, if you knew but all. This riding by night, by the bye, is cursedly tiresome. It has shook me worse than the basket of a stage-coach.

HASTINGS But how? Where did you leave your fellow travellers? Are they in safety? Are they housed?

TONY Five and twenty miles in two hours and a half is no such bad driving. The poor beasts have smoaked for it: Rabbet me, but I'd rather ride forty miles after a fox, than ten with such *varment.*

HASTINGS Well, but where have you left the ladies? I die with impatience.

TONY Left them. Why where should I leave them, but where I found them.

HASTINGS This is a riddle.

TONY Riddle me this then. What's that goes round the house, and round the house and never touches the house?

HASTINGS I'm still astray.

TONY Why that's it, mon. I have led them astray. By jingo, there's not a pond or slough within five miles of the place but they can tell the taste of.

HASTINGS Ha, ha, ha, I understand; you took them in a round, while they supposed themselves going forward. And so you have at last brought them home again.

TONY You shall hear. I first took them down Feather-bed-lane, where we stuck fast in the mud. I then rattled them crack over the stones of Up-and-down Hill – I then introduc'd them to the gibbet on Heavy-tree Heath, and from that, with a circumbendibus, I fairly lodged them in the horse-pond at the bottom of the garden.

HASTINGS But no accident, I hope.

TONY No, no. Only mother is confoundedly frightened. She thinks herself forty miles off. She's sick of the journey, and the cattle can scarce crawl. So if your own horses be ready, you may whip off with cousin, and I'll be bound that no soul here can budge a foot to follow you.

HASTINGS My dear friend, how can I be grateful?

TONY Ay, now its dear friend, noble 'Squire. Just now, it was all ideot, cub, and run me though the guts. Damn *your* way of fighting, I say. After we take a knock in this part of the country, we kiss and be friends. But if you had run me through the guts, then I should be dead, and you might go kiss the hangman.

HASTINGS The rebuke is just. But I must hasten to relieve Miss Neville; if you keep the old lady employed, I promise to take care of the young one.   *Exit Hastings*.

TONY Never fear me. Here she comes. Vanish. She's got from the pond, and draggled up to the waist like a mermaid.

Enter Mrs Hardcastle.

MRS HARDCASTLE Oh, Tony, I'm killed. Shook. Battered to death. I shall never survive it. That last jolt that laid us against the quickset hedge has done my business.

TONY Alack, mama, it was all your own fault. You would be for running away by night, without knowing one inch of the way.

MRS HARDCASTLE I wish we were at home again. I never met so many accidents in so short a journey. Drench'd in the mud, overturn'd in a ditch, stuck fast in a slough, jolted to a jelly, and at last to lose our way. Whereabouts do you think we are, Tony?

TONY By my guess we should be upon Crackskull common, about forty miles from home.

MRS HARDCASTLE O lud! O lud! the most notorious spot in all the country. We only want a robbery to make a complete night on't.

TONY Don't be afraid, mama, don't be afraid. Two of the five that kept here are hanged, and the other three may not find us. Don't be afraid. Is that a man that's galloping behind us? No; its only a tree. Don't be afraid.

MRS HARDCASTLE The fright will certainly kill me.

TONY Do you see any thing like a black hat moving behind the thicket?

MRS HARDCASTLE O death!

TONY No, it's only a cow. Don't be afraid, mama; don't be afraid.

MRS HARDCASTLE As I'm alive, Tony, I see a man coming towards us. Ah! I'm sure on't. If he perceives us we are undone.

TONY (*Aside.*) Father-in-law, by all that's unlucky, come to take one of his night walks. (*To her.*) Ah, it's a highwayman, with pistils as long as my arm. A damn'd ill-looking fellow.

MRS HARDCASTLE Good heaven defend us! He approaches.

TONY Do you hide yourself in that thicket, and leave me to manage him. If there be any danger I'll cough and cry hem. When I cough be sure to keep close.

Mrs Hardcastle hides behind a tree in the back scene.

Enter Hardcastle.

HARDCASTLE I'm mistaken, or I heard voices of people in want of help. Oh, Tony, is that you. I did not expect you so soon back. Are your mother and her charge in safety?

TONY Very safe, Sir, at my aunt Pedigree's. Hem.

MRS HARDCASTLE (*From behind.*) Ah death! I find there's danger.

HARDCASTLE Forty miles in three hours; sure, that's too much, my youngster.

TONY Stout horses and willing minds make short journies, as they say. Hem.

MRS HARDCASTLE (*From behind.*) Sure he'll do the dear boy no harm.

HARDCASTLE But I heard a voice here; I should be glad to know from whence it came?

TONY It was I, Sir, talking to myself, Sir. I was saying that forty miles in four hours was very good going. Hem. As to be sure it was. Hem. I have got a sort of cold by being out in the air. We'll go in, if you please. Hem.

HARDCASTLE But if you talk'd to yourself, you did not answer yourself. I am certain I heard two voices, and am resolved (*raising his voice*) to find the other out.

MRS HARDCASTLE (*From behind.*) Oh! he's coming to find me out. Oh!

TONY What need you go, Sir, if I tell you. Hem. I'll lay down my life for the truth – hem – I'll tell you all, Sir.

Detaining him.

HARDCASTLE I tell you, I will not be detained. I insist on seeing. It's in vain to expect I'll believe you.

MRS HARDCASTLE (*Running forward from behind.*) O lud, he'll murder my poor boy, my darling. Here, good gentleman, whet your rage upon me. Take my money, my life, but spare that young gentleman, spare my child, if you have any mercy.

HARDCASTLE My wife! as I'm a Christian. From whence can she come, or what does she mean!

MRS HARDCASTLE (*Kneeling.*) Take compassion on us, good Mr Highwayman. Take our money, our watches, all we have, but spare our lives. We will never bring you to justice, indeed we won't, good Mr Highwayman.

HARDCASTLE I believe the woman's out of her senses. What, Dorothy, don't you know me?

MRS HARDCASTLE Mr Hardcastle, as I'm alive. My fears blinded me. But who my dear, could have expected to meet you here, in this frightful place, so far from home? What has brought you to follow us?

HARDCASTLE Sure, Dorothy, you have not lost your wits? So far from home, when you are within forty yards of your own door. (*To him.*) This is one of your old tricks, you graceless rogue you. (*To her.*) Don't you know the gate, and the mulberry-tree; and don't you remember the horsepond, my dear?

MRS HARDCASTLE Yes, I shall remember the horsepond as long as I live; I have caught my death in it. (*To Tony.*) And is it to you, you graceless varlet, I owe all this. I'll teach you to abuse your mother, I will.

TONY Ecod, mother, all the parish says you have spoil'd me, and so you may take the fruits on't.

MRS HARDCASTLE I'll spoil you, I will.

Follows him off the stage. Exit.

HARDCASTLE There's morality, however, in his reply.   *Exit.*

Enter Hastings and Miss Neville.

HASTINGS My dear Constance, why will you deliberate thus? If we delay a moment, all is lost for ever. Pluck up a little resolution, and we shall soon be out of the reach of her malignity.

MISS NEVILLE I find it impossible. My spirits are so sunk with the agitations I have suffered, that I am unable to face any new danger. Two or three years patience will at last crown us with happiness.

HASTINGS Such a tedious delay is worse than inconstancy. Let us fly, my charmer. Let us date our happiness from this very moment. Perish fortune. Love and content will encrease what we possess beyond a monarch's revenue. Let me prevail.

MISS NEVILLE No, Mr Hastings; no. Prudence once more comes to my relief, and I will obey its dictates. In the moment of passion, fortune may be despised, but it ever produces a lasting repentance. I'm resolved to apply to Mr Hardcastle's compassion and justice for redress.

HASTINGS But tho' he had the will, he has not the power to relieve you.

MISS NEVILLE But he has influence, and upon that I am resolved to rely.

HASTINGS I have no hopes. But since you persist, I must reluctantly obey you.   *Exeunt.*

SCENE: *Changes.*

Enter Sir Charles and Miss Hardcastle.

SIR CHARLES What a situation am I in. If what you say appears, I shall then find a guilty son. If what he says be true, I shall then lose one that, of all others, I most wish'd for a daughter.

MISS HARDCASTLE I am proud of your approbation, and to shew I merit it, if you place yourselves as I directed, you shall hear his explicit declaration. But he comes.

SIR CHARLES I'll to your father, and keep him to the appointment.   *Exit Sir Charles.*

Enter Marlow.

MARLOW Tho' prepar'd for setting out, I come once more to take leave, nor did I, till this moment, know the pain I feel in the separation.

MISS HARDCASTLE (*In her own natural manner.*) I believe those sufferings cannot be very great, Sir, which you can so easily remove. A day or two longer, perhaps, might lessen your uneasiness, by shewing the little value of what you now think proper to regret.

MARLOW (*Aside.*) This girl every moment improves upon me. (*To her.*) It must not be, Madam. I have already trifled too long with my heart. My very pride begins to submit to my passion. The disparity of education and fortune, the anger of a parent, and the contempt of my equals, begin to lose their weight; and nothing can restore me to myself, but this painful effort of resolution.

MISS HARDCASTLE Then go, Sir. I'll urge nothing more to detain you. Tho' my family be as good as her's you came down to visit, and my education, I hope, not inferior, what are these advantages without equal affluence? I must remain contented with the slight approbation of imputed merit; I must have only the mockery of your addresses, while all your serious aims are fix'd on fortune.

Enter Hardcastle and Sir Charles from behind.

SIR CHARLES Here, behind this screen.

HARDCASTLE Ay, Ay, make no noise. I'll engage my Kate covers him with confusion at last.

MARLOW By heavens, Madam, fortune was ever my smallest consideration. Your beauty at first caught my eye; for who could see that without emotion. But every moment that I converse with you, steals in some new grace, heightens the picture, and gives it stronger expression. What at first seem'd rustic plainness, now appears refin'd simplicity. What seem'd forward assurance, now strikes me as the result of courageous innocence, and conscious virtue.

SIR CHARLES What can it mean! He amazes me!

HARDCASTLE I told you how it would be. Hush!

MARLOW I am now determined to stay, Madam, and I have too good an opinion of my father's discernment, when he sees you, to doubt his approbation.

MISS HARDCASTLE No, Mr Marlow, I will not, cannot detain you. Do you think I could suffer a connexion, in which there is the smallest room for repentance? Do you think I would take the mean advantage of a transient passion, to load you with confusion? Do you think I could ever relish that happiness, which was acquired by lessening your's?

MARLOW By all that's good, I can have no happiness but what's in your power to grant me. Nor shall I ever feel repentance, but in not having seen your merits before. I will stay, even contrary to your wishes; and tho' you should persist to shun me, I will make my respectful assiduities atone for the levity of my past conduct.

MISS HARDCASTLE Sir, I must entreat you'll desist. As our acquaintance began, so let it end, in indifference. I might have given an hour or two to levity; but seriously, Mr Marlow, do you think I could ever submit to a connexion, where I must appear mercenary, and you imprudent? Do you think I could ever catch at the confident addresses of a secure admirer?

MARLOW (Kneeling.) Does this look like security. Does this look like confidence. No, Madam, every moment that shews me your merit, only serves to encrease my diffidence and confusion. Here let me continue –

SIR CHARLES I can hold it no longer. Charles, Charles, how hast thou deceived me! Is this your indifference, your uninteresting conversation!

HARDCASTLE Your cold contempt; your formal interview. What have you to say now?

MARLOW That I'm all amazement! What can it mean!

HARDCASTLE It means that you can say and unsay things at pleasure. That you can address a lady in private, and deny it in public; that you have one story for us, and another for my daughter.

MARLOW Daughter! – this lady your daughter!

HARDCASTLE Yes, Sir, my only daughter. My Kate, whose else should she be.

MARLOW Oh, the devil.

MISS HARDCASTLE Yes, Sir, that very identical tall squinting lady you were pleased to take me for. (*Curtesying.*) She that you addressed as the mild, modest, sentimental man of gravity, and the bold forward agreeable rattle of the ladies club; ha, ha, ha.

MARLOW Zounds, there's no bearing this; it's worse than death.

MISS HARDCASTLE In which of your characters, Sir, will you give us leave to address you. As the faultering gentleman, with looks on the ground, that speaks just to be heard, and hates hypocrisy; or the loud confident creature, that keeps it up with Mrs Mantrap, and old Miss Biddy Bucksin, till three in the morning; ha, ha, ha.

MARLOW O, curse on my noisy head. I never attempted to be impudent yet, that I was not taken down. I must be gone.

HARDCASTLE By the hand of my body, but you shall not. I see it was all a mistake, and I am rejoiced to find it. You shall not stir, I tell you. I know she'll forgive you. Won't you forgive him, Kate. We'll all forgive you. Take courage, man.

They retire, she tormenting him to the back scene.

Enter Mrs Hardcastle, Tony.

MRS HARDCASTLE So, so, they're gone off. Let them go, I care not.

HARDCASTLE Who gone?

MRS HARDCASTLE My dutiful niece and her gentleman, Mr Hastings, from Town. He who came down with our modest visitor here.

SIR CHARLES Who, my honest George Hastings? As worthy a fellow as lives, and the girl could not have made a more prudent choice.

HARDCASTLE Then, by the hand of my body, I'm proud of the connexion.

MRS HARDCASTLE Well, if he has taken away the lady, he has

not taken her fortune, that remains in this family to console us for her loss.

HARDCASTLE Sure Dorothy you would not be so mercenary?

MRS HARDCASTLE Ay, that's my affair, not your's.

HARDCASTLE But you know if your son, when of age, refuses to marry his cousin, her whole fortune is then at her own disposal.

MRS HARDCASTLE Ay, but he's not of age, and she has not thought proper to wait for his refusal.

Enter Hastings and Miss Neville.

MRS HARDCASTLE (*Aside.*) What, returned so soon, I begin not to like it.

HASTINGS (*To Hardcastle.*) For my late attempt to fly off with your niece, let my present confusion be my punishment. We are now come back to appeal from your justice to your humanity. By her father's consent, I first paid her my addresses, and our passions were first founded in duty.

MISS NEVILLE Since his death, I have been obliged to stoop to dissimulation to avoid oppression. In an hour of levity, I was ready even to give up my fortune to secure my choice. But I'm now recover'd from the delusion, and hope from your tenderness what is denied me from a nearer connexion.

MRS HARDCASTLE Pshaw, pshaw, this is all but the whining end of a modern novel.

HARDCASTLE Be it what it will, I'm glad they're come back to reclaim their due. Come hither, Tony boy. Do you refuse this lady's hand whom I now offer you?

TONY What signifies my refusing. You know I can't refuse her till I'm of age, father.

HARDCASTLE While I thought concealing your age, boy, was likely to conduce to your improvement, I concurred with your mother's desire to keep it secret. But since I find she turns it to a wrong use, I must now declare, you have been of age these three months.

TONY Of age! Am I of age, father?

HARDCASTLE Above three months.

TONY Then you'll see the first use I'll make of my liberty. (*Taking Miss Neville's hand.*) Witness all men by these presents, that I, Anthony Lumpkin, Esquire, of BLANK place, refuse you, Constantia Neville, spinster, of no place at all, for my true and lawful wife. So Constance Neville may marry whom she pleases, and Tony Lumpkin is his own man again.

SIR CHARLES O brave 'Squire.

HASTINGS My worthy friend.

MRS HARDCASTLE My undutiful offspring.

MARLOW Joy, my dear George, I give you joy sincerely. And could I prevail upon my little tyrant here to be less arbitrary, I should be the happiest man alive, if you would return me the favour.

HASTINGS (*To Miss Hardcastle.*) Come, Madam, you are now driven to the very last scene of all your contrivances. I know you like him, I'm sure he loves you, and you must and shall have him.

HARDCASTLE (*Joining their hands.*) And I say so too. And Mr Marlow, if she makes a good wife as she has a daughter, I don't believe you'll ever repent your bargain. So now to supper, to-morrow we shall gather all the poor of the parish about us, and the Mistakes of the Night shall be crowned with a merry morning; so boy take her; and as you have been mistaken in the mistress, my wish is, that you may never be mistaken in the wife.

Epilogue

BY DR GOLDSMITH

Well, having stoop'd to conquer with success,
And gain'd a husband without aid from dress,
Still as a Bar-maid, I could wish it too,
As I have conquer'd him to conquer you:
And let me say, for all your resolution,
That pretty Bar-maids have done execution.
Our life is all a play, compos'd to please,
'We have our exits and our entrances.'
The first act shews the simple country maid,
Harmless and young, of ev'ry thing afraid;
Blushes when hir'd, and with unmeaning action,
I hopes as how to give you satisfaction.
Her second act displays a livelier scene, –
Th' unblushing Bar-maid of a country inn.
Who whisks about the house, at market caters,
Talks loud, conquets the guests, and scolds the waiters.
Next the scene shifts to town, and there she soars,
The chop house toast of ogling connoissieurs.
On 'Squires and Cits she there displays her arts,
And on the gridiron broils her lover's hearts –
And as she smiles, her triumphs to compleat,
Even Common Councilmen forget to eat.
The fourth act shews her wedded to the 'Squire,
And Madam now begins to hold it higher;
Pretends to taste, at Operas cries *caro*,
And quits her Nancy Dawson, for *Che Faro*.
Doats upon dancing, and in all her pride,
Swims round the room, the *Heinel* of Cheapside:
Ogles and leers with artificial skill,
Till having lost in age the power to kill,
She sits all night at cards, and ogles at spadille.

Such, thro' our lives, the eventful history —
The fifth and last act still remains for me.
The Bar-maid now for your protection prays,
Turns Female Barrister, and pleads for Bayes.

THE SCHOOL FOR
SCANDAL

Dramatis Personæ

AS ORIGINALLY ACTED
AT DRURY LANE THEATRE IN 1777

SIR PETER TEAZLE	Mr King
SIR OLIVER SURFACE	Mr Yates
SIR TOBY BUMPER	Mr Gaudry
SIR BENJAMIN BACKBITE	Mr Dodd
JOSEPH SURFACE	Mr Palmer
CHARLES SURFACE	Mr Smith
CARELESS	Mr Farren
SNAKE	Mr Packer
CRABTREE	Mr Parsons
ROWLEY	Mr Aickin
MOSES	Mr Baddeley
TRIP	Mr LaMash
LADY TEAZLE	Mrs Abington
LADY SNEERWELL	Miss Sherry
MRS CANDOUR	Miss Pope
MARIA	Miss P. Hopkins

Gentlemen, Maid, and Servants

SCENE
London

Prologue

WRITTEN BY MR GARRICK

A School for Scandal! tell me, I beseech you,
Needs there a school – this modish art to teach you?
No need of lessons now; – the knowing think –
We might as well be taught to eat and drink;
Caus'd by a dearth of scandal, should the vapours
Distress our fair ones – let 'em read the papers;
Their powerful mixtures such disorders hit;
Crave what you will – there's *quantum sufficit*.
'Lord!' cries my Lady *Wormwood* (who loves tattle,
And puts much salt and pepper in her prattle),
Just ris'n at noon, all night at cards, when threshing
Strong tea and scandal – 'Bless me, how refreshing!
Give me the papers, *Lisp* – how bold and free!   *Sips.*
Last night Lord L. (*sips*) was caught with Lady D.
For aching heads what charming *sal volatile!*   *Sips.*
If Mrs B. will still continue flirting,
We hope she'll *draw*, or we'll *undraw* the curtain.
Fine satire, poz – in public all abuse it,
But, by ourselves, (*sips*) our praise we can't refuse it.
Now, *Lisp*, read you – there, at that dash and star.'
'Yes, ma'am – A certain Lord had best beware,
Who lives not twenty miles from Grosv'nor Square;
For should he Lady W – find willing, –
Wormwood is bitter' – 'Oh! that's me! the villain!
Throw it behind the fire, and never more
Let that vile paper *come within my door.*'
Thus at our friends we laugh, who feel the dart;
To reach *our* feelings, we ourselves must smart.
Is our young bard so young – to think that he
Can stop the full spring-tide of calumny?

Knows he the world so little, and its trade?
Alas! the devil's sooner *rais'd* than *laid*.
So strong, so swift, the monster there's no gagging:
Cut Scandal's head off, still the tongue is wagging.
Proud of your smiles once lavishly bestow'd,
Again our young Don Quixote takes the road;
To show his gratitude he draws his pen,
And seeks this Hydra, Scandal, in his den.
From his fell gripe the frighted fair to save –
Tho' he should fall th' attempt must please the brave.
For your applause all perils he would through –
He'll fight – that's write – a cavalero true,
Till every drop of blood – that's ink – is spilt for you.

Act I

SCENE I

SCENE: *Lady Sneerwell's house.*

Lady Sneerwell at the dressing-table. Mr Snake drinking chocolate.

LADY SNEERWELL The paragraphs, you say, Mr Snake, were all inserted?

SNAKE They were, madam; and as I copied them myself in a feigned hand, there can be no suspicion whence they came.

LADY SNEERWELL Did you circulate the report of Lady Brittle's intrigue with Captain Boastall?

SNAKE That's in as fine a train as your ladyship could wish. In the common course of things, I think it must reach Mrs Clackit's ears within four-and-twenty hours; and then, you know, the business is as good as done.

LADY SNEERWELL Why, truly, Mrs Clackit has a very pretty talent, and a great deal of industry.

SNAKE True, madam, and has been tolerably successful in her day. To my knowledge she has been the cause of six matches being broken off, and three sons disinherited; of four forced elopements, and as many close confinements; nine separate maintenances, and two divorces. Nay, I have more than once traced her causing a *tête-à-tête* in the *Town and Country Magazine*, when the parties, perhaps, had never seen each other's face before in the course of their lives.

LADY SNEERWELL She certainly has talents, but her manner is gross.

SNAKE 'Tis very true – She generally designs well, has a free tongue and a bold invention; but her colouring is too dark, and her outlines often extravagant. She wants that delicacy of tint, and mellowness of sneer, which distinguish your lady-ship's scandal.

LADY SNEERWELL You are partial, Snake.

SNAKE Not in the least — everybody allows that Lady Sneerwell can do more with a word or look, than many can with the most laboured detail, even when they happen to have a little truth on their side to support it.

LADY SNEERWELL Yes, my dear Snake; and I am no hypocrite to deny the satisfaction I reap from the success of my efforts. Wounded myself, in the early part of my life, by the enven-omed tongue of slander, I confess I have since known no pleasure equal to the reducing others to the level of my own injured reputation.

SNAKE Nothing can be more natural. But, Lady Sneerwell, there is one affair in which you have lately employed me, wherein, I confess, I am at a loss to guess your motives.

LADY SNEERWELL I conceive you mean with respect to my neighbour, Sir Peter Teazle, and his family?

SNAKE I do. Here are two young men, to whom Sir Peter has acted as a kind of guardian since their father's death; the eldest possessing the most amiable character, and universally well spoken of; the youngest, the most dissipated and extrava-gant young fellow in the kingdom, without friends or charac-ter: the former an avowed admirer of your ladyship's, and apparently your favourite; the latter attached to Maria, Sir Peter's ward, and confessedly beloved by her. Now, on the face of these circumstances, it is utterly unaccountable to me, why you, the widow of a city knight, with a good jointure, should not close with the passion of a man of such character and expectations as Mr Surface; and more so why you should be so uncommonly earnest to destroy the mutual attachment subsisting between his brother Charles and Maria.

LADY SNEERWELL Then at once to unravel this mystery, I must inform you, that love has no share whatever in the intercourse between Mr Surface and me.

SNAKE No!

LADY SNEERWELL His real attachment is to Maria, or her fortune; but finding in his brother a favoured rival, he has been obliged to mask his pretensions, and profit by my assistance.

SNAKE Yet still I am more puzzled why you should interest yourself in his success.

LADY SNEERWELL How dull you are! Cannot you surmise the weakness which I hitherto, through shame, have concealed even from you? Must I confess that Charles, that libertine, that extravagant, that bankrupt in fortune and reputation, that he it is for whom I'm thus anxious and malicious, and to gain whom I would sacrifice everything?

SNAKE Now, indeed, your conduct appears consistent; but how came you and Mr Surface so confidential?

LADY SNEERWELL For our mutual interest. I have found him out a long time since. I know him to be artful, selfish, and malicious – in short, a sentimental knave; while with Sir Peter, and indeed with all his acquaintance, he passes for a miracle of prudence, good sense, and benevolence.

SNAKE Yes; yet Sir Peter vows he has not his equal in England, and above all, he praises him as a man of sentiment.

LADY SNEERWELL True – and with the assistance of his sentiment and hypocrisy he has brought Sir Peter entirely into his interest with regard to Maria, while poor Charles has no friend in the house, though, I fear, he has a powerful one in Maria's heart, against whom we must direct our schemes.

Enter Servant.

SERVANT Mr Surface.

LADY SNEERWELL Show him up. (*Exit Servant.*) He generally calls about this time. I don't wonder at people giving him to me for a lover.

Enter Joseph Surface.

JOSEPH SURFACE My dear Lady Sneerwell, how do you do today? Mr Snake, you most obedient.

LADY SNEERWELL Snake has just been rallying me on our mutual attachment; but I have informed him of our real views. You know how useful he has been to us, and, believe me, the confidence is not ill-placed.

JOSEPH SURFACE Madam, it is impossible for me to suspect a man of Mr Snake's sensibility and discernment.

LADY SNEERWELL Well, well, no compliments now; but tell me when you saw your mistress, Maria – or, what is more material to me, your brother.

JOSEPH SURFACE I have not seen either since I left you; but I can inform you that they never meet. Some of your stories have taken a good effect on Maria.

LADY SNEERWELL Ah! my dear Snake! the merit of this belongs to you: but do your brother's distresses increase?

JOSEPH SURFACE Every hour. I am told he has had another execution in the house yesterday. In short, his dissipation and extravagance exceed anything I have ever heard of.

LADY SNEERWELL Poor Charles!

JOSEPH SURFACE True, madam; notwithstanding his vices, one can't help feeling for him. Aye poor Charles, indeed! I'm sure I wish it were in my power to be of any essential service to him; for the man who does not share in the distresses of a brother, even though merited by his own misconduct, deserves —

LADY SNEERWELL O Lud! you are going to be moral, and forget that you are among friends.

JOSEPH SURFACE Egad, that's true! — I'll keep that sentiment till I see Sir Peter; — however, it is certainly a charity to rescue Maria from such a libertine, who, if he is to be reclaimed, can be so only by a person of your ladyship's superior accomplishments and understanding.

SNAKE I believe, Lady Sneerwell, here's company coming: I'll go and copy the letter I mentioned to you. — Mr Surface, your most obedient.   *Exit Snake.*

JOSEPH SURFACE Sir, your very devoted. — Lady Sneerwell, I am very sorry you have put any further confidence in that fellow.

LADY SNEERWELL Why so?

JOSEPH SURFACE I have lately detected him in frequent conference with old Rowley, who was formerly my father's steward, and has never, you know, been a friend of mine.

LADY SNEERWELL And so you think he would betray us?

JOSEPH SURFACE Nothing more likely: take my word for't, Lady Sneerwell, that fellow hasn't virtue enough to be faithful even to his own villainy. — Ah! Maria!

Enter Maria.

LADY SNEERWELL Maria, my dear, how do you do? — What's the matter?

MARIA O there's that disagreeable lover of mine, Sir Benjamin

Backbite, has just called at my guardian's, with his odious uncle, Crabtree; so I slipped out, and ran hither to avoid them.

LADY SNEERWELL Is that all?

JOSEPH SURFACE If my brother Charles had been of the party, madam, perhaps you would not have been so much alarmed.

LADY SNEERWELL Nay, now you are severe; for I dare swear the truth of the matter is, Maria heard *you* were here. — But, my dear, what has Sir Benjamin done, that you would avoid him?

MARIA Oh, he has done nothing — but 'tis for what he has said: his conversation is a perpetual libel on all his acquaintance.

JOSEPH SURFACE Ay, and the worst of it is, there is no advantage in not knowing him — for he'll abuse a stranger just as his best friend; and his uncle is as bad.

LADY SNEERWELL Nay, but we should make allowance — Sir Benjamin is a wit and a poet.

MARIA For my part, I confess, madam, wit loses its respect with me, when I see it in company with malice. — What do you think, Mr Surface?

JOSEPH SURFACE Certainly, madam; to smile at the jest which plants a thorn in another's breast is to become a principal in the mischief.

LADY SNEERWELL Pshaw! — there's no possibility of being witty without a little ill nature: the malice of a good thing is the barb that makes it stick. — What's your opinion, Mr Surface?

JOSEPH SURFACE To be sure, madam; that conversation, where the spirit of raillery is suppressed, will ever appear tedious and insipid.

MARIA Well, I'll not debate how far scandal may be allowable; but in a man, I am sure, it is always contemptible. We have pride, envy, rivalship, and a thousand motives to depreciate each other; but the male slanderer must have the cowardice of a woman before he can traduce one.

Enter Servant.

SERVANT Madam, Mrs Candour is below, and, if your lady-ship's at leisure, will leave her carriage.

LADY SNEERWELL Beg her to walk in. — (*Exit Servant.*) Now, Maria, here is a character to your taste; for, though Mrs

Candour is a little talkative, everybody allows her to be the best-natured and best sort of woman.

MARIA Yet with a very gross affectation of good nature and benevolence, she does more mischief than the direct malice of old Crabtree.

JOSEPH SURFACE I'faith 'tis true, Lady Sneerwell: whenever I hear the current running against the characters of my friends, I never think them in such danger as when Candour undertakes their defence.

LADY SNEERWELL Hush! – here she is! –

Enter Mrs Candour.

MRS CANDOUR My dear Lady Sneerwell, how have you been this century? – Mr Surface, what news do you hear? – though indeed it is no matter, for I think one hears nothing else but scandal.

JOSEPH SURFACE Just so, indeed, ma'am.

MRS CANDOUR Ah! Maria child, – what, is the whole affair off between you and Charles? – His extravagance, I presume – the town talks of nothing else.

MARIA I am very sorry, ma'am, the town has so little do do.

MRS CANDOUR True, true, child: but there's no stopping people's tongues. I own I was hurt to hear it, as I indeed was to learn, from the same quarter, that your guardian, Sir Peter, and Lady Teazle have not agreed lately as well as could be wished.

MARIA 'Tis strangely impertinent for people to busy themselves so.

MRS CANDOUR Very true, child; – but what's to be done? People will talk – there's no preventing it. Why, it was but yesterday I was told that Miss Gadabout had eloped with Sir Filagree Flirt. – But, Lord! there is no minding what one hears; though, to be sure, I had this from very good authority.

MARIA Such reports are highly scandalous.

MRS CANDOUR So they are, child – shameful! shameful! But the world is so censorious, no character escapes. – Lord now! who would have suspected your friend, Miss Prim, of an indiscretion? Yet such is the ill-nature of people, that they say her uncle stopped her last week, just as she was stepping into the York diligence with her dancing-master.

MARIA I'll answer for't there are no grounds for the report.

MRS CANDOUR O no foundation in the world, I dare swear: no

more, probably, than for the story circulated last month, of Mrs Festino's affair with Colonel Cassino; – though to be sure, the matter was never rightly cleared up.

JOSEPH SURFACE The licence of invention some people take is monstrous indeed.

MARIA 'Tis so; but, in my opinion, those who report such things are equally culpable.

MRS CANDOUR To be sure they are; tale-bearers are as bad as the tale-makers – 'tis an old observation, and a very true one: but what's to be done, as I said before? How will you prevent people from talking? Today, Mrs Clackit assured me, Mr and Mrs Honeymoon were at last become mere man and wife, like the rest of their acquaintance. She likewise hinted that a certain widow, in the next street, had got rid of her dropsy and recovered her shape in a most surprising manner. And at the same time Miss Tattle, who was by, affirmed, that Lord Buffalo had discovered his lady at a house of no extraordinary fame; and that Sir Harry Bouquet and Tom Saunter were to measure swords on a similar provocation. But, Lord, do you think that I would report these things! No, no! tale-bearers, as I said before, are just as bad as the tale-makers.

JOSEPH SURFACE Ah! Mrs Candour, if everybody had your forbearance and good nature!

MRS CANDOUR I confess, Mr Surface, I cannot bear to hear people attacked behind their backs; and when ugly circumstances come out against our acquaintance I own I always love to think the best. – By-the-by, I hope 'tis not true that your brother is absolutely ruined?

JOSEPH SURFACE I am afraid his circumstances are very bad indeed, madam.

MRS CANDOUR Ah! I heard so – but you must tell him to keep up his spirits; everybody almost is in the same way – Lord Spindle, Sir Thomas Splint, Captain Quinze, and Mr Nickit – all up, I hear, within this week; so if Charles is undone, he'll find half his acquaintance ruined too, and that, you know, is a consolation.

JOSEPH SURFACE Doubtless, ma'am – a very great one.

Enter Servant.

SERVANT Mr Crabtree and Sir Benjamin Backbite.

Exit Servant.

LADY SNEERWELL So, Maria, you see your lover pursues you; positively you shan't escape.

Enter Crabtree and Sir Benjamin Backbite.

CRABTREE Lady Sneerwell, I kiss your hand – Mrs Candour, I don't believe you are acquainted with my nephew, Sir Benjamin Backbite? Egad! ma'am, he has a pretty wit, and is a pretty poet too; isn't he, Lady Sneerwell?

SIR BENJAMIN Oh, fie, uncle!

CRABTREE Nay, egad it's true: I back him at a rebus or a charade against the best rhymer in the kingdom. – Has your ladyship heard the epigram he wrote last week on Lady Frizzle's feather catching fire? – Do Benjamin, repeat it, or the charade you made last night extempore at Mrs Drowzie's conversazione. Come now; – your first is the name of a fish, your second a great naval commander, and –

SIR BENJAMIN Uncle, now – prythee –

CRABTREE I'faith, ma'am, 'twould surprise you to hear how ready he is at all these things.

LADY SNEERWELL I wonder, Sir Benjamin, you never publish anything.

SIR BENJAMIN To say truth, ma'am, 'tis very vulgar to print; and, as my little productions are mostly satires and lampoons on particular people, I find they circulate more by giving copies in confidence to the friend of parties. However, I have some love elegies, which, when favoured with this lady's smiles, I mean to give the public.

CRABTREE 'Fore heaven, ma'am, they'll immortalize you! – you will be handed down to posterity, like Petrarch's Laura, or Waller's Sacharissa.

SIR BENJAMIN Yes, madam, I think you will like them, when you shall see them on a beautiful quarto page, where a neat rivulet of text shall meander through a meadow of margin. 'Fore Gad, they will be the most elegant things of their kind!

CRABTREE But, ladies, that's true – have you heard the news?

MRS CANDOUR What, sir, do you mean the report of –

CRABTREE No, ma'am, that's not it. – Miss Nicely is going to be married to her own footman.

MRS CANDOUR Impossible!

CRABTREE Ask Sir Benjamin.

SIR BENJAMIN 'Tis very true, ma'am: everything is fixed, and the wedding liveries bespoke.

CRABTREE Yes – and they do say there were pressing reasons for it.

LADY SNEERWELL Why, I have heard something of this before.

MRS CANDOUR It can't be – and I wonder any one should believe such a story, of so prudent a lady as Miss Nicely.

SIR BENJAMIN O Lud! ma'am, that's the very reason 'twas believed at once. She had always been so cautious and so reserved, that everybody was sure there was some reason for it at bottom.

MRS CANDOUR Why, to be sure, a tale of scandal is as fatal to the credit of a prudent lady of her stamp as a fever is generally to those of the strongest constitutions. But there is a sort of puny sickly reputation, that is always ailing, yet will outlive the robuster characters of a hundred prudes.

SIR BENJAMIN True, madam, – there are valetudinarians in reputation as well as constitution, who, being conscious of their weak part, avoid the least breath of air, and supply their want of stamina by care and circumspection.

MRS CANDOUR Well, but this may be all a mistake. You know, Sir Benjamin, very trifling circumstances often give rise to the most injurious tales.

CRABTREE That they do, I'll be sworn, ma'am. – Did you ever hear how Miss Piper came to lose her lover and her character last summer at Tunbridge? – Sir Benjamin, you remember it?

SIR BENJAMIN Oh, to be sure! – the most whimsical circumstance.

LADY SNEERWELL How was it, pray?

CRABTREE Why, one evening, at Mrs Ponto's assembly, the conversation happened to turn on the difficulty of breeding Nova Scotia sheep in this country. Says a young lady in company, I have known instances of it; for Miss Letitia Piper, a first cousin of mine, had a Nova Scotia sheep that produced her twins. What! cries the Lady Dowager Dundizzy (who you know is as deaf as a post), has Miss Piper had twins? – This mistake, as you may imagine, threw the whole company into a fit of laughter. However, 'twas the next day everywhere reported, and in a few days believed by the whole town, that Miss Letitia Piper had actually been brought to bed of a fine boy and girl.

LADY SNEERWELL Strange, indeed!

CRABTREE Matter of fact, I assure you. – O Lud! Mr Surface, pray is it true that your uncle, Sir Oliver, is coming home?

JOSEPH SURFACE Not that I know of, indeed, sir.

CRABTREE He has been in the East Indies a long time. You can scarcely remember him, I believe – Sad comfort, whenever he returns, to hear how your brother has gone on!

JOSEPH SURFACE Charles has been imprudent, sir, to be sure; but I hope no busy people have already prejudiced Sir Oliver against him – he may reform.

SIR BENJAMIN To be sure he may: for my part, I never believed him to be so utterly void of principle as people say; and though he has lost all his friends, I am told nobody is better spoken of by the Jews.

CRABTREE That's true, egad, nephew. If the Old Jewry was a ward, I believe Charles would be an alderman: no man more popular there, 'fore Gad! I hear he pays as many annuities as the Irish tontine; and that, whenever he is sick, they have prayers for the recovery of his health in all the synagogues.

SIR BENJAMIN Yet no man lives in greater splendour. They tell me, when he entertains his friends he will sit down to dinner with a dozen of his own securities; have a score of tradesmen waiting in the antechamber, and an officer behind every guest's chair.

JOSEPH SURFACE This may be entertainment to you, gentlemen, but you pay very little regard to the feelings of a brother.

MARIA Their malice is intolerable! – Lady Sneerwell, I must wish you a good morning: I'm not very well. *Exit Maria.*

MRS CANDOUR O dear! she changes colour very much.

LADY SNEERWELL Do, Mrs Candour, follow her; she may want assistance.

MRS CANDOUR That I will, with all my soul, ma'am. – Poor dear creature, who knows what her situation may be! *Exit.*

LADY SNEERWELL 'Twas nothing but that she could not bear to hear Charles reflected on, notwithstanding their difference.

SIR BENJAMIN The young lady's *penchant* is obvious.

CRABTREE But, Benjamin, you must not give up the pursuit for that: follow her, and put her into good humour. Repeat her some of your own verses. Come, I'll assist you.

SIR BENJAMIN Mr Surface, I did not mean to hurt you; but depend on't your brother is utterly undone.

CRABTREE O Lud, ay! undone as ever man was. Can't raise a guinea!

SIR BENJAMIN Everything sold, I am told, that was movable.

CRABTREE I have seen one that was at his house. Not a thing left but some empty bottles that were overlooked, and the family pictures, which I believe are framed in the wainscot. –

SIR BENJAMIN And I'm very sorry also to hear some bad stories against him. *Going.*

CRABTREE O! he has done many mean things, that's certain.

SIR BENJAMIN But, however, as he's your brother – *Going.*

CRABTREE We'll tell you all another opportunity. *Exeunt.*

LADY SNEERWELL Ha! ha! 'tis very hard for them to leave a subject they have not quite run down.

JOSEPH SURFACE And I believe the abuse was no more acceptable to your ladyship than to Maria.

LADY SNEERWELL I doubt her affections are further engaged than we imagine. But the family are to be here this evening, so you may as well dine where you are, and we shall have an opportunity of observing further; in the meantime, I'll go and plot mischief, and you shall study sentiment. *Exeunt.*

SCENE 2

SCENE: *Sir Peter Teazle's house.*

Enter Sir Peter.

SIR PETER When an old bachelor marries a young wife, what is he to expect? 'Tis now six months since Lady Teazle made me the happiest of men – and I have been the most miserable dog ever since that ever committed wedlock! We tiffed a little going to church, and came to a quarrel before the bells had done ringing. I was more than once nearly choked with gall during my honeymoon, and had lost all comfort in life before my friends had done wishing me joy. Yet I chose with caution – a girl bred wholly in the country, who never knew luxury beyond one silk gown, nor dissipation above the annual gala of a race ball. Yet she now plays her part in all the extravagant fopperies of the fashion and the town, with as ready a grace as if she never had seen a bush or a grass-plot out of Grosvenor Square! I am sneered at by all my acquaintance, and paragraphed in the newspapers. She dissipates my fortune, and contradicts all my humours; yet the worst of it is, I doubt I love her, or I should never bear all this. However, I'll never be weak enough to own it.

Enter Rowley.

ROWLEY O! Sir Peter, your servant; how is it with you, sir?

SIR PETER Very bad, Master Rowley, very bad. I meet with nothing but crosses and vexations.

ROWLEY What can have happened to trouble you since yesterday?

SIR PETER A good question to a married man!

ROWLEY Nay, I'm sure, Sir Peter, your lady can't be the cause of your uneasiness.

SIR PETER Why, has anybody told you she was dead?

ROWLEY Come, come, Sir Peter, you love her, notwithstanding your tempers don't exactly agree.

SIR PETER But the fault is entirely hers, Master Rowley. I am, myself, the sweetest-tempered man alive, and hate a teasing temper; and so I tell her a hundred times a day.

ROWLEY Indeed!

SIR PETER Ay; and what is very extraordinary, in all our disputes she is always in the wrong! But Lady Sneerwell, and the set she meets at her house, encourage the perverseness of her disposition. – Then, to complete my vexation, Maria, my ward, whom I ought to have the power of a father over, is determined to turn rebel too, and absolutely refuses the man whom I have long resolved on for her husband; meaning, I suppose, to bestow herself on his profligate brother.

ROWLEY You know, Sir Peter, I have always taken the liberty to differ with you on the subject of these two young gentlemen. I only wish you may not be deceived in your opinion of the elder. For Charles, my life on't! he will retrieve his errors yet. Their worthy father, once my honoured master, was, at his years, nearly as wild a spark; yet, when he died, he did not leave a more benevolent heart to lament his loss.

SIR PETER You are wrong, Master Rowley. On their father's death, you know, I acted as a kind of guardian to them both, till their uncle Sir Oliver's eastern liberality gave them an early independence – of course, no person could have more opportunities of judging of their hearts, and I was never mistaken in my life. Joseph is indeed a model for the young men of the age. He is a man of sentiment, and acts up to the sentiments he professes; but, for the other, take my word for't, if he had any grain of virtue by descent, he has dissipated it with the rest of his inheritance. Ah! my old friend, Sir Oliver, will be deeply mortified when he finds how part of his bounty has been misapplied.

ROWLEY I am sorry to find you so violent against the young man, because this may be the most critical period of his fortune. I came hither with news that will surprise you.

SIR PETER What! let me hear.

ROWLEY Sir Oliver is arrived, and at this moment in town.

SIR PETER How! you astonish me! I thought you did not expect him this month.

ROWLEY I did not: but his passage has been remarkably quick.

SIR PETER Egad, I shall rejoice to see my old friend. 'Tis sixteen years since we met. — We have had many a day together: but does he still enjoin us not to inform his nephews of his arrival?

ROWLEY Most strictly. He means, before it is known, to make some trial of their dispositions.

SIR PETER Ah! There needs no art to discover their merits — he shall have his way; but, pray, does he know I am married?

ROWLEY Yes, and will soon wish you joy.

SIR PETER What, as we drink health to a friend in a consumption! Ah! Oliver will laugh at me. We used to rail at matrimony together, but he has been steady to his text. — Well, he must be soon at my house, though! — I'll instantly give orders for his reception. But, Master Rowley, don't drop a word that Lady Teazle and I ever disagree.

ROWLEY By no means.

SIR PETER For I should never be able to stand Noll's jokes; so I'll have him think, Lord forgive me! that we are a very happy couple.

ROWLEY I understand you: but then you must be very careful not to differ while he is in the house with you.

SIR PETER Egad, and so we must — and that's impossible. Ah! Master Rowley, when an old bachelor marries a young wife, he deserves — no — the crime carries its punishment along with it. *Exeunt.*

Act II

SCENE I

SCENE: *Sir Peter Teazle's house.*

Enter Sir Peter and Lady Teazle.

SIR PETER Lady Teazle, Lady Teazle, I'll not bear it!

LADY TEAZLE Sir Peter, Sir Peter, you may bear it or not, as you please; but I ought to have my own way in everything, and what's more, I will too. What! though I was educated in the country, I know very well that women of fashion in London are accountable to nobody after they are married.

SIR PETER Very well, ma'am, very well; — so a husband is to have no influence, no authority?

LADY TEAZLE Authority! No, to be sure: if you wanted authority over me, you should have adopted me, and not married me: I am sure you were old enough.

SIR PETER Old enough! — aye, there it is! Well, well, Lady Teazle, though my life may be made unhappy by your temper, I'll not be ruined by your extravagance!

LADY TEAZLE My extravagance! I'm sure I'm not more extravagant than a woman of fashion ought to be.

SIR PETER No, no, madam, you shall throw away no more sums on such unmeaning luxury. 'Slife! to spend as much to furnish your dressing-room with flowers in winter as would suffice to turn the Pantheon into a greenhouse, and give a *fête champêtre* at Christmas.

LADY TEAZLE Lord, Sir Peter, am I to blame, because flowers are dear in cold weather? You should find fault with the climate, and not with me. For my part, I'm sure, I wish it was spring all the year round, and that roses grew under one's feet!

SIR PETER Oons! madam — if you had been born to this, I

shouldn't wonder at your talking thus; but you forget what your situation was when I married you.

LADY TEAZLE No, no, I don't; 'twas a very disagreeable one, or I should never have married you.

SIR PETER Yes, yes, madam, you were then in somewhat an humbler style: the daughter of a plain country squire. Recollect, Lady Teazle, when I saw you first, sitting at your tambour, in a pretty figured linen gown, with a bunch of keys at your side, your hair combed smooth over a roll, and your apartment hung round with fruits in worsted, of your own working.

LADY TEAZLE Oh, yes! I remember it very well, and a curious life I led! my daily occupation to inspect the dairy, superintend the poultry, make extracts from the family receipt-book, and comb my Aunt Deborah's lapdog.

SIR PETER Yes, yes, madam, 'twas so indeed.

LADY TEAZLE And then, you know, my evening amusements! To draw patterns for ruffles, which I had not the materials to make up; to play Pope Joan with the curate; to read a sermon to my aunt; or to be stuck down to an old spinet to strum my father to sleep after a fox-chase.

SIR PETER I am glad you have so good a memory. Yes, madam, these were the recreations I took you from; but now you must have your coach – vis-à-vis – and three powdered footmen before your chair; and, in the summer, a pair of white cats to draw you to Kensington Gardens. No recollection, I suppose, when you were content to ride double, behind the butler, on a dock'd coach-horse?

LADY TEAZLE No – I swear I never did that; I deny the butler and the coach-horse.

SIR PETER This, madam, was your situation; and what have I done for you? I have made you a woman of fashion, of fortune, of rank; – in short, I have made you *my wife*.

LADY TEAZLE Well, then, – and there is but one thing more you can make me to add to the obligation, that is –

SIR PETER My widow, I suppose?

LADY TEAZLE Hem! hem!

SIR PETER I thank you, madam – but don't flatter yourself; for, though your ill conduct may disturb my peace of mind, it shall never break my heart, I promise you: however, I am equally obliged to you for the hint.

LADY TEAZLE Then why will you endeavour to make yourself so disagreeable to me, and thwart me in every little elegant expense?

SIR PETER 'Slife, madam, I say, had you any of these little elegant expenses when you married me?

LADY TEAZLE Lud, Sir Peter! would you have me be out of the fashion?

SIR PETER The fashion, indeed! what had you to do with the fashion when you married me?

LADY TEAZLE For my part, I should think you would like to have your wife thought a woman of taste.

SIR PETER Aye – there again – taste – Zounds! madam, you had no taste when you married me!

LADY TEAZLE That's very true, indeed, Sir Peter; and, after having married you, I am sure I should never pretend to taste again. But now, Sir Peter, since we have finished our daily jangle, I presume I may go to my engagement at Lady Sneerwell's?

SIR PETER Aye, there's another precious circumstance – a charming set of acquaintance you have made there!

LADY TEAZLE Nay, Sir Peter, they are all people of rank and fortune, and remarkably tenacious of reputation.

SIR PETER Yes, egad, they are tenacious of reputation with a vengeance; for they don't choose anybody should have a character but themselves! – Such a crew! Ah! many a wretch has rid on a hurdle who has done less mischief than these utterers of forged tales, coiners of scandal, and clippers of reputation.

LADY TEAZLE What, would you restrain the freedom of speech?

SIR PETER Oh! they have made you just as bad as any one of the society.

LADY TEAZLE Why, I believe I do bear a part with a tolerable grace. But I vow I bear no malice against the people I abuse. When I say an ill-natured thing, 'tis out of pure good humour; and I take it for granted, they deal exactly in the same manner with me. But, Sir Peter, you know you promised to come to Lady Sneerwell's too.

SIR PETER Well, well, I'll call in just to look after my own character.

LADY TEAZLE Then, indeed, you must make haste after me or you'll be too late. So good-bye to you.   *Exit Lady Teazle.*

SIR PETER So — I have gained much by my intended expostula-
tion: yet with what a charming air she contradicts everything
I say, and how pleasantly she shows her contempt for my
authority! Well, though I can't make her love me, there is
great satisfaction in quarrelling with her; and I think she
never appears to such advantage as when she is doing
everything in her power to plague me.   *Exit.*

SCENE 2

SCENE: *Lady Sneerwell's house.*

*Lady Sneerwell, Mrs Candour, Crabtree, Sir Benjamin
Backbite, and Joseph Surface discovered, Servants attending
with tea.*

LADY SNEERWELL Nay, positively, we will hear it.
JOSEPH SURFACE Yes, yes, the epigram, by all means.
SIR BENJAMIN Oh, plague on't, uncle! 'tis mere nonsense.
CRABTREE No, no; 'fore Gad, very clever for an extempore!
SIR BENJAMIN But, ladies, you should be acquainted with the
circumstances. You must know, that one day last week, as
Lady Betty Curricle was taking the dust in Hyde Park, in a
sort of a duodecimo phaeton, she desired me to write some
verses on her ponies; upon which I took out my pocket-book,
and in one moment produced the following:

> *Sure never were seen two such beautiful ponies;*
> *Other horses are clowns, but these macaronies:*
> *To give 'em this title I am sure isn't wrong.*
> *Their legs are so slim, and their tails are so long.*

CRABTREE There, ladies, done in the smack of a whip, and on
horseback too.
JOSEPH SURFACE A very Phoebus, mounted — indeed, Sir
Benjamin!
SIR BENJAMIN Oh dear sir, — trifles — trifles.

Enter Lady Teazle and Maria.

MRS CANDOUR I must have a copy.
LADY SNEERWELL Lady Teazle, I hope we shall see Sir Peter?
LADY TEAZLE I believe he'll wait on your ladyship presently.

LADY SNEERWELL Maria, my love, you look grave. Come, you shall sit down to cards with Mr Surface.

MARIA I take very little pleasure in cards – however, I'll do as your ladyship pleases.

LADY TEAZLE I am surprised Mr Surface should sit down with her; I thought he would have embraced this opportunity of speaking to me, before Sir Peter came.   *Aside.*

MRS CANDOUR Now, I'll die, but you are so scandalous, I'll forswear your society.

LADY TEAZLE What's the matter, Mrs Candour?

MRS CANDOUR They'll not allow our friend Miss Vermillion to be handsome.

LADY SNEERWELL Oh, surely she's a pretty woman.

CRABTREE I am very glad you think so, madam.

MRS CANDOUR She has a charming fresh colour.

LADY TEAZLE Yes, when it is fresh put on.

MRS CANDOUR Oh, fie! I'll swear her colour is natural: I have seen it come and go!

LADY TEAZLE I dare swear you have, ma'am: it goes off at night, and comes again in the morning.

SIR BENJAMIN True, ma'am, it not only comes and goes, but, what's more – egad, her maid can fetch and carry it!

MRS CANDOUR Ha! ha! ha! how I hate to hear you talk so! But surely, now, her sister *is*, or *was*, very handsome.

CRABTREE Who? Mrs Evergreen? O Lord! she's six-and-fifty if she's an hour!

MRS CANDOUR Now positively you wrong her; fifty-two or fifty-three is the utmost – and I don't think she looks more.

SIR BENJAMIN Ah! there's no judging by her looks, unless one could see her face.

LADY SNEERWELL Well, well, if Mrs Evergreen *does* take some pains to repair the ravages of time, you must allow she effects it with great ingenuity; and surely that's better than the careless manner in which the widow Ochre caulks her wrinkles.

SIR BENJAMIN Nay, now, Lady Sneerwell, you are severe upon the widow. Come, come, 'tis not that she paints so ill – but, when she has finished her face, she joins it on so badly to her neck, that she looks like a mended statue, in which the connoisseur may see at once that the head's modern, though the trunk's antique!

CRABTREE Ha! ha! ha! Well said, nephew!

MRS CANDOUR Ha! ha! ha! Well, you make me laugh; but I vow I hate you for it. – What do you think of Miss Simper?

SIR BENJAMIN Why, she has very pretty teeth.

LADY TEAZLE Yes, and on that account, when she is neither speaking nor laughing (which very seldom happens), she never absolutely shuts her mouth, but leaves it always on a jar, as it were, thus –   *Shows her teeth.*

MRS CANDOUR How can you be so ill-natured?

LADY TEAZLE Nay, I'll allow even that's better than the pains Mrs Prim takes to conceal her losses in front. She draws her mouth till it positively resembles the aperture of a poor's-box, and all her words appear to slide out edgewise. As it were thus: *How do you do, madam? Yes, madam.*

LADY SNEERWELL Very well, Lady Teazle; I see you can be a little severe.

LADY TEAZLE In defence of a friend it is but justice. – But here comes Sir Peter to spoil our pleasantry.

Enter Sir Peter Teazle.

SIR PETER Ladies, your most obedient. – Mercy on me! here is the whole set! a character dead at every word, I suppose.

Aside.

MRS CANDOUR I am rejoiced you are come, Sir Peter. They have been so censorious – they will allow good qualities to nobody; not even good nature to our friend Mrs Pursy.

LADY TEAZLE What, the fat dowager who was at Mrs Codrille's last night?

MRS CANDOUR Nay, her bulk is her misfortune; and, when she takes so much pains to get rid of it, you ought not to reflect on her.

LADY SNEERWELL That's very true, indeed.

LADY TEAZLE Yes, I know she almost lives on acids and small whey; laces herself by pulleys; and often, in the hottest noon in summer, you may see her on a little squat pony, with her hair plaited up behind like a drummer's, and puffing round the Ring on a full trot.

MRS CANDOUR I thank you, Lady Teazle, for defending her.

SIR PETER Yes, a good defence, truly.

MRS CANDOUR But Sir Benjamin is as censorious as Miss Sallow.

CRABTREE Yes, and she is a curious being to pretend to be censorious – an awkward gawky, without any one good point under heaven.

MRS CANDOUR Positively you shall not be so very severe. Miss Sallow is a relation of mine by marriage, and as for her person, great allowance is to be made; for, let me tell you, a woman labours under many disadvantages who tries to pass for a girl at six-and-thirty.

LADY SNEERWELL Though, surely, she is handsome still – and for the weakness in her eyes, considering how much she reads by candle-light, it is not to be wondered at.

MRS CANDOUR True, and then as to her manner; upon my word I think it is particularly graceful, considering she never had the least education; for you know her mother was a Welch milliner, and her father a sugar-baker at Bristol.

SIR BENJAMIN Ah! you are both of you too good-natured!

SIR PETER Yes, damned good-natured! This their own relation! mercy on me!   *Aside.*

MRS CANDOUR For my part, I own I cannot bear to hear a friend ill spoken of.

SIR PETER No, to be sure!

SIR BENJAMIN And Mrs Candour is of so moral a turn, she can sit for an hour and hear Lady Stucco talk sentiment.

LADY TEAZLE Nay, I vow Lady Stucco is very well with the dessert after dinner; for she's just like the French fruit one cracks for mottoes – made up of paint and proverb.

MRS CANDOUR Well, I never will join in ridiculing a friend; and so I constantly tell my cousin Ogle, and you all know what pretensions she has to be critical on beauty.

CRABTREE Oh, to be sure! she has herself the oddest counten-ance that ever was seen; 'tis a collection of features from all the different countries of the globe.

SIR BENJAMIN So she has, indeed – an Irish front –

CRABTREE Caledonian locks –

SIR BENJAMIN Dutch nose –

CRABTREE Austrian lips –

SIR BENJAMIN Complexion of a Spaniard –

CRABTREE And teeth *à la Chinoise* –

SIR BENJAMIM In short, her face resembles a *table d'hôte* at Spa – where no two guests are of a nation –

CRABTREE Or a congress at the close of a general war – wherein all the members, even to her eyes, appear to have a different interest, and her nose and chin are the only parties likely to join issue.

MRS CANDOUR Ha! ha! ha!

SIR PETER Mercy on my life! – a person they dine with twice a week!   *Aside.*

LADY SNEERWELL Go, go; you are a couple of provoking toads.

MRS CANDOUR Nay, but I vow you shall not carry the laugh off so – for give me leave to say, that Mrs Ogle –

SIR PETER Madam, madam, I beg your pardon – there's no stopping these good gentlemen's tongues. – But when I tell you, Mrs Candour, that the lady they are abusing is a particular friend of mine, I hope you'll not take her part.

LADY SNEERWELL Well said, Sir Peter! but you are a cruel creature – too phlegmatic yourself for a jest, and too peevish to allow wit in others.

SIR PETER Ah! madam, true wit is more nearly allied to good-nature than your ladyship is aware of.

LADY TEAZLE True, Sir Peter: I believe they are so near akin that they can never be united.

SIR BENJAMIN Or rather, madam, suppose them to be man and wife, because one seldom sees them together.

LADY TEAZLE But Sir Peter is such an enemy to scandal, I believe he would have it put down by Parliament.

SIR PETER 'Fore heaven, madam, if they were to consider the sporting with reputation of as much importance as poaching on manors, and pass an Act for the Preservation of Fame, I believe there are many who would thank them for the bill.

LADY SNEERWELL O Lud! Sir Peter; would you deprive us of our privileges?

SIR PETER Aye, madam; and then no person should be permitted to kill characters and run down reputations, but qualified old maids and disappointed widows.

LADY SNEERWELL Go, you monster.

MRS CANDOUR But, surely, you would not be quite so severe on those who only report what they hear?

SIR PETER Yes, madam, I would have Law-Merchant for them too; and in all cases of slander currency, whenever the drawer of the lie was not to be found, the injured parties should have a right to come on any of the indorsers.

CRABTREE Well, for my part, I believe there never was a scandalous tale without some foundation.

LADY SNEERWELL Come, ladies, shall we sit down to cards in the next room?

Enter Servant, who whispers Sir Peter.

SIR PETER I'll be with them directly. I'll get away unperceived.
Apart.

LADY SNEERWELL Sir Peter, you are not going to leave us?

SIR PETER Your ladyship must excuse me; I'm called away by particular business. But I leave my character behind me.
Exit Sir Peter.

SIR BENJAMIN Well – certainly, Lady Teazle, that lord of yours is a strange being: I could tell you some stories of him would make you laugh heartily – if he were not your husband.

LADY TEAZLE Oh, pray don't mind that; come, do let's hear them. *Lady Teazle joins the rest of the company, going into the next room.*

JOSEPH SURFACE Maria, I see you have no satisfaction in this society.

MARIA How is it possible I should? If to raise malicious smiles at the infirmities and misfortunes of those who have never injured us be the province of wit or humour, Heaven grant me a double portion of dullness!

JOSEPH SURFACE Yet they appear more ill-natured than they are – they have no malice at heart.

MARIA Then is their conduct still more contemptible; for, in my opinion, nothing could excuse the intemperance of their tongues, but a natural and uncontrollable bitterness of mind.

JOSEPH SURFACE But can you, Maria, feel thus for others, and be unkind to me alone? Is hope to be denied the tenderest passion?

MARIA Why will you distress me by renewing the subject?

JOSEPH SURFACE Ah! Maria! you would not treat me thus, and oppose your guardian, Sir Peter's will, but that I see that profligate Charles is still a favoured rival.

MARIA Ungenerously urged! – But whatever my sentiments are for that unfortunate young man, be assured I shall not feel more bound to give him up, because his distresses have lost him the regard even of a brother.

Enter Lady Teazle and comes forward.

JOSEPH SURFACE Nay, but Maria, do not leave me with a frown: by all that's honest, I swear – Gad's life, here's Lady Teazle. – (*Aside*). – You must not – no, you shall not – for, though I have the greatest regard for Lady Teazle –

MARIA Lady Teazle!

JOSEPH SURFACE Yet were Sir Peter once to suspect –

LADY TEAZLE What is this, pray? Do you take her for me? – Child, you are wanted in the next room. – (*Exit Maria.*) – What is all this, pray?

JOSEPH SURFACE O, the most unlucky circumstance in nature! Maria has somehow suspected the tender concern I have for your happiness, and threatened to acquaint Sir Peter with her suspicions, and I was just endeavouring to reason with her when you came in.

LADY TEAZLE Indeed! but you seemed to adopt a very tender mode of reasoning – do you usually argue on your knees?

JOSEPH SURFACE Oh, she's a child, and I thought a little bombast. – But, Lady Teazle, when are you to give me your judgement on my library, as you promised?

LADY TEAZLE No, no; I begin to think it would be imprudent, and you know I admit you as a lover no farther than fashion requires.

JOSEPH SURFACE True – a mere platonic cicisbeo – what every London wife is entitled to.

LADY TEAZLE Certainly, one must not be out of the fashion. However, I have so many of my country prejudices left, that, though Sir Peter's ill-humour may vex me ever so, it never shall provoke me to –

JOSEPH SURFACE The only revenge in your power. Well – I applaud your moderation.

LADY TEAZLE Go – you are an insinuating wretch. – But we shall be missed – let us join the company.

JOSEPH SURFACE But we had best not return together.

LADY TEAZLE Well – don't stay; for Maria shan't come to hear any more of your reasoning, I promise you.

Exit Lady Teazle.

JOSEPH SURFACE A curious dilemma, truly, my politics have run me into! I wanted, at first, only to ingratiate myself with Lady Teazle, that she might not be my enemy with Maria; and I have, I don't know how, become her serious lover. Sincerely I begin to wish I had never made such a point of gaining so very good a character, for it has led me into so many cursed rogueries that I doubt I shall be exposed at last.

Exit.

SCENE 3

SCENE: *Sir Peter Teazle's house.*

Enter Rowley and Sir Oliver Surface.

SIR OLIVER Ha! Ha! ha! so my old friend is married, hey? – a young wife out of the country. – Ha! ha! ha! that he should have stood bluff to old bachelor so long, and sink into a husband at last!

ROWLEY But you must not rally him on the subject, Sir Oliver: 'tis a tender point, I assure you, though he has been married only seven months.

SIR OLIVER Then he has been just half a year on the stool of repentance! – Poor Peter! – But you say he has entirely given up Charles, – never sees him, hey?

ROWLEY His prejudice against him is astonishing, and I am sure greatly increased by a jealousy of him with Lady Teazle, which he had been industriously led into by a scandalous society in the neighbourhood, who have contributed not a little to Charles's ill name. Whereas the truth is, I believe, if the lady is partial to either of them, his brother is the favourite.

SIR OLIVER Aye, I know there are a set of malicious, prating, prudent gossips, both male and female, who murder characters to kill time; and will rob a young fellow of his good name, before he has years to know the value of it. – But I am not to be prejudiced against my nephew by such, I promise you. – No, no, – if Charles has done nothing false or mean, I shall compound for his extravagance.

ROWLEY Then, my life on't, you will reclaim him. – Ah, sir, it gives me new life to find that *your* heart is not turned against him, and that the son of my good old master has one friend, however, left.

SIR OLIVER What, shall I forget, Master Rowley, when I was at his years myself? Egad, my brother and I were neither of us very prudent youths; and yet, I believe, you have not seen many better men than your old master was.

ROWLEY Sir, 'tis this reflection gives me assurance that Charles may yet be a credit to his family. – But here comes Sir Peter.

SIR OLIVER Egad, so he does! – Mercy on me! – he's greatly altered – and seems to have a settled married look! One may read *husband* in his face at this distance!

Enter Sir Peter.

SIR PETER Ha! Sir Oliver – my old friend! Welcome to England a thousand times!

SIR OLIVER Thank you – thank you, Sir Peter! and i'faith I am glad to find you well, believe me!

SIR PETER Oh! 'tis a long time since we met – sixteen years, I doubt, Sir Oliver, and many a cross accident in the time.

SIR OLIVER Aye, I have had my share. But what! I find you are married, hey, my old boy? Well, well – it can't be helped – and so – I wish you joy with all my heart!

SIR PETER Thank you, thank you, Sir Oliver. – Yes, I have entered into – the happy state; – but we'll not talk of that now.

SIR OLIVER True, true, Sir Peter; old friends should not begin on grievances at first meeting – no, no, no.

ROWLEY Take care, pray, sir.   *To Sir Oliver.*

SIR OLIVER Well – so one of my nephews is a wild young rogue, hey?

SIR PETER Wild! – Ah! my old friend, I grieve for your disappointment there; he's a lost young man, indeed. However, his brother will make you amends; Joseph is, indeed, what a youth should be. Everybody in the world speaks well of him.

SIR OLIVER I am sorry to hear it; he has too good a character to be an honest fellow. Everybody speaks well of him! – Pshaw! then he has bowed as low to knaves and fools as to the honest dignity of genius and virtue.

SIR PETER What, Sir Oliver! do you blame him for not making enemies?

SIR OLIVER Yes, if he has merit enough to deserve them.

SIR PETER Well, well – you'll be convinced when you know him. 'Tis edification to hear him converse; he professes the noblest sentiments.

SIR OLIVER Oh! plague of his sentiments! if he salutes me with a scrap of morality in his mouth, I shall be sick directly. – But, however, don't mistake me, Sir Peter; I don't mean to defend Charles's errors: but, before I form my judgement of either of them, I intend to make a trial of their hearts; and my friend Rowley and I have planned something for the purpose.

ROWLEY And Sir Peter shall own he has been for once mistaken.

SIR PETER Oh, my life on Joseph's honour.

SIR OLIVER Well – come, give us a bottle of good wine, and we'll drink your lady's health, and tell you our scheme.

SIR PETER *Allons*, then!

SIR OLIVER And don't, Sir Peter, be so severe against your old friend's son. Odds my life! I am not sorry that he has run out of the course a little: for my part, I hate to see prudence clinging to the green suckers of youth; 'tis like ivy round a sapling, and spoils the growth of the tree.   *Exeunt.*

Act III

SCENE: *Sir Peter Teazle's house.*

Enter Sir Peter Teazle, Sir Oliver, and Rowley.

SIR PETER Well, then, we will see this fellow first, and have our wine afterwards: but how is this, Master Rowley? I don't see the jet of your scheme.

ROWLEY Why, sir, this Mr Stanley, whom I was speaking of, is nearly related to them by their mother. He was once a merchant in Dublin, but has been ruined by a series of undeserved misfortunes. He has applied, by letter, since his confinement, both to Mr Surface and Charles: from the former he has received nothing but evasive promises of future service, while Charles has done all that his extravagance has left him power to do; and he is, at this time, endeavouring to raise a sum of money, part of which, in the midst of his own distresses, I know he intends for the service of poor Stanley.

SIR OLIVER Ah! – he is my brother's son.

SIR PETER Well, but how is Sir Oliver personally to –

ROWLEY Why sir, I will inform Charles and his brother that Stanley has obtained permission to apply personally to his friends, and, as they have neither of them ever seen him, let Sir Oliver assume his character, and he will have a fair opportunity of judging, at least, of the benevolence of their dispositions: and believe me, sir, you will find in the youngest brother one who, in the midst of folly and dissipation, has still, as our immortal bard expresses it,

> *a tear for pity, and a hand*
> *Open as day, for melting charity.*

SIR PETER Pshaw! What signifies his having an open hand or purse either, when he has nothing left to give? Well, well — make the trial, if you please. But where is the fellow whom you brought for Sir Oliver to examine, relative to Charles's affairs?

ROWLEY Below, waiting his commands, and no one can give him better intelligence. This, Sir Oliver, is a friendly Jew, who, to do him justice, has done everything in his power to bring your nephew to a proper sense of his extravagance.

SIR PETER Pray let us have him in.

ROWLEY Desire Mr Moses to walk upstairs.

Calls to Servant.

SIR PETER But, pray, why should you suppose he will speak the truth?

ROWLEY Oh! I have convinced him that he has no chance of recovering certain sums advanced to Charles, but through the bounty of Sir Oliver, who he knows is arrived; so that you may depend on his fidelity to his own interests. I have also another evidence in my power, one Snake, whom I have detected in a matter little short of forgery, and shall shortly produce him to remove some of your prejudices, Sir Peter, relative to Charles and Lady Teazle.

SIR PETER I have heard too much on that subject.

ROWLEY Here comes the honest Israelite.

Enter Moses.

— This is Sir Oliver.

SIR OLIVER Sir, I understand you have lately had great dealings with my nephew, Charles.

MOSES Yes, Sir Oliver, I have done all I could for him; but he was ruined before he came to me for assistance.

SIR OLIVER That was unlucky, truly; for you have had no opportunity of showing your talents.

MOSES None at all; I hadn't the pleasure of knowing his distresses till he was some thousands worse than nothing.

SIR OLIVER Unfortunate, indeed! — But I suppose you have done all in your power for him, honest Moses?

MOSES Yes, he owns that: this very evening I was to have brought him a gentleman from the city, who does not know him, and will, I believe, advance him some money.

SIR PETER What, – one Charles has never had money from before?

MOSES Yes, – Mr Premium, of Crutched Friars, formerly a broker.

SIR PETER Egad, Sir Oliver, a thought strikes me! – Charles, you say, does not know Mr Premium?

MOSES Not at all.

SIR PETER Now then, Sir Oliver, you may have a better opportunity of satisfying yourself than by an old romancing tale of a poor relation: go with my friend Moses, and represent Premium, and then, I'll answer for it, you'll see your nephew in all his glory.

SIR OLIVER Egad, I like this idea better than the other, and I may visit Joseph afterwards as Old Stanley.

SIR PETER True – so you may.

ROWLEY Well, this is taking Charles rather at a disadvantage, to be sure; – however, Moses, you understand Sir Peter, and will be faithful?

MOSES You may depend upon me. – This is near the time I was to have gone.

SIR OLIVER I'll accompany you as soon as you please, Moses. – But hold! I have forgot one thing – how the plague shall I be able to pass for a Jew?

MOSES There's no need – the principal is Christian.

SIR OLIVER Is he? I am very sorry to hear it. But, then again, an't I rather too smartly dressed to look like a money-lender?

SIR PETER Not at all; 'twould not be out of character, if you went in your carriage – would it, Moses?

MOSES Not in the least.

SIR OLIVER Well – but how must I talk? – there's certainly some cant of usury and mode of treating that I ought to know.

SIR PETER Oh! there's not much to learn. The great point, as I take it, is to be exorbitant enough in your demands – hey, Moses?

MOSES Yes, that's a very great point.

SIR OLIVER I'll answer for't I'll not be wanting in that. I'll ask him eight or ten per cent on the loan, at least.

MOSES If you ask him no more than that, you'll be discovered immediately.

SIR OLIVER Hey! – what, the plague! – how much then?

MOSES That depends upon circumstances. If he appears not very anxious for the supply, you should require only forty or fifty per cent; but if you find him in great distress and want the moneys very bad, you must ask double.

SIR PETER A good honest trade you're learning, Sir Oliver!

SIR OLIVER Truly I think so – and not unprofitable.

MOSES Then, you know, you haven't the moneys yourself, but are forced to borrow them for him of a friend.

SIR OLIVER Oh! I borrow it of a friend, do I?

MOSES And your friend is an unconscionable dog; but you can't help it!

SIR OLIVER My friend an unconscionable dog, is he?

MOSES Yes, and he himself has not the moneys by him, but is forced to sell stock at a great loss.

SIR OLIVER He is forced to sell stock at a great loss, is he? Well, that's very kind of him.

SIR PETER I'faith, Sir Oliver – Mr Premium, I mean, you'll soon be master of the trade. But, Moses! would not you have him run out a little against the Annuity Bill? That would be in character, I should think.

MOSES Very much.

ROWLEY And lament that a young man now must be at years of discretion before he is suffered to ruin himself?

MOSES Aye, great pity!

SIR PETER And abuse the public for allowing merit to an Act whose only object is to snatch misfortune and imprudence from the rapacious relief of usury, and give the minor the chance of inheriting his estate without being undone by coming into possession.

SIR OLIVER So – so – Moses shall give me further instructions as we go together.

SIR PETER You will not have much time, for your nephew lives hard by.

SIR OLIVER Oh! never fear: my tutor appears so able, that though Charles lived in the next street, it must be my own fault if I am not a complete rogue before I turn the corner.

Exeunt Sir Oliver and Moses.

SIR PETER So, now, I think Sir Oliver will be convinced: you are partial, Rowley, and would have prepared Charles for the plot.

ROWLEY No, upon my word, Sir Peter.

SIR PETER Well, go bring me this Snake, and I'll hear what he has to say presently. – I see Maria, and want to speak with her. (*Exit Rowley*.) I should be glad to be convinced my suspicions of Lady Teazle and Charles were unjust. I have never yet opened my mind on this subject to my friend Joseph – I am determined I will do it – he will give me his opinion sincerely.

Enter Maria.

So, child, has Mr Surface returned with you?

MARIA No, sir; he was engaged.

SIR PETER Well, Maria, do you not reflect, the more you converse with that amiable young man, what return his partiality for you deserves?

MARIA Indeed, Sir Peter, your frequent importunity on this subject distresses me extremely – you compel me to declare, that I know no man who has ever paid me a particular attention whom I would not prefer to Mr Surface.

SIR PETER So – here's perverseness! No, no, Maria, 'tis Charles only whom you would prefer. 'Tis evident his vices and follies have won your heart.

MARIA This is unkind, sir. You know I have obeyed you in neither seeing nor corresponding with him: I have heard enough to convince me that he is unworthy my regard. Yet I cannot think it culpable, if, while my understanding severely condemns his vices, my heart suggests pity for his distresses.

SIR PETER Well, well, pity him as much as you please; but give your heart and hand to a worthier object.

MARIA Never to his brother!

SIR PETER Go – perverse and obstinate! but take care, madam; you have never known what the authority of a guardian is: don't compel me to inform you of it.

MARIA I can only say, you shall not have a just reason. 'Tis true, by my father's will, I am for a short period bound to regard you as his substitute; but must cease to think you so when you would compel me to be miserable.   *Exit Maria*.

SIR PETER Was ever man so crossed as I am? everything conspiring to fret me! I had not been involved in matrimony a fortnight, before her father, a hale and hearty man, died, on purpose, I believe, for the pleasure of plaguing me with the care of his daughter. But here comes my helpmate – she appears in great good humour. How happy I should be if I could tease her into loving me, though but a little!

Enter Lady Teazle.

LADY TEAZLE Lud! Sir Peter, I hope you haven't been quarrelling with Maria? It is not using me well to be ill-humoured when I am not by.

SIR PETER Ah, Lady Teazle, you might have the power to make me good-humoured at all times.

LADY TEAZLE I am sure I wish I had; for I want you to be in a charming sweet temper at this moment. Do be good-humoured now, and let me have two hundred pounds, will you?

SIR PETER Two hundred pounds; what, an't I to be in a good humour without paying for it? But speak to me thus, and i'faith there's nothing I could refuse you. You shall have it; but seal me a bond for the repayment.

LADY TEAZLE Oh, no – there – my note of hand will do as well.
Offering her hand.

SIR PETER And you shall no longer reproach me with not giving you an independent settlement. I mean shortly to surprise you; – but shall we always live thus, hey?

LADY TEAZLE If you please. I'm sure I don't care how soon we leave off quarrelling, provided you'll own you were tired first.

SIR PETER Well – then let our future contest be, who shall be most obliging.

LADY TEAZLE I assure you, Sir Peter, good nature becomes you. You look now as you did before we were married, when you used to walk with me under the elms, and tell me stories of what a gallant you were in your youth, and chuck me under the chin, you would; and ask me if I thought I could love an old fellow, who would deny me nothing – didn't you?

SIR PETER Yes, yes, and you were as kind and attentive –

LADY TEAZLE Ay, so I was, and would always take your part, when my acquaintance used to abuse you, and turn you into ridicule.

SIR PETER Indeed!

LADY TEAZLE Ay, and when my cousin Sophy has called you a stiff, peevish old bachelor, and laughed at me for thinking of marrying one who might be my father, I have always defended you, and said, I didn't think you so ugly by any means.

SIR PETER Thank you.

LADY TEAZLE And I dared say you'd make a very good sort of a husband.

SIR PETER And you prophesied right; and we shall certainly now be the happiest couple –

LADY TEAZLE And never differ again?

SIR PETER No, never – though at the same time, indeed, my dear Lady Teazle, you must watch your temper very narrowly; for in all our little quarrels, my dear, if you recollect, my love, you always began first.

LADY TEAZLE I beg your pardon, my dear Sir Peter: indeed, you always gave the provocation.

SIR PETER Now, see, my angel! take care – contradicting isn't the way to keep friends.

LADY TEAZLE Then, don't you begin it, my love!

SIR PETER There, now! you – you are going on. You don't perceive, my life, that you are just doing the very thing which you know always makes me angry.

LADY TEAZLE Nay, you know if you will be angry without any reason – my dear –

SIR PETER There! now you want to quarrel again.

LADY TEAZLE No, I am sure I don't: but if you will be so peevish –

SIR PETER There now, who begins first?

LADY TEAZLE Why, you, to be sure. I said nothing – but there's no bearing your temper.

SIR PETER No, no, madam; the fault's in your own temper.

LADY TEAZLE Aye, you are just what my Cousin Sophy said you would be.

SIR PETER Your Cousin Sophy is a forward, impertinent gipsy.

LADY TEAZLE You are a great bear, I am sure, to abuse my relations. How dare you abuse my relations?

SIR PETER Now may all the plagues of marriage be doubled on me, if ever I try to be friends with you any more!

LADY TEAZLE So much the better.

SIR PETER No, no, madam: 'tis evident you never cared a pin for me, and I was a madman to marry you – a pert, rural coquette, that had refused half the honest 'squires in the neighbourhood!

LADY TEAZLE And I am sure I was a fool to marry you – an old

dangling bachelor, who was single at fifty, only because he
never could meet with anyone who would have him.

SIR PETER Aye, aye, madam; but you were pleased enough to
listen to me: you never had such an offer before.

LADY TEAZLE No! didn't I refuse Sir Tivy Terrier, who everybody said would have been a better match? for his estate is
just as good as yours, and he has broke his neck since we have
been married.

SIR PETER I have done with you, madam! You are an unfeeling,
ungrateful – but there's an end of everything. I believe you
capable of everything that is bad. Yes, madam, I now believe
the reports relative to you and Charles, madam. – Yes,
madam, you and Charles are – not without grounds –

LADY TEAZLE Take care, Sir Peter! you had better not insinuate
any such thing! I'll not be suspected without cause, I promise
you.

SIR PETER Very well, madam, very well! a separate maintenance
as soon as you please. Yes, madam, or a divorce! I'll make an
example of myself for the benefit of all old bachelors. – Let us
separate, madam.

LADY TEAZLE Agreed! agreed! – And now, my dear Sir Peter,
we are of a mind once more, we may be the happiest couple –
and never differ again, you know – ha! ha! ha! Well, you are
going to be in a passion, I see, and I shall only interrupt you
– so, bye! bye!   *Exit.*

SIR PETER Plagues and tortures! Can't I make her angry either!
Oh, I am the miserablest fellow! But I'll not bear her presuming to keep her temper: no! she may break my heart, but she
shan't keep her temper.   *Exit.*

SCENE 2

SCENE: *At Charles's house, a chamber.*

Enter Trip, Moses, and Sir Oliver.

TRIP Here, Master Moses! if you'll stay a moment I'll try
whether Mr – what's the gentleman's name?

SIR OLIVER Mr – (*Apart.*) Moses, what is my name?

MOSES Mr Premium.

TRIP Premium – very well.   *Exit, taking snuff.*

SIR OLIVER To judge by the servants, one wouldn't believe the master was ruined. But what! – sure, this was my brother's house?

MOSES Yes, sir; Mr Charles bought it of Mr Joseph, with the furniture, pictures, etc., just as the old gentleman left it. Sir Peter thought it a piece of extravagance in him.

SIR OLIVER In my mind, the other's economy in selling it to him was more reprehensible by half.

Enter Trip.

TRIP My master says you must wait, gentlemen: he has company, and can't speak with you yet.

SIR OLIVER If he knew who it was wanted to see him, perhaps he would not have sent such a message?

TRIP Yes, yes, sir; he knows you are here – I did not forget little Premium: no, no, no –

SIR OLIVER Very well; and I pray, sir, what may be your name?

TRIP Trip, sir; my name is Trip, at your service.

SIR OLIVER Well, then, Mr Trip, you have a pleasant sort of place here, I guess?

TRIP Why, yes – here are three or four of us pass our time agreeably enough; but then our wages are sometimes a little in arrear – and not very great either – but fifty pounds a year, and find our own bags and bouquets.

SIR OLIVER Bags and bouquets! halters and bastinadoes!

Aside.

TRIP And *à propos*, Moses, have you been able to get me that little bill discounted?

SIR OLIVER Wants to raise money, too! – mercy on me! Has his distresses too, I warrant, like a lord, and affects creditors and duns. *Aside.*

MOSES 'Twas not to be done, indeed, Mr Trip.

TRIP Good lack, you surprise me! My friend Brush has endorsed it, and I thought when he put his name at the back of a bill 'twas as good as cash.

MOSES No! 'twouldn't do.

TRIP A small sum – but twenty pounds. Hark'ee, Moses, do you think you couldn't get it me by way of annuity?

SIR OLIVER An annuity! ha! ha! a footman raise money by way of annuity! Well done, luxury, egad! *Aside.*

MOSES Well, but you must insure your place.

TRIP Oh, with all my heart! I'll insure my place, and my life too, if you please.

SIR OLIVER It's more than I would your neck.   *Aside*.

TRIP But then, Moses, it must be done before this d—d Register takes place; one wouldn't like to have one's name made public, you know.

MOSES No, certainly. But is there nothing you could deposit?

TRIP Why, nothing capital of my master's wardrobe has dropped lately; but I could give you a mortgage on some of his winter clothes, with equity of redemption before November – or you shall have the reversion of the French velvet, or a post-obit on the blue and silver: these, I should think, Moses, with a few pair of point ruffles, as a collaterial security – hey, my little fellow?

MOSES Well, well.   *Bell rings*.

TRIP Egad, I heard the bell! I believe, gentlemen, I can now introduce you. Don't forget the annuity, little Moses! This way, gentlemen: insure my place, you know.

SIR OLIVER If the man be a shadow of the master, this is the temple of dissipation indeed!   *Exeunt*.

SCENE 3

Charles Surface, Careless. Sir Toby Bumper,
etc., discovered at a table, drinking wine.

CHARLES SURFACE 'Fore heaven, 'tis true! – there's the great degeneracy of the age. Many of our acquaintance have taste, spirit, and politeness; but, plague on't, they won't drink.

CARELESS It is so, indeed, Charles! they give in to all the substantial luxuries of the table, and abstain from nothing but wine and wit.

CHARLES SURFACE Oh, certainly society suffers by it intolerably; for now, instead of the social spirit of raillery that used to mantle over a glass of bright Burgundy, their conversation is become just like the Spa water they drink, which has all the pertness and flatulence of champagne without its spirit or flavour.

FIRST GENTLEMAN But what are they to do who love play better than wine?

CARELESS True! there's Harry diets himself for gaming, and is now under a hazard regimen.

CHARLES SURFACE Then he'll have the worst of it. What! you wouldn't train a horse for the course by keeping him from corn? For my part, egad, I'm never so successful as when I am a little merry; let me throw on a bottle of champagne, and I never lose – at least I never feel my losses, which is exactly the same thing.

SECOND GENTLEMAN Ay, that I believe.

CHARLES SURFACE And, then, what man can pretend to be a believer in love, who is an abjurer of wine? 'Tis the test by which the lover knows his own heart. Fill a dozen bumpers to a dozen beauties, and she that floats to the top is the maid that has bewitched you.

CARELESS Now then, Charles, be honest, and give us your real favourite.

CHARLES SURFACE Why, I have withheld her only in compassion to you. If I toast her, you must give a round of her peers, which is impossible – on earth.

CARELESS Oh! then we'll find some canonized vestals or heathen goddesses that will do, I warrant!

CHARLES SURFACE Here then, bumpers, you rogues! bumpers! Maria! Maria –

FIRST GENTLEMAN Maria who?

CHARLES SURFACE Oh, damn the surname! – 'tis too formal to be registered in Love's calendar – but now, Sir Toby, beware, we must have beauty superlative.

CARELESS Nay, never study, Sir Toby: we'll stand to the toast, though your mistress should want an eye, and you know you have a song will excuse you.

SIR TOBY Egad, so I have! and I'll give him the song instead of the lady.

SONG

Here's to the maiden of bashful fifteen;
 Here's to the widow of fifty;
Here's to the flaunting extravagant quean,
 And here's to the housewife that's thrifty.

Chorus: Let the toast pass, –
  Drink to the lass,
I'll warrant she'll prove an excuse for a glass.

> Here's to the charmer whose dimples we prize;
> Now to the maid who has none, sir;
> Here's to the girl with a pair of blue eyes;
> And here's to the nymph with but *one*, sir.

Chorus: Let the toast pass, —
> Drink to the lass,
> I'll warrant she'll prove an excuse for a glass.

> Here's to the maid with a bosom of snow:
> Now to her that's as brown as a berry:
> Here's to the wife with her face full of woe,
> And now to the damsel that's merry.

Chorus: Let the toast pass, —
> Drink to the lass,
> I'll warrant she'll prove an excuse for a glass.

> For let 'em be clumsy, or let 'em be slim,
> Young or ancient, I care not a feather;
> So fill a pint bumper quite up to the brim,
> And let us e'en toast them together.

Chorus: Let the toast pass, —
> Drink to the lass,
> I'll warrant she'll prove an excuse for a glass.

ALL Bravo! Bravo!

Enter Trip and whispers to Charles.

CHARLES SURFACE Gentlemen, you must excuse me a little. Careless, take the chair, will you?

CARELESS Nay, prithee, Charles, what now? This is one of your peerless beauties, I suppose, has dropt in by chance?

CHARLES SURFACE No, faith! To tell you the truth, 'tis a Jew and a broker, who are come by appointment.

CARELESS Oh, damn it! let's have the Jew in.

FIRST GENTLEMAN Ay, and the broker too, by all means.

SECOND GENTLEMAN Yes, yes, the Jew and the broker.

CHARLES SURFACE Egad, with all my heart! — Trip, bid the gentlemen walk in. — (*Exit Trip.*) Though there's one of them a stranger, I can tell you.

CARELESS Charles, let us give them some generous Burgundy, and perhaps they'll grow conscientious.

CHARLES SURFACE Oh, hang 'em, no! wine does but draw forth a man's natural qualities; and to make them drink would only be to whet their knavery.

Enter Trip, Sir Oliver, and Moses.

CHARLES SURFACE So, honest Moses, walk in: walk in, pray, Mr Premium – that's the gentleman's name, isn't it, Moses?

MOSES Yes, sir.

CHARLES SURFACE Set chairs, Trip – sit down, Mr Premium – glasses, Trip. – Sit down, Moses. Come, Mr Premium, I'll give you a sentiment; here's *Success to usury* – Moses, fill the gentleman a bumper.

MOSES *Success to usury!*

CARELESS Right, Moses – usury is prudence and industry, and deserves to succeed.

SIR OLIVER Then – *here's all the success it deserves!*

CARELESS No, no, that won't do, Mr Premium; you have demurred to the toast, and must drink it in a pint bumper.

FIRST GENTLEMAN A pint bumper, at least.

MOSES Oh, pray, sir, consider – Mr Premium's a gentleman.

CARELESS And therefore loves good wine.

SECOND GENTLEMAN Give Moses a quart glass – this is mutiny, and a high contempt for the chair.

CARELESS Here, now for't! I'll see justice done, to the last drop of my bottle.

SIR OLIVER Nay, pray, gentlemen – I did not expect this usage.

CHARLES SURFACE No, hang it, you shan't! Mr Premium's a stranger.

SIR OLIVER Odd! I wish I was well out of their company.

Aside.

CARELESS Plague on 'em then! if they won't drink, we'll not sit down with them. Come, Harry, the dice are in the next room – Charles, you'll join us when you have finished your business with these gentlemen?

CHARLES SURFACE I will! I will! – (*Exeunt Gentlemen.*) Careless!

CARELESS (*Returning.*) Well!

CHARLES SURFACE Perhaps I may want you.

CARELESS Oh, you know I am always ready: word, note, or bond, 'tis all the same to me.   *Exit.*

MOSES Sir, this is Mr Premium, a gentleman of the strictest honour and secrecy; and always peforms what he undertakes. Mr Premium, this is –

CHARLES SURFACE Pshaw! have done. – Sir, my friend Moses is a very honest fellow, but a little slow at expression: he'll be an hour giving us our titles. Mr Premium, the plain state of the matter is this: I am an extravagant young fellow who wants to borrow money – you I take to be a prudent old fellow, who has got money to lend. I am blockhead enough to give fifty per cent sooner than not have it; and you, I presume, are rogue enough to take an hundred if you can get it. Now, sir, you see we are acquainted at once, and may proceed to business without further ceremony.

SIR OLIVER Exceeding frank, upon my word. – I see, sir, you are not a man of many compliments.

CHARLES SURFACE Oh, no, sir! plain dealing in business I always think best.

SIR OLIVER Sir, I like you the better for it – however, you are mistaken in one thing; I have no money to lend, but I believe I could procure some of a friend; but then he's an unconscionable dog. Isn't he, Moses? And must sell stock to accommodate you, mustn't he, Moses?

MOSES Yes, indeed! You know I always speak the truth, and scorn to tell a lie!

CHARLES SURFACE Right. People that speak truth generally do: but these are trifles, Mr Premium. What! I know money isn't to be bought without paying for't!

SIR OLIVER Well – but what security could you give? You have no land, I suppose?

CHARLES SURFACE Not a mole-hill, nor a twig, but what's in beau-pots out of the window!

SIR OLIVER Nor any stock, I presume?

CHARLES SURFACE Nothing but live stock – and that's only a few pointers and ponies. But pray, Mr Premium, are you acquainted at all with any of my connexions?

SIR OLIVER Why, to say the truth, I am.

CHARLES SURFACE Then you must know that I have a dev'lish rich uncle in the East Indies, Sir Oliver Surface, from whom I have the greatest expectations?

SIR OLIVER That you have a wealthy uncle, I have heard; but how your expectations will turn out is more, I believe, than you can tell.

CHARLES SURFACE Oh, no! – there can be no doubt. They tell me I'm a prodigious favourite, and that he talks of leaving me everything.

SIR OLIVER Indeed! this is the first I've heard of it.

CHARLES SURFACE Yes, yes, 'tis just so. Moses knows 'tis true; don't you, Moses?

MOSES Oh, yes! I'll swear to't.

SIR OLIVER Egad, they'll persuade me presently I'm at Bengal.
Aside.

CHARLES SURFACE Now I propose, Mr Premium, if it's agreeable to you, a post-obit on Sir Oliver's life: though at the same time the old fellow has been so liberal to me, that I give you my word, I should be very sorry to hear that anything had happened to him.

SIR OLIVER Not more than I should, I assure you. But the bond you mention happens to be just the worst security you could offer me – for I might live to a hundred and never recover the principal.

CHARLES SURFACE Oh, yes, you would – the moment Sir Oliver dies, you know, you would come on me for the money.

SIR OLIVER Then I believe I should be the most unwelcome dun you ever had in your life.

CHARLES SURFACE What! I suppose you're afraid that Sir Oliver is too good a life?

SIR OLIVER No, indeed I am not; though I have heard he is as hale and healthy as any man of his years in Christendom.

CHARLES SURFACE There again, now, you are misinformed. No, no, the climate has hurt him considerably, poor uncle Oliver. Yes, yes, he breaks apace, I am told – and is so much altered lately that his nearest relations wouldn't know him.

SIR OLIVER No! ha! ha! ha! so much altered lately that his nearest relations wouldn't know him! That's droll! egad – ha! ha! ha!

CHARLES SURFACE Ha! ha! – you're glad to hear that, little Premium?

SIR OLIVER No, no, I'm not.

CHARLES SURFACE Yes, yes, you are – ha! ha! ha! – you know that mends your chance.

SIR OLIVER But I'm told Sir Oliver is coming over; nay, some say he is actually arrived.

CHARLES SURFACE Pshaw! Sure I must know better than you whether he's come or not. No, no, rely on't he's at this moment at Calcutta – isn't he, Moses?

MOSES Yes, certainly.

SIR OLIVER Very true, as you say, you must know better than I, though I have it from pretty good authority – haven't I, Moses?

MOSES Yes, most undoubted!

SIR OLIVER But, sir, as I understand you want a few hundreds immediately – is there nothing you could dispose of?

CHARLES SURFACE How do you mean?

SIR OLIVER For instance, now, I have heard that your father left behind him a great quantity of massy old plate.

CHARLES SURFACE O Lud! – that's gone long ago. – Moses can tell you how better than I can.

SIR OLIVER Good lack! all the family race-cups and corporation bowls! – (*Aside.*) Then it was also supposed that his library was one of the most valuable and complete –

CHARLES SURFACE Yes, yes, so it was – vastly too much so for a private gentleman. For my part, I was always of a communicative disposition, so I thought it a shame to keep so much knowledge to myself.

SIR OLIVER Mercy upon me! Learning that had run in the family like an heirloom! – (*Aside.*) Pray, what are become of the books?

CHARLES SURFACE You must inquire of the auctioneer, master Premium, for I don't believe even Moses can direct you.

MOSES I never meddle with books.

SIR OLIVER So, so, nothing of the family property left, I suppose?

CHARLES SURFACE Not much, indeed; unless you have a mind to the family pictures. I have got a room full of ancestors above, and if you have a taste for old paintings, egad, you shall have them a bargain!

SIR OLIVER Hey! what the devil! sure, you wouldn't sell your forefathers, would you?

CHARLES SURFACE Every man of 'em, to the best bidder.

SIR OLIVER What! your great-uncles and aunts?

CHARLES SURFACE Aye, and my grandfathers and grandmothers too.

SIR OLIVER Now I give him up! (*Aside*.) – What the plague, have you no bowels for your own kindred? Odd's life, do you take me for Shylock in the play, that you would raise money of me on your own flesh and blood?

CHARLES SURFACE Nay, my little broker, don't be angry: what need you care, if you have your money's worth?

SIR OLIVER Well, I'll be the purchaser: I think I can dispose of the family canvas. – Oh, I'll never forgive him this! never!

Aside.

Enter Careless.

CARELESS Come, Charles, what keeps you?

CHARLES SURFACE I can't come yet; i'faith, we are going to have a sale above stairs; here's little Premium will buy all my ancestors!

CARELESS Oh, burn your ancestors!

CHARLES SURFACE No, he may do that afterwards, if he pleases. Stay, Careless, we want you: egad, you shall be auctioneer: so come along with us.

CARELESS Oh, have with you, if that's the case. I can handle a hammer as well as a dice-box – a-going – a-going.

SIR OLIVER Oh, the profligates!   *Aside*.

CHARLES SURFACE Come, Moses, you shall be appraiser, if we want one. Gad's life, little Premium, you don't seem to like the business?

SIR OLIVER Oh, yes, I do, vastly! Ha! ha! ha! yes, yes, I think it a rare joke to sell one's family by auction – ha! ha! – Oh, the prodigal!   *Aside*.

CHARLES SURFACE To be sure! when a man wants money, where the plague should he get assistance, if he can't make free with his own relations?   *Exeunt*.

Act IV

SCENE I

SCENE: *Picture room at Charles's house.*

Enter Charles, Sir Oliver, Moses, and Careless.

CHARLES SURFACE Walk in, gentlemen, pray walk in; — here they are, the family of the Surfaces, up to the Conquest.

SIR OLIVER And, in my opinion, a goodly collection.

CHARLES SURFACE Ay, ay, these are done in the true spirit of portrait-painting; no *volunteer grace* or expression. Not like the works of your modern Raphael, who gives you the strongest resemblance, yet contrives to make your portrait independent of you; so that you may sink the original and not hurt the picture. No, no; the merit of these is the inveterate likeness — all stiff and awkward as the originals, and like nothing in human nature besides.

SIR OLIVER Ah! we shall never see such figures of men again.

CHARLES SURFACE I hope not. — Well, you see, Master Premium, what a domestic character I am; here I sit of an evening surrounded by my family. — But come, get to your pulpit, Mr Auctioneer; here's an old gouty chair of my grandfather's will answer the purpose.

CARELESS Ay, ay, this will do. But, Charles, I haven't a hammer; and what's an auctioneer without his hammer?

CHARLES SURFACE Egad, that's true. What parchment have we here? *Richard heir to Thomas.* Oh, our genealogy in full. Here, Careless — you shall have no common bit of mahogany, here's the family tree for you, you rogue, — this shall be your hammer, and now you may knock down my ancestors with their own pedigree.

SIR OLIVER What an unnatural rogue! — an *ex post facto* parricide! *Aside.*

CARELESS Yes, yes, here's a list of your generation indeed; — faith, Charles, this is the most convenient thing you could have found for the business, for 'twill not only serve as a hammer, but a catalogue into the bargain. But come, begin. — A-going, a-going, a-going!

CHARLES SURFACE Bravo, Careless! Well, here's my great-uncle, Sir Richard Raveline, a marvellous good general in his day, I assure you. He served in all the Duke of Marlborough's wars, and got that cut over his eye at the battle of Malplaquet. — What say you, Mr Premium? — look at him — there's a hero for you, not cut out of his feathers, as your modern clipt captains are, but enveloped in wig and regimentals, as a general should be. — What do you bid?

SIR OLIVER Bid him speak.   *Aside to Moses.*

MOSES Mr Premium would have *you* speak.

CHARLES SURFACE Why, then, he shall have him for ten pounds, and I'm sure that's not dear for a staff-officer.

SIR OLIVER Heaven deliver me! his famous Uncle Richard for ten pounds! — (*Aside.*) Very well, sir, I take him at that.

CHARLES SURFACE Careless, knock down my Uncle Richard. — Here, now, is a maiden sister of his, my great-aunt Deborah, done by Kneller, in his best manner, and esteemed a very formidable likeness. — There she is, you see, a shepherdess feeding her flock. — You shall have her for five pounds ten — the sheep are worth the money.

SIR OLIVER Ah! poor Deborah! a woman who set such value on herself! (*Aside.*) — Five pounds ten — she's mine.

CHARLES SURFACE Knock down my Aunt Deborah! — Here, now, are two that were a sort of cousins of theirs. — You see, Moses, these pictures were done some time ago, when beaux wore wigs, and the ladies their own hair.

SIR OLIVER Yes, truly, head-dresses appear to have been a little lower in those days.

CHARLES SURFACE Well, take this couple for the same.

MOSES 'Tis a good bargain.

CHARLES SURFACE This, now, is a grandfather of my mother's, a learned judge, well known on the western circuit. — What do you rate him at, Moses?

MOSES Four guineas.

CHARLES SURFACE Four guineas! — Gad's life, you don't bid me the price of his wig. – Mr Premium, you have more respect for the woolsack; do let us knock his lordship down at fifteen.

SIR OLIVER By all means.

CARELESS Gone!

CHARLES SURFACE And there are two brothers of his, William and Walter Blunt, Esquires, both members of Parliament, and noted speakers, and what's very extraordinary, I believe, this is the first time they were ever bought or sold.

SIR OLIVER That is very extraordinary, indeed! I'll take them at your own price, for the honour of Parliament.

CARELESS Well said, little Premium! – I'll knock them down at forty.

CHARLES SURFACE Here's a jolly fellow – I don't know what relation, but he was mayor of Norwich: take him at eight pounds.

SIR OLIVER No, no; six will do for the mayor.

CHARLES SURFACE Come, make it guineas, and I'll throw you the two aldermen there into the bargain.

SIR OLIVER They're mine.

CHARLES SURFACE Careless, knock down the mayor and aldermen. – But, plague on't, we shall be all day retailing in this manner; do let us deal wholesale: what say you, little Premium? Give me three hundred pounds for the rest of the family in the lump.

CARELESS Aye, aye, that will be the best way.

SIR OLIVER Well, well, anything to accommodate you; – they are mine. But there is one portrait which you have always passed over.

CARELESS What, that ill-looking little fellow over the settee?

SIR OLIVER Yes, sir, I mean that; though I don't think him so ill-looking a little fellow, by any means.

CHARLES SURFACE What, that? – oh; that's my uncle Oliver; 'twas done before he went to India.

CARELESS Your uncle Oliver! Gad, then you'll never be friends, Charles. That, now, to me, is as stern a looking rogue as ever I saw; an unforgiving eye, and a damned disinheriting countenance! an inveterate knave, depend on't. Don't you think so, little Premium?

SIR OLIVER Upon my soul sir, I do not; I think it is as honest a looking face as any in the room, dead or alive; – but I suppose uncle Oliver goes with the rest of the lumber?

CHARLES SURFACE No, hang it! I'll not part with poor Noll. The old fellow has been very good to me, and, egad, I'll keep his picture while I've a room to put it in.

SIR OLIVER The rogue's my nephew after all! (*Aside.*) — But, sir, I have somehow taken a fancy to that picture.

CHARLES SURFACE I'm sorry for't, for you certainly will not have it. Oons, haven't you got enough of them?

SIR OLIVER I forgive him everything! (*Aside.*) — But sir, when I take a whim in my head, I don't value money, I'll give you as much for that as for all the rest.

CHARLES SURFACE Don't tease me, master broker; I tell you I'll not part with it, and there's an end of it.

SIR OLIVER How like his father the dog is. — Well, well, I have done. — I did not perceive it before, but I think I never saw such a striking resemblance. — (*Aside.*) — Here is a draft for your sum.

CHARLES SURFACE Why, 'tis for eight hundred pounds!

SIR OLIVER You will not let Sir Oliver go?

CHARLES SURFACE Zounds! no! — I tell you, once more.

SIR OLIVER Then never mind the difference, we'll balance that another time — but give me your hand on the bargain; you are an honest fellow, Charles — I beg pardon, sir, for being so free. — Come, Moses.

CHARLES SURFACE Egad, this is a whimsical old fellow! But hark'ee, Premium, you'll prepare lodgings for these gentlemen.

SIR OLIVER Yes, yes, I'll send for them in a day or two.

CHARLES SURFACE But hold; do now send a genteel conveyance for them, for I assure you, they were most of them used to ride in their own carriages.

SIR OLIVER I will, I will — for all but Oliver.

CHARLES SURFACE Aye, all but the little nabob.

SIR OLIVER You're fixed on that?

CHARLES SURFACE Peremptorily.

SIR OLIVER A dear extravagant rogue! (*Aside.*) — Good-day! — Come, Moses. — Let me hear now who dares call him profligate!   *Exeunt Sir Oliver Surface and Moses.*

CARELESS Why, this is the oddest genius of the sort I ever met with!

CHARLES SURFACE Egad, he's the prince of brokers, I think. I wonder how the devil Moses got acquainted with so honest a fellow. – Ha! here's Rowley; do, Careless, say I'll join the company in a moment.

CARELESS I will – but don't let that old blockhead persuade you to squander any of that money on old musty debts, or any such nonsense; for tradesmen, Charles, are the most exorbitant fellows.

CHARLES SURFACE Very true, and paying them is only encouraging them.

CARELESS Nothing else.

CHARLES SURFACE Aye, aye, never fear. (*Exit Careless.*) So! this was an odd old fellow, indeed. – Let me see, two-thirds of this is mine by right, – five hundred and thirty odd pounds. 'Fore Heaven! I find one's ancestors are more valuable relations than I took them for! – Ladies and gentlemen, your most obedient and very grateful servant.

Enter Rowley.

Ha! old Rowley! egad, you are just come in time to take leave of your old acquaintance.

ROWLEY Yes, I heard they were a-going. But I wonder you can have such spirits under so many distresses.

CHARLES SURFACE Why, there's the point! my distresses are so many, that I can't afford to part with my spirits; but I shall be rich and splenetic, all in good time. However, I suppose you are surprised that I am not more sorrowful at parting with so many near relations; to be sure, 'tis very affecting; but rot 'em, you see they never move a muscle, so why should I?

ROWLEY There's no making you serious a moment.

CHARLES SURFACE Yes, faith, I am so now. Here, my honest Rowley, here, get me this changed directly, and take a hundred pounds of it immediately, to old Stanley.

ROWLEY A hundred pounds! consider only –

CHARLES SURFACE Gad's life, don't talk about it: poor Stanley's wants are pressing, and, if you don't make haste, we shall have someone call that has a better right to the money.

ROWLEY Ah! there's the point! I never will cease dunning you with the old proverb –

CHARLES SURFACE 'Be just before you're generous.' – Why, so I would if I could; but Justice is an old hobbling beldame, and I can't get her to keep pace with Generosity for the soul of me.

ROWLEY Yet, Charles, believe me, one hour's reflection –

CHARLES SURFACE Aye, aye, it's all very true; but, hark'ee, Rowley, while I have, by Heaven I'll give; so, damn your economy, and now for hazard.   *Exeunt.*

SCENE 2

SCENE: *The parlour.*

Enter Sir Oliver and Moses.

MOSES Well, sir, I think, as Sir Peter said, you have seen Mr Charles in high glory; 'tis great pity he's so extravagant.

SIR OLIVER True, but he would not sell my picture.

MOSES And loves wine and women so much.

SIR OLIVER But he would not sell my picture.

MOSES And games so deep.

SIR OLIVER But he would not sell my picture. – Oh, here's Rowley.

Enter Rowley.

ROWLEY So, Sir Oliver, I find you have made a purchase –

SIR OLIVER Yes, yes, our young rake has parted with his ancestors like old tapestry.

ROWLEY And here has he commissioned me to re-deliver you part of the purchase-money – I mean, though, in your necessitous character of old Stanley.

MOSES Ah! there is the pity of all: he is so damned charitable.

ROWLEY And I left a hosier and two tailors in the hall, who, I'm sure, won't be paid, and this hundred would satisfy them.

SIR OLIVER Well, well, I'll pay his debts, and his benevolence too. – But now I am no more a broker, and you shall introduce me to the elder brother as old Stanley.

ROWLEY Not yet awhile; Sir Peter, I know, means to call there about this time.

Enter Trip.

TRIP Oh, gentlemen, I beg pardon for not showing you out; this way – Moses, a word.   *Exeunt Trip and Moses.*

SIR OLIVER There's a fellow for you – would you believe it, that puppy intercepted the Jew on our coming, and wanted to raise money before he got to his master!

ROWLEY Indeed!

SIR OLIVER Yes, they are now planning an annuity business. – Ah, Master Rowley, in my days servants were content with the follies of their masters, when they were worn a little threadbare; but now, they have their vices, like their birthday clothes, with the gloss on. *Exeunt.*

SCENE 3

SCENE: *A library.*

Joseph Surface and a Servant.

JOSEPH SURFACE No letter from Lady Teazle?

SERVANT No, sir.

JOSEPH SURFACE I am surprised she has not sent, if she is prevented from coming. Sir Peter certainly does not suspect me. Yet I wish I may not lose the heiress, through the scrape I have drawn myself into with the wife; however, Charles's imprudence and bad character are great points in my favour.

Knock without.

SERVANT Sir, I believe that must be Lady Teazle.

JOSEPH SURFACE Hold! – See whether it is or not, before you go to the door: I have a particular message for you if it should be my brother.

SERVANT 'Tis her ladyship, sir; she always leaves the chair at the milliner's in the next street.

JOSEPH SURFACE Stay, stay: draw that screen before the window – that will do; – my opposite neighbour is a maiden lady of so curious a temper. – (*Servant draws the screen, and exit*). I have a difficult hand to play in this affair. Lady Teazle has lately suspected my views on Maria; but she must by no means be let into that secret, – at least, till I have her more in my power.

Enter Lady Teazle.

LADY TEAZLE What, sentiment in soliloquy? Have you been very impatient now? – O Lud! don't pretend to look grave – I vow I couldn't come before.

JOSEPH SURFACE Oh, madam, punctuality is a species of constancy very unfashionable in a lady of quality.

LADY TEAZLE Upon my word, you ought to pity me. Do you

know Sir Peter is grown so ill-tempered to me of late, and so jealous of Charles, too; that's the best of the story, isn't it?

JOSEPH SURFACE I am glad my scandalous friends keep that up.
Aside.

LADY TEAZLE I am sure I wish he would let Maria marry him, and then perhaps he would be convinced; don't you, Mr Surface?

JOSEPH SURFACE Indeed I do not. (*Aside.*) – Oh, certainly I do! for then my dear Lady Teazle would also be convinced how wrong her suspicions were of my having any design on the silly girl.

LADY TEAZLE Well, well, I'm inclined to believe you. But isn't it provoking, to have the most ill-natured things said of one? – And there's my friend Lady Sneerwell has circulated I don't know how many scandalous tales of me, and all without any foundation, too – that's what vexes me.

JOSEPH SURFACE Aye madam, to be sure, that is the provoking circumstance – without foundation; yes, yes, there's the mortification, indeed; for, when a scandalous story is believed against one, there certainly is no comfort like the consciousness of having deserved it.

LADY TEAZLE No, to be sure, then I'd forgive their malice; but to attack me, who am really so innocent, and who never say an ill-natured thing of anybody – that is, of my friends; and then Sir Peter, too, to have him so peevish, and so suspicious, when I know the integrity of my own heart – indeed 'tis monstrous!

JOSEPH SURFACE But, my dear Lady Teazle, 'tis your own fault if you suffer it. When a husband entertains a groundless suspicion of his wife, and withdraws his confidence from her, the original compact is broke, and she owes it to the honour of her sex to endeavour to outwit him.

LADY TEAZLE Indeed! – So that, if he suspects me without cause, it follows, that the best way of curing his jealousy is to give him reason for't?

JOSEPH SURFACE Undoubtedly – for your husband should never be deceived in you, – and in that case it becomes you to be frail in compliment to his discernment.

LADY TEAZLE To be sure, what you say is very reasonable, and when the consciousness of my innocence –

JOSEPH SURFACE Ah! my dear madam, there is the great

mistake; 'tis this very conscious innocence that is of the greatest prejudice to you. What is it makes you negligent of forms, and careless of the world's opinion? – why, the consciousness of your own innocence. What makes you thoughtless in your conduct, and apt to run into a thousand little imprudences? – why, the consciousness of your own innocence. What makes you impatient of Sir Peter's temper, and outrageous at his suspicions? – why, the consciousness of your innocence.

LADY TEAZLE 'Tis very true!

JOSEPH SURFACE Now, my dear Lady Teazle, if you would but once make a trifling *faux pas*, you can't conceive how cautious you would grow, and how ready to humour and agree with your husband.

LADY TEAZLE Do you think so?

JOSEPH SURFACE Oh, I'm sure on't; and then you would find all scandal would cease at once, for, in short, your character at present is like a person in a plethora, absolutely dying from too much health.

LADY TEAZLE So, so; then I perceive your prescription is, that I must sin in my own defence, and part with my virtue to preserve my reputation?

JOSEPH SURFACE Exactly so, upon my credit, ma'am.

LADY TEAZLE Well, certainly this is the oddest doctrine, and the newest receipt for avoiding calumny!

JOSEPH SURFACE An infallible one, believe me. Prudence, like experience, must be paid for.

LADY TEAZLE Why, if my understanding were once convinced –

JOSEPH SURFACE Oh, certainly, madam, your understanding should be convinced. – Yes, yes – Heaven forbid I should persuade you to do anything you thought wrong. No, no, I have too much honour to desire it.

LADY TEAZLE Don't you think we may as well leave *honour* out of the argument?

JOSEPH SURFACE Ah, the ill effects of your country education, I see, still remain with you.

LADY TEAZLE I doubt they do indeed; and I will fairly own to you, that if I could be persuaded to do wrong, it would be by Sir Peter's ill usage sooner than your *honourable logic*, after all.

JOSEPH SURFACE Then, by this hand, which he is unworthy of — *Taking her hand.*

Enter Servant.

'Sdeath, you blockhead — what do you want?

SERVANT I beg pardon, sir, but I thought you would not choose Sir Peter to come up without announcing him.

JOSEPH SURFACE Sir Peter! — Oons and the devil!

LADY TEAZLE Sir Peter! O Lud — I'm ruined — I'm ruined!

SERVANT Sir, 'twasn't I let him in.

LADY TEAZLE Oh! I'm quite undone! What will become of me now, Mr Logic? Oh! he's on the stairs — I'll get behind here — and if ever I'm so imprudent again —

Goes behind the screen.

JOSEPH SURFACE Give me that book.

Sits down, Servant pretends to adjust his chair.

Enter Sir Peter Teazle.

SIR PETER Aye, ever improving himself. Mr Surface, Mr Surface —

JOSEPH SURFACE Oh, my dear Sir Peter, I beg your pardon. (*Gaping, throws away the book.*) I have been dozing over a stupid book. — Well, I am much obliged to you for this call. You haven't been here, I believe, since I fitted up this room. — Books, you know, are the only things I am a coxcomb in.

SIR PETER 'Tis very neat indeed. — Well, well, that's proper; and you can make even your screen a source of knowledge — hung, I perceive, with maps.

JOSEPH SURFACE Oh, yes, I find great use in that screen.

SIR PETER I dare say you must, certainly, when you want to find anything in a hurry.

JOSEPH SURFACE Aye, or to hide anything in a hurry either.

Aside.

SIR PETER Well, I have a little private business —

JOSEPH SURFACE You need not stay.   *To Servant.*

SERVANT No, sir.   *Exit.*

JOSEPH SURFACE Here's a chair, Sir Peter — I beg —

SIR PETER Well, now we are alone, there is a subject, my dear friend, on which I wish to unburthen my mind to you — a point of the greatest moment to my peace; in short, my good friend, Lady Teazle's conduct of late has made me very unhappy.

JOSEPH SURFACE Indeed! I am very sorry to hear it.

SIR PETER Aye, 'tis but too plain she has not the least regard for me; but, what's worse, I have pretty good authority to suspect she has formed an attachment to another.

JOSEPH SURFACE You astonish me!

SIR PETER Yes; and, between ourselves, I think I've discovered the person.

JOSEPH SURFACE How! you alarm me exceedingly.

SIR PETER Ah, my dear friend, I knew you would sympathize with me!

JOSEPH SURFACE Yes – believe me, Sir Peter, such a discovery would hurt me just as much as it would you.

SIR PETER I am convinced of it. – Ah! it is a happiness to have a friend whom we can trust even with one's family secrets. But have you no guess who I mean?

JOSEPH SURFACE I haven't the most distant idea. It can't be Sir Benjamin Backbite!

SIR PETER Oh no! What say you to Charles?

JOSEPH SURFACE My brother! impossible! O no, Sir Peter, you must not credit the scandalous insinuations you may hear. No, no, Charles to be sure has been charged with many things of this kind, but I can never think he would meditate so gross an injury.

SIR PETER Ah, my dear friend, the goodness of your own heart misleads you. You judge of others by yourself.

JOSEPH SURFACE Certainly, Sir Peter, the heart that is conscious of its own integrity is ever slow to credit another's treachery.

SIR PETER True; but your brother has no sentiment – you never hear him talk so.

JOSEPH SURFACE Yet I can't but think Lady Teazle herself has too much principle.

SIR PETER Aye, but what is principle against the flattery of a handsome, lively young fellow?

JOSEPH SURFACE That's very true.

SIR PETER And then, you know, the difference of our ages makes it very improbable that she should have any great affection for me; and if she were to be frail, and I were to make it public, why the town would only laugh at me – the foolish old bachelor, who had married a girl.

JOSEPH SURFACE That's true, to be sure – they *would* laugh.

SIR PETER Laugh – aye, and make ballads, and paragraphs, and the devil knows what of me.

JOSEPH SURFACE No – you must never make it public.

SIR PETER But then again – that the nephew of my old friend, Sir Oliver, should be the person to attempt such a wrong, hurts me more nearly.

JOSEPH SURFACE Aye, there's the point. – When ingratitude barbs the dart of injury, the wound has double danger in it.

SIR PETER Aye – I, that was, in a manner, left his guardian: in whose house he had been so often entertained; who never in my life denied him – my advice!

JOSEPH SURFACE Oh, 'tis not to be credited! there may be a man capable of such baseness, to be sure; but, for my part, till you can give me positive proofs, I cannot but doubt it. However, if it should be proved on him, he is no longer a brother of mine – I disclaim kindred with him: for the man who can break the laws of hospitality, and attempt the wife of his friend, deserves to be branded as the pest of society.

SIR PETER What a difference there is between you! What noble sentiments!

JOSEPH SURFACE Yet, I cannot suspect Lady Teazle's honour.

SIR PETER I am sure I wish to think well of her, and to remove all ground of quarrel between us. She has lately reproached me more than once with having made no settlement on her; and, in our last quarrel, she almost hinted that she should not break her heart if I was dead. Now, as we seem to differ in our ideas of expense, I have resolved she shall have her own way, and be her own mistress in that respect for the future; and, if I were to die, she will find I have not been inattentive to her interest while living. Here, my friend, are the drafts of two deeds, which I wish to have your opinion on. – By one, she will enjoy eight hundred a year independent while I live; and, by the other, the bulk of my fortune at my death.

JOSEPH SURFACE This conduct, Sir Peter, is indeed truly gener-ous. – I wish it may not corrupt my pupil.   *Aside.*

SIR PETER Yes, I am determined she shall have no cause to complain, though I would not have her acquainted with the latter instance of my affection yet awhile.

JOSEPH SURFACE Nor I, if I could help it.   *Aside.*

SIR PETER And now, my dear friend, if you please, we will talk over the situation of your hopes with Maria.

JOSEPH SURFACE Oh, no, Sir Peter; another time, if you please.

SIR PETER I am sensibly chagrined at the little progress you seem to make in her affections.

JOSEPH SURFACE I beg you will not mention it. What are my disappointments when your happiness is in debate! – (*Softly.*) 'Sdeath, I shall be ruined every way!   *Aside*.

SIR PETER And though you are averse to my acquainting Lady Teazle with your passion, I'm sure she's not your enemy in the affair.

JOSEPH SURFACE Pray, Sir Peter, now, oblige me. I am really too much affected by the subject we have been speaking of, to bestow a thought on my own concerns. The man who is entrusted with his friend's distresses can never –

Enter Servant.

Well, sir?

SERVANT Your brother, sir, is speaking to a gentleman in the street, and says he knows you are within.

JOSEPH SURFACE 'Sdeath, blockhead, I'm not within – I'm out for the day.

SIR PETER Stay – hold – a thought has struck me: you shall be at home.

JOSEPH SURFACE Well, well, let him up. – (*Exit Servant.*) He'll interrupt Sir Peter, however.   *Aside*.

SIR PETER Now, my good friend, oblige me, I entreat you. Before Charles comes, let me conceal myself somewhere – then do you tax him on the point we have been talking on, and his answer may satisfy me at once.

JOSEPH SURFACE Oh, fie, Sir Peter! would you have me join in so mean a trick? – to trepan my brother too?

SIR PETER Nay, you tell me you are *sure* he is innocent; if so, you do him the greatest service by giving him an opportunity to clear himself, and you will set my heart at rest. Come, you shall not refuse me: here, behind the screen will be – hey! what the devil! there seems to be one listener here already – I'll swear I saw a petticoat!

JOSEPH SURFACE Ha! ha! ha! Well, this is ridiculous enough. I'll tell you, Sir Peter, though I hold a man of intrigue to be a most despicable character, yet you know, it does not follow that one is to be an absolute Joseph either! Hark'ee, 'tis a little French milliner, – a silly rogue that plagues me, – and having some character to lose, on your coming, sir, she ran behind the screen.

SIR PETER Ah! you rogue! But, egad, she has overheard all I have been saying of my wife.

JOSEPH SURFACE Oh, 'twill never go any farther, you may depend upon it!

SIR PETER No! then, faith, let her hear it out. – Here's a closet will do as well.

JOSEPH SURFACE Well, go in there.

SIR PETER Sly rogue! sly rogue.   *Goes into the closet.*

JOSEPH SURFACE A narrow escape, indeed! and a curious situation I'm in, to part man and wife in this manner.

LADY TEAZLE (*Peeping.*) Couldn't I steal off?

JOSEPH SURFACE Keep close, my angel!

SIR PETER (*Peeping.*) Joseph, tax him home.

JOSEPH SURFACE Back, my dear friend!

LADY TEAZLE Couldn't you lock Sir Peter in?

JOSEPH SURFACE Be still, my life!

SIR PETER (*Peeping.*) You're sure the little milliner won't blab?

JOSEPH SURFACE In, in, my dear Sir Peter! – 'Fore Gad, I wish I had a key to the door.

Enter Charles Surface.

CHARLES SURFACE Holla! brother, what has been the matter? Your fellow would not let me up at first. What! have you had a Jew or a wench with you?

JOSEPH SURFACE Neither, brother, I assure you.

CHARLES SURFACE But what has made Sir Peter steal off? I thought he had been with you.

JOSEPH SURFACE He *was*, brother; but, hearing you were coming, he did not choose to stay.

CHARLES SURFACE What! was the old gentleman afraid I wanted to borrow money of him!

JOSEPH SURFACE No, sir; but I am sorry to find, Charles, you have lately given that worthy man grounds for great uneasiness.

CHARLES SURFACE Yes, yes, yes, they tell me I do that to a great many worthy men. – But how so, pray?

JOSEPH SURFACE To be plain with you, brother – he thinks you are endeavouring to gain Lady Teazle's affections from him.

CHARLES SURFACE Who, I? O Lud! not I, upon my word. Ha! ha! ha! ha! so the old fellow has found out that he has got a young wife, has he? – or, what is worse, has her ladyship discovered she has an old husband?

JOSEPH SURFACE This is no subject to jest upon, brother. He who can laugh –

CHARLES SURFACE True, true, as you were going to say – then, seriously, I never had the least idea of what you charge me with, upon my honour.

JOSEPH SURFACE Well, it will give Sir Peter great satisfaction to hear this.   *Aloud*.

CHARLES SURFACE To be sure, I once thought the lady seemed to have taken a fancy to me; but, upon my soul, I never gave her the least encouragement: – besides, you know my attachment to Maria.

JOSEPH SURFACE But sure, brother, even if Lady Teazle had betrayed the fondest partiality for you –

CHARLES SURFACE Why, look'ee, Joseph, I hope I shall never deliberately do a dishonourable action; but if a pretty woman was purposely to throw herself in my way – and that pretty woman married to a man old enough to be her father –

JOSEPH SURFACE Well –

CHARLES SURFACE Why, I believe I should be obliged to borrow a little of your morality, that's all. – But, brother, do you know now that you surprise me exceedingly, by naming *me* with Lady Teazle; for i'faith, I always understood *you* were her favourite.

JOSEPH SURFACE Oh, for shame, Charles! This retort is foolish.

CHARLES SURFACE Nay, I swear I have seen you exchange such significant glances –

JOSEPH SURFACE Nay, nay, sir, this is no jest.

CHARLES SURFACE Egad, I'm serious. Don't you remember one day, when I called here –

JOSEPH SURFACE Nay, prithee, Charles –

CHARLES SURFACE And found you together –

JOSEPH SURFACE Zounds, sir, I insist –

CHARLES SURFACE And another time, when your servant –

JOSEPH SURFACE Brother, brother, a word with you! – Gad, I must stop him.   *Aside*.

CHARLES SURFACE Informed, I say, that –

JOSEPH SURFACE Hush! I beg your pardon, but Sir Peter has overheard all we have been saying. I knew you would clear yourself, or I should not have consented.

CHARLES SURFACE How, Sir Peter! Where is he?

JOSEPH SURFACE Softly; there!   *Points to the closet.*

CHARLES SURFACE Oh, 'fore Heaven, I'll have him out. Sir Peter, come forth!

JOSEPH SURFACE No, no –

CHARLES SURFACE I say, Sir Peter, come into court. – (*Pulls in Sir Peter.*) What! my old guardian! – What! turn inquisitor, and take evidence, incog?

SIR PETER Give me your hand, Charles – I believe I have suspected you wrongfully; but you mustn't be angry with Joseph – 'twas my plan!

CHARLES SURFACE Indeed!

SIR PETER But I acquit you. I promise you I don't think near so ill of you as I did: what I have heard has given me great satisfaction.

CHARLES SURFACE Egad, then, 'twas lucky you didn't hear any more. Wasn't it, Joseph?

SIR PETER Ah! you would have retorted on him.

CHARLES SURFACE Aye, aye, that was a joke.

SIR PETER Yes, yes, I know his honour too well.

CHARLES SURFACE But you might as well have suspected *him* as *me* in this matter, for all that. Mightn't he, Joseph?

SIR PETER Well, well, I believe you.

JOSEPH SURFACE Would they were both out of the room!

Enter Servant, and whispers to Joseph Surface.

SIR PETER And in future, perhaps, we may not be such strangers.

SERVANT Lady Sneerwell is below, and says she will come up.

JOSEPH SURFACE (*To the Servant.*) Lady Sneerwell! Gad's life, she mustn't come here. Gentlemen, I beg pardon – I must wait on you downstairs; here's a person come on particular business.

CHARLES SURFACE Well, you can see him in another room. Sir Peter and I have not met a long time, and I have something to say to him.

JOSEPH SURFACE (*Aside.*) They must not be left together. – (*To

Charles.) I'll send this man away, and return directly. – Sir
Peter, not a word of the French milliner.

SIR PETER Oh, not for the world! – (*Exit Joseph.*) Ah, Charles,
if you associated more with your brother, one might indeed
hope for your reformation. He is a man of sentiment. – Well,
there is nothing in the world so noble as a man of sentiment.

CHARLES SURFACE Pshaw! he is too moral by half; – and so
apprehensive of his good name, as he calls it, that I suppose
he would as soon let a priest into his house as a girl.

SIR PETER No, no, – come, come, – you wrong him. No, no,
Joseph is no rake, but he is no such saint in that respect either.
– I have a great mind to tell him – we should have a laugh.

Aside.

CHARLES SURFACE Oh, hang him! he's a very anchorite, a young
hermit!

SIR PETER Hark'ee – you must not abuse him: he may chance
to hear of it again, I promise you.

CHARLES SURFACE Why, you won't tell him?

SIR PETER No – but – this way. – Egad, I'll tell him. – (*Aside.*)
Hark'ee, have you a mind to have a good laugh at Joseph?

CHARLES SURFACE I should like it of all things.

SIR PETER Then, i'faith, we will! – I'll be quit with him for
discovering me. He had a girl with him when I called.

Whispers.

CHARLES SURFACE What! Joseph? You jest.

SIR PETER Hush! – a little French milliner – and the best of the
jest is – she's in the room now.

CHARLES SURFACE The devil she is!   *Looking at the closet.*

SIR PETER Hush! I tell you.   *Points to the screen.*

CHARLES SURFACE Behind the screen! Odds life, let's unveil her!

SIR PETER No, no – he's coming – you shan't, indeed!

CHARLES SURFACE Oh, egad, we'll have a peep at the little
milliner!

SIR PETER Not for the world! – Joseph will never forgive me.

CHARLES SURFACE I'll stand by you –

SIR PETER Odds, here he is!

*Joseph Surface enters just as Charles Surface throws down the
screen.*

CHARLES SURFACE Lady Teazle, by all that's wonderful!
SIR PETER Lady Teazle, by all that's damnable!

CHARLES SURFACE Sir Peter, this is one of the smartest French milliners I ever saw. Egad, you seem all to have been diverting yourselves here at hide and seek, and I don't see who is out of the secret. Shall I beg your ladyship to inform me? Not a word! – Brother, will you be pleased to explain this matter? What! is Morality dumb too? – Sir Peter, though I found you in the dark, perhaps you are not so now! All mute! Well – though I can make nothing of the affair, I suppose you perfectly understand one another – so I'll leave you to yourselves. – (*Going.*) Brother, I'm sorry to find you have given that worthy man grounds for so much uneasiness. – Sir Peter! there's nothing in the world so noble as a man of sentiment! *Exit Charles. They stand for some time looking at each other.*

JOSEPH SURFACE Sir Peter – notwithstanding – I confess – that appearances are against me – if you will afford me your patience – I make no doubt – but I shall explain everything to your satisfaction.

SIR PETER If you please, sir.

JOSEPH SURFACE The fact is, sir – that Lady Teazle, knowing my pretensions to your ward, Maria – I say, sir, Lady Teazle, being apprehensive of the jealousy of your temper – and knowing my friendship to the family – she, sir, I say – called here – in order that – I might explain these pretensions – but on your coming – being apprehensive – as I said – of your jealousy – she withdrew – and this, you may depend on it, is the whole truth of the matter.

SIR PETER A very clear account, upon my word; and I dare swear the lady will vouch for every article of it.

LADY TEAZLE For not one word of it, Sir Peter!

SIR PETER How! don't you think it worth while to agree in the lie?

LADY TEAZLE There is not one syllable of truth in what that gentleman has told you.

SIR PETER I believe you, upon my soul, ma'am!

JOSEPH SURFACE (*Aside.*) 'Sdeath, madam, will you betray me?

LADY TEAZLE Good Mr Hypocrite, by your leave, I'll speak for myself.

SIR PETER Aye, let her alone, sir; you'll find she'll make out a better story than you, without prompting.

LADY TEAZLE Hear me, Sir Peter! – I came here on no matter relating to your ward, and even ignorant of this gentleman's pretensions to her. But I came, seduced by his insidious arguments, at least to listen to his pretended passion, if not to sacrifice your honour to his baseness.

SIR PETER Now, I believe, the truth is coming out indeed!

JOSEPH SURFACE The woman's mad!

LADY TEAZLE No, sir — she has recovered her senses, and your own arts have furnished her with the means. — Sir Peter, I do not expect you to credit me — but the tenderness you expressed for me, when I am sure you could not think I was a witness to it, has penetrated so to my heart, that had I left the place without the shame of this discovery, my future life should have spoken the sincerity of my gratitude. As for that smooth-tongued hypocrite, who would have seduced the wife of his too credulous friend, while he affected honourable addresses to his ward — I behold him now in a light so truly despicable, that I shall never again respect myself for having listened to him.   *Exit.*

JOSEPH SURFACE Notwithstanding all this, Sir Peter, Heaven knows —

SIR PETER That you are a villain! and so I leave you to your conscience.

JOSEPH SURFACE You are too rash, Sir Peter; you *shall* hear me. The man who shuts out conviction by refusing to —

SIR PETER O damn your sentiments.

> *Exeunt, Surface following and speaking.*

Act V

SCENE: *The library.*

Enter Joseph Surface and Servant.

JOSEPH SURFACE Mr Stanley! – and why should you think I would see him? you must know he comes to ask something.

SERVANT Sir, I should not have let him in, but that Mr Rowley came to the door with him.

JOSEPH SURFACE Pshaw! blockhead! to suppose that I should now be in a temper to receive visits from poor relations! – Well, why don't you show the fellow up?

SERVANT I will, sir. – Why, sir, it was not my fault that Sir Peter discovered my lady –

JOSEPH SURFACE Go, fool! – (*Exit Servant.*) Sure Fortune never played a man of my policy such a trick before! My character with Sir Peter, my hopes with Maria, destroyed in a moment! I'm in a rare humour to listen to other people's distresses! I shan't be able to bestow even a benevolent sentiment on Stanley. – So! here he comes, and Rowley with him. I must try to recover myself, and put a little charity into my face, however.   *Exit.*

Enter Sir Oliver and Rowley.

SIR OLIVER What! does he avoid us? – That was he, was it not?

ROWLEY It was, sir. But I doubt you are come a little too abruptly. His nerves are so weak, that the sight of a poor relation may be too much for him. I should have gone first to break it to him.

SIR OLIVER Oh, plague of his nerves! Yet this is he whom Sir Peter extols as a man of the most benevolent way of thinking!

ROWLEY As to his way of thinking, I cannot pretend to decide, for, to do him justice, he appears to have as much speculative benevolence as any private gentleman in the kingdom, though he is seldom so sensual as to indulge himself in the exercise of it.

SIR OLIVER Yet he has a string of charitable sentiments, I suppose, at his fingers' ends.

ROWLEY Or, rather, at his tongue's end, Sir Oliver; for I believe there is no sentiment he has more faith in than that 'Charity begins at home.'

SIR OLIVER And his, I presume, is of that domestic sort which never stirs abroad at all.

ROWLEY I doubt you'll find it so; — but he's coming. I mustn't seem to interrupt you; and you know, immediately as you leave him, I come in to announce your arrival in your real character.

SIR OLIVER True; and afterwards you'll meet me at Sir Peter's.

ROWLEY Without losing a moment.   *Exit.*

SIR OLIVER I don't like the complaisance of his features.

Enter Joseph Surface.

JOSEPH SURFACE Sir, I beg you ten thousand pardons for keeping you a moment waiting. — Mr Stanley, I presume.

SIR OLIVER At your service.

JOSEPH SURFACE Sir, I beg you will do me the honour to sit down — I entreat you, sir.

SIR OLIVER Dear sir — there's no occasion. — Too civil by half.
                                                           Aside.

JOSEPH SURFACE I have not the pleasure of knowing you, Mr Stanley; but I am extremely happy to see you look so well. You were nearly related to my mother, I think, Mr Stanley?

SIR OLIVER I was sir; — so nearly that my present poverty, I fear, may do discredit to her wealthy children, else I should not have presumed to trouble you.

JOSEPH SURFACE Dear sir, there needs no apology: He that is in distress, though a stranger, has a right to claim kindred with the wealthy. I am sure I wish I was one of that class, and had it in my power to offer you even a small relief.

SIR OLIVER If your uncle, Sir Oliver, were here, I should have a friend.

JOSEPH SURFACE I wish he was, sir, with all my heart: you should not want an advocate with him, believe me, sir.

SIR OLIVER I should not need one – my distresses would recommend me. But I imagined his bounty had enabled you to become the agent of his charity.

JOSEPH SURFACE My dear sir, you were strangely misinformed. Sir Oliver is a worthy man, a very worthy sort of man; but avarice, Mr Stanley, is the vice of age. I will tell you, my good sir, in confidence, what he has done for me has been a mere nothing; though people, I know, have thought otherwise, and, for my part, I never chose to contradict the report.

SIR OLIVER What! has he never transmitted you bullion – rupees – pagodas?

JOSEPH SURFACE Oh, dear sir, nothing of the kind! – No, no – a few presents now and then – china, shawls, congou tea, avadavats, and Indian crackers – little more, believe me.

SIR OLIVER Here's gratitude for twelve thousand pounds! – Avadavats and Indian crackers!   *Aside*.

JOSEPH SURFACE Then, my dear sir, you have heard, I doubt not, of the extravagance of my brother; there are very few would credit what I have done for that unfortunate young man.

SIR OLIVER Not I, for one!   *Aside*.

JOSEPH SURFACE The sums I have lent him! – Indeed I have been exceedingly to blame; it was an amiable weakness – however – I don't pretend to defend it – and now I feel it doubly culpable, since it has deprived me of the pleasure of serving *you*, Mr Stanley, as my heart dictates.

SIR OLIVER Dissembler! – (*Aside*.) Then, sir, you can't assist me?

JOSEPH SURFACE At present, it grieves me to say, I cannot; but, whenever I have the ability, you may depend upon hearing from me.

SIR OLIVER I am extremely sorry –

JOSEPH SURFACE Not more than I, believe me; – to pity, without the power to relieve, is still more painful than to ask and be denied.

SIR OLIVER Kind sir, your most obedient humble servant.

JOSEPH SURFACE You leave me deeply affected, Mr Stanley. – William, be ready to open the door.

SIR OLIVER O, dear sir, no ceremony.

JOSEPH SURFACE Your very obedient.

SIR OLIVER Your most obsequious.

JOSEPH SURFACE You may depend upon hearing from me, whenever I can be of service.

SIR OLIVER Sweet sir, you are too good.

JOSEPH SURFACE In the meantime I wish you health and spirits.

SIR OLIVER Your ever grateful and perpetual humble servant.

JOSEPH SURFACE Sir, yours as sincerely.

SIR OLIVER Charles! – you are my heir. *Aside. Exit.*

JOSEPH SURFACE This is one bad effect of a good character; it invites application from the unfortunate, and there needs no small degree of address to gain the reputation of benevolence without incurring the expense. The silver ore of pure charity is an expensive article in the catalogue of a man's good qualities; whereas the sentimental French plate I use instead of it makes just as good a show, and pays no tax.

Enter Rowley.

ROWLEY Mr Surface, your servant: I was apprehensive of interrupting you, though my business demands immediate attention, as this note will inform you.

JOSEPH SURFACE Always happy to see Mr Rowley. – How! – (*Reads the letter.*) Oliver Surface! – My uncle arrived!

ROWLEY He is, indeed: we have just parted – quite well, after a speedy voyage, and impatient to embrace his worthy nephew.

JOSEPH SURFACE I am astonished! – William! stop Mr Stanley, if he's not gone.

ROWLEY Oh! he's out of reach, I believe.

JOSEPH SURFACE Why did you not let me know this when you came in together?

ROWLEY I thought you had particular business; – but I must be gone to inform your brother, and appoint him here to meet his uncle. He will be with you in a quarter of an hour.

JOSEPH SURFACE So he says. Well, I am strangely overjoyed at his coming. – Never, to be sure, was anything so damned unlucky! *Aside.*

ROWLEY You will be delighted to see how well he looks.

JOSEPH SURFACE Oh! I'm rejoiced to hear it. – Just at this time! *Aside.*

ROWLEY I'll tell him how impatiently you expect him.

JOSEPH SURFACE Do, do; pray give my best duty and affection. Indeed, I cannot express the sensations I feel at the thought of seeing him. – (*Exit Rowley.*) Certainly his coming just at this time is the cruellest piece of ill fortune.   *Exit.*

SCENE 2

SCENE: *Sir Peter Teazle's.*

Enter Mrs Candour and Maid.

MAID Indeed, ma'am, my lady will see nobody at present.

MRS CANDOUR Did you tell her it was her friend Mrs Candour?

MAID Yes, ma'am; but she begs you will excuse her.

MRS CANDOUR Do go again. – I shall be glad to see her, if it be only for a moment, for I am sure she must be in great distress. – (*Exit Maid.*) Dear heart, how provoking! I'm not mistress of half the circumstances! We shall have the whole affair in the newspapers, with the names of the parties at full length, before I have dropped the story at a dozen houses.

Enter Sir Benjamin Backbite.

Oh, Sir Benjamin! you have heard, I suppose –

SIR BENJAMIN Of Lady Teazle and Mr Surface –

MRS CANDOUR And Sir Peter's discovery –

SIR BENJAMIN Oh, the strangest piece of business, to be sure!

MRS CANDOUR Well, I never was so surprised in my life. I am so sorry for all parties, indeed.

SIR BENJAMIN Now, I don't pity Sir Peter at all: he was so extravagantly partial to Mr Surface.

MRS CANDOUR Mr Surface! Why, 'twas with Charles Lady Teazle was detected.

SIR BENJAMIN No such thing! – Mr Surface is the gallant.

MRS CANDOUR No, no! Charles is the man. 'Twas Mr Surface brought Sir Peter on purpose to discover them.

SIR BENJAMIN I tell you I had it from one –

MRS CANDOUR And I have it from one –

SIR BENJAMIN Who had it from one, who had it –

MRS CANDOUR From one immediately – but here comes Lady Sneerwell; perhaps she knows the whole affair.

Enter Lady Sneerwell.

LADY SNEERWELL So, my dear Mrs Candour, here's a sad affair of our friend Teazle!

MRS CANDOUR Aye, my dear friend, who could have thought it?

LADY SNEERWELL Well, there is no trusting to appearances; though indeed, she was always too lively for me.

MRS CANDOUR To be sure, her manners were a little too free; but then she was very young!

LADY SNEERWELL And had, indeed, some good qualities.

MRS CANDOUR So she had, indeed. But have you heard the particulars?

LADY SNEERWELL No; but everybody says that Mr Surface –

SIR BENJAMIN Aye, there; I told you Mr Surface was the man.

MRS CANDOUR No, no, indeed, the assignation was with Charles.

LADY SNEERWELL With Charles! You alarm me, Mrs Candour!

MRS CANDOUR Yes, yes, he was the lover. Mr Surface, to do him justice, was only the informer.

SIR BENJAMIN Well, I'll not dispute with you, Mrs Candour; but, be it which it may, I hope that Sir Peter's wound will not –

MRS CANDOUR Sir Peter's wound! Oh, mercy! I didn't hear a word of their fighting.

LADY SNEERWELL Nor I, a syllable.

SIR BENJAMIN No! what, no mention of the duel?

MRS CANDOUR Not a word.

SIR BENJAMIN Oh Lord, yes, yes: they fought before they left the room.

LADY SNEERWELL Pray let us hear.

MRS CANDOUR Aye, do oblige us with the duel.

SIR BENJAMIN 'Sir,' says Sir Peter, immediately after the discovery, 'you are a most ungrateful fellow.'

MRS CANDOUR Aye, to Charles –

SIR BENJAMIN No, no – to Mr Surface – 'a most ungrateful fellow; and old as I am, sir,' says he, 'I insist on immediate satisfaction.'

MRS CANDOUR Aye, that must have been to Charles; for 'tis very unlikely Mr Surface should fight in his own house.

SIR BENJAMIN 'Gad's life, ma'am, not at all – 'giving me immediate satisfaction,' – On this, ma'am, Lady Teazle, seeing Sir Peter in such danger, ran out of the room in strong hysterics, and Charles after her, calling out for hartshorn and water; then, madam, they began to fight with swords –

Enter Crabtree.

CRABTREE With pistols, nephew – pistols: I have it from undoubted authority.

MRS CANDOUR Oh, Mr Crabtree, then it is all true!

CRABTREE Too true, indeed, madam, and Sir Peter dangerously wounded –

SIR BENJAMIN By a thrust in *seconde* quite through his left side –

CRABTREE By a bullet lodged in the thorax.

MRS CANDOUR Mercy on me! Poor Sir Peter!

CRABTREE Yes, madam; though Charles would have avoided the matter, if he could.

MRS CANDOUR I knew Charles was the person.

SIR BENJAMIN My uncle, I see, knows nothing of the matter.

CRABTREE But Sir Peter taxed him with the basest ingratitude –

SIR BENJAMIN That I told you, you know –

CRABTREE Do, nephew, let me speak! and insisted on immediate –

SIR BENJAMIN Just as I said –

CRABTREE Odds life, nephew, allow others to know something too! A pair of pistols lay on the bureau (for Mr Surface, it seems, had come home the night before late from Salthill, where he had been to see the Montem with a friend, who has a son at Eton), so, unluckily, the pistols were left charged.

SIR BENJAMIN I heard nothing of this.

CRABTREE Sir Peter forced Charles to take one, and they fired, it seems, pretty nearly together. Charles's shot took effect, as I tell you, and Sir Peter's missed; but, what is very extraordinary, the ball struck against a little bronze Shakespeare that stood over the fireplace, grazed out of the window at a right angle, and wounded the postman, who was just coming to the door with a double letter from Northamptonshire.

SIR BENJAMIN My uncle's account is more circumstantial, I confess; but I believe mine is the true one, for all that.

LADY SNEERWELL I am more interested in this affair than they imagine, and must have better information.   *Aside. Exit.*

SIR BENJAMIN (*After a pause, looking at each other.*) Ah! Lady Sneerwell's alarm is very easily accounted for.

CRABTREE Yes, yes, they certainly *do* say – but that's neither here nor there.

MRS CANDOUR But, pray, where is Sir Peter at present?

CRABTREE Oh! they brought him home, and he is now in the house, though the servants are ordered to deny him.

MRS CANDOUR I believe so, and Lady Teazle, I suppose, attending him.

CRABTREE Yes, yes; and I saw one of the faculty enter just before me.

SIR BENJAMIN Hey! who comes here?

CRABTREE Oh, this is he: the physician, depend on't.

MRS CANDOUR Oh, certainly! it must be the physician; and now we shall know.

Enter Sir Oliver.

CRABTREE Well, doctor, what hopes?

MRS CANDOUR Aye, doctor, how's your patient?

SIR BENJAMIN Now, doctor, isn't it a wound with a small-sword?

CRABTREE A bullet lodged in the thorax, for a hundred.

SIR OLIVER Doctor! a wound with a small-sword! and a bullet in the thorax? What! are you mad, good people?

SIR BENJAMIN Perhaps, sir, you are not a doctor?

SIR OLIVER Truly, I am to thank you for my degree, if I am.

CRABTREE Only a friend of Sir Peter's, then, I presume. But, sir, you must have heard of his accident?

SIR OLIVER Not a word!

CRABTREE Not of his being dangerously wounded?

SIR OLIVER The devil he is!

SIR BENJAMIN Run through the body –

CRABTREE Shot in the breast –

SIR BENJAMIN By one Mr Surface –

CRABTREE Aye, the younger.

SIR OLIVER Hey! what the plague! you seem to differ strangely in your accounts: however, you agree that Sir Peter is dangerously wounded.

SIR BENJAMIN Oh, yes, we agree there.

CRABTREE Yes, yes, I believe there can be no doubt in that.

SIR OLIVER Then, upon my word, for a person in that situation, he is the most imprudent man alive; for here he comes, walking as if nothing at all was the matter.

Enter Sir Peter.

Odds heart, Sir Peter, you are come in good time, I promise you; for we had just given you over!

SIR BENJAMIN Egad, uncle, this is the most sudden recovery!

SIR OLIVER Why, man, what do you do out of bed with a small-sword through your body, and a bullet lodged in your thorax?

SIR PETER A small-sword and a bullet!

SIR OLIVER Aye, these gentlemen would have killed you without law or physic, and wanted to dub me a doctor, to make me an accomplice.

SIR PETER Why, what is all this?

SIR BENJAMIN We rejoice, Sir Peter, that the story of the duel is not true, and are sincerely sorry for your other misfortune.

SIR PETER So, so; all over the town already.   *Aside.*

CRABTREE Though, Sir Peter, you were certainly vastly to blame to marry at all at your years.

SIR PETER Sir, what business is that of yours?

MRS CANDOUR Though, indeed, as Sir Peter made so good a husband, he's very much to be pitied.

SIR PETER Plague on your pity, ma'am! I desire none of it.

SIR BENJAMIN However, Sir Peter, you must not mind the laughing and jests you will meet with on the occasion.

SIR PETER Sir, sir, I desire to be master in my own house.

CRABTREE 'Tis no uncommon case, that's one comfort.

SIR PETER I insist on being left to myself: without ceremony – I insist on your leaving my house directly!

MRS CANDOUR Well, well, we are going; and depend on't, we'll make the best report of you we can.   *Exit.*

SIR PETER Leave my house!

CRABTREE And tell how hardly you've been treated.   *Exit.*

SIR PETER Leave my house!

SIR BENJAMIN And how patiently you bear it.   *Exit.*

SIR PETER Fiends! vipers! furies! Oh! that their own venom would choke them!

SIR OLIVER They are very provoking indeed, Sir Peter.

Enter Rowley.

ROWLEY I heard high words: what has ruffled you, sir?

SIR PETER Pshaw! what signifies asking? Do I ever pass a day without my vexations?

SIR OLIVER Well, I'm not inquisitive. I come only to tell you, that I have seen both my nephews in the manner we proposed.

SIR PETER A precious couple they are!

ROWLEY Yes, and Sir Oliver is convinced that your judgement was right, Sir Peter.

SIR OLIVER Yes, I find Joseph is indeed the man, after all.

ROWLEY Aye, as Sir Peter says, he is a man of sentiment.

SIR OLIVER And acts up to the sentiments he professes.

ROWLEY It certainly is edification to hear him talk.

SIR OLIVER Oh, he's a model for the young men of the age! — But how's this, Sir Peter? you don't join us in your friend Joseph's praise, as I expected.

SIR PETER Sir Oliver, we live in a damned wicked world, and the fewer we praise the better.

ROWLEY What! do you say so, Sir Peter, who were never mistaken in your life?

SIR PETER Pshaw! plague on you both! I see by your sneering you have heard the whole affair. I shall go mad among you!

ROWLEY Then, to fret you no longer, Sir Peter, we are indeed acquainted with it all. I met Lady Teazle coming from Mr Surface's so humbled, that she deigned to request me to be her advocate with you.

SIR PETER And does Sir Oliver know all too?

SIR OLIVER Every circumstance.

SIR PETER What, of the closet — and the screen, hey?

SIR OLIVER Yes, yes, and the little French milliner. Oh, I have been vastly diverted with the story! Ha! ha! ha!

SIR PETER 'Twas very pleasant.

SIR OLIVER I never laughed more in my life, I assure you: ha! ha! ha!

SIR PETER Oh, vastly diverting! ha! ha! ha!

ROWLEY To be sure, Joseph with his sentiments! ha! ha! ha!

SIR PETER Yes, his sentiments! Ha! ha! ha! Hypocritical villain!

SIR OLIVER Aye, and that rogue Charles to pull Sir Peter out of the closet: ha! ha! ha!

SIR PETER Ha! ha! 'twas devilish entertaining, to be sure!

SIR OLIVER Ha! ha! ha! Egad, Sir Peter, I should like to have seen your face when the screen was thrown down: ha! ha!

SIR PETER Yes, my face when the screen was thrown down: ha! ha! ha! Oh, I must never show my head again!

SIR OLIVER But come, come, it isn't fair to laugh at you neither, my old friend; though, upon my soul, I can't help it.

SIR PETER Oh, pray don't restrain your mirth on my account: it does not hurt me at all! I laugh at the whole affair myself. Yes, yes, I think being a standing jest for all one's acquaintance a very happy situation. Oh, yes, and then of a morning to read the paragraphs about Mr S—, Lady T—, and Sir P—, will be so diverting! I shall certainly leave town to-morrow and never look mankind in the face again.

ROWLEY Without affectation, Sir Peter, you may despise the ridicule of fools: but I see Lady Teazle going towards the next room; I am sure you must desire a reconciliation as earnestly as she does.

SIR OLIVER Perhaps my being here prevents her coming to you. Well, I'll leave honest Rowley to mediate between you; but he must bring you all presently to Mr Surface's, where I am now returning, if not to reclaim a libertine, at least to expose hypocrisy.

SIR PETER Ah, I'll be present at your discovering yourself there with all my heart; though 'tis a vile unlucky place for discoveries.

ROWLEY We'll follow.   *Exit Sir Oliver.*

SIR PETER She is not coming here, you see, Rowley.

ROWLEY No, but she has left the door of that room open, you perceive. See, she is in tears.

SIR PETER Certainly a little mortification appears very becoming in a wife. Don't you think it will do her good to let her pine a little?

ROWLEY Oh, this is ungenerous in you!

SIR PETER Well, I know not what to think. You remember the letter I found of hers evidently intended for Charles!

ROWLEY A mere forgery, Sir Peter, laid in your way on purpose. This is one of the points which I intend Snake shall give you conviction of.

SIR PETER I wish I were once satisfied of that. She looks this way. What a remarkably elegant turn of the head she has! Rowley, I'll go to her.

ROWLEY Certainly.

SIR PETER Though, when it is known that we are reconciled people will laugh at me ten times more.

ROWLEY Let them laugh, and retort their malice only by showing them you are happy in spite of it.

SIR PETER I'faith, so I will! and, if I'm not mistaken, we may yet
be the happiest couple in the country.

ROWLEY Nay, Sir Peter, he who once lays aside suspicion –

SIR PETER Hold, Master Rowley! if you have any regard for me,
never let me hear you utter anything like a sentiment: I have
had enough of them to serve me the rest of my life.

Exeunt.

SCENE 3

SCENE: *The library.*

Enter Joseph Surface and Lady Sneerwell.

LADY SNEERWELL Impossible! Will not Sir Peter immediately be
reconciled to Charles, and of consequence no longer oppose
his union with Maria? The thought is distraction to me.

JOSEPH SURFACE Can passion furnish a remedy?

LADY SNEERWELL No, nor cunning either. Oh! I was a fool, an
idiot, to league with such a blunderer!

JOSEPH SURFACE Surely, Lady Sneerwell, I am the greatest
sufferer; yet you see I bear the accident with calmness.

LADY SNEERWELL Because the disappointment doesn't reach
your heart; your interest only attached you to Maria. Had
you felt for her what I have for that ungrateful libertine,
neither your temper nor hypocrisy could prevent your showing the sharpness of your vexation.

JOSEPH SURFACE But why should your reproaches fall on me
for this disappointment?

LADY SNEERWELL Are you not the cause of it? What had you to
bate in your pursuit of Maria to pervert Lady Teazle by the
way? Had you not a sufficient field for your roguery in
blinding Sir Peter, and supplanting your brother, but you
must endeavour to seduce his wife? I hate such an avarice of
crimes; 'tis an unfair monopoly, and never prospers.

JOSEPH SURFACE Well, I admit I have been to blame. I confess I
deviated from the direct road of wrong, but I don't think
we're so totally defeated neither.

LADY SNEERWELL No!

JOSEPH SURFACE You tell me you have made a trial of Snake since we met, and that you still believe him faithful to us?

LADY SNEERWELL I do believe so.

JOSEPH SURFACE And that he has undertaken, should it be necessary, to swear and prove, that Charles is at this time contracted by vows and honour to your ladyship, which some of his former letters to you will serve to support?

LADY SNEERWELL This, indeed, might have assisted.

JOSEPH SURFACE Come, come; it is not too late yet. (*Knocking at the door.*) But hark! this is probably my uncle, Sir Oliver: retire to that room; we'll consult further when he's gone.

LADY SNEERWELL Well, but if *he* should find you out too?

JOSEPH SURFACE Oh, I have no fear of that. Sir Peter will hold his tongue for his own credit's sake – and you may depend on it I shall soon discover Sir Oliver's weak side!

LADY SNEERWELL I have no diffidence of your abilities: only be constant to one roguery at a time.   *Exit Lady Sneerwell.*

JOSEPH SURFACE I will, I will! – So! 'tis confounded hard, after such bad fortune, to be baited by one's confederate in evil. Well, at all events, my character is so much better than Charles's, that I certainly – hey! – what – this is not Sir Oliver, but old Stanley again. Plague on't that he should return to tease me just now – I shall have Sir Oliver come and find him here – and –

Enter Sir Oliver.

Gad's life, Mr Stanley, why have you come back to plague me at this time? You must not stay now, upon my word.

SIR OLIVER Sir, I hear your uncle Oliver is expected here, and though he has been so penurious to you, I'll try what he'll do for me.

JOSEPH SURFACE Sir, 'tis impossible for you to stay now, so I must beg. – Come any other time, and I promise you, you shall be assisted.

SIR OLIVER No: Sir Oliver and I must be acquainted.

JOSEPH SURFACE Zounds, sir! then I insist on your quitting the room directly.

SIR OLIVER Nay, sir –

JOSEPH SURFACE Sir, I insist on't: – here, William! show this gentleman out. Since you compel me sir, not one moment – this is such insolence.

Enter Charles.

CHARLES SURFACE Heyday! what's the matter now? What the devil, have you got hold of my little broker here? Zounds, brother, don't hurt little Premium. What's the matter, my little fellow?

JOSEPH SURFACE So! he has been with you, too, has he?

CHARLES SURFACE To be sure he has. Why, he's as honest a little – But sure, Joseph, you have not been borrowing money too, have you?

JOSEPH SURFACE Borrowing! no! But, brother, you know we expect Sir Oliver here every –

CHARLES SURFACE O Gad, that's true! Noll mustn't find the little broker here, to be sure.

JOSEPH SURFACE Yet, Mr Stanley insists –

CHARLES SURFACE Stanley! why his name's Premium.

JOSEPH SURFACE No, no, Stanley.

CHARLES SURFACE No, no, Premium.

JOSEPH SURFACE Well, no matter which – but –

CHARLES SURFACE Aye, aye, Stanley or Premium, 'tis the same thing, as you say; for I suppose he goes by half a hundred names, besides A. B. at the coffee-house.   *Knocking.*

JOSEPH SURFACE 'Sdeath! here's Sir Oliver at the door. Now I beg, Mr Stanley –

CHARLES SURFACE Aye, aye, and I beg, Mr Premium –

SIR OLIVER Gentlemen –

JOSEPH SURFACE Sir, by heaven you shall go!

CHARLES SURFACE Aye, out with him, certainly.

SIR OLIVER This violence –

JOSEPH SURFACE 'Tis your own fault.

CHARLES SURFACE Out with him, to be sure.

Both forcing Sir Oliver out.

Enter Sir Peter and Lady Teazle, Maria, and Rowley.

SIR PETER My old friend, Sir Oliver – hey! What in the name of wonder! – here are dutiful nephews – assault their uncle at his first visit!

LADY TEAZLE Indeed, Sir Oliver, 'twas well we came in to release you.

ROWLEY Truly, it was; for I perceive, Sir Oliver, the character of old Stanley was not a protection to you.

SIR OLIVER Nor of Premium either: the necessities of the former could not extort a shilling from that benevolent gentleman; and with the other I stood a chance of faring worse than my ancestors, and being knocked down without being bid for.

JOSEPH SURFACE Charles!

CHARLES SURFACE Joseph!

JOSEPH SURFACE 'Tis now complete!

CHARLES SURFACE Very.

SIR OLIVER Sir Peter, my friend, and Rowley too, look on that elder nephew of mine. You know what he has already received from my bounty; and you also know how gladly I would have regarded half my fortune as held in trust for him: judge, then, my disappointment in discovering him to be destitute of truth, charity, and gratitude!

SIR PETER Sir Oliver, I should be more surprised at this declaration, if I had not myself found him to be selfish, treacherous, and hypocritical.

LADY TEAZLE And if the gentleman pleads not guilty to these, pray let him call *me* to his character.

SIR PETER Then, I believe, we need add no more: if he knows himself, he will consider it as the most perfect punishment that he is known to the world.

CHARLES SURFACE If they talk this way to Honesty, what will they say to me, by-and-by?   *Aside.*

SIR OLIVER As for that prodigal, his brother, there –

CHARLES SURFACE Aye, now comes my turn: the damned family pictures will ruin me.   *Aside.*

JOSEPH SURFACE Sir Oliver – uncle, will you honour me with a hearing?

CHARLES SURFACE Now, if Joseph would make one of his long speeches, I might recollect myself a little.   *Aside.*

SIR OLIVER I suppose you would undertake to justify yourself?
                                             To Joseph.

JOSEPH SURFACE I trust I could.

SIR OLIVER Pshaw! – nay, if you desert your roguery in this distress and try to be justified, you have even less principle than I thought you had. (*Turns from him in contempt.*) Well, sir! (*To Charles.*) – and you would justify yourself too, I suppose?

CHARLES SURFACE Not that I know of, Sir Oliver.

SIR OLIVER What! – Little Premium has been let too much into the secret, I suppose?

CHARLES SURFACE True, sir; but they were *family* secrets, and should not be mentioned again, you know.

ROWLEY Come, Sir Oliver, I know you cannot speak of Charles's follies with anger.

SIR OLIVER Odd's heart, no more I can; nor with gravity either. – Sir Peter, do you know the rogue bargained with me for all his ancestors; sold me judges and generals by the foot, and maiden aunts as cheap as broken china.

CHARLES SURFACE To be sure, Sir Oliver, I did make a little free with the family canvas, that's the truth on't. My ancestors may rise in judgement against me, there's no denying it; but believe me sincere when I tell you – and upon my soul I would not say so if I was not – that if I do not appear mortified at the exposure of my follies, it is because I feel at this moment the warmest satisfaction at seeing you, my liberal benefactor.

SIR OLIVER Charles, I believe you. Give me your hand again: the ill-looking little fellow over the settee has made your peace.

CHARLES SURFACE Then, sir, my gratitude to the original is still increased.

LADY TEAZLE Yet, I believe, Sir Oliver, here is one whom Charles is still more anxious to be reconciled to.

SIR OLIVER Oh, I have heard of his attachment there; and with the young lady's pardon, if I construe right – that blush –

SIR PETER Well, child, speak your sentiments.

MARIA Sir, I have little to say, but that I shall rejoice to hear that he is happy; for me, – whatever claim I had to his attention, I willingly resign to one who has a better title.

CHARLES SURFACE How, Maria!

SIR PETER Heyday! what's the mystery now? – While he appeared an incorrigible rake, you would give your hand to no one else; and now that he is likely to reform I'll warrant you won't have him.

MARIA His own heart and Lady Sneerwell know the cause.

CHARLES SURFACE Lady Sneerwell!

JOSEPH SURFACE Brother, it is with great concern I am obliged to speak on this point, but my regard to justice compels me, and Lady Sneerwell's injuries can no longer be concealed.

Goes to door.

Enter Lady Sneerwell.

ALL Lady Sneerwell!

SIR PETER So! another French milliner! Egad, he has one in every room in the house, I suppose!

LADY SNEERWELL Ungrateful Charles! Well may you be surprised, and feel for the indelicate situation your perfidy has forced me into.

CHARLES SURFACE Pray, uncle, is this another plot of yours? For, as I have life, I don't understand it.

JOSEPH SURFACE I believe, sir, there is but the evidence of one person more necessary to make it extremely clear.

SIR PETER And that person, I imagine, is Mr Snake. – Rowley, you were perfectly right to bring him with you, and pray let him appear.

ROWLEY Walk in, Mr Snake.

Enter Snake.

I thought his testimony might be wanted; however, it happens unluckily, that he comes to confront Lady Sneerwell, not to support her.

LADY SNEERWELL A villain! Treacherous to me at last! – Speak, fellow, have you too conspired against me?

SNAKE I beg your ladyship ten thousand pardons: you paid me extremely liberally for the lie in question; but I unfortunately have been offered double to speak the truth.

LADY SNEERWELL The torments of shame and disappointment on you all! *Going.*

LADY TEAZLE Hold, Lady Sneerwell – before you go, let me thank you for the trouble you and that gentleman have taken, in writing letters from me to Charles, and answering them yourself; and let me also request you to make my respects to the Scandalous College, of which you are president, and inform them, that Lady Teazle, licentiate, begs leave to return the diploma they granted her, as she leaves off practice, and kills characters no longer.

LADY SNEERWELL You too, madam – provoking – insolent – May your husband live these fifty years! *Exit.*

SIR PETER Oons! what a fury!

LADY TEAZLE A malicious creature it is.

SIR PETER Hey! not for her last wish?

LADY TEAZLE Oh, no!

SIR OLIVER Well, sir, and what have you to say now?

JOSEPH SURFACE Sir, I am so confounded, to find that Lady Sneerwell could be guilty of suborning Mr Snake in this manner, to impose on us all, that I know not what to say: however, lest her revengeful spirit should prompt her to injure my brother, I had certainly better follow her directly. *Exit.*

SIR PETER Moral to the last drop!

SIR OLIVER Ay, and marry her, Joseph, if you can. Oil and vinegar, egad! you'll do very well together.

ROWLEY I believe we have no more occasion for Mr Snake at present?

SNAKE Before I go, I beg pardon once for all, for whatever uneasiness I have been the humble instrument of causing to the parties present.

SIR PETER Well, well, you have made atonement by a good deed at last.

SNAKE But I must request of the company that it shall never be known.

SIR PETER Hey! – what the plague! – Are you ashamed of having done a right thing once in your life?

SNAKE Ah, sir, consider, – I live by the badness of my character; and, if it were once known that I had been betrayed into an honest action, I should lose every friend I have in the world.

SIR PETER Here's a precious rogue!

SIR OLIVER Well, well – we'll not traduce you by saying anything in your praise, never fear. *Exit Snake.*

LADY TEAZLE See, Sir Oliver, there needs no persuasion now to reconcile your nephew and Maria.

SIR OLIVER Aye, aye, that's as it should be, and, egad, we'll have the wedding to-morrow morning.

CHARLES SURFACE Thank you, my dear uncle.

SIR PETER What, you rogue! don't you ask the girl's consent first?

CHARLES SURFACE Oh, I have done that a long time – a minute ago – and she has looked *yes.*

MARIA For shame, Charles! – I protest, Sir Peter, there has not been a word.

SIR OLIVER Well, then, the fewer the better: may your love for each other never know abatement.

SIR PETER And may you live as happily together as Lady Teazle and I – intend to do.

CHARLES SURFACE Rowley, my old friend, I am sure you congratulate me; and I suspect that I owe you much.

SIR OLIVER You do, indeed, Charles.

ROWLEY If my efforts to serve you had not succeeded you would have been in my debt for the attempt; but deserve to be happy, and you overpay me.

SIR PETER Aye, honest Rowley always said you would reform.

CHARLES SURFACE Why, as to reforming, Sir Peter, I'll make no promises, and that I take to be a proof that I intend to set about it. But here shall be my monitor – my gentle guide. – Ah! can I leave the virtuous path those eyes illumine?

Though thou, dear maid, shouldst waive thy beauty's sway,
Thou still must rule, because I will obey:
An humble fugitive from Folly view,
No sanctuary hear but Love (*to the audience*) and you:
You can, indeed, each anxious fear remove,
For even Scandal dies if you approve.

Epilogue

BY MR COLMAN

Spoken by Mrs Abington in the character of Lady Teazle.

I, who was late so volatile and gay,
Like a trade wind must now blow all one way,
Bend all my cares, my studies, and my vows,
To one dull rusty weathercock – my spouse!
So wills our virtuous bard – the motley Bayes
Of crying epilogues and laughing plays!
Old bachelors, who marry smart young wives,
Learn from our play to regulate your lives:
Each bring his dear to town, all faults upon her –
London will prove the very source of honour.
Plung'd fairly in, like a cold bath it serves,
When principles relax, – to brace the nerves:
Such is my case – and yet I must deplore
That the gay dream of dissipation's o'er:
And say, ye fair, was ever lively wife,
Born with a genius for the highest life,
Like me untimely blasted in her bloom,
Like me condemn'd to such a dismal doom?
Save money – when I just knew how to *waste* it!
Leave London – just as I began to taste it!

Must I then watch the early-crowing cock,
The melancholy ticking of a clock;
In a lone rustic hall for ever pounded.
With dogs, cats, rats, and squalling brats surrounded?
With humble curate can I now retire
(While good Sir Peter boozes with the squire),
And at backgammon mortify my soul,

That pants for loo, or flutters at a vole.
Seven's the main! Dear sound! that must expire,
Lost at hot cockles round a Christmas fire;
The transient hour of fashion too soon spent,
Farewell the tranquil mind, farewell content!
Farewell the *plumèd* head, the cushion'd *tête*,
That takes the cushion from its proper seat!
That spirit-stirring drum! – card-drums I mean,
Spadille – odd trick – pam – basto – king and queen!
And you, ye knockers, that, with brazen throat,
The welcome visitors' approach denote;
Farewell! – all quality of high renown,
Pride, pomp, and circumstance of glorious Town!
Farewell! your revels I partake no more,
And Lady Teazle's occupation's o'er!
And this I told our bard; he smiled, and said 'twas clear,
I ought to play deep tragedy next year.
Meanwhile he drew wise morals from his play,
And in these solemn periods stalk'd away:
'Blest were the fair like you; her faults who stopt,
And closed her follies when the curtain dropt!
No more in vice or error to engage,
Or play the fool at large on life's great stage.'

SUGGESTIONS FOR FURTHER READING

The standard historical account of English dramatic literature in the eighteenth century is: Allardyce Nicoll, *A History of English Drama 1660–1900*, volume 2, *Early Eighteenth Century Drama*; volume 3, *Late Eighteenth Century Drama* (Cambridge: Cambridge University Press, 1952).

A less comprehensive but more up-to-date account can be found in the following two volumes: John Loftis, Richard Southern, Marion Jones and Arthur H. Scouten, *The Revels History of Drama in English*, volume 5, *1660–1750* (London: Methuen, 1976); Michael R. Booth, Richard Southern, Frederick and Lise-Lone Marker and Robertson Davies, *The Revels History of Drama in English*, volume 6, *1750–1880* (London: Methuen, 1975).

A concise but illuminating survey is available in the relevant volumes of *The Oxford History of English Literature*: Bonamy Dobrée, *English Literature in the Early Eighteenth Century, 1700–1740* (Oxford: Clarendon Press, 1959); John Butt and Geoffrey Carnall, *The Mid-Eighteenth Century* (Oxford: Clarendon Press, 1979).

Introductory studies of a general kind include: Frederick S. Boas, *An Introduction to Eighteenth-Century Drama, 1700–1780* (Oxford: Clarendon Press, 1953); Arthur H. Scouten and others, *Restoration and Eighteenth-Century Drama* (London: Macmillan, 1980).

Informative studies of important aspects of the subject include: Ian Donaldson, *The World Upside-Down: Comedy from Jonson to Fielding* (Oxford: Clarendon Press, 1970); Robert D. Hume, *The Rakish Stage: Studies in English Drama 1660–1800* (Carbondale: Southern Illinois University Press, 1983); Jacqueline Pearson, *The Prostituted Muse: Images of Women and Women Dramatists 1642–1737* (Hemel Hempstead: Harvester Wheatsheat, 1988); John Loftis, *Comedy and Society from Congreve to Fielding* (Stanford: Stanford University Press, 1959); Frederick W. Bateson, *English Comic Drama 1700–1750* (Oxford: Clarendon Press, 1929); John Loftis, *The Politics of Drama in Augustan England* (Oxford: Clarendon Press, 1963); Jean B. Kern, *Dramatic Satire in the Age of Walpole* (Ames: Iowa State University Press, 1976); Leo Hughes, *A Century of English Farce* (Princeton: Princeton University Press, 1956); Arthur Sherbo, *English Sentimental Drama* (East Lansing: Michigan State University Press, 1957); Frank H. Ellis, *Sentimental Comedy: Theory and Practice* (Cambridge: Cambridge University Press, 1991); Richard Bevis, *The Laughing Tradition: Stage Comedy in Garrick's Day* (London: George Prior, 1981).

The most comprehensive work on the acting profession in Restoration and eighteenth-century England is: Philip H. Highfill Jr., Kalman A. Burnim, and Edward A. Langhans, *A Biographical Dictionary of Actors, Actresses, Musicians, Dancers, Managers and Other Stage Personnel in London, 1660–1800* (Carbondale: Southern Illinois University Press, 16 volumes, 1973–93).

The most comprehensive source of information about productions in the London theatres is: William Van Lennep, general editor, *The London Stage 1660–1800* (Carbondale: Southern Illinois University Press, 11 volumes, 1965–1968).

A more concise and accessible account of the same subject is: Robert D. Hume, editor, *The London Theatre World 1660–1800* (Carbondale: Southern Illinois University Press, 1980).

A substantial and well-edited collection of documents relevant to theatrical history is: David Thomas, editor, *Theatre in Europe, A Documentary History: Restoration and Georgian England, 1660–1788* (Cambridge: Cambridge University Press, 1989).

A detailed and well-illustrated history of the two major theatrical buildings can be found in: *Survey of London*, volume 35: *The Theatre Royal Drury Lane and the Royal Opera House Covent Garden* (London: Athlone Press for the Greater London Council, 1970).

A valuable and readable contemporary account of theatrical history from 1690 to 1740 is available in: Colley Cibber, *An Apology for the Life of Colley Cibber, with an Historical View of the Stage during His Own Time*, edited by B. R. S. Fone (Ann Arbor: University of Michigan Press, 1968).

A witty and enlightening survey of actors and acting circa 1760 is offered in: Charles Churchill, *The Rosciad*, in *The Poetical Works*, edited by Douglas Grant (Oxford: Clarendon Press, 1956).

Other informative studies of theatrical history include: Kenneth Richards and Peter Thomson, editors, *The Eighteenth-Century English Stage* (London: Methuen, 1972); Allardyce Nicoll, *The Garrick Stage: Theatres and Audience in the Eighteenth Century* (Manchester: Manchester University Press, 1980); Cecil Price, *Theatre in the Age of Garrick* (Oxford: Basil Blackwell, 1973); Carola Oman, *David Garrick* (London: Hodder & Stoughton, 1958); Shirley Strum Kenny, editor, *British Theatre and the Other Arts, 1660–1800* (Washington: The Folger Shakespeare Library, 1984).

The following items are relevant to the study of Addison: Joseph Addison, *The Dramatic Works* (Glasgow: R. Urie, 1750); *The Spectator*, edited by Donald F. Bond (Oxford: Clarendon Press, 5 volumes, 1965); Peter Smithers, *The Life of Joseph Addison* (London: Clarendon Press, 1968); John Dennis, *Remarks upon Cato: A Tragedy*, in *The Critical Works* edited by Edward Niles Hooker (Baltimore, 2 volumes, 1939); John Loftis, 'The London Theatres in Early Eighteenth-Century Politics', *Huntington Library Quarterly* volume 18, 1955; M. M. Kelsall, 'The Meaning of Addison's *Cato*', *Review of English Studies*, new series, volume 17, 1966; F. M. Little, 'Addison's *Cato* in the Colonies', *William and Mary Quarterly* volume 23, 1966.

The following items are relevant to the study of Steele: Richard Steele, *The Plays*, edited by Shirley Strum Kenny (Oxford: Clarendon Press, 1971); *The Tatler*, edited by Donald F. Bond (Oxford: Clarendon Press, 3 volumes, 1987); Richard Steele, *The Theatre 1720*, edited by John Loftis (Oxford: Clarendon Press, 1962); John Dennis, *Remarks on a Play, Call'd, The Conscious Lovers, a Comedy*, in *The Critical Works*, edited by Edward Niles Hooker (Baltimore, 2 volumes, 1939); Calhoun

Winton, *Captain Steele: The Early Career of Richard Steele* (Baltimore: Johns Hopkins Press, 1964); Calhoun Winton, *Sir Richard Steele M.P.: The Later Career* (Baltimore: Johns Hopkins Press, 1970); John Loftis, *Steele at Drury Lane* (Berkeley: University of California Press, 1952).

The following items are relevant to the study of Gay: John Gay, *Dramatic Works*, edited by John Fuller (Oxford: Clarendon Press, 2 volumes, 1983); John Gay, *Poetry and Prose*, edited by Vinton A. Dearing (Oxford: Clarendon Press, 2 volumes, 1974); William Eben Schultz, *Gay's Beggar's Opera, Its Content, History and Influence* (New Haven: Yale University Press, 1923); William Empson, *Some Versions of Pastoral* (London: Chatto & Windus, 1935); Sven M. Armens, *John Gay, Social Critic* (New York: King's Crown Press, 1954); J. J. Sherwin, 'The World Is Mean and Man Uncouth', *Virginia Quarterly Review* volume 35, 1959; Patricia Meyer Spacks, *John Gay* (New York: Twayne, 1965); David Nokes, *John Gay: A Profession of Friendship* (Oxford: Oxford University Press, 1995).

The following items are relevant to the study of Fielding: Henry Fielding, *The Works*, edited by Arthur Murphy (London: J. Johnson and others, 10 volumes, 1806); Henry Fielding, *Tom Thumb and The Tragedy of Tragedies*, edited by L. J. Morrissey (Edinburgh: Oliver & Boyd, 1970); Pat Rogers, *Henry Fielding: A Biography* (London: Paul Elek, 1979); Martin C. Battestin, *Henry Fielding: A Life* (London: Routledge, 1989); Donald Thomas, *Henry Fielding* (London: Weidenfeld & Nicolson, 1990); Robert D. Hume, *Henry Fielding and the London Theatre, 1728–1737* (Oxford: Clarendon Press, 1988); Albert J. Rivero, *The Plays of Henry Fielding: A Critical Study of His Dramatic Career* (Charlottesville: University Press of Virginia, 1989).

The following items are relevant to the study of Lillo: George Lillo, *Dramatic Works*, edited by James L. Steffenson and Richard Noble (Oxford: Clarendon Press, 1993); George Lillo, *The London Merchant*, edited by William H. McBurney (London: Edward Arnold, 1965); George Lillo, *Fatal Curiosity*, edited by William H. McBurney (London: Edward Arnold, 1967); Cleanth Brooks and Robert B. Heilman, editors, *Understanding Drama: Twelve Plays* (London: Harrap, 1947); L. M.

Prince, 'George Barnwell Abroad', *Comparative Literature* volume 2, 1950; J. Hamard, 'Le drame bourgeois: l'influence de Lillo', *Revue de littérature comparée* volume 39, 1965; William H. McBurney, 'What Lillo Read: A Speculation', *Huntington Library Quarterly* volume 29, 1966.

The following items are relevant to the study of Goldsmith: Oliver Goldsmith, *Collected Works*, edited by Arthur Friedman (Oxford: Clarendon Press, 5 volumes, 1966); Oliver Goldsmith, *Poems and Plays*, edited by T. Davies (London: Dent, 1990); Ralph M. Wardle, *Oliver Goldsmith* (Lawrence: University of Kansas Press, 1957); Ricardo Quintana, *Oliver Goldsmith: A Georgian Study* (London: Weidenfeld & Nicolson, 1969); John Ginger, *The Notable Man: The Life and Times of Oliver Goldsmith* (London: Hamish Hamilton, 1977); Andrew Swarbrick, editor, *The Art of Oliver Goldsmith* (London: Vision Press, 1984); Elmar Lehmann, '*Not Merely Sentimental*': *Studien zu Goldsmiths Komödien* (Munich: Wilhelm Fink, 1974).

The following items are relevant to the study of Sheridan: Richard Brinsley Sheridan, *The Dramatic Works*, edited by Cecil Price (Oxford: Clarendon Press, 2 volumes, 1973); R. Crompton Rhodes, *Harlequin Sheridan: The Man and the Legends* (Oxford: Basil Blackwell, 1933); Madeleine Bingham, *Sheridan: The Track of a Comet* (London: Allen and Unwin, 1972); Stephen Ayling, *A Portrait of Sheridan* (London: Constable, 1985); James Morwood, *The Life and Works of Richard Brinsley Sheridan* (Edinburgh: Scottish Academic Press, 1985); John Loftis, *Sheridan and the Drama of Georgian England* (Oxford: Basil Blackwell, 1976); Mark S. Auburn, *Sheridan's Comedies: The Contexts and Achievements* (Lincoln: University of Nebraska Press, 1977).

NOTES

_____

Cato

p. 1 l.1 CATO: the younger Cato (95–46 B.C.) resisted the attacks of Julius Cæsar and his associates on the Roman Republic. After Cæsar's victory Cato withdrew to Utica in North Africa, where he committed suicide rather than risk the consequences of capture. His stoic and constitutional principles made him a hero to later critics of imperial rule, including the poet Lucan.

p. 3 l.2 MR POPE: Alexander Pope (1688–1744) was the greatest English poet of the eighteenth century. In 1713 his political affiliations, unlike Addison's, were with the Tory régime rather than the Whig opposition.

p. 3 l.3 _Mr Wilks_: Robert Wilks, who acted Juba, was celebrated principally for his performances as 'a gay, splendid, generous, easie, fine young Gentleman'.

p. 3 l.21 Plato: the Greek philosopher, whose arguments for the immortality of the soul Cato ponders in Act V Scene 1.

p. 3 l.26 little Senate: Pope later adapted this phrase for his attack on Addison in lines 193–214 of _An Epistle to Dr Arbuthnot_.

p. 3 l.30 proud Cæsar: after his return to Rome, Cæsar rode in four triumphal processions, the last of which celebrated his victory in Africa. According to Appian (II: 101), the crowds were restrained by fear but groaned when they saw a picture of Cato 'torn open by himself like a wild beast'.

p. 4 l.11 the first famed Cato: the elder Cato (234–149 B.C.) was the great-grandfather of the play's central character. As Censor in 184 B.C. he resisted the Greek influence on Latin culture and sought to re-establish traditional Roman values.

p. 4 l.14 French translation: the many English versions of French plays which were performed in the London theatres around this time include Sir John Vanbrugh's *The Confederacy* (1705), which was based on Dancourt's *Les Bourgeoises à la mode*, Colley Cibber's *Ximena* (1712), which was based on Corneille's *Le Cid*, and Ambrose Philips' *The Distressed Mother* (1712), which was based on Racine's *Andromaque*. In the preface to *A Bold Stroke for a Wife* (1718), Susannah Centlivre proclaimed her originality:

> Our plot is new, and regularly clear,
> And not one single Tittle from *Molière*.

p. 4 l.14   Italian song: Italian opera was introduced on to the English stage in 1705, and its popularity thereafter aroused indignant protests from John Dennis and others. The most celebrated composers were the Italian Marcantonio Buononcini and the German Georg Friedrich Händel.

p. 5 l.3   Mr Booth: Barton Booth, who acted Cato, later became one of the three actor-managers of Drury Lane.

p. 5 l.6   JUBA: Juba, the son of Hiempsal II of Numidia, fought with Pompey against Cæsar and later joined forces with Cato and Metellus Scipio. He died in 46 B.C. in a suicide pact with Marcus Petreius. His son, also named Juba, was an infant in 46 B.C. and was subsequently brought up in Italy. Addison envisages the younger Juba as adult at the time of Cato's death.

p. 5 l.6   *Numidia*: the north-eastern portion of modern Algeria, which became a Roman province in 46 B.C.

p. 5 l.6   Mr Wilks: see note on p. 3 l.3 above.

p. 5 l.7   SYPHAX: the historical Syphax was a Numidian chief who fought against Rome in the second Punic War.

p. 5 l.7   Mr Cibber: Colley Cibber (1671–1747) was a talented actor, a competent dramatist, a bad poet, and the dominant figure among the actor-managers of Drury Lane. He published an illuminating autobiography in 1740, and was ridiculed by Pope in the final version of *The Dunciad*.

p. 5 l.13   Mrs Oldfield: Anne Oldfield took leading roles in the comedies of George Farquhar, and was the principal actress in the Drury Lane company during its heyday under the management of Cibber, Wilks, and Booth.

p. 5 l.16   Utica: a coastal town thirty miles from Carthage, best known as the scene of Cato's death.

p. 7 l.22   Pharsalia: the decisive battle of the war between Pompey and Cæsar was fought near the town of Pharsalus in Thessaly in 48 B.C. Book VII of Lucan's historical epic, sometimes designated *Pharsalia*, gives a lurid description of the bloodshed, and provides a model for Addison's anti-Cæsarian rhetoric.

p. 10 l.7   *solus*: alone.

p. 11 l.17   *Solus*: alone.

p. 13 l.13   *Solus*: alone.

p. 14 l.7   Zama: a town in North Africa, celebrated as the site of the elder Scipio's victory over Hannibal. Addison treats it as the capital of Numidia.

p. 15 l.24   stoicism: a major philosophical tradition of ancient Greece, whose theories of knowledge and virtue were taken up in republican Rome by the younger Cato and in imperial Rome by the younger Seneca.

p. 15 l.27   a slave's hand: See note on p. 5 l.6 above. Petreius was a Roman citizen, but not a member of the patrician élite.

p. 18 l.6   the gods and Cato: a pious Addisonian re-fashioning of Lucan's more incisive statement that 'the victorious cause pleased the gods, but the defeated cause pleased Cato'.

p. 21 l.3   *The Senate*: Cato's 'little Senate', the surviving emblem of republican legitimacy, is meeting not in Rome but in Utica.

p. 21 l.18   the whole Nile: after his victory at Pharsalus, Cæsar followed Pompey to Egypt, where he deposed Ptolemy XIII and established Cleopatra as queen.

p. 21 l.19   Juba's overthrow: the reference is to the elder Juba. See note on p. 5 l.6.

p. 21 l.20   Scipio's death: the reference here is to Metellus Scipio, who fought against Cæsar at Pharsalus and was subsequently killed in North Africa.

p. 22 l.10   corps: dead bodies.

p. 22 l.11   Thessaly: the district of northern Greece in which the battle of Pharsalus was fought.

p. 22 l.17   Pompey: Gnaeus Pompeius (106–48 B.C.), Cæsar's opponent in the civil war of 50–48 B.C.

p. 22 l.18   Scipio's ghost: see note on p. 21 l.20 above.

p. 22 l.33   Scythia: this region between the Carpathians and the Don lay outside the boundaries of the Empire, but was invaded by Pompey in 66–64 B.C.

p. 25 l.14   the Capitol: the Capitoline Hill in Rome was in reality a citadel and a religious centre, but Addison envisages it as the meeting-place of the Senate.

p. 28 l.7   Hannibal: the Carthaginian leader who defeated the Romans at Cannae in 216 B.C., but was defeated by the elder Scipio Africanus at Zama in 202 B.C. He spent his last years in exile, seeking support from enemies of Rome in Syria and Asia Minor.

p. 30 l.27   Your Scipios: the celebrated men of that name were the elder Scipio Africanus, who defeated Hannibal at Zama, and the younger Scipio Africanus, who captured and destroyed Carthage in 146 B.C.

p. 30 l.29   Sabines: according to legend, the male founders of Rome saved their race from extinction by abducting women from the nearby territory of the Sabini.

p. 32 l.17   Punic: Numidia was close to Carthage, the Phoenician or Punic colony which had been Rome's chief enemy in the western Mediterranean.

p. 32 l.36   *Solus*: alone.

p. 33 l.12   Atlas: the highest peak of the Atlas Mountains, associated with the Titan who held up the sky.

p. 45 l.1   Pluto, seized of Proserpine: in Book V of the *Metamorphoses* Ovid relates how Proserpina (Greek Persephone) was carried off by Pluto (Greek Dis) and followed into the Underworld by Ceres (Greek Demeter).

p. 49 l.15   Elysium: the 'happy fields' which are the dwelling-place of the virtuous dead.

p. 53 l.23   **the self-devoted Decii:** members of this family over three generations were said to have ensured the success of Roman armies by 'devoting' themselves to the gods of the Underworld and then charging the enemy lines.

p. 53 l.24   **the Fabii:** a family who played a leading role in the military campaigns of the Roman Republic, and especially in the Second Punic War of 218–201 B.C.

p. 53 l.24   **the great Scipios:** see note on p. 30 l.27 above.

p. 54 l.11   **Thy virtues ... Cato's friend:** the younger Juba was educated in Italy, and ruled much of North Africa under Augustus. He wrote many books, and introduced Graeco-Roman culture into his kingdom.

p. 54 l.20   **the Sabine field:** the writings of the elder Cato include a treatise on agriculture, but it was Horace (65–8 B.C.) who established the literary tradition of the 'Sabine farm' as a place of civilised retirement.

p. 54 l.21   **the great Censor:** see notes on p. 4 l.11 and p. 54 l.20 above.

p. 56 l.3   *solus*: alone.

p. 56 l.6   **Plato:** the popularity of this scene caused Bernard Lintot to publish in 1713 a translation of the *Phaedo* by Lewis Theobald under the title *Plato's Dialogue of the Immortality of the Soul*.

p 60 1.13   **Pompey's son:** probably Sextus Pompeius, the younger son of Cæsar's opponent, who was with his father in Egypt and later raised forces against Cæsar in Spain.

p. 61 l.38   **And robs ... life:** this line is said to have been written by Pope to replace Addison's final line

And oh! 'twas this that ended Cato's life.

p. 62 l.2   **DR GARTH:** the Whig poet and physician Sir Samuel Garth published a mock-epic entitled *The Dispensary* in 1699, and made a large contribution to the collaborative translation of Ovid's *Metamorphoses* which appeared in 1717.

p. 62 l.3   *Mrs Porter*: Mary Porter, who acted Lucia, was an established member of the Drury Lane company.

p. 62 l.28   **the Ring:** a promenade in Hyde Park.

The Conscious Lovers

p. 66 l.1   To the King: Steele, as a loyal supporter of the House of Hanover, dedicates his most ambitious play to George I.

p. 66 l.19   Our King ... his Displeasure: this passage alludes to a Jacobite plot which was discovered in April 1722 and led to arrests and trials over the following months.

p. 68 l.21   *Goths* and *Vandals*: Steele implies that duelling, like unruly behaviour in the theatre, is a habit worthy of the barbarians who destroyed the Roman Empire.

p. 69 l.10   Sig. *Carbonelli*: a celebrated Italian violinist.

p. 69 l.26   *Terence*: Publius Terentius Afer (?195–159 B.C.), the Latin dramatist whose *Andria* is the principal source for Steele's play.

p. 69 l.27   Mr *Cibber*: see note on p. 5 l.7 above.

p. 69 l.34   *Terence*'s celebrated Funeral: see note on p. 76 l.31 below.

p. 71 l.2   MR WELSTED: Leonard Welsted (1688–1747), an associate of Addison and Steele, whose poetry is ridiculed in *The Dunciad* Book III lines 169–72.

p. 71 l.3   *Mr Wilks*: see note on p. 3 l.3 above.

p. 71 l.11   Pinkey's face: the comic actor William Penkethman was celebrated by Steele in *Spectator* 370 for his ability to 'represent a Sense of Pleasure and Pain at the same time'.

p. 71 l.29   a Smithfield show: an entertainment typical of Bartholomew Fair, which was held in the Smithfield district near the church of St Bartholomew the Great.

p. 73 l.5   Mr Booth: see note on p. 5 l.3 above.

p. 73 l.6   Mr Wilks: see note on p. 3 l.3 above.

p. 73 l.9   Mr Cibber: see note on p. 5 l.7 above.

p. 73 l.10   Mr Theo. Cibber: see note on p. 265 l.2 below.

p. 73 l.14   Mrs Oldfield: see note on p. 5 l.13 above.

p. 75 l.3   SCENE I: this scene between Sir John Bevil and Humphrey closely follows the opening dialogue between Simo and Sosia in the *Andria*.

p. 76 l.31 **at the masquerade:** in the *Andria* this incident took place at a funeral. The change was suggested by Cibber, and Steele made it reluctantly.

p. 77 l.5 **Cymon in the Fable:** the principal character of 'Cymon and Iphigenia', an adaptation from Boccaccio published in John Dryden's *Fables* (1700).

p. 79 l.16 **shams:** false shirt-fronts.

p. 79 l.18 **frock:** frock-coat.

p. 80 l.2 **the Painted Chamber:** a room in Parliament where waiting servants addressed one another by the names of their masters.

p. 80 l.4 **the Court of Requests:** the building used as meeting-place for the House of Lords.

p. 80 l.6 ***nemine contradicente*:** with no one speaking against it.

p. 80 l.24 **Ridotto's:** musical entertainments introduced in 1722 at the Opera House in the Haymarket.

p. 80 l.25 **Bellsize:** an estate in the Hampstead area, used in summer for public entertainments.

p. 82 l.3 **twire:** throw concealed glances.

p. 83 l.2 **Crispo:** the principal character of an opera composed by Buononcini in 1721.

p. 83 l.5 *Se vedette*: the first words of an aria in Buononcini's *Crispo*, part of which may be translated as follows: 'If you see/ My Thoughts/ Ye just gods, defend/ The Innocence of my Heart.'

p. 84 l.17 **after death:** Joseph Addison died in 1719.

p. 84 l.18 **This charming vision of Mirza!:** an oriental tale by Addison, published in *Spectator* 159.

p. 88 l.24 **Toulon:** a seaport and naval base in southern France.

p. 100 l.23 **Crispo:** see note on p. 83 l.2 above.

p. 100 l.23 **Griselda:** another opera composed by Buononcini in 1721.

p. 100 l.32 *dolce sogno*: 'Sweet Sleep', an aria sung by the heroine in *Griselda*.

p. 101 l.7   Otway: Thomas Otway (1652–85), author of *The Orphan* and *Venice Preserved*.

p. 106 l.22   You took ... my undoing: Steele had already described such an incident in *Guardian* 87.

p. 106 l.29   Pyramus and Thisbe: the Babylonian lovers whose story is told by Ovid in Book IV of the *Metamorphoses*.

p. 108 l.16   liquorish: lecherous.

p. 111 l.24   Lycurgus: the reference is to the semi-legendary founder of the Spartan constitution, not to the Athenian statesman of the fourth century B.C.

p. 111 l.25   Lacedæmonians: Spartans.

p. 111 l.31   Sparta: city-state in southern Greece, noted for the severity of its military training and the austerity of its social customs.

p. 111 l.40   I have observ'd her: a letter published in the *St James's Journal* in November 1722 complained that Cimberton's conversation offended against the rules which Steele himself had prescribed for 'the Entertainment of a polite Audience'. The complaint presumably related to this scene, which seems to have been less decorous in the first acting version than it is in the published text.

p. 114 l.13   *Bramble and Target*: the *Freeholder's Journal* declared in November 1722 that these two lawyers were 'not to be match'd in all the Inns, or the Courts at Westminster'.

p. 114 l.32   messuage: house, outbuildings and adjacent lands.

p. 115 l.37   Westminster: trials were held in Westminster Hall.

p. 120 l.9   a tyrant custom: Steele denounced duelling in similar terms in *Spectator* 84 and 97.

p. 123 l.20   cocker: breeder of fighting-cocks.

p. 124 l.41   *incognita*: unidentified woman.

p. 125 l.9   John Dryden: the couplet occurs both in Dryden's prologue for Thomas Southerne's *The Disappointment* (1684) and in his epilogue for Sir John Vanbrugh's *The Pilgrim* (1700).

p. 136 l.21   commode: accommodating.

p. 143 l.2   MR WELSTED: see note on p. 71 l.2 above. When the play was published, this epilogue was substituted for that which had been spoken on the first night.

The Beggar's Opera

p. 146 l.19 Miss Fenton: Lavinia Fenton's performance as Polly Peachum was received with such enthusiasm that her fame almost surpassed that of the opera itself. She later married the Duke of Bolton.

p. 147 l.6 St Giles's: the parish of St Giles-in-the-Fields, which was notorious as a haunt of beggars and prostitutes.

p. 147 l.23 a nice impartiality between our two ladies: this alludes to the rivalry between the opera-singers Faustina Bordoni and Francesca Cuzzoni.

p. 149 l.7 *Through all the employments of life*: an early tradition ascribes this lyric to Jonathan Swift.

p. 149 l.16 a double capacity: Peachum, like the master-criminal Jonathan Wild who was condemned to death in 1725, collects rewards for the recovery of 'lost' property which his agents have stolen. When an agent's ability to supply goods begins to decline, Peachum informs against him and thus collects another reward under the Highwayman Act of 1692.

p. 150 l.24 The bonny grey-eyed morn: the lyric familiar to Gay's audience can be found in Thomas Durfey's *Wit and Mirth or Pills to Purge Melancholy* (III 234) under the heading 'A Song'. The singer recounts how Jockey seduced her not with money but with 'pretty tales of love'.

p. 150 l.33 Newgate: the main prison in the City of London from the thirteenth century to the nineteenth.

p. 151 l.31 Robin of Bagshot: this name and the four that follow invite the audience to see Sir Robert Walpole as a subordinate figure in a gang of highwaymen. Bagshot was a heath where highwaymen operated.

p. 152 l.9 Cold and raw: the original lyric is in *Pills to Purge Melancholy* (II 167) under the title 'The Farmer's Daughter'. The singer recalls how he met a farmer's daughter who was going to town to sell her barley. He offered her £20 for the barley, and another £20 if she would spend the night with him. She rejected both offers, telling him to keep his 'Purse' for his 'poor Spouse at home'. In the lyric which Mrs Peachum sings to the same tune, rural virtue and agricultural imagery have been replaced with mythological imagery and urban corruption.

p. 152 l.10 Venus's girdle: according to Homer (*Iliad* XIV), anyone who wore this girdle immediately became desirable.

p. 152 l.17 Adonis: a young man who was loved by Venus and killed by a wild boar.

p. 153 l.3 quadrille: a fashionable card-game.

p. 153 l.5 Marybone: a district frequented by gamblers.

p. 153 l.26 Why is your faithful slave disdained ?: the original lyric is in *Pills to Purge Melancholy* (III 211) under the heading 'A Song'. Its central stanza reads:

> When I behold your Lips, your Eyes,
> Your snowy breasts that fall and rise,
>   Fanning my raging Flame;
> That Shape so made to be imbrac't,
> What would I give I might but taste
>   Of what I dare not name!

Mrs Peachum's version replaces eroticism with worldly wisdom.

p. 153 l.34 a Temple coffee-house: the Temple is a centre for legal education between the Strand and the Thames.

p. 154 l.18 cambric: cloth from Cambrai in Flanders.

p. 154 l.28 Of all the simple things we do: the original lyric, in which a married man laments his situation, appears in *Pills to Purge Melancholy* (I 250) as 'The Mouse Trap: Made to a Comical Tune in *The Country Wake*'.

p. 155 l.9 at the opera: outside the Opera House in the Haymarket.

p. 155 l.14 Redriff: Rotherhithe, a district on the south bank of the Thames below London Bridge.

p. 155 l.24 Hockley-in-the-Hole: a centre for bull and bear baiting near Clerkenwell Green. A quarter-staff contest there was described by Steele in *Spectator* 436.

p. 155 l.28 the Old Bailey: the meeting-place of the Central Criminal Court.

p. 155 l.33 the ordinary's paper: the ordinary is the Newgate chaplain. The reference is probably not to a text connected with benefit of clergy, but rather to the Newgate biographies allegedly based on the chaplain's record of criminals' confessions.

p. 156 l.31 *Covent Garden*: a district noted at this date both for its vegetable market and for its prostitutes.

p. 157 l.13 *As men should serve a cowcumber*: eighteenth-century physicians were said to recommend that a cucumber should be carefully sliced and dressed, and then thrown away.

p. 159 l.5 O Jenny, O Jenny, where hast thou been?: the original lyric is in *Pills to Purge Melancholy* (I 169) under the title 'The Willoughby Whim: A Scotch Song in a Dialogue between Two Sisters'.

p. 160 l.8 Drury Lane: the major centre for prostitution, and the site of London's most prestigious theatre.

p. 160 l.11 Tunbridge: Tunbridge Wells, a fashionable spa south-east of London, was the subject of a poem by Rochester and a play by Rawlins.

p. 160 l.33 'A soldier and a sailor': the original lyric, which is in *Pills to Purge Melancholy* (III 221) under the heading 'A Song', declares that the sailor surpasses the soldier, the tailor and the tinker in the art of seduction. Similarly, Peachum's song declares that the lawyer surpasses the fox, the whore, the daughter, the wife and the thief in the art of robbery.

p. 161 l.12 Nimming: thieving.

p. 162 l.17 'Now ponder well, ye parents dear': the tune identified by this opening line is that of the popular ballad about the children in the wood, which Addison praised in *Spectator* 85 as 'a plain simple Copy of Nature'. The text was later included in Thomas Percy's *Reliques of Ancient English Poetry* (1765), where it was identified as a ballad version of a tragedy published in 1601. Lavinia Fenton's rendering of Gay's lyric is said to have been the turning-point in the reception of *The Beggar's Opera* on its first performance: the audience was 'much affected' by her 'innocent looks' when she came to the 'painful and ridiculous image' of the last two lines.

p. 162 l.27 'Le printemps rappelle aux armes': 'Spring recalls men to battle.' The original lyric is in *Pills to Purge Melancholy* (I 189) under the heading 'Chanson en Francois'. It is followed by an English translation, which begins: 'Spring invites, the Troops are going, let Tears be flowing.' In the following lines the singer begs Flora and Zephyrus not to return, because the end of winter will mean the renewal of military activity and the departure of her lover.

p. 163 l.34 Holborn: the route from Newgate to the place of execution at Tyburn passed through Holborn.

p. 164 l.1 Jack Ketch: a traditional name for the hangman.

p. 164 l.15 'Pretty parrot, say': the original lyric is in *Pills to Purge Melancholy* (V 280) under the heading 'A New Song: Translated from the French'. Whereas Macheath's questions are addressed to Polly and answered in her professions of love, the man's questions in the original were answered by an observant parrot who reported the woman's infidelity.

p. 164 l.33 'Pray, fair one, be kind': the reference is to a ditty sung by Captain Plume in George Farquhar's comedy *The Recruiting Officer* (1706). Plume's last verse sounds a minatory note which is absent from Macheath's song:

> I still will adore
> And love more and more,
> But by Jove, if you chance to prove cruel,
> I'll get me a miss
> That freely will kiss,
> Though I afterwards drink water gruel.

p. 165 l.12 'Over the hills, and far away': the original is in *Pills to Purge Melancholy* (V 317) under the title 'Jockey's Lamentation'. The second verse reads:

> *Jockey* was a bonny Lad,
>   As e'er was born in *Scotland* fair;
> But now poor *Jockey* is run mad,
>   For *Jenny* causes his Despair;
> *Jockey* was a Piper's Son,
>   And fell in Love while he was young:
> But all the Tunes that he could play,
>   Was, *O'er the Hills, and far away*,
> And, *'Tis o'er the Hills and far away*,
> *'Tis o'er the Hills and far away*,

> 'Tis o'er the Hills and far away,
> The Wind has blown my Plad away.

In *The Recruiting Officer* both Captain Plume and Sergeant Kite occasionally sing verses of another lyric to the same tune, and a full text of that lyric is printed in *Pills to Purge Melancholy* (V 319) under the title 'The Recruiting Officer: Or, The Merry Volunteers: Being an Excellent New Copy of Verses upon Raising Recruits'. There are allusions to these songs in Gay's eclogue-sequence *The Shepherd's Week* (1714) and his tragi-comi-pastoral farce *The What D'Ye Call It* (1715). A text obviously derived from them can be found on page 408 of *The Oxford Dictionary of Nursery Rhymes*.

p. 167 l.13 otamies: when bodies taken from the gallows had been used for anatomy lessons, their 'otamies' or skeletons were put on display. See Hogarth's *The Four Stages of Cruelty*.

p. 168 l.6 Fill ev'ry glass: the original is in *Pills to Purge Melancholy* (I 180 and 182) under the headings 'A Drinking Song, in Praise of our Three fam'd Generals' and 'Translated from the French'. The French version begins:

> Que chacun remplisse son verre,
> Pour boire a nos trois Generaux.

The English version begins:

> Fill ev'ry Glass, and recommend 'em,
> We'll drink our three Generals' Healths at large.

The reference is to the War of the Spanish Succession, and the three Generals are Marlborough, Eugene and Auverquerque. The song also celebrates Queen Anne and mocks the Young Pretender.

p. 169 l.20 Moorfields: a district frequented by highwaymen and other criminals.

p. 169 l.23 March in Rinaldo: Handel's *Rinaldo* had its first performance at the Haymarket in 1711. In Gay's version the highwaymen not only prepare for action like 'great heroes' but also plan like alchemists to turn the lead of their bullets into the gold of their booty.

p. 170 l.6 Would you have a young virgin: the original is in *Pills to Purge Melancholy* (I 133) under the heading 'A Song in the First Act of *The Modern Prophets*. Sung by Mr. Pack'. The first verse reads:

> Would ye have a young Virgin of fifteen Years,
> You must tickle her Fancy with sweets and dears,
> Ever toying, and playing, and sweetly, sweetly,
> Sing a Love Sonnet, and charm her Ears:
> Wittily, prettily talk her down,
> Chase her, and praise her, if fair or brown,
> > Sooth her, and smooth her,
> > And teaze her, and please her,
> And touch but her Smicket, and all's your own.

The second and third verses give similar advice on the best approaches to 'a Widow well known in a Man' and 'a Punk of a Humour free'.

p. 170 l.24   Hockley-in-the-Hole: see note on p. 155 l.24 above.

p. 170 l.25   Vinegar Yard: a court near the Drury Lane theatre.

p. 170 l.26   Lewkner's Lane: the location of a brothel founded by Jonathan Wild.

p. 171 l.21   If music be the food of love, play on!: this is the first line of Shakespeare's *Twelfth Night*. There is also a song in *Pills to Purge Melancholy* (III 75) which begins 'If Musick be the Food of Love, / Sing on, sing on, sing on.'

p. 171 l.27   Cotillon: an elaborate French dance involving frequent changing of partners.

p. 172 l.19   lute-string ... padesoy: lustring and paduasoy were expensive silks imported from France and Holland.

p. 172 l.20   Lock: warehouse for stolen goods.

p. 172 l.23   cambric: see note on p. 154 l.18 above.

p. 174 l.23   Was this well done, Jenny?: cf. Shakespeare's *Antony and Cleopatra* Act V Scene 2 line 320, and Dryden's *All for Love* Act V Scene 2, 'Charmian, is this well done?'

p. 175 l.31   garnish: newcomers were expected to 'buy drinks' for the other prisoners.

p. 177 l.25   'Twas when the sea was roaring: the reference is to a lyric in Gay's *The What D'Ye Call It* (1715), which was said to have been set to music by Handel.

p. 179 l.12 This long arrear of the Government: the reference is to the delays in payment of rewards under the Highwayman Act.

p. 179 l.22 like great statesmen: the quarrel between Peachum and Lockit, which alludes to that between Walpole and his brother-in-law Townshend, is precipitated by the insult contained in these words.

p. 179 l.32 *That was levelled at me*: it is said that this song was encored in Walpole's presence, and that he responded by encoring it a second time, which 'brought the audience into so much good humour with him, that they gave him a general huzza from all parts of the house'.

p. 182 l.29 All in the Downs: these are the opening words of a lyric by Gay himself entitled 'Sweet William's Farewell to Black-Ey'd Susan'. By using the same tune in this new context, Gay relates Polly's feelings about Macheath's imminent execution to Susan's feelings about William's departure for the war.

p. 185 l.8 AIR 20: the quarrel between Lucy and Polly alludes to that between the rival opera-singers Faustina Bordoni and Francesca Cuzzoni.

p. 185 l.10 *And are for flinging dirt*: the monosyllable 'dirt' is extended over several notes in the manner of Italian opera.

p. 186 l.30 'The Lass of Patie's Mill': there is a song with this title in the volume of poems which Allan Ramsay published in 1721.

p. 190 l.4 a shotten herring: a herring whose supply of sperm has been exhausted.

p. 190 l.16 Lock: warehouse for stolen goods.

p. 190 l.31 'Lillibulero': the reference is to a ballad written in 1688, when James II appointed the Earl of Tyrconnel as Lord Lieutenant of Ireland. 'Lillibulero' and 'bullen a-la' were said to be Irish words which the Catholics had used for purposes of identification during the massacre of Protestants in 1641. The text was re-printed, with explanatory comments, in Thomas Percy's *Reliques of Ancient English Poetry* (1765).

p. 192 l.5 the Coronation account: this refers both to the items stolen during the coronation of George II, and to the large Civil List with which Walpole won the new king's favour.

p. 192 l.9 instalments: days on which a new Lord Mayor was installed.

p. 193 l.26 A shepherd kept sheep: the original is in *Pills to Purge Melancholy* (V 35) under the heading 'A Song'.

p. 194 l.1 chap: purchaser, fence.

p. 194 l.9 The Act for destroying the mint: an Act of 1722, which abolished the status of the Mint as a debtors' sanctuary.

p. 194 l.14 the Act ... against imprisonment for small sums: an Act of 1725, which sought to prevent arrest for debts of less than ten pounds.

p. 196 l.5 I have the ratsbane ready: poisoning was a common motif in Italian opera, but the poison being used here is a notably vulgar one.

p. 196 l.6 gin: the consumption of gin by the lower classes was regarded as a threat to public health. See Hogarth's *Beer Street and Gin Lane*.

p. 196 l.17 spleen: this was the name given to a form of depression associated with ladies of high rank. See 'The Spleen: A Pindaric Poem' by Anne Finch Countess of Winchilsea (1701), Pope's *The Rape of the Lock* (1714) Canto IV lines 11–78, and Matthew Green's poem *The Spleen* (1737).

p. 197 l.23 'O Bessy Bell': the narrative ballad 'Bessy Bell and Mary Gray', which is No. 128 in the 1969 edition of *The Oxford Book of Ballads*, tells a grim story about two women who died of the plague. The song of the same title which Ramsay included in his 1721 collection is a dramatic lyric about a man unable to choose between two 'bonny lasses'. A still more attenuated version can be found on page 31 of *The Oxford Dictionary of Nursery Rhymes*. Gay's text invites comparison with Ramsay's, which was presumably the 'Scotch Song' of the same title performed around this time by 'Miss Robinson' at the Haymarket opera-house.

p. 198 l.12 Come, sweet lass: the original is in *Pills to Purge Melancholy* (III 217) under the heading 'A Song'. The merry inanity of its pastoralism makes it a suitably incongruous vehicle for Lucy's offer of rat-poison.

p. 202 l.21 'Of all the girls that are so smart': this is the first line of 'The Ballad of Sally in our Alley' by Henry Carey, a very popular song whose happy innocence is appropriate neither to the 'condemned hold' nor to the 'brimmer' which Macheath is addressing.

p. 202 l.29 Chevy Chase: this narrative ballad about border warfare is No. 104 in the 1969 edition of *The Oxford Book of Ballads*.

p. 203 l.1 'To old Sir Simon, the king': the original, which is in *Pills to Purge Melancholy* (III 143), is an anti-Puritan celebration of drink and song. In *Tom Jones* (Book IV Chapter 5) Fielding identifies it as the song which Squire Western asks his daughter to play on the harpsichord when he is drunk.

p. 203 l.6 Joy to great Cæsar: this is the first line of a text which appears in *Pills to Purge Melancholy* (II 155) under the heading 'The King's Health: Set to Farinel's Ground. In Six Parts'. In its celebration of Charles II and the Duke of York, and its condemnation of Shaftesbury and Oates, it is clearly a Tory response to the Exclusion Bill crisis.

p. 203 l.7 *If thus ... brandy*: in rhyming 'can die' with 'brandy', Gay improves on an antiquated model which rhymed 'Cæsar' with 'pleasure'.

p. 203 l.13 'Did you ever hear of a gallant sailor?': the original is in *Pills to Purge Melancholy* (V 80) under the title 'The Unconstant Woman'.

p. 203 l.19 'Green Sleeves': the reference is to the Elizabethan love-song entitled 'A New Courtly Sonnet of the Lady Greensleeves'. The melody and original words of this song were still familiar in 1856, when Dickens brought Gay's text to bear on his own version of the great man as criminal in Book II Chapter 12 of *Little Dorrit*. An eighteenth-century tradition attributed this lyric to Swift, but its argument was introduced in Peachum's first song and is to be reiterated in the Beggar's last speech.

p. 203 l.24 *Tyburn tree*: the gallows on the place of execution near the present site of the Marble Arch.

p. 205 l.6 *The toll of the bell*: the bell of St Sepulchre's Church near Newgate began tolling five minutes before the procession was due to set out for Tyburn.

p. 205 l.31 Through the whole piece ... punished for them: the Beggar's final speech clarifies the implications of his new lyric for

'Green Sleeves', and identifies the argument of that lyric as the argument of his opera as a whole.

The Tragedy of Tragedies

p. 209 l.1   H. Scriblerus Secundus: Henry Fielding here identifies himself as the second Scriblerus, the first being the pedantic editor responsible for the *Dunciad Variorum* of 1729.

p. 209 l.11   *egregium . . . anteponendum*: 'an excellent work of great value, far superior to both ancient and modern tragedies'.

p. 209 l.13   Dr B—: Richard Bentley (1662–1742), the great classical scholar satirised by Pope.

p. 209 l.13   *Citiùs . . . dubitârim*: 'I should more readily believe that Mævius wrote the *Aeneid* than that the notorious Scriblerus wrote this tragedy, whose author I firmly believe to have handed on [a work by] Seneca himself.' Maevius was a bad poet satirised by Horace.

p. 209 l.16   Burman: Pieter Burman, the Professor of Greek under whom Fielding had studied in the University of Leyden.

p. 209 l.16   *Heroum . . . principem*: 'Easily the first of all tragic heroes'.

p. 209 l.24   Mr D—: John Dennis, an intelligent but irascible critic who attacked works by Addison, Steele and Pope.

p. 210 l.24   Clariss. Bentleium: the illustrious Bentley. (See note on p. 209 l.13 above).

p. 210 l.40   Edward M—r: the narrative ballad about Tom Thumb was printed and published by Edward Midwinter. In *A Tale of a Tub* (1704), Jonathan Swift declared that its author was 'a Pythagorean philosopher' and that the work contained 'the whole scheme of the Metempsychosis'.

p. 211 l.7   Mr C—l: Edmund Curll, the bookseller who wins the urination contest in *The Dunciad* Book II lines 179–90.

p. 211 l.16   Sophonisba: a Carthaginian princess, sister of Hannibal, who married the Numidian Syphax in order to win him over to the Carthaginian cause. According to Livy (30:12–15) she later took poison sent to her by her lover Masinissa rather than face captivity in Rome. Tragic dramatists who had written about Sophonisba before Fielding's time include Giangiorgio Trissino (1524), John Marston (1605), Jean Mairet (1634), Pierre Corneille (1663), and Nathaniel Lee (1675). James Thomson's *Sophonisba* was acted at Drury Lane in February 1730, just two months before the first performance of *Tom Thumb* at the Little Theatre in the Haymarket.

p. 211 l.23   the Brutus of Voltaire: Voltaire's tragedy about Lucius Junius Brutus was performed in French in 1730. An English adaptation by William Duncombe was acted at Drury Lane in 1734.

p. 211 l.24   the Marius Jun. of Otway: for *The History and Fall of Caius Marius*, which was acted at the Dorset Garden theatre in 1679, Otway incorporated large portions of Shakespeare's *Romeo and Juliet* in a dramatisation of the conflict between Marius and Sulla. As Otway's version of Romeo, Marius Junior is a very different character from the austere Brutus of Voltaire.

p. 212 l.8   Mr D—: see the note on p. 209 l.24 above.

p. 212 l.11   Aristotle: John Dennis was strongly committed to the concept of tragedy expounded by Aristotle in the *Poetics*.

p. 212 l.15   Sergeant Kite: a character in George Farquhar's comedy *The Recruiting Officer*, first acted at Drury Lane in 1706.

p. 212 l.17   physiognominical: the usual form of the adjective from 'physiognomy' is 'physiognomical'. The extra syllable could be a joke, but is probably an error.

p. 212 l.36   Mr Dryden: in the essay 'Of Heroic Plays' which was prefixed to the published version of his two-part heroic play *The Conquest of Granada*, Dryden argued that those who used blank verse for serious drama had already 'forsaken the imitation of ordinary converse', and should therefore commit themselves to 'the last perfection of art' by writing in couplets. To remain where they were, he contended, was 'to lodge in the open field, betwixt two Inns'.

p. 213 l.1   Telephus ... sesquipedalia verba: 'Telephus and Peleus, when poor and in exile, reject bombastic phrases and polysyllabic words.' Telephus was the hero of a tragedy by Euripides. The sufferings of Peleus are a common subject in Greek art. The quotation is from lines 96–7 of Horace's *Ars Poetica*.

p. 213 l.10   dolere sermone pedestri: 'to grieve in a colloquial style'. The phrase is adapted from line 95 of the *Ars Poetica*.

p. 213 l.13　*sermo pedestris*: 'A colloquial style'. This is the nominative form of the phrase quoted in p. 213 l.10.

p. 213 l.15　Cicero: Marcus Tullius Cicero, the Roman statesman and orator.

p. 213 l.15　*Quid ... scientiâ*: 'what is so passionate, or so appropriate for tragedy, as the empty sound of words, containing no meaning and no understanding?' Fielding is quoting, amending, and misinterpreting an ironic question from Cicero's *De Oratore* (I xii).

p. 213 l.20　Longinus: the supposed author of a Greek treatise entitled *On the Sublime*, probably written in the first century A.D.

p. 213 l.22　*Omne ... vincit.*: 'tragedy surpasses every other form of writing in seriousness.' The quotation is from *Tristia* II 381.

p. 213 l.24　Bathos: this Greek word means 'depth', but is used in English by the Scriblerians to designate the opposite of the sublime, the quality which occasions a sudden and ludicrous descent. Pretending that 'gravitate' means not 'in seriousness' but 'in weight', Fielding attributes to Ovid the view that tragedy is more frequently absurd than any other genre.

p. 214 l.5　the *Earl of Essex*: *The Unhappy Favourite or The Earl of Essex* (1681) by John Banks, whose 'she-tragedies' were scorned by critics but enjoyed by theatrical audiences.

p. 214 l.11　*Quæ ... legerim*: 'which I do not condemn, since I have never read them'.

p. 215 l.7　Mr Mullart: in the years 1729–34 William and Elizabeth Mullart acted on many stages, from Bartholomew Fair and Southwark Fair to Drury Lane and Lincoln's Inn Fields. They joined John Rich's troupe at Covent Garden in 1734, and remained there until their deaths in 1742 and 1745 respectively.

p. 216 l.7　Mrs Mullart: see note on p. 215 l.7 above.

p. 217 l.15　*Cato*: by Joseph Addison, 1713.

p. 217 l.15　*Mariamne*: by Elijah Fenton, 1723.

p. 217 l.15　*Tamerlane*: by Nicholas Rowe, 1701.

p. 217 l.22　Caes. Borg.: *Caesar Borgia or The Son of Pope Alexander the Sixth*, by Nathaniel Lee, 1679.

p. 217 l.23   the new *Sophonisba*: by James Thomson, 1730.

p. 217 l.28   the *Persian Princess*: *The Persian Princess or The Royal Villain*, by Lewis Theobald, 1708.

p. 218 l.16   State of Innocence: *The State of Innocence and The Fall of Man*, an opera by John Dryden based on Milton's *Paradise Lost* and published in 1677.

p. 218 l.17   Don Sebastian: *Don Sebastian King of Portugal* by John Dryden, 1689.

p. 218 l.18   Sophonisba: by James Thomson, 1730.

p. 218 l.19   Revenge: *The Revenge* by Edward Young, 1721.

p. 218 l.20   Dr B—y: see note on p. 209 l.13 above.

p. 218 l.20   Mr D—s: see note on p. 209 l.24 above.

p. 218 l.21   Mr T—d: Lewis Theobald (1688–1744), who exposed the errors of Pope's edition of Shakespeare and was satirised in the first version of *The Dunciad*.

p. 218 l.23   Mr S—n: the reference is probably to the Whig historian and antiquary Nathanael Salmon (1675–1742).

p. 218 l.26   the *Royal Villain*: see note on p. 217 l.28 above.

p. 218 l.27   Petrus Burmanus: see note on p. 209 l.16 above.

p. 218 l.28   Hercules: Latin name for the Greek Heracles, a demigod who undertook and completed twelve seemingly impossible tasks.

p. 218 l.30   Hermes Trismegistus: the supposed author of religio-philosophical treatises and other works composed in Hellenistic Egypt.

p. 218 l.32   Justus Lipsius: a Flemish scholar of the late sixteenth century, whose works included an edition of Tacitus.

p. 218 l.33   *Thomam ... constat*: 'It is generally agreed that Tom Thumb was none other than Hercules.'

p. 218 l.34   Mr Midwinter: the publisher of the ballad, whom Fielding here treats as its author.

p. 218 l.36   Dr B—y: see note on p. 209 l.13 above.

p. 218 l.37   *Spenser*: the lines quoted occur in *The Faerie Queene* Book II Canto x Stanzas 7 and 73.

p. 218 l.45   *Risum teneatis, Amici*: 'Control your laughter, friends.' A proverbial phrase, usually followed by a question-mark and interpreted 'Can you control your laughter, friends?'

p. 218 l.46   Mr D—s: see note on p. 209 l.24 above.

p. 218 l.48   the *Persian Princess*: see note on p. 217 l.28 above.

p. 218 l.49   *Aurengzebe*: by John Dryden, 1675.

p. 218 l.50   Emmeline in Dryden: a character in the dramatic opera *King Arthur*, by John Dryden and Henry Purcell, which was first performed in 1691.

p. 219 l.21   *Cyrus*: *Cyrus the Great or The Tragedy of Love* by John Banks, 1695.

p. 219 l.23   Mr D—s: see note on p. 209 l.24 above.

p. 219 l.25   Mary Queen of Scots: the reference is to a tragedy by John Banks, which was published in 1684 as *The Rival Queens or The Death of Mary Queen of Scotland*, and acted in a revised version in 1704 as *The Albion Queens or The Death of Mary Queen of Scots*.

p. 219 l.27   Liberty Asserted: by John Dennis, 1704.

p. 219 l.28   *Omne ... potest*: 'The greater always contains the lesser, but the lesser cannot contain the greater.'

p. 219 l.29   Scaliger: Julius Caesar Scaliger (1484–1558), humanist and controversialist, or his son Joseph Justus Scaliger (1540–1609), editor and student of chronology.

p. 219 l.29   in *Thumbo*: in his commentary on *Tom Thumb*.

p. 219 l.30   the *Earl of Essex*: see note on p. 214 l.5 above.

p. 219 l.35   Aurengzebe: see note on p. 218 l.49 above.

p. 219 l.38   Earl of Essex: see note on p. 214 l.5 above.

p. 219 l.40   Mr Banks: see note on p. 214 l.5 above.

p. 220 l.16   the *Captives*: *The Captives* by John Gay, 1724.

p. 220 l.24   Sophonisba: by James Thomson, 1730.

p. 220 l.27   Busiris: by Edward Young, 1719.

p. 220 l.28   Earl of Essex: see note on p. 214 l.5 above.

p. 220 l.32   Lee's Sophonisba: *Sophonisba or Hannibal's Overthrow* by Nathaniel Lee, 1675.

p. 220 l.35   Mithridates: by Nathaniel Lee, 1678.

p. 220 l.38   Cyrus the Great: see note on p. 219 l.21 above.

p. 220 l.41   Royal Villain: see note on p. 217 l.28 above.

p. 220 l.44   Anna Bullen: *Vertue Betray'd or Anna Bullen* by John Banks, 1682.

p. 221 l.23   Cyrus the Great: see note on p. 219 l.21 above.

p. 221 l.24   Mr D—s: see note on p. 209 l.24 above.

p. 221 l.27   Mithridates: see note on p. 220 l.35 above.

p. 221 l.28   the new Sophonisba: By James Thomson, 1730.

p. 221 l.33   Mr Tate: From *Injur'd Love or The Cruel Husband* by Nahum Tate, 1707.

p. 221 l.37   Gloriana: by Nathaniel Lee, 1676.

p. 221 l.39   Cleomenes: *Cleomenes the Spartan Hero* by John Dryden, 1692.

p. 221 l.41   Victim: *The Victim* by Charles Johnson, 1714.

p. 221 l.42   Busiris: see note on p. 220 l.27 above.

p. 222 l.25   the Captives: see note on p. 220 l.16 above.

p. 222 l.28   Nero: by Nathaniel Lee, 1674.

p. 222 l.29   Sebastian: see note on p. 218 l.17 above.

p. 222 l.33   Lu. Ju. Brut.: *Lucius Junius Brutus, Father of his Country* by Nathaniel Lee, 1680.

p. 222 l.35   'This is a man!': from *The Duke of Guise* by John Dryden and Nathaniel Lee, 1682.

p. 222 l.42   All for Love: by John Dryden, 1677.

p. 222 l.43   Banks: see note on p. 214 l.5 above.

p. 222 l.46   Mr W—: the author to whom Fielding attributes this inanely flattering comment on a notably clumsy line is Leonard Welsted. See note on p. 71 l.2 above.

p. 223 l.36   Mithridates: see note on p. 220 l.35 above.

p. 223 l.37   Injured Love: see note on p. 221 l.33 above.

p. 223 l.38   the *Persian Princess*: see note on p. 217 l.28 above.

p. 223 l.40   the *Captives*: see note on p. 220 l.16 above.

p. 224 l.28   *Love Triumphant*: the quotation is not from *Love Triumphant* by John Dryden (1694) but from *The Indian Queen* by John Dryden and Sir Robert Howard (1664).

p. 224 l.30   the *Revenge*: see note on p. 218 l.19 above.

p. 224 l.36   Anna Bullen: see note on p. 220 l.44.

p. 224 l.37   Cyrus the Great: see note on p. 219 l.21 above.

p. 224 l.39   Duke of Guise: see note on p. 222 l.35 above.

p. 224 l.41   New Sophonisba: by James Thomson, 1730.

p. 225 l.31   *Anna Bullen*: see note on p. 220 l.44 above.

p. 225 l.34   Liberty Asserted: see note on p. 219 l.27 above.

p. 225 l.35   *A bride ... by your side*: from *Anna Bullen*. See note on p. 220 l.44 above.

p. 225 l.38   Albion Queens: see note on p. 219 l.25 above.

p. 225 l.39   *The Tragedy of Love*: see note on p. 219 l.21 above.

p. 225 l.43   Conquest of Granada: *Almanzor and Almahide or The Conquest of Granada by the Spaniards: In Two Parts* by John Dryden, 1670 and 1671.

p. 226 l.30   *Earl of Essex*: see note on p. 214 l.5 above.

p. 226 l.35   *Cyrus*: see note on p. 219 l.21 above.

p. 227 l.33   Mary Queen of Scots: see note on p. 219 l.25 above.

p. 227 l.34   the *Naval Lyric*: *Imperium Pelagi: A Naval Lyric Written in imitation of Pindar's Spirit, Occasion'd by his Majesty's Return September 1729 and the Succeeding Peace* by Edward Young, 1730.

p. 227 l.39   State of Innocence: see note on p. 218 l.16 above.

p. 227 l.40   *Earl of Essex*: see note on p. 214 l.5 above.

p. 227 l.43   *Cyrus*: see note on p. 219 l.21 above.

p. 228 l.25 Tothill-Bridewell: a London prison in which female prisoners were required to beat hemp.

p. 228 l.29 Aristotle: the reference is to the *Poetics*, but Fielding's summary is a mischievous distortion of Aristotle's argument.

p. 228 l.35 Injur'd Love: see note on p. 221 l.33 above.

p. 228 l.38 *King Arthur*: see note on p. 218 l.50 above.

p. 228 l.41 *Sebastian*: see note on p. 218 l.17 above.

p. 229 l.25 Mr Rowe: Bajazet is a character in *Tamerlane* by Nicholas Rowe, which was first acted in 1701. When Scriblerus says that Rowe owes little to the author of *Tom Thumb*, Fielding means that Rowe's tragedies are relatively free from those faults which his burlesque-play was designed to ridicule.

p. 230 l.28 *Sebastian*: see note on p. 218 l.17 above.

p. 230 l.34 Mr D—s: see note on p. 209 l.24 above.

p. 230 l.35 *Busiris*: see note on p. 220 l.27 above.

p. 230 l.44 Mary Queen of Scots: see note on p. 219 l.25 above.

p. 231 l.32 Aurengzebe: see note on p. 218 l.49 above.

p. 231 l.33 the *Persian Princess*: see note on p. 217 l.28 above.

p. 231 l.35 Anthony: Act I line 228 of Dryden's *All for Love* in fact reads:

> Give me some music; look that it be sad.

p. 232 l.4 Bantam: Fielding is inventing a heroic ancestor for the breed of fighting cocks known as bantams, which were thought to have originated in Java.

p. 232 l.5 the King of Brentford, Old or New: the two kings of Brentford appear in Act I Scene 2 of *The Rehearsal*, a burlesque of Dryden's heroic plays which was written by the Duke of Buckingham and others and acted at the Theatre Royal in Bridges Street in 1671.

p. 232 l.32 *Oh! Marius, Marius; wherefore art thou Marius?*: Fielding quotes this line from *The History and Fall of Caius Marius* by Thomas Otway. See note on p. 211 l.24 above.

p. 232 l.34 Victim: see note on p. 221 l.41 above.

p. 232 l.35 Noah's Flood: *Noah's Flood or The Destruction of the World* by Edward Ecclestone, 1679.

p. 233 l.15 Terrâ Incognitâ: the phrase commonly used on maps to designate unknown territory, and in particular the still-unexplored continent of Australia.

p. 233 l.26 Gloriana: see note on p. 221 l.37 above.

p. 233 l.28 Conquest of Granada: see note on p. 225 l.43 above.

p. 233 l.32 Banks's Earl of Essex: see note on p. 214 l.5 above.

p. 233 l.35 Lucifer in the State of Innocence: see note on p. 218 l.16 above.

p. 233 l.36 Mr D—s: see note on p. 209 l.24 above.

p. 233 l.43 Cleomenes: see note on p. 221 l.39 above.

p. 234 l.29 Lee's Sophonisba: see note on p. 220 l.32 above.

p. 234 l.30 *Liberty Asserted*: see note on p. 219 l.27 above.

p. 234 l.38 Gloriana: see note on p. 221 l.37 above.

p. 235 l.28 Mr W—: see note on p. 222 l.46 above.

p. 235 l.29 the new *Sophonisba*: by James Thomson, 1730.

p. 235 l.32 *Duke upon Duke*: the reference is to 'an excellent new play-house ballad' beginning 'To lordings proud I tune my song', which was published in 1720. See the Twickenham edition of the poems of Pope, Volume VI pages 217-24.

p. 235 l.35 the *Bloody Brother*: the reference is to the play printed in 1639 as *The Bloody Brother: A Tragedy* and in 1640 as *The Tragedy of Rollo Duke of Normandy*. This was included in the Beaumont and Fletcher Folio of 1679, but like many plays in that collection was commonly regarded as the unaided work of John Fletcher.

p. 235 l.39 Hannibal: see note on p. 220 l.32 above.

p. 236 l.32 Albion Queens: see note on p. 219 l.25 above.

p. 236 l.35 Hannibal: see note on p. 220 l.32 above.

p. 236 l.37 Duke of Guise: the quotation comes not from *The Duke of Guise* by John Dryden and Nathaniel Lee (1682) but from *Caesar*

Borgia or The Son of Pope Alexander the Sixth by Nathaniel Lee (1679).

p. 236 l.38   **Gloriana:** see note on p. 221 l.37 above.

p. 237 l.15   **Aurengzebe:** see note on p. 218 l.49 above.

p. 237 l.16   **Busiris:** see note on p. 220 l.27 above.

p. 237 l.21   **State of Innocence:** see note on p. 218 l.16 above.

p. 237 l.25   **All for Love:** see note on p. 222 l.42 above.

p. 237 l.29   **Cleomenes:** see note on p. 221 l.39 above.

p. 237 l.31   **Sebastian:** see note on p. 218 l.17 above.

p. 237 l.33   **Anna Bullen:** see note on p. 220 l.44 above.

p. 237 l.40   **King Arthur:** see note on p. 218 l.50 above.

p. 237 l.42   **the new *Sophonisba*:** by James Thomson, 1730.

p. 238 l.31   **Conquest of Granada:** see note on p. 225 l.43 above.

p. 238 l.32   **Mr Dryden:** the reference is to *All for Love* III. 2. 416 ff.

p. 238 l.33   **Mr Addison:** in *Guardian* 110, Addison comments: 'Let any one read the Dialogue between *Octavia* and *Cleopatra*, and he will be amazed to hear a *Roman* Lady's mouth filled with such obscene raillery.'

p. 238 l.36   **Mr D—:** see note on p. 209 l.24 above.

p. 238 l.39   **Injured Love:** see note on p. 221 l.33 above.

p. 239 l.28   **Mr L—:** the reference may perhaps be to Bernard Lintot (1675–1736), the publisher of many poems and plays by living authors. Although he was the publisher of Pope's Homer, Lintot also brought out works critical of Pope and his friends. He plays a leading role in *The Dunciad Variorum*, most notably in Book II lines 49–64 and the accompanying notes.

p. 239 l.29   **Shakespeare, Jonson and Fletcher:** these dramatists were still commonly regarded as the masters of 'the last age'.

p. 239 l.33   **Earl of Essex:** see note on p. 214 l.5 above.

p. 239 l.34   ***Sophonisba*:** by James Thomson, 1730.

p. 239 l.35   **Aurengzebe:** see note on p. 218 l.49 above.

p. 239 l.36   Cleomenes: see note on p. 221 l.39 above.

p. 239 l.39   Anna Bullen: see note on p. 220 l.44 above.

p. 239 l.40   *Verba tragica*: the phrase means 'tragic words', and suggests that the five nouns so designated epitomise the character of modern tragedy.

p. 240 l.20   Love Triumphant: by John Dryden, 1694.

p. 240 l.25   Sebastian: see note on p. 218 l.17 above.

p. 240 l.27   Aurengzebe: see note on p. 218 l.49 above.

p. 240 l.29   New Sophonisba: by James Thomson, 1730.

p. 240 l.31   Anna Bullen: see note on p. 220 l.44 above.

p. 240 l.37   *Eurydice*: by David Mallet, 1731. This tragedy was first performed at Drury Lane in February 1731, after the acting of *Tom Thumb* but just before the acting of *The Tragedy of Tragedies*. Fielding's *Eurydice Hiss'd* was acted in 1737.

p. 240 l.37   Dr Young: Edward Young, the poet of *Night Thoughts*, was also responsible for the sensational tragedies *Busiris* (1719) and *The Revenge* (1721).

p. 240 l.40   *Curæ leves loquuntur, ingentes stupent*: 'Light sorrows speak, great sorrows are silent.' This is line 607 of the play by Seneca variously known as the *Hippolytus* or the *Phaedra*.

p. 240 l.41   Herodotus: the Greek historian Herodotus (III: 14) tells the story of the deposed Egyptian king Psammenitus, who endured his own sufferings without complaint, but was moved to tears by those of a stranger.

p. 240 l.42   Montaigne: the paradox defined by Seneca and Herodotus is further explored by Michel de Montaigne (1533–1592) in his essay 'On Sadness' (*Essais* I: 2).

p. 240 l.46   Don Carlos: these lines come not from the tragedy *Don Carlos* (1676) by Thomas Otway but from the 'tragi-comi-pastoral farce' *The What D'Ye Call It* (1715) by John Gay.

p. 241 l.18   *Busiris*: see note on p. 220.27 above.

p. 241 l.19   Gloriana: see note on p. 221 l.37 above.

p. 241 l.25   Duke of Guise: see note on p. 222 l.35 above.

p. 241 l.27   Conquest of Granada: see note on p. 225 l.43 above.

p. 241 l.31   State of Innocence: see note on p. 218 l.16 above.

p. 241 l.34   Earl of Essex: see note on p. 214 l.5 above.

p. 241 l.37   Sophonisba: by James Thomson, 1730.

p. 242 l.38   The tottering ... its props: from *The Persian Princess*. See note on p. 217 l.28 above.

p. 241 l.39   Busiris: see note on p. 220.27 above.

p. 241 l.41   Medea: *The Tragedy of Medea* by Charles Johnson, 1730.

p. 241 l.42   *She seemed the sad effigies of herself*: this line is from *The Albion Queens* by John Banks. See note on p. 219 l.25 above.

p. 241 l.43   *Assist me, Zulema ... against me*: these two lines come not from *The Albion Queens* but from the first part of *The Conquest of Granada* by John Dryden. See notes on p. 219 l.25 and p. 225 l.43 above.

p. 242 l.16   the wonderful bitch: a French dog that played cards.

p. 242 l.29   Mr F—: Scriblerus Secundus attributes this vulgar jest about the Welsh enthusiasm for cheese to Henry Fielding. See Chapter 26 of *Roderick Random* (1748) by Tobias Smollett.

p. 242 l.33   Love Triumphant: see note on p. 240 l.20 above.

p. 242 l.35   Albion Queens: see note on p. 219 l.25 above.

p. 242 l.38   Conquest of Granada: see note on p. 225 l.43 above.

p. 242 l.39   All for Love: see note on p. 222 l.42 above.

p. 242 l.40   the new *Sophonisba*: by James Thomson, 1730.

p. 243 l.33   Aurengzebe: see note on p. 218 l.49 above.

p. 243 l.35   Mr D—s: see note on p. 209 l.24 above.

p. 243 l.36   Cyrus: see note on p. 219 l.21 above.

p. 243 l.39   *Love Triumphant*: see note on p. 240 l.20 above.

p. 244 l.25   Virtue Betrayed: see note on p. 220 l.44 above.

p. 244 l.26   The *Persian Princess*: see note on p. 217 l.28 above.

p. 244 l.41   Conquest of Granada: see note on p. 225 l.43 above.

p. 244 l.42   **My Lord Bacon:** in Book VIII of *De Augmentis Scientia-rum* Francis Bacon declares that the Proverbs of Solomon include 'not a few excellent civil precepts and cautions, springing from the inmost recesses of wisdom and extending to much variety of occasions'.

p. 245 l.4   *solus:* 'alone'.

p. 245 l.23   ψυχὴ ὁ μῦθος τῆς τραγῳδίας: 'The plot is the soul of tragedy.' This dictum occurs in Aristotle's *Poetics* VI 19. Scriblerus' contention that μῦθος is equivalent to the Latin *fabula* and therefore means 'ghost' is patently absurd.

p. 245 l.24   **M Dacier:** André Dacier (1651–1722) published a com-mentary on Aristotle's *Poetics* in 1692.

p. 245 l.26   *Te premet nox, fabulæque Manes:* 'Night and the fabled spirits close in upon you.' As Scriblerus indicates, this line comes from Horace (*Odes* I. 4.16). Modern commentators disagree about the case, number and significance of *fabulæ*, but clearly it does not mean 'ghosts'.

p. 245 l.28   **foreign critic:** the reference to a 'learned and judicious foreign critic' could perhaps mean that a Leyden acquaintance contrib-uted the following sentence.

p. 245 l.29   *Nec quidquam . . . prætulerim:* 'And nothing in this work is more admirable than a certain horrid ghost, which (if I may venture to disagree with the very learned Mr D—s) I greatly prefer to all the other spectres in which English tragedy abounds.' The phrase 'D—isii V. Doctiss.' can be expanded as 'Dionysii Viri Doctissimi'.

p. 246 l.27   **Conquest of Granada:** see note on p. 225 l.43 above.

p. 246 l.28   **Mr D—:** see note on p. 209 l.24 above.

p. 246 l.30   *Liberty Asserted:* see note on p. 219 l.27 above. Fielding here endorses Dennis' condemnation of puns in order to strengthen his attack on Dennis' practice as a dramatist.

p. 246 l.35   the *Victim:* see note on p. 221 l.41 above.

p. 246 l.42   **Cyrus the Great:** see note on p. 219 l.21 above.

p. 246 l.45   **Almanzor:** see note on p. 225 l.43 above.

p. 247 l.24   **Pluto:** the Roman god of the underworld.

p. 247 l.34   *Cyrus:* see note on p. 219 l.21 above.

p. 247 l.38 **Conquest of Granada:** see note on p. 225 l.43 above.

p. 247 l.41 **Mr Dryden:** these lines occur in the Dryden-Purcell opera *King Arthur*. See note on p. 218 l.50 above.

p. 248 l.35 **Ind. Emp.:** *The Indian Emperour or The Conquest of Mexico by the Spaniards* by John Dryden, 1665.

p. 249 l.5 **In Dryden's Ovid's Metamorphoses:** *Ovid's Metamorphoses in Fifteen Books, Translated by the Most Eminent Hands* was published in 1717. The sections which had been translated by Dryden, before his death in 1700, were Books 1 and 12 and parts of Books 8, 9, 10, 11, 13, and 15.

p. 249 l.6 **Jove:** the king of the gods was known in Greek as Zeus. The English forms Jupiter and Jove are derived from the nominative and genitive forms of his Latin name.

p. 249 l.7 **Danae:** Danaë was confined to a brazen chamber by her father Acrisius, but the king of the gods had intercourse with her in the shape of a stream of gold which poured through the roof into her lap. This story, which inspired many Renaissance paintings, is briefly alluded to by Danaë's son Perseus in Book IV of the *Metamorphoses*. The story of Danaë and Perseus is told in full by Apollodorus of Athens in Book II of his *Biblioteca*.

p. 249 l.29 **Sophonisba:** by James Thomson, 1730.

p. 249 l.31 **Mr D—:** see note on p. 209 l.24 above.

p. 250 l.21 ***Credat Judaeus Apella / Non ego:*** 'Let Apella the Jew believe it, for I do not.' The sentence is from Horace (*Satires* I 5 100–101).

p. 250 l.22 **Mr D—:** see note on p. 209 l.24 above.

p. 250 l.24 **all the Samsons and Herculeses of antiquity:** both Samson in the Old Testament and Heracles or Hercules in Graeco-Roman mythology possessed superhuman strength.

p. 250 l.26 **Mr Dryden's defence of his Almanzor:** in the 'Essay of Heroic Plays', which he prefixed to the published text of *The Conquest of Granada*, Dryden sought to justify the 'over-boiling courage' of his hero.

p. 250 l.30 ***O son of Atreus:*** Atreus was the father of Agamemnon, the Greek commander in the Trojan War, and of Menelaus, the husband of Helen.

p. 250 l.32   Victim: see note on p. 221 l.41 above.

p. 250 l.36   Love Triumph.: see note on p. 240 l.20 above.

p. 250 l.40   Injured Love: see note on p. 221 l.33 above.

p. 250 l.42   new *Sophonisba*: by James Thomson, 1730.

p. 250 l.45   the *Revenge*: see note on p. 218 l.19 above.

p. 251 l.19   Elysian shades: see note on p. 49 l.15 above. The replacement of 'fields' with 'shades' shows Grizzle's hostile intent.

p. 251 l.26   *cum suis*: 'With their forces'.

p. 251 l.30   Conq. of Granada: see note on p. 225 l.43 above.

p. 251 l.33   K. Arthur: see note on p. 218 l.50 above.

p. 251 l.36   Gloriana: see note on p. 221 l.37 above.

p. 251 l.37   the *Indian Emperor*: see note on p. 248 l.35 above.

p. 252 l.37   Female Warrior: *Friendship Improv'd or The Female Warriour* by Charles Hopkins, 1699.

p. 252 l.38   *History of Tom Thumb*: see note on p. 210 l.40 above. These four stanzas from the ballad had been quoted by William Wagstaffe in *A Comment upon the History of Tom Thumb* (1711), with the ironic note: 'There is nothing more common throughout the Poets of the finest Taste, than to give an Account of the Pedigree of their Hero.' By introducing this ludicrous passage of ballad-narrative into the text of his burlesque-play, Fielding shows that his attack on modern tragedy is not an Addisonian plea for nature and simplicity. Like Wagstaffe, who had enlisted the absurdity of the Tom Thumb ballad to question Addison's celebration of *Chevy-Chase*, Fielding here invokes classical principles in order to expose the naïvety and extravagance which the ballad and the heroic play have in common.

p. 252 l.41   Persian Princess: see note on p. 217 l.28 above.

p. 253 l.27   K. Arthur: see note on p. 218 l.50 above.

p. 253 l.33   Busiris: see note on p. 220 l.27 above.

p. 253 l.36   Mr D—: see note on p. 209 l.24 above.

p. 253 l.39 Liberty Asserted: see note on p. 219 l.27 above. Here again Fielding enlists Dennis's intelligently aggressive critical writings to expose the weaknesses of Dennis's plays.

p. 253 l.42 Hannibal: see note on p. 220 l.32 above.

p. 254 l.28 *Busiris*: see note on p. 220 l.27 above.

p. 254 l.34 *Mandane*: Mandane is a female character in Young's *Busiris*.

p. 254 l.39 Conq. of Granada: see note on p. 225 l.43 above.

p. 254 l.40 *My soul ... its way*: this is an abbreviated version of a speech uttered by Almanzor in Act V of *The Conquest of Granada Part Two*:

> My Soul should, ev'n for your last accent, stay
> And then shoot out, and with such speed obey;
> It should not bait at Heav'n to stop its way.

To 'bait' is to break a journey for the benefit of the horses. See note on p. 225 l.43 above.

p. 254 l.44 Gloriana: see note on p. 221 l.37 above.

p. 255 l.6 To Hampstead or to Highgate: villages outside London where citizens and their wives could escape from the noise and dirt of the city.

p. 255 l.29 Cleomenes: see note on p. 221 l.39 above.

p. 255 l.30 *Some kind sprite ... at hand*: this quotation is from *Don Sebastian*. See note on p. 218 l.17 above.

p. 255 l.33 Conq. of Granada: see note on p. 225 l.43 above.

p. 255 l.34 *And in ... his soul*: this line is from *Cleomenes*. See note on p. 221 l.39 above.

p. 255 l.36 *Sebastian*: see note on p. 218 l.17.

p. 256 l.36 *Coffee-House Politician*: *Rape upon Rape or The Justice Caught in his Own Trap* was acted at the Little Theatre in the Haymarket in June 1730, and published in the same year as *The Coffee-House Politician or The Justice Caught in his Own Trap*. The author was Henry Fielding, but the published text did not give his name.

p. 256 l.38 *King Arthur,* or *The British Worthy*: see note on p. 218 l.50 above.

p. 256 l.41 Cleomenes: see note on p. 221 l.39 above.

p. 257 l.15 Dryden: these lines are from *The Conquest of Granada.* See note on p. 225 l.43 above.

p. 257 l.19 *Cleomenes*: see note on p. 221 l.39 above.

p. 257 l.21 *I ask ... they lie*: these lines are from *Cleomenes.* See note on p. 221 l.39 above.

p. 257 l.24 *Rival Ladies*: by John Dryden, 1664.

p. 257 l.32 *Essay on Dramatic Poetry*: Dryden's *Of Dramatic Poesy: An Essay* was written around 1665 and published in 1668. The sentence which Scriblerus quotes is uttered by Neander, who represents Dryden, when he is considering the differences between French and English drama. After making this initial concession, Neander proceeds to defend the English dramatists against the charge that they present 'incredible actions' on stage. Adopting a cruder version of patriotism, Scriblerus interprets the sentence as an admission that English audiences have a barbarous appetite for violent spectacle. On that basis, he proceeds to celebrate this appetite as the quality which enables Britain to win military victories over France. As Fielding's burlesque-play finished with a ridiculous accumulation of corpses, so the learned commentary of Scriblerus ends with an appropriately ludicrous assertion that the Battle of Blenheim was won in the heroic tragedies of Drury Lane.

The London Merchant

p. 261 l.1 To Sir John Eyles: Eyles was a Member of Parliament under three monarchs, and was elected Lord Mayor in 1727.

p. 261 l.5 Mr Dryden: in *A Discourse on Satire,* which he prefixed to a collaborative translation of Juvenal and Persius in 1693, Dryden attributed to Aristotle the view that tragedy was 'the most perfect work of poetry' because it was 'the most united' and thus allowed the mind to comprehend 'the whole beauty of it without distraction'.

p. 261 l.29 I am far from denying that tragedies ... are without their use: the logic of this sentence seems to require 'suggesting' rather than 'denying'.

p. 262 l.2 **a Tamerlane and a Bajazet:** as the spelling indicates, Lillo is thinking not of Marlowe's *Tamburlaine* but of Nicholas Rowe's *Tamerlane* (1701), in which the two characters named were commonly seen as portraits of William III and Louis XIV.

p. 262 l.8 **Cato:** the reference is to the *Cato* of Joseph Addison, whose values both Whigs and Tories claimed as their own.

p. 262 l.22 *Hamlet*: all the passages quoted are from the soliloquy at the end of Act II.

p. 263 l.23 **The proprietors in the South Sea Company:** Eyles was appointed Sub-Governor in January 1721, when the company was being re-organised.

p. 263 l.30 **the Court:** Eyles and other directors of the South Sea Company were 'received with great distinction' by George II in 1729.

p. 265 l.2 *Mr Cibber, junior:* Theophilus Cibber (1703–58), son of the actor-manager Colley Cibber, was patentee of Drury Lane for ten months in 1731–2. His first wife was the actress Jane Johnson, and his second wife the singer and actress Susanna Maria Arne. He acted at Drury Lane, Lincoln's Inn Fields, Covent Garden, the Little Theatre in the Haymarket, and the Theatre Royal in Dublin. In 1753 he published *The Lives of the Poets* in five volumes.

p. 265 l.18 **In Southerne's, Rowe's, or Otway's moving strains:** Thomas Otway was the author of *The Orphan* (1680) and *Venice Preserved* (1682). Thomas Southerne was the author of *The Fatal Marriage* (1694) and *Oroonoko* (1695). Nicholas Rowe was the author of *The Fair Penitent* (1703) and *The Tragedy of Jane Shore* (1714). These six plays were commonly praised for their melodious verse, their representation of women's sufferings in male-dominated societies, and their power to 'draw tears from the eyes of the auditors'.

p. 265 l.24 **the famed old song:** according to Thomas Percy, who included 'George Barnwell' in his *Reliques of Ancient English Poetry*, the text had been printed 'at least as early as the middle of the seventeenth century'.

p. 267 l.5 **Mr Cibber, Jun.:** see note on p. 265 l.2 above.

p. 267 l.9 **Mrs Cibber:** Jane Johnson (1706–33), the first wife of Theophilus Cibber, acted regularly at Drury Lane from 1723 to 1732.

p. 267 l.11 **Mrs Charke:** Charlotte Charke, the youngest daughter of

Colley Cibber, acted between 1730 and 1737 at Drury Lane and at the Little Theatre in the Haymarket. After breaking off relations with her family, she dressed in men's clothes and called herself 'Mr Brown'. She published *A Narrative of the Life of Mrs Charlotte Charke* in 1755.

p. 269 l.6   **packet:** a vessel with regular sailing-dates.

p. 269 l.9   **our royal mistress:** Elizabeth I. The action of the play is envisaged as taking place about 1587.

p. 270 l.5   **the bank of Genoa:** Genoa was one of the great banking centres of the time, but this episode appears to be unhistorical.

p. 270 l.9   **Walsingham:** Sir Francis Walsingham, Elizabeth's Secretary of State.

p. 271 l.12   **dispense with:** excuse.

p. 280 l.15   **the grand apostate:** Satan.

p. 282 l.32   **We have heard ... consuming flames:** The events mentioned here are recorded in Joshua 10:13, Isaiah 38:8, 1 Kings 17:17–22, Luke 7:15, John 11:22, Numbers 20:11, Exodus 16:21, Daniel 6:22, and Daniel 3:25.

p. 283 l.30   **prevented:** anticipated.

p. 298 l.33   **SCENE 5:** a comparison of this scene and the next two with the corresponding section of the ballad will show how Lillo reworks his material:

> Unto his uncle then
>   He rode with might and main,
> Who with a welcome and good cheer
>   Did Barnwell entertain.
> One fortnight's space he stayed,
>   Until it chanced so,
> His uncle with his cattle did
>   Unto a market go.
> His kinsmen rode with him,
> Where he did see right plain,
> Great store of money he had took:
>   When coming home again,
> Sudden within a wood,
>   He struck his uncle down,
> And beat his brains out of his head;

> So sore he crackt his crown.
> Then seizing fourscore pound,
>   To London straight he hyed,
> And unto Sarah Millwood all
>   The cruell fact descryed.

Although the text is presented as if it was in ballad stanzas, it actually consists of alternating six-foot and seven-foot iambic lines rhyming in couplets. This is the form which the Elizabethans called 'poulter's measure', and its use suggests that the poem may be of sixteenth-century origin.

p. 299 l.8 Just Heaven! Then what should I be! For him that was: two pirated editions of 1737 alter this to read 'Just Heaven! Then what should I feel for him that was'. The altered text makes better sense, but the incoherence of the original text could be interpreted as an expression of the speaker's mental condition.

p. 301 l.19 Cain: see Genesis 4.

p. 301 l.21 Nero: the emperor Nero had his mother Agrippina killed in A.D. 59.

p. 301 l.27 *The rich man thus . . . remains for all*: the reference is to the story of Dives and Lazarus in Luke 16:19–31, and in particular to the rejection of Dives' prayer that Abraham should send Lazarus to warn his five brothers.

p. 305 l.19 Where shall I hide me?: compare Psalms 139:7, 'Whither shall I go from thy spirit? or whither shall I flee from thy presence?'

p. 312 l.2 suburb-magistrates: magistrates outside the City of London, who were accused of encouraging vice because their incomes depended on it.

p. 322 l.12 devoted: doomed.

p. 324 l.4 devoted: doomed.

p. 326 l.2 COLLEY CIBBER: see note on p. 5 l.7 above.

p. 326 l.3 *Mrs Cibber*: see note on p. 267 l.9 above.

p. 326 l.11 cocked up in cue: with his hair drawn up into a 'queue' or tail.

She Stoops to Conquer

p. 328 l.5   Mr Shuter: Edward Shuter, commonly known as Ned, was one of the leading comic actors of the day.

p. 329 l.1   To Samuel Johnson: the great poet, critic, essayist, biographer, and lexicographer was, like Goldsmith, an advocate of 'laughing comedy'.

p. 329 l.11   Mr Colman: George Colman the Elder, dramatist and manager of the Covent Garden theatre.

p. 331 l.2   DAVID GARRICK: the most celebrated actor and theatre-manager of the eighteenth century.

p. 331 l.3   Mr Woodward: Henry Woodward, who turned down the part of Tony Lumpkin, is nonetheless represented in this prologue as a comic actor mourning the death of the Comic Muse.

p. 331 l.7   'Tis not alone ... that within: the quotations are from *Hamlet* Act I Scene 2 lines 77 and 85.

p. 331 l.16   *Shuter* and *I*: see notes on p. 328 l.5 and p. 331 l.3 above.

p. 331 l.19   Poor *Ned* and *I*: see notes on p. 328 l.5 and p. 331 l.3 above.

p. 331 l.22   a hearty cup: Shuter had been accused of appearing drunk on stage.

p. 332 l.7   A *doctor* comes: Goldsmith had studied medicine in Edinburgh and Leyden, but his claim to a degree is dubious.

p. 332 l.9   *five draughts*: the classical principle that a play should have five acts stems from Horace (*Ars Poetica* 189).

p. 333 l.18   rumbling: this form of the word 'rambling' was as old-fashioned in 1773 as the Hardcastles' house.

p. 333 l.22   Prince Eugene and the Duke of Marlborough: the leaders of the Austrian and British forces in the War of the Spanish Succession.

p. 338 l.30   Allons: let us go.

p. 338 l.32   Would it were bed time and all were well: compare Falstaff's words in *1 Henry IV* V. 1. 125, 'I would 'twere bed-time, Hal, and all were well'.

p. 338 l.39   knock himself down: Tony, using the mallet as symbol of his authority, is going to announce the next item on the programme as a song by himself.

p. 339 l.8   genus: a vulgar mispronunciation of 'genius'.

p. 339 l.10   *Their Lethes, their Styxes, and Stygians*: the Lethe and the Styx are two of the rivers of the classical underworld. 'Stygian' is the adjective from 'Styx'.

p. 339 l.11   *Their Quis, and their Quæs, and their Quods*: the words 'qui', 'quae' and 'quod' are the nominative singular masculine, feminine, and neuter forms of the Latin relative pronoun.

p. 339 l.12   *Pigeons*: simpletons.

p. 339 l.14   *Methodist preachers*: the travelling preachers associated with the Methodist movement were noted for their hostility to drink.

p. 339 l.23   *jorum*: a large drinking-bowl, especially a bowl of punch.

p. 339 l.28   *bustards*: large edible birds.

p. 339 l.28   *widgeons*: wild ducks.

p. 339 l.35   nothing that's *low*: Goldsmith's previous comedy, *The Good-Natured Man*, had been criticised for its 'low' humour.

p. 340 l.6   Water Parted: a song in the opera *Artaxerxes* by Thomas Augustine Arne (1762).

p. 340 l.6   the minuet in Ariadne: Porpora's *Ariadne* and Handel's *Arianna* dealt with same subject, and were both performed in 1734. The reference here is to the minuet at the end of Handel's overture.

p. 341 l.26   We wanted no ghost to tell us that: compare *Hamlet* I. 5. 129:

> There needs no ghost, my lord, come from the grave
> To tell us this.

p. 342 l.27   we could as soon find out the longitude: an act of 1713 offered rewards totalling £20,000 for an accurate method of determining a ship's longitude. The full reward was paid three months after the first performance of *She Stoops to Conquer*.

p. 345 l.9   the story of Ould Grouse in the gun-room: 'Grouse' was a name commonly given to sporting dogs in Ireland.

p. 347 l.34 prepossessing: prompting initially unfavourable judgments.

p. 347 l.36 the dutchesses of Drury-lane: the prostitutes of the Drury Lane area called themselves by aristocratic titles.

p. 348 l.22 Denain: Hardcastle's uncompleted anecdote refers to the period before Marlborough's dismissal, when the allied forces were preparing to besiege the fortress of Denain near Valenciennes. Marlborough was not present in July 1712, when the siege was ended by a French victory.

p. 348 l.23 the *ventre d'or* waistcoat: A waistcoat whose front portions are of gold-coloured material.

p. 349 l.5 Here's cup, Sir: not punch, but a sweetened and flavoured wine.

p. 349 l.24 *for us that sell ale*: the third dialogue of Swift's *Polite Conversation* contains the sentence: 'Thus it must be, if we sell ale'. This commonplace saying is here being used metaphorically but interpreted literally.

p. 349 l.30 *Heyder Ally*: a maharaja of Mysore.

p. 349 l.31 *Ally Cawn*: a ruler of Bengal, deposed in 1761.

p. 349 l.32 *Ally Croaker*: a character in a popular Irish song.

p. 349 l.39 Westminster-hall: in Westminster Hall, the building where major trials were held, one might expect to hear ingenious but sometimes dubious arguments.

p. 350 l.10 the battle of Belgrade: Prince Eugene defeated the Turks near Belgrade in 1717. In 1772 Johnson, Boswell and Goldsmith dined with General Oglethorpe, and the General described the battle of Belgrade by pouring wine on the table and explaining everything 'with a wet finger'.

p. 351 l.9 the whole Joiners Company, or the Corporation of Bedford: the rich banquets enjoyed by trade associations and municipal authorities had long been a subject for Tory jests. Compare Pope's account (in *The Dunciad* I 91–2) of the night following the installation of the Lord Mayor:

> Now May'rs and Shrieves all hush'd and satiate lay,
> Yet eat, in dreams, the custard of the day.

p. 351 l.14   **pruin sauce:** prune sauce.

p. 351 l.28   **a florentine:** a kind of pie or tart, usually of meat baked in a dish with a cover of paste.

p. 351 l.28   **a shaking pudding:** see Robert May, *The Accomplisht Cook or The Art and Mystery of Cookery* (1665) p. 180. The nearest modern equivalent is a jelly.

p. 351 l.28   **tiff – taff – taffety cream:** taffety cream was a dish of cream and eggs, supposed to resemble taffety silk in texture.

p. 351 l.31   **a green and yellow dinner:** these are the colours of the china, which was more memorable than the food.

p. 353 l.3   **the laws of marriage:** this was interpreted by early audiences as a hostile comment on the Royal Marriage Act of 1772.

p. 355 l.1   **Cicero never spoke better:** the Roman orator is here cited as an emblem of supreme eloquence.

p. 357 l.3   *sola*: alone.

p. 357 l.29   **Ranelagh, St James's, or Tower Wharf:** Ranelagh Gardens were still frequented by the aristocracy. St James's was the fashionable district around St James's Palace. Tower Wharf was an unfashionable district east of the City.

p. 357 l.34   **the Pantheon:** A domed building on Oxford Street, opened in 1772 as a 'Receptacle of fashionable Pleasure'.

p. 357 l.34   **the Grotto Gardens:** the Grotto Gardens, located in St George's Fields, competed with Ranelagh but had lower admission charges.

p. 357 l.34   **the Borough:** the Borough of Southwark had once been a residence of the aristocracy, but was inhabited in Goldsmith's time by 'tradesmen and manufacturers'.

p. 357 l.37   **the Scandalous Magazine:** the *Town and Country Magazine* printed accounts of sexual liaisons in high society, illustrating each report with an engraved 'tête-à-tête'.

p. 358 l.3   *degagée*: the French adjective 'dégagé' means 'easy' or 'unconstrained'.

p. 358 l.4   *friseur*: hairdresser.

p. 358 l.6   the Ladies Memorandum-book: an advertisement in *Lloyd's Evening Post* for 6–8 January 1773 announces that *The Ladies Own Memorandum Book or Daily Pocket Journal for the Year 1773* is embellished with 'twelve of the genteelest head-dresses'.

p. 358 l.10   inoculation: inoculation against smallpox, which was introduced by Lady Mary Wortley Montagu after her return from Turkey in 1718, not only saved lives but also prevented damage to the complexion.

p. 358 l.18   his great flaxen wig: the large full-bottomed wig was even more out-of-date than Mrs Hardcastle's hairstyle.

p. 358 l.24   Gothic: barbarous.

p. 358 l.25   tête: a fashionable lady's wig.

p. 359 l.12   crack: lie.

p. 359 l.32   *The Complete Huswife*: the reference is to *The Compleat Housewife* (3rd edition 1729), which included 'a Collection of Two Hundred Family Receipts of Medicines'.

p. 359 l.33   *Quincy*: John Quincy was the author of *A Compleat English Dispensatory* (1718).

p. 361 l.6   Anon?: 'What are you saying?'

p. 362 l.2   *Solus*: alone.

p. 363 l.5   *mauvaise honte*: bashfulness, shyness, timidity.

p. 363 l.13   Bully Dawson: in *Spectator* 2 Steele reports that Sir Roger de Coverly 'kick'd Bully *Dawson* in a publick Coffee-house for calling him Youngster'.

p. 364 l.23   bobs: Pendants.

p. 364 l.24   my genus: see note on p. 339 l.8 above.

p. 365 l.12   Morrice. Prance.: 'Clear out, disappear.'

p. 365 l.25   Marcasites: ornaments made from a crystallized form of iron pyrites.

p. 365 l.36   A parcel of old-fashioned rose and table-cut things: the reference is to two ways of cutting diamonds, both of which Mrs Hardcastle believes to be old-fashioned.

p. 365 l.38   king Solomon at a puppet-shew: in 'The Adventures of a
Strolling Player' Goldsmith referred to the young drummer of a puppet-
show as the 'interpreter to Punch and king Solomon'.

p. 368 l.18   Cherry in the Beaux Stratagem: Cherry is the landlord's
daughter in George Farquhar's comedy *The Beaux Stratagem* (1706).

p. 369 l.1   Attend the Lion there ... this half hour: these are the
names of the rooms at the inn where Miss Hardcastle imagines herself
serving.

p. 370 l.36   the Ladies Club in town: in 1770 Horace Walpole
reported that 'a club of both sexes' was 'to be created at Almac's, on
the model of that of the men of White's'.

p. 371 l.27   I never nick'd seven that I did not throw ames ace three
times following: 'I have never had a winning throw that was not
followed by three losing throws.' The reference is to hazard, in which
the winning throws were seven and eleven and the lowest possible
throw was a double ace.

p. 376 l.18   liberty and Fleet-street for ever: this may be a radical
slogan, alluding to the bookseller John Williams who sold the banned
No. 45 of *The North Briton* from his shop in Fleet Street.

p. 377 l.17   *The Rake's Progress*: a series of engravings based on
Hogarth's paintings. Hardcastle is suggesting that Marlow resembles
the principal character of Hogarth's work.

p. 378 l.18   The Dullissimo Maccaroni: the reference is to the series of
satirical portraits known as 'Darly's Macaronis', which was completed
in January 1773 and then advertised for sale in five volumes. See also
the note on p. 421 l.24 below.

p. 379 l.33   Whistle-jacket: a famous racehorse which was in the news
because it had sired many horses that won races in 1771–3.

p. 380 l.22   haspicholls: harpsichord.

p. 381 l.24   *izzard*: an old name for the letter Z.

p. 381 l.30   feeder: trainer of fighting cocks.

p. 381 l.33   The gentlemen of the Shake-bag club has cut the gentlemen of Goose-green quite out of feather: The news which Miss Neville
is inventing concerns the victory of one cock-fighting club over another.

A shake-bag was a large fighting cock, and goose-green was one of the preferred shades of plumage.

p. 383 l.5 **old Bedlam:** the Hospital of St Mary of Bethlehem in Bishopsgate was incorporated in 1547 as a royal foundation for the reception of lunatics. It was replaced in 1675 by a new hospital in Moorfields.

p. 383 l.18 **with baskets:** the weapons with which Tony proposes to fight are single-sticks with basket hilts, which would put his genteel opponents at some disadvantage.

p. 388 l.35 **Rabbet me, but:** a slang expression meaning approximately 'Confound it'.

p. 388 l.37 *varment*: presumably Tony's corruption of 'vermin'.

p. 390 l.15 **kept here:** 'operated as highwaymen in this area'.

p. 390 l.29 **pistils:** Tony means 'pistols', but the botanical associations of 'pistils' suggest that the highwayman's weapons are integral parts of his body.

p. 398 l.10 **We have our exits and our entrances:** this is a modified version of Jacques' line 'They have their exits and their entrances' in *As You Like It* II. 7. 141. Goldsmith's epilogue as a whole is modelled on Jacques' speech about the ages of man.

p. 398 l.27 *caro*: an Italian term of approbation, meaning literally 'dear', but in practice equivalent to 'bravo' or 'encore'.

p. 398 l.28 **Nancy Dawson:** a popular song celebrating a horn-pipe dancer.

p. 398 l.28 *Che Faro*: 'Che farò senza Euridice?' is the best-known aria in Gluck's opera *Orfeo* (1764).

p. 398 l.30 **the *Heinel* of Cheapside:** Anne Heinel was one of the leading dancers at the Haymarket opera-house. Cheapside was the commercial centre of the City of London.

p. 398 l.33 **spadille:** the ace of spades.

p. 399 l.4 **Bayes:** because the poet's crown was made of bay-leaves, the name Bayes became the conventional designation first for the Poet Laureate and then for any poet or dramatist.

The School for Scandal

p. 402 l.4 **Mr King:** Thomas King (1730–1805) acted at Drury Lane from 1748 to 1802. He was also involved with Garrick's Shakespeare Jubilee at Stratford in 1769, and with the development of the theatre at Sadler's Wells.

p. 402 l.8 **Mr Palmer:** John Palmer (1744–98) acted at Drury Lane from the 1760s to the 1790s, and also travelled extensively in the British Isles as actor and touring lecturer. His everyday personality was Sheridan's model for the character who became Joseph Surface. Charles Lamb in his essay 'On the Artificial Comedy of the Last Century', remembers 'the gay boldness, the graceful solemn plausibility, the measured step, the insinuating voice . . . the downright *acted* villainy of the part'. In the years 1785–8 Palmer tried unsuccessfully to challenge the authority of the patentees by establishing a new theatre in Wellclose Square.

p. 402 l.9 **Mr Smith:** William Smith acted at Covent Garden from 1754 to 1774, and at Drury Lane from 1774 to his retirement in 1788. According to Boaden he was 'fair and noble' in appearance and 'dignified and manly' in his deportment. Charles Surface was his most famous role.

p. 402 l.16 **Mrs Abington:** Frances Barton (1737–1815) began her theatrical career in 1756 and married James Abington in 1759. After acting in Ireland from 1759 to 1765, she returned to London and joined the Drury Lane company. She gave her most celebrated performance as Lady Teazle, and James Boaden described her as 'the most brilliant satirist of her sex'. She moved to Covent Garden in 1782, and retired in 1799.

p. 403 l.2 **MR GARRICK:** after dominating the theatrical world for some thirty-five years, Garrick transferred the management of Drury Lane to Sheridan in 1776. He died in 1779.

p. 403 l.10 *quantum sufficit:* 'as much as is needed'.

p. 403 l.17 *sal volatile:* smelling salts; a solution of ammonium carbonate used as a restorative in fainting fits.

p. 403 l.20 **poz:** an abbreviation of 'positively', used colloquially to mean 'certainly' or 'indeed'.

p. 404 l.6 **Don Quixote:** Garrick, who has retired from the fray, professes to see his young successor's attack on a fashionable vice as naïvely idealistic.

p. 404 l.8 Hydra: the killing of this many-headed snake was one of the labours of Hercules.

p. 404 l.12 a cavalero true: Garrick follows up his allusion to Cervantes by using the Spanish term for a knight or horseman.

p. 405 l.24 *Town and Country Magazine*: see note on p. 357 l.37 above.

p. 408 l.7 execution: seizure of property.

p. 410 l.38 diligence: stage-coach.

p. 411 l.33 Lord Spindle, Sir Thomas Splint, Captain Quinze, and Mr Nickit: the improbable names suggest that the principal cause of financial ruin is gambling.

p. 412 l.9 a rebus: an 'ingenious kind of conceit' condemned by Addison in *Spectator* 59.

p. 412 l.25 love elegies: poems resembling the *Love Elegies* published in 1743 by James Hammond.

p. 412 l.28 Petrarch's Laura: the Italian poet Francesco Petrarca, known in English as Petrarch, addressed his sonnets to a woman he called 'Laura'.

p. 412 l.29 Waller's Sacharissa: Edmund Waller (1606–87) wrote poems to Lady Dorothea Sidney, whom he called 'Sacharissa'.

p. 413 l.26 Tunbridge: see note on p. 160 l.11 above.

p. 414 l.15 the Old Jewry: a street in London whose residents still included some Jewish money-lenders. Ben Jonson used it as the setting for much of the anglicised version of *Every Man in his Humour*.

p. 414 l.18 the Irish tontine: a tontine was a form of lottery named after the Neapolitan banker Lorenzo Tonti. From 1773 onwards the Irish government used this method to pay off its debts.

p. 414 l.23 officer: the officer in question is a bailiff.

p. 414 l.36 *penchant*: 'inclination'.

p. 418 l.24 the Pantheon: see note on p. 357 l.34 above.

p. 418 l.24 *fête champêtre*: this phrase for an outdoor entertainment or rural festival was new to English usage in the 1770s.

p. 419 l.8 tambour: embroidery frame.

p. 419 l.19 Pope Joan: a card-game, known by this name from the 1730s to the 1830s.

p. 419 l.24 *vis-à-vis*: a light carriage for two people sitting face to face.

p. 419 l.25 cats: either a printer's error for 'cobs', or an otherwise unrecorded term for 'ponies'.

p. 420 l.26 hurdle: a rudimentary cart used for transporting prisoners to the gallows.

p. 421 l.19 taking the dust: Sir Benjamin modifies the common phrase 'taking the air' in the interests of malice and accuracy.

p. 421 l.19 Hyde Park: the park had been opened to the public in James I's reign, and was much frequented by ladies and gentlemen on horse-back.

p. 421 l.20 a duodecimo phaeton: a phaëton is a carriage resembling the sun-chariot once driven by Apollo's son Phaëton. A duodecimo is a book for which each sheet has been folded to make twelve pages. A duodecimo phaëton is therefore a diminutive carriage.

p. 421 l.24 *macaronies*: fops or dandies who imitate continental tastes and fashions.

p. 421 l.29 A very Phoebus, mounted: Phoebus Apollo was the god of poetry and the sun.

p. 423 l.36 the Ring: see note on p. 62 l.28.

p. 424 l.33 Irish front: a front is a band of false hair worn over the forehead.

p. 424 l.38 teeth *à la Chinoise*: the manifestations of beauty admired by the Chinese were said to include black teeth.

p. 424 l.39 a *table d'hôte* **at Spa**: Spa was an internationally celebrated watering-place near Liège, whose name later became a common noun. A *table d'hôte* was a table for individual customers, who might well be of different nationalities.

p. 425 l.37 Law-Merchant: Sir Peter is arguing that reputation should be protected by a legal code analogous to that which safeguards property rights in international trade.

p. 427 l.24 cicisbeo: this Italian word for the recognised male escort of a married woman was later replaced by the phrase 'cavalier servente'. Compare stanza 37 of Byron's *Beppo* (1817).

p. 428 l.11 stood bluff to old bachelor: obstinately remained a bachelor as he grew older.

p. 430 l.11 *Allons:* see note on p. 338 l.30 above.

p. 431 l.7 jet: 'point' or 'purpose'.

p. 431 l.29 *a tear for pity ... melting charity:* the 'bard' is Shakespeare. The quotation is from *2 Henry IV* IV. 4. 32.

p. 433 l.3 Crutched Friars: Crutched Friars was a continuation of Jewry Street.

p. 434 l.19 the Annuity Bill: the Annuity Bill, which sought to protect the financial interests of minors, was passed four days after the first performance of *The School for Scandal.*

p. 439 l.22 bags: a bag is a silk pouch which holds the tail of a bagwig.

p. 440 l.4 this d—d Register: the Annuity Bill required that all life annuities should be registered.

p. 440 l.12 a post-obit: a bond which takes effect after death.

p. 440 l.33 Spa water: see note on p. 424 l.39 above.

p. 440 l.38 under a hazard regimen: playing no other game than hazard.

p. 444 l.33 beau-pots: usually large vases for cut flowers, but here clearly window-boxes.

p. 447 l.5 Shylock in the play: Charles Macklin acted Shylock in Shakespeare's *The Merchant of Venice* for the first time on 14 February 1741, and for the last time on 7 May 1789. He had appeared in the role six times in the theatrical season 1776–7 before the production of *The School for Scandal.*

p. 448 l.10   your modern Raphael: Sheridan applies this phrase elsewhere to Sir Joshua Reynolds.

p. 448 l.20   an old gouty chair: probably a chair designed for people suffering from gout.

p. 448 l.30   an *ex post facto* parricide: Sir Oliver sees Charles's sale of the family portraits as a retrospective massacre of his ancestors.

p. 449 l.9   Malplaquet: a battle fought on 11 September 1709, in which the British forces were commanded by the Duke of Marlborough.

p. 449 l.22   Kneller: Sir Godfrey Kneller, the leading portrait-painter in England from 1680 to his death in 1723.

p. 450 l.2   the woolsack: the Lord Chancellor's cushion in the House of Lords, and hence the judiciary as a whole.

p. 450 l.14   Norwich: the MS variants 'Manchester' and 'Bristol' suggest that the acting text may have been adapted at this point to suit different audiences.

p. 451 l.32   nabob: the governor of a town or district in India, hence a man who has returned from India after making a fortune.

p. 454 l.5   birthday clothes: ceremonial dress for the king's birthday.

p. 457 l.20   *throws away the book*: Palmer in the London production threw the book 'to the end of the room'. William Wyatt Dimond in the Bath production of 1777 'carefully pulled down the page he was reading and gave it to his servant'.

p. 460 l.31   trepan: 'deceive'.

p. 461 l.1   Joseph: see Genesis 39, and compare Fielding's *Joseph Andrews* (1742).

p. 463 l.12   incog: incognito, without revealing one's identity.

p. 469 l.10   rupees: silver coins from India.

p. 469 l.11   pagodas: gold coins from India.

p. 469 l.13   congou tea: a kind of black tea from China.

p. 469 l.14   avadavats: small black and red song-birds from India.

p. 469 l.14   Indian crackers: not biscuits but fireworks.

p. 472 l.39   hartshorn: carbonate of ammonia, smelling-salts.

p. 473 l.7   in *seconde*: using the second of eight parries recognised in swordplay.

p. 473 l.24   the Montem: the 'processus ad montem', a three-yearly procession of Eton schoolboys to Salthill, which is now a part of Slough.

p. 486 l.2   MR COLMAN: see note on p. 329 l.11 above.

p. 486 l.3   *Mrs Abington*: see note on p. 402 l.16 above.

p. 486 l.8   Bayes: see note on p. 399 l.4 above.

p. 486 l.9   crying epilogues: Colman is referring to Sheridan's epilogue for George Ayscough's adaptation of Voltaire's *Semiramis*, acted at Drury Lane on 14 December 1776. Sheridan there expresses gratitude to the ladies for 'the chrystal incense of each falling tear', and expresses the hope that they will leave the theatre with these 'graceful' tears still 'ling'ring' in their eyes.

p. 486 l.26   pounded: imprisoned.

p. 487 l.1   loo: a card-game.

p. 487 l.1   a vole: winning of all the tricks in a deal.

p. 487 l.2   Seven's the main: a phrase called out by the 'caster' in the game of hazard.

p. 487 l.3   hot cockles: a rustic game, mentioned by Gay in the Monday eclogue of *The Shepherd's Week* and by Goldsmith in Chapter 11 of *The Vicar of Wakefield*.

p. 487 l.5   Farewell the tranquil mind ... Lady Teazle's occupation's o'er: these eleven lines parody a speech in Shakespeare's *Othello* (III. 3. 353–62).

p. 487 l.6   *tête*: see note on p. 358 l.25 above.

p. 487 l.8   Card-drums: card parties at private houses.

p. 487 l.9   spadille: see note on p. 398 l.33 above.

p. 487 l.9   pam – basto: Pam and Basto are the knave and ace of clubs.

p. 487 l.10   ye knockers: brass door-knockers were a recent innovation in London, and were almost unknown in the country.